QUEERLY PHRASED

OXFORD STUDIES IN SOCIOLINGUISTICS
Edward Finegan, *General Editor*

Editorial Advisory Board

Douglas Biber
Alessandro Duranti
John R. Rickford
Suzanne Romaine
Deborah Tannen

QUEERLY PHRASED

Language, Gender, and Sexuality

Edited by

ANNA LIVIA

and

KIRA HALL

New York   Oxford
OXFORD UNIVERSITY PRESS
1997

Oxford University Press

Oxford   New York

Athens   Auckland   Bangkok   Bogota   Bombay   Buenos Aires
Calcutta   Cape Town   Dar es Salaam   Delhi   Florence   Hong Kong
Istanbul   Karachi   Kuala Lumpur   Madras   Madrid   Melbourne
Mexico City   Nairobi   Paris   Singapore   Taipei   Tokyo   Toronto   Warsaw

and associated companies in
Berlin   Ibadan

Library of Congress Cataloging-in-Publication Data
Queerly phrased : language, gender, and sexuality / edited by Anna
   Livia and Kira Hall.
      p.   cm.
   ISBN 0-19-510470-6; ISBN 0-19-510471-4 (pbk.)
   1. Language and languages—Sex differences.   2. Gays—Language.
I. Livia, Anna.   II. Hall, Kira, 1962–
P120.S48Q44   1997
408'.6'64—dc21   97-6284

9 8 7 6 5 4 3 2 1

Printed in the United States of America
on acid-free paper

SERIES FOREWORD

Sociolinguistics is the study of language in use. With special focus on the relationships between language and society, its principal concerns address the forms and functions of variation across social groups and across the range of communicative situations in which women and men deploy their verbal repertoires. In short, sociolinguistics examines discourse as it is constructed and co-constructed, shaped and reshaped, in the interactions of everyday life and as it reflects and creates the social realities of that life.

While some linguists examine the structure of sentences independent of who is speaking or writing and to whom, independent of what precedes and what follows in a discourse, and independent of setting, topic, and purpose, sociolinguists investigate linguistic expression embedded in its social and situational contexts in everyday life. Interest in linguistic matters among language observers who are *not* professional linguists also focuses on language in use, for it is only there that the intricacies of social structure are reflected and the situational and strategic influences that shape our discourse are mirrored.

With *Queerly Phrased*, Oxford Studies in Sociolinguistics presents its first volume addressing the intersection in the web of language, gender, and sexuality. The volume editors, Anna Livia and Kira Hall, have commissioned essays that are mostly anthropological-linguistic or sociolinguistic but also literary/critical. In an era when queer theory and feminist theory have played increasingly prominent roles in furthering out understanding of the place of language in literature and, more important, in everyday interactions between members of sometimes subtly different social groups, *Queerly Phrased* is a notable contribution to linguists' understanding of issues ranging from the indexical value of language choices and the interconnectedness of dialect and register to the critical link between language and power. Linguistic studies often focus on the formal properties of language or on correlations between linguistic expression and demographic categories such as sex, ethnicity, and socioeconomic status. In these essays, by contrast, readers will find analyses that tug at tidy definitions of social groupings based on demographic categories, which have shaped orthodox thinking about connections between sex and gender, sexuality and social status, and language and identity, as well as about the constructions of social reality and personal identity. *Queerly Phrased* is about the place of language in the lives of human beings and their integration within more fluid and less demographic social groups than are traditionally treated by variation studies.

The perspectives represented in *Queerly Phrased* are those principally of linguists and anthropological linguists, but the authors include literary scholars, fiction writers, interpreters, a historian, a psychotherapist, and an activist. With its striking diversity and prideful queerness, the collection is intellectually provocative, socially diverse, humanly affecting, and sociolinguistically innovative. Above all, *Queerly Phrased* is important to linguistic and sociolinguistic scholarship. It is also important to people whose lives are affected by queer expression, and as the essays in this book document and demonstrate, that category includes us all.

Offering a platform for studies of language use in communities around the globe, Oxford Studies in Sociolinguistics invites synchronic or diachronic treatments of discourse and of social dialects and registers, whether oral, written, or signed. The series is host to studies that are descriptive or theoretical, interpretive or analytical. While the volumes in the series generally report original research, an occasional one synthesizes or interprets existing knowledge. The series aims for a style that is accessible beyond linguists to other humanists and social scientists. Some volumes will hold appeal for educated readers keenly interested in the language of human affairs—for example, in the discourse of doctors or lawyers engaging their clients and one another with their specialist registers, or of women and men striving to fathom the sometimes baffling character of their shared interactions. By providing a forum for innovative and valuable studies of language in use, Oxford Studies in Sociolinguistics aims to influence the agenda for linguistic research in the twenty-first century and provide an array of provocative analyses to help launch that agenda. We are pleased to have *Queerly Phrased* as the latest volume in the series.

Edward Finegan

ACKNOWLEDGMENTS

We owe a substantial debt to those who have helped provide an intellectual community in which we could discuss our own ideas and become acquainted with those of others, let people know about this book, seek contributions to it, and, most important, receive confirmation that queer linguistics was a field needing to be launched. This is a community that is physically present at conferences like those of the Berkeley Women and Language Group, the American Association of Applied Linguistics, and the American Anthropological Association, as well as the annual Lavender Language Weekends at American University, and that reconvenes between times in the less material reaches of cyberspace, notably on the OUTiL (OUT in Linguistics) list organized by Arnold Zwicky. We would therefore like to thank our colleagues and predecessors in the field, without whom this volume would have remained another interesting project scribbled on the back of another bus ticket: William Leap, organizer of the Lavender Language Weekends; Arnold Zwicky of OUTiL; Gregory Ward, who has compiled an impressive bibliography of articles on gay and lesbian language; Mary Bucholtz, on whom we tried out many of our ideas; and Jennifer Coates and Kathy Wood, who were unfailingly enthusiastic about the book.

All the world's queer,

save thee and me,

and thee's a bit funny.

—an old Yorkshire saying

CONTENTS

II   QUEERSPEAK

III   LINGUISTIC GENDER-BENDING

CONTRIBUTORS

James D. Armstrong is associate professor of anthropology at SUNY Plattsburgh. He has done extensive fieldwork on identity and social organization in modern-day Israel, and has published articles on mainstream Israeli culture, extensionist semantics, and engaged pedagogy. He is co-author (with R. Robbins) of *Anthropology and Global Issues* (forthcoming) and co-editor (with Philip DeVita) of *Distant Mirrors: America as a Foreign Culture* (1993).

Bruce Bagemihl completed his doctorate in linguistics from the University of British Columbia. He has spoken widely on transgender issues and the lesbian and gay response to the transgender community. He is currently finishing work on a major new book, the first comprehensive account of the natural history of homosexuality and transgenderism.

Rusty Barrett is a Ph.D. candidate in the department of linguistics at the University of Texas at Austin. His dissertation is a grammar of Sipakapense, a Mayan language of Guatemala. He has also conducted research on the intersections of language and identity in the speech of African American drag queens.

Marie-Jo Bonnet specializes in cultural history. She has been a member of the Women's Liberation Movement since 1971 and was active in the creation of the Gouines Rouges. She received her Ph.D. in history in 1979 from the University of

Paris VII. She is the author of *Un choix sans équivoque* (1981, republished in 1995 as *Les relations amoureuses entre les femmes du XVIè au XXè siècle*).

Jennifer Coates is professor of English language and linguistics at Roehampton Institute, London University, and was a visiting scholar at Melbourne University, Australia, in 1994–1995. Her most important works include *Women, Men and Language: A Sociolinguistic Account of Gender Differences in Language* (1986, 1993), *Women in Their Speech Communities: New Perspectives on Language and Sex* (1989), and *Women Talk: Conversation between Women Friends* (1996).

Randy Conner is a writer, educator, and activist. His works include *Blossom of Bone: Reclaiming the Connections between Homoeroticism and the Sacred* (1993) and *The Encyclopedia of Queer Myth, Symbol and Spirit* (1996) which he co-authored with his companion, David Hatfield-Sparks, and their daughter, Mariya Sparks.

Rudolf Gaudio teaches linguistic anthropology at the University of Arizona. His latest project, on the gender-bending practices of Hausa-speaking *yan-daudu*, connects his interest in African studies, Islam, and the discursive construction of gender and sexuality. He plans to do further research in the subaltern spaces of Islam.

Kira Hall is assistant professor of linguistic anthropology at Yale University, specializing in the study of language and gender. She is currently writing on the language practices of Hindi-speaking *hijras* (eunuchs) in North India. Her previous research includes the gendered nature of computer-mediated communication and the interpretation of language and gender theory by transsexual communities in the United States. With Mary Bucholtz she is co-editor of *Gender Articulated: Language and the Socially Constructed Self* (1995).

Mary Ellen Jordan recently completed her degree in linguistics at the University of Melbourne and is currently working in the publishing industry.

Mala S. Kleinfeld is project coordinator and instructor at Nova Community College and a freelance interpreter in the Washington D.C. area. She interprets as a volunteer for HIV/AIDS workshops and other issues in the gay community. She received her master's degree in linguistics from Gallaudet University in 1995. In 1997 she will attend the University of New Mexico for her doctorate in educational linguistics.

William L. Leap is professor of anthropology and a member of the women's/gender studies core faculty at American University (Washington D.C.). He is author of *Word's Out: Gay Men's English* (1996) and editor of *Beyond the Lavender Lexicon* (1995) and (with Ellen Lewin) *Out in the Field: Reflections of Lesbian and Gay Anthropologists* (1996). His current research examines connections between language, place, and space in urban gay experience.

A. C. Liang received her undergraduate degree from MIT in chemical engineering. She is currently writing her doctoral dissertation on the construction of coherence in coming out stories in the department of linguistics at the University of California at Berkeley. She and her brother, a law professor at Pepperdine University, are editing an anthology of articles on cultural models in language and law.

Anna Livia is assistant professor of French linguistics at the University of Illinois, Champaign-Urbana, specializing in the linguistic analysis of literary texts. Her previous research includes the fictional representation of butch/femme lesbian speech and literary experiments with linguistic gender. She is also a novelist and short story writer and has translated two books by 1920s lesbians, Lucie Delarue-Mardrus and Natalie Clifford Barney.

Ian Lucas researched "Gay Theatrical Maneuvers" at the University College of Wales, Aberystwyth. Recent publications include *Impertinent Decorum: Gay Theatrical Manoeuvres* (1994) and *Growing Up Positive: Stories from a Generation of Young People Affected by AIDS* (1995). *Kiss and Tell*, a book about the direct action group OutRage!, will be published in 1997.

Birch Moonwomon-Baird is a linguist in the department of English at Ohio State University. She received her Ph.D. in linguistics from the University of California at Berkeley. Funded by a research grant from Ohio State University, Moonwomon has been working on an ethnographic project with Lindsay Welcome on lesbian lives, which focuses on the life stories of self-identified lesbians in Berkeley, California, and Columbus, Ohio.

Elizabeth Morrish is subject leader of linguistics at Nottingham Trent University, Nottingham, United Kingdom. She obtained her Ph.D. from Leeds University in 1985. Her research interests include phonetic theory and lexical access, as well as queer linguistics. Her publications include papers on lesbian representation, the pragmatics of outing, and the linguistic erasure of identity.

M. Lynne Murphy is a lexical semanticist and lexicologist in the department of linguistics at the University of Witwatersrand, having completed her Ph.D. on lexical organization at the University of Illinois at Champaign-Urbana. She is working on a book of cognitive and social constraints on social labeling, which will build on issues she discusses in this volume as well as her work on racial labeling in the United States and South Africa.

Tina M. Neumann received her M.A. degree in linguistics, with a concentration in American Sign Language (ASL) from Gallaudet University in 1994. Currently she is researching figurative language use in ASL poetry, as well as teaching American Sign Language.

Naoko Ogawa is a doctoral student in linguistic anthropology at the University of California, Davis. Her interests include language attitude, language and gender, and geolinguistics. Her dissertation is on the linguistic indexicalization of gender identity, focusing on that of Japanese speakers with atypically gendered identities such as gay males and lesbians.

Geneviève Pastre has an Agrégation in Grammar. Since 1989 she has been director of the first lesbian publishing house in France—les Editions Geneviève Pastre. She is a poet, dramatist, and essayist and has written many articles, poems, and stories on female (and male) homosexuality in both the ancient world and the present day.

Robin M. Queen is an assistant professor of linguistics in the English department at Kent State University. She recently completed her dissertation at the University of Texas at Austin. She is interested in further exploring the relationship between language and identity in and across a variety of different types of speech communities.

Janet S. (Shibamoto) Smith is professor of anthropology, University of California, Davis. Among her principal interests are Japanese sociolinguistics and language and gender. Publications include *Japanese Women's Language* (1985) and numerous articles on Japanese language and gender. Present projects include work on the speech of Japanese women in positions of authority, as well as on gay male speech.

Michael J. Sweet received doctorates in Buddhist studies and psychology from the University of Wisconsin-Madison. He is a psychotherapist at the Madison VA Hospital and clinical assistant professor in the department of psychiatry at the University of Wisconsin-Madison. Publications include articles on Buddhism, psychotherapy, and sexuality; current projects include books about queerness in classical India and Buddhist meditation.

James Valentine is lecturer in sociology in the department of applied social science at the University of Stirling, Scotland. After his Ph.D. on the sociology of literature, he carried out research in Japan and since 1986 has focused on representations of marginality in Japanese culture. He co-edited *Unwrapping Japan* (1990) and is now working on marginality and framing of identity.

Noni Warner is a Deaf lesbian who was born deaf and learned sign language when she was nineteen years old. She is currently involved in sign language research related to phonology and literacy. She has an MA in linguistics from Gallaudet University.

Diane Watt is lecturer in the department of English at the University of Wales, Aberystwyth. She gained her D.Phil. from the University of Oxford in 1993. Her main research interests are English women writers before 1700, feminist theory, queer theory, and gender studies.

Kathleen M. Wood is assistant professor in the English department at Gallaudet University. She has published and presented on lesbian coming out stories and on lesbian communication. Her Ph.D. work at Georgetown focused on how Deaf students of English create literate identities in the telling of their literacy life stories.

Arnold M. Zwicky is Distinguished University Professor (Emeritus) at Ohio State and visiting professor at Stanford. He has served as president of the Linguistic Society of America and is manager of the OUTiL mailing list. His research focuses on morphology/syntax/phonology relationships. Outside of the academy he writes fiction on themes of gay male sensuality.

INTRODUCTION

"It's a Girl!"

Bringing Performativity Back to Linguistics

ANNA LIVIA AND KIRA HALL

We began collecting articles for this volume in March 1994 while preparations for the third Berkeley Women and Language Conference (BWLC) were at their height. In our own papers for the 1994 conference, we were each grappling with recent developments in queer theory and its uneasy, often antagonistic, relation to feminist theory. So, as it turned out, were several of the other conference participants that year. During the two previous decades, although a substantial body of research had been carried out on language and gender, few of these studies had taken sexuality, or sexual orientation, as a criterion for analysis, and the vast majority assumed gender as an unproblematic category indexically linked to the sex of the speaker or writer.

The small amount of research carried out on language and sexual orientation in the 1960s and 1970s tended to concentrate on the lexical level. During this period, a number of gay glossaries and lexicons were compiled, including Cory and LeRoy, "A Lexicon of Homosexual Slang" (1963), Strait and Associates, *The Lavender Lexicon: Dictionary of Gay Words and Phrases* (1964), Rodgers, *The Queens' Vernacular* (1972), and Farrel, "The Argot of the Homosexual Subculture" (1972). Although most of these works spotlighted white gay male speech in the United States, a few, like Giallombardo's *Society of Women: A Study of a Woman's Prison* (1966), presented the language of lesbians, while others included terms from languages other than English, such as the tongue-in-cheek "Gay Girl's Guide to the

U.S. and the Western World" (published as early as 1949), which has sections on French, German, and Russian.

The narrow range of gay-focused linguistic scholarship stands in stark contrast to the blossoming of interest and research on (heterosexual) men's and women's language in the same period, a topic that has been studied at every linguistic level from phonology and phonetics to morphosyntax, semantics, lexicon, and discourse. This research has covered such different areas as silencing and verbosity; topic choice and topic take-up; gaps and overlap; use of diminutives, superlatives, and hypocoristics; hedges and indirect speech acts; stress, pitch, and intonation patterns; semantic derogation; code-switching; and ethnic speech patterns. In the absence of explicit statements as to why sexuality was not included as a criterion of analysis in these studies, one is left to suppose that gay male speakers were included among the class of male respondents, while lesbians were placed with the women, a classification based on the unspoken assumption that shared gender provides a commonality that overrides considerations of sexual orientation.

One of the earliest gay glossaries, Gershon Legman's "The Language of Homosexuality: An American Glossary" (1941), listing 329 terms, appeared as appendix 7 to *Sex Variants: A Study of Homosexual Patterns* by one George Henry, M.D. Legman's glossary includes only gay male slang, and the author's explanation for this focus is interesting. Legman imputes the absence of lesbian terms not to the limitations of his own methods of data collection (he consulted other dictionaries, rather than conducting his own fieldwork) but to the "tradition of gentlemanly restraint among lesbians" (quoted in Hayes 1978: 204). This apparently simple statement contains a complex folk theory of the relationship among gender, sexuality, and language. Far from assuming that lesbians speak like women, Legman categorizes them among men, and gentlemen at that, a subsection of "restrained" (i.e., reticent) male speakers whose speech is marked by the absence of debasing slang. If the lack of lesbian slang indicates that lesbians speak like gentlemen, the abundance of gay male slang (329 items) must indicate that gay men's speech resembles that of women—working-class women, presumably, not "ladies."[1] It would seem that Legman accepted the folk linguistic view of women's verbosity, which more than twenty years of linguistic research has since been at pains to disprove. The association of lesbian speech with upper-class masculinity and gay male speech with lower-class femininity is strikingly at odds with the feminist-informed studies of the 1970s and 1980s, which, as mentioned, classified lesbians with women and paid little attention to class distinctions.

Commenting on the difficulty of obtaining copies of Legman's glossary, Charles Clay Doyle notes that the 1941 edition of *Sex Variants* is almost inaccessible, and the more easily available edition of 1948 excludes Legman's appendix. Doyle reports that it took considerable time and effort to obtain the 1941 edition on interlibrary loan. Six institutions refused to send their copy, a refusal that Doyle imputes to the fact that the book contains "numerous frontal photographs of naked human beings, which are intended to illustrate various physical types among homosexuals" (1982: 74–75). A grave, somewhat titillating warning appears on the title page: "The material in this book has been prepared for the use of the medical and allied professions only."

We have, perhaps, moved beyond the time when gay language could safely be studied only by persons holding medical degrees and the inclusion of pictures of naked, reputed homosexuals was grounds for the noncirculation of a work.[2] The glossaries and lexicons were followed by studies of lesbian and gay discourse (e.g., Hayes 1976[3]); ethnographic research into the defining aspects of gay and lesbian milieux (e.g., Ponte 1974[4]); the meaning of paralinguistic phenomena such as eye gaze and body posture (e.g., Webbink 1981); and gay code-switching (e.g., Lumby 1976). Birch Moonwomon's 1985 study "Toward the Study of Lesbian Speech" (reprinted this volume) was probably the first work to focus on perceptions of specifically lesbian speech and stress patterns. Although several scholars emerged in the 1970s as prominent researchers in the field—Julia Penelope (Stanley) (1970) working on the specificity of lesbian as opposed to gay male lexicon; Stephen O. Murray (1979) working on semantics and ritual insult; Joseph Hayes, who compiled a twenty-two-page annotated bibliography on the "language and language behavior of lesbian women and gay men" (1978, 1979)—the field itself failed to emerge. The first book-length collection of articles on lesbian and gay language issues, Chesebro's *Gayspeak: Gay Male and Lesbian Communication*, was published in 1981 and addresses questions of rhetoric and communication rather than linguistics as such. *Queer Words, Queer Images: Communication and the Construction of Homosexuality*, which came out in 1994, also concentrates on communication and rhetoric, as well as on media images of gays and lesbians and the process of coming out. It was not until William Leap began collecting articles for his edited volume, *Beyond the Lavender Lexicon*, that a book-length work concentrating on language issues as such was conceived.

Queer Theory

In this volume are collected a series of articles that approach the study of language from the twin perspectives of gender and sexuality, conceived as separate but intricately linked categories. In fact, the separation of sexuality and gender forms one of the cornerstones of queer theory, neatly encapsulated in Eve Kosofsky Sedgwick's Axiom Two:

> The study of sexuality is not co-extensive with the study of gender; correspondingly, antihomophobic inquiry is not coextensive with feminist inquiry. (1990: 27)

If the separation of sexuality and gender is a key element of queer theory, the separation of sex and gender, or biological sex and the social production of male and female identities, is a key element of feminism. As Sedgwick observes, although many gender-based analyses do involve accounts of intragender relations, their definitional appeal "must necessarily be to the diacritical frontier between different genders" (1990: 31); hence the privileging of heterosexual relations that lesbian theorists have criticized within feminism.[5] Since Sedgwick's formulation of the limitations of gender-based analysis (and therefore, albeit covertly, of the shortcomings of feminism) is both clear and beautifully expressed, we quote it here:

"The analytic bite of a purely gender-based account will grow less incisive and direct as the distance of its subject from a social interface between different genders increases. It is unrealistic to expect a close, textured analysis of same-sex relations through an optic calibrated in the first place to the coarser stigmata of gender difference" (1990: 32).

In this introduction we propose not to present or explicate the whole, complex developing field of queer theory but rather to point out those of its tenets that are most useful to linguistics and a study of language in context and, conversely, the contribution linguistics has made to queer theory. In some ways, queer theory, with its concern for hegemonic social forces rather than individual speakers—a position it largely inherits from postmodernism—may be seen as a reaction against the identity politics of feminism. *Identity politics*, a label most commonly applied from without and used to disparage the political position thus described, revolves around the recognition of one's identity as a member of a specific (typically oppressed) group: *women, blacks, the working class, the disabled*. Linked to the notion of community based on personal identity rather than on political allegiance is the more radical belief that only the people directly involved have the authority to speak for that community; that it is for gay men to theorize and combat gay oppression, while lesbians speak out against lesbian oppression. This belief, if pushed to its logical conclusion, would reduce scholarship (and, incidentally, creative production) to participant observation (and autobiography).

One of the most important criticisms of identity politics is that it is essentialist; that is, it assumes that personal identity is an unproblematic category and that all social relations may be derived from it. Linguistic studies of men's and women's speech that do not take into account other social parameters, such as class, race, age, occupation, or political affiliation, might be considered essentialist in outlook, informed by a brand of identity politics that assumes that gender is the superordinate category of which the other parameters are mere subdivisions. In the last chapter of *Man Made Language* (1980), for example, a volume that is composed mainly of commentary on previous studies, Dale Spender quotes various feminist critics who have pointed out the absence of representations of working-class and black women from the literary canon: "Working class women, literate or illiterate, play virtually no part in the conversion of raw material into literature" (Glastonbury 1979: 173; quoted in Spender 1980: 226); "Black women's existence, experience and culture and the brutally complex systems of oppression which shape these are in the 'real world' of white and/or male consciousness beneath consideration, invisible, unknown" (Smith 1979: 183, quoted in Spender 1980: 227). Yet Spender makes no comment on the absence of working-class and black speakers in the linguistic studies she outlines in the main body of the book.

We wish not to reduce feminism to identity politics, revolving around gender as the most salient category, or even to assert that feminist theory necessarily prioritizes identity politics but only to point out that it has been thus characterized and that it is, in part, against this categorization that queer theory has evolved. Clearly, a theory that is unable to focus on relations between members of the same sex is as inadequate to the study of lesbian, gay, bisexual or transgender discourse as is a theory that focuses on homosexual and homosocial discourse to the exclusion of cross-sex discourse. The former will be unable to analyze differences between same-sex versus cross-sex discourse, while the latter will downplay gender differences between gay men and lesbians. It may seem trite to state that both feminism and queer theory provide useful tools for linguistic research, but it is nevertheless true.

Although intersubjective relations have been well theorized by feminist linguists (see, for example, Coates and Cameron 1989 or Eckert and McConnell-Ginet 1995), intersubjectivity remains inadequately conceptualized within queer theory. Judith Butler, who, with Sedgwick, is the foremost and most frequently quoted queer theorist, considers the individual *I* who speaks as "a citation of the place of the 'I' in speech" (1993: 226). There is, Butler insists, "no 'I' who stands behind discourse" (1993: 225). According to Butler, there is no referent for *I* that precedes the moment of speech. The deictic 'I' and 'you' *interpellate* each other, in Louis Althusser's term, which has been widely borrowed in both postmodernism and queer theory. That is to say both *I* and *you* call upon (hail) and call into being the other term in the dyad. Jacques Derrida, linchpin philosopher of poststructuralism, asserts that there is no transcendental signified that might lock referent to signifier. Indeed, he coined the term *différance*—a wordplay on the French noun *différence* (difference), spelled with an *e* taken from the Latin present participle (an etymology now opaque to most French speakers), and the verb *différer* (to differ), of which the French present participle is spelled *différant*. The neologism *différance*, whose participial origin is made transparent in its spelling, emphasizes the ongoing nature of the play of the signifier in the signifying chain, a process that is seen as unending since, in Derridean thought, the signifier cannot "acquire representational authority" (1976: 379). A theory that postulates the nonexistence of a referent behind the *I* will be unable to deal with the relationship between groups of speaking subjects or their addressees and interlocutors. Instead, this theory of language accords priority to the relationship between words, to the virtual exclusion of relationships between referents. Speakers are both created and constricted by the endless iterability (another Derridean keyword) of discourse. One is trapped within the limits of the sayable.

To linguists this claim must seem not only erroneous but unscientific. In his work on the linguistic aspects of translation, Roman Jakobson has shown that any cognitive experience may be conveyed in any existing language (Jakobson 1971: 264). John Searle, working in the philosophy of language, has formulated a similar insight in his Principle of Expressibility: "Whatever can be meant can be said" (Searle 1969: 68). While we might not wish to accept the extreme limitations on individual agency suggested by the Derridean scheme, nevertheless Derrida's prioritizing of the relationship between signifiers—a move in which Roland Barthes, Claude Lévi-Strauss, and Michel Foucault (to name but a few) preceded him— proves a useful analytical tool if one considers it an emphasis, not an absolute. Most utterances are not unique, never previously formulated phrases, but things said before on other, similar occasions. Conference papers in recent years (at conventions as varied as the Modern Language Association meetings and the Kentucky Narrative Conference) have begun to feature the term *ventriloquism* in their titles: "The Ventriloquized Subject of Mimetic Narrative Identity," for example—

not a resurgence of a dying vocal art but a reference to the way speakers "channel" previous speakers, as texts make intertextual reference to preceding texts. This iterability points to the importance of preexisting discourses, not only to the final shape of the utterance, but also to its authority as a speech act. Think of a girl trying to get her younger brother ready for school, handing him the clothes their mother has left out for him on a chair, giving him the packed lunch their mother has prepared, and using the words and phrases their mother uses, as though they were her own: "Come on, hurry up, and get dressed, or you'll be late for school. You are an old slowcoach," she scolds, just as her mother does. Her brother, recognizing the term *slowcoach* as a favorite of his mother, acknowledges the directive to "hurry up" as originating in a superior, preestablished authority. Derrida and, following him, Butler argue that it is the citational aspect of an utterance that makes it authoritative. In Butler's articulation, if a performative speech act succeeds, it is because "that action echoes prior action, and accumulates the force of authority through the repetition or citation of a prior, authoritative set of practices" (1993: 226–227). We will discuss the importance of speech acts, and especially performativity, to queer theory later.

As linguists we are familiar with the indexical properties of deictics which necessarily gain their meaning from the context of utterance. *I* is the person saying *I*; *you* is/are the person/s addressed; *here* is the place of utterance; *now* is the moment of utterance. It seems that in the postmodern queer theory espoused by Butler, deictics are no longer a limited set, and deixis is itself a constituting principle of language: words have no meaning in and of themselves except as meaning is constructed in discourse. Once the initial shock of the disappearance of the referent has passed, it is possible to discern the theoretical apparatus behind the disappearance. A key tenet of postmodernism, which Butler has inherited, is that of an extreme cultural and linguistic relativity that finds its most explicit expression in the writings of Foucault. "We must not forget that the psychological, psychiatric, medical category of homosexuality was *constituted* from the moment it was *characterized*" (our emphasis), writes Foucault in his *History of Sexuality* (1990: 43). For him it is the act of naming *homosexuality* as such that brings it into being. He remarks elsewhere that discourses should be considered not simply as groups of signs or signifying elements that refer to contents or representations but as "practices that systematically form the object of which they speak" (1972: 49). When Butler quotes the argument that "the category of 'sex' is the instrument or effect of 'sexism' . . . , that 'race' is the instrument and effect of 'racism' . . . , that gender only exists in the service of heterosexism" (1993: 123), she too is referring to the idea that categorizing creates or constitutes that which it refers to—though she points out that one can reverse and displace the usual meanings of such culturally loaded terms.

Linguists will probably be more familiar with the concept of linguistic determinism as articulated by Edward Sapir and Benjamin Whorf, an axiom commonly referred to as the "Sapir-Whorf hypothesis." In its strong version, linguistic determinism—a position that seems closest to that of Foucault and his followers in queer theory—the Sapir-Whorf hypothesis posits that the language one speaks determines one's perception of reality. In its weak version, linguistic relativity, it states that one's native language exerts a strong influence over one's perception of reality. The concept of linguistic relativity is most clearly formulated in Sapir's statement repudiating earlier beliefs in a correlation between linguistic morphology and cultural development.

Linguistic relativity
It is quite an illusion to imagine that one adjusts to reality essentially without the use of language and that language is merely an incidental means for solving specific problems of communication and reflection. The fact of the matter is that the "real" world is to a large extent unconsciously built on the language habits of the group. (Sapir 1929, quoted in Mühlhaüsler and Harré 1990: 3)

Linguistic determinism
Such categories as ... gender ... are systematically elaborated in language and are not so much discovered in experience as imposed upon it because of the tyrannical hold that linguistic form has upon our orientation in the world. (1970: 68)

It might seem that while Foucault is talking about the constitutive power of discourse, Sapir is more concerned with the lexical and morphosyntactic levels of language, a distinction that might be mapped onto the Saussurean *parole*, on the one hand, and *langue*, on the other. However, when Sapir insists on the importance of the "language habits of the group," the distinction becomes blurred, and Foucault's conception of the power of discourse becomes strikingly similar to Sapir's hypothesis of the centrality of language to perception.

The strong version of the Sapir-Whorf hypothesis has been disproven by numerous experiments concerning, particularly, color terminology considered from a cross-linguistic perspective. In the 1960s, Brent Berlin and Paul Kay showed that although color distinctions are coded differently in different languages, the terms are not arbitrary, nor is the spectrum divided up at random. The color spectrum is an objective fact with consistent, identifiable, physical properties, and human cognition is so similar, whatever one's culture or native language, that we approach the spectrum in the same way. Berlin and Kay have shown, for example, that all languages have at least two color terms that express the concepts of *black* and *white* (or *dark* and *light*). If the language also possesses a third term, it will be *red*; the fourth and fifth terms will be *yellow* and *green* (in either order); the sixth and seventh terms will be *blue* and then *brown*. After these come terms like *gray, pink, orange*, and *purple* (in any order) (Berlin & Kay 1969). The nonexistence of a particular term in one's native language does not prevent one from distinguishing the main divisions of the color spectrum. Although there will be great disagreement about where to draw demarcation lines between *blue* and *green*, for example, speakers have little difficulty indicating a *typical blue* or a *typical green* and do so with remarkable uniformity.

For many queer theorists, linguistic determinism still appears to be a highly influential concept, though scholars familiar with French structuralist and poststructuralist thought and largely ignorant of American linguistic anthropology would probably credit Foucault with its original formulation. Related to the concept of linguistic determinism is Benjamin Whorf's infamous Eskimo snow hoax. The claim that Eskimo (Inuit? Yupik?) has three, nine, four dozen, fifty, one hundred, two hundred words for snow (figures taken from Geoffrey Pullum's *The Great Eskimo Vocabulary Hoax* 1991: 159–171) is intended to show that the existence of a multitude of lexical items within the same semantic field demonstrates the cultural importance of the field (a point made by Dell Hymes in 1964: 16). Conversely, the absence of discrete lexical items is understood to indicate that the concept itself is lacking from the culture under investigation, as we saw earlier in reference to the term *homosexuality*, which, as Foucault pointed out, was not coined till the late nineteenth century. Sedgwick wittily ironizes this conception of the power of the lexicon: "Same-sex genital relations may have been perfectly common during the period under discussion—but since there was no language about them, *they* must have been completely meaningless" (1990: 52). To be fair, some linguists have also assumed that without its own denotative term, a concept must be lacking from a culture. In his study of homosexuality in Maori (spoken in New Zealand), L. K. Gluckman postulates that "homosexual expression was unknown to the pre-European Maori. Ancient Maori had no word for sodomy" (quoted in Hayes 1978: 205). It should be noted, however, that this stance would be atypical of contemporary linguistics.

Sedgwick's irony points up a conceptual weakness in social constructionism, an analytical perspective widely used within queer theory. If homosexuality (or lesbianism) is constructed within and by its specific cultural context, then the term cannot be applied cross-culturally or transhistorically, for this would be to posit a homosexual "essence" independent of material circumstance. As we have shown in our earlier discussion of Derrida's prioritization of the relationship between signifiers, for postmodern and queer theorists cultural concepts are deeply dependent on the discourse in which they are embedded. Social constructionism, with its extreme sensitivity toward cultural context, risks falling into a similar logical short circuit as linguistic determinism due to its inability to draw parallels between cultures.

It was in order to show up the falsity of any claim that morphological structure reflects the culture of its speakers that Sapir first formulated the axiom of cultural and linguistic relativism. He intended this as a warning against earlier assumptions that "primitive" peoples speak structurally "primitive" languages. With similar concern for cultural specificity, respect for the diversity of different cultures, and fear of perpetuating that assimilationist tactic that perceives only those elements in another culture that correspond to elements in the researchers' own, queer-theorist historians and literary critics are turning away from the platitudinous affirmations of the gay liberationist 1970s and 1980s: "Gays have existed throughout history"; "There are lesbians in every culture and every society." The lesbian philosopher Claudia Card, for example, points out the problems of an essentialist position: "The concept of 'lesbian culture' . . . seems to presuppose that we can extract lesbian culture from many cultures. Is that supposition nonsensical? Arrogant? Culturally imperialistic?" (1995: 16).

In his discussion of gay history, David Halperin asks, "Is there a history of sexuality?," pointing out that "the history of sexuality, in order to qualify as a genuinely historical enterprise, must treat sexuality not as a purely conceptual and therefore timeless category of historical analysis but as an object of historical scrutiny in its own right" (1993: 416). Halperin goes on to describe how sex in classical Athens was seen not as a mutual enterprise but as an action performed by a social superior (adult male citizen) upon a social inferior (boy, woman, slave). Erotic desires and sexual object-choices were determined not by anatomical sex but by "the social articulation of power" (420). Distinctions between homosexuality and heterosexuality had little meaning, Halperin argues, for the distinction between male and female sexual partners was not culturally important compared with that between citizens and noncitizens.

Clearly, one cannot study gay, lesbian, bisexual, or transsexual discourse cross-culturally or transhistorically if the terms are defined in such a narrowly culture-specific way as to be ungeneralizable. It is here that the notion of the performativity of gender, articulated by Judith Butler, demonstrates its utility. With the theory of gender performativity we move away from the social construction of sexuality to the discursive construction of gender. Since this is an important point, it will prove useful to take a little time to elaborate it. Linguists will have no trouble recognizing the term *performativity* as Austinian or in tracing its origin to Austin's pithy little volume, *How to Do Things with Words* (conceived 1939, presented at Harvard 1955, first published 1962). As Butler asserts, gender is performative because it calls itself into existence by virtue of its own felicitous pronunciation. This pronunciation is felicitous, as we recall from Austin's little book, if it is made in the required social circumstances. A marriage is successfully performed by the declaration "I now pronounce you man and wife" if the speaker is a member of the clergy duly vested with the power to perform the marriage ceremony and the couple of whom he pronounces these words consists of one man and one woman, of whom neither is already married to someone else, each is in sound mind, and both are of age. The declaration is performative because it is by the pronunciation of the words that the marriage is performed. "I now pronounce you man and wife" is not a commentary on a marriage; it is the marriage itself.

Austin begins his discussion of performativity by considering the traditional constative, beloved of the logical positivists, and its verifiability or truth value. The classic constative "snow is white" is descriptive, and descriptively true or false. Austin introduces the performative as a new and separate category of utterance that has no truth value, since it does not describe the world but acts upon it—a way of "doing things with words." For Butler the marriage ceremony is not simply one example among many but is central to the "heterosexualization of the social bond" (1993: 224). She cites the midwife's pronouncement "It's a girl" as another, similar performative, one that "initiates the process by which a certain girling is compelled" (232). Performatives work through the power of citation; "it is through the citation of the law that the figure of the judge's *will* is produced . . . ; it is through the invocation of convention that the speech act of the judge [I sentence you to be hanged from the neck until you are dead, for example] derives its binding power" (225). In Austin's terms, it is the very "felicity conditions" that ensure a successful outcome to the performative declaration that give that declaration its authoritative status.

Gender, then, is said to be performative because, as with the classic utterance "It's a girl," statements of gender are never merely descriptive but prescriptive, requiring the referent to act in accordance with gender norms and, moreover, to create the appropriate gender in every culturally readable act she performs, from the way she combs her hair to the way she walks, talks, or smiles. Gender is considered not simply to fit the appropriate "words to the world," in the manner of a classic constative characterized by truth or falsity but, in important ways, to call that situation into being under certain, felicitous conditions, fitting "the world to the words uttered" (to use John Searle's terms, borrowed from Elizabeth Anscombe: Searle 1979).

Butler argues that the utterers of performative speech acts only think they are initiating an action when in fact they are merely reproducing regulatory norms (ventriloquizing the previous speech acts of previous speakers). For Butler, it is discourse that produces the speaker and not the other way around, because the performative will be intelligible only if it "emerges in the context of a chain of binding conventions." Even activities like gender impersonation are reiterative, because the impersonator must invoke the very essence of these "binding conventions" in order for the performance to be comprehensible. Such performances should therefore be analyzed not so much as innovative discourses of resistance but as focused appropriations of existing norms. As Butler reminds us (1993: 228), self-determination does not necessarily result from self-naming, since the names themselves have their own historicity, which precedes our use of them. No movement for the reclamation of pejorative epithets such as *dyke*, *faggot*, and *queer* ever succeeds in eradicating their pejorative force entirely; indeed, it is in part due to their emotive charge that we are moved to reclaim them in the first place. Drag, in its deliberate misappropriation of gender attributes, serves to queer not only the gender performance of the speaker but, by implication, all the other terms in the gender paradigm, according none the innocence of the natural or the merely descriptive. When one of the Sisters of Perpetual Indulgence conducts a marriage ceremony between two gay men, he is accused by members of the Christian Right of "bringing the holy sacrament into disrepute," a criticism that points up the inherent weakness of the institution of heterosexuality.

These premises provide us with the conceptual background to see our way out of the social constructionist dilemma. As linguists, we would not wish to confine our research to the discourse of cultures and historical periods so like our own that the terms used to refer to key concepts such as *sex, gender, homosexuality, lesbianism* cover more or less the same ground as in our own, but neither would we wish to be accused of assimilationism or incomprehension of local specificity. This ethical quandary seems to foredoom any attempt at a multicultural perspective on gay and lesbian speech. However, if we turn the idea around and consider *sex, gender, homosexuality*, and *lesbianism* in our own culture as concepts that are performative rather than constative (or descriptive), then we begin to see that any study of gender or sexuality, of men's, women's, gay, lesbian, transsexual, bisexual, hijra, or 'yan daudu speech, whether in our own dialect or in the ancient Sumerian women's language Eme-sal, will necessarily (1) create its own object of research and (2) need to pay acute attention to the historical moment and specific community involved. The concept of performativity points both to the historicity of key cultural terms and to the possibility of queering the traditional meanings. It also places emphasis on the localized practice of gender (performed at each moment by every culturally readable act), for speakers incorporate local as well as dominant ideals of linguistic gender into their "communities of practice" (Eckert and McConnell-Ginet 1995). Gender as a reiterative performance has access to a variety of scripts, not all of which may be intelligible to the culture at large and some of which may be in conflict with others.

It is time to bring performativity back to its disciplinary origins. Cultural theorists have neglected what we consider to be the most revolutionary point of Austin's little book, a book that begins in characteristic humility: "What I shall have to say here is neither difficult nor contentious; the only merit I should like to claim for it is that of being true, at least in parts." Considering the enormous contemporary interest in speech act theory in general and in performatives in particular, this humble beginning must be waved aside as about as modest as Jonathan Swift's "Modest Proposal." Austin seemingly sets out to resolve an odd little anomaly that gets in the way of the truth value of utterances in ordinary language: The performative acts upon the world; it does not merely describe it and is therefore neither true nor false. During the course of the next 160 pages, performatives slowly move across an imagined graph, from a marginal position occupying only a thin sliver of territory grudgingly given up by the constative to a new superordinate position outside the chart. For, as Austin makes plain, "to state," the classic constative, "is every bit as much to perform an illocutionary act as, say, to warn or to pronounce" (134). With the tumbling of this final barrier, performatives are promoted to the level of the speech act itself, since all utterances turn out to be performative, of which constatives are merely a subsection, on a par with directives or commissives. If even statements rely on regulatory norms in order to be felicitous, the class of performative speech acts encompasses much more than the select set beloved of queer theorists. Applying the same extension to gender performativity, the gendered act that may be recognized as intelligible cannot be reduced to a dominant set of hegemonic heterosexual conventions. The chapters in this volume seek to uncover more localized gender conventions and the contradictions within the norms themselves that, when skillfully manipulated, may provide the locus for change. Lesbian, gay, and other sexually liminal speakers are often obliged to become adept at such manipulation, thereby demonstrating their comprehension of prevailing conventions.

Queerly Phrased

This, then, is the theoretical background that informs the editing of this volume. To see what practical applications it may have, let us turn to the articles themselves. The book is divided into three sections: liminal lexicality, queerspeak, and linguistic gender-bending. Articles in the first section focus on culturally and ideologically significant lexical items denoting alternative sexual identities. The terms discussed come from Renaissance French and English, as well as from present-day

Japanese, Yiddish, Polari, and American Sign Language. They denote lesbian, gay, and bisexual behavior and include both ingroup terms used by the community and outgroup terms used by heterosexuals and other outsiders. Read together as a cohesive unit, the articles in this section demonstrate, not only that changes in the prevailing sexual mores of the wider society have a profound impact on perceptions of marginal groups and are reflected in the terms used to describe them, but also that group members have considerable power to define themselves and that these definitions play an important role in creating the sexual climate of the times. Each time there is a movement toward political correctness in speech, an outlawing of specific lexical items as demeaning to a particular group, there will be a countermove among members of the group seen as marginalized aimed at reclaiming the terms at issue because of their affective force.

Articles in the queerspeak section discuss gay and lesbian discourse strategies, asking what characteristics are specific to the speech of gay men or lesbians and whether these traits must be found exclusively in such speech for them to be classified "gay." Linguistic data have been taken from a wide range of contexts, including gay men's graffiti on bathroom walls, coming-out stories, lesbian comics, the conversation of women friends, and homophobic slang. The discourse in question is not only that of the spoken word but also that of sign language, computer-mediated text, literary language, and media reports. Subjects include the Deaf as well as the hearing, Asian Americans as well as Australians and British participants. The implicit thesis of this section is that, while certain types of speech may indeed be labeled lesbian or gay in character, this classification requires recognition of a complex network of cultural, contextual, and textual factors. An utterance becomes typically lesbian or gay only if the hearer/reader understands that it was the speaker's intent that it should be taken up that way.[6] Queerspeak should thus be considered an essentially intentional phenomenon, sharing some of the echoic or polyphonic structure of irony.

In the section on linguistic gender-bending, the focus moves away from gay and lesbian discourse to the uses made of the linguistic gender system by ambiguously sexed subjects such as transsexuals, hermaphrodites, the hijras of India, and the 'yan daudu of Nigeria, as well as by Parisian gays and Japanese couples. This section is crucial to the argument of the book as a whole. It demonstrates that, while grammatical gender in different languages may enforce a vision of the world as inherently gendered, the linguistic gender system also provides a means to express one's relationship to the concept of gender. Hermaphrodites, for example, compelled in the modern era to declare "their one true sex" despite their ambiguous anatomy, are considered to be monsters whose monstrosity is highlighted by the grammatical conundrum they present. Yet, at the same time, their physical ambiguity, and the impossibility of assigning them without doubt to one gender or the other, causes an intolerable breach in the gender system, a breach that will be filled by new, previously unthinkable terms. The articles in this section emphasize the ludic aspects of linguistic gender, demonstrating that speakers may consciously refer to themselves in terms deemed appropriate for the opposite sex in order to display a lack of allegiance to prevailing norms.

The rhetorical force of this volume progresses thus: It begins in a minute anatomization of particular lexical items denoting marginal sexualities. It shows that these items cannot be taken as given but depend for their meaning on a whole network of terms for human sexuality, including *heterosexuality*, which is thereby revealed as a linguistic construct like *homosexuality*, *monosexuality*, and *bisexuality*. The focus then widens to an examination of language at the discourse level and an insistence on the importance of speaker intent and hearer uptake (the illocutionary and perlocutionary force of any speech act). The final section shows that the concept of gender is itself fluid and insists on speaker agency and conscious use of language, revealing gender to be a process rather than a state. With the publication of *Queerly Phrased*, we hope not only to establish a place in linguistics for queer theory but also to encourage queer theorists to look again at the linguistic roots of many of the tenets of queer theory.

NOTES

1. Legman's association of lesbian speech with upper-class masculinity runs counter to current cultural mappings, as indicated by Livia (1995) in her account of literary representations of lesbian speech and Queen (this volume) in her discussion of comic-book representations of lesbian speech. Livia demonstrates that butch lesbians in fiction adopt the vocal traits of a stereotyped working class, while Queen shows that lesbian characters like Hothead Paisan employ nonstandard phonetic variants stereotypically associated with working-class males.

2. But not, alas, on e-mail. Witness the current debate in the U.S. Congress and in the press concerning which words and images may be sent via the Internet. See, for example, "On-Line Service Blocks Access to Topics Called Pornographic," *New York Times*, December 29, 1995 (A1, col. 1; C4, col. 4), which reports Compuserve's global block on access to more than 200 computer discussion groups and pictures in response to a new legal ruling in Germany (to mention only my tea-break reading while writing this introduction— A. L.). According to the *Times* report, "some of the banned Usenet areas include discussion groups devoted to topics like homosexuality that were not necessarily pornographic or a threat to children" (C4, col. 5–6).

3. Hayes's 1976 article "Gayspeak" shows that some features of gay men's verbal style are similar to those found in prototypical "women's speech," extending the domain of "gay linguistics" from the lexical to the discursive. His article features a lively analysis of a highly camp paragraph from *Data-Boy*, a biweekly tabloid distributed free in gay bars in Los Angeles, in which "the girls" are described as "just running pitter patter up and down the Blvd with their smart umbrellas and raincoats" (260).

4. One is pleased to imagine that this researcher at least must have gained a certain satisfaction from his work. Here is Hayes's annotation to Ponte's "Life in a Parking Lot: An Ethnography of a Homosexual Drive-in": "A heterosexual male sociologist observes the socializing and pickup activities of gay men in a California beach parking lot and adjacent area. Field notes record the nonverbal activity (car maneuvering and parking, eye contact, sexual posturing, cigarette lighting) and verbal exchanges in the parking area and restroom (daytime) and adjacent beach (night) for 5 days in early 1970" (1979: 303).

5. Most noteworthy of these criticisms must surely be that of Monique Wittig, famous for her proclamation that "lesbians are not women" (1992: 32). See also Hoagland and Penelope 1988 for other specifically lesbian critiques of feminism and Penelope 1990 for a lesbian critique of language and linguistics.

6. The importance of hearer recognition of speaker intent has been formulated most neatly and most notably by H. P. Grice in his discussion of meaning$_{NN}$ (nonnatural), a groundbreaking argument which Grice, with a humility akin to Austin's, presents by remarking "all this is very obvious" (1990: 78). Austin's theory of perlocutionary force or speaker uptake (1962) covers similar terrain.

REFERENCES

Austin, John L. (1975). *How to Do Things with Words.* Cambridge, MA: Harvard University Press.

Berlin, Brent, and Paul Kay (1969). *Basic Color Terms: Their Universality and Evolution.* Berkeley, CA: University of California Press.

Butler, Judith (1990). *Gender Trouble: Feminism and the Subversion of Identity.* New York: Routledge.

——— (1993). *Bodies that Matter.* New York: Routledge.

Card, Claudia (1995). *Lesbian Choices.* New York: Columbia University Press.

Chesebro, James W. (1981). *Gayspeak: Gay Male and Lesbian Communication.* New York: Pilgrim Press.

Coates, Jennifer, and Deborah Cameron (eds.) (1989). *Women in Their Speech Communities.* London: Longman.

Cory, Donald Webster, and John P. LeRoy (1963). "A Lexicon of Homosexual Slang." *The Homosexual and His Society: A View from Within.* New York: Citadel Press.

Derrida, Jacques (1976). *Of Grammatology,* trans. Gayatri Spivak. Baltimore, MD: Johns Hopkins University Press.

Doyle, Charles Clay (1982). "Homosexual Slang Again." *American Speech* 57, no. 1: 74–76.

Eckert, Penelope, and Sally McConnell-Ginet (1995). "Communities of Practice: Where Language, Gender, and Power All Live." In Kira Hall and Mary Bucholtz (eds.), *Gender Articulated.* London: Routledge.

Farrel, Ronald A. (1972). "The Argot of the Homosexual Subculture." *Anthropological Linguistics* 14: 97–109.

Foucault, Michel (1972). *The Archeology of Knowledge and the Discourse on Language.* New York: Pantheon.

——— (1990). *The History of Sexuality: An Introduction.* New York: Random House.

Giallombardo, R. (1966). *Society of Women: A Study of a Woman's Prison.* New York: Wiley.

Glastonbury, Marion (1979). "The Best Kept Secret—How Working Class Women Live and What They Know." *Women's Studies International Quarterly* 2, no. 2: 171–183.

Gluckman, L. K. (1974). "Transcultural Consideration of Homosexuality with Special Reference to the New Zealand Maori. *Australian and New Zealand Journal of Psychiatry* 8, no. 2 (June): 121–125.

Grice, H. P. (1990). "Meaning." In A. P. Martinich (ed.), *The Philosophy of Language,* 2d ed. New York: Oxford University Press, pp. 72–78.

Halperin, David (1993). "Is There a History of Sexuality?" In Henry Abelove, Michèle Barale, and David Halperin (eds.), *The Lesbian and Gay Studies Reader.* New York: Routledge, pp. 416–431.

Hayes, Joseph (1976). "Gayspeak." *Quarterly Journal of Speech* 62 (October): 256–266. Reprinted in Chesebro 1981.

——— (1978). "Language and Language Behavior of Lesbian Women and Gay Men: A Selected Bibliography (Part 1)." *Journal of Homosexuality* 4, no. 2 (Winter): 201–212.

——— (1979). "Language and Language Behavior of Lesbian Women and Gay Men: A Selected Bibliography (Part 2)." *Journal of Homosexuality* 4, no. 3 (Spring): 299–309.

Hoagland, Sarah Lucia, and Julia Penelope (1988). *For Lesbians Only*. London: Only-women Press.

Hymes, Dell (1964). *Language in Culture and Society*. New York: Harper & Row.

Jakobson, Roman (1971). "On Linguistic Aspects of Translation." *Selected Writings*, Vol. 2: *Word and Language*. The Hague: Mouton, pp. 260–266.

Leap, William (ed.) (1995). *Beyond the Lavender Lexicon: Authenticity, Imagination, and Appropriation in Lesbian and Gay Languages*. Buffalo, NY: Gordon and Breach.

Legman, Gershon (1941). "The Language of Homosexuality: An American Glossary." In George Henry (ed.), *Sex Variants: A Study of Homosexual Patterns*. New York: Hoeber [Harper & Bros.].

Livia, Anna (1995). "'I Ought to Throw a Buick at You': Fictional Representations of Butch/Femme Speech." In Kira Hall and Mary Bucholtz (eds.), *Gender Articulated*. New York: Routledge.

Lumby, Malcolm (1976). "Code Switching and Sexual Orientation: A Test of Bernstein's Sociolinguistic Theory." *Journal of Homosexuality* 1, no. 4 (Summer): 383–399.

Mühlhäusler, Peter, and Rom Harré (1990). *Pronouns and People: The Linguistic Construction of Social and Personal Identity*. Oxford: Blackwell.

Murray, Stephen O. (1979). "The Art of Gay Insulting." *Anthropological Linguistics* 21: 211–223.

Murray, Stephen O. (1982). "Labels and Labelling: Prototype Semantics of 'Gay Community'." *Working Papers of the Language Behavior Research Laboratory* 51.

Nerf S., P. Asti, and D. Dilldock (eds.) [pseuds] (1949). *The Gay Girl's Guide to the U.S. and the Western World*. N.p. [San Francisco?]

Penelope, Julia [as Stanley, Julia] (1970). "Homosexual Slang." In *American Speech* 45, nos. 1–2: 45–59.

Penelope, Julia (1990). *Speaking Freely*. New York: Pergamon.

———— (1992). *Call Me Lesbian: Lesbian Lives, Lesbian Theory*. Freedom, CA: Crossing Press.

Ponte, M. (1974). "Life in a Parking Lot: An Ethnography of a Homosexual Drive-in." In J. Jacobs (ed.), *Deviance: Field Studies and Self-Disclosure*. Palo Alto, CA: National Press Books.

Pullum, Geoffrey (1991). *The Great Eskimo Vocabulary Hoax and Other Irreverent Essays on the Study of Language*. Chicago: University of Chicago Press.

Ringer, R. Jeffrey (1994). *Queer Words, Queer Images: Communication and the Construction of Homosexuality*. New York: New York University Press.

Rodgers, B. (1972). *The Queens' Vernacular: A Gay Lexicon*. San Francisco: Straight Arrow Books.

Sapir, Edward (1970). "The Status of Linguistics as a Science." In D. G. Mandelbaum (ed.), *Selected Writings of Edward Sapir*. Berkeley: University of California Press.

Searle, John (1969). *Speech Acts: An Essay in the Philosophy of Language*. Cambridge: Cambridge University Press.

———— (1979). *Expression and Meaning: Studies in the Theory of Speech Acts*. Cambridge: Cambridge University Press.

Sedgwick, Eve Kosofsky (1990). *The Epistemology of the Closet*. Berkeley: University of California Press.

Smith, Barbara (1979). "Toward a Black Feminist Criticism." *Women's Studies' International Quarterly* 2, no. 2: 183–194.

Spender, Dale (1980). *Man Made Language*. London: Routledge & Kegan Paul.

Strait and Associates (1964). *The Lavender Lexicon: Dictionary of Gay Words and Phrases*. San Francisco: Strait.

Webbink, Patricia (1981). "Nonverbal Behavior and Lesbian/Gay Orientation." In Clara
    Mayo and Nancy Henley (eds.), *Gender and Non-verbal Behavior*. New York: Springer,
    pp. 253–259.
Wittig, Monique (1992). "The Straight Mind." *The Straight Mind and Other Essays*.
    Boston: Beacon, pp. 21–32.

I

LIMINAL LEXICALITY

1

Two Lavender Issues for Linguists

ARNOLD M. ZWICKY

Some questions about sexual orientation are naturals for professional linguists—for theoretical linguists, phoneticians, sociolinguists, psycholinguists, discourse analysts, and anthropological linguists, for instance. One natural topic (which I look at in the following section) concerns the lexical items that are available for referring to sexual orientations and to people of various orientations. A second topic which I look at in the following section concerns differences in the language and speech of people of different orientations.

As with early studies of language and the sexes, the first approaches to these questions about language and sexuality tended toward the anecdotal and personal. Linguists have been inclined to behave like ordinary speakers, citing usages that happen to have attracted their attention and formulating hypotheses on the basis of unexamined folk theories, rather than using the analytical tools of their trade. This behavior can be observed almost any day on the Internet, for instance in the Usenet newsgroups *sci.lang* (for discussion of issues about language) and *soc.motss* (for discussion of issues about homosexuality) and on the LINGUIST, ADS-L (American Dialect Society), and OUTiL (OUT in Linguistics) mailing lists.

Linguistics does have analytic tools for approaching these questions, but they are only beginning to be used, and it seems tremendously hard to get answers. In this chapter, I survey those tools and suggest reasons why answers have been so hard to come by.

Lexical Issues

What lexical items are available for referring to sexual orientations and to people of various orientations? In modern English, for example, there are an enormous number of lexical choices in the domain of sexual orientation. Virtually every one is publicly contested; not only do speakers differ as to which lexical items are appropriate in which social contexts, but many are aware of these differences and are willing to retail their folk theories about such matters, often with considerable heat. The public forums of lgb life are full of such wrangling.

In fact, early in the history of the OUTiL list, in October 1992 (I started the list in 1991 to bring lgb linguists together both socially and intellectually), a dozen subscribers worked pretty thoroughly over this ground, after one subscriber quoted a problematic passage about the word *queer* in an article by Jeffrey Schmalz, "Gay Politics Goes Mainstream," in the 9 October 1992 issue of the *New York Times Sunday Magazine*: "The word is in vogue now, with some lesbians preferring it to 'gay,' which, despite common usage, technically applies only to men."

Here I provide a small sampling of these contested choices, with brief comments on a few of them. (Most of this inventory will be boringly familiar to lgb readers.)

1. *Homosexual* versus *gay*. Some would insist on one, some on the other, and many see a distinction (behavior vs. identity, identity vs. sensibility, whatever) between the two.
2. *Lesbian* versus *dyke*. Here, too, many see a distinction, of behavior versus identity or in a neutral versus an "in your face" stance or in degree of "butchness." *Dyke* is also a reclaimed epithet, a term of derision that has been to some extent rescued as an expression of pride.
3. Reclaimed epithets. *Dyke* has fairly recently been reclaimed; for some speakers in some contexts and for some purposes, it is no longer an epithet. Attempts to reclaim *faggot* have met with mixed responses; while I was in Washington for the 1994 Lavender Languages conference, the *Washington Blade* (16 September, pp. 18, 22) was reporting (largely negative) responses in San Francisco to the gay Seattle newspaper columnist Dan Savage's use of the word in his columns, in which every letter begins with "Hey Faggot." The issue for all such lexical items is: For which speakers, in which contexts, and for which purposes has the word been reclaimed?
4. *Gay*$_{ADJ}$ versus *gay*$_N$. Many who are comfortable with the former are not with the latter. There are similar, though not necessarily identical, objections to *straight* and *queer* used as nouns; and, in general, to the zero conversion of adjectives to count nouns; and, even more generally, to the choice of predicate adjectives like *Jewish* versus predicate nouns like *Jew*. The usual objection is that the nouns denote an all-embracing, essential property, while the adjectives denote one characteristic among many.[1]
5. *Queer*, especially in its adjectival use, as in the Digital Queers slogan "We're here, we're queer, we have e-mail." Another reclaimed epithet, it is

also another item that many judge to refer to sensibility or culture rather than sexual behavior or orientation.[2] A generational clash is evident here, with many older speakers finding it irredeemable and many younger speakers preferring it to *gay*. In addition, some have seized on *queer* as an umbrella label for the "sexual minorities," taking in not only homosexuals and bisexuals but also transgender and transsexual people, tranvestites, leatherfolk, the BDSM (bondage and discipline, sadism and masochism) community, fetishists, and so on; others protest that this extension bleaches any useful meaning from the term and in addition devalues gay people and their interests by burying them in a loose collection of sexually transgressive types.

6. *Gay* as a superordinate term, including both women and men, versus *gay* as either a subordinate term, taking in men only, or an ambiguous term (like *animal*, with a superordinate sense that includes human beings and a subordinate sense in which it is opposed to *human being*); this conflict contrasts the *gay* of Gay Activists Alliance with the *gay* of The National Organization of Gay and Lesbian Scientists and Technical Professionals.

7. *Gay* as a superordinate term, including both homosexual (in some sense!) and bisexual people in opposition to *straight*, versus *gay* as a subordinate term, in a ternary opposition with *bi(sexual)* and *straight*.

8. *Admitted, avowed, confessed,* or *self-confessed* (all of which are perceived by many to have negative connotations) versus *open* or *out* as modifiers with reference to lgb people who have disclosed their orientation (not to mention *in your face* for those whose behavior or costumes make their orientation more or less constantly visible).

9. *Out* itself as covering disclosure by others (*outing*) in addition to various degrees and kinds of self-disclosure (recognition of one's own orientation, the first same-sex sexual experience, announcing to someone else, announcing publicly). There is often no easy, or single, answer to a question like "Is Sandy out?"

10. Various lexical taxonomies referring to behavior, appearance, or personality: for example, *butch* versus *fem(me)*[3] (applied to both women and men), *stud* versus *queen, bear* versus *twink* versus *clone, dyke* versus *lipstick lesbian*.

11. *Straight-acting, masculine, athletic,* and similar terms used (especially in Men-Seeking-Men personals ads) to pick out Butch types.

Note that the first lexical choices, (1)–(7), make it extremely difficult to refer to lgb folk in any way that most hearers or readers will accept, or even understand as intended. My own use of lgb as a modifier in this article, as in lgb people and lgb folk, makes yet another choice, one that, perhaps predictably, many find either ludicrous or offensive.

What to do? The instinct to try to uncover meanings by simply thinking about what words mean to you or asking other people just to think about what words mean to them is understandable, and from the ethnographic or sociological point of view it can be enormously revealing. Certainly, it is a place for linguists to start. But as a technique for the scientific study of meanings, this approach is hopeless and has long been known to be so. It is especially problematic in domains that speakers are likely to be uneasy about, or where speakers already have explicitly formulated folk theories about the meanings and uses of words, or where the lexical choices are as likely a matter of context and use as of semantics, strictly speaking. All of these problems arise in the domain of sexual orientation.

In any case, we are dealing here with systems of folk (in this case, lgb folk) classification, systems of the sort studied by anthropologists and anthropological linguists. See, for example, the bibliography of early research in this area by Harold Conklin (1972), which covers the domains of kinship, plants, animals, orientation in time and space, anatomy and disease (the domain that is probably most comparable to the domain of sexual orientation), color, and other sensations, or the work of Cecil Brown (Brown 1984, for instance) on the folk classification of plants and animals, or the review by John Lucy (1992: ch. 5) of studies of lexical coding in the domain that has gotten by far the most attention, color.[4]

Admittedly, much of this research has focused on domains that can be seen as intrinsically structured to a considerable degree by human physiology (color) or anatomy (spatial orientation) or by nature itself (plants and animals). But there are domains—kinship and disease are two notable ones—where a significant portion of the structure is surely imposed on the domain or, as we say, "constructed" by particular cultures, and these can serve as models for the analysis of the lexical domain of sexual orientation.

Experimental studies—involving tasks like labeling, sorting, discrimination, similarity judgments, concept learning, and memory—are not usually possible in such domains, because these tasks call attention to the distinctions under study and so are likely to evoke explicit folk theories and produce artifactual behavior. But there are two kinds of research, systematic observation and directed interviewing, that can be pursued.

In systematic observation, large amounts of text are collected naturalistically on occasions where people are quite likely to be discussing the domain under study. In directed interviewing, texts are collected under prompting by an interviewer, who introduces topics that are quite likely to provoke discussion of the domain under study. In either case, the analyst needs to record considerable information about the speakers and the settings they are in. Ideally, the extracted data should be subjected to statistical analysis, though the enormous number of potentially relevant variables may preclude that.

In my opinion, linguists should be approaching the lexical domain of sexual orientation by means of systematic observation and directed interviewing, following the lead of, for instance, Geneva Smitherman (1991) and John Baugh (1991) on (in Baugh's careful phrasing) "terms of self-reference among American slave defendants" and of some of the articles in this volume, such as M. Lynne Murphy on the term *bisexual* and its relatives and Kleinfeld and Warner on signs for lgb people. It is not an easy task, but it is doable.

What makes such investigations difficult is a constellation of problems, which are shared with other situations where social diversification and change are reflected by, and realized in, lexical change:

1. As with slang, we are dealing with shifting, local usages. Rapid change divides the generations, and locally restricted usages produce intergroup misunderstandings.
2. As with ethnic and racial labels, language names, personality type labels, and names for subgroupings in small social groups (e.g., the *jocks* versus *burnouts* distinction in an American high school studied by Penelope Eckert 1989), by their choice of words, people are actively negotiating conceptualizations, as personal and political acts. Even when I was (as I am no longer) by inclination and behavior bisexual, I spoke of myself as gay in most public contexts, preferring to ally myself with those whose orientation was entirely toward members of their own sex rather than risk being seen as some sort of straight person.
3. There are sometimes large gaps in the coverage of the set of lexical items. When there is a large gap, many individuals in the domain do not fall easily into any of the opposed categories. Gaps within domains are not in any way unusual—they can be found even in very large sets of basic color words, for example—but they are especially prominent in domains where the folk ideology of binary opposition holds sway, as it certainly does in the domains of sex and sexuality. A great many people will be located at some considerable distance from the "ideal types" (butch versus fem(me), for instance).
4. There are often fuzzy boundaries between categories, even within a social group that has relatively stable usage. For many lgb speakers of English, the boundaries between gay and bisexual, on the one hand, and between straight and bisexual, on the other, seem to be not at all clear; certainly, they are the focus of considerable discussion in public lgb forums.
5. There are audience and other context effects. Whether I speak of myself, or refer to some other man, as gay or queer or homosexual or a queer or a homosexual or a faggot might depend very much on the person I am talking to and the nature of our interaction.

All of these facts make investigating the lexicon of sexual orientation a hard task, requiring serious fieldwork within lgb subcultures. Not an impossible one, but very far from an armchair, or coffee table, exercise—though I should remind you that the lexicon is in many ways the easiest part of a language to study; the social meanings of other linguistic variables are even harder to get at.

Phonetics is the aspect of language that has by far the best-developed methods for experimentation and for naturalistic data collection, so it is natural for linguists interested in the second issue I'm focusing on in this chapter—differences between people of different orientations—to look to phonetics for answers. I turn now to this second issue.

Differences between Gay and Straight

It is a widespread folk belief that you can pick out nonstraight people, or at least nonstraight men, by their behavior, in particular by their speech. This belief is probably a corollary of another folk belief, that homosexuality is an (inappropriate) identification with the other sex, that lesbians think and act like men and that gay men think and act like women. Since people are in fact quite good at discriminating the sexes on the basis of speech alone, it follows that dykes and faggots should be detectable by a disparity between their appearance and their speech, or in fact merely by contradictory signals in their speech. In actual practice this belief seems to be restricted to men; for straight people, there appears to be no female equivalent to The Voice.

The idea that "you can spot 'em" coexists uneasily with the astonishment many straight people have felt on discovering that some acquaintance, friend, or family member is gay. Such experiences could be taken to mean that only a certain number (perhaps a small number) of homosexual people—the "blatant" ones—are identifiable by their behavior.

Lgb people themselves differ as to how much "gaydar," how much ability to spot gay people in public, they believe themselves to have. My partner and I have notably defective gaydars; mine hardly ever goes off, and his goes off far more often than could conceivably be right. Many lgb people believe that their gaydar works only on members of their own sex (where it might be said to have real value). In any case, it is not clear how much of anyone's gaydar uses cues of speech and language, as opposed to visual cues.

Note that there are two different questions here, the second of which depends on having an answer to the first. First, there is the question of difference: Are gay people—in general, or some distinguishable subgroup of them—different in their speech or language from straight people of their sex? Then, there is the question of discriminability: Assuming that there are at least sometimes significant differences, can people—in general, or some distinguishable subgroup of them—detect these differences and use them to discriminate gay from straight at better than chance?

Difficulties

Even if we restrict ourselves to the question of difference, it is clear that there are serious difficulties in investigating these matters. Here is a brief inventory of five of these.

1. There are difficulties in identifying the groups to be compared and obtaining suitable subjects. Who counts as gay? Who counts as straight? Does using only "out" gay people as subjects bias the results, or are such subjects actually to be preferred? The problems here surround any sort of research of gay/straight differences, of course.
2. There is great variability within both the gay and the straight populations on matters of behavior in general, and speech and language in particular.

Recall that most differences between the sexes involve rather small (though significant) differences between means for two populations that exhibit both enormous overlap and great variability; yet we perceive these differences as large and obvious. Given that people are only rarely surprised to discover someone's sex but are fairly often surprised to discover someone's sexuality, differences between groups of different sexualities (but the same sex) will quite likely be smaller, and variances larger, even than between the sexes.

3. It is tempting to choose as subjects representing a group the most recognizable members of that group; these are either the purest subjects or the most extreme, depending on your point of view. Just as traditional dialectology tended to seek out older rural informants who had lived in one place all their lives, and quantitative studies of social varieties tend to favor young urban informants with a high degree of identification with vernacular (or "street") culture, so we might approach the gay population by selecting the most (stereo) typical informants: diesel dykes and flaming queens. This is relatively easy to do, but it would skew the data enormously, and it cannot give us a picture of variation throughout the speech community.

4. Within these groups we want to investigate, there are different, sometimes overlapping, sometimes vaguely delineated "communities of practice" (Eckert & McConnell-Ginet 1992). It would be foolish to suppose that for the purposes of research on behavior there is a single "gay community" from which subjects can be randomly sampled (or, for that matter, a single "straight community"). The norms of behavior can be expected to differ quite considerably from one community of practice to another, and people can be expected to shift quite considerably as they move from one community of practice to another. Many lgb people clearly shift among a number of speech styles and modes of self-presentation. Which of these do we want to tap, and how? (The problem is familiar from research on vernacular speech and creole continua, of course.)

5. There are problems in selecting the characteristics to be examined. I assume here that lexical items, like *gaydar* (glossed earlier) and *twink* (a cute young thing, male), that are almost entirely used by lgb people will be set aside in investigating these questions. The focus of such investigations will be on more subtle aspects of speech or language:

   - on matters of grammar (especially on phonetic variables, especially prosodic characteristics)
   - on pragmatic strategies (e.g., those considered in the work of William Leap, in this volume, on gay male talk: probing, cooperation and competition, offers and invitations)
   - on discourse organization (e.g., what devices are used to make discourses coherent and how information is conveyed, and shared beliefs reinforced, by indirect means rather than by direct assertions)
   - on rhetoric (via content analysis or studies of audience effects)
   - on other global properties of discourse (e.g., authenticity and risk taking/revelation, again as considered by Leap)

The literature on the characteristics of lgb talk is very heavily focused on rhetorical matters rather than on grammatical ones. In fact, the two collections that would appear from their titles to be most relevant to linguists (Chesebro 1981 and Ringer 1994) are almost entirely taken up with rhetorical and lexical questions. The rhetorical issues are often fascinating, but for the most part they are not questions that linguists, or at least linguists engaged in their usual modes of research, are prepared to answer.

Discourse and pragmatics

Let me briefly traverse the middle ground between grammar and rhetoric. Staying close to home, I inventory some of the discourse-organizing and pragmatic strategies that have been suggested (in one place or another in the literature or by colleagues) as characteristic of gay male talk and writing:

- subjective stance
- irony, sarcasm (distancing, saying and not saying, "not taking seriously")
- resistance, subversiveness
- double/triple/etc. vision, metacommentary
- embeddedness, discursiveness
- open aggression
- seductiveness
- reversal, inversion

Some of these are stereotypically "feminine" (subjective stance, resistance and subversiveness, seductiveness), some stereotypically "masculine" (distancing, open aggression). Some—resistance and subversiveness, multiple vision, reversal—are associated with powerlessness and marginality. Some—subjective stance, distancing—hint at hidden or stigmatized identities.[5] Many are simply the common coin of postmodern discourse—most of the characteristics in the list above are to be found in the writing of Donald Barthelme, for instance, as well as in the writing of Robert Glück—and are scarcely to be directly connected to gender, sexuality, marginality, or stigma.

Again, there is much of interest here, and linguistics can certainly provide indispensable conceptual tools for analysis, but as in poetics (Zwicky 1986) the methods that linguists use in their ordinary practice will not provide an analysis of the phenomena. Subjectivity, reversal, multiple vision, and the rest are realized (in part) in speech and writing, but they are not themselves properties of speech or writing, in the way that having only front vowels and being an instance of the agentless passive construction and containing a cataphoric pronoun and presupposing the truth of some proposition are.

The state of the art

Previous linguistic research on the grammatical characteristics of lgb talk is, in fact, inconclusive. Before the publication of this volume, two studies (both small in scale and modest as to their claims) considered the questions of difference and discriminability using standard linguistic methods.

In Gaudio's (1994) study on men "sounding gay," judges (not selected on the basis of orientation) were asked to evaluate various characteristics (including "gay" versus "straight") of eight male speakers, four gay and four not, but all reading the same passages; the judges turned out to be good at distinguishing gay men from straight men on the basis of their speech.

Gaudio also investigated the pitch properties of the gay speakers' productions compared to those of the straight speakers. These included several properties that had been investigated in the literature comparing women's and men's speech. It turned out to be not at all clear what phonetic properties allowed the judges to discriminate. There were several suggestive differences, but they did not reach statistical significance.

It does seem clear, even from Gaudio's small study, that gay men's speech is not particularly similar to women's speech, at least with respect to those prosodic characteristics that have often been claimed to differentiate women from men.

Moonwomon's study (1985, reprinted in this volume), which paired two lesbian and two straight female speakers, examined only the difference question and not the discriminability question. Though there were suggestive differences again, with the lesbians tending to have lower-pitched voices and a narrower pitch range, these didn't reach statistical significance. As a result, it is not even clear that lesbians are distinguishable in their speech from straight women: lesbian inaudibility as well as invisibility. Moonwomon suggests that whatever differences do exist might be subtle and might lie more in discourse organization than in prosody.

Why are these questions so hard to answer?

I suggest that the source of the difficulties, and also of the apparent differences between women and men, may lie in the ways gender roles are acquired.[6] From the literature on the reasons for differences in women's and men's use of more vernacular and more standard variants (Cameron & Coates 1988; Deuchar 1988, for instance), we can extract at least four important psychosocial mechanisms in the acquisition of a gender identity and its associated norms of behavior:

1. *Modeling*: We use the people around us as models for our own behavior (and so will not acquire norms for which we have no or few models).
2. *Identification*: From the available potential models, we choose people we believe ourselves to be, or wish to be, like.
3. *Avoidance*: We avoid behaviors that are associated with people we do not believe ourselves to be, or do not wish to be, like.
4. *Enforcement*: Other people in our social groups maintain norms by rewarding conformity and punishing nonconformity—sometimes openly and explicitly, but more often covertly and tacitly.

The mechanisms of modeling and enforcement are provided externally, by the social context we grow up in, while the mechanisms of identification and avoidance are, in an important sense, internal. It is these two internal mechanisms that I am suggesting might give rise to a significant difference between the sexes in the way a gay identity develops.

My suggestion is that for many lesbians, what is most important is identification with the community of women—becoming a "woman-identified woman" in several ways—while for many gay men, what is most important is distancing themselves from straight men, that is, from the societally masculine norms. This difference in the primary mechanism—identification for lesbians, avoidance for gay men—would be consonant with the larger societal inclination to take masculine pursuits and priorities as the only really significant ones and so to subvert women's identification with the community of women, which lesbians would then have to work to maintain. In addition, this difference is consonant with the often-observed tendency for masculine roles to be much more rigidly enforced than feminine roles; almost any American man can recall a set of gender shibboleths—men cross their legs this way, carry their books this way, strike a match this way, and so on—that are not only explicitly articulated as part of general boy lore but are also enforced by taunting and jeering. (There is no real parallel in the socialization of girls to their gender roles.) Gay men will consequently be inclined to see their sexuality as a rejection of gender norms.

Insofar as these broad generalizations are valid, it would follow that many lesbians might not in fact be distinguishable in speech from straight women. Admittedly, a sense of difference, distinctness, deviation will play a role in the acquisition of a lesbian identity as it does in the acquisition of a gay male identity; given this sense of difference, we should expect real but subtle differences between lesbians and straight women. It is also true that gay men are reared as men and so can be expected to conform to a great many (though not all) masculine norms; given this shared history, we should expect there to be many similarities between gay and straight men.

We would then have no reason to expect that differences between gay men and straight men would involve the display of specifically feminine behaviors. It would be sufficient for a gay man merely to be different from the masculine norms in any way whatsoever, not necessarily in any way that is associated specifically with women. However, the well-known effect that I like to think of as the "throwing-like-a-girl phenomenon"—anything that does not accord with the specifically, often highly culture-specific, masculine norms is likely to be interpreted as feminine—will lead to the widespread impression that gay men "act like girls."

In any case, a gay man can mark himself as gay, and can easily be detected to be doing so, by observers gay or straight, by diverging in his behavior, speech and language included, in almost any way from straight men. That would make "the gay voice" very hard indeed to detect by phonetic investigation; if there are just five or ten ways in which gay men could deviate from masculine norms, and if different gay men choose different ways to do so, then the mean deviation from any individual norm for the group as a whole could be quite small, and that difference would be hard to detect except with enormous numbers of subjects (not to mention analytic techniques that recognize the possibility of multiple norms). Seeming lack of difference could then coexist quite happily with very easy discriminability.

There are some parallel lessons from speech studies at the segmental level. For a great many, probably nearly all, categorizations of segments in language—as velar versus labial, or voiced versus voiceless, say—perception of the categories uses many cues other than the obvious and primary one. There are cues provided by other segments in the context, and there are cues provided by properties of the relevant segment other than the primary cue.[7] Indeed, there is often considerable individual variation as to which properties are the most reliable cues in speech production, and also considerable individual variation as to which properties are the most salient cues in speech perception. These individual differences do not usually interfere with understanding, since it is sufficient for some cue to be produced and perceived most of the time. And it is usually the case that most speakers agree, in both production and perception, as to which cues are the most important. But careful analysis reveals more individual variation than might at first have been expected.

Similarly, studies of how people convey and detect structural ambiguity in expressions like *big cats and dogs* (*big* + *cats and dogs* versus *big cats* + *and dogs*) and *The hostess greeted the girl with a smile* (*greeted* + *the girl with a smile* versus *greeted the girl* + *with a smile*) indicate that different speakers choose different prosodic properties to mark off constituent boundaries and tend to rely on different properties in deciding where those boundaries are in other people's productions (Lehiste 1973; Lehiste et al. 1976). The end of a constituent can be marked by pausing, by having the pitch fall towards the end, by lengthening the sounds at the end, or by using variants of these final sounds that would be expected at the end of an utterance. Any one of several properties, or a combination of several of them, will do the job. Interestingly, different people have different preferences for boundary signals.

In these phonetic studies we see a multiplicity of concomitants and of possible cues, just as in the displaying and detection of a gay identity. In fact, in the case of gay identity there are surely many more possible cues than there are in the phonetic examples, and there is no reason to expect general (tacit) agreement as to which cues are most salient. When I poll linguists about the phonetic characteristics of The Voice for gay men, I get a very wide range of suggestions: the prosodic characteristics considered by Gaudio (wide pitch range and frequent fluctuation in pitch), frequent use of a specific pitch pattern (high rising-falling), concentration of pitches toward the high end of a speaker's range, large fast falls in pitch at the ends of phrases, breathiness (often associated with "sexiness"), lengthening of fricatives (especially *s* and *z*), affrication of *t* and *d*, even dentalization of alveolar *t/d/s/z/n* (which, thanks to its association with the white working class in some northeastern U.S. cities, is often taken to be a marker of masculinity). It is entirely possible that everyone is right—but for different speakers, in different places, on different occasions.

In any case, the more cues there are, and the less agreement there is as to which cue is the most important, the more difficult it will be for linguists to discover the cues at all. Much larger sample sizes are required than the ones that have so far been used in what are essentially pilot studies, and analysts must be prepared to subclassify their subject populations, in the expectation that some of them are doing very different things from others. When these conditions are satisfied, I expect that gay-straight differences in phonetics will emerge, probably more easily for men than for women, but eventually for both.

Conclusion

Linguists have the tools to investigate the lexicon of the lgb world and to discover phonetic differences between the speech of gay and straight people. Neither task is easy, for reasons I have detailed here, but they are doable, and excellent beginnings have been made on both of these lavender issues.

ACKNOWLEDGMENTS   An earlier version of this article was presented at the Second American University Conference on Lavender Languages and Linguistics, 17 September 1994. I am indebted to the audience there—in particular, Kira Hall, William Leap, Birch Moonwomon, Ruth Morgan, and Keith Walters—for many helpful and thought-provoking comments and to Hall and Moonwomon for detailed comments on a postconference draft of this article.

NOTES

1. See Wierzbicka (1986) for a nuanced discussion of this difference.

2. Writers who try to clarify their intent in using *queer* often find themselves merely entangled. Doty (1993), for instance, has a diffuse introductory chapter explaining that, as he uses the word, *queer* isn't about sex, but then it isn't entirely not about sex, either. Then, still not fully satisfied, he explores the question some more at the beginning of his first chapter.

3. As applied to women, the two spellings have a history and cultural setting that would not be obvious from inspecting dictionaries of slang, sexual slang in particular, which all seem to treat *fem* and *femme* as mere variants. Yet Kennedy and Davis (1992: 77) observe in their first footnote about lesbian life in the 1940s and 1950s: "We are using the spelling *fem* rather than *femme* on the advice of our narrators. They feel that *fem* is a more American spelling, and that *femme* has an academic connotation with which they are uncomfortable." *Femme*, however, has become the spelling of choice; this is the spelling Nestle uses in the subtitle of her 1992 book and throughout her own contributions to the volume.

4. Color, of course, with its (relatively) easily measurable dimensions, is not a very good model for other sorts of folk classifications.

5. Here is a typical observation, by Morris Dickstein, writing in a *New York Times Book Review* (23 July 1995, p. 6) review of Edmund White's *Skinned Alive*: "Before the 1970's, when direct professions of homosexuality were taboo, writers from Oscar Wilde to Cocteau to Genet made their mark with works that were often theatrical, oblique, florid and artificial. The strategies of concealment many gay people used in their lives were turned into richly layered artistic strategies by gifted writers, choreographers, directors and set designers. For the writers, wit and paradox became more important than sincerity, since sincerity meant self-acceptance (which could be difficult) and self-exposure (which could be dangerous); style, baroque fantasy and sensuous detail were disguises that suited them far better than verisimilitude or realism."

6. Like the studies I have cited, these remarks concern modern European and North American cultures. I make no claims here about sexuality and gender cross-culturally.

7. This particular topic seems to fall uncomfortably in the area between phonetics and psycholinguistics, which means that introductory textbooks tend not to discuss it. Among the psycholinguistics texts, at least two—Clark & Clark (1977: ch. 5) and Garman (1990: sec. 4.2), with a chart of speech cues (192–193) based on Borden & Harris (1980: 184–186)—do, however.

REFERENCES

Baugh, John (1991). "The Politicization of Changing Terms of Self-Reference among American Slave Descendants." *American Speech* 66, no. 2: 133–146.

Borden, Gloria Jo, and Katherine S. Harris (1980). *Speech Science Primer: Physiology, Acoustics, and Perception of Speech.* Baltimore: Williams and Wilkins.

Brown, Cecil H. (1984). *Language and Living Things: Uniformities in Folk Classification and Naming.* New Brunswick, NJ: Rutgers University Press.

Cameron, Deborah, and Jennifer Coates (1988). "Some Problems in the Sociolinguistic Examination of Sex Differences." In Jennifer Coates and Deborah Cameron (eds.), *Women in Their Speech Communities.* London: Longman, pp. 13–26.

Chesebro, James (ed.) (1981). *Gayspeak: Gay Male and Lesbian Communication.* New York: Pilgrim Press.

Clark, Herbert H., and Eve V. Clark (1977). *Psychology and Language.* New York: Harcourt Brace Jovanovich.

Conklin, Harold C. (1972). *Folk Classification: A Topically Arranged Bibliography of Contemporary and Background References through 1971.* New Haven, CT: Yale University Department of Anthropology.

Deuchar, Margaret (1988). "A Pragmatic Account of Women's Use of Standard Speech." In Jennifer Coates and Deborah Cameron (eds.), *Women in Their Speech Communities.* London: Longman, pp. 27–32.

Doty, Alexander (1993). *Making Things Perfectly Queer: Interpreting Mass Culture.* Minneapolis: University of Minnesota Press.

Eckert, Penelope (1989). *Jocks and Burnouts.* New York: Teachers College Press.

Eckert, Penelope, and Sally McConnell-Ginet (1992). "Communities of Practice: Where Language, Gender, and Power All Live." In Kira Hall, Mary Bucholtz, and Birch Moonwomon (eds.), *Locating Power: Proceedings of the Second Berkeley Women and Language Conference.* Berkeley, CA: Berkeley Women and Language Group.

Garman, Michael (1990). *Psycholinguistics.* Cambridge: Cambridge University Press.

Gaudio, Rudolf P. (1994). "Sounding Gay: Pitch Properties in the Speech of Gay and Straight Men." *American Speech* 69, no. 1: 30–57.

Kennedy, Elizabeth Lapovsky, and Madeline Davis (1992). "'They Was No One to Mess With': The Construction of the Butch Role in the Lesbian Communities of the 1940s and 1950s." In Joan Nestle (ed.), *The Persistent Desire: A Femme-Butch Reader.* Boston: Alyson, pp. 62–79.

Kleinfeld, Mala S., and Noni Warner (this volume). "Lexical Variation in the Deaf Community."

Leap, William L. (this volume). "Performative Effect in Three Gay English Texts."

Lehiste, Ilse (1973). "Phonetic Disambiguation of Syntactic Ambiguity." *Glossa* 7, no. 2: 107–122.

Lehiste, Ilse, Joseph P. Olive, and Lynn A. Streeter (1976). "Role of Duration in Disambiguating Syntactically Ambiguous Sentences." *JASA* 60, no. 5: 1199–1202.

Lucy, John A. (1992). *Language Diversity and Thought: A Reformulation of the Linguistic Relativity Hypothesis.* Cambridge: Cambridge University Press.

Moonwomon, Birch (1985). "Toward the Study of Lesbian Speech." In Sue Bremner, Noelle Caskey, and Birch Moonwomon (eds.), *Proceedings of the First Berkeley Women and Language Conference*. Berkeley, CA: Berkeley Women and Language Group, pp. 96–107 (reprinted in this volume).

Murphy, M. Lynne (this volume). "The Elusive Bisexual: Social Categorization and Lexico-Semantic Change."

Nestle, Joan (ed.) (1992). "The Persistent Desire: A Femme-Butch reader." Boston: Alyson.

Ringer, R. Jeffrey (ed.) (1994). *Queer Words, Queer Images: Communication and the Construction of Homosexuality*. New York: New York University Press.

Smitherman, Geneva (1991). "What Is Africa to Me?: Language, Ideology, and *African American*. *American Speech* 66, no. 2: 115–132.

Wierzbicka, Anna (1988). "What's in a Noun? (or: How Do Nouns Differ in Meaning from Adjectives?)." In Anna Wierzbicka (ed.), *The Semantics of Grammar*. Amsterdam: John Benjamins, pp. 463–497.

Zwicky, Arnold M. (1986). "Linguistics and the Study of Folk Poetry." In Peter Bjarkman and Victor Raskin (eds.), *The Real-World Linguist: Linguistic Applications in the 1980s*. Norwood, NJ: Ablex, pp. 57–73.

2

$\mathcal{T}$he Elusive Bisexual

Social Categorization and
Lexico-Semantic Change

M. LYNNE MURPHY

This chapter focuses on some of the "lavender lexical issues" raised by Arnold Zwicky in Chapter 1. In particular, it examines the inclusiveness and the exclusiveness of sexual minority labels—asking to whom speakers mean to refer when they use labels like *gay* and *queer* and whom hearers understand to be referred to when these words are used. Special attention is paid to the inclusion or exclusion of those labeled *bisexual* in the extensions of other labels, to see whether the emergence of bisexual activism since the 1970s has had an effect on lexical innovation and semantic change in sexual category labels. Certainly, the emergence of bisexual identity has encouraged much lexical innovation (e.g., *bi, biphobia, monosexual, gay-identified bisexual, byke*—Geller 1990; Hutchins and Kaahumanu 1991). Furthermore, as a bisexual identity (or identities) has developed and been asserted, so have debates about whether categories such as *gay, lesbian, dyke,* and *queer* include people who identify as bisexual, as well about who counts as *bisexual.*

The realm of interest here is limited to the use of sexual category labels within and among sexual minority communities, so my discussion focuses on how people who do not consider themselves part of the social/sexual mainstream use and, in the process, effect change in these words. The disparity in the use of such labels within and outside (or *at*) sexual minority communities justifies this narrow focus, although a study of what words like *gay* and *bisexual* mean to people who identify as neither might yield some interesting data for comparison. The analysis, later in this chapter, of a cursory survey of sexual orientation label-use/attitudes supports this intuition. For instance, respondents who do not identify as sexual minority members say they use the word *lesbian* to refer to women who have had sexual relations with or desires toward only women, whereas people who identified as gay, lesbian, or bisexual were about five times as likely to claim that their use of the word includes reference to women whose relations and desires have been predominantly (but not exclusively) same-sex oriented. Furthermore, the connotations of words such as *queer* and *dyke* (as well as *gay* and *lesbian*) differ according to the users of the words and their intentions, so limiting the set of users makes this project more coherent and manageable.

The question this paper addresses is not just "What do sexual category labels mean?" but "What *can* sexual category labels mean?"—that is, what social or cognitive forces limit the senses of these labels? The approach is derived from work in social psychology on cognitive constraints on social categorization, discrimination, and stereotyping. This chapter tests whether the constraints on social categorization have linguistic correlates. Since social categorization is frequently achieved through labeling, one would expect to find such correlates. However, most research in this area has been based on ethnic, racial, or sex categorization, raising doubt about the validity of its conclusions across sources of social labeling. Considering that in the last few decades minority sexual orientation identities have developed into quasi-ethnic identities (at least in the United States, but to some degree in other first-world, Anglophonic countries) (Altman 1982; Epstein 1987), one might expect that sexual orientation labels are subject to the same sorts of semantic constraints as, say, the pseudoracial categories represented by labels like *black*, *Asian*, and *Hispanic*. This chapter shows that although ethnic and sexual categorization have much in common, use of sexual category labels by sexual minority members contradicts some predictions derived from the social psychology literature, especially where bisexuality is concerned.

Notes on Terminology

Writing about social category labels provides particular problems, since the writer cannot hide from the fact that all labels are polysemous, fraught with connotation, and frequently used misleadingly. So, a few words on the vocabulary in this chapter are necessary.

Labels such as *gay*, *black*, or *disabled* are termed *social category labels*. For expediency, labels based on sexual/affectional orientation, preference, identity, or activity are here termed *sexual category labels*, although the term *sexual* is certainly not an unloaded word.

Italics indicate that a token of a word is intended to refer to the word itself. Single quotation marks indicate reference to the category that a word denotes. When labels such as *bisexual* or *gay* are used without italics, they refer to people who self-identify by those labels. When referring to behaviors or identities that are not self-imposed or not associated with a particular lexical item, the terms *same-sex*, *other-sex*, and *either-sex* are used. The last is perhaps not the best description of bisexual orientation, which may be better described as *sex-immaterial* (Ross and

Paul 1992). However, since these terms are being used here to reflect identities and behavior as well as orientations, *either-sex* is used. The other terms, *same-sex* or *other-sex*, can be exclusive or not—that is, people whose orientation is either-sex are included in both the same-sex and the other-sex category. The terms *exclusively-same-sex* and *exclusively-other-sex*, on the other hand, exclude either-sex orientations.

Sexual minority is used here to encompass all orientation and identity categories that include same-sex orientation. Again, the words *sexual* and *minority* are problematic, and some other-sex-oriented groups could count as sexual minorities, but restrictions of space and legibility encourage use of this term.

Sexual Categories, Ethnicity, and Cognition: Some Hypotheses

It has been politically (and perhaps cognitively) expedient for sexual minority members to use the model of ethnicity in forming identities, analyzing their cultures, and arguing for civil rights. Associating sexual and ethnic minority status provides sexual minorities with models for a civil rights advocacy and for the formation of sexual minority cultures with particular customs, aesthetics, and values. Since the concept of "ethnicity" is a rather problematic one, the position that sexual minority groups constitute ethnicities can be supported by a number of seemingly contradictory arguments, and even within individuals these identities may be based upon inconsistent beliefs (Epstein 1987).

A naïve equation of sexual orientation with ethnicity could be based on an essentialist understanding of sexual orientation: that sexual object-choice orientation is innate and sexual identity derives from sexual object-choice. Thus, one could be born into such an identity just as one is born into a Zulu or Thai ethnicity. However, this folk notion of identity and ethnicity is problematic from both sides. First, while sexual object-choice may or may not be determined or influenced by physiological factors, object-choice does not determine identity. While throughout history (and, so far as we can tell, prehistory), same-sex sex has taken place, only recently has sexual object-choice been so influential in the development of so many peoples' identities (Katz 1995). At the same time, it is grossly simplistic and incorrect to claim that "race" or "ethnicity" is the product of nature and not socially constructed. While most people cannot choose to adopt a different race or ethnicity from their parents', the racial identities that people adopt are not natural ones but socially constructed categories with intricate and sometimes inescapable histories. The categories are based on certain prototypes, with socioeconomic forces constraining their application so that, for example, people of mixed African/ European heritage belong to differently defined social groups in the United States, Brazil, and South Africa.

While the constructionist position, claiming that sexual identity is developed socially, is also consistent both with the politically expedient ethnicity model and with recent theoretical work on sexual identity (especially "Queer Theory"), the essentialist position seems to inform most nonacademic thought and rhetoric on the matter. As Stephen Epstein notes: "While constructionist theorists have been preaching the gospel that the hetero/homosexual distinction is a social fiction, gays and lesbians, in everyday life and in political action, have been busy hardening the categories. Theory, it seems, has not been informing practice" (1987: 12). The hardening of these categories began after the initial organization of the post-Stonewall movement. In the early 1970s, the movement was focused more on abolishing categorization of people into "pathological" homosexual/heterosexual categories than on reifying those categories. With such slogans as "Any woman can be a lesbian" and "Feminism is the theory, lesbianism is the practice," lesbian feminists, in particular, argued that sexual orientation is mutable. However, by the mid- to late 1970s, a more essentialist view was on its way in.

It seems no coincidence that the firming of gay and lesbian identities as essential conditions coincided with the birth of the bisexual movement, since the bisexual is "a walking example of constructionism" (Udis-Kessler 1990: 59). With sexual identity categories seen as fixed and narrower than previously held, less room was available in them for people whose self-concepts included, but were not limited to, same-sex orientation. It is a chicken-and-egg question, however, whether the increased essentialism in gay and lesbian identity politics was the cause or the effect of an increase in self-categorizations as bisexual. Although the bisexual political movement chronologically followed the rise in essentialism, a trend of (mostly apolitical) bisexual identification occurred in the early 1970s, which *Newsweek* (24 May 1974) termed "Bisexual Chic." It is possible that the rise in gay and lesbian essentialism was in part inspired by the desire to dissociate the gay and lesbian political identities from "sexual tourists."

So, how does bisexuality fit into the ethnic model of sexual identity? In comparing sexual categorization to race-based ethnic categorization, one might assume that the categories 'homosexual' and 'heterosexual' are comparable to 'black' and 'white', since they are the most diametrically opposed and salient of the categories. Following this analogy, then, is the 'bisexual' category a mixture of the two, like 'mulatto', or a separate category altogether, on par with 'Asian' or 'Native American'? Both analogies are found in bisexual literature (Shuster 1991 and Murphy 1992, respectively). However, the default situation is to view bisexuals as having 'mixed' sexuality. This is reflected in epithets (*AC/DC*, *switch-hitter*, *fence-sitter*) and assumed in most scalar views of sexuality.

The hypotheses discussed here come from a particular orientation of social psychology, sometimes called the Cognitive Orientation (Ashmore and Del Boca 1981). This body of research assumes that social categorization and stereotypes are not special classes of concepts but instead are constrained by the same cognitive structures and processes as other types of concepts. This approach to the investigation of social categories is well suited to a linguistic investigation of the names of these categories, since the necessity of integrating theories of word meaning and conceptual structure is, if not always successfully achieved, acknowledged by most lexical semanticists and cognitive psychologists. Furthermore, this approach is as objective as possible for such an endeavor, in that it involves no assumptions that categorization itself is an intrinsically bad process.

Within this tradition, many generalizations about categorization processes have been offered. These generalizations constitute hypothesized constraints on category development, which in turn propose hypotheses about constraints on the meanings and uses of social category labels. Of these, I concentrate on five, listed here with illustrations from racial classification.

I   The existence of a social category depends on the existence of another category to compare it to (Tajfel and Turner 1979).

For example, 'people of color' is cohesive only to the extent that it contrasts with 'white'.

II   There is a tendency to preserve the status quo in categorization systems, even if there is evidence that the system is inadequate (Tajfel and Forgas 1981).

For example, many Americans, due to the popularization of a particular pseudoracial categorization system (Caucasoid, Mongoloid, Negroid), believe that there are three races even if they know of people who are not easily placed in those categories (e.g., native Australians, South American Indians).

III   Categorization heightens the perception of differences between categories and minimizes the perception of differences within categories (Campbell 1956; Taylor 1981).

Thus, categorization leads to stereotyping; for example, outgroup members generalize that all Asian people are hard-working, all African people are good dancers, and so on.

IV   The greater the difference in social value between categories, "the more likely it is that errors of assignment into a negatively valued category will be in the direction of overinclusion, and errors of assignment into a positively valued category will be in the direction of overexclusion" (Tajfel and Forgas 1981: 121).

Thus, people of mixed race tend to be classified with the more negatively valued group, as in the United States, where people with any African ancestry at all are categorized as black (Davis 1991).

V   In striving for positive social identity, people seek to belong to groups that compare favorably to other groups; if, for "objective" reasons (e.g., appearance, descent) they must be categorized with a particular group, then they will change their interpretations of the group's attributes and/or attempt to force societal change to improve their situation (Tajfel 1978); thus, people have a general stereotype of their own group as good and deserving and of outgroups as bad and undeserving (Brewer 1979).

While some people try to "pass" as part of a more positively valued category, people almost never try to pass as part of a group that they consider a step down from their own. If people are not free to recategorize themselves (or if the cost of joining another category is too great), they will find virtue in being part of a negatively valued group. For example, people from a negatively valued group may feel that the traditions of their group are more meaningful or their experience more valid than those of the outgroup.

Since lexical items are used to represent and maintain categories, these hypotheses about categorization suggest the following hypotheses concerning the lexical items that are used to represent social categories.

I'   If a category name is introduced, an opposite will also be introduced.

II' New category names that are incompatible with an accepted categorization system either will not gain acceptance (and thus become obsolete) or will undergo semantic change in order to be compatible with the existing system.

III' Category names will be most closely associated with members of the category that are least like members of a relevant contrast category.

IV' Names for positively valued groups will be associated with more exclusive senses than are names for negatively valued groups.

V'   People who identify within a category (and thus are likely to value that category positively in comparison to others) will use narrower senses of that category's name than will outgroup members.

All of the categorization hypotheses and some of the linguistic correlates have been supported by experimental investigations. However, past research investigated visible characteristics, like sex and race, rather than categories that have behavioral or intrapsychic cues, such as sexual orientation or intellectual ability. So, in investigating Hypotheses I'–V', two issues are at stake. The first is whether the psychological hypotheses are supported by linguistic evidence. The second is whether the hypotheses are supported by evidence from a type of categorization with invisible membership criteria.

Sexual Category Labeling: Testing the Hypotheses

The hypotheses make predictions about what will happen if a new social category is added to the culture's repertoire: The new category will be constrained in part by the old categories (since there is resistance to abandoning old categorizing systems), and the system will tend toward the starkest possible contrasts. Two recent changes in sexual categorization provide opportunity to investigate these hypotheses. First, a bisexual political and cultural identity movement has made it more relevant to differentiate people who identify as exclusively-same-sex oriented from those who identify as either-sex oriented. Second, the word *queer* has been reclaimed for ingroup reference, with strong claims by many parties about why the word has been adopted and what it means. Frequent among the claims about *queer* is that it refers to members of all sexual minorities, with varying interpretations of what constitutes a sexual minority. As is shown later, the hypotheses' predictions are mostly borne out, *except* for use of the words for people who identify as bisexual. The nature and possible causes of these unexpected findings are considered later in the chapter. In short, the ambiguity of the category 'bisexual' with reference to the ethnicity model of sexual orientation hinders parallel treatment of sexual orientation and ethnicity in the cognitive social psychology model.

Before looking at the linguistic evidence, let us look briefly at the role of bisexual identity politics in the development and maintenance of sexual orientation categories. The hypothesis that bisexual identity politics has affected sexual category vocabulary is based on two assumptions. First, I assume that bisexual identity politics challenges many popular understandings of sexual identity and related strategies for self-conceptualization. Particularly, acknowledging bisexuality challenges the notions that same-sex orientation is biologically determined and immutable. The second assumption is that bisexual identity politics have had an impact on gay and lesbian identity politics in a way that has stimulated lexico-semantic change in sexual category labels. This assumption is upheld by the fact that many organizations of and for sexual minority members have changed their names in recent years to include the word *bisexual*, while new organizations often include *bisexual* in their names or missions, and even more have debated the possibility of including *bisexual* in their names. However, inclusion of the word *bisexual* tends to occur in local and new organizations, not in long-standing national and international organizations, such as the National Gay and Lesbian Task Force or the International Lesbian and Gay Association, although these organizations do address bisexuality in their policies and actions.[1] This is attributable not only to the fact that such organizations have more invested in their names but also to the nature of the bisexual movement, which has tended to be locally organized, without much national or international structure. (For histories of the bi movement, see Weise 1992 and Hutchins and Kaahumanu 1990.)

Political activism by bisexual organizations is often directed within the sexual minority communities. While on the one hand bisexual activists argue that "the oppression of bisexuals is lesbian and gay oppression [by the mainstream culture]" (Shuster 1991: 269), they also argue that the sexual minority community's politics must address the fact that bisexuals have particular needs and suffer particular prejudices. (The term *biphobia* reflects this position.) These two perspectives assert both similarity with and difference from gay and lesbian identities. While these two assertions need not be contradictory, in that they do not claim absolute identity or difference, in practice they often seem that way.

Caveats on resources

For practical reasons, electronic media were extensively used as sources of data for this research. The use of such sources necessitates several caveats. In order to investigate hypothesized patterns of word use, I administered a questionnaire on perceptions of word use to several sexual minority e-mail lists, including GayNet, the Gay, Lesbian, and Bisexual People of Color list (GLBPOC), and the Bisexual

Activists list (BiAct-L). The preamble to the survey included a request that the recipient pass the survey on to interested parties, so long as queer theory or linguistics lists were not contacted. I received ninety-eight usable surveys.

The questionnaire was divided into two parts. The first section was intended to gauge perceptions of the denotations and connotations of *gay, lesbian, bisexual, homosexual,* and *queer.* The first five questions were of the form: "When I use the word X, I intend to include . . . ," followed by a number of options such as "only women," "people whose sexual relations/desires have been ONLY same-sex," "people whose HISTORY OF SEXUAL RELATIONS includes ANY same-sex experience." The question for *queer* included options for including transsexuals, transvestites, people who enjoy sadomasochism and/or bondage and dominance activities, and fetishists, regardless of their sexual (object) orientation. Respondents were asked to respond to every option, using a scale of always (4), usually (3), sometimes (2), occasionally (1), and never (0). Responses were tabulated by sexual identity group, and average answers for each group were calculated. The next three questions were similar to the earlier ones for *queer, bisexual,* and *gay,* except that these three asked "When OTHERS use the word X, I assume they are including . . . ." The last three questions asked the respondent to choose which items from a list of sexual identity labels (including the ones just given, plus *bi, dyke, heterosexual,* and *straight*) were (a) offensive to their referents, (b) self-labels for the respondent, and (c) words the respondent would not use to label others. The second section asked for basic demographic data, recent sexual history, membership in sexual minority organizations, and the respondents' degree of openness about their sexual identities.

The results of this questionnaire are of limited use for the following reasons. First, since respondents were self-selected, the results cannot be assumed to be broadly representative. (Self-selection of respondents is a nearly necessary feature of research involving sexual minorities, however.) Second, the responses are even less representative of the public at large because the questionnaire was administered by computer. Thus, many respondents were associated with universities, and almost half (45) have graduate degrees. E-mail administration of the survey may also account for the fact that most respondents were male and between twenty-two and forty years of age. Furthermore, since most respondents received the questionnaire through a sexual minority mailing list, they may be more informed about or concerned with sexual identity politics than the average same-sex oriented person. Third, due to some oversights in writing the survey, some questions led to weaker conclusions than might otherwise be available. The worst oversight was not asking respondents what sexual identity label they *most* identify with, in addition to asking them to choose "as many as apply" from a list of labels for themselves. It was thus not possible to divide the surveys into groups of strictly self-identified bisexual men, bisexual women, gay men, lesbians, and others. Responses were placed in one of the bisexual categories only if: (a) the respondent selected the label *bisexual* and/or *bi* but not *gay* or *lesbian,* or (b) the respondent selected *bisexual* and/or *bi* in addition to *gay* and/or *lesbian and* claimed either to belong to a bisexual-only organization or to have had other-sex-oriented desires or sexual activity in the last twelve months. With these criteria, the surveys were divided into twenty-two bisexual male, ten bisexual female, forty gay male, thirteen lesbian, and thirteen "other"—mostly straight-identified, but including three who chose not to label themselves and one who did not answer the question.[2]

The questionnaire results reflect perceptions of word use and meaning, not word use itself. The intention was to gauge (a) whether people in different sexual identity categories perceive themselves as using these words in a particular way, (b) whether they feel their use of the words are in conflict with others', and (c) whether these attitudes coincide with actual usage. Although the results cannot be claimed to be representative, they do aid in discovering some trends and bringing evidence against some of the hypotheses to be tested here.

The other electronic source of information here is a corpus drawn from the GayNet Digest e-mail list in May 1993. The GayNet Digest is intended as a forum for discussing gay-, lesbian-, and bisexual-relevant news; however, some people use it for social networking as well. The corpus includes signed and anonymous informal electronic communication, articles from the gay and the mainstream press, press releases, and radio transcripts. Examples from GayNet Digest are marked "GN."[3]

Dichotomies: Us versus Them

Hypothesis I' predicts that social category labels will coincide with (or spur introduction of) labels for contrasting categories. Sexual category labels support this hypothesis. Furthermore, the contrasts tend to be dichotomized, giving every label a unique antonym.

Homosexual and *heterosexual* seem to have entered the English language at the same time, through the 1892 translation of Krafft-Ebing's *Psychopathia Sexualis*. However, *heterosexual* is not as old as *homosexual* in Hungarian and German, into which *homosexual* was introduced two decades earlier. Nevertheless, *homosexual* has always had some antonym, if not the present one, including *normalsexual* (Dynes 1985). Interestingly, *homosexual* was only one of a number of synonymous words introduced in the latter half of the nineteenth century, and one of the reasons that Wayne Dynes (1985) cites for its success was that, unlike *Uranian* and *die konträre Sexualempfindung*, contrasting items were easily morphologically derived for it.

Today, *straight* is the catch-all antonym for all of the colloquial same-sex orientation and identity labels (*gay, lesbian, dyke, queer*). The use of *straight* as an antonym for this range of labels may have begun with its contrast to *queer* in counterfeiting slang (Dynes 1985) and/or through the contrast of *gay* ('promiscuous, prostituting') and *straight* ('chaste, virtuous, respectable') (Oxford English Dictionary [OED], v. XVI: 818). *Straight* is available as a contrast category for all of these labels since it is and was highly polysemous. The particular sense 'other-sex oriented' is relatively recent (the first OED citation is from 1941), but its long-held senses associated with virtue and normality allow it to contrast in particular with *queer*, even when *queer* denotes people who are other-sex oriented (e.g., transvestites or S/M practitioners).

Hypothesis I' does not preclude the existence of more than two contrasting labels in a semantic field; however, there is a definite tendency to polarize (Hypothesis III') and dichotomize the field. In racial labeling in the United States, any middle ground between *black* and *white* is not usually lexically differentiated (although lexical items are available). Similarly, an item like *disabled* is contrasted with *able-bodied*; *able-bodied* is not the opposite of *partially abled*. (This phenomenon is not in the least restricted to social categorizing. See Horn 1989.) So, although *bisexual* is not ruled out from the field containing *homosexual* and *heterosexual* (or *gay* and *straight*), as a nonpolar label, it is less salient. For those who identify using this label, this fact is bound to cause some disquiet. In identifying with a label, one develops an identity based on contrast with another group, but to contrast oneself with more than one group simultaneously is not easy, since different criteria for comparison usually exist. So, it is natural that people who identify with a nonpolar label contrast their category primarily with only one other category. This may be seen in the seemingly Janus-like political claims of activists in bisexual politics. Sometimes, ingroup members contrast their group with one extreme ("[like gays and lesbians,] we're not straight"), sometimes to the other ("we're not gays or lesbians").

But within bisexual political rhetoric, the burden of double comparison is sometimes abandoned through use of the label *monosexual,* which denotes both exclusively-same-sex and exclusively-other-sex orientation. Thus the criterion for differentiation of the groups is not sexual-object orientation but the *rigidity* of that orientation. Although the word has a history dating to at least 1922 (Montgomery 1993),[4] it has not garnered widespread use outside the bisexual activist community and occasional psychological texts. In fact, *monosexual* may not have developed in any steady manner, since the word seems to be re-coined repeatedly. Thus, *monosexual* exists solely for the contrastive function described in Hypothesis I', since no one uses the label as primary self-reference.

In summary, the evidence from sexual category labeling supports Hypothesis I': Lexical items for a social category coexist with items with contrasting denotations. Furthermore, it seems to support a stronger hypothesis: Ingroup members will have lexical items that refer to outgroup members in general. In other words, an "us versus them" mentality is lexicalized.

Incompatibility with the extant system: The moribund monosexual

Hypothesis II' states that new category names that are incompatible with an accepted categorization system will either become obsolete or undergo semantic change in order to be compatible with the extant system. *Monosexual* may demonstrate the obsolescence option.

Incompatibility can be analyzed in terms of semantic fields of the sort described by Adrienne Lehrer (1974). Such diagrams delineate contrast relations horizontally and hyponymy relations vertically. A field for sexual category labels includes (1).[5]

(1)

(people)			
queer, LesBiGay			straight heterosexual
homosexual, gay$_1$		bisexual	
gay$_2$	lesbian		

The field itself is quite mutable, within its own limits. For example, it would not be a major burden on the field to add a word (*byke*) that denotes only women with either-sex orientation. We could also change the field so that another sense of *queer* includes some heterosexuals (so that one could be *heterosexual* but not *straight*). Such expansions of the field have, in fact, occurred, and are shown in (2). The changes in

(2)

(people)				
queer$_1$			straight$_1$	
queer$_2$, LesBiGay			heterosexual straight$_2$	
homosexual, gay$_1$		bisexual		
gay$_2$	lesbian		byke	

(2) are possible because they do not interfere with the extant senses in (1). However, to introduce a word, for example, that is intended to denote exclusively-same-sex-oriented women and other-sex-oriented people would require abandonment of this field, since its criteria for contrast would no longer be valid. In other words, such a category could not supersede *lesbian* and *straight* because other categories intervene in this system. Hypothesis II′ predicts the lexical failure of such a category: The extant field will be maintained, and words that do not fit into it will not be used.

Although I may be greatly exaggerating the death of *monosexual* (a word in my own active vocabulary), the resistance to its usage among the people it denotes indicates that it will remain bisexual jargon. Assuming that the social situation will continue to progress in the same direction it has been progressing in for the past twenty years, exclusively same- and other-sex-identified people have no reason to adopt a label that groups them together and differentiates them from what is now a much less visible sexual category. Without broad-based support, *monosexual* will become, if not obsolete, at least stunted.

The problem for *monosexual* is the conceptualization of the category 'bisexual' as mediating between the exclusively same- or other-sex orientations, as reflected in the field in (1) but also in scales of sexual behavior or orientation, such as the Kinsey scale (Kinsey et al. 1948), in which exclusively-other-sex orientation is on one extreme, exclusively same sex orientation is on the other extreme, and either-sex orientation is in the middle, as in (3).

(3)

<exclusively-other-sex   <either-sex>   exclusively-same-sex>

The *bisexual* / *monosexual* dichotomy necessitates a scale in which the middle of (3) is an extreme, as in (4) (Ross and Paul 1992).

(4)

<gender-immaterial object-choice   gender-specific object-choice>

Furthermore, *monosexual* forces the abandonment of the semantic field in (1), since it does not observe the highest level of contrast in that field: exclusively other-sex orientation versus same-sex orientation. The subcategories it encompasses are not contiguous and encompass different levels in the taxonomy, as shown in (5).

(5)

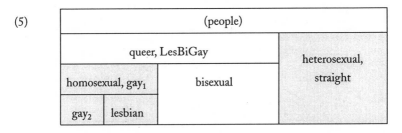

Thus, if *monosexual* does gain usage, it will be at the expense of other categories such as 'queer'. At this point, such a development seems highly unlikely, except within some bisexual-identified groups, who may prefer scale (4) to scale (3).

Polarization: The making of queer queers

Hypothesis III' proposes that category names are most closely associated with members of the category that are least like members of a relevant contrast category. This hypothesis is supported by the use of *queer* as synonymous with *lesbian and gay*.

When sexual minority activists began reclaiming *queer* in print, debates about the denotations, connotations, and usage of the word followed. As a derisive label, *queer* denoted anyone who was other than *straight*. Reclaimed *queer* is also used in strict contrast to *straight*—meaning "anyone who is not part of the heterosexual mainstream." In this vein, bisexuals have adopted *queer* as a label of self-reference, as in Hutchins and Kaahumanu's (1991: 216) assertion that a bisexual in the gay and lesbian community is "a queer among queers." Academics promoting a constructionist view of sexual identity use *queer* to indicate any break from the mainstream ideal of sexual behavior or desire. People defend their use of *queer* by arguing that it is expediently inclusive. For example, Gabriel Rotello claimed "When you're trying to describe the community, and you have to list gays, lesbians, bisexuals, drag queens, transsexuals (post-op and pre-), it gets unwieldy. Queer says it all" (Stanley 1991: 24).

However, in its reclamation by an essentially essentialist political movement, *queer* has also gained popularity as a synonym for *gay/lesbian* or *homosexual*, albeit with different affect. For example, *queer* is used synonymously with *lesbian and gay*, as in (6), and contrasted with *bisexual*, as in (7), in the manifesto distributed at the 1990 New York Pride Parade. In (8), it is contrasted with *not hetero*, indicating a polar interpretation.

(6) When a lot of lesbians and gay men wake up in the morning, we feel angry and disgusted, not gay. So we've decided to call ourselves queer. (Queers Read This 1990)
(7) I also hate the medical and mental health establishments, particularly the psychiatrist who convinced me not to have sex with men for three years in until we (meaning *he*) could make me bisexual rather than queer. (Queers Read This 1990)
(8) If she is not queer, at least tell me she is not hetero! (GN 12 Aug 94)

Similarly, many authors who use *queer* address only exclusively-same-sex issues and use *queer* as a synonym for *gay/lesbian* (Signorile 1993; de Lauretis 1991; Kopkind et al. 1993). We also must assume that when someone claims that 10 percent of the population is *queer* (GN), that person is substituting *queer* for *homosexual* for different affect, not because he or she is abandoning any denotational differences among the words.

So, while *queer* retains its 'anything but straight' sense, it is also used as a synonym for *homosexual*. The table in (9) shows the extent to which this is true in the GN corpus.

(9) *Queer in the GN corpus*

Sense	Tokens
'exclusively-same-sex male' (= *gay man*)	1
'exclusively-same-sex' (= *gay/lesbian*)	5
'same-sex-inclusive (= *gay/lesbian/bisexual*)	10
'any radical sexual minority member'	8[6]
'other-sex-oriented gay-rights supporter'	1
reference to the word itself	7
indeterminable reference	22

Inclusive and exclusive uses of *queer* may coexist for some time, since people with other-sex orientation (especially bisexuals) are claiming it for themselves and people who use it exclusively often do so unintentionally. For example, when called on his very exclusive use of *queer*, one GN participant apologized, shown in (10). The narrowing of *queer* to be equivalent to *gay male* was, in this case, subintentional.

(10) A: . . . half the queers, dykes, and bi's in America were there.
      B: I thought dykes and bis *were* queer.
      A: [B] brought up the fact that dykes and bi's are also queer. He's right, and I'm sorry for the mistake.

Hypothesis III', then, is supported by the patterns of polysemy in *queer* as well as by the gradability of *queer* based on a polar interpretation, as noted by Blasingame (1992: 50): "Bisexuals are often viewed as less queer because they do not identify as exclusively gay or lesbian. . . . [A] system that oppresses us now has us fighting over who is 'truly' queer." Although *queer* is contrasted with *straight*, its narrower senses follow the prediction that the word will be associated with people who are most different from those in the contrasting category. The people who are most steadily associated with the label *queer* are just those at the farthest pole from those considered *straight*, that is, people with exclusively-same-sex orientation.

Narrowing of definitions: Who counts in a queer census?

Hypotheses IV' and V' lead to seemingly contradictory but well-supported predictions. Hypothesis IV' predicts that positively valued groups will be exclusive categories, while negatively valued groups will be more inclusive categories. In cultures where hetero- versus homosexuality is a basis for identity building, exclusively-other-sex identity is generally valued over same-sex identity. Thus, narrower senses are predicted for labels like *straight* and *heterosexual* than for *gay, lesbian, bisexual*, and *queer*. However, Hypothesis V' predicts that among exclusively-same-sex-identified people, self-referential labels will carry narrower senses, and for the either-sex identified, *bisexual* and *bi* will have narrower senses than the other labels.

Exclusive senses for the labels of both the other-sex-identified outgroup (which is positively valued in the mainstream culture) and the ingroups are found in the language of same-sex-oriented communities. These different usages can be seen to fulfill different political, social, or rhetorical aims. However, it is not as common to find exclusive uses of *bisexual* and *bi* among the people who self-identify through those labels.

Inclusive *queer, lesbian, gay*

Let us first consider *queer, gay*, and *lesbian* with reference to Hypothesis IV', by which *straight* and *heterosexual* are predicted to represent exclusive categories. This is reflected in mainstream culture. If one is called *straight*, one is assumed to have no romantic or sexual feelings whatsoever toward members of the same sex. Among same-sex-identified people, *straight* may also have an exclusive sense, thus forcing *queer* or *gay* and *lesbian* to be more inclusive. In this case, anyone who has ever had same-sex desires or experience is *queer* and, in some cases, *gay* or *lesbian*.

Queer in its 'not exclusively straight' sense certainly bears out this point. In some contexts, the word is applied broadly enough to refer to anyone with same-sex orientation and sometimes even to those without same-sex orientation, such as other-sex-oriented people who partake in cross-dressing, sadomasochism, or bondage practices or who identify politically with sexual minorities, as in (11) and (12).

(11)   Gay, lesbian, bi, hetero or undefined, all the anarchists were queer in their own way.
        (GN, from *Love & Rage*, an anarchist magazine)

(12)   SJP was featured in an Advocate cover story several months back, and she's as queer as they come (meaning friendly-hetero rather than lesbian or bi). (GN— parentheses in original)

The inclusive use of *queer* is also seen in self-identification. Bisexuals in the survey especially self-identified with *queer*, indicating that they do not believe that the word excludes them. The responses of bisexuals to the question "What labels do you apply to yourself?" support this point, as shown in (13). Among bisexual re- spondents, 84.3 percent identify themselves as *queer*. The remainder do not nec- essarily view *queer* as exclusive, since many people choose not to use *queer* for other reasons.

(13)

	Total (n = 98)	Gay Male (n = 40)	Lesbian (n = 13)	Bi Male (n = 22)	Bi Female (n = 10)	Other (n = 13)
Queer	56.1	55.0	46.2	81.8	90.0	0
Homosexual	45.9	72.5	53.8	27.3	30.0	0
Gay	68.3	95.0	76.9	68.1	40.0	
Lesbian	17.3	0	92.3	4.5	40.0	0
Dyke	20.4	0	84.7	4.5	80.0	0
Bisexual	32.6	5.0	23.1	86.3	80.0	0
Bi	33.7	7.5	15.4	90.9	80.0	0
Heterosexual	11.2	2.5	0	13.6	10.0	46.2
Straight	9.2	0	0	18.2	0	38.4
no label[7]	8.1	3.1	0	4.5	0	30.8

Some bisexuals also use *gay* and *lesbian* inclusively in self-identifying, since signif- icant proportions of bisexuals used these labels for self-reference. Similarly, Hutchins and Kaahumanu (1991: 214) include a photograph of badges with slo- gans, two of which are "Bisexual and Proud to Be Lesbian" and "Bisexual and Proud to Be Gay."

Inclusive application of *gay* and *lesbian* by same-sex-oriented people is partic- ularly evident in arguments for civil rights aimed at the outgroup. The intent is ev- ident: to assert that same-sex-oriented people are so numerous that "gay and les- bian" rights must be addressed. Sometimes, it is not clear whether the intention is to include either-sex-oriented people or whether the existence of either-sex- oriented people is not acknowledged, as in the contrast between *gay* and *straight* in (14).

(14)   Whether we are black, Latino, white, straight, or gay, we must unite to make the administration listen. (GN, from Cornell University student newspaper)

Either-sex orientation does seem to be included in the use of *gay* or *lesbian* to describe historical figures. Usually, such claims are made in spite of the fact that the historical figure is not known to have identified with those labels, and often these claims are made in the face of evidence that the person was also involved with members of the other sex. As such, a claim that "Eleanor Roosevelt was a les- bian" (GN) may be asserted using the interpretation of *straight* as a category to be reserved for the exclusively-other-sex-oriented, while *gay* and *lesbian* refer inclusively to any same-sex-oriented people.

Exclusive *queer, lesbian, gay*

Application of the labels *queer, gay* and *lesbian* to people who are not exclusively same-sex oriented does not prove that the words have inclusive senses. Instead, some speakers may not be using the labels inclusively but may be rationalizing the application of narrow senses of the labels to people who might not belong in that narrow extension. In the case of historical figures, one might claim, "Yes, Eleanor Roosevelt was married, but this doesn't mean she was other-sex oriented, since she was under enormous pressure to marry." Thus, the speaker would apply a narrow sense of *lesbian* to Roosevelt ('exclusively-same-sex oriented'). Such strategies are not limited to historical figures. Rust (1992b: 369) shows that "Within the lesbian community, individuals are assumed to be homosexual in the absence of and often in spite of evidence to the contrary." If *gay* and *lesbian* had only inclusive meanings, they would not contrast with *bisexual*, and therefore it would not be a problem to consider people's other-sex experiences as equivalent to their same-sex experiences in labeling them *gay* or *lesbian*. However, *gay* and *lesbian* clearly do have narrow, polarized senses. Hypothesis V', that within the group, labels are used exclusively is supported by the evident need within the gay and lesbian communities to reframe people's other-sex-oriented experiences as irrelevant to their sexual orientation ("I had crushes on boys, but they don't count"; "I'm attracted to my wife, but not in the same way as men").

Other evidence favors Hypothesis V' as well. To return to *queer*, its polarization, described earlier, shows that it is used in a narrower sense by sexual-minority members. Furthermore, *gay* and *lesbian* are used exclusively in ingroup rhetoric. This is found in discussions of who is a "real" or "pure" gay or lesbian, as in (15).

(15) I am a True Lesbian. . . . This means I have no fantasies about having sex with men and I am faithful in relationships with women. (from a letter in *Lesbian Connection*, quoted in Young 1992: 79)

This narrow interpretation of *lesbian* or a similarly exclusive interpretation of *gay* is usually implicit in self-referential discourse. If one responds "I'm gay" to the romantic advances of a person of the other sex, one implicates that other-sex attraction is out of the question for a gay person. Further evidence of exclusive use of *gay* and *lesbian* can be found in situations where these labels are used synonymously with *homosexual* (which, by virtue of its morphological contrast with *bisexual*, is usually interpreted as exclusively-same-sex oriented).

Finally, exclusive use of *gay* and *lesbian* is found in many examples where these two labels are used in contrast with *bisexual*, as in (16).

(16) But we (gay, lesbian and bisexual people) need a safe space where we can feel comfortable being ourselves! (GN)

In contrast to the observation that (some) bisexuals use *lesbian* and *gay* inclusively, lobbying by bisexual individuals and organizations to have the word *bisexual* included in organization and event titles indicates either that some bisexuals view *gay* and *lesbian* as overwhelmingly exclusive or that they believe that others interpret these labels exclusively. On the same page of Hutchins and Kaahumanu (1991: 214) that shows the "Bisexual and Proud to Be Gay" badge, another badge says "Bi the way, don't assume I'm gay." Bisexuals seem to disagree as to whether 'bisexual' is a subtype of 'gay and lesbian' or a contrasting category.

Survey respondents indicated that they do not use the labels *gay* and *lesbian* to refer to people whose history of sexual relations includes any same-sex experience.[8] On a scale of 0 (never) to 4 (always), the average response indicates that people believe they only occasionally use *gay* and *lesbian* for people who might not be considered 'straight' in the mainstream culture by virtue of their having some consensual same-sex experience. In contrast, respondents said they are more likely to use *queer* inclusively. Average responses by group are given in (17).

(17)   HISTORY OF SEXUAL RELATIONS includes ANY same-sex experience

	All	Gay Male	Lesbian	Bi Male	Bi Female	Other
Gay	0.956	1.076	0.692	1.15	0.777	0.666
Lesbian	0.978	1.153	1.166	0.95	0.666	0.5
Queer[9]	1.904	1.705	2.416	2.368	2.6	0.857

Lesbian seems to be more exclusive than *gay*, although that is not reflected in the self-reported usage in (17). For example, two complementary magazines advertised in *Exit*, a South African gay and lesbian newspaper (1994), are "for lesbian and bi women" and "for gay guys." Since the company provides no magazine "for bi men," one is left to assume that *gay* is inclusive of *bi*, while *lesbian* is not. This intuition is reflected by the reporting of self-labels in the questionnaire (see 13). While more than 68 percent of bisexual-identified men also labeled themselves *gay*, only four out of ten bisexual women called themselves *lesbian*. This may be explainable by the relative social positions of bisexuals in the gay and lesbian communities. As Rust (1992b: 367–368) notes, among lesbians "bisexuality is seen as a personal, social, and political threat." If the gay male community is more tolerant of bisexual members than the lesbian community, it would stand to reason that its label would be more inclusive.

To conclude, Hypothesis IV', that 'straight' is an exclusive category, is borne out in the use of *gay* and *lesbian*, at least in rhetoric directed at outgroup members. Hypothesis V', that *lesbian* and *gay* have exclusive senses among same-sex-oriented people, is borne out as well. The narrowing of these senses is generally achieved by polarization. Of course, sexual category labeling is affected by more than just sexual orientation and behavior. Most important, it reflects identification with a sexual minority group or its culture, as shown in Rust's (1992b) work on lesbian and bisexual category differentiation. In her study (p. 373), "only one-third of lesbian-identified respondents stated that they were 100% attracted to women," the rest being 50 to 95 percent attracted to women. Similarly, in their study of men, Philip Blumstein and Pepper Schwartz (1976: 342) found "little coherent relationship between the amount and 'mix' of homosexual and heterosexual behavior in a person's biography and that person's choice to label himself or herself as bisexual, homosexual, or heterosexual."

Inclusive/exclusive *bisexual*: Is everyone bi? Is anyone bi?

The sexual category labels considered so far behave according to the hypotheses. However, the use of self-referential terms by bisexual people does not fit well with Hypothesis V', which states that a label's meaning will be more exclusive among the ingroup than among the outgroups. On the contrary, *bisexual* is more often used to mean 'anyone who has had both same- and other-sex experience or desires' by bisexual-identified people than by gay- or lesbian-identified people. Thus, the label is more exclusive as used by outgroup members than as used by ingroup members. Similarly, Rust (1992a: 292) reports that twice as many bisexual women as lesbians in her study stated that everyone is or is potentially bisexual (30 percent vs. 15 percent). The self-reported use of *bisexual* shown in (18) can be compared to the items in (17). Respondents believe they use *bisexual* less inclusively than *queer*, but more inclusively than *gay* or *lesbian*.

(18)   HISTORY OF SEXUAL RELATIONS includes ANY same-sex experience

	All	Gay Male	Lesbian	Bi Male	Bi Female	Other
Bisexual	1.813	1.567	1.923	2.15	2.666	1.25

There are several possible explanations for why Hypothesis V' is not supported by bisexual use of *bisexual*. First, the status of bisexual identity and the visibility of the bisexual movement are not as well established as are gay and lesbian identities and movements. While people have been organizing on the basis of gay or lesbian identity since at least the 1950s, organizations based on bisexual identity have flourished only since the early 1980s. Furthermore, the existence of gay and lesbian identities have been acknowledged and thus strengthened by outgroup members, while the same cannot be said of bisexual identity. Thus, one might conclude that bisexuals do not have sufficient social power to be exclusive in their definition of *bisexual*. Rather than take the exclusive sense of *bisexual* that Hypothesis V' predicts, bisexuals may feel the need to be inclusive in order to strengthen their numbers. This explanation suggests that if the bisexual movement has the same success in bringing attention to its identity that the gay and lesbian movement has had, then *bisexual* will become a more exclusive category.

However, another possible explanation is that Hypotheses V and V' are not applicable to categories that are not in polar contrast to another category in the field. In order for this explanation to hold for *bisexual*, it must be the case that bisexuals generally view themselves as being between gay and straight on a scalar view of sexuality. This has certainly been the historical estimation of the 'bisexual' category. However, if bisexuals come to view themselves in opposition to a 'monosexual' category rather than to the 'homosexual' and 'heterosexual' categories, then the extension of the word is predicted to become more exclusive. The view of 'bisexual' as a category independent from 'homosexual' and 'heterosexual' has been promoted by several bisexual activists and theorists (Rust 1992a, Eridani 1992). If such a view becomes more generally accepted among bisexuals, we will have the opportunity to test this hypothesis and see whether a contrast between the "true bisexual" and the "pseudobisexual" arises.

Another possible explanation is that Hypotheses V and V' are not valid for groups whose members believe that group membership is chosen. This explanation assumes that the behaviors identified by Hypothesis V are caused by the perception that one is forced into one particular category rather than another. While it is common to hear that "we have no choice in being gay or lesbian," it is less common to hear people saying that they have no choice in being bisexual. The "no-choice" position for those who identify as gay or lesbian has been given support by recent discoveries linking same-sex orientation with particular neurological development. However, such studies have not been received by the bisexual community with the same sort of interest (or sometimes relief) that is seen in gay and lesbian communities. On the contrary, in bisexual political circles, such studies are seen as misguided or threatening in that they reify a polar view of sexuality that delegitimizes bisexual identity.

Choice seems to be a core concept to bisexual identity, not just in terms of choice of sexual partner, but in terms of identity, community, and lifestyle. Many people who identify as bisexual acknowledge that they could identify as *gay/lesbian* or *straight* if they chose to express their sexualities and politics in certain ways, although they feel that identification as *bisexual* is more "honest" (Ripley 1992; Zipkin 1992). This view of sexual categories conflicts with the ethnicity model of sexual categorization. While one cannot get away with claiming "Although my parents are Greek and I grew up in New Jersey, I'm Maori," one can get away with claiming "I'm lesbian, even though I sleep with men" or "I'm bi, although I date only women."

If the notion of choice is what keeps *bisexual* from having an exclusive meaning in the bisexual community, then we must establish why. How do the dynamics of identity and labeling change depending on whether group membership is choice-based or inherited and imposed? The crucial difference between these types of groups is the possibility of recruitment. Bisexuals who acknowledge that they chose their identity must also view at least some members of other sexual categories as having chosen their present identities, since they know that others, when presented with the 'bisexual'/'homosexual'/'heterosexual' choice, might take different options. Thus, the bisexual movement may increase its numbers not by encouraging people to announce an identity that they presumably already have (as in coming out of the closet) but by encouraging people to choose an identity different from the one they already have. In order to investigate the role of choice, other choice-based categories must be examined (e.g., political, occupational, and belief categories).

A final possible explanation for the oddness of the bisexual category with regard to Hypothesis V' is that the data presented here are not representative. It could be the case that an exclusive use of *bisexual is* used in the bisexual community to a greater degree than in the outgroup. Certainly, exclusive senses are available and used. In the context of a bisexual organization to which I belonged, members some-times discussed whether a new member was "really" bisexual or whether the person had joined the group to fulfill other aims, such as living out a *ménage à trois* fantasy or denying the exclusivity of his or her same-sex attractions. However, the exclu-sive sense of *bisexual* seems stronger among those who identify as *gay* or *lesbian*. Such exclusive senses can be seen in the questioning of others' identifications as *bi-sexual*. For example, in an article about a musician who is out as having a "flexible" sexual orientation, the editor of a South African gay and lesbian magazine says:

> In my opinion, Kerkorrel seems to be playing a bit of media gymnastics. Seems a lit-tle bit reminiscent of the David Bowie–Mick Jagger closet-with-a-revolving door to me. Anyway, he says he talks through his music. Well, what does *River of Love* say to you? I know what it says to me. [gives the lyrics of a love song with masculine pro-nouns] (Rose 1995: 63)

The insinuation here is that if a man is oriented toward men, he must be gay; the message is that it is insincere to claim an either-sex orientation. At the other ex-treme, people who claim to be bisexual are sometimes forced out of the gay and lesbian categories through use of an exclusive sense of *gay* and *lesbian* in combina-tion with a view of sexual orientation as a strictly complementary domain: Either you are straight or you are gay or lesbian. This view is seen in the statement of a twenty-two-year-old lesbian quoted in *Mademoiselle* magazine (1993): "Bis use lesbianism as a sex toy." In such views, any middle ground between *gay* and *straight* is excluded—so that the outgroup use of *bisexual* is not just exclusive; it is nearly mythical. *Bisexual* becomes the sexual *square circle*, an expression with a sense, but, for many people, an impossible extension.

Conclusions—New Directions

Since sexual minority category status is often conceptualized in terms of an eth-nicity model, it is not altogether surprising that sexual and ethnic/racial categories and their labels have similar characteristics, since, to some extent, sexual minority categorization may mimic ethnic and racial categorization. However, the 'bisexual' category challenges the cognitive social psychology model. Considering that bi-sexuality has an ambiguous place in the folk ethnicity model, this may not be sur-prising. However, no single obvious explanation of this deviation presents itself. Thus, the work presented here calls for further work to determine why *bisexual* has an inclusive meaning among ingroup members.

Another area of interest is the continued use of *monosexual*. As exclusively same- and other-sex-identified people hear this label more (through increased vis-ibility of a bisexual identity), will it be rejected or change in meaning? Will its con-tinued use in the bisexual community encourage self-conceptualization in terms of the gender-material/gender-immaterial scale? (And will this have any effect on gay/lesbian and straight self-concepts?)

Needless to say, this chapter raises at least as many questions as it answers.

ACKNOWLEDGMENTS   Writing this chapter in South Africa has been challenging, and I'm grateful to all those who have helped me overcome this challenge. Thanks to all on the GayNet and BiAct-L lists who answered queries. Kath Pennavaria of the Kinsey Institute, Michael Montgomery, and Loraine Hutchins were especially informative and helpful. Thanks to Kira and Anna for their patience, encouragement, and comments. Responsibility for any errors or misinterpretations herein is my own.

NOTES

1. The topic of name change has been raised, but not pursued, in these organizations. The discussion in ILGA is illustrative of the differences in sexual identities across national or linguistic groups, since one reaction to the proposal of name change has been "But everyone is bisexual!" This is contrary to the argument one hears in many Anglophonic nations—that every bisexual is gay.

2. Those who chose not to label themselves reported strictly other-sex-oriented desires and experience. Thus, the "Other" category may be interpreted as a "Heterosexual" category.

3. The GayNet archives are available to the public through majordomo@queernet.org.

4. From *Bi-Sexual Love* by Wilhelm Stekel, translated by James S. van Teslaar (quoted in Montgomery 1993): "All persons are bisexual. But persons repress either the homosexual or heterosexual components on account of certain motives or because they are compelled by particular circumstances and consequently act as if they were monosexual."

5. The field representation is simplified in several ways. Only the terms considered in this paper are included (thus, *transsexual* is not), and overlaps among categories are not shown, such as the overlap between *gay*$_1$ and *bisexual*.

6. Seven of these eight tokens are from the anarchist magazine *Love and Rage*.

7. Except for the "Other" category, respondents were assigned to categories according to their own self-labeling. Thus, people in any category but "Other" who selected the "no label" option *did* label themselves.

8. *Sexual relations* was defined to include consensual dating, touching, and sex.

9. Respondents who checked 0 (never) because they don't use the word *queer* were tabulated as nonresponses and therefore do not lower the average.

REFERENCES

Altman, Dennis (1982). *The Homosexualization of America, The Americanization of the Homosexual*. New York: St. Martin's.

Ashmore, Richard D., and Frances K. Del Boca (1981). "Conceptual Approaches to Stereotypes and Stereotyping." In Hamilton 1981: 1–35.

Blasingame, Brenda Marie (1992). "The Roots of Biphobia: Racism and Internalized Heterosexism." In Weise 1992: 47–53.

Blumstein, Philip W., and Pepper Schwartz (1976). "Bisexuality in Men." *Urban Life* 5: 339–358.

Brewer, M. B. (1979). "In-group Bias in the Minimal Intergroup Situation: A Cognitive-Motivational Analysis." *Psychological Bulletin* 86: 307–323.

Campbell, Donald T. (1956). "Enhancement of Contrast as a Composite Habit." *Journal of Abnormal and Social Psychology* 53: 350–355.

Davis, F. James (1991). *Who Is Black? One Nation's Definition*. University Park: Pennsylvania State University Press.

de Lauretis, Teresa (ed.) (1991). *Queer Theory: Lesbian and Gay Sexualities.* Special issue of *differences: A Journal of Feminist Cultural Studies* 3: 2.

Dynes, Wayne (1985). *Homolexis: A Historical and Cultural Lexicon of Homosexuality.* New York: Scholarship Committee of the Gay Academic Union.

Epstein, Steven (1987). "Gay Politics, Ethnic Identity: The Limits of Social Constructionism." *Socialist Review* 17: 9–54.

Eridani. 1992. "Is Sexual Orientation a Secondary Sex Characteristic?" In Weise 1992: 173–181.

Geller, Thomas (ed.) (1990). *Bisexuality: A Reader and Sourcebook.* Ojai, CA: Times Change Press.

Hamilton, David L. (ed.) (1981). *Cognitive Processes in Stereotyping and Intergroup Behavior.* Hillsdale, NJ: Lawrence Erlbaum.

Horn, Laurence R. (1989). *A Natural History of Negation.* Chicago: University of Chicago Press.

Hutchins, Loraine, and Lani Kaahumanu (eds.) (1991). *Bi Any Other Name: Bisexual People Speak Out.* Boston: Alyson.

Katz, Jonathan Ned (1995). *The Invention of Heterosexuality.* New York: Dutton.

Kinsey, Alfred C., Wardell B. Pomeroy, and Clyde E. Martin (1948). *Sexual Behavior in the Human Male.* Philadelphia: W. B. Saunders.

Kopkind, Andrew et al. (eds.) (1993). *A Queer* Nation. Special issue of *The Nation* 271: 1.

Lehrer, Adrienne (1974). *Semantic Fields and Lexical Structure.* Amsterdam: North Holland.

Montgomery, Michael (1993). Letter to the Editor of the Oxford English Dictionary Project. Posted to the Bisexual Theory List (bithry-l@brownvm.brown.edu), 16 December.

Murphy, Peggy Boucher (1992). "A letter to Opra *(sic).*" *The BiMonthly: The Champaign-Urbana Bisexual Network Newsletter* 1, no. 3: 3–4.

Nunberg, Geoffrey D. (1978). *The Pragmatics of Reference.* Bloomington: Indiana University Linguistics Club.

Oxford English Dictionary, 2d ed. (1989). Oxford: Clarendon.

"Queers Read This" (1990). Leaflet distributed at the New York Lesbian and Gay Pride Parade, June.

Ripley, Rebecca (1992). "The Language of Desire: Sexuality, Identity and Language." In Weise 1992: 91–102.

Rose, Madeleine (1995). "Labels Can Hurt." *Outright* (April): 63.

Ross, Michael W., and Jay P. Paul (1992). "Beyond Gender: The Basis of Attraction in Bisexual Men and Women." *Psychological Reports* 71, 3: 1283–1290.

Rust, Paula C (1992a). "Who Are We and Where Do We Go from Here? Conceptualizing Bisexuality." In Weise 1992: 281–310.

Rust, Paula C. (1992b). "The Politics of Sexual Identity: Sexual Attraction and Behavior among Lesbian and Bisexual Women." *Social Problems* 39, no. 4: 366–386.

Shuster, Rebecca (1991). "Beyond Defense: Considering Next Steps for Bisexual Liberation." In Hutchins and Kaahumanu 1991: 266–274.

Signorile, Michelangelo (1993). *Queer in America: Sex, the Media, and the Closets of Power.* London: Abacus.

Stanley, Alessandra (1991). "Militants Back 'Queer', Shoving 'Gay' the Way of 'Negro.'" *New York Times* 6 April: L23–24.

Tajfel, Henri (1978). *The Social Psychology of Minorities.* London: Minority Rights Group.

Tajfel, Henri, and Joseph P. Forgas (1981). "Social Categorization: Cognitions, Values, and

Groups." In Joseph P. Forgas (ed.), *Social Cognition: Perspectives on Everyday Understanding*, New York: Academic Press, pp. 113–140.

Tajfel, Henri, and John Turner (1979). "An Integrative Theory of Intergroup Conflict." In William G. Austin and Stephen Worchel (eds.), *The Social Psychology of Intergroup Relations*, Monterey, CA: Brooks/Cole, pp. 33–47.

Taylor, Shelley E. (1981). "A Categorization Approach to Stereotyping." In Hamilton 1981: 83–113.

Udis-Kessler, Amanda (1990). "Bisexuality in an Essentialist World: Toward an Understanding of Biphobia." In Geller 1990: 51–63.

Weise, Beth Reba (ed.) (1992). *Closer to Home: Bisexuality and Feminism*. Seattle: Seal Press.

Young, Stacey (1992). "Breaking Silence about the "B-word": Bisexual Identity and Lesbian-Feminist Discourse." In Weise 1992: 75–87.

Zipkin, Dvora (1992). "Why Bi?" In Weise 1992: 55–73.

3

*L*exical Variation in the Deaf Community Relating to Gay, Lesbian, and Bisexual Signs

MALA S. KLEINFELD AND NONI WARNER

During the past decade speakers of American Sign Language (ASL), in keeping with current trends in language use, have developed strong opinions about the appropriateness of certain politically charged signs. These opinions have in turn influenced people who interpret the language for the hearing community. This chapter focuses on Deaf community members, both deaf[1] and hearing, and the variation in their use of signs for gay, lesbian, and bisexual persons. Since research on American Sign Language began only in 1960, there is a limited literature available on gay terminology and variations thereof. The purpose of the present study is to discover the sociolinguistic rules affecting the employment of signs for gay identity; we examine the signs that speakers have used in the past, the signs that speakers use now, and the current attitude toward these signs both within and without the ASL-using community.

Within the Deaf community in the United States, ASL is becoming more and more accepted as the language of the Deaf. People from all over the world are coming to America to learn ASL; in 1989, for instance, Gallaudet University hosted "Deaf Way," an international Deaf conference attended by speakers of many different sign languages from around the world. This contact with other sign languages had a strong influence on the ASL-speaking participants, particularly at the lexical level, for many people in the American Deaf community have now adopted the native signs for certain countries. A sign resembling the Japanese Sign Language sign for *Japan*, for example, has been adopted by ASL signers and is now more commonly used than the original ASL sign. The former sign, produced on the outer corner of the eye with a "J" handshape,[2] was seen as offensive to Japanese people because it brought attention to an anatomical difference (i.e., eye shape). The new sign, in contrast, is produced in the space in front of the signer's chest, with an "L" handshape on each hand like an outline of the shape of Japan. The decision to use this sign as opposed to the older sign appears to be based on considerations of political correctness.

Signs referring to gay identity have undergone comparable transformations in recent years. In the eastern part of the United States, for example, the sign GAY has traditionally been produced on the chin using the "G" or "Q" handshape. Within the past few years, a more neutral sign, #GAY,[3] has been adopted by many members of the gay community. (In written notation, the sign's gloss is preceded by the crosshatch # to indicate that this is a lexicalized form of a fingerspelled sequence.) Again, the choice of sign is conditioned by the speaker's attitude toward the community in question.

This fact is corroborated by James Woodward (1979) in his book *Signs of Sexual Behavior*. Woodward, a hearing researcher, emphasizes how important it is for hearing people to be careful with their English-to-ASL translations, listing a number of variations of signs used in the Deaf community for the terms *gay* and *lesbian*. He writes of the need to find out which signs are considered politically correct by asking Deaf people directly, and his work serves as a collection of such data. Since many Deaf people are reluctant to show hearing people their signs for intimate activities or concepts, Woodward published his book in order to benefit hearing professionals working in the field of deafness. Much has changed since 1979, however, especially with respect to Deaf people's willingness to discuss ASL openly with hearing people. The present study reflects this development.

A survey was conducted at Gallaudet University in 1981 by William Rudner and Rachelle Butowsky, who interviewed twelve heterosexual men and women, ten homosexual men, and eleven homosexual women (all Deaf). Photographs of fourteen signs were shown to the different groups in the study, and their English glosses were compared to those in other groups. Researchers studied the attitudes and connotations that were attached to each of the signs. In 1993, as a follow-up to this earlier study, approximately thirty-five members of the Deaf gay community from the areas of Washington, D.C., Virginia, and Maryland gathered for a day to discuss linguistic and cultural issues relating to those Deaf people in the gay community.[4] The participants were divided into groups to discuss lexical signs commonly used in the gay community and to identify which signs were seen as politically correct or incorrect. Although the results of this conference have not yet been published, the present article and the small body of work reviewed in it represent the most up-to-date information regarding the corpus of lexical signs used in the gay community and the attitudes surrounding their usage.

A number of factors influence the choice of sign in ASL, among them community, register, and context. In *Sociolinguistic Aspects of the Black Deaf Community*, Anthony Aramburo (1989) shows that members of the Black Deaf community have their own corpus of lexical items not seen when they converse with nonmembers of the community. The lexical item SCHOOL used in the Black Deaf community, for instance, is different from the sign for *school* used outside the community. Not only do members have their own dialect, then, but also they employ this dialect only when speaking to other community members. Register variation is similarly influential. In *Towards a Description of Register Variation in ASL,* June Zimmer (1989) argues that signed messages differ at all levels (i.e., phonological, morphological, lexical, syntactic, discursive) and that the differences perceived are related to register. Indeed, the meaning of an utterance can be altered in the translation process if the languages are not matched for register. Context, too, is an important factor, as signers use language differently in different situations. Looking at the different uses of Signed English and ASL, for example, Zimmer pointed out that what was considered a form of diglossia in the Deaf community had in fact been misidentified. While it was thought that Signed English represented a high-prestige dialect and ASL a low-prestige dialect, the former is in fact a manual communication system invented approximately two decades ago as an attempt to teach deaf people English. During the 1970s, Signed English was used in the education of deaf children, and it is still used today, although not so extensively as before. ASL, on the other hand, is a natural sign language of the Deaf; it has its own morphosyntactic structure and is quite different from English.

Methodology

Informants

This research involved thirteen hearing interpreters and twelve Deaf signers at Gallaudet University. The Deaf informants were randomly selected among the faculty, staff, and students, although we made sure to include an equal number of gay and straight people; six men (two gay, one bisexual, three straight) and six women (three gay, three straight) participated in the study. The only criteria used in selection were that participants should be fluent signers and deaf. The hearing group consisted of thirteen randomly chosen interpreters also employed at Gallaudet University: four men (two gay, two straight) and nine women (six straight, two lesbians, and one bisexual).[5] Table 3-1 describes relevant aspects of the respondents' backgrounds.

It is interesting to note that only two interpreters were native signers. This proportion is a good representation of the proportion of native signers among interpreters in the United States. At Gallaudet, approximately 10 percent of the interpreters are native signers. Six of the interpreters for this study hold certification from the Registry of Interpreters for the Deaf (RID). Forty percent of the interpreters acquired sign language on the West Coast; 30 percent learned sign language in the Midwest, and 30 percent on the East coast. All the Deaf participants grew up deaf, eight are native signers, and four learned ASL later in life, usually in their late teens. Two were from the West Coast, five from the East Coast, three from the northern Midwest, and two from the South.

Table 3-1. Informants' demographics. (Letters are used to represent Deaf people and numbers to represent hearing people)

Subjects	Gender	Sexual Orientation[a]	Years Since Acquiring ASL/ Age ASL Acquired	Geographic Location	Type of School[b]	Family Status[c]
1	M	S	10	California		H
2	M	G	11	Florida		H
3	F	S	3	Wisconsin		H
4	F	S	8	Ohio		H of H
5	F	B	2	Florida		H
6	F	L	10	California		H
7	F	S	2	Illinois		H
8	F	S	3	California		H
9	M	G	13	Indiana		H
10	F	L	6	Oregon		H
11	F	S	15	Maryland/DC		H
12	F	S	15	Illinois		D
13	M	S	1	Vermont		H
A	M	G	at birth	North Carolina	RES	D
B	M	G	age 3	Massachusetts	RES	H
C	M	B	age 3.5	Wisconsin	MS	H
D	M	S	at birth	New Mexico	RES	D
E	M	S	age 11	Minnesota	H/MS	H
F	M	S	at birth	Maryland/DC	RES	D
G	F	L	age 5	New York	RES/H	H
H	F	L	age 20	California	H	H
I	F	L	at birth	Wisconsin	RES	D
J	F	S	age 15	Ontario	H/RES	H
K	F	S	age 14	Kentucky	RES/MS	H
L	F	S	age 5	Pennsylvania	RES/MS	H

a. M = male, F = female, S = straight, G = gay, B = bisexual

b. RES = residental schools, MS = mainstream programs, H = hearing public school

c. H = hearing, D = deaf, H of H = hard of hearing

Interview process for Deaf and hearing informants

The interviews were conducted separately by each researcher; all data collection sessions and interviews were videotaped. Pictures were used to encourage the production of lexical items by Deaf informants and to avoid the use of fingerspelling by the interviewer so that signers would focus on ASL and not be influenced by English (see Appendix A). The interpreters listened to an audiotape of a lecture incorporating several key lexical items (see Appendix B).

While we were eliciting information in response to the photographs and audiotapes, we took note of specific lexical items employed by the participants in order to refer to them later in the interview section. After the data collection, the informants were asked to discuss what they had signed and to respond to a series of questions:

1. Do you know of other variants for the lexical items used in the lecture?
2. Why did you choose not to use those variants during the interpretation or description of photographs?
3. Do you feel that some of the signs have specific connotations attached to them?
4. Do you consider one sign more appropriate than another?

Findings

In our study we found a great deal of variation in the signs used to describe gay people and aspects of the life of a gay person. There is strong evidence that certain signs are not acceptable for use by nonmembers of the community. The range of signs used in the Deaf community that occurred in this study is shown in Figure 3-1. Note that ASL signs are expressed by all capital letters (e.g. GAY) while fingerspelled terms incorporate hyphens (e.g. D-R-A-G). Lower-case letters are used to express concepts in ASL; several lexical signs may be associated with any one concept. This taxonomic tree illustrates that ASL has a variety of signs to designate the same referent. In recent years, however, some of those variations have adopted new meanings and can no longer be substituted for other variations.

Our analysis is divided into three sections. The first section explores the differences in interpretation of the twelve English words used by the two groups of informants.[6] The second section deals with the phonological variations for the sign LESBIAN. The third section discusses representations of the term *gay*.

Differences in Interpretation

Bisexual

The term *bisexual* varies according to the region where a person learned to sign or first interacted with gay individuals. The first variant involves fingerspelling B-I-S-E-X-U-A-L in its entirety. Some straight informants chose to fingerspell "bisexual"; however, the sign used most consistently by other informants was the lexicalized fingerspelled sign #BI. Another variation is used by interpreters on the West Coast. This sign is produced with the handshape "V" contacting the side of the eye with the index finger and moving downward to a bent "V," ending contact at the side of the mouth (see Figure 3-2). Other respondents from the West coast signed NUM-TWO + GENDER; participants trained on the East Coast, however, found these two signs to be "ugly," "strange," and "awkward to produce."

The final variation of *bisexual* is a verb, lexically speaking. Although many people who produce it are unaware of its grammatical class, some informants agreed that this sign functions as a verb and not a noun. The sign is produced at chest level, with the weak hand facing inward toward the signer with the "V" handshape and the dominant hand moving back and forth with a bent "V" (see Figure 3-3); it can also be produced with both handshapes in a bent "V" formation

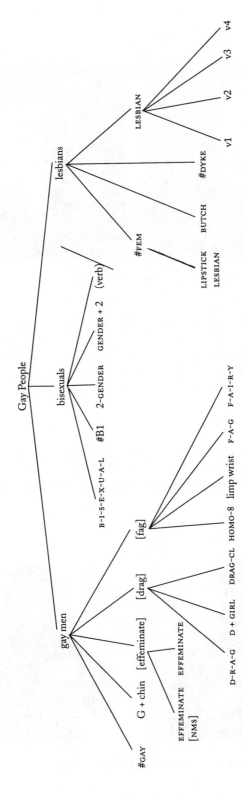

Figure 3-1. Taxonomic tree for terms found in the research. NMS = Nonmanual signals (i.e., linguistic information not on the hands)

a   b

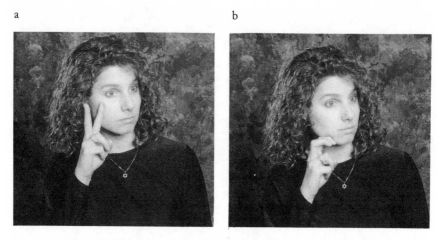

Figure 3-2a, b. The sign BISEXUAL: NUM-TWO + GENDER.

(see Figure 3-4). The sign connotes an individual who has more than one sexual partner at a time: The dominant hand is seen as representing the bisexual, while the weak hand represents the partners. It is also seen as being derived from the sign SLUT. Many of the participants considered this variant an inappropriate sign choice since it describes a person's actions rather than the person him- or herself.

Butch/Dyke

The next lexical item is the term *butch*, which is fingerspelled by most straight informants. Most gay informants signed MACHO or B-U-T-C-H. The sign MACHO (see Figure 3-5) is also glossed as GANG by some respondents, who

a   b

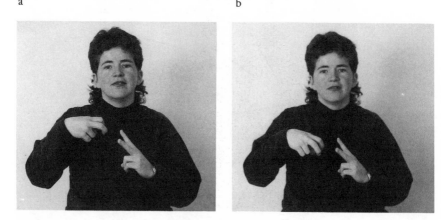

Figure 3-3a, b. Alternative sign for BISEXUAL: BISEXUAL (verb 1).

a
b

Figure 3-4a, b. Another alternative sign for BISEXUAL: BISEXUAL (verb 2).

also felt that this sign was not an appropriate reference for a lesbian. Ninety percent of the straight interpreters chose to fingerspell B-U-T-C-H rather than risk offending anyone. There seems to be some confusion among all groups with regard to the precise connotations of this sign. In the same way that hearing society does not view the term *dyke* in a positive way, the Deaf community disagrees about what a "dyke" is and what the term means. Our research shows that the stylistic way of producing D-Y-K-E has become lexicalized into #D-(Y)-K-E (where the Y dips and the K is not fully formed). There were no straight

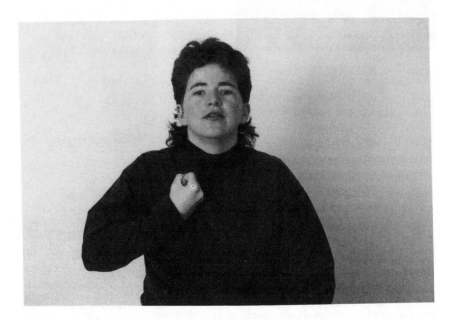

Figure 3-5. The sign MACHO.

a   b

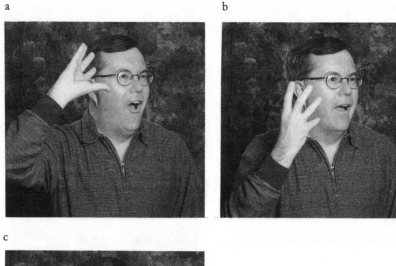

c

Figure 3-6a, b, c. The sign DRAG-CL.

people in either study (Deaf or hearing) who used the lexicalized fingerspelled #DYKE.

Drag

Within the past few years a new sign for *drag* has been borrowed from Germany. Some of the gay interpreters in this study consider the new sign DRAG-CL[7] trendy (see Figure 3-6), commenting that it is appropriate for the glamorous life style it depicts. Before this European sign was introduced into the American Deaf community, both Deaf and hearing informants used an initialized sign influenced by the English system D + GIRL (see Figure 3-7). The D + GIRL is not accepted by individuals who perform in drag shows or dress in drag on occasion. Most of the gay males in both groups (as well as a few lesbians) produced

a   b

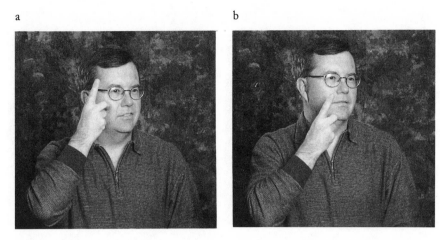

Figure 3-7a, b. The sign DRAG: D + GIRL.

DRAG-CL. All other informants, Deaf and hearing alike, chose to fingerspell *drag*.

Effeminate/Feminine

The terms *effeminate* and *feminine* are frequently used in the gay community to describe characteristics of gays and lesbians. The sign EFFEMINATE (Figure 3-8) when used by Deaf people in the study describes feminine women, but for men it indicates effeminate behavior. The interpreters participating in the study

Figure 3-8. The sign EFFEMINATE.

a

b

c

Figure 3-9a, b, c. The sign HOMO-8.

reported that EFFEMINATE refers to men only, stating that they never produced this sign to describe a woman. The hearing subjects used #FEM to refer to
women when describing very feminine characteristics. A small percentage of the
Deaf subjects used #FEM to refer to women. The Deaf and hearing lesbians said
that they preferred #FEM to EFFEMINATE.

The gay and lesbian participants in the study strongly felt that the terms for
fag and *fairy* should not be used by the heterosexual community, indicating that
such use was very derogatory. They also felt that members of the gay community
should employ them only as a form of teasing, much like HOMO-8 (discussed
later in this chapter; see Figure 3-9). When these terms are signed, the fingerspelling is lexicalized to #FAG and #FAIRY. While some respondents sign these
terms like HOMO-8, others use the gesture LIMP-WRIST to indicate effeminate behavior.

Homosexual

In our research, we found that many informants fingerspelled H-O-M-O-S-E-X-U-A-L. (Another variant, HOMO-8, will be discussed later in this chapter). When the context required the labeling of a group of people, as in the lecture, some gay and straight informants said they would use other variants. It was clear among the gay respondents that *homosexual* is considered a medical term and is not equivalent to *gay*, and they generally chose to fingerspell it. Others used the compound G+chin^LESBIAN or LESBIAN^#GAY (lesbi-gay) to show respect for both genders. A parallel may be seen within the Deaf community in the use of the terms *homosexual* versus *gay* and *hearing-impaired* versus *deaf*. While *hearing-impaired* is a medical term referring to the audiological status of a person and tends to be broadly defined, *Deaf* is a cultural term referring to the person's cultural status within the Deaf community and tends to be more specific.

Come-out

One important facet of life in the gay, lesbian, and bisexual community is *coming out*, or openly recognizing oneself as a homosexual or bisexual. In recent years there has been a strong movement toward coming out in both the hearing and the Deaf communities. Several signs have emerged in relation to this topic, each of which encodes different social attitudes. In talking with the different informants, we discovered that there were many different opinions about which sign is most appropriate. In the first place, the term *coming out* can mean several different things. One may be "coming out" to oneself, for instance, in which case most respondents would use the sign glossed as ADMIT (either one or two handed) plus a labeling sign such as LESBIAN or GAY. This sign is very popular among signers from the West Coast. Another sign, used by straight and gay informants alike, is ANNOUNCE, which also needs an identifier such as GAY or LESBIAN. The interpreters who used these two signs (ADMIT or ANNOUNCE) felt that they represented a conceptual translation. Both were seen as politically correct and were accepted by Deaf informants.

There is a more general sign for *coming out*, a sign that is glossed as RESIGN (see Figure 3-10). The interpreters surveyed believed that this sign used the base sign for CLOSET, changing the dominant hand to show the movement of "coming out." Deaf and hearing informants felt this sign choice was not only English-based but insulting to gay people because of its iconic imagery. Another general sign used by Deaf and hearing people on the East Coast is 2H-OPEN^COAT (see Figure 3-11). A straight female informant, however, claimed that this sign portrayed gay people as "people who will take their clothes off without hesitation," preferring the sign ADMIT or ANNOUNCE.

a   b

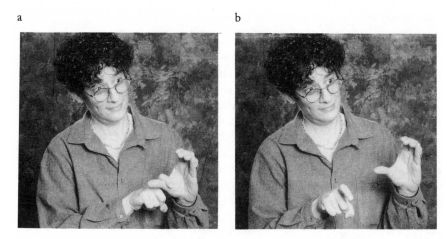

Figure 3-10a, b. The sign COME OUT (RESIGN).

Phonological Variations for the Sign LESBIAN

The first set of signs consists of the phonological variations for the term *lesbian*.[8]
Videotapes, questionnaires, and background sheets of informants from Kleinfeld
and Warner (1994) were further analyzed to investigate the usage of the four variants of the sign LESBIAN. Further interviews with some informants were necessary to provide a stronger foundation for our findings.

Phonetic notation[9] of the four variants of LESBIAN[10] was prepared and appears in Figures 3-12–3-15. The taxonomic tree in Figure 3-16 shows the variations of the sign LESBIAN. Figure 3-12 shows Variant 1 (henceforth V1), which
is produced at the chin with an "L"- shaped handshape, having contact at the chin
with the web of the thumb and index finger. The production of this sign has a
Movement Hold (M-H) structure. All MHMH patterns are initially just that, but

a   b

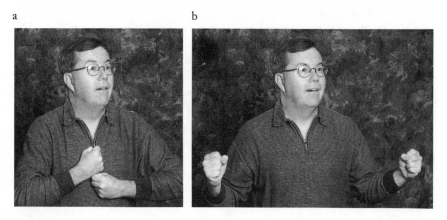

Figure 3-11a, b. The sign COME OUT: 2H-OPEN^COAT.

LESBIAN[web,MH]
Variant 1

		M	H
MajCl		M	H
cont		str	
ThRot	u		
ThExt	+		
FgSel	l		
FgExt	+		
AA-A	WBTH		
Sprel-A	ant		cont
Loc/Hgt-A	CN		
Rotat	thup		

Figure 3-12. Variant sign: LESBIAN (MH).

they go through a morphological process known as "Hold Deletion and Movement Empenthesis," which ends up looking like MMMH. (In Figure 3-12 MH is +Reduplication; the remaining Figures 3-13 to 3-15 are MMMH.) It is important to note the difference of the movement in V1 in contrast with that of V2, shown in Figure 3-13. This sign is produced in the same fashion as V1, except that the movement of the sign is Movement-Hold-Movement-Hold (M-H-M-H). Figures 3-12 and 3-13 appear to be the same, except for the nonmanual signals that accompany V1. A majority of nouns in ASL follow the M-H-M-H structure. V2 is the sign depicted in Sign language dictionaries and in all other books in which LESBIAN is discussed, and it is known as the citation form for LESBIAN. We will see later how it differs from the Movement-Hold pronunciation.

The third variant (V3), shown in Figure 3-14, is produced with the same handshape as V1 and V2, except that the contact point is at the joint of the index

LESBIAN[web,MMMH]

Variant 2							
MajCl		M		M		M	H
cont		str		str		str	
ThRot	u						
ThExt	+						
FgSel	l						
FgExt	+						
AA-A	WBTH						
Sprel-A	ant		cont		ant		cont
Loc/Hgt-A	CN						
Rotat	thup						

Figure 3-13. Variant sign: LESBIAN (MMMH).

finger or the middle phalanx. The structure of this sign also follows the M-H-M-H pattern before the phonological processes have applied. There is a range of possible contact points for this sign, from the proximal bone to the middle bone of the index finger. The final variant (V4) (see Figure 3-15) is produced with the tip of the index finger contacting the chin, while all other features are exactly the same as for V1 through V3. The structure of the tip version is M-H-M-H, and the point of contact can range from the middle bone through the distal bone, to the tip or pad of the index finger.

Data Analysis

We now move on to an analysis of the information provided by respondents. Table 3-2 shows the informants' usage of the variants for LESBIAN. Only one infor-

LESBIAN[joint,MMMH]

Variant 3						
MajCl		M		M		M	H
cont		str		str		str	
ThRot	u					
ThExt	+					
FgSel	l					
FgExt	+					
AA-A	INFl					
Sprel-A	ant		cont		ant		cont
Loc/Hgt-A	CN					
Rotat	thup					

Figure 3-14.   Variant sign: LESBIAN joint (MMMH).

mant, a straight woman (J), produced V1. V2, however, was produced by one straight male (D), three straight women (#7, K, L), one lesbian (#10), and one gay man (C). V3 was produced by five straight men (1, 13, D, E, F), five straight women (3, 4, 8, J, L), and five lesbians (5, 10, G, H, I). V4 was not produced by any straight men; four straight women did produce it (4, 11, 13, K), one of whom also produced V3 (#4). Three of the four straight women interpreters have been in the field much longer than the other three female interpreters and have evidently increased their knowledge of signs and their usage. Four lesbians (5, 6, G, H) and four gay men (2, 9, A, B) produced V4.

A number of questions began to arise that we, as researchers, needed to answer: Did the informants choose these variants over others? If so, why? Were the informants selecting specific variants for particular situations, or were they influ-

LESBIAN[tip,MMMH]
Variant 4

MajCl		M	M	M	H
cont		str	str	str	
ThRot	u				
ThExt	+				
FgSel	l				
FgExt	+				
AA-A	PDFI				
Sprel-A	ant	cont	ant		cont
Loc/Hgt-A	CN				
Rotat	thup				

Figure 3-15.   Variant sign: LESBIAN tip (MMMH).

enced by the observers' paradox? The presence of another person in the room, particularly when that person is hearing as in this case, may influence the signer's lexical choice. In order to get answers to these questions, we asked informants about their responses during the interview process. Informants were asked, for example: "You used this particular sign LESBIAN [we showed which variant they had used]. Do you know of any other ways to sign that?" If the person was uncertain about what we were asking, the question was restated: "You used this particular sign LESBIAN; have you seen *this* sign?" (another variation of the sign was then shown). Table 3-3 shows that most of the informants were aware of all existing variants. Interestingly, though, the straight men's knowledge appears to be more limited. Only one straight man (F) knew all variants; three straight men (1, 13, D) knew of only two variants, V2 and V3, although neither of the two

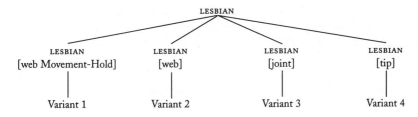

Figure 3-16. Taxonomic tree for the variations of LESBIAN.

hearing signed V2 in the lecture portion of the study. One bisexual (C) did not know all the variations either; this may have been due to his sexual orientation, since he was not as involved with the gay community as the gay men were.

The more experienced straight women interpreters (4, 11, 12) knew all four variants, whereas the interpreters who had been in the field only a few years (3, 8) knew only of V2 and V3, a pattern similar to that of the straight men. The four gay men (2, 9, A, B), the two lesbian interpreters (5, 6), and all the deaf lesbians knew all four variations, except for #10, who only knew of two (V2 and V3). In the interview portion of the study, however, #10 commented that she did not

Table 3-2. The sign LESBIAN produced by informants.

Respondents	V1 (web, MH)	V2 (web)	V3 (joint)	V4 (tip)
Straight Male		D	1, 13, D, E, F	
Straight Female	J	7, K, L	3, 4, 8, J, L	4, 11, 12, K
Lesbian Female		(10)*	5, (10), G, H, I	5, 6, G, H
Gay Male		C	A, B, C	2, 9, A, B

*No. 10 classifies herself as a lesbian but does not socialize with signers who are gay; her manner of producing the sign LESBIAN, as well as the meanings she attributes to different variants, strongly suggest that she is only loosely associated with the community. We have therefore put parentheses around her number.

Table 3-3. Knowledge of variations for the sign LESBIAN.

Respondents	V1 (web, MH)	V2 (web)	V3 (joint)	V4 (tip)
Straight Male	F	1, 13, D, F	1, 13, D, E, F	F
Straight Female	4,11,12, J, L	3, 4, 7, 8, 11, 12, J, K, L	3, 4, 8, 11, 12, J, K, L	4, 11, 12, K
Lesbian Female	5, 6, G, H, I	5, 6, (10)*, G, H, I	5, 6, (10), G, H, I	5, 6, G, H, I
Gay Male	2, 9, A, B	2, 9, A, B, C	2, 9, A, B, C	2, 9, A, B

*No. 10 classifies herself as a lesbian but does not socialize with signers who are gay; her manner of producing the sign LESBIAN, as well as the meanings she attributes to different variants, strongly suggest that she is only loosely associated with the community. We have therefore put parentheses around her number.

"know much about gay or lesbian things." Table 3-4 thus demonstrates that sign usage is not based on knowledge alone; many of the signers knew more varieties than they used.

The last grouping of data shows the connotations of the variants, which appear to determine why some interpreters choose one sign over another. Table 3-4, which indicates the connotations that interpreters reported for each variant, was compiled by reviewing the videotapes and questionnaires and conducting a follow-up meeting after the researchers had compiled the data. This collection of data helped discover the specific connotations of the variants and the social attitudes toward them. The informants were asked to indicate if they felt that a particular variant had a positive (+), neutral (ø), or negative (−) meaning attached to it. We also asked if the signs that they did not use had any negative connotations and if that connotation was the reason they chose not to use them.

One straight Deaf man (F) believed V1 and V2 were negative; he knew V3 to be neutral and V4 to be positive. The other two straight Deaf men had little to say except that E believed V3 to be positive and D believed V2 and V3 to be neutral. Two straight Deaf women (J, L) considered V1 and V2 to be negative but V3 to be positive. The other straight Deaf woman (K) thought V2 negative as well but said she had learned that she should sign V4 because it was a positive sign for lesbians; she considered V3 to be neutral. The two straight male interpreters felt that V2 and V3 were positive representations of the sign LESBIAN, as far as they could tell. The same three straight women (4, 11, 12) who had knowledge of all four variants also agreed on their meanings and the connotations associated with each variant (V1 and V2 negative, V3 neutral, V4 positive).

There seemed to be some confusion among the three other straight women as to the appropriateness of V2. Since V2 is the citation form used in dictionaries, the two interpreters with only two or three years of experience seemed to feel that "if it is in the dictionary, then it must be right," whereas #3 chose to be neutral about both the signs that she knew. This interpreter said that she had never been in a situation where she had needed to use these types of signs and that, moreover, she would not accept an assignment if it was of this nature because she did not feel comfortable with all the meanings. All of the lesbian and gay informants (with the exception of #10 and C; see table 3-4) agreed that V1 was a sign used to describe a stereotypical lesbian as seen by heterosexual society and that it had negative connotations. V1 with its Movement-Hold structure gives the sign more emphasis and is usually accompanied with negative nonmanual signals, shown in Figure 3-12. Within the gay community this variant is used in ingroup teasing, as when members call one another a "dyke" or indicate that someone is "macho" or a lesbian with "pride." There is a strong tendency to associate this sign with oral sex, due to its phonetic structure. Informants who were members of the gay community viewed this sign as very derogatory if signed by an outsider.

Table 3-4. Attitudes of informants towards variations of LESBIAN.

Respondents	V1			V2			V3			V4		
	+	ø	−	+	ø	−	+	ø	−	+	ø	−
Straight Male	F	1, 13		D	F, 1, 13, E			D, F		F		
Straight Female	4, 11, 12, J, L	7, 8		3	4, 11, 12, J, K, L		J, L	3, 4, 7, 8, 11, 12, K		4, 11, 12, K		
Lesbian Female	5, 6, G, H, I	10		5, 6, G, H, I	10		5, 6, G, H, I			5, 6, G, H, I		
Gay Male	2, 9, A, B			2, 9, A, B, C			2, 9, A, B, C			2, 9, A, B		

Summary

Given the choice between V1 and V2, V2 is more acceptable to members of the gay community because they realize that this is the sign that appears in sign language dictionaries and the one that the majority of sign language instructors teach as the citation form. The fact that most teachers, hearing or Deaf, teach V2 as the sign for *lesbian* and that this is the sign that appears in dictionaries and is used by Woodward in *Signs of Sexual Behavior*, as well as in Rudner and Butowsky's (1981) article "Signs Used in the Deaf Gay Community," nevertheless causes problems in itself. This is a sensitive issue, and the present research needs to be incorporated into the ASL curriculum. If ASL students become interpreters or members of the Deaf community and a Deaf gay person sees them producing this variant (V2), the gay person will probably question whether the signer is closed-minded, homophobic, or just straight and ignorant of the preferred sign choice. This may present a level of discomfort for the gay individual. There are no instructional materials that inform straight people of the negative connotations associated with this sign; signers who do not interact with gay people may have never had the opportunity for this kind of input.

Members of the Deaf gay community, as well as people who support and interact with them, say that they feel comfortable using V3 as a general label for lesbians. This sign is seen as respectful whether used by a straight person or by another gay person. It may be considered neutral or positive, although most interpreters surveyed evaluated it as neutral. V4 is the most acceptable variant in all situations promoting gay and lesbian rights. It is seen as the most appropriate, and perhaps the most politically correct, variant for LESBIAN, and it seems to be moving away from its iconic relation to the sign for oral sex. Everyone who was aware of the existence of this sign labeled it the most positive.

A safe sign to use, if one is not sure of the connotations of all variants, is V3 (see Figure 3-14). This sign is said to be neutral in describing a woman or group of women who are lesbians, although it does not show as much respect to the person described as V4. Asking people on Gallaudet campus at random, not knowing their sexual identity or hearing status, showed that they generally sign with the joint contacting the chin (V3). In this study, V4 (Figure 3-15) was seen as the sign that the majority of gay men and lesbians prefer to use. Some lesbians in the D.C. area, Deaf and hearing alike, stated that when a straight person signs using the "web," they sense a negative stigma attached to that sign and may be a little leery about what the person's ideas are about lesbians. Some lesbians, who are a bit more feminine than others, prefer to use the tip version to describe themselves. Some of these women call themselves *lipstick lesbians* and would associate the "web" with descriptions of dykes.

In conclusion, the hearing informants seem to be very aware of the correct ways of designating a gay person or a characteristic of a member of the gay community. Those who were members of the gay community felt that they knew the politically correct signs and were confident of their ability to act as interpreter in any situation that called for those lexical items to be used. There was one female interpreter (#10), however, who felt she knew what was appropriate, when in fact some of her choices were better categorized with those of straight people. One might assume that if an interpreter is gay, he or she would naturally know the "right" signs to use. Our study reveals, however, that this is not always the case.

We are not aware of any other studies that have been conducted on this topic to date. This area of linguistics is very new to the Deaf community, and more studies will prove to be beneficial in the interpreting field. Interpreters are the people who relay information to many deaf individuals, and it is therefore imperative that they know the changes in the language as they surface.

Variations for the Term Gay

This section deals with the three variations of the lexical item *gay*: G + chin, #GAY, and HOMO-8. Following the same format that we used for the sign LESBIAN, these items are analyzed for production, knowledge, and connotations. (Keep in mind that the letters represent Deaf people and numbers represent hearing people). (See Tables 3-5 and 3-6.)

When the term *gay* appeared in either the audiotape or with the photographs, there were two methods of production. The first is a "G" or "Q" handshape that contacts the chin with the index finger and thumb, henceforth the G + chin (see Figure 3-17) The second variation is a lexicalized fingerspelled sign (Liddell &

Table 3-5. Signs produced by Deaf informants for the concept *gay*.

Respondents	G + chin	#GAY	HOMO-8
Straight Male	D, E	D, F	
Straight Female	J, K, L	K, L	
Lesbian Female	H, I	G, H, I	
Gay Male	A, B, C	A, B, C	

Table 3-6. Knowledge of variations for the concept *gay*.

Respondents	G + chin	#GAY	HOMO-8
Straight Male	D, E, F, 1, 13	D, F, 1, 13	D, E, F, 1, 13
Straight Female	J, K, L, 3, 4, 7,8 ,11, 12	J, K, L, 4, 8, 11, 12	J, K, L, 3, 4, 7, 8, 11,12
Lesbian Female	G, H, I, 5, 6, 10	G, H, I, 5, 6	G, H, I, 5, 6, 10
Gay Male	A, B, C, 2, 9	A, B, C, 2, 9	A, B, C, 2, 9

Johnson 1989) G-(A)-Y[11] (henceforth #GAY), formerly referred to as a finger-spelled loan sign (Battison 1979). #GAY was used by the largest majority of each group compared to other signs.

Most people felt strongly that #GAY was a friendly sign to use when referring to gay men (or lesbians, in some cases) and to the gay community. Gay men at the Lavender Languages and Linguistics Conference, held at American University in 1993, stated that #GAY was used to identify others but that, if they were to identify themselves in the first person, they would use G + chin. G + chin is seen as an

Figure 3-17. The sign GAY: G + CHIN.

Table 3-7. Respondents' attitudes toward different variants of *gay*.

Respondents	G + chin			#GAY			HOMO-8		
	+	ø	−	+	ø	−	+	ø	−
Straight Male		1		1	D				1
		13		13					13
		D		F					D
		E							E
		F							F
Straight Female	3	K	8	4	L				3
	7		11	8					4
	J		12	11					7
			L	12					8
				J					11
				K					12
									J
									K
									L
Lesbian Female	10	6	G	5					5
		I	H	6					6
				G					10
				H					G
				I					H
									I
Gay Male		A		2					2
		B		9					9
		C		A					A
				B					B
				C					C

NOTE: The responses of gay men and lesbians depend on who is producing the sign, but G + chin and #GAY are both seen as positive by all gay people.

ingroup sign; gay men prefer that straight people (either Deaf or hearing) use #GAY. Some gay people take offense when a straight person uses G + chin, perceiving negative connotations.[12] Table 3-7 shows the attitudes of the informants toward the different variations for *gay* and *homosexual*.

Some lesbian informants said they refer to themselves as #GAY instead of using one of the variations for LESBIAN, although they do occasionally call themselves V3 or V4. Their reason was that #GAY applies to both men and women. Most straight people mentioned that they were taught by others (gay people, school system, family) that to say HOMO-8 was negative and felt that #GAY has come to be considered a more appropriate sign in recent years. HOMO-8 (Figure 3-9) is considered a very derogatory sign for *homosexual*, and no one in either the Deaf or hearing group produced this sign in our study; some Deaf men and one Deaf woman, however, said they would use this sign among straight friends. In contrast, gay informants stated that it should not be used by straight people, regardless of their acceptance by members of the gay community. The use of this sign in ASL is perhaps analogous with the use of the word *fag* in English, which carries strong negative connotations. Both gay and lesbian informants would use the HOMO-8 variant only with other gay people in the community as ingroup teasing or mocking. All interpreters said that they would never use this sign in an interpreting situation unless the speaker meant it to be derogatory. An individual who wanted to refer to gay people in a respectful manner would use any of the compounds mentioned earlier or #GAY to include the entire community.

There is some controversy in both the straight and the gay communities as to what #GAY designates. Most informants used #GAY to refer to the community, while a few used it to refer to men only. #GAY carries the least negative connotations of all the signs discussed, and it crosses the boundary comfortably between gay and straight. V4 is the least politically charged of the three variations of the sign LESBIAN. The trend seen in the use of #GAY versus G+chin and the various locations and meanings for LESBIAN may indicate a wish to use those signs that produce the least negative reaction; that is, when given a lexical choice, signers use those signs that convey the least negative meaning.

Conclusion

This survey has only touched on issues of variation in American Sign Language relating to the lesbian and gay community; more research clearly needs to be done with a larger number of informants. From our research at Gallaudet, it appears that the signs considered most acceptable and used most widely are #GAY, V3, and V4. But according to the background forms filled out by participants, people from Washington State, Los Angeles, and other parts of the West Coast do not use #GAY, perceiving G + chin to have neutral, not negative, connotations. It is possible that these attitudes are limited to the East Coast or even to Washington D.C.; #GAY may be just a regional variant. We nevertheless suspect that #GAY may become the national standard. It is spreading swiftly at Gallaudet and in the surrounding area, and as Deaf people travel to different parts of the United States to attend conferences or events, neutral signs of this nature will become more widely used. #GAY had not appeared at California State University, Northridge, as of July 1994 (Kleinfeld);[13] but interested parties may nevertheless begin to use #GAY after discussing the research done at Gallaudet.

Appendix A
Pictures

The pictures involved are from greeting cards and postcards obtained from Lambda Rising, a gay bookstore in Washington, D.C. Numbers 1 through 10 include descriptions of the pictures shown to Deaf informants.

1. two "feminine" women in a bathtub, kissing each other
2. two "butch" women, separate, each looking the part of the tough person
3. two "feminine" women hugging each other
4. one woman with short hair, in men's cotton pants, sitting on a motorbike
5. woman with short cropped hair with a widow's peak, wearing a leather jacket
6. two men
7. two men, one holding the other, the other holding flowers, looking at each other
8. a man in high-heeled shoes, lifting a dumbbell
9. a man dressed like a woman with a blonde wig, a dress, and a frilly scarf
10. a boy between two men, in a family-like picture, one man wearing a T-shirt that reads "gay father," the other wearing a T-shirt that reads "gay stepfather"

Appendix B
Model Lecture: "Gay and Lesbian Youth in Crisis"

Lesbian and *gay* youth grow up with several strikes against them before they even discover or name their sexual orientation. At a young age, children observe society's dislike and disapproval of "*homosexuals*." Children learn that they may not fit society's expectations of the heterosexual.

Often these youth are afraid to '*come-out*' in fear that they won't be accepted because of the awful stereotypes that society has for *homosexuals*. The community of *gays*, *lesbians*, and *bisexuals* is still a community of people, not sick, unfit, weirdos that should be condemned to hell!

It is understandable that it would be difficult for a parent to look at their son dressed up like a *drag queen*, or to look at their daughter in men's clothing all the time. However, the community goes way beyond just sexual orientation. Being *gay* is not a bedroom issue only; these people are *gay* twenty-four hours a day. Within the community there are different groups of individuals. As mentioned earlier there are the *gay men*, *lesbian women*, and *bisexuals*. There is a lot of controversy in both the heterosexual and *homosexual* community as to the validity of a *bisexual*. Is it just a phase, or can a person actually be attracted to both sexes? We will not attempt to answer this question today.

What about the *gays* and *lesbians* in the community who dress a little different? The *femmes* who are referred to as *lipstick lesbians*, who often wear dresses, have long hair, long nails, make up and high heels—do people on the streets label them "*lesbian*"? Not usually, these are 'invisible,' who could live amongst the straight people without any doubt that they will be looked at as any different. On the opposite scale, there are the *butches* who may dress in men's clothing and have short hair. Or the *dykes*, who may be like a *butch*, but wear men's cologne, undergarments, body piercing, and may not shave any body hair. These may be generalizations, but statistics have not be done, and we can only draw conclusions on what we have seen.

What about the men who dress like *GQ* models, and perhaps have a higher pitched voice than most—do we call him a *fag, fairy,* or *effeminate*? More than likely he will be labeled that way, but how do we know what role he plays in his *homosexual* relationship? He may be very manly or macho in his personal life and we would never know. In fact it is really none of our business, just as the person walking down the street would offend you if they made assumptions about your personal life just because you may be "different" than they expected.

Appendix C
Lexical Items Used for Both Deaf and Hearing

HOMOSEXUAL	FEMININE
BISEXUAL	BUTCH
GAY	DYKE
LESBIAN	FAG (FAIRY)
DRAG	COME OUT
EFFEMINATE	

ACKNOWLEDGMENTS   An earlier version of this paper appeared in Lucas (1996). We would like to thank Robert E. Johnson for giving us his time during the summer and the school year to help us construct our graphs and for his all-around support and humor, which kept us sane; Ceil Lucas for being open-minded and for allowing us to explore this avenue in American Sign Language and for her essential feedback on our work; Jessica Chaiken for editing our orginal paper and for volunteering her time for more editing; Robert Hahn for his feedback and for being a sign model; Jody Dunn and E. Lynn Jacobowitz for being sign models; Robert Herbold, a computer technician, for his technical assistance with the computer; and our informants for their patience and help. Without you, this chapter would not have been possible. Last but not least, we would like to thank each other.

NOTES

1. James Woodward (1972) proposed that *deaf* be used when referring to the audiological condition of not hearing and that *Deaf* be used when referring to a particular group of deaf people who share a language. When we refer to deaf people in this chapter, we may use either 'Deaf' or 'deaf'; both terms refer to a person who uses ASL and/or a community of people including those who are hearing.

2. *Handshape* refers here to fingerspelling. The *J* handshape mentioned indicates the ASL form of the English letter *J*.

3. According to Battison (1979), this sign was coined as a fingerspelled loan sign. The term *lexicalized fingerspelling*, introduced by Liddell and Johnson in 1989, is now used in place of the term *fingerspelled loan sign*.

4. This information was collected from a videotape of the First ASL Linguistics Conference, supplied by Clayton Valli. The conference, held for the deaf gay and lesbian community, took place at the Old Post Office Pavilion in Washington, D.C.

5. These labels for sexual orientation were taken from a background sheet that infor-

mants filled out prior to the interview; bisexual women were classified with lesbians for the purpose of this study.

6. A full description of these signs is to be found in Kleinfeld and Warner (1994), "Prescriptivism in the Deaf Community Related to Gay, Lesbian, and Bisexual Signs."

7. CL indicates a classifier.

8. Analysis of data from the hearing interpreters in this section was taken from Kleinfeld (ms.), "Variation among Sign Language Interpreters: The Case of LESBIAN," Department of Linguistics, Georgetown University.

9. From Liddell and Johnson (1989). Johnson's (ms.) phonological notation is used to describe each variant and will be used throughout this chapter.

10. Analysis of the variations for the sign LESBIAN was taken from Kleinfeld (ms.).

11. Parentheses are used for letters that are not produced in the lexicalized finger-spelled sign.

12. This is a small pool of informants, and the signs and connotations reported in this section could be regional variations.

13. Mala Kleinfeld, the researcher for the hearing interpreters, surveyed some certified interpreters at the National Center on Deafness at California State University, Northridge, during a three-week period in June 1994.

REFERENCES

Aramburo, Anthony J. (1989). "Sociolinguistic Aspects of the Black Deaf Community." In Ceil Lucas (ed.), *The Sociolinguistics of the Deaf Community*. San Diego: Academic Press, pp. 103–119.

Battison, Robbin (1979). *Lexical Borrowing in American Sign Language*. Silver Spring, MD: Linstok, pp. 107–141.

Johnson, Robert E. (ms.). Lecture notes, "American Sign Language Morphology," Spring 1994. Department of Linguistics and Interpreting, Gallaudet University.

Kleinfeld, Mala S. (ms.). "Variation among Sign Language Interpreters: The Case of LESBIAN." Department of Linguistics, Georgetown University.

Kleinfeld, Mala S., and Noni Warner (1994). "Prescriptivism in the Deaf Community Relating to Gay, Lesbian, and Bisexual Signs." In Elizabeth Winston (ed.), *Communication Forum*. Washington, D.C.: Gallaudet University Press, pp. 67–97.

Liddell, Scott, and Robert E. Johnson (1989). "American Sign Language: The Phonological Base." *Sign Language Studies* 64: 195–277.

Lucas, Ceil, ed. (1996). *Multicultural Aspects in Deaf Communities*. Washington D.C.: Gallaudet Press.

Rudner, William A., and Rochelle Butowsky (1981). "Signs Used in the Deaf Gay Community." *Sign Language Studies* 30: 36–48.

Woodward, James (1972). "Implications for Sociolinguistics Research among the Deaf." *Sign Language Studies* 1: 1–7.

Woodward, James (1979). *Signs of Sexual Behavior: An Introduction to Some Sex-related Vocabulary in American Sign Language*. Silver Spring, MD: T. J. Publishers.

Zimmer, June (1989). "Towards a Description of Register Variation of Registers in ASL." In Ceil Lucas (ed.), *The Sociolinguistics of the Deaf Community*. San Diego: Academic Press, pp. 253–272.

4

*T*he Color of His Eyes

Polari and the Sisters of Perpetual Indulgence

IAN LUCAS

In 1950 a series of notes written on Christmas cards to friends became the basis for an article on the theatrical vocabulary known as *polari*. Yet even at such an early stage in its study, the writer Eric Partridge was warning:

> Parlyaree . . . is a glossary, a vocabulary, not a complete language. Little remains. Even that little may disappear. (1950: 116)

What, then, is polari, and what is its significance in British gay and theatrical culture?

Background

Polari is the most comprehensive extant form of British gay slang. It is derived from a variety of sources, including rhyming slang, circus backslang, Romany, Latin, and criminal cant. Its high renaissance occurred during the 1950s and 1960s, when it was popularized in the mainstream in England by the larger-than-life characters of Julian and Sandy in the BBC Radio series *Round the Horne*.

Gay slang in Britain dates back to the involvement of the homosexual subculture with the criminal "underworld." The homosexual subculture of the eighteenth century mixed with the gypsies, tramps, and thieves of popular song to pro-

85

duce a rich cross-fertilization of customs, phrases, and traditions. As the Industrial Revolution dramatically changed settlement patterns, more and more people drifted away from villages and small communities and moved to the larger towns in search of work and opportunity. In these larger urban locations, the scope for the development of nontraditional communities—communities of outcasts— substantially increased. The growth of molly houses (private spaces for men to meet, drink, have sex together, and practice communal rituals) encouraged the creation of a *molly* identity, culture, and language in the eighteenth century (Norton 1992: 99). A linguistic culture among the "outcasts" of society emerged and developed, feeding into that profession traditionally associated with poofs and whores: theater.

Much of Parlarey, the traveling showmen's language, appears to be derived from the *lingua franca* or the vocabulary of traveling actors and showmen during the eighteenth and early nineteenth centuries. Specifically, theatrical Parlarey included phrases such as *joggering omee* (street musician, possibly from the French *jongleurs*), *slang a dolly to the edge* (to show and work a marionette on a small platform outside the performance booth in order to attract an audience), and *climb the slang-tree* (to perform onstage). *Nanty dinarly* (having no money) also had a peculiarly theatrical translation in the phrase "There's no treasury today, the ghost doesn't walk." The disappearance of large numbers of traveling costermongers and cheapjacks by the early twentieth century effectively denied the language its breathing space. As many of the traveling entertainers moved sideways into traveling circus shows, so the language moved with them, kept alive as a living and changing language within circus culture.

By the mid-twentieth century, there had also been a crossover to a recognizably gay form of slang, with Polari used by the gay community to communicate in code in elaborate forms. Words such as *trade* and *ecaf* (backslang for *face*, shortened to *eek)* became part of gay subculture. *Blagging trade* (picking up sexual partners), *zhoosing your riah* (doing your hair), *trolling to a bijou bar* (stepping into a gay club), and *dishing the dirt* (recounting gossip) all became popular coded phrases to describe and encode an emerging homosexual lifestyle (Burton 1985: 39). By the 1960s, with secret homosexual clubs emerging in swinging London and the Wolfenden Committee discussing the possibility of law reform around (homo)sexuality, in line with changing social attitudes towards divorce, premarital sex, and abortion, it seems appropriate that Polari should rear its irreverent head as a code for an exciting and important period in gay history.

Polari became an appropriate theatrical manoeuvre with which to confuse and confound the *naff omees* (straight men).[1] It traveled the world via the sea queens, who incorporated navy slang into a new version of the language and also accommodated local dialects and phrases. Polari, by its furtive nature, attracted the bawdy and ribald—something as innocent-sounding as *varda the colour of his eyes* actually meant "check out the size of his penis" and *nanty curtain* meant that an *omee* (man) was circumcised. The capacity for innuendo that accompanied the bawdy nature of Polari naturally endeared the language to camp and comedy, and this is how the language crossed over into mainstream British radio comedy during the 1960s.

Jules and Sand: It's the Smut that Sells

> Omies and palones of this borough! We are poised at a moment in history. The future could be naff, or it could be bona. The time has come for a frank and honest varda at our awkward position. I am questing after this seat for the good of my fellow omies. Let us not mince words. Let us put our best lallie forward and with our eeks shining with hope, troll together towards the fantabulosa futurette! (Jules's maiden speech as a prospective member, *Keep Britain Bona*, BBC Radio)

The most famous and popular use of Polari came with *Round the Horne*, written by Marty Feldman and Barry Took. The program was a series of sketches performed by a regular team of comic actors, revolving around a number of regular characters that included such eccentric creations as Rambling Syd Rumpo, Daphne White-thigh, and Seamus Android. Among the menagerie of queer fellows were Julian and Sandy, two out-of-work actors who "made do" with a series of odd jobs and occupations. Jules and Sand, played by Kenneth Williams and Hugh Paddock, developed a cult following and, at the prime time of two-thirty on Sunday afternoons, titillated and astounded listeners with double (or quadruple) innuendos.

Jules and Sand were not, however, Polari purists. Theirs was a mixture of camp, innuendo, Polari, improvisation, and irony. Their presentation was safe, and their language reflected this; their Polari was accessible and used for comic timing. Although the innuendo behind their trips to Tangiers, a fashionable gay resort at that time, was (to a contemporary British audience) perverse, Julian and Sandy were recognizable as harmless, effeminate *omiepalones* making do. To this extent, they were sympathetic but not pitied: Jules's maiden speech for the "Keep Britain Bona" party represents not only the naiveté of the common man but also a radical desire to "make Great Britain Fairyland." Their language enabled them to encode the homosexual lifestyles of 1960s Britain—Jules and Sand were, at different times, dancers, musicians, caterers, lawyers, mediums, pet-shop owners, and book publishers—but it was also a language that set them apart. Kenneth Horne, the show's lynchpin, represented the *omie* on the street, both fascinated by and suspicious of Jules and Sand. Ostensibly straight, his own play with Polari—"Bold!"—demonstrated both the power and the vulnerability of the code. The language defined who was part of Jules's and Sand's social and, by implication, homosexual circle, but once the code had been broken, once Polari had been understood, codified, *blagged*, or picked up, it became ineffective as a defense mechanism against outside interrogation.

And here is a dilemma for Polari: The very nature of the language, its obliqueness, its anachronistic sense of time and place, mean that as a code or theatrical manoeuvre, it is very limited. What made it successful on radio—its ability to encode and diffuse the sexual and social experience of homosexuals through comedy—meant that in and of itself, Polari could only be a glossary, a collection of words and phrases that could be strategically employed either to create a sense of belonging (as would probably have been the case for itinerant actors and homosexual coteries) or to exclude *naff omees* from pointed conversations. As a language and form in itself, it never successfully developed to the point where it could be distanced from its context. With traveling showman, and later with the homosexual subculture of 1960s Britain, Polari was reinvented and reconstituted in order to serve a new purpose and to serve a community of interests based on exclusion and secrecy. *Round The Horne* had to dilute Polari through a comic, heterosexual filter in order to exoticize (and therefore make sense of) the language for its ostensibly heterosexual listeners. At the same time, the ubiquity of Polari bestowed on it a status and reverie that divorced it from its common roots. What used to be about the bawdy, the ribald, the everyday, and the irreverent become sanctioned as entertainment by none other than the country's national broadcasting institution, the BBC.

Polari then became exposed and, ultimately, vulnerable. Its success predicted its downfall. Polari's raison d'être had self-exploded; it was no longer needed as a theatrical manoeuvre in communities that had become legitimized or sanctioned, however restricted such acceptance might be. As a novel form of comedy, it had limited appeal for a larger audience, and once Britain had grown out of its penchant for smut in the harsh political realism of the 1980s, Polari faced exile from community and textbook, never having been fully recorded in the first place. Partridge's *Cinderella among Languages* lost her ticket to the Prince's Ball.

Una Lexicon Peroney!

Polari now occupies an almost mythical place in modern British gay culture. Terms such as *eek, riah, trade, troll, cottage* (a public place for cruising or picking up, such as public toilets) remain in common parlance. A gay freebie magazine emerged several years ago under the title *Varda*, and *Bona* magazine, launched in 1994 (to almost immediate failure), also echoed an earlier soft gay porn magazine of the same name.[2] Queens of a certain age and background are likely to retain Polari as part of their heritage, although opportunities for passing on the *bona lavs* are limited by the increasing polarization of the commercial queer scene, where marketing dictates a style and orientation based on premises of youth and beauty that create different and exclusive worlds for different ages. Where once community initiatives such as the London Lesbian and Gay Centre offered meeting spaces for cultures and heritages outside the commercial scene, the very failure of such resources indicates that an interest in the present, as opposed to the past, is what drives current queer markets. Polari can be marketed by androgynous and noncommittal pop idols such as Morrissey in titling an album *Bona Drag*, but his lyrics also ultimately alienate the language and culture: "The Piccadilly palare/ was just silly slang / between me and the boys in my gang."[3]

So the place for Polari is not now in the everyday, the ordinary, or the surreptitious. Instead, its role as the Cinderella among languages needs to be magically transformed—to become part of the extraordinary, the fabulous. And it is here that perhaps Polari has finally come home—in the ironic spirituality of the Sisters of Perpetual Indulgence, whose inventive gay liturgy requires a paradoxical, and entertaining, spiritual language. In Britain, the London Order of the Sisters of Perpetual Indulgence—America's most successful export of gay male nuns—was founded by Mother Ethyl Dreads-A-Flashback in autumn 1990. Already steeped in quasi-religious language from the Australian and American Orders, the profession to expiate Stigmatic Guilt and promulgate Universal Joy soon also became a mission to bring to the British gay community rituals and events that sponsored a sense of belonging, tradition, and spirituality. Here, the Sisters' events might best be understood by Dr. Elizabeth Stuart's literal definition of liturgy as "people's work" (1992: 10). The context for events such as blessings and canonizations had already been identified in America and Australia by the respective National Orders of Sisters. Fairly soon after the establishment of an Order in Britain, the need for a suitable British interpretation of New World initiatives was felt.

In Polari, the Sisters found a replacement for Latin, the traditional liturgical language of Western Christianity. It married the sacred and the profane in the language of the event. Polari, the occasional language, became the Language of the Occasion. It represented in itself a sacrament, revered and passed down from generation to generation of initiates. Yet it is more than a mystical language, half-forgotten and only half-understood. It is also the language of irony and parody, as are the Sisters' celebrations themselves. They work on many levels. As events, they are transformed into communal and cultural celebrations by the presence of a recognizable lesbian and gay community. At the same time, many of the ceremonies are parodies of traditional institutionalized events—marriages, blessings, honors. But parody itself can create only a vacuum. It does not replace that which it usurps. Its role is to subvert or usurp, not to create alternative or revitalized structures. The Sisters of Perpetual Indulgence aim to provide valid and resonant rituals while using traditional forms to criticize and/or reclaim notions of spirituality and "virtue." They are twenty-first-century nuns, putting the virtue into Virtual Reality.

The Polari used in these events is a version of Jules's and Sand's high-camp comedy but also of more traditional (historical) Polari *lavs*. In order to illustrate this textually, it is necessary to look at one such ceremony in some detail, while, one hopes, not betraying or overanalyzing the event itself to the point of collapse. The first major event conducted by the Sisters of Perpetual Indulgence, and therefore possibly the first-ever use of Polari in an organized public ritual, was the canonization of the film maker Derek Jarman at his home, Prospect Cottage, in Dungeness, Kent, under the shadow of a nuclear power station.

The canonization took place in the light of Ian McKellen's knighthood for services to theater by the same government that had introduced the notorious Section 28 (which made it illegal for local authorities to use public funds in order to "promote" homosexuality), against which both he and Derek Jarman had publicly campaigned. Derek Jarman had also publicly identified himself as HIV-positive, while at the same time celebrating what the mainstream press saw and criticized as a promiscuous irresponsibility in *blagging trade* on Hampstead Heath, an infamous (and very popular) gay cruising ground in North London.

Canonization of St. Derek

In many ways, Derek Jarman's canonization was a very traditional, structured honors ceremony. It was broadly divided into sections and events that self-consciously parodied themselves. In order, these were the Baying of Derek; the Giving Away of Derek; Procession to the Altar; Welcoming; First Reading; Second Reading; Sermon; Laying on of Hands; Crowning and Hailing of the Saint; Closing. Polari was used intermittently but was also treated as one of the structuring elements of the ceremony; it helped formalize responses between the Sister Celebrant and the Gathered Faithful. In this sense, it helped define the event itself. Responses were conditioned and directed through the formal use of Polari as High Polari, a ceremonial language. For those members of the Gathered Faithful who were unsure about the sincerity of the canonization, the use of Polari offered a refuge, a semicomprehensible sanctioning and mystifying of the Event. The Baying of Derek consisted of the calling of Derek from within his cottage, in order to be presented to the Sisters by the Best Man (or the nearest available thing). The simple chanting of "Derek! Derek! Derek! Out! Out! Out!" echoed political rallies against Section 28, the Gulf War, and the poll tax, where the British government was shouted "Out! Out! Out!" A hymn parody, "Derek's Windy Garden," led to the Giving Away of Derek:

> BEST MAN   Bona Sisters of Perpetual Indulgence, I plead with you to take this naked and unblessed omipalone into your fertile bosom and make of him a man.
>
> (*The Sisters reject him*)
>
> (*The Best Man repeats his petition*)
>
> (*The Sisters again reject him*)
>
> BEST MAN   Sisters, you little witches, I plead with you for a third and final time, to take this naked and unblessed omipalone and make of him a man.
>
> SISTERS   Yes! We shall make a man of him.

The symbolic rejections and repetitions simply acted as manoeuvers to formalize and structure the ceremony, in the same way that during the opening of Parliament every year, the Queen's petition to enter Parliament is traditionally denied and then allowed. It naturally followed that in the Canonization, Derek should then process to the altar, a reconstituted ceremonial space in front of the Gathered Faithful, and then join the Sisters in what would later become a traditional Polari welcome for the Order:

> SISTER CELEBRANT   Omies and palonies of the Gathered Faithful, how bona to varda your dolly old eeks.
>
> SISTERS   Bona to vada you,
>
> GATHERED FAITHFUL   To vada you bona.

The Welcoming is itself not only a parody of the traditional welcome with which Julian and Sandy used to greet Kenneth Horne on BBC Radio; it also translates into Polari the mainstream comedian Bruce Foryth's (camp) catchphrase for his primetime television game show *The Generation Game*: "Nice to see you, to see you nice!" In continuing the welcome, the Sister Celebrant invoked spiritual imagery and phraseology but also undermined the seriousness of the event by juxtaposing the reverential tone with the "spirit" of an early cult children's television show, *Muffin The Mule*, underlining the irony behind the ceremony:

> We've all trolled down here to honour this bona omipalone, Derek. We, the Sisters of Perpetual Indulgence and Gathered Faithful, do hereby invoke the spirit of our beloved Muffin the Mule, to recognise the bona works and practises of Mr. Derek Jarman in promulgating Universal Joy within the Community and outside of it, in his bona bijou celluloid masterpiecettes, and in his promulgations off screen. But most of all, in honour of his fantabulosa nose.

In order to put the Canonization in context, Derek was reminded "that this canonization means fuck all." After the first reading from *Miss Manner's Book Of Etiquette*, and a second reading from a national paper of the day, a self-consciously long-winded and ironic sermon was given by the Sister Celebrant, who ruminated on the similarities between multicultural society and the making of tea, culminating in the Laying on of Hands:

> Sissies and Omies and palonies of the Gathered Faithful, we're now getting to the kernel, the nub, the very thrust of why we're gathered here today at Derek's bona bijou lattie. The reason being that Dezzie, bless his little heart-face, is very dear to our heart. Look at him, his little lallies trembling with anticipation, heart of gold, feet of lead, and a knob of butter. So, perhaps we could take a little time to reach out and touch, to handle for a moment Dezzie's collective parts.

At the same time as Derek Jarman, as a person living with AIDS, was having his own body revered, he was also the object of ridicule. He had become, through the use of Polari in an irreligious manner, the site of the sacred and the profane. This was furthered by the Crowning of the Saint with "a bona helmet on his riah" and a necklace made of cock-rings and pornographic pictures. Sister Celebrant said:

> And now, with this bona crown, we, the Sisters of Perpetual Indulgence, are proud to name this humble omipalone as "St. Derek of Dungeness, of the Order Of Celluloid Knights."

It seems appropriate that it was Derek Jarman, whose film *Sebastiane* was performed entirely in Latin, who should be the first British saint to be canonized in Polari. That the ceremony had an effect on him is certain. When asked to pick his favorite readings for BBC Radio's *Open Book* series, where celebrities discuss their favorite pieces of literature, Jarman asked for a recording of the Canonization to be included. And, on his death in 1994, most of his obituaries mentioned his canonization as an important event in his life. He himself saw it as defining the 1990s.[4]

And so Polari becomes part of the Sisters' mission in expiating Stigmatic Guilt and promulgating Universal Joy. It becomes part of the canon of lesbian and gay ritual and celebration, working not as a functional but as a ceremonial language and heritage. Polari gains protection from a raising of its status. It is fragile, broken, and vulnerable, but it is possible for us to preserve remnants, *natty fakements*, unrestricted by a language whose structures have to be negotiated, reclaimed, fought for, in the way that much heterospeak has been. The most eloquent and urgent call to arms for Polari comes from an "internal" communiqué within the Sisterhood, as Sister Dolores Fanchon reminds the Order of its responsibility in promulgating Polari:

> Cant the parlary in the Bungeries, cant the parlary in the charvering carseys and the drags. One lexicon peroney and the bona lavs of dolly parlary can be detected by the hearing cheats of all those incognitos and margeries in Eine. Tell your bencoves and beanpeas, when acting the bougereau quality or doing the rights, our lavs of parlary will bespangle us like natty fakements, and do the rights to all those mace gloaks who cant the naf, and still expect the parkering ninty of the high camp existance [*sic*].

No translation will be given!

ACKNOWLEDGMENTS   With thanks to all those who have helped contribute words and phrases, especially the Sisters of Perpetual Indulgence and Sister Dolores Fanchon.

Appendix
A Simple Polari Glossary

1 *una*
2 *dewey*
3 *tray*
4 *quattro (quater)*
5 *chinker*
6 *say*
7 *setter*
8 *otter*
9 *nobba*
10 *daiture*

acting dickey   temporary work
badge cove   pensioner
balonie   rubbish
barney   fight

battyfang   to hit and bite
beancove   young queen
bencove   close friend
bevie   public house, also a drink
billngsgate   bad language
bingey   penis

blag   pick up
bloke   man, any fellow
bolus   chemist
bona   good
bona nochy   goodnight
booth   room

bougereau quality outrageously nellie
bungery pub
buvare a drink
cackle talk/gossip
cant to talk
caravansera railway station
carsey house
charver to have sex
chavies boys, children
climb the slanging tree perform
clobber clothes
corybungus arse
cottage public toilet
cove friend, mate
diddle gin
dilly Picadilly Circus
dinarly money
do the rights seek revenge
dolly dear
ecaf (eek) face
Eine London
fakements personal adornments
fantabulosa marvelous
farting crackers trousers
feeliers girls, children
flatties men (in audience)
fungus old man
gaffer showman
gillie woman (in audience)
hearing cheat ear
lally leg
lattie home/house
lally covers trousers

lav word
lily law police
lucoddy body
metzes money
mince walk effeminately
mish shirt
moey mouth
multi many
mungaree food
naff uninteresting (straight)
nanty not, none, negative
nanty dinarlee penniless
omie man
omiepalone homosexual
on your tod by yourself
palone woman
parkering ninty wages/ salary
parlary to talk in Polari
peroney for each one
pig elephant
ponging somersaulting
rattling cove taxi driver
riah hair
scarper escape, to do a Johnny Scarper
stampers shoes
strillers piano
strillers omie/palone pianist
thews arms
trade sexual partner
troll to walk, look for trade
trundling cheat car
varda to look
yews eyes

NOTES

1. Peter Burton records *naff* in this sense as meaning "normal as fuck," although *naff* is most often derivative of "naive." It is worth noting that a few years ago the Prince of Wales, Prince Charles, caused a controversy when he allegedly used the phrase *naff off*. Perhaps the British monarchy are secret Polari speakers?

2. *Bona* here means good, an exclamation. It has been suggested that it is a pun on *boner*, i.e., erection, although I have only rarely heard the phrase in England. A more likely suggestion for the origins of *Bona* as a title for a glossy gay lifestyle magazine lies in the success of the popular women's magazine, *Bella*, whose formula *Bona* followed. One suggestion for *Bona*'s title was *Fella*, but this was thought too explicit a cross-reference, and so *Bona* seemed an appropriate second choice.

3. "Piccadilly Palare" by Morrissey, from the album *Bona Drag*.

4. Comment made by Derek Jarman on a 1992 touring exhibition of photographs of the Sisters and the canonization, *In A Perfect World*, by the photographer Denis Doran.

REFERENCES

Burton, Peter (1985). *Parallel Lives*. London: GMP.

Jarman, Derek (1992). *At Your Own Risk: A Saint's Testimony*. London: Hutchinson.

Lucas, Ian (1994). *Impertinent Decorum: Gay Theatrical Manoeuvres*. London: Cassell.

Norton, Rictor (1992). *Mother Clap's Molly House: The Gay Subculture in England 1700–1830*. London: GMP.

———. (1984). In Paul Beale (ed.), *Dictionary of Slang and Unconventional English*, 8th ed. London: Routledge & Kegan Paul.

Partridge, Eric (1950). "Parlyaree—Cinderella among Languages." In *Here, There and Everywhere: Essays: Upon Language*. London: Hamish Hamilton.

Seago, Edward (1924). *Sons of Sawdust — With Paddy O'Flynn's Circus in Western Ireland*. London: Putnam.

Watson, Oscar (1990). "Polare as a Second Language." *Square Peg*, no. 27.

5

*P*ots and Pans

Identification of Queer Japanese
in Terms of Discrimination

JAMES VALENTINE

Japanese and Western people commonly define each other as queer. The peculiarity is considered to apply generally to the "other" people but also includes particular notions of sexual strangeness.[1]

Increasingly, and especially with the breakup of the Soviet Union and the consequent search for new solidarities and scapegoats, notions of national or cultural identity are constructed in an occidental-oriental contrast that commonly sets "the Japanese" against "the West," each representing outsiders beyond the circle of those who belong. Japan and the United States, in particular, have come to perceive each other as mutually defining opposites (Robertson 1990: 188). A special construction of Japan as Other has thus become predominant in the various possible "Othernesses of Japan"[2] that can be set up.

The overriding Western image of Japan is one of mystery and inscrutability. Japanese people are seen as weird and wonderful, the strangest of strangers. The peculiarity of "the Japanese" is seen to lie in their homogeneity and their conformity. Their queer qualities are seen as quaint, doomed to die out in a modernization process, or (like quality control) as virtues to be copied in the international economic competition, in which the Japanese (seen in racist terms) are thought to have an unfair advantage, since they are "naturally" group-oriented and cooperative.

In this characterization, Japanese theories tend to agree. Indeed, *Nihonjinron*, theories of the Japanese people, are constructed in academic and media circles both outside and inside Japan, with remarkable agreement on the peculiar nature of "the Japanese," whatever positive or negative evaluations may be placed thereon (Breger 1992: 191). Westerners, in turn, are seen as queer, from a Japanese point of view, in terms of individual peculiarity and the peculiarity of Western individualism, as distinguished from the kind of individuality that is consistent with Japanese spirit (Hendry 1992: 56; Moeran 1984: 262–263).

The queer qualities of the contrasting culture incorporate conceptions of sexual queerness. Western views of "oriental" men may characterize them as failing to conform to Western codes of masculinity, and this combination of sexism and racism intersects with imperialist and colonialist fantasies, promoting the idea that "good natives are feminized—submissive and grateful—and that the passive, exotic and feminized East is eager to submit to the domination of the masculine West" (Garber 1992: 124–125).[3]

Similarly, Japanese people tend to view homosexuality as something foreign. The predominant image of homosexuality in Japan is Western,[4] as when the few television programs referring explicitly to gay men give Western examples (Valentine in press), and when *shōjo manga* (girls' comics) portray androgynous Western youths in aristocratic affairs (Aoyama 1988: 195; Buruma 1985: 125). In the same way, AIDS is seen as a foreign threat; since 1986 gay saunas in Japan have put up notices barring foreigners, as if only foreign gay men were likely to be HIV-positive and Japanese men were somehow by definition safe.

The combination of sexism and racism in the mutually defining orientalist-occidentalist discourse further defines the women of the opposing culture from a male heterosexist point of view as sexually ideal and ideally sexual. They are seen as the acme of sexualized womanhood and as supersexual in appetite and availability.

The sexual strangeness of foreigners from a male heterosexist standpoint renders the epithet *queer* particularly appropriate. The equivalent Japanese term is *hen*. Although of itself this lacks the immediate homosexual connotation of the English term, it can, as noted later, refer to sexual strangeness. The Japanese word is commonly applied to foreigners, as in the phrase *hen-na gaijin* (queer/strange foreigner[s]), and to other outsiders: the term *gaijin* (foreigner) is itself a combination of *gai* (outside) and *jin* (person). Foreigners who stay outside Japan are not strange. Foreigners in Japan, or more specifically Japanized foreigners, foreigners who try to act Japanese, appear queer (Lebra 1976: 25; Hendry 1993a).[5] Outsiders who remain clearly outside do not pose the problem of marginality; it is within an insider context that their peculiarity is perceived. Those who are neither properly inside nor out are thus especially liable to characterization as queer.

In a society where pure, unambiguous belonging is paramount (Lebra 1976: 24) and homogeneity is (falsely) assumed, outsiders within gain extra significance[6] and are seen as especially strange, quintessentially queer.[7] Outsiders within consist of those whose belonging is uncertain, incomplete, or improper, including those who transgress the conventional categories of gender and sexuality. Queers are queer in Japan, too.

Gendered Identification and Erotic Practice

The identification of lesbians and gay men[8] in Japan has to be understood in terms of the predominant conflation of sex, gender, and sexuality. Sexuality (unlike gender) is not a major source of identity, and those whose sexual orientation is toward the same sex are identified as differently gendered. This must be seen in the context of the tradition of erotic relations between men and androgynous youths.

In Japan, until the Meiji Restoration (1868), a tradition of same-sex relations was able to continue without identification of the person as a type of sexual being. Yet even the acknowledgement of same-sex relations was variable, with greater recognition for men than women. Lesbian relations went largely uncategorized, and lesbians are still relatively ignored today, having fewer labels than their male counterparts.

Although males who had sexual relations with other males were not normally identified in terms of their sexuality, younger males were often conceived in terms of gender marginality: "not women, but not men either" (Schalow 1991: 120). Those who were identified in sexual terms were either the youths who were the objects of erotic attention or males who were working as prostitutes. Sexual identification was thus generally ignored except in terms of the objects of male desire and in terms of those in sexual employment.[9]

Eroticism between males was nonetheless acknowledged (even where the males were not identified with it) and was known as *nanshoku* (or *danshoku*)—literally 'male color': color (*shoku* or *iro*) is often used in Japanese to indicate eroticism or sensual desire. *Nanshoku* can be conceived as a distinctive Edo tradition of "male homosexuality" obliterated since Meiji (Aoyama 1988: 195). This tradition was both conventionalized and idealized; the encouragement of particular forms (for example, those consistent with samurai virtues) did not, however, prevent their adaptation and transgression, and hence there existed a "tremendous range of sexual behaviors" (Schalow 1991: 128).

From the Meiji Restoration, there was a particular concern in official circles about eradicating homosexuality (Takada 1994: 196). For a short time (1873–1883), this even meant the establishment of a specific law against male homosexual practice (Watanabe 1989: 121–122). The modernization process was seen as one of Westernization, equivalent to civilization (Mita 1992: 220n), and it was not only the technological, legal, and political apparatus that was adopted from abroad; Western conceptions of sexuality were imported, too.[10]

In relation to male homosexuality, this meant the exchange of colorful and romantic terms for designations that either translated Western concepts or focused on gender ambiguity rather than sexuality. Prewar popular terms tended to refer to gender rather than sexuality, so a man seen as feminine might be called *oyama*, referring (as does *onnagata*) to the male actors of female roles in Kabuki (Watanabe 1989: 84), again drawing on the tradition of androgyny. Most commonly, however, homosexual activity went unlabeled, unacknowledged.

Unspecified Strangeness

Identification of homosexuality in terms of gender transgression means that the sexuality, unspecified and subsumed under gender, is not fully acknowledged in sexual terms; the sexuality remains implicit, if not completely desexualized. Recognition is, however, greater for men than for women. Lesbian relations are still accorded less acknowledgement and visibility and face a more restricted battery of concepts.

Unspecified sexuality is in some senses freer, escaping the confines of categorization; yet it is at the same time more invisible and lacking in subcultural support. Even so, it may not escape all categories. Relationships and identities are still regarded as gendered, and sexuality may be implicitly acknowledged as strange, yet unspecified. There may be qualms about references to queers and sensitivity to specifically sexual terms, not out of concern for the objects of definition but for the sake of decency and decorum. Thus, direct sexual reference may be avoided, but indirect terms of discrimination may be applied.

In Japanese society, where concerns for polite speech and etiquette are highly developed,[11] euphemistic expressions flourish. In some cases, decency may make it very difficult to refer at all to particular people, for no words can be sufficiently euphemistic. Here, verbal specification may be avoided through the use of hand gestures. In the West, a common gesture to refer to gay men is the limp wrist, combining notions of effeminacy with a faint put-down: damning with faint gestures. In Japan, the equivalent gesture involves raising the hand to shield the mouth, in a movement similar to that required by Japanese etiquette of women laughing, but in the case of gay men this gesture is reversed, so that the palm turns outwards instead of inwards—a twisted reversal of feminine modesty. Lesbians, however, are not even accorded a gesture.

In verbal terms, the most common indirect discriminatory designation of otherness in Japanese is the already mentioned equivalent of *queer*—*hen*—which has negative connotations and can also mean suspicious-looking. *Hen* has an all-purpose usage in referring to peculiar difference and is thus less specifically related to sexuality than *queer* has become in English.

Japanese writing uses *kanji* (Chinese characters), most of which have multiple readings, thus permitting ambiguity and allusion without preventing specification where needed.[12] *Hen* is written with the *kanji* 変, which can also be read as the first one or two syllables of words such as *kawari* and *kawatta*, implying change, difference, inconstancy, becoming other: becoming other renders one queer and perhaps unpredictable. *Hen* and *kawari* can further refer to accident, calamity, something going wrong; something queer has happened.

In combination words, *hen* carries connotations of change and strange. With *jin* (person) it forms *henjin* (strange person, 'queer fish'). The *hen* of *henjin* is, however, occasionally written with a different *kanji* (偏), which can be read as *katayo(ru)/(ri)*, implying one-sidedness, bias, unbalance, deviation. This is also the *kanji* used in *henken* (prejudice). The idea of an odd person being unbalanced or one-sided is also found in the discriminatory word *katawa*, whose closest English equivalent is 'cripple'. *Katawa* can be written with two *kanji* that combine 'one/side' and 'wheel', conveying the image of a (vehicle with a) single wheel and thus not operating "properly." It is noteworthy that *katawa* is sometimes used by the older generation today to refer to an unmarried man, implying that the other half is needed for one to function properly and that to be unmarried is a form of disability. Not to be properly paired up is clearly odd.

With its alternative written forms, *henjin* may imply not only someone strange but someone unbalanced. In English the notion of a person being unbalanced hints at mental illness. This meaning is also found in *kawatta*, which, when used to describe a person (*hito*) as in *kawatta hito*, is a euphemistic way of referring to mental illness (Hendry 1988: 410).

Although the "queer" connotations of *hen* are general, rather than specifically sexual, *hen/kawatta* can be used to refer to sexual strangeness. This reference becomes more direct and explicit in combinations such as *henshitsu* and *hentai*.

Henshitsu (literally 'change in quality') has the meaning of degeneration, so that *henshitsu-sha* (*sha* meaning 'person') comes to mean a degenerate or deviant, especially a sexual "pervert."

Hentai (denoting change in state, condition, or appearance and hence metamorphosis or transformation) carries the additional meaning of perversion or abnormality, especially when used as an adjective. *Hentai-sha* is an abnormal person, especially a sexual "pervert," and is used as a shortened term for the more explicit *hentai-seiyoku-sha* (*seiyoku* meaning 'sexual desire').

An even shorter version of this, which would have begun as a euphemism, is *etchi*, meaning 'lewd' or 'indecent'. *Etchi*, written in *katakana* (the Japanese syllabary generally used for writing foreign words), is the Japanese pronunciation of the Roman letter *H*, which is the first letter of *hentai* (when written in the Roman alphabet). *Etchi* (which would be a little like using *Q* to stand for *queer* in English) can be used for several kinds of sexual indecency or lasciviousness, such as when men make use of crowded subway trains to touch women sexually, but it can also refer to queer sexuality, so a lesbian schoolteacher may be referred to as *etchi* by her pupils.

Hen, in its various forms and combinations, thus highlights a difference and judges it queer: an odd otherness. Although an all-purpose term for peculiarity, in particular contexts it refers to queer sexuality, but with less specific implication of homosexuality than its English counterpart now carries. The unspecified strangeness of *hen* is suitable for implying queerness, while at the same time avoiding explicit sexual reference. For more direct identification of queer sexuality in Japan, foreign terms have been adopted.

Foreign Forms

In Japan the majority of terms used to refer specifically to lesbians and gays have been imported. Imported concepts, which in many cases retain a recognizably foreign form in the Japanese language, convey the notion of alien forms of sexuality.[13]

In the Meiji era, Western legal and political forms were introduced, together with Western specialisms and notions of expertise. These institutions promote lengthy bureaucratic formulations, including categories of sexuality and deviation, often conceived in medical and legal terms. The expansion of categories increases the scope for both discrimination and euphemism. The adoption of Western concepts of sexuality has resulted in a proliferation of terms for lesbians and, especially, gay men in Japan. These include the coining of new Japanese terms and the translation, borrowing, and adaptation of Western terms. Many of these discriminating concepts, dressed for the sake of decency in their metaphorical or foreign form,[14] are passed or cut down into popular terms of abuse.

The concept of homosexuality, as constructed in the West, acquired its most direct translation into Japanese as *dōseiai*, a formal or bureaucratic term, not much used in common parlance. Interestingly, the Japanese term is closer to 'homophilia', as *ai* means 'love' rather than 'sex' (so that the literal meaning is 'same-sex love'), but this may merely reflect a Japanese preference for euphemisms. The 'same-sex' can be either female or male, as is the case in principle with 'homosexuality', though *dōseiai*, in contrast to the English term, is not always in practice assumed to refer only to male homosexuality. *Dōseiai* is found with reference to female couples in early-twentieth-century Japan (Robertson 1989: 57). This usage for either sex survives in contemporary Japan. For example, the third episode of the television drama serial *Kōkō Kyōshi* (High school teacher), shown on Japanese television in January 1993, was entitled *Dōseiai*, referring to lesbianism.

Although *dōseiai* can refer to both male and female homosexuality, the term *lesbian* was also imported from the West, becoming in Japanese *rezubian*. This is another formal term that was introduced without achieving common usage: through its foreign form and formality it both makes and masks reference.

The formal terms *dōseiai* and *rezubian* are rather long and clumsy: to mean a homosexual, *dōseiai* has to become *dōseiai-sha* or *dōseiai no hito*. This is an interesting contrast with the English term (and its equivalents in other European languages), where the shorter term (homosexual rather than homosexual*ity*) identifies the person. Unwieldy translated and transliterated terms, employed as bureaucratic definitions, fail to gain popularity in everyday parlance and are to some extent protected from derogatory commonsense overtones. Long terms last long-term. Abbreviations, however, enable wider usage; thereby the currency changes more rapidly and is more readily degraded.

Thus, for lesbians the abbreviation *rezu* is much more widely known and used than the longer, formal term *rezubian*. The parallel term for gay men is *homo*. Both *rezu* and *homo* are commonly used in a discriminatory manner. *Homo* is an abbreviation of homosexual, but the abbreviated term (as in English) refers only to male homosexuals. An alternative would be *gei* (gay), but here, as so often, the import of an alien term is accompanied by a change of meaning and limited applicability.

In Japanese use of foreign terms over time we can trace the process of adoption of a term and its change of signification. The English word *gay* (*gei*), for instance, first came to mean, during the postwar period in Japan, a male prostitute (*gei-bōi*/gay-boy), especially one who was cross-dressed. Its reference was thus to sexual employment rather than to sexual preference. More recently, the term has come to be used in its Western sense. Indeed, it tends to be confined to describing Western people and situations, as well as aspects of the commercial scene, as in gay bars (*gei-bā*) and magazines. In terms of identification, *gei* carries implications of a political stance or movement, of sexuality defining self, and hence of coming out. Thus, in Japan identification as "gay" is unlikely for those who are not part of the gay commercial scene or who do not conceptualize themselves primarily in terms of sexuality.

Even terms of sexual identification can become desexualized, as in a recent adaptation of the meaning of *homo*[15] in the coining of a new concept *semi-homo*, reported in the 31 March 1993 issue of the popular weekly Japanese magazine *Spa*. The report suggests that in Japan there is a new phenomenon of single men living together, who can be described as *semi-homo*. Although their sexual orientation is toward women, they have lost interest in sex. They find that modern independent Japanese women expect or demand too much of them, and so they retreat from dating and the prospect of marriage and instead live with other men as couples, though without sleeping together. The link with homosexuality is thus simultaneously devised and denied by the media: "In name and situation [homo and semi-homo] look partly the same, but they are completely different" (*Kotoba to jōtai ichibu nite iru ga, mattaku kotonaru mono da*) (1993: 50). In this case, an apparently sexual term is employed to describe marital status rather than sexuality, thus revealing the continuing emphasis on marriage in Japanese society.

Whatever their change of meaning, the imported short terms of reference for lesbians and gay men retain their visibly foreign form in Japanese. Terms borrowed from foreign languages (except Chinese) are kept visibly apart by using a special script, *katakana* (or, less frequently, by maintaining their original foreign script). Thus, same-sex relations, designated in foreign terms and marked out by distinct script, can be kept apart from Japanese ways, confirming a prejudice (relying on a neglect of history) that these queer forms are not Japanese but those of foreigners.

Apart from the offspring of a Japanese and a non-Japanese (called *hāfu*, meaning 'half' and written in *katakana*), lesbians and gay men are the only minority in Japan to be commonly identified in visibly foreign terms.[16] Borrowed words in *katakana* script do not, of course, necessarily convey negative evaluations. Foreign forms may be adopted for euphemism, fashion, or fun. Indeed, the terms adopted to refer to lesbians and gay men are often initially euphemistic: lack of familiarity holds off contemptuous connotations, while suggesting something originally unfamiliar. Borrowed terms are ideal for clothing strange sexualities, providing them with an outside coat of decency.

Thus, an effective way of dealing with queers is to define them in foreign forms. These forms may become familiar with frequency of usage and, as short or shortened terms (in particular *rezu* and *homo*), take on a discriminatory coloring that the lengthy formal euphemisms largely manage to avoid.

Kin and Kitchen

In contrast, native Japanese terms may (like the generic *hen*) euphemize by referring to a general oddness, not specifically sexual, or they may try to understand the strange in the comforting conceptions of kin and kitchen.

The domestic sphere of kin and kitchen is called on to provide familiar forms for conceptualizing queers in Japan. A province thought appropriate to women is especially suitable for the identification of gay men, who are primarily conceived as transgressing gender boundaries.

The most popular Japanese-derived term for gay men places them in the kitchen. They are called *okama*, which has become a familiar term of discrimination. *Kama* literally means 'cauldron', 'kettle', or 'pot', as in a pot for cooking rice. When the *o* prefix is added, the expression becomes more indirect, polite, and feminized, and it is in this version that the term is used to designate gay men. The softened expression is for the ears of straight society. Its tasteful allusion does not imply respect for the feelings of those designated.

Okama does not just associate gay men with the kitchen. The pot is considered to be shaped like a bottom, and its use in cooking further connotes a hot bottom. This image is confirmed by a portrayal of an *okama* in the popular 1990 film comedy *Byōin e ikō* (Let's go to hospital), in which the *okama* was shown in one scene with a firework up his bottom. Although the *kama* part of *okama* can be written with the *kanji* for pot 釜, it is commonly written phonetically in the Japanese *hiragana* syllabary. The *o* prefix is almost always written in *hiragana* but may occasionally be written with the *kanji* 阿. In Japanese, the choice of written character, from among several homophones, can carry special connotations. The character 阿 tends to have negative references such as flattery and fawning, or it may be used patronizingly as a prefix in naming a woman or child. The *O* of Okuni, the rather disreputable female founder of Kabuki, is written this way.[17]

The meaning of *okama* has changed since Meiji, when it was used to refer to a male prostitute. Its popularity declined after the war but revived in the 1970s through its use as a term of ridicule in the media. On Japanese television it is still the most common way of referring to gay men. Although its usage is wide, its reference is restricted to those seen as feminine in manner and dress, thereby carrying further connotations of transvestism. Its general application to gay men reveals the conflation of gender and sexuality in Japan. A sexual orientation to the same sex implies transgression to the opposite gender.

To find an equivalent term in English, it would be necessary to emphasize either the connotations of femininity (as in *queen* or, especially, *drag-queen*, with its reference to transvestism) or of passivity (if a relatively indirect and delicate slang term could be found for a person practicing so-called passive anal intercourse).

In parallel to *okama*, and as a kind of afterthought,[18] a term was adopted for lesbians: *onabe*. Just as *kama* means 'pot', *nabe* means 'pan' and, as in English, is shallower and has a wider opening than a pot. Like *pots and pans* in English, *nabe-kama* suggests basic kitchen utensils. In their metaphorical use, pots and pans are placed together in a conceptual opposition that indicates their common but contrasting transgressions. *Onabe* was promoted by the media in the early 1970s,[19] but despite attempts to popularize it, it has never really caught on, which further indicates that lesbians are accorded less recognition than gay men in Japan. Their conception is derivative of prior constructions of gay men as *okama*.

The subsequent and subsidiary conception of *onabe* suggests less concern with and about lesbians, while its parallel to the more popular *okama* further demonstrates that identifications in Japan are still primarily in terms of gender rather than sexuality. The restricted acknowledgement of queer sexuality in Japan is even more scant for lesbians. Sexual relationships between women, even where on occasion suggested or represented in the media, as in television dramas, tend to go unlabeled (Valentine in press). Lesbians are thus denied credibility, passing untermed and unrecognized,[20] except in the odd derogatory reference to *rezu* or in terms like *onabe*, which are conceived through gender, mirroring the pattern by which gay men are characterized.

Onabe is the stereotype of lesbian that most Japanese have: a woman who acts and dresses in "masculine" style and uses masculine language. It is thus the opposing echo of *okama*. Beyond the media, *onabe* became part of the commercial scene. The first reported *onabe* bar, called *Kikōshi* (Young noble), opened in the Roppongi district of Tokyo in 1973, and its customers included *dansō rezubian* (masculine-attired lesbians) (Nanami 1990: 102). In the 1980s, though, *onabe* bars became scarce. In 1993 Yomiuri Television presented a program billed as a debate (*tōron*) of *Okama vs. Onabe*, in which two opposing sides were set up to consider issues of sex, gender, and sexuality, in a discussion managed by three straight men at the top table (Valentine in press). This "debate" suggests that the concept of *onabe* has not disappeared, at least in the media.

In yet a further development of the pots and pans metaphor, there is a subcultural term, *okoge*, that has gained wider usage in Japan since being used as the title for a 1992 film about a woman who develops an attachment to a gay male couple. *Okoge* refers to the burnt food (rice) that sticks to the bottom of a pot (*kama*) and thus indicates metaphorically a woman who likes being in the company of gay men and sticks to or with them. *Okoge*, in its original culinary sense, is sometimes appreciated for its taste, despite its scorched nature, and its metaphorical use is less offensive than the English translation 'fag-hag'.

The adoption of *onabe* and *okoge* is clearly derivative of the prior conception of *okama*, which places gay men significantly in the kitchen.[21] As in other representations, the implication is that gay men belong in a province that is proper to women. Thus, television and film portrayals of gay men commonly represent them in terms of female kin roles, such as mother or elder sister (Valentine in press). Assignment of *okama* to the realm of kinship, and to feminine family roles that suit their supposed gender, allows them to act as surrogate mothers, as in the 1990 television drama *And Yet I Want to Be a Mother* (*Soredemo haha ni naritai*) and the 1989 film *Kitchen* (*Kitchin*). Representation as *okama* puts the queer where he belongs: in the feminine sphere as defined by domesticity.

In media portrayals, *okama* look like fakes, trying to be women but noticeably failing. They are, in more than one sense, "made up" (Valentine in press). The construction here could be seen in terms of kitsch rather than kitchen. The media appeal is artifice, rather than genuine gender transformation. Not really men, not really women, they are, moreover, not really sexual. They are defined in terms of gender rather than sexuality, and insofar as any sexuality is recognized it is domesticated, tamed rather than wild, kept within the confines of kin and kitchen.

This domestic confinement of homosexuality, however, fails to acknowledge lesbians. Their construction as "masculine" does not fit in the domestic sphere, which may help to explain why *onabe* has failed to become a popular term. Attempts made to conceptualize lesbians in terms of kin and kitchen in Japan do not carry conviction; their incorporation is either secondary and contradictory or else, as noted in the next section, they are desexualized into sisterhood, which removes even the threat of gender marginality that is recognized in the constructed femininity of gay men.

Yet, as we shall see, sisterhood can be taken up and used as a province for the protection of identity against both sexualization and desexualization—a domain for defense against declamation.

Defensive Definitions

Those oppressed by dominant definitions are not doomed to accept them passively; they may attempt resistance to summation or suppression of self—the twin problems faced by queers, of having sexuality sum up one's whole identity or, alternatively, of having sexuality unspoken and stifled, denied any recognition. A strategy against this double danger is to develop defensive definitions, ways of calling "us" that cannot be read by "them." Carefully coded language can avoid public announcements and denouncements. Self-definitions are coded away from public consumption, comprehension, and incorporation.[22]

Proclamation of sexuality has never been an easy option for queers and has sometimes scarcely been an option at all. The secrecy essential for many to survive has left a whole history of coded names that permit identification and solidarity among those in the know. In Japan, the use of foreign and familiar forms to designate queer sexuality has not been confined to dominant definitions. Alien terms have been adopted, and kin concepts such as sisterhood have been adapted, to allow coded identification.

A common method of coding is to use the initial letters of the name of an organization. Thus, a gay group in Osaka is known as OGC, which stands for Osaka Gay Community. The positive-sounding English terms *gay* and *community* are included in the name of the organization, which in public can be openly designated by its initials, without this convenience making the name or the purpose of the organization inaccessible to those who wish to make contact or read relevant publications. Similarly, TLGDC stands for Tokyo Lesbian and Gay Deaf Community, YL is used to refer to young lesbians, and the sexist label OL (office lady) can be wonderfully subverted (as in the 1996 Tokyo Lesbian and Gay Parade) to indicate office lesbian. Some apparent acronyms are simply oblique identifications: OCCUR (transliterated into *katakana* script as *akā*) designates a group with an English name that bears no obvious relationship to its gay activist aims; this group has gained considerable publicity since 1990 by fighting a legal case against exclusion from a youth recreation house in the Tokyo suburb of Fuchū.

Foreign names, initials, or acronyms can provide positive coding for lesbian and gay organizations. An alternative is to use Japanese syllables in abbreviation, as in *Regumi* (which could be translated as 'Le[sbian]-group'), a lesbian group in Tokyo. While *gumi* here refers to group, *re* is short for *rezubian* (lesbian). The abbreviation not only is useful as partial coding but also avoids the slightly longer and derogatory abbreviation *rezu* and even eschews the name *lesbian*, which is thought by some to have been spoiled by heterosexual male misuse; lesbian sexuality is commonly represented in straight men's pornography, which is one of the restricted provinces in which lesbian relations are recognized, though at the same time denied existence beyond the sphere of the male gaze.[23]

The coding of such organizations, which are at least partly political in aim, is not meant to be impenetrable; it is a matter of caution and convenience in public communication, in contrast to a genuine concern for concealment from all except those who belong. It would not be appropriate to give examples of groups that wish to maintain full secrecy through careful coding.

Some coding is, however, well known, yet regarded in some sense as "innocent." It is here that the concept of sisterhood can be appropriated to allow definition without defamation. Although *sister* may desexualize a relationship, it does acknowledge closeness and solidarity. In Japan, since the early twentieth century, sexual relationships between schoolgirls have been indicated by the initial *S*, written as the Roman letter *S* or as *esu* in *katakana*. In this usage, which has now declined, *S* stood for the English word *sister* or *sex* or the Japanese word *shōjo* (girl), or all three.[24] The use of initials is here combined with a suggestion of sisterhood. Thus, young women in sexual relations could be conceived in familiar terms as sisters, enabling dispositions to be revealed without being reviled. Kin terms can be used to provide positive and apparently "innocent" designations of sexual relationships.

Sister is also used by some gay men in Japan as an appellation for oneself or others. In particular, *onē-san* (elder sister), is used to address a gay man considered feminine. Similarly, a "feminine" style of speech used by some gay men is known as *onē-kotoba* (sister language: 'sissy speech' may come closer to the idiom).[25]

The adaptation of expressions of sisterhood by lesbians and gay men for their own ends shows their active role in constructing their identity and their world, albeit using available cultural conventions.[26] In this way they may develop identifications that confound clear-cut categories or defy dominant definitions of their nature and value.

Defying Definitions

Discriminatory definitions can be openly defied, challenging their unreflective currency and advancing alternative epithets and evaluations, or they can be indirectly defied by escaping or undermining their application. Foiling the application of prevailing conceptions may proceed through the already noted defensive definitions, which can evade extensive comprehension or can "wrap"[27] for suitable consumption, appealing to an appropriate audience or to a wider public in terms that defy defamation.

Among Japanese lesbians and gay men, the general preference is to defy definitions by avoiding them altogether, to go as far as possible undefined. Yet this leaves prevailing conceptions unchallenged. Ironically, this in itself can be an effective way of remaining out of the reach of controlling classifications, which connote stereotypes enabling the unfitting to pass unnoticed. *Okama* stereotypes in the media can operate this way; those who do not fit the media stereotype of *okama* can pass unremarked in everyday life. Stereotyped representations thus become decoys for the concealment of a sexuality that goes unrecognized in mainstream terms (Valentine in press). Although dominant definitions may act as decoys that divert attention from one who does not readily fit the bill, they are thereby able to persist unchecked. Discrimination may be avoided by those who pass, but terms of discrimination abide and abuse those who do not elude their application.

An alternative way of defying definitions is to challenge them openly by flaunting or flouting them: wearing the label with pride (and hence challenging any derogatory connotation) or proclaiming a new and positive appellation. Defiant definitions of this type are not common in Japan, but they are sometimes used by those who are already publicly defined.

Those who are public figures in the world of entertainment, and visible by virtue of transvestism, sometimes adopt new terms that circumvent the negative connotations of dominant definitions that would otherwise be used. Some of those identified as *okama* find *nyū hāfu* preferable as a new and modish name that lacks the derogatory overtones of *okama*.[28] *Nyū hāfu* (new half) is a fashionable term for male-to-female transvestite homosexuals. This designation stems from the early 1980s: it is significant that *hāfu* is employed again for a marginal category. Another currently popular term with similar reference is *misutā redi* (mister lady), which arose in the late 1980s. While the implication of transvestism or indeed transsexuality is stronger in *nyū hāfu* and *misutā redi* than in *okama*, these terms are not clearly distinguished by the majority of Japanese, and they are often used and understood interchangeably. Although the new expressions (made up of imported words and written in *katakana* script) are proposed as alternatives to *okama*, they still share the primary reference to gender rather than to sexuality.

This may help to explain why defiant definitions are rarely favored in Japan outside the world of entertainment[29] and the recently amplified but still small voice of lesbian and gay politics. Prevailing conceptions view queers primarily in terms of transgressions of gender, rather than of sexuality. To wear such labels with pride is a restricted option, available only to those who regard themselves in terms of gender marginality. Alternatively, to proclaim a same-sex sexual orientation, in borrowed Western terms, may mean primary identification (by others at least, if not by self) in terms of sexuality. To most Japanese, of whatever sexuality, such an identification seems strange. It is queer to be identified primarily in sexual terms.

Queer Identifications

The available terms for queer identification in Japan are all, in some respect, unsuitable. No term escapes the poles of ponderous officialese[30] and popular discrimination or avoids imposing a desexualizing or essentially sexualizing identity.

Lesbian (*rezubian*) and *gay* (*gei*) are sometimes used in Japan as terms announcing sexual identity, but they are rejected by many who would like a balance (as would most of us) between having their sexuality totally unrecognized, and having only their sexuality recognized as if it were their sole or primary defining attribute.[31] To sum up a person in terms of sexuality is not very discriminating, but it may be highly discriminatory.

Thus, Japanese and non-Japanese queers have much in common—not only the oppression of discriminatory terms but also the aspiration for nonexclusive and nonfundamentalist recognition of sexuality in terms that will inevitably remain queer as long as dominant definitions circumscribe character in fixed confining forms of gender and sexuality. In rejecting identity fundamentalism, queers who transgress boundaries can join in solidarity with other discriminated groups, in terms that assign no fundamental identity but recognize a common and nonexclusive queerness.

The attempt to take up *queer* and use it positively and defiantly in the English-speaking world has not so far been paralleled in Japan with the adoption of *hen*, partly because of its general reference to peculiarity rather than to specifically sexual strangeness. The discriminatory term may have to become more closely confined to sexual peculiarity before it can be appropriated in defiance. *Hentai* (abnormal) has, however, been used as an advertising slogan, attracting attention to a gay publication with the notion of fashionable perversion (Lunsing 1995: 75). As for the imported term *queer* (*kuia*), its recent adoption in Japanese sexual politics and queer studies (Noguchi et al. 1996) does not retain in Japanese the discriminatory connotations that it has in English; only the initiated would recognize any defiance in its use. Similarly, *daiku* (dyke) and *bian* (reclaiming the part dropped from *rezubian* when abbreviated to the discriminatory *rezu*) appear defiant but in practice act as coded identifications in public.

Defiant declarations of queer sexuality in Japan are rare in any terms. In contrast, defensive definitions find favor, not only to escape being pinned down by prevailing categories, but also because they suit Japanese conceptions of self. In particular, conceptualizing self in terms of sexuality is considered alien in Japan, as this makes doing into being, practice into essence, in that what you do defines what you are. In Japan, what you are, your self, tends to be defined through interaction, where you belong with others, your socially recognized networks of relationships.[32] Traditionally, the relationships that define you are those of family/household (not necessarily kin-related) and work: areas of obligation beyond which lie secondary and marginalized provinces. Gender also defines you, along with the household relationships that pertain to gender. This is an area for prime belonging and hence prime identification in Japan. Gender marginality is defined in contrast as improper belonging.

The primacy given to these forms of belonging renders alternative bearings difficult to establish and awkward to acknowledge openly in terms of identification. At the same time, this encourages hidden selves, which are not involved in the principal and publicly recognized modes of belonging. The inner self is thus particularly prized in Japan and even accorded "moral superiority" (Lebra 1992: 112); indeed, Japanese culture permits and promotes the concealment of less public selves through the strength of the cultural dichotomies between front and back, appearance and feeling. The socially sanctioned practice of adopting a suitable front (*omote*) for keeping inappropriate selves back (*ura*), of hiding one's true feelings or motives (*honne*) behind an official stance or formal appearance (*tatemae*), gives considerable rein to secret selves and divergent definitions. In this way, Japanese society comfortably accommodates compartmentalization.

Defensive definitions are thus prevalent in Japanese society, and not only among queers. Are we to make the presumption that this is a cultural quirk, a historical phase that will pass, as Japan joins the rest of "us" in advancing open identification and, more particularly, in proclaiming sexual identity? Surely it should not be assumed that Japan will have to move through an evolutionary pattern that we might want to impose on the basis of Western history.[33] Why should Japan have to go through the "stage" of defining self in terms of sexuality, when it could be considered already in the postmodern mode of eschewing essentialist identifications on the basis of actions?[34] Nevertheless, in another sense, Japan is a long way from the promised postmodern paradise,[35] which to queers everywhere can seem elusive and illusory: homosexualities, where recognized, are marginalized. The center is still strong, and those in the margins are lumped together (Valentine 1994: 13).

The multitude of designations in Japan for queer sexualities may sound as if there are subtle discriminations being made between different types of sexual orientation. Yet the assorted categories tend to be interchangeable; the mainstream fails to discriminate between different types of difference except on gender grounds, thus allowing a blanket discrimination against difference. Queers are basically all queer.

Here it is apparent that Japanese society is not so strange after all. The notion of queers as outsiders within is common to Japanese and Western societies. Among such outsiders, lesbians and gay men are quintessentially queer, the model of marginality, and may act as metaphors for other discriminated groupings in representations that demonstrate the connections between diverse oppressions and exclusions.[36] Japanese people are thus not peculiar in seeing outsiders, and queers in particular, as queer. The pattern of using foreign forms for supposedly alien sexualities, with the implication that they belong elsewhere, is shared by other societies, including the very societies in the West that are most regularly contrasted with Japan and from which the foreign expressions for sexualities have been borrowed. The myth of Japan's cultural peculiarity, itself characterized as queer in Western conceptions, is both promoted and punctured by the common use of discriminatory terms for the identification of queer sexualities.

NOTES

1. Parallels between Japanese and Western usage of discriminatory terms for queer sexualities were explored in the paper "Terms of Abuse, Terms of Defence: Discriminated Sexualities in Japan," which I delivered at a conference on Lesbian and Gay Studies in Scotland at the University of Glasgow, October 1993. The Japanese material has been expanded for the present chapter, while comparison and contrast with Western societies will be pursued elsewhere. I am grateful to Okada Kimie, Daphne Hamilton, and Wim Lunsing for their comments on the Glasgow paper.

2. Befu notes that "Othernesses of Japan" vary according to the viewer: "Taking Japan

as the 'Other', the nature of this 'Other', in reality, has less to do with who the 'Other' is than with the identity of the subject who is gazing at the 'Other'" (1992: 17).

3. Cobham similarly notes "the process within orientalist discourse by which the subaltern 'other' was constructed as feminine or effeminate as a way of representing the power balance in the relationship between Europe and its colonies" (1992: 47).

4. Alternatively, homosexuality in Japan is sometimes believed to pertain to those of Korean origin, while Mihashi Osamu, a sociologist who has conducted research among Korean residents in Japan, informed me of the Koreans' conviction, that homosexuality is not a Korean but a Japanese phenomenon. The view of homosexuality as a foreign import into Japan goes back even further, with popular tradition dating its introduction (from China, Japan's occidental Other at the time) to the ninth century (Watanabe 1989: 31). The belief that homosexuality is a foreign way is found in many cultures: for example, Sweet, in a paper in this volume, reports a rabbinical view that places Jews above the suspicion of same-sex sexuality.

5. Similarly, Ohnuki-Tierney (1990: 199) notes that unambiguous foreigners, especially Chinese or Western, may be regarded as a source of purity, while minority groups within Japan may be deemed impure and scapegoated.

6. See Valentine (1990: 38–39). The pervasive inside/outside (*uchi/soto*) distinction in Japan can be seen as a continuum, where boundaries are flexible (Bachnik 1986: 69; Hamabata 1990: 48). Some boundaries, however, are more intractable, and those who transgress become awkward and peculiar outsiders within, their excluded marginality in turn used to define cardinal borders. "The homo in relation to the hetero, much like the feminine in relation to the masculine, operates as an indispensable interior exclusion—an outside which is inside interiority making the articulation of the latter possible, a transgression of the border which is necessary to constitute the border as such" (Fuss 1991: 3).

7. For example, Imamura (1989: 17) argues that foreign wives of Japanese can be seen as quintessential strangers.

8. There are, of course, no neutral unconstructed terms that avoid historical and cultural connotations; this is one of the main points in this article. Yet, at the same time, I have to use some designation to refer to those with a same-sex sexual orientation; this is not to assume, however, that current connotations of these terms are applicable universally. Boswell suggests that, in the disputed application of words such as *homosexual* and *gay*, we should avoid the extremes of nominalism or realism, constructionism or essentialism, that would render us "paralyzed by words" (1991: 22).

9. Young men continue to be identified in this way in Japan; there is an ongoing tradition of *bishōnen*, beautiful androgynous youths, who are objects of desire in *manga*, theater and film. In contrast with feudal Japan, these youths are now considered to be principally the objects of young women's attention. It is significant that the term *bishōnen* is an outgroup designation (it is not a term one would use for oneself). Moreover, *bishōnen* are constructed as ambiguous in terms of both gender and sexuality.

10. "Outdoor nudity was prohibited by a proclamation which stated that it was offensive to visiting Westerners and reflected poorly upon the country. The same justification appeared in a proclamation banning mixed bathing, pornography and tattoos—'barbarous customs which Westerners look down upon'" (Mita 1992: 212). Homosexuality could be seen as such a barbarous custom, but ironically both a native Japanese one (offensive to Westerners) and a barbarous non-Japanese one, eventually even attributable to Westerners. Same-sex sexual relations are thus disdained and disclaimed on both sides, relying on historical oblivion and contemporary ignorance.

11. Kondo notes the complexity of politeness considerations in Japanese, "the layers of distance and intimacy encoded in language" (1990: 31). Linguistic layering can be seen as

part of the wider regard for "wrapping" in Japanese culture, as in the presentation of elaborately wrapped gifts, expressing both care and distance (Hendry 1993b: 64).

12. This is generally evident in terms of identification, and more particularly in personal names, as Ogawa points out: "the very complexity of reading and writing Japanese names is an advantage for the purposes of identification" (1992: 34).

13. The use of alien terms does not imply that modern Japanese views of homosexuality are solely the result of imported concepts. Watanabe relates these views to the "continuous development of capitalism, the formation of an industrialized society" (1989: 124).

14. This merely makes the discrimination latent rather than blatant. As Mihashi argues, "[T]he degree of discrimination is greater today than in the Edo period. It is also more covert, and this has much to do with the change in character of the discriminatory language" (1987: S24).

15. Elsewhere in this volume Armstrong notes that, in certain contexts, American derogatory uses of *homo* may imply stereotypically feminine behavior, such as caring and cooking, rather than referring to sexuality as such.

16. It is important to be able to identify ourselves in terms of our own language, as Islam points out: "The word *shamakami* is from my native Bengali language and it means 'love for your equal or same'. . . . I personally feel very good about the word *lesbian*. It is a powerful word, yet I think it's important to convey the same meaning and power in our own language" (1993: 43).

17. Although the connotations of *okama* can be traced, this does not mean that they are known to the majority of its users. Most Japanese would not know the way in which the *o* of *okama* is written in *kanji*, nor would they be aware of its implications. Many would also be unconscious of making an oblique anatomical reference when using *okama*. Similarly, most English speakers would not know the original meaning of *faggot*. The derogatory sense of the term remains, even while its specific connotations have lapsed.

18. A similar sequence of constructs can be traced in nineteenth-century European medicine. Subsequent to "male homosexuality," (con)fused with gender transgression, came an analogous conception of lesbianism. "The masculine female invert was perhaps an analogous afterthought" (Newton 1991: 287).

19. Watanabe Tsuneo, whose work on gender and sexuality in Japanese society is ground-breaking, informed me of the media promotion of the term *onabe*. A Japanese feminist bookseller told me in an interview that, at elementary school in the mid-1970s, she and a boy exchanged insults of *okama* and *onabe*; she used *okama* to deride him for effeminacy, and he retaliated with *onabe*. Robertson suggests that the term was originally coined in the early 1900s "as the 'gender' opposite of *okama*" (1992: 176).

20. This is, of course, not unique to Japan: Swann notes that feminists have "identified several 'lexical gaps'—an absence of words to refer to women's experiences. Many of these relate to women's sexuality. . . . When women get into the language, they are often portrayed negatively, or in relation to men" (1992: 57). Butler argues that the oppression of lesbians "works through the production of a domain of unthinkability and unnameability. Lesbianism is not explicitly prohibited in part because it has not even made its way into the thinkable, the imaginable, that grid of cultural intelligibility that regulates the real and the nameable" (1991: 20).

21. Interestingly, in usage now considered archaic, both *onabe* and *okama* could refer to maidservants. The kitchen association remains strong for gay men conceived as *okama*. It is worth noting that *Kitchen* (*Kitchin*) is the title of the most famous recent novel that focuses on an *okama*. The novel, by Yoshimoto Banana, was made into a popular film by Morita Yoshimitsu.

22. Similarly, Hebdige (1979) notes the ideological and commercial incorporation of subcultures and their attempts to resist this by coding away.

23. Waterhouse suggests that, in Anglo-American culture, outside of objectification by the male gaze "lesbian desire and lesbian identities have already been rendered invisible" (1993: 114).

24. See Robertson (1989: 57). Here Robertson notes other designations, especially associated with Takarazuka, that conceive of lesbian relations in masculine-feminine (hetero-gender) kinship terms, such as older brother and younger sister (*aniki* and *imōto*).

25. Japanese is especially rich in the capacity to express gender identity. *Onē-kotoba* may be simply feminine style, or it may be ultra-feminine (more than most women would use). Hirano (1990) contends that *onē-kotoba* may be used to make fun, implying the wickedness of women. In a similar vein, but without the critique of sexism, the program accompanying the film *Okoge* suggests that *onē* refers to a gay man who appears like an elder sister, who is "bitchy" "catty," or "waspish," but who takes good care of one. The paper by Ogawa and Smith in the present volume explores in detail the use of gendered speech by Japanese gay men and notes that, contrary to the impression among heterosexuals, it is far from the case that all gay men speak in *onē-kotoba*. Instead of conforming to a stereotype, gay men's speech is found to adapt existing conventions and invent new ones.

26. The available terms are a site for struggle: Dyer tells of living life "in those terms, though in constant struggle within and against them" (1992: 161).

27. Hendry sees wrapping as a pervasive principle of Japanese culture but also as a more or less pronounced feature of all societies (1993b: 171–172).

28. This is not to say that *okama* cannot be worn with pride. Some who celebrate their gender marginality may find the search for a new designation irrelevant, preferring, as did participants in the television "debate" of *Okama vs. Onabe*, to be recognized openly in a common category.

29. In the liminal world of entertainment, it can pay to draw attention to one's peculiarity. There are, however, limits to curiosity value. Mass popularity can be undermined by an inappropriate revelation, as happened with the singer Sagara Naomi when "her lesbian lover told all in a television talk show" (Buruma 1985: 45).

30. Official terms developed by "experts" are often too awkwardly erudite for everyday queer self-definition: Dyer notes that "homosexual" and its equivalents have a "learned feel where one wants a colloquial term to trip off the mouth" (1993: 7).

31. Butler argues against the oppression of "abjects," the (un)subjects that are unnamed and unviable (1991: 20), but she also remarks, "I'm permanently troubled by identity categories, consider them to be invariable stumbling-blocks" (1991: 14). Dyer is similarly ambivalent about such categories: "Having a word for oneself and one's group . . . contains and fixes identity. It is significant to most aspects of who I am that I am gay but all the same it is only part of who I am; yet the label, and the very real need to make a song and dance about it, is liable to suggest that it is all that I am, that it explains everything about me. It has the effect of suggesting that sexuality is fixed, that it consists of clear, unchanging categories, which is untrue both for individuals and for the historical constructions of sexuality" (1993: 9). Jarman stresses how we are limited by terms: "These names—gay, queer, homosexual—are limiting. I would love to finish with them" (1993: 30).

32. Nakane conceptualizes this as Japanese defining self through "frame" rather than "attribute" (1973: 2).

33. Similarly, Fadi, in a paper in this volume, questions the cross-cultural inevitability and relevance of the linguistic progression of North American sexual identities.

34. Kondo suggests that relationally defined selves in Japan "mount a radical challenge to our own assumptions about fixed, essentialist identities" (1990: 33).

35. Postmodernists proclaim that beyond modernity we reach a realm of dispersed power and fluid identities. Progress toward this promised land seems uneven and far from inevitable. The postmodern project can be seen as Utopian: it "disregards (or fails to acknowledge) the political struggles necessary to bring about change" (Harding 1992: 348). Mainstream power to pin down identities of "others" has not dissolved.

36. As Cook notes, in a review of a queer performance: "Like all the best queer art, it employs homosexuality as a metaphor for outsiders of every hue" (1994: 5).

REFERENCES

Armstrong, James (this volume). "Homophobic Slang as Coercive Discourse among College Students."
Aoyama, Tomoko (1988). "Male Homosexuality as Treated by Japanese Women Writers." In Gavan McCormack and Yoshio Sugimoto (eds.), *The Japanese Trajectory: Modernization and Beyond*. Cambridge: Cambridge University Press, pp. 186–204.
Bachnik, Jane M. (1986). "Time, Space and Person in Japanese Relationships." In Joy Hendry and Jonathan Webber (eds.), *Interpreting Japanese Society*. Oxford: JASO, pp. 49–75.
Befu, Harumi (1992). "Introduction: Framework of Analysis." In Harumi Befu and Josef Kreiner (eds.), *Othernesses of Japan*. Munich: Iudicium, pp. 15–35.
Boswell, John (1991). "Revolutions, Universals and Sexual Categories." In Martin Bauml Duberman, Martha Vicinus, and George Chauncey Jr. (eds.), *Hidden from History: Reclaiming the Gay and Lesbian Past*. London: Penguin, pp. 17–36.
Breger, Rosemary (1992). "The Discourse on Japan in the German Press: Images of Economic Competition." In Roger Goodman and Kirsten Refsing (eds.), *Ideology and Practice in Modern Japan*. London: Routledge, pp. 171–195.
Buruma, Ian (1985). *A Japanese Mirror: Heroes and Villains of Japanese Culture*. Harmondsworth: Penguin.
Butler, Judith (1991). "Imitation and Gender Insubordination." In Diana Fuss (ed.), *Inside/Out*. New York: Routledge, pp. 13–31.
Cobham, Rhonda (1992). "Misgendering the Nation: African Nationalist Fictions and Nuruddin Farah's *Maps*." In Andrew Parker, Mary Russo, Doris Sommer, and Patricia Yaeger (eds.), *Nationalisms and Sexualities*. New York: Routledge, pp. 42–59.
Cook, William (1994). Review of Scott Capurro: "Risk gay." *Guardian* (II) (August 16): 5.
Dyer, Richard (1992). *Only Entertainment*. London: Routledge.
——— (1993). *The Matter of Images: Essays on Representations*. London: Routledge.
Fuss, Diana (1991). "Inside/Out." In Diana Fuss (ed.), *Inside/Out*. New York: Routledge, pp. 1–10.
Garber, Marjorie (1992). "The Occidental Tourist: *M. Butterfly* and the Scandal of Transvestism." In Andrew Parker, Mary Russo, Doris Sommer, and Patricia Yaeger (eds.), *Nationalisms and Sexualities*. New York: Routledge, pp. 121–146.
Hamabata, Matthews M. (1990). *Crested Kimono: Power and Love in the Japanese Business Family*. Ithaca: Cornell University Press.
Harding, Sandra (1992). "The Instability of the Analytical Categories of Feminist Theory." In Helen Crowley and Susan Himmelweit (eds.), *Knowing Women: Feminism and Knowledge*. Cambridge: Polity Press, pp. 338–354.
Hebdige, Dick (1979). *Subculture: The Meaning of Style*. London: Methuen.
Hendry, Joy (1988). "Sutorenjā toshite no minzoku-gakusha—Nihon no tsutsumi bunka o megutte." In Yoshida Teigo and Miyake Hitoshi (eds.), *Kosumosu to shakai*. Tokyo: Keiō Tsūshin, pp. 407–425.

————. (1992). "Individualism and Individuality: Entry into a Social World." In Roger Goodman and Kirsten Refsing (eds.), *Ideology and Practice in Modern Japan.* London: Routledge, pp. 55–71.

————. (1993a). "El extraño en la educación japonesa y los problemas del extraño en Japón." Paper presented at conference on *El extraño.* La Casa de Velázquez, Madrid, November.

————. (1993b). *Wrapping Culture.* Oxford: Oxford University Press.

Hirano, Hiroaki (1990). "Josō, onē." *Fujin Minshū Shimbun* (May 25).

Imamura, Anne E. (1989). "Interdependence of Family and Education: Reactions of Foreign Wives of Japanese to the School System." In James J. Shields Jr. (ed.), *Japanese Schooling: Patterns of Socialization, Equality, and Political Control.* University Park: Pennsylvania State University Press, pp. 16–27.

Islam, Sarmeen (1993). "Toward a Global Network of Asian Lesbians." In Rakesh Ratti (ed.), *A Lotus of Another Color: An Unfolding of the South Asian Gay and Lesbian Experience.* Boston: Alyson, pp. 41–46.

Jarman, Derek (1993). *At Your Own Risk.* London: Vintage.

Kondo, Dorinne (1990). *Crafting Selves: Power, Gender and Discourses of Identity in a Japanese Workplace.* Chicago: University of Chicago Press.

Lebra, Takie Sugiyama (1976). *Japanese Patterns of Behavior.* Honolulu: University of Hawaii Press.

———— (1992). "Self in Japanese Culture." In Nancy R. Rosenberger (ed.), *Japanese Sense of Self.* Cambridge: Cambridge University Press, pp. 105–120.

Lunsing, Wim (1995). "Japanese Gay Magazines and Marriage Advertisements." *Journal of Gay and Lesbian Social Services* 3: 71–87.

Mihashi, Osamu (1987). "The Symbolism of Social Discrimination." *Current Anthropology* 28: S19–29.

Mita, Munesuke (1992). *Social Psychology of Modern Japan.* Kegan Paul International: London.

Moeran, Brian (1984). "Individual, Group and *seishin*: Japan's Internal Cultural Debate." *Man* 19: 252–266.

Nakane, Chie (1973). *Japanese Society.* Harmondsworth: Penguin.

Nanami, Kaori (1990). "Rezubian bā no yoru to yoru." *Bessatsu Takarajima* 64: *Onna o aisuru onnatachi no monogatari.* Tokyo: JICC Shuppankyoku, pp. 100–110.

Newton, Esther (1991). "The Mythic Mannish Lesbian: Radclyffe Hall and the New Woman." In Martin Bauml Duberman, Martha Vicinus, and George Chauncey Jr. (eds.), *Hidden from History: Reclaiming the Gay and Lesbian Past.* London: Penguin, pp. 281–293.

Noguchi, Katsuzō, Shiki Reiko, Torai Masae, and Satō Anna (eds.) (1996). *Kuia sutadīzu '96: kuia jenerēshon no tanjō.* Tokyo: Nanatsumori Shokan.

Ogawa, Ryō (1992). "Some Problems Concerning Personal Names." In Umesao Tadao, J. Marshall Unger, and Sakiyama Osamu (eds.), *Japanese Civilization in the Modern World,* Vol. 7, *Language, Literacy, and Writing.* Osaka: National Museum of Ethnology, pp. 23–37.

Ohnuki-Tierney, Emiko (1990). "The Ambivalent Self of the Contemporary Japanese." *Cultural Anthropology* 5: 197–216.

Robertson, Jennifer (1989). "Gender-bending in Paradise: Doing 'Female' and 'Male' in Japan." *Genders* 5: 50–69.

————. (1992). "Doing and Undoing 'Female' and 'Male' in Japan: The Takarazuka Review." In Takie Sugiyama Lebra (ed.), *Japanese Social Organization.* Honolulu: University of Hawaii Press, pp. 165–193.

Robertson, Roland (1990). "Japan and the USA: The Interpenetration of National Identities and the Debate about Orientalism." In Nicholas Abercrombie, Stephen Hill, and Bryan S. Turner (eds.), *Dominant Ideologies*. London: Unwin Hyman, pp. 182–198.

Schalow, Paul Gordon (1991). "Male Love in Early Modern Japan: A Literary Depiction of the 'Youth.' In Martin Bauml Duberman, Martha Vicinus, and George Chauncey Jr. (eds.), *Hidden from History: Reclaiming the Gay and Lesbian Past*. London: Penguin, pp. 118–128.

" 'Semi-homo' genshō to wa nani ka. Tettei bunseki suru." (1993). *Spa* (March 31), 50–53.

Swann, Joan (1992). "Ways of Speaking." In Frances Bonner, Lizbeth Goodman, Richard Allen, Linda Janes, and Catherine King (eds.), *Imagining Women: Cultural Representations and Gender*. Cambridge: Polity Press and Open University, pp. 56–66.

Takada, Masatoshi (1994). "Changing Patterns of Sexuality and Sex-based Roles." In Ueda Atsushi (ed.), *The Electric Geisha: Exploring Japan's Popular Culture*. Tokyo: Kodansha, pp. 195–203.

Valentine, James (1990). "On the Borderlines: The Significance of Marginality in Japanese Society." In Eyal Ben-Ari, Brian Moeran, and James Valentine (eds.), *Unwrapping Japan: Society and Culture in Anthropological Perspective*. Manchester: Manchester University Press, pp. 36–57.

———— (1994). "Shared Selves: Solidarities Constructed through Representations of Boundary Transgressors in Japan." Paper presented at World Congress of Sociology, "Contested Boundaries and Shifting Solidarities." University of Bielefeld, Germany, July.

———— (in press). "Skirting and Suiting Stereotypes: Representations of Marginalised Sexualities in Japan." *Theory, Culture and Society*.

Watanabe, Tsuneo (1989). *The Love of the Samurai*. London: Gay Men's Press.

Waterhouse, Ruth (1993). "The Inverted Gaze." In Susan Scott and David Morgan (eds.), *Body Matters*. London: Falmer Press, pp. 105–121.

Yoshimoto, Banana (1988). *Kitchin*. Tokyo: Fukutake Shoten.

6

*T*alking about *Feygelekh*

A Queer Male Representation in Jewish American Speech

MICHAEL J. SWEET

This chapter is an extended reflection on the Yiddish word *feygele* (plural: *feygelekh*), literally 'little bird' or 'birdie,' used in North American Yiddish and American Jewish (Eastern Ashkenazic) English to denote a gay or effeminate male. It attempts to shed some light on the obscure history of this term and to unravel its significations. In so doing, the chapter necessarily touches on more general related matters, such as the valuation of same-sex sexuality in Jewish culture and on kindred words in Yiddish and other Jewish and non-Jewish languages. It begins with the origin of this inquiry and the sources used in its pursuit; after a brief overview of the representation of male same-sex sexuality and gender nonconformity in Jewish culture, it looks at the main question at hand—the origins and the meanings of the word *feygele* and its social functions. Finally, it considers the prospects for finding adequate self-representational terms for gay men in Yiddish and American Jewish English.

Beginnings and Sources

While I do not have a specific memory of first hearing the word *feygele*, it seems to me that I have always known it. Its exact denotation may have been unclear to me as a child, but it had a palpably strong negative charge, indicating contemptuous disparagement of a failure to meet cultural expectations of maleness. Its impact is well described in "Caravans," a short story by Lev Raphael, in which the teenage protagonist overhears his bitter father speaking about him: "'Hah' he said. 'He dresses like a girl! A *feygele*.' That was Yiddish for faggot: little birdie.... I cringed at *feygele*.... It was not what I wanted *anyone* to think of me" (1990: 70).

With the passage of time and geographical and sociocultural distance from the intensely Eastern European Jewish working-class environment of my youth, I seldom heard or thought of the word *feygele*, although I occasionally sighted it in print, in a variety of spellings, such as "fagola," feigele, and faygeleh, etc.[1] However, I happened to send out an inquiry about this word on *Mendele*, the Internet Yiddish language and culture discussion list, since I had wondered whether this word might not be useful as a self-designation by Jewish gay men. This query proved to be a productive one, and spawned an interesting conversational thread resulting in a language column being devoted to this subject in the major national Jewish-interest newspaper, *Forward* (Philologos 1994). All of this piqued my curiosity, and I began to research this topic from printed sources on Yiddish and American language, gay culture in the United States, and other relevant areas, as well as in discussions with others interested in queer studies. The result brings together disparate literary, nonliterary, and personal testimony about this word; archival research in diaries or letters may yet unearth contemporary references that will better clarify when and how this word came into being and its meanings for those who originally used it.

Jewish Culture and Male Queerness

The ruling attitude toward same-sex sexuality within Jewish religious culture has been one of denial and the enforcement of invisibility. The well-known condemnatory passages in Leviticus (18: 22; 20: 13) express disgust and hostility toward male-male sex, especially with the breaching of gender boundaries that was believed to occur therein.[2] Normative gender roles were very distinctly demarcated among Jews, and cross-dressing was prohibited except during the carnivalesque Purim holiday (Sandrow 1986: 1–20). At the other end of the attitudinal spectrum, there is homoerotic Hebrew poetry from Muslim Spain, which speaks in very positive terms of the emotional and spiritual sides of male-male relations, if not explicitly of their physical component (Roth 1982). Aside from these references, and rabbinical commentaries on the passages in Leviticus, there are very few mentions of male-male eroticism in Jewish scholastic and secular literature. Same-sex relations were so invisible, at least to elite authorities, that later rabbis felt confident in abrogating earlier Talmudic prohibitions against unmarried men teaching males or sleeping under the same cloak, because Jews were considered as being above the suspicion of same-sex sexuality.[3] Female-female sexuality is not mentioned in the Hebrew scriptures at all, and very rarely even in the vast commentarial corpus (Satlow 1994: 15–17); Hebrew lacks even a word for women who have sex with women, except for the contemporary *lesbit*, adapted from the international term and used as a general imprecation toward sexually transgressive women (Freedman 1989: 230).

Despite its generally secularist and more cosmopolitan outlook, Yiddish literature largely lacks overt representation of same-sex sexuality. Some notable exceptions include the prominent lesbian theme in Sholem Asch's controversial 1907 play *Got fun Nekome* (*God of Vengeance*; Siegel 1976: 37), and stories dealing directly with this topic in the work of Isaac Bashevis Singer, such as "Zeitl and Rickel,"[4] "Two,"[5] and "Disguised" (Singer 1986), as well as the homosexual subtext in his "Yentl the Yeshiva Boy" (Singer 1981: 149–169). While same-sex love may be sympathetically depicted, its practice is invariably shown as leading to death or degradation. The word *feygele* is not found, in its queer sense, in any of these works. The obscurity surrounding the origins and development of this word is matched by the silence of most Yiddish-speaking Jews about the phenomenon of male-male sex, which this word at least partially indicates. A linguistic researcher who surveyed a few native Yiddish-speaking secular intellectuals about this word summarized their responses in two prototypical phrases: "It didn't exist among us" (*bay undz iz dos nit geven*) and "We didn't know about such things" (*intsome nish gevist fin azelkhe zakhn*).[6] Awareness of homoeroticism may have been greater among the less educated masses, as evidenced by a proverb collected by an early twentieth-century folklorist: "A lad is bashful with a man" (*a bokher mit a zokher shayt zikh*; Bernstein 1908: 6), which the collector explained as a reference to the possibility of male homosexuality (*mishkav-zokher*).

Birds and Fairies

In its more general uses, *feygele* is the diminutive of *foygl* (bird) and is a term of endearment for a small child or a beloved female, in which sense it is frequently found in Yiddish love songs and lullabies (Rubin 1979: 34–36, 82, 318). In its avian sense, this word connotes freedom, for obvious reasons, in songs about people in prison, for example (Lehman 1928: 123–34). It is also the diminutive of Feyge, a name that was common among Eastern European Jewish women. While its formation as a diminutive is somewhat irregular, similar vowel changes occur in the diminutive of other Yiddish words: *moyd<meydl, hoyz<heyzl* (Schaechter 1986: 189; D. Katz 1987: 66-67).

In its queer sense *feygele* denotes an effeminate and usually homosexual male and is best translated by *fairy*. *Feygele* and *fairy* cover an identical semantic range; the latter was the most commonly used label for a category of gender and sexual nonconformity that was widely current in America from the turn of the twentieth century through the 1940s and is attested in print as early as the 1890s (Chauncey 1994: 47–63; Legman 1983: 577). In contrast, I have found no printed or anecdotal sources that attest to the use of *feygele* as a synonym for *fairy* before the 1930s, or outside of North America. A particularly telling bit of negative evidence is the absence of this meaning of the word in Harkavy's still authoritative 1928 *Yiddish-English-Hebrew Dictionary*, especially since Harkavy was highly descriptivist in his approach to Yiddish, thoroughly familiar with American Yiddish, and boldly inclusive of terms for body parts and sexual functions that were then widely considered unprintable. It appears, therefore, most logical to view *feygele* as primarily influenced by the preexisting and widespread *fairy*, and as having arisen in the urban immigrant neighborhoods in which persons labeled as fairies by self and others were the most visible embodiments of nonnormative gender role and sexual orientation (Chauncey 1994: 16–17, 72–76, 202). Effeminate men in their social role as escorts to married women are matter-of-factly described in Sholem Asch's 1918 naturalistic novel of American Jewish immigrant life, *Onkel Mozes*, in a scene set at a middle-class Jewish beach resort: "Here and there a young man was also seen in a huddle of women, also in swimming clothes. But they were so fat and dressed in such a way, that they were also regarded as matronly women" (104).[7]

The most specific early reference to *feygele* was in the 1940 Yiddish film *Der Amerikaner Shadkhn* (*The American Matchmaker*), directed by Edgar Ulmer (Sicular 1994: 42–43). The protagonist of this film is a "confirmed bachelor," whose bachelor butler in one scene addresses their canary as *feygele* and compares its bachelor state to his master's and his own, indicating its (and their) gender ambiguity. The scene clearly presupposes the audience's knowledge of the double meaning of *feygele*. A number of informants on *Mendele* and elsewhere also attested to the wide awareness of this word among second-generation Eastern European Jewish males in North American urban neighborhoods from the 1930s through the 1960s. As one informant stated, it was often used as a slur against any boy who exhibits even small signs of gender role deviance, such as "walking funny."[8] It was also used in the sense of homosexual orientation, a highly salient characteristic in assessing the marriageability of young men, as in one person's recollection of her mother's telling a relative that she was happy that the only gentile male in her daughter's tour group going to France was "*a feygele, got tsi dank* (a fairy, thank god).[9] Disparagement and shame are often associated with the use of this term; this is illustrated in the dialogue from a confrontational scene in a comic series featuring a Jewish gay man as a central character (Barella 1993: 103)—the gay character's straight brother says: "*I* certainly don't want to *advertise* to *all of Los Angeles, the world* and the members of *my synagogue* that *my* little brother is *a feygeleh*!!"

It is not my contention that *feygele* is a direct translation of *fairy* but merely that it took on a similar meaning under its direct influence. There is a Yiddish word for *fairy* in its storybook sense, *fee*, but this is a rare and literary word, not even included in rather comprehensive lexicons such as Stutchkoff's and Harkavy's and thus unlikely to be familiar to the average Eastern European Jewish immigrant. Furthermore, the fairy as a species of folkloristic fauna was unknown in Yiddish folktales and children's stories (Silverman Weinreich 1954: 199). However, these creatures would have been known to the generation born in America or brought here at an early age from the plethora of American fairy tales, other literature (e.g., *Peter Pan*), and folklore (e.g., the "tooth fairy"). *Feygele* would have been a natural candidate to describe the "fairies" who were visible on the streets of immigrant neighborhoods; its nonsexual connotations are nearly identical to those of the folkloristic fairy—a winged, flying, free-living, bright, and delicate creature. The use of the diminutive suggests daintiness and femininity—among birds, perhaps a sparrow, canary, or even a hummingbird; the sterotypically "masculine" birds, such as eagles, hawks, or owls, would never be called *feygelekh*.

Etymologies and Lexicography

There are other associative connections that may have had a secondary role in the revaluation of *feygele* as fairy. Birds have sexual and erotic associations in many languages; in Yiddish *nakht-feygele* (night-birdie) can mean *streetwalker* (Stutchkoff 1950: 597). Perhaps the strongest avian-queer association in Yiddish is a kindred bird diminutive, *gendzl* (gosling), which is the probable etymon of the American English tramp and underworld term *gunsel*, a derisive term for a young man as a catamite or receptive sexual partner, among other meanings. This use of the word was first attested in a 1918 compilation of prison slang and was known by the 1930s (Lighter 1994: 996), at least in the underworld milieu, which was an important source for transmitting Yiddish words to English (Steinmetz 1986: 43). Its queer sense was knowingly alluded to in Dashiel Hammet's popular mystery novel *The Maltese Falcon* (1992: 110) and in the two movies subsequently based on it.

Another metaphorical analogy between flying creatures and gay/nelly men is, of course, the butterfly, associated in many cultures with frivolity and sexual license—"flitting from flower to flower." The fairies of folklore are also sometimes depicted with butterfly wings (Dulac 1928: 9). According to the files of the *Language and Culture Atlas of Ashkenazic Jewry* (LCAAJ),[10] the most widely distributed word in spoken Yiddish for butterfly is *zumerfeygele* 'summer birdie.' Despite my initial supposition that *feygele* was related to *zumerfeygele*, I have not been able to trace any queer connotations for this word in Yiddish, or in any of its coterritorial languages. *Birdie, little dove,* and *butterfly* [*ptíchka, golúbka,* and *bábochka*] have been reported as terms for gay males in Russian,[11] but these are recent prison slang, not in wide and common usage.[12] Mexican Spanish uses *mariposa* as a synonym for an effeminate gay man, and the Hebrew word for butterfly, *parpar,* has been reported as carrying the same meaning;[13] however, the Hebrew and the Spanish do not appear to have a common source, in that Ladino (or more properly, Judezmo), which has influenced Hebrew through the Sephardic communities in Israel, does not use any lepidopterous terms in relation to queer men (Arditti 1987: 217). Moreover, it is extremely unlikely that there was any direct relationship between either Israeli Hebrew or Mexican Spanish and American Yiddish.

A much more likely source of influence is German, which was widely understood by secularly educated Yiddish speakers; it was also coterritorial with Yiddish in Galicia, Latvia, and elsewhere in Eastern Europe and thus likely to be known to ordinary Yiddish-speakers engaged in business with non-Jewish suppliers or customers. German does use words cognate with *feygele,* i.e., *Vogel* and its derivatives, in very sexual senses, notably *vögeln* 'to fuck', *vögelchen* (the German equivalent of *feygele*) 'streetwalker', *vogelhaus* 'brothel', and so on (Küpper 1984: 3017); particularly salient is *arschvögeln* 'to butt-fuck'.[14] These expressions may have influenced *feygele*'s taking on a sexual connotation, especially in view of the widespread homologizing of fairies and prostitutes in the popular imagination (J. N. Katz 1983: 379–380, 401–402).

Despite its wide currency among Jewish Americans, *feygele* has hardly been noticed by serious lexicographers of Yiddish or American English. Perhaps its first mention in an English dictionary was its definition as "a pervert, fairy, homosexual, fag" in a 1966 work by an amateur lexicographer (Kogos 1966: 35). The word hardly fared better in its next appearance, in the enormously popular book by the writer and humorist Leo Rosten (1968), *The Joy of Yiddish*, in which it is given an entirely specious etymology from a nonexistent German word, *Vögele*. It is coyly stated to be "quite common (the word, not the libidinal arrangement) in the American-Jewish vernacular" and accurately defined as "homosexual . . . A synonym for the English 'fairy' or 'fag.' (114). Rosten's false etymology was subsequently repeated *in toto* in Wayne Dynes's 1985 lexicon (54). In his later book *Hooray for Yiddish* (1982: 123–124), Rosten, this time correctly, notes that *feygele* is the diminutive of the Yiddish *foygl* and adds another definition, otherwise unattested, as 'jailbird'. In both books Rosten notes that *feygele* was a discreet or euphemistic way of describing homosexuals, especially when others were listening. The term does not appear in any of the major unabridged English dictionaries or in dictionaries of American slang or dialect, with the exception of the *Dictionary of American Regional English*, where it is said to be "perhaps influenced by English fag" (Cassidy 1991: 373), following Rosten's (1968: 114) speculation.

The near absence of queer men in Yiddish literature is mirrored by the exclusion of *feygele* from Yiddish philological works. As mentioned earlier, the queer sense of *feygele* is not to be found in Harkavy's 1928 dictionary (1987); nor is it in Stutchkoff's thesaurus, published in 1950, long after this word had gained wide currency in North American Yiddish. It is not recorded even later in Uriel Weinreich's highly prescriptivist 1968 dictionary; Steinmetz's (1968) otherwise excellent work on American Yiddish and American Jewish English also ignores this common Jewish-American word.

The question must still be asked: Why *feygele* and not some other Yiddish word that could have served the same function? Did it fill a niche in the language that could not be met by a preexisting term? The latter is not an absolute requirement, as American Yiddish adopted numerous English words and calque translations, even in cases where perfectly good, common Yiddish words were available (Feinsilver 1970: 373; Mark 1938). There are two Yiddish words that may have been suitable to designate gender and sexual deviance in Yiddish, *androginos* and *tumtum*. The first of these, however, was an uncommon learned word (from the Greek *andrógynos*) and specifically denoted a biological hermaphrodite. The second, *tumtum* (*timtim* in some dialects), seems a more likely possibility for rendering *fairy*. *Tumtum* is found under the rubric of "exceptions" in Stutchkoff's thesaurus (1950: 597), between *androginos* and an expression meaning "neither fish nor fowl"; it is variously defined as "sexless person" (Harkavy 1987: 237), "shy, beardless adolescent or a hermaphrodite" (Rosten 1982: 124), and "a person with underdeveloped secondary sexual characteristics,"[15] and it is mistakenly rendered in various translations of Bashevis Singer's short stories (e.g., Singer 1981: 171; Singer 1969: 160) as "eunuch"; the Yiddish for a true eunuch is *soris*. *Tumtum* is a word of Hebrew-Aramaic origin, found in the Talmud (TB Yevemot 99B; TB Baba Batra 140b) and is used as an equivalent of *fairy* and *feygele* by at least some American Jews.[16] If, as Rosten (1968: 114; 1982: 124) claims, *feygele* was used for purposes of concealment, it is puzzling that *tumtum* was not adopted, as it would seem to provide greater discretion (e.g., in the presence of children or non-Jews) than *feygele*, with its closeness in sound to *fag* and *fairy*.

Feygele *as Gender Borderguard*

The rise of the *feygele* as a deprecated Other among North American Jews in the 1930s doubtless relates to the radical changes in the definition of the masculine that had begun among less traditional Eastern European Jews. These reflected the idealization of strenuous masculinity by the non-Jewish European cultures to which they were acculturating; the traditional scholarly male ideal-type of the rabbinical elite appeared decidedly feminine in light of the warrior/athlete traits valued by the dominant cultures among which Jews had lived since Roman times,[17] and this version of the masculine was greatly reinforced and elaborated in nineteenth-century Europe (Mosse 1985: 31–36); assimilation in America only accelerated the process of change. Modernizing and secularizing Jews, and especially Zionists, rejected the image of the bookish, passive ghetto or diaspora Jew, linked by some anti-Semites and Jewish intellectuals alike to abnormal sexuality (Biale 1992: 178–180; Gilman 1992: 228–229), in favor of the new, strenuously virile ideal of "muscular Judaism" (Biale 1992: 177–182). This concept was also found within the non-Zionist Jewish socialist movement, epitomized by "back to the land" movements among the immigrants (Howe 1976: 84–87; Kann 1993; Eisenberg 1995), and symbolized by the Yeshiva scholar-turned-farmer hero of Peretz-Hirshbein's very popular play *Grine Felder* (*Green Fields,* 1977), which was first presented around 1910. The average Jewish immigrant man, as a laborer for others, sterotypically mild, nebbishy, and henpecked (the character of Myron Berger, the protagonist's father in Odets's *Awake and Sing*, is prototypical in this regard), found himself in a precarious position as far as masculine identity was concerned.

This was especially true during the period when gender and sexual boundaries were hardening in the non-Jewish American culture as well (Chauncey 1994: 111–127). Jews and queers had in common a certain marginality vis-à-vis WASP male middle-class culture, and Jewish comedians were especially prominent in playing with ambiguities of sexuality and gender: for example, Milton Berle's cross-dressing act, the near-queer persona of Jack Benny (McFadden 1993: 120–122, 127–130), and the *feygele*-like shticks of Eddie Cantor and the early Jerry Lewis. The *feygele*, whose qualities were assimilated to those of women, formed a disowned Other in contrast to whom even the economically, socially, and physically weak Jewish male, the stereotypical "sexual schlimiel" (Biale 1992: 205–210), might view himself as strong and manly. The contempt in which the *feygele* was held formed a strong disincentive to openly crossing gender boundaries in the closely interwoven, shame-based first- and second-generation Eastern European Jewish communities; this remains the situation for Orthodox Jewish gay men, who must remain deeply closeted or face severe social sanctions (Brudner 1994).

Conclusions: The Future of Feygele

Turning at last to my original question on *Mendele*, which began this inquiry: Can *feygele* be transformed into a proud self-designation by Jewish gay men, as other pejorative terms such as *queer*, *dyke*, and indeed *fairy* itself (Hay 1996: 238–264) have been by American lesbians and gay men? The only word for gay males that is presently available in standard Yiddish is the coldly medical international term *homoseksualist*; in contrast, *little bird*, with its pleasant connotations of freedom and brightness, would seem to offer a welcome alternative.

Feygele has been used positively in at least two instances that I have found, in an autobiographical essay, "Confessions of a Feygele-Boichik" (Schuman 1989) and in a gay comic (Cruse 1990). Schuman, who was raised in a conservative, Orthodox milieu, recounts his struggles to come to terms with his gayness, which culminate in his acknowledging himself, unashamedly and matter-of-factly, as a *"feygele boychik,"* best translated in this context as a *gay boy*. The Cruse comic, which focuses on the adventures of its gay male protagonist Wendel and his mainly lesbian and gay male circle of friends, presents *feygele* in a very positive, and ethnically nonspecific, context. In a scene at a gay rights rally that has been disrupted by homophobes, Wendel observes his friend Sterno (not ethnically identified but depicted as either African American or mixed race) tackling a homophobe and comments admiringly, "The fleeing fagbasher has failed to reckon with the force of a flying fagola!"

However, the suggestion that *feygele* be used in an affirmative manner was not greeted with enthusiasm by the members of *Mendele*, one of whom compared it as a hate term to *kike*, suggesting that it indicates self-hatred.[18] The morpheme "gay" probably cannot be incorporated into Yiddish, as it has been into so many other languages, because of its frequent use as a Yiddish lexeme ("go," in the first person singular and second singular imperative). A possible option would be the calque translation of gay, *freylekh*, which has been used in this connection by some gay and lesbian Jews[19] and which was historically used (*freylekhe yidn*) to refer to the socially ambiguous role of the Jewish professional "merrymaker." (Lifschultz 1952: 51). In the end, of course, the matter will be decided by those who speak and write Yiddish, including the small population of secular Yiddish speakers, together with the wider anglophone American Jewish community in which numerous Yiddish words and phrases are used as markers of ethnic identity (Steinmetz 1986: 8–9). There is some evidence that young gay Jews are reclaiming Yiddish, finding it, according to Tony Kushner, "less butch and macho" than Hebrew-Israeli culture (Rosen 1996: 27). There are also the ultra-orthodox Khasidic communities, with a growing number of Yiddish speakers; however, as yet there are no data on which words these communities use to refer to queer men. It will be these speakers and writers, both secular and pious, who will determine whether *feygele* will fly proudly into the next century.

ACKNOWLEDGMENTS   I would like to thank the following for their help and suggestions: Patrick Hamilton, Marvin Herzog, Simon Karlinsky, Eve Sicular,

George Talbot, Leonard Zwilling, and all the members of *Mendele* who joined in this discussion. This chapter is dedicated to the memory of Alfred James, *zikhroyne-livrokhe: mayn tayere feygele, azamin zise un sheyne.*

NOTES

1. The spelling of *feygele*, along with all other Yiddish words in this essay, accords with the YIVO transliteration system (Weinreich xx–xxv), except for words with well-accepted English spellings. All translations from the Yiddish are by the author, unless otherwise noted.

2. On the meaning of these passages in their philological and sociocultural context, see Olyan (1994); for later commentators' understanding of these matters see Satlow (1994).

3. TB Quiddushin, 82A. Translated in Neusner (1992: 174–75).

4. English version: "Zeitl and Rickel," trans. Mirra Ginsburg, in Singer (1975b: 111–124). Yiddish original: "Tsaytl un Rikl," in Singer (1975a: 88–100).

5. Isaac Bashevis Singer, "Two," trans. Joseph Singer, in Singer (1979: 33–47). No reference has been given here, or in other Singer bibliographies that have been consulted, for the Yiddish original for this story; Roberta Saltzman, who is currently compiling a complete bibliography of Singer's work, stated that this story probably does not have a published Yiddish original (personal communication, March 1995).

6. Marvin Herzog. *Mendele* 3.246, 24 February 1994.

7. "Vu nit vu hot zikh bay a krentsel froyen oykh bavizn a yunger man, oykh in a bodkostyum. Nor er is oykh geven azoy fet un azoy ongeton, as men hot gemeynt az er iz oykh a yidene."

8. Norton Stoler, personal communication, November 1994.

9. Ellen Prince. *Mendele* 3.253, 28 Febrary 1994.

10. This data was obtained thanks to the kindness of the editor-in-chief of the LCAAJ, Marvin Herzog, and reflects answers to a question that elicited Yiddish words for *butterfly* (personal communication, 21 November 1994).

11. David Greenberg, personal communication, December 1994.

12. Simon Karlinsky, personal communication, 2 December 1994. Karlinsky also stated that the contemporary Russian equivalent of *gay*, *golubói*, although etymologically related to *golub* ('dove'), connotes only "pale blue" to Russian speakers (see also Corten 1992: 52).

13. Daniella HarPaz. *Mendele* 3.286, 14 March 1994.

14. Anno Siegal, personal communication, 2 January 1995. Siegal reports that this is a vulgar but common expression, not necessarily disparaging, referring to the active role in anal intercourse.

15. "Glossary," in Singer (1975b: 300).

16. See testimony on this matter in Shandler (1989: 99) and from Dan Leeson, *Mendele* 3.252, 25 February 1994, who reports its use as interchangeable with *feygele* in the early 1940s in Paterson, New Jersey. Its use in the sense of *impotent* by contemporary East European Jews (who use *mishkav-zokhernik* to mean a homosexual) was reported by Dovid Katz (personal communication, 10 November 1996). See also I. J. Singer (1996: 46).

17. This point was forcefully made by Daniel Boyarin, in a lecture at the University of Wisconsin at Madison, 28 March 1995: "Rabbis and Their Pals: Cross-Dressing and the Homosocial Couple in Babylonian Judaism." See his forthcoming book *Unheroic Conduct*, to be published by the University of California Press.

18. Mitchell Brown. *Mendele* 3.252, 2 February 1994.

19. For example, its use on a poster in a gay pride march, *freylekhe folk* (gay people), depicted in Faith Rogow (1990); also see the mention of a punning name for a lesbian

klezmer band, "Lebedyke un Freylekh" (=*lebedik un freylekh* 'lively and gay') in *Bridges* 4, no. 1 (1994): 57.

REFERENCES

Arditti, Adolfo (1987). "Some 'Dirtywords' in Modern Salonika, Istanbul, and Jerusalem Judezmo." *Jewish Language Review* 7A: 209–218.

Asch, Sholem (1940). *Onkel Mozes*, rev. ed., ed. Yudel Mark. New York: Workmens' Circle Mittleshul.

Barella, Tim (1993). *Domesticity Isn't Pretty*. Minneapolis: Palliard Press.

Bernstein, Ignaz (1908). *Jüdische Sprichwörter und Redensarten* [Jewish proverbs and sayings]. Vienna: Beir Löwit Verlag.

Biale, David (1992). *Eros and the Jews: From Biblical Israel to Contemporary America*. New York: Basic Books.

Brudner, Jim (1994). "Closeted by the Curse of Sexual 'Abomination.'" *Forward* (May 6): 12.

Cassidy, Frederic (ed.) (1991). *Dictionary of American Regional English*. Vol. 2. Cambridge, Mass.: Belknap Press.

Chauncey, George (1994). *Gay New York*. New York: Basic Books.

Corten, Irina H. (1992). *Vocabulary of Soviet Society and Culture*. Durham, NC: Duke University Press.

Cruse, Howard (1990). *Wendel Comix #1*. Princeton, WI: Kitchen Sink Press.

Dulac, Edmund (1928). *A Fairy Garland*. London: Cassell.

Dynes, Wayne (1985). *Homolexis*. New York: Gay Academic Union.

Eisenberg, Ellen (1995). *Jewish Agricultural Colonies in New Jersey, 1882–1920*. Syracuse, NY: Syracuse University Press.

Feinsilver, Lilian Mermin (1970). *The Taste of Yiddish*. S. Brunswick, NJ: A. S. Barnes.

Freedman, Marcia (1989). "A Lesbian in the Promised Land." In Evelyn T. Beck (ed.), *Nice Jewish Girls: A Lesbian Anthology*, rev. ed. Boston: Beacon Press, pp. 230–240.

Gilman, Sander (1992). "The Jewish Body: A Foot-note." In Howard Eilberg-Schwartz (ed.), *People of the Body: Jews and Judaism from an Embodied Perspective*. Albany, NY: State University of New York Press, pp. 223–241.

Hammet, Dashiel (1992). *The Maltese Falcon*. New York: Vintage Press.

Harkavy, Alexander (1987). *Yiddish-English-Hebrew Dictionary*, 2d ed. New York: Schocken Books.

Hay, Harry (1996). In Will Roscoe (ed.), *Radically Gay*. Boston: Beacon Press.

Hirshbein, Peretz (1977). "Grine Felder." In Hyman Bass (ed.), *Di Yidishe Drame fun 20stn Yorhundert*, vol. 2. New York: Congress for Jewish Culture, pp. 61–106.

Howe, Irving (1976). *World of Our Fathers*. New York: Harcourt Brace Jovanovich.

Kann, Kenneth (1993). *Comrades and Chicken Ranchers: The Story of a California Jewish Community*. Ithaca, NY: Cornell University Press.

Katz, Dovid (1987). *Grammar of the Yiddish Language*. London: Duckworth.

Katz, Jonathan Ned (1983). *Gay/Lesbian Almanac: A New Documentary*. New York: Harper & Row.

Kogos, Fred (1966). *A Dictionary of Yiddish Slang and Idioms*. New York: Castle Books,.

Küpper, Heinz (1984). *Illustriertes Lexikon der Deutschen Umgangssprache*, vol. 8. Stuttgart: Ernest Klett.

Legman, Gershon (1983). "The Language of Homosexuality: An American Glossary." In Jonathan Ned Katz (ed.), *Gay/Lesbian Almanac: A New Documentary*. New York: Harper.

Lehman, Shmuel (1928). *Ganeyvim Lider.* Warsaw: Farlag Pinkhas Graubard.

Lifschultz, E. (1952). "Merrymakers and Jesters among Jews," *Yivo Annual of Jewish Social Science* 7: 43–83.

Lighter, Jonathan (1994). *Random House Historical Dictionary of American Slang*, vol. 1. New York: Random House.

Mark, Yudel (1938). "Yidishe Anglitisismen." In A. Mukduni and Yankev Shatski (eds.), *Yorbukh fun Amoptayl*, vol. 1. New York: Yiddish Scientific Institute, American Branch, pp. 296–321.

McFadden, Margaret T. (1993). "'America's Boyfriend Who Can't Get a Date': Gender, Race, and the Cultural Work of the Jack Benny Program, 1932–1946." *Journal of American History* 80: 113–134.

Mosse, George (1985). *Nationalism and Sexuality.* New York: Howard Fertig.

Neusner, Jacob (1992). *The Talmud of Babylonia: An American Translation.* vol 19B. Atlanta: Scholars Press.

Odets, Clifford (1982). "Awake and Sing!" *Six Plays.* London: Methuen, pp. 33–101.

Olyan, Saul M. (1994). "'And with a Male You Shall Not Lie the Lying Down of a Woman': On the Meaning and Significance of Leviticus 18: 22 and 20: 13." *Journal of the History of Sexuality* 5: 179–206.

Philologos (1994). "An E-Mail Fairy Tale." *Forward*, 11 March, p. 16.

Raphael, Lev (1990). "Caravans." *Dancing on Tisha B'av.* New York: St. Martin's Press, pp. 69–82.

Rogow, Faith (1990). "A Look at the Rise of Lesbian Feminism." *Bridges* 1, no. 1: 67–79.

Rosen, Jonathan (1996). "A Dead Language, Yiddish Lives. And So Does the Fight over Why." *New York Times Magazine* (26 July), pp. 26–27.

Rosten, Leo (1968). *The Joy of Yiddish.* New York: McGraw-Hill.

Rosten, Leo (1982). *Hooray for Yiddish.* New York: Simon and Schuster.

Roth, Norman (1982). "'Deal Gently with the Young Man': Love of Boys in Medieval Hebrew Poetry of Spain." *Speculum* 57, no. 1: 20–51.

Rubin, Ruth (1979). *Voices of a People.* Philadelphia: Jewish Publication Society of America.

Sandrow, Nahma (1986). *Vagabond Stars: A World History of Yiddish Theater.* New York: Seth Press.

Satlow, Michael L. (1994). "'They Abused Him Like a Woman': Homoeroticism, Gender Blurring, and the Rabbis of Late Antiquity." *Journal of the History of Sexuality* 5: 1–25.

Schaechter, Mordkhe (1986). *Yidish Tvey: A lernbikhl far mitndike kursn* [Yiddish II: A textbook for intermediate courses]. Philadelphia: Institute for the Study of Human Issues.

Schuman, Burt (1989). "Confessions of a 'Feygele-Boichik.'" In Christie Balka and Andy Rose (eds.), *Twice Blessed: On Being Lesbian, Gay, and Jewish.* Boston: Beacon Press, pp. 12–20.

Shandler, Jeffrey (1989). "Gerry's Story: An Oral History." In Christie Balka and Andy Rose (eds.), *Twice Blessed: On Being Lesbian, Gay, and Jewish.* Boston: Beacon Press, pp. 92–102.

Sicular, Eve (1994). "'A Yingl mit a Yingl Hot Epes a Tam': The Celluloid Closet of Yiddish Film." *Jewish Folklore and Ethnology Review* 16: 40–45.

Siegel, Ben (1976). *The Controversial Sholem Asch: An Introduction to His Fiction.* Bowling Green, OH: Bowling Green University Popular Press.

Silverman Weinreich, Beatrice (1954). "Four Yiddish Variants of the Master-Thief Tale." In Uriel Weinreich (ed.), *The Field of Yiddish.* New York: Linguistic Circle of New York, pp. 199–213.

Singer, Isaac Bashevis (1975a). "Tsaytl un Rikl." In Chone Shmeruk (ed.), *Der Shpigl un Andere Dertseylungen* [The mirror and other stories]. Jerusalem: Magnes Press.

—— (1975b). "Zeitl and Rickel." Trans. Mirra Ginsburg. In *The Seance and Other Stories*. New York: Farrar, Straus & Giroux.

—— (1979). "Two." Trans. Joseph Singer. In *Old Love*. New York: Farrar, Straus & Giroux.

—— (1981). "Yentl the Yeshiva Boy." Trans. Marion Magid and Elizabeth Pollet. *The Collected Stories*. New York: Farrar, Straus & Giroux.

Singer, Isaac Bashevis (1986). "Disguised." Trans. Deborah Menashe. *New Yorker* (September 22), 34–38.

Singer, Israel Joshua (1996). "In Heyse Teg" [In the hot days]. Reprinted in *The Pakn Treger* 22: 44–53.

Steinmetz, Sol (1986). *Yiddish and English: A Century of Yiddish in America*. University, AL: University of Alabama Press.

Stutchkoff, Nahum (1950). In Max Weinreich (ed.), *Der Oytser fun der Yidisher Sprakh* [*Thesaurus of the Yiddish language*]. New York: Yiddish Scientific Institute (YIVO).

Weinreich, Uriel (1977). *Modern English-Yiddish–Yiddish-English Dictionary*. New York: Schocken Books.

7

Les Molles et les chausses

Mapping the Isle of Hermaphrodites
in Premodern France

RANDY CONNER

"*C'est le langage 'fricassé,*'" Pauline M. Smith writes of the French language as spoken and written in the sixteenth century in her introduction to Henri Estienne's *Deux dialogues du nouveau langage françois* (1578), "with its mania for adverbs, extravagant metaphors, outrageous obscenities" (Estienne 1980: 23). In Philibert-Joseph Le Roux's *Dictionnaire comique* (1786), we find that to " 'faire une fricassée' signifie faire une mêlange de plusieurs choses ensemble," that is, "[it] signifies 'to create a mixture by blending several items together'" (Le Roux 1786: v. I, 546). Late-twentieth-century writers, including Terence Cave in *The Cornucopian Text: Problems of Writing in the French Renaissance* (1979) and Giancarlo Maiorino in *The Cornucopian Mind and the Baroque Unity of the Arts* (1990), have, as one may decipher from their respective titles, described the sensibility that produced this "*langage fricassé*" as "cornucopian." To arrive at his conception of "cornucopian" language, Cave draws on the works of the philosopher Erasmus (1469–1536), who tells us, "Nature herself rejoices particularly in variety, for there is nothing anywhere in the immense multitude of things which she has left unpainted with the wonderful coat of variety" (22), and on the image of Gargantua's codpiece in Rabelais's (1490–ca. 1553) satire *Gargantua and Pantagruel.* This giant's codpiece, we learn, "took twenty-four and a quarter yards" of cloth and was "set with rich diamonds, precious rubies, rare turquoises, magnificent emeralds, and Persian pearls (Rabelais 1981: 55)." If you had seen it, we are told, "you would have compared it to one of those grand Horns of Plenty that you see on ancient monuments, one

such as Rhea gave to the two nymphs. . . . For it was always . . . green, always flourishing . . . full of flowers, full of fruit, full of every delight" (Rabelais 1981: 55).

A language *fricassé*, a cornucopian language, suggests, as Cave explains, "a
rich, many-faceted discourse springing from a fertile mind and powerfully affecting its recipient" (5). Cave continues, "cornucopian movement depends primarily
on lexical productivity . . . on . . . an exuberant display of . . . terms seeming to initiate an open-ended movement, via the multiplicity of phenomena, towards plenitude" (1979: 184–185).

It is wise to remember this cornucopian, this *fricassé*[ed] sensibility as we
search the culture(s) of premodern France for earlier incarnations of ourselves, that
is, of persons who have engaged in same-sex eroticism and/or who have performed behaviors regarded as "androgynous/gynandrous," "gender variant," or
"transgendered."

In premodern France, from antiquity until the nineteenth century (as well as
thereafter), transgenderism, gender-variant behavior, and homoerotic/lesbian inclination were often conflated both in popular consciousness and in texts and
other artistic productions. Persons perceived to be transgendered or as engaging in
gender-variant behavior were—reflecting cornucopian sensibility—referred to by
various names; they were *androgynes*, *garson-fillettes*, *hermaphrodites*, and *ma(s)le-
femelles* (Cotgrave 1971). Terms also emerged for the behavior of such persons; a
woman who behaved in a "masculine" manner was described as *hommasse* (*hom-
mace*) or *viragine*; for a man who behaved in a "feminine" or an "effeminate" manner, *mollet*, *muliebre*, and other terms were employed (Cotgrave 1971; Greimas and
Keane 1992).

In a subtle manner, the medieval writer Jean Gerson (1363–1429) linked
same-sex eroticism and androgyny by speaking of "voluptuous" acts and invoking,
in the *Vivat Rex*, the image of the fountain of the nymph Salmacis, believed to
transform those who bathed in its waters into hermaphrodites (Smith 1966: 50).
Shortly thereafter, the poet Eustace Deschamps (d. 1406) poetically railed "*Contre les hermaphrodites*," in a work that the French literary scholar Pauline M. Smith
has described as "a hostile portrait of homosexuals" (1966: 50). In 1532 Antoine
Du Saix (1505–1579) wrote in *L'Espernon de discipline*:

> But the *douillet* [an effeminate male] disguises and
>   transforms himself [*se desguise & transforme*],
> In this his pleasure consists,
>   He who is male, in short, a woman he becomes [*Que
> qui est homme, en brief, femme il devient*]. (Smith 1966: 87)

For many persons inhabiting premodern France, folklore, linked to the myths
and religions of their forebears, continued to contribute profoundly to notions of
erotic or gendered identity. They were mindful of the fact that "a person might
change sex while passing under the rainbow" [*une personne peut changer de sexe en
passant sous l'arc-en-ciel*] (Sébillot 1968: v. I, 91).

Just as many persons living in premodern France believed transgenderism to
be an "essential" trait bestowed by a divine force (as, for example, by the rainbow),

many felt that the inclination toward same-sex eroticism or love was also divinely inspired. Many were convinced, it seems, by Agnolo Firenzuola's (1493–1543) Neoplatonic treatise *On the Beauty of Women* (1541). In this text, Firenzuola recounts the tale found in the *Symposium* of Plato, which describes the primordial creation of three double-sexed beings, one male-female or androgynous, one male-male, and one female-female. Apparently accepting the mythic truth of this tale, he explains that "[t]hose who were female in both halves, or are descended from those who were, love each other's beauty," that is, these are women-loving women by nature, or by divine creation (Firenzuola 1992: 17).

As concerns same-sex eroticism, I suggest that *fricassé*[ed] or cornucopian sensibility and late-twentieth-century cultural relativism—represented by social constructionist texts including Jonathan Goldberg's *Sodometries: Renaissance Texts, Modern Sexualities* (1992)—are *not* equivalent. That is to say, in a nutshell, while it may be difficult in terms of premodern French language or culture to discover a single term, such as *sodomite*, to cover all persons engaging in same-sex eroticism, this is not to say that no such terms, or persons designated by them, existed or that, as Goldberg and other constructionists have suggested, such terms as *sodomy* (in French, *sodomie*) represent "utterly confused categor[ies]" (Goldberg, 1992: 18). Indeed, there is little doubt in my mind that when Claude Desainliens (a.k.a. Claudius Hollyband), a French teacher living in London during the second half of the sixteenth century, exclaimed in his *Dictionarie French and English* (1593), "Bougre, *he that committed such a fact* [i.e., 'bougrerie, *buggery*'] [the previous entry] *and sodomite villanie: a buggerer: burne them all*," he knew—as we now know—exactly what he meant (Desainliens 1970).

Goldberg speaks wisely, however, when he states that it is "virtually impossible to believe that anyone might self-identify as a sodomite" in the Renaissance. Indeed, to have done so would have meant to risk one's execution (Goldberg 1992: 19). Nevertheless, persons engaging in same-sex eroticism and transgendered behavior inhabited a world in which, despite the relative absence of verbalized self-identification, they were identified and categorized by others in terms with which many of them must have been familiar.

Sodomie

As concerns *sodomie*, while the term, in premodern France, exemplary of cornucopian or *fricassé*[ed] sensibility, possessed numerous meanings, it was not by any means an "utterly confused category." From dictionaries and other texts, we may discern, from the medieval period onward, three significations: (1) erotic activity, primarily anal in nature but also other forms of nonprocreative sexuality, including oral sex and bestiality, undertaken between any two parties; (2) anal intercourse between any two persons; and (3) same-sex—male-male or female-female—erotic activity, including but not limited to anal intercourse (Cotgrave 1971; Desainliens 1970; Greimas and Keane 1992; Huguet 1925–1967; Le Roux 1786; Ranconet 1960; Courove 1985: 189–205). As early as 1260 C.E., however, (and perhaps even earlier), *sodomite* referred primarily to a man accused of engaging in male-male anal eroticism and thus also committing heresy by performing an act held to exist "outside the realm of God"—"He who is a sodomite [*sodomite*] must lose his testicles; and if he is found to be such a second time, he must lose his penis; and if he is found such a third time, he must be burned alive [*il doit être brûlé*]" (Courove 1985: 191). This basic classification holds true for *sodomite* as well, except that here we are focusing on a person who engages in the behavior just mentioned, with one important addition: *Sodomite* frequently refers to a male who takes the "active" or penetrating role in anal intercourse or the "active" role in oral or interfemoral intercourse. Employing a typical constructionist strategy, Goldberg foregrounds those occasions when "sodomy" and "sodomite" have been used too generally or inappropriately rather than those occasions—much more abundant in the literature—when they have been employed to refer directly to same-sex—often, although not always, anal and male-male—eroticism.

In his *Apologie pour Herodote* (1566), Henri Estienne makes it quite clear that when he uses the term *sodomie*, he is referring not to anal or any other nonreproductive form of intercourse undertaken by male-female couples but only to erotic activity undertaken by same-sex partners. In speaking of the Celts, for instance, he writes: "[W]e read in the 13th book of Athenaeus (*The Deipnosophists*) that in his time the Celts, notwithstanding the fact that there lived among them much more beautiful women than among other barbarians, were given to sodomy [*sodomie*]" (Estienne 1879: v. I, ch. 10, 140).

That Estienne refers to same-sex eroticism rather than to heterosexual anal intercourse or to bestiality when he employs the term *sodomie* becomes even clearer when he recounts the tale of a young woman of his era who married another woman. In doing so, moreover, he links homoerotically inclined males to lesbian females in an association that has often gone unnoticed. Living at Fontaines, located between Blois and Rommorantin, the young woman, who had begun to dress in men's clothes, took a job as a stablekeeper at a hostelry in the Faubourg du Foye, where she worked for seven years, apparently without anyone suspecting that she might not be what she seemed. There she met, fell in love with, and was married to another young woman. Leaving her job at the inn, she planted and tended a vineyard. The two women lived happily together for two years. Then, tragically, the identity of the first was somehow discovered. She confessed and was burned at the stake. Estienne, believing Sappho to have been bisexual—although he does not use this term—distinguishes the poetess from this woman, whom he believes has loved other women only. It is for this reason that he classifies her and her wife's relationship as one of *sodomie* (Estienne 1879: v. I, ch. 13, 177–178).

That the term *sodomie* stresses same-sex erotic behavior rather than bestiality or the act of anal intercourse undertaken by persons of the opposite sex is borne out by other French writers, as well. In Philippe de Marnix de Sainte-Aldegonde's (1538–1598) *Tableau des différends de la religion*, for example, we find *sodomie* clearly linked to other terms connoting same-sex eroticism, including *bardasseau*, *Ganimedes*, and *bougres* (Marnix 1857: v. IV, 155–157). That lesbian women and homoerotically inclined men were sometimes linked by way of same-sex eroticism is supported by the equation of *lesbin* and *bardache* (these terms are discussed later in this chapter) in a 1640 translation of Lucian's *Dialogues of the Courtesan*s and in Le Roux's *Dictionnaire comique* (Le Roux 1786: v. II, 82).

Indeed, when heterosexual sodomy is referred to in premodern French texts, it is described as a substitute for homosexual sodomy, as in the work of Pierre Brantôme. He tells us of men who, "becoming enamoured of some handsome Adonis, abandon their wives to take pleasure with these young men [*amourachez de quelque bel Adonis, leur abandonnent leurs femmes pour jouir d'eux*]" (Brantôme 1886: v. IX, 176). When they are not courageous enough to do so, they plan escapades in which they offer young men to their wives in order—allegedly much to the surprise of the young men—to make love to them after their wives have been satiated. When this scenario backfires, as when the young man rejects the husband's advances—being neither "*b*—— [i.e., *bougre*], *ny bardasche*" [the "receptive" partner in a relationship; see later discussion]—or when neither scenario occurs, the husband then sodomizes his wife. In one particular instance, however, when a young man rejects the husband's advances, the wife supports him, telling him that her husband wouldn't dare report this event, because he knows she might accuse him of sodomizing her. This, she suggests, might well reveal his secret desire—to enjoy erotic relations with males—which might consequently lead to his execution. Brantôme suggests, incidentally, that such women should perhaps have the right to indulge in extramarital affairs (Brantôme 1886: v. IX, 176).

The term *bougrerie*, like the term *sodomie*, was subject to cornucopian interpretation. Yet, like *sodomie*, its multiple significations did not permit it to become an "utterly confused category." *Bougrerie* emerged in the Middle Ages as a term identifying Bogomilism, a pagano-Christian religious heresy originating in the vicinity of Bulgaria, the practitioners of which were alleged to practice male-male anal eroticism. From the thirteenth century on, when *bougre* (as *bogresse*) was employed to refer to a "person who committed the sin against nature" [*la débauche contre nature*], *bougrerie* and its relations were, until the twentieth century, only rarely employed in contexts in which—despite the usual foregrounding of one— all of these significations—anal or other same-sex eroticism, religious heresy, and foreign influence—were not meant to be taken into consideration when defining an erotic act or person(s) involved (Ranconet 1960; Courove 1985: 70–78). In the *Dictionnaire comique*, we find this definition: "He who has young men in his devotion with whom he commits sodomy" [*Qui a de jeunes garçons à sa dévotion avec lesquels il commet la sodomie*] (Le Roux 1786: v. I, 138). While Gilles Ménage (1613–1692), in his *Dictionnaire etymologique*, offers a couple of rather controversial theories concerning both the origin and the development of the term—including its origin in *boyaux* and *boiau cullier*, "intestines" and "anus," rather than in Bogomilism, and its linkage of anal eroticism and heresy due to the possibly mistaken attribution to Betisach, the treasurer of Jean de France, the duc de Berry (1340–1416), of both of these sins/crimes—even he (Ménage) stays within the parameters of anal or same-sex eroticism, spiritual deviation, and foreign influence (Ménage 1750: v. I, 221–222; Greimas and Keane 1992).

What most lucidly establishes the homoerotic significations of these terms— *bougre*/*bougrerie*, *sodomite*/*sodomie*—is their linkage to each other and to other terms signifying homoerotic and/or gender variant behavior. While it must be admitted that these associations are often made implicitly rather than explicitly, often by employing only one or, in some cases, none of the implied terms, it is nevertheless the case that these links are meant to be forged in the minds of hearers or listeners. From the work of the *jongleur* Gautier le Leu, for instance, we know that by the mid-thirteenth century, the association of the terms *bougre*, *(h)érite* (heretic), and *sodomite* must have been well established. The evidence lies in his work *La Veuve* (The Widow). Here, a widow accuses her second husband of not fulfilling his manly duties; she complains:

> This scoundrel shows me less regard
> than he does the dungheap in the yard.
> However, by Saint Loy I know
> His moral code is just as low
> as that of those on Mount Wimer;
> for woman's love he doesn't care. (Harrison 1974: 369).[1]

While none of the three terms—*(h)érite*, *bougre*, *sodomite*—appears overtly in the lyric, all lie behind the three last-quoted lines, that is, in the connection between the husband's "moral code"—"for woman's love he doesn't care"—and that of "those on Mont Wimer." Mont Wimer, also called Mont Aimé, lies in Champagne and was well known as the scene of a mass execution of a group of 183 Cathars. The Cathars, a congregation of antinomian mystics historically linked to the Bogomils of Eastern Europe, were known in medieval France primarily as *Bougres* (Bogomils) and *(h)érites*, because their practices had been deemed heretical by the Catholic Church. The Cathars, like the Bogomils, were widely believed to participate in same-sex eroticism. Thus, we are not surprised when Gautier le Leu's widow compares her husband's lack of interest in heterosexuality with that of the Cathar heretics of Mont Wimer, mentally linking *bougre*, *(h)érite*, and *sodomite* (Livingston 1951: 95–96; Loos 1974: 197; Bailey 1975: 139–141).

A similar linkage is observed in his lyric *Du Sot Chevalier* (The Foolish Knight). This is an absurd tale of several knights who decide, it being a stormy night, to accept the hospitality of a wealthy chevalier even after they have misinterpreted his description of making love to his wife as a desire to have intercourse with one or more of them. At one point, the tallest knight, Wales, says to the others:

> "Milords, I know it's true
> I'm taller than the rest of you;
> I'll not go near this sodomite
> who does his work with such delight!
> I'd rather hang upon a rood
> than go and let myself be screwed." (Harrison 1974: 331)

The term that appears in the French for "this sodomite" is *cel erite* 'this heretic'. It is abundantly clear, however, that it is male-male eroticism that is here signified by *cel erite*. While the term *bougre* remains unspoken here, it is nevertheless present in the joining of "heretic" to "one who practices anal intercourse" (Harrison 1974: 331–341).

In other, especially Renaissance, texts, these associations are explicitly stated, as in Estienne's usage of *bougre Sodomiticque* in the *Apologie* (Estienne 1879: v. I, ch. 13, 176) and in this passage, dating from 1587, describing the love of Anthony Bacon (1558–1601; the diplomat brother of Francis) for the young Isaac Burgades:

> Mr. Bacon, the English gentleman, caressed Isaac Burgades, his page, sojourning with him often in a room in his lodgings. . . . sodomy [*sodomie*] was not found to be wrong. . . . Bacon assured him [M. de Bèze, the minister of Geneva, or M. Constant, the minister of Montauban] that there was nothing wrong in being a bugger and a sodomite [*d'être bougre et sodomite*]. (Courove 1985: 195)

Clearly, if one fails to note such linkages, observing terms like *sodomie* only in isolation, one will not see how these terms are used in connection to lessen any doubt in a hearer or reader's mind as to specific contextual definitions. It must be remembered, however, that a link such as that between *sodomite/sodomie* and *bougre/bougrerie* represents only one link in a vast, cornucopian chain.

Berdaches *and Others*

In contrast to the error of finding *sodomy* and such terms to be "utterly confused categories," we must beware of the error of seeking to find a *single* term that covers all "gay"—and here I refer to homoerotically or lesbian-inclined—or "queer" —and here I add the elements of gender-variant or transgendered behavior and bi- or pansexuality—persons. In erring in this way, we tend to disregard a crucial element in the historical construction of same-sex and gendered relations in many Western and non-Western societies prior to the emergence of the political philosophies of egalitarian (as opposed to Greek) democracy and socialism, which is to say that many of us, driven by our own ideals, disregard the splitting in many societies of persons engaged in relationships into "active" and "passive" (I prefer and will henceforth employ the term "receptive") roles, which are typically gendered as "masculine" and "feminine" or "effeminate" (or "butch" and "femme," in late-twentieth-century gay slang) and which are often performed by older and younger persons, respectively. Such relationships may be further categorized along economic class and even ethnic lines.

The premodern French, like those of other Western cultures, must have received or appropriated this basic pattern of male-male erotic organization from their Greco-Roman forebears, who classified the active partner (performing penetration) as a *paedicator*, a *paedico*, or a *draucos*, and the receptive partner as a *pathicus*, *catamitus* (allegedly derived from "Ganymede"), *cinaedus* (Grk., kinaidos, kinaidos; Fr., *cinède*; It., *cinèdo*), *badas* (Grk., badas, from which *bardache* may ultimately derive) *mollis delicatus*. If the receptive partner had reached adulthood, he was referred to as an *exoletus* (Forberg 1966: v. I, 81).

In premodern French, the active partner became the *sodomite*, the *bougre*, the *pédareste*, the *jean-foutre*, while the receptive partner became the *bardache*, the *ragasch*, the *mignon*, the *ganymedes*. Of these, *ganymedes* is drawn directly from the myth of the Greek god Zeus's love for the youth Ganymede. Randle Cotgrave (d. 1634) defines *ganymedes* as "The name of a Trojan boy, whom Jupiter so loved . . . ; hence, any boy thats loved for carnall abuse; an Ingle" (Cotgrave 1971). The term *ingle*, often employed by English writers when referring to *ganymedes* (and to *bardaches*; discussed later) and in general to those males taking the receptive role, signifies a "boy-favourite; a catamite." To "ingle" boys means to "play wantonly with boyes against nature."

Cotgrave defines *bardache* (*berdache*, *bredache*), which, as mentioned earlier, may ultimately be derived from *baδas* (badas), a Greek synonym for *cinaedus* found in Hesychius (Hesychius 1867; Ménage 1750) that perhaps later merged with, or became confused with, *bardaj*, an Arabic term for *slave* and was reintroduced by sailors speaking Polari (Hancock 1984: 384, 391–395; Rodgers 1979; Sainéan 1922–1923: v. I, 146; Conner 1993: 173–174; Lucas this volume), as "an Ingle; a youth kept, or accompanied for Sodomie." To *bardachiser* a young male, he explains, is to "commit Sodomie [with him]; to bugger, to ingle." From the onset of its reemergence in sixteenth-century French, *bardache* was linked to the realm of myth. Pierre Le Loyer, sieur de la Brosse, in his *Discours des spectres, ou visions et apparitions d'esprits* (1605), invoked the Greco-Roman goddess Cotys as the "tutelary Goddess of *bardaches* and prostitutes [*Deesse tutelaire des bardaches et des putains*]." Indeed, he appears to have accepted a mythic origin of the term: "Agdistis [an androgynous being of Greco-Roman myth], who was the lover of Attis [a young man primarily known as the consort of the goddess Cybele] of whom Arnobius speaks, derives from *Hasdesch*, which signifies '*bardache*,' 'effeminate' [*effeminé*], as were those of the band and troop of Cybele [i.e., the *galli* priests]" (Le Loyer 1605–1608; VII. 3, 8; Huguet 1925–1967; Conner 1993: 186). It is perhaps for this reason that the term *bardache* (usually as *berdache*) may have later been chosen from among so many others to serve as a general designation for indigenous Americans who engaged in same-sex eroticism and served spiritual functions.

We have already spoken of the importance of observing linkages of terms in order both to avoid the error of assuming that such terms as *sodomy* are "utterly confused" categories and to appreciate the cornucopian mind's complex structuring and/or revealing of erotic and/or gendered identity. Having now considered the terms *bardache* and *ganymedes*, I offer this quote from *La somme des péchés*, by the sixteenth-century French Franciscan theologian Jean Benedicti. Having already mentioned the terms *molles* ("effeminates") and *pathiques* ("receptive partners in anal eroticism"), in explaining the words of St. Paul, he states:

And it seems to me that these were *bardaches*, [dwelling in] the brothel destroyed by King Josiah. He demolished, says the Scripture, the houses of the effeminates [*effeminés*], thus are they called in our common version. The Hebrews called them *Kadeschim* [*Qadeshim*], the Ethnics [i.e., the Greeks] named them *cinaedos*, that is to say, *cinèdes*. Such was Ganymede, with whom Jupiter was enamoured, if the poets speak truly.

Such was Julius Caesar when he was yet a youth, loved by King Nicomedes. (Courove 1985: 61)

The term *ragasch* is derived from the Italian *ragazzo*, signifying a youth who lives in the streets; both became synonymous with *bardache* (It., *bardassa*) and *cinaedus* in the sixteenth century. The term *mignon*, signifying a "favorite, wanton, dilling, darling," will be discussed later.

The term *bougiron* (*bougeron*), depending on the context in which it was employed, could refer either to the active role, as when opposed to *bardache*, or to the receptive role, as when opposed to *bougre*. In André Thevet's (1502–1590) *Cosmographie universelle* (1575), for instance, we find, "If he is a male, he is called a *Bardache* or a *Bougeron*" (Thevet XXI. 10), whereas in an anonymous poem written in April 1583 and recorded by Pierre de l'Estoile in his *Journal*, we find:

> They are advised, and very wise
> To thus have hidden their faces
> Or one would see, among the good
> The *bougres* and the *bougirons*. (L'Estoile 1875–1876: v. II, 115)

Thus far, other than recounting Estienne's tale of the lesbian-inclined transvestite, I have said little concerning women. In part, this is due to the fact that my research has focused primarily on males. Beyond this, information concerning lesbian and gender-variant women appears to have been suppressed even more successfully than that concerning their male counterparts. Nevertheless, accounts are to be found (Bonnet, Watt this volume).

Lesbiennes *and* Fricarelles

In his *Journal*, Montaigne recounts a tale of a female transvestite, a woman-loving woman named Marie, from Vitry-le-François, who, along with six or seven other women, decided to dress as a man in order to become a professional in the weaving industry. As a young "man," Marie came to be well liked by her fellow workers. Eventually, she met a young woman to whom she became engaged; in the end, however, the two did not marry. (This woman, Montaigne notes, was still alive when he heard this tale.) Some time later, she fell in love with another woman, and shortly thereafter the two were married [*épousée*]. Unfortunately, they had been married for only four or five months when someone apparently recognized Marie as a female he or she had previously known. Marie was condemned to be hanged [*à estre pendu*], in part because she preferred to suffer death than to return to the state of traditional womanhood [*ce qu'elle disoit aymer suffrir que de se remettre en estat de fille*] and in part because she used, or was alleged to use, a dildo when making love to her wife [*des inventions illicites à supplier au défaut de son sexe*] (Montaigne 1903: 35–37; Montaigne 1946: 87–88).

In Brantôme, we encounter a Spanish courtesan living at Rome in the late sixteenth century who had named herself Isabelle de Lune, apparently after the heroine of a novella by Bandello (1485–1561). She fell in love with another courtesan, a beautiful woman who took the nickname La Pandore. Although Isabelle married, she did not end her affair with La Pandore; it was said that she thereby gave her husband "cuckold's horns" (Brantôme 1886: v. IX, 194).

While women-loving women were occasionally associated with men-loving men, as revealed by the passage from Estienne's *Apologie* mentioned earlier, being described as *sodomites*, they were, as mirrors of cornucopian sensibility, also called *tribades* and *lesbiennes*, the erotic descendants of their Greco-Roman forebears, as well as *fricarelles* (*friquarelles*) and *fricatrices*, referring to the "rubbing" of their bodies together. Nor was their lovemaking to be satiated by a single term; *donna con donna, s'entrefriquer, s'entrefrotter, freyer, fricarelle, friquer*, and *geminos committere cunnos* were among those terms employed to describe lesbian eroticism, arising from impassioned *amitié* (Brantôme 1886: v. IX, 193–206; Huguet 1925–1967; Le Roux 1786: v. II, 547). As concerns the roles taken in lesbian lovemaking, my research suggests that while such roles probably existed, they do not seem to have been organized as rigidly as those involving male couples.

Brantôme recounts a tale he apparently received from M. [Henri, the Count] de Clermont [et de Tonnere]-Tallard the Younger (d. 1573) in which the terms *se frotter* and *s'entrefriquer* are employed:

> [B]eing a young boy, and having the honor of accompanying M. d'Anjou, since then our King Henri III, into his study, and often studying with him, their instructor being M. de Gournay; one day, being at Thoulouze, studying with his master in his chambers, and being seated in a corner . . . , he saw, through a little chink [in the wood], into another chamber, where two very powerful women, all curled up and their hose (*callesons*, Italian hose, derived from *calzone*) lowered, lying one on top of the other, kissing in the manner of doves, *se frotter, s'entrefriquer*. . . . And he said that he saw this game (*jeu*) being played on other occasions . . . I do not say that this is true . . . it is very believable; since these two women have always carried this reputation, of continuing to make love in this manner, of passing their time thus. (Brantôme 1886: v. IX, 197–198)

Elsewhere, he employs the terms *lesbiennes* and *fricarelles*:

> [T]here are in numerous spots and regions such women and lesbians (*telles dames et lesbiennes*), in France, in Italy and in Spain, in Turkey, Greece, and other sites. And where these women are reclusive, and do not possess their freedom entirely, this practice continues strongly. . . . The Turks go to the baths more for this wantonness (*paillardise*) than for anything else. . . . Even the courtesans, who have men at their command at all hours, still they make use of these *fricarelles*. . . . In our France, such women are common enough . . . the fashion has been carried here from Italy by a lady of high standing [he may be referring here to Catherine de Médicis] whom I shall by no means name. (Brantôme 1886: v. IX, 195)

While the premodern French employed terms to designate directly same-sex eroticism, gender variance, and the persons engaging in these behaviors, they were much more fascinated with a fricassee, a cornucopia of words and phrases less directly linking these behaviors and persons, terms drawn from the realms of myth, the theater, courtly life, life at sea, and elsewhere.

When speaking of lesbian or bisexual and gender-variant women, writers (unfortunately, often hostile) invoked the legendary women of Juvenal's *Satires*, Martial's *Epigrams*, and Lucian's *Dialogues of the Courtesans*: Bassa, Clonarium, Leana, Laufella, Medullina, and Philaenis (Brantôme 1886: v. IX, 193–195). Catherine de Médicis, perceived as gender variant and possibly lesbian, was deemed "*Catheris Medicaea Virago*" (Catherine de Médicis, the virago) and compared to the Roman goddess Cybele (L'Estoile 1875–1876: v. I, 79–80). Most frequently, however, writers called on the Greek poet Sappho. Brantôme, describing the lesbian women of his own time as enjoying "*donna con donna*, in imitation of the learned lesbian [*lesbienne*] Sappho," wrote: "They say that Sappho of Lesbos was a very powerful mistress in this profession [*mestier*], indeed, they say that she invented it, and that since [that time] lesbian women [*les dames lesbiennes*] have imitated her in this, and have continued to do so up to this day" (Brantôme 1886: v. IX, 195).

Sotties

To refer to gender-variant and/or homoerotically or bisexually inclined men, writers (like those mentioned earlier, often hostile) chanted the names of Adonis, Alexander the Great, Amour, Eros, the *galli* priests of the goddess Cybele, Ganymede (as already mentioned), Heliogabalus, Hercules (as the cross-dressing servant of his amazonian captor Queen Omphale), Hermaphroditus, and Sardanapalus (Smith 1966: 50, 86–87, 180, 190–191; Brantôme 1886: v. IX, 176; L'Estoile 1875–1876: v. I, 79–80, 252, 281; Marnix 1857: v. IV, 155, 157; Estienne 1980: 186). The gods, heroes, and rulers were joined by biblical figures: Absalom, Ammon, the men of Sodom, Saint Luke (Luc—as Saint-Luc, a *mignon* of Henri III, as well as *cul*, "ass," spelled backwards) (Marnix 1857: v. IV, 157; L'Estoile 1875–1876: v. I, 245; Sainéan 1922–1923: v. II, 301), as well as fairy spirits. For instance, by way of the "*mignon*" terms—we shall examine these in greater depth later—*folat*, meaning "wanton," and *folet*, meaning "a prettie foole, a little fop," gender-variant, homoerotically inclined *mignons* were linked to the *follets*. These are the "descendants of elves," a "merry, independent group" who are "not beyond making crude practical jokes" and who "cannot be driven away by exorcisms or holy water" (Arrowsmith 1977: 217–218).

This delight in cornucopian, frequently indirect, identification of gender-variant and sexually variant behaviors and persons had emerged sometime prior to or during the late Middle Ages, in the realm of the theater, with the performance, by clerics and by itinerant fools called *sots*, of burlesque plays called *sotties*. *Sotties* celebrated sex, food, games, and other pastimes, while ridiculing church and state. Bawdy and outrageous, the *sotties*, says Ida Nelson, "were founded on gay (*gai*), homosexual desire." The *sotties*, through their characters, reveal a complex medieval French categorization of homoerotic activities and relationships. In terms of roles, the *sot* himself signifies the receptive partner, while the *galant* represents the active partner. The *fol* 'fool' signifies a bisexual male. The plays overflow with terms that possess rich connotations relating to homoeroticism and gender variance; for instance, *brodié* 'to be embroidered or embellished', via its relation to *brode* 'broth', *langage brode* 'an effeminate language or speech', and *brodier* 'arse, bumme, taile', connotes playing the receptive role in homoerotic relations (Cotgrave 1971; Nelson 1976: 60, 66), while *lard* 'bacon fat' and its derivatives (abundant also in Rabelais), by way of *lardasse* 'stick, thrust, great pricke,' *lardé* 'pricked, or pierced into, as with a larding pricke', *faire du lard* 'to live idly, fare deliciously, fatten with pleasure', and *frotter leur lard ensemble* 'to leacher it' or 'to beat their bacon together' connotes, in culinary terms, both the actors and the act (Cotgrave 1971; Nelson 1976: 54, 56, 58, 62, 67, 68).

Life at Sea

When we speak of the association of same-sex eroticism, gender variance, and life at sea, we must, I believe, risk speculation if we wish to arrive at the heart of the cornucopian perception of role or identity. Several maritime roles may have been associated with male homoerotic and/or gender variant behavior. These may have included the *mouche*, the *fadrin*, the *calfat*, and the *matelot*. The *mouche* is an apprentice sailor, like his Spanish and Italian cousins, the *mozo* and the *mozzo*, respectively (Sainéan 1922–1923: v. I, 121). As *mousche de lippée*, it carries the connotation of a "lickorous and saucie," in other words, a "wanton" or "lustful" companion. It is conceivable, by way of the term *lippée*, derived from *lippe* 'lip', that the expression might refer connotatively to kissing or even to oral intercourse. The term *mouche* has survived into the twentieth century as *moussaillon*, a young sailor (Sizaire 1976: 192). The *fadrin* is a "young sailor, a novice" (Sainéan 1922–1923: v. I, 110) and as such is synonymous with the *mouche* (also *mousche*, *mousse*), a "skipper, or ship-boy." The term *fadrin* has the connotative meaning of foolish and is in this way related to the terms *fat, fadas, fadeses, fatras*; it is further related to *fatrouiller*, 'to play the fop' and 'to copulate' (Sainéan 1922–1923: v. II, 300; Cotgrave 1971). The preceding terms are also linked to the world of the fairies. *Fadas, fadhas, fadet*, and *farfadet* appear to have been Portuguese-derived terms for fairies, and more particularly for those types of fairies referred to as *follets*, mentioned earlier, and *lutins*. The *calfat* (also *calfateur, calfatreur, galefretier*) was responsible for the caulking, mending, trimming, and rigging of ships. He often had a servant, a young man known as the *calfatin*. According to Sainéan in *La Langue de Rabelais*:

> We have already mentioned the nautical term *freté*, in the expression *fin freté*. The *calfat*, whom Rabelais calls by the southern (French) name *gallefretier* (Book III, Chapter 27), is perceived as a *goujat*, a soldier's boy, and a *vaurien*, a rascal or rogue; the *calfat* has the reputation of leading a debauched life. This pejorative connotation is still used [in the twentieth century] by speakers in central and western France. (Sainéan 1922–1923: v. II, 284–285)

The erotic behavior of, and the relationship between, the *calfat* and the *calfatin* may have been suggested to sixteenth-century French speakers by way of the connotative meanings of terms related to *calfat, calfatin,* and so on. The terms *calfeutrer* 'to caulk a ship' and *freter* 'to load a ship', for example, may have signified the active partner in male same-sex erotic behavior or in a relationship, while *calfeutré* 'to be caulked', *fretaillé* 'to be cut, hacked, notched', *freté* 'to be loaded, as a ship', and *galefreté* 'to be rigged, or trimmed up, as a ship', may have signified the receptive partner in erotic relations. This hypothesis is supported by a number of related terms that were applied to persons who participated in sexually variant relations. These terms include *fretillant* 'lascivious, wanton, lustful, ticklish, wriggling, frigging, itching . . . wagging, nimble' and *fretillard* (or *fretilleur*), which Cotgrave defines as a "lascivious, wanton, ticklish, lustful companion . . . a restless fop . . . [who] figs up and down, as if he had an itch on his breech." *Fretillard/fretilleur* appears to be further linked to another term possibly connoting sexually variant behavior, *gale-fesson*, describing a male with a "scratcht-bum, or scabd-arse."

A *matelot* was generally depicted as a sailor, specifically as an apprentice sailor "attached to another" of higher rank or as one taking orders "from officers and masters." Employed as early as 1357 and surviving as "mate" in the literature of pirates, the term *matelot* also came to have the connotative meaning of "loving friend." By the sixteenth century, the term, in its Dutch spelling of *mattenoot*, came to mean "two *matelots* sharing a single hammock" or simply, "bed companions." These significations persisted into the nineteenth century, when the affectionate or erotic nature of the relation became especially emphasized. "Two men . . . who loved each other deeply" were depicted as mirroring the "powerful friendship of *matelots*." *Mon matelot* persisted well into the nineteenth century as a term of male-male affection (Ranconet 1960).

In *Sodomy and the Pirate Tradition,* B. R. Burg (1984) explains that, among pirates or buccaneers in the seventeenth century (and perhaps earlier), *matelotage* was an institution "linking . . . a buccaneer and another male—most often a youth—a relationship with clearly homosexual characteristics" (128). While the bond of *matelotage* among pirates, as opposed to sailors, was sometimes tainted with abuse—violence was a way of life for many pirates—"the generally recognized bond it created between men and the understanding that an inviolable attachment existed between the two as long as the master wanted it to remain so gave *matelotage,* a sacrosanct aura among buccaneers" (Burg 1984:128). In some cases, even among pirates, the relationship of *matelotage* appears to have taken a marriage-like form, with the two *matelots* sharing all property in common and with the one inheriting all property on the death of the other (Burg 1984: 128). It is conceivable that the term *bardache,* often used, as mentioned earlier, to refer to a male who takes the receptive role in male-male erotic relations, may have been applied to one of the partners in the relationship of *matelotage,* since we find in *La Langue de Rabelais* that *bardache* was a term of "jargon common among *matelots*" (Sainéan 1922–1923: v. I, 146). Finally, in association with sailing, we find the term *bougeron,* in its alternate spelling of *boujarron.* Although in the twentieth century the once understood popular linkage between life at sea and homoeroticism appears to have been largely forgotten, its memory has been preserved in two items referred to as *boujarrons*: the sailor's blue linen jersey and a small measure of tafia rum offered to calm the crew in stormy weather (Sizaire 1976:192).

Life at Court

From 1498 until 1539 the French were locked in battle with the Italians. This period came to an end with the marriage of Catherine de Médicis (1519–1589) to Henri II (1519–1559), leading to great Italian influence, especially in the fine arts and the philosophy of Neoplatonism. Italian influence made its mark especially on courtly life, and perhaps, beyond philosophy and the fine arts, most powerfully in the arenas of language, fashion, and gendered behavior (Smith 1966: 76–95, 122). The rise of Italian influence was matched by the rise of anti-Italian, and also anti-Catholic, sentiment. Italian Catholics were accused of engaging in many "evil" practices, not surprisingly including homoeroticism. Both Joachim DuBellay (ca. 1525–1560), in *Ample Discours au roy sur ses quatre estats* and Gabriel Du Puyherbault, in *Theotimus* (1549), condemned Italians—whom they felt were continuing to indulge in the vices of the ancient Romans—for bringing homosexuality and effeminacy to the French court (Smith 1966: 122). Indeed, when one reads a text written during this period, one must be careful not to interpret accusations of sodomy as observations; one must conduct further research to determine if historical and other data support or bring into question such accusations.

With this warning in mind, we may nevertheless assert that the court of Henri III (1551–1589) and his mother, Catherine de Médicis—who, more than any other individuals, were popularly blamed for transporting the vices of Italy to France—offers ample evidence of a cultural celebration of excessive elegance, the carnivalesque, the power of women, and the beauty of men. If one were to choose a single female figure to signify this era, one might well choose the Queen herself, described as *viragine*, compared to the great goddess Cybele, and honored as a patron of androgynous males. If I were to choose a single male figure, it would be Henri.

We learn in Estienne's *Deux Dialogues* that Henri III was frequently referred to as "*elle*" (she). In part, this proto-"camp" appellation derived from a revived usage of "*Sa Majesté*," rather than "*Sire*," to refer to the King; the French nobles and courtiers of this period seem to have become acutely aware of the different relationships of gender and language in French and in other tongues such as English, and, as we might expect, they delighted in playing on such differences. In L'Estoile's *Journal* we find, "They speak at court only of his (her) Majesty, / She goes, she comes, she is, she was" (*On ne parle en la Cour que de sa Majesté, / Elle va, elle vient, elle est, ell'a esté*) (Estienne 1980: 223, n.653).[2] In July 1576, on the occasion of Henri's alleged marriage to Quélus (or Caylus), one of his *mignons*, Agrippa D'Aubigné (1552–1630) wrote:

> [H]e wore all that day
> The monstrous costume, matching his lover's,

So that at first sight, one would have been at pains
To say whether he'd seen a female King [*Roy femme*] or
a male Queen [*homme Royne*].

(D'Aubigné, *Tragiques: Princes*, quoted in Estienne 1980:
181–182, n. 517)

It is possible, furthermore, that persons closer to the King than D'Aubigné referred to Henri as the *homme Royne*, that is, as the "male Queen." What is more, in Renaissance France, the term for *queen*, especially when spelled *Royne* rather than *Reyne*, referred not only to a female ruler but also to a bawdy or bohemian woman imagined to be a Gypsy (Greimas and Keane 1992).

If I were to choose an archetypal male figure to signify this era, however, rather than a single individual, I would choose the figure of the *mignon*, a class to which Henri III certainly belonged. Once merely a "favorite, wanton, dilling, darling," the *mignon* had become the beloved friend of kings (and of certain women also), the youthful, dying god, the arbiter of language and of fashion. He pronounced "*affection*" in an Italian manner, as "*affettionné*," and "*je vais*" (I go) as "*j'allions*." Such pronunciations, in the view of Estienne, would destroy the French language by effeminizing it and, by extension, would aid in the destruction of France (Estienne 1980: 403, 407). A *mignon* required a vocabulary as rich, as cornucopian as Gargantua's codpiece. Not satiated with *mignon*, he became *beau fils, bedaud, besiat, couchette, damoiseau, dorelot, folat, ganimede(s), marjolet, muguetz, popelin*. His erotic behavior was generally referred to as *impudique* (translating into sixteenth-century English as 'impudent, wanton, lascivious'), *endemené, gai* [or *gay*], or *joyeux*, and, more specifically, as *sardanapale*. His costume, referred to in the verse above, included the infamous *chausses à la bougrine* (hose fit for buggery)—that is, tights worn without a codpiece. (L'Estoile 1875–1876: v. I, 147; Smith 1966: 190). As a beloved or lover of another man, he became an *androgame* 'male spouse'. His lover may have affectionately termed him *mon ami, mon bedon, mon cousin, mon mistigouri*.[3]

Conclusion

One of the primary features of the language of premodern France was its "*fricassé*[ed]" or "cornucopian" quality, that is, its passion, especially in terms of definitions and descriptions, for mixing terms from various tongues and arenas of life, especially multivalent terms abundant in connotative meaning, and for multiplying these terms in an attempt to arrive at a near-perfect, *bien qualifié* (well qualified) definition or description, signifying, on a symbolic plane, the richness of that which is being defined or described. As far as words and phrases designating same-sex eroticism, transgenderism, and persons engaging in these behaviors are concerned, this suggests that if we are to discover expressions relating to these acts or persons, we cannot limit ourselves to examining the presence, absence, or use in isolation of one or two terms, such as *sodomy* (*sodomie*). Rather, while we should observe terms such as *sodomy* in context, we must focus on seeking out texts (linguistic as well as paralinguistic or metalinguistic) that depict situations in which such behaviors or persons might be located; doing so, we must pay careful attention to words and expressions that may be meant to be read both denotatively and connotatively, especially observing metaphoric terms that associate one code or sign system with another, such as terms linking the code of erotic terminology with that of costume or cuisine. The premodern French, in attempting to describe same-sex eroticism and gender-variant behavior and the persons engaging in these, blended terms drawn from numerous codes or sign systems, including those from the realms of myth and religion (such as Adonis, Cybele, Ganymede, and Saints Luke and Mathurin), ancient history and classical literature (Alexander the Great, Sappho, Sardanapalus), foreign cultures (*bardache, ragasch*), the maritime professions (*matelot*), costume (*chausses à la bougrine*), and cuisine (*lard*), in their effort to arrive at a definition or description that would capture the "essence" of that behavior or person without sacrificing copiousness or plenitude.

Many of the terms and expressions formulated or employed by the premodern French were in use until the late nineteenth century—*androgyne, bardache, cousin(e), fricarelle, ganimede, mignon*, and *tribade*, to name only a few. A very few, like *bougre*, continued to be used but diminished in terms of homoerotic significance. Others, like *lesbienne*, are still in use today (Bruant 1905; Delesalle 1895; Delvau 1968; Larchey 1861).

I have often wondered what the premodern French might have thought of our agonizing, late-twentieth-century debate concerning the relationship between nurture and nature. Inhabiting a world that no longer employs myriad names (but merely half a dozen) to designate sexual and gender variance, that no longer believes that one may change sex by passing under the rainbow, I can only imagine. What I am certain of, however, is that if we are to discover our "queer" ancestors in premodern France, we must reach far into the cornucopia, far into Gargantua's codpiece; there, great treasures wait.

Appendix

Here are several definitions of terms given in the text that are associated with *mignon* behavior or identity. I have taken the liberty of paraphrasing some of the definitions, being careful not to alter their meanings.

androgame: the male spouse of a male (Huguet 1925–1967; Ranconet 1960).

beau-fils: a youth or a young man who is handsome and well mannered; also employed ironically to designate a man who takes on the role of the *dameret* (an apparently heterosexual role roughly equivalent to that of the *damoiseau*) or the *damoiseau*, who perfumes himself, affects effeminate manners, and uses makeup (Le Roux 1786).

bedaud/bedon: *bedaud*: a fed(d)le, minion, favorite; a dilling, or darling. *Mon petit bedaud*: My prettie ape, my little bullie. *mon bedon*: my prettie rogue, my sweet bully (Cotgrave 1971). (Sometimes translated into English as *feddle*.)

besiat: a *mignon*, a delicate young man (Le Roux 1786).

couchette: a monk's or nun's cot; figuratively, a *mignon* of one's bed (*un mignon de couchette*). Used to designate a young man who is well mannered and somewhat effeminate (Le Roux 1786).

cousin: A term of politeness or tenderness; *mon cousin*, a title bestowed by Henri III not only on princes but on other dignitaries (Greimas and Keane 1992).

damoiseau, damoisel: a neat fellow, spruce yonker, effeminate youth (Cotgrave 1971); an effeminate male (Greimas and Keane 1992). Also *teinct damoiselet*: an effeminate complexion; a face of a hue more womanlie than manlike (Cotgrave 1971); *endamoysellé*: disguised as a maiden (Huguet 1925–1967).

dorelot: a darling, dilling, sweet heart; wanton, fed[d]le (Cotgrave 1971). (See OED for "darling/dereling," "dilling," "feddle").

endemené: wanton. *Vous êtes fort Endemené* [you play the wanton] (Desainliens 1970). Wanton, livelie, stirring, waggish, lascivious, that loves to be fisking, fidging, or frigging (Cotgrave 1971). lascivious, voluptuous (Le Roux 1786).

folat: wanton, lascivious . . . effeminate (Cotgrave 1971) *folastrément*: wantonness . . . lascivious, toying, effeminacy; foolish dalliance (Cotgrave 1971); *folastrer*: to play the wanton (Cotgrave 1971); *folatreries*: fond tricks, lascivious pranks, wanton fashions, effeminate actions (Cotgrave 1971); *folet*: a prettie foole, a little fop (Cotgrave 1971); *esprit folet*: an hobgoblin, Robin-goodfellow (Cotgrave 1971); *poil folet*: a young mossie beard (Cotgrave 1971).

gai/gay: *gay & joyeux*: mer[r]y, lusty (Desainliens 1970). Merrie, frolicke, blithe, jollie . . . lustie . . . (Cotgrave 1971). (Also see Nelson 1976: 44–45).

ganimede(s), ganymede(s): the name of a Trojan boy, whom Jupiter so loved (say the poets) as he tooke him up to heaven, and made him his cup-bearer; hence, any boy thats loved for carnall abuse; an Ingle (Cotgrave 1971). For *bardache*, a youth who gives pleasure, with whom one commits sodomy (Le Roux 1786); *ganimedique*: after the manner of Ganymede, of a *mignon* (Huguet 1925–1967); *ganymedien*: Of a *ganymede*, a *mignon* (Huguet 1925–1967).

impudique: lascivious, wanton, unchaste, obscene, shameless, incontinent, uncleane (Cotgrave 1971).

marjolet: as *c'est un petit marjolet*, he is a fine darling (Desainliens 1970). For *damoiseau, dameret, mignon* . . . effeminate, delicate (Le Roux 1786); a lascivious and impudent male (Greimas and Keane 1992).

mistigouri: My pillococke, my prettie rogue (Cotgrave 1971); penis (Le Roux 1786); the penis; flattering word for a young boy: 1598, Florio, *Zugo* . . . a pillicocke, a darling, or a wanton, or a minion (OED).

muguet(z): A young, elegant lover (Greimas and Keane 1992). Synonymous with *damoiseau*, for a male who decks himself out like a woman; an "Adonis" (Le Roux 1786).

popelin: a little finicall [i.e., affected, overly refined] darling (Cotgrave 1971); related to *popin*: spruce . . . trimme . . . daintie, prettie; *se popiner*: to trimme, or tricke up himself; *populo*: a prettie, plump-faced, and cherrie-cheekt boy; and *pouper*: to dandle, feddle, cocker, cherish much (Cotgrave 1971).

sardanapale: Sardanapalisme: Filthie, and effeminate sensualitie (Cotgrave 1971). For debauched, effeminate, one who leads a life of luxury (Le Roux 1786). (Marnix 1857: v. IV, p. 157, links Sardanapalus to *bougres*).

NOTES

The title of this essay, which means "The Effeminates [*Les Molles*] and the Hose [*Les Chausses*]," puns on the expression "words [*les mots*] and things [*et les choses*]." The essay is dedicated to the courageous Pierre Guiraud, whose study *Le Jargon de Villon, ou le gai savoir de la Coquille* (Paris: Gallimard, 1968), while controversial, remains to date one of the few explorations of premodern French language and culture in terms of homoeroticism. This essay is also dedicated to Dr. Ida Nelson, author of *La Sottie sans souci: Essai d'interprétation homosexuelle* (Paris: Honoré-Champion, 1976), another early, illuminating gay/queer studies text, which I am currently translating. Her inspiration, support, and delightful wit are greatly appreciated.

> 1. Et cis ribaus me tient plus vil
>   Que le femier de son cortil
>   Mais je sai bien, par Saint Eloi
>   Qu'il n'est mie de bone loi,
>   Ains est de çaus del Mont Wimer.
>   Il n'a soing de dames amer. (Livingston 1951: 95)

This translation is Harrison's; translations in this article are primarily my own unless otherwise noted.

2. See the discussion of the language of the Hermaphrodites of Thomas Artus's *Description de l'Isle des Hermaphrodites*.

3. Further study of the employment of the terms listed in the glossary (see appendix), as well as of *bardache*, *bougre*, and kindred terms not only in French but in other European languages as well might greatly enhance our understanding of the manner in which roles, identities, and (sub-)cultures relating to same-sex eroticism and gender variance emerged, survived, and were transformed in the West. For instance, one intriguing passage from Sir Thomas Urquhart's and Peter Le Motteaux's translation of Chapter 5 of Rabelais's *Pantagrueline Prognostication* merits such study. When Rabelais's narrator sarcastically classifies *boulgrins* (*bougres*) as one of those groups of persons (also including prostitutes) patronized by the planet/goddess Venus, Urquhart and Le Motteux translate this single term—employing "cornucopian" sensibility—into English as "Ganymedes, Bardachoes, Huflers, Ingles, Fricatrices[!], He-whores and Sodomites" (Rabelais, *Gargantua and Pantagruel*, trans. Urquhart: v. III, 397). One might explore in depth Gregorio Leti's *Il Putanismo Di Roma/ Il Puttanismo Romano* (1669), a text that became important to late-seventeenth- and eighteenth-century French scholars like Le Roux (*Dictionnaire comique*) and that establishes an association between the French terms and the English and the Italian terms.

REFERENCES

Arrowsmith, Nancy, with George Morse (1977). *A Field Guide to the Little People*. New York: Hill and Wang.

Bailey, Derrick Sherwin (1975). *Homosexuality and the Western Christian Tradition*. Hamden, Connecticut: Archon Books.

Bonnet, M. J. (this volume). "Sappho . . . ou l'importance de la culture dans le langage de l'amour."

Brantôme, Pierre de Bourdeille, seigneur de (1886). *Oeuvres complètes*, ed. Ludovic Lalanne. Paris: Mme. Ve. Jules Renouard.

Bruant, Aristide (1905). *L'Argot au XXe siècle: Dictionnaire français=argot*. Paris: Librairie Ernest Flammarion.

Burg, B. R. (1984). *Sodomy and the Pirate Tradition*. New York: New York University Press.

Cave, Terence (1979). *The Cornucopian Text: Problems of Writing in the French Renaissance*. Oxford: Clarendon Press.

Conner, Randy P. (1993). *Blossom of Bone: Reclaiming the Connections between Homoeroticism and the Sacred*. San Francisco: HarperCollins.

Cotgrave, Randle (1971). *A Dictionarie of the French and English Tongues*. New York: Da Capo Press.

Courove, Claude (1985). *Vocabulaire de l'homosexualité masculine*. Paris: Payot.

Delesalle, Georges (1895). *Dictionnaire argot-français*. Paris.

Delvau, Alfred (1968). *Dictionnaire erotique moderne*. Genève: Slatkine Reprints.

Desainliens, Claude (1970). *A Dictionary (Dictionarie) French and English*. Menston, England: Scolar Press.

Estienne, Henri (1879). *Apologie pour Herodote*, ed. P. Ristelhuber. Paris: Isidore Liseux.

———— (1980). *Deux dialogues de nouveau langage françois italianizé*, ed. P. M. Smith. Genève: Editions Slatkine.

Firenzuola, Agnolo (1992). *On the Beauty of Women*, trans., ed. Konrad Eisenbichler and Jacqueline Murray. Philadelphia: University of Pennsylvania Press.

Forberg, Frederick Charles (1966). *Manual of Classical Erotology*. New York: Grove Press.

Goldberg, Jonathan (1992). *Sodometries: Renaissance Texts, Modern Sexualities*. Stanford: Stanford University Press.

Greimas, Algirdas Julien, and Teresa Mary Keane (1992). *Dictionnaire du moyen français: La Renaissance*. Paris: Larousse.

Guiraud, Pierre (1968). *Le Jargon de Villon, ou le gai savoir de la Coquille*. Paris: Gallimard.

———— (1982). *Dictionnaire des étymologies obscures*. Paris: Payot.

Hancock, Ian (1984). "Shelta and Polari." *Language in the British Isles*, ed. Peter Trudgill. New York: Cambridge University Press.

Harrison, Robert L. (ed., trans.) (1974). *Gallic Salt: Eighteen Fabliaux Translated from the Old French*. Berkeley: University of California Press.

Hesychius (Hesychii Alexandrini) (1867). *Lexicon*, ed. Mauricius Schmidt. Jenae (Genève): Sumptibus Hermanni Dufftii.

Huguet, Edmond (1925–1967). *Dictionnaire de la langue française du seizième siècle*. Paris: Librairie Ancienne Edouard Champion.

Katz, Jonathan, ed. (1976). *Gay American History: Lesbians and Gay Men in the U.S.A.* New York: Thomas Y. Crowell.

Larchey, Loredan (1961). *Dictionnaire historique, etymologique et anecdotique de l'argot parisien*. Paris: F. Polo.

Le Loyer, Pierre (1605). *A Treatise of Spectres or Straunge Sights*. London.

———— (1605–1608). *Discours des spectres, ou visions et apparitions d'esprits*. Paris.

Le Roux, Philibert-Joseph (1786). *Dictionnaire comique, satyrique, critique, burlesque, libre et proverbial*. Paris: Pampelune.

L'Estoile, Pierre de (1875–1876). *Mémoires: Journaux: Journal de Henri III*. Paris: Librairie des Bibliophiles.

Livingston, Charles H. (1951). *Le Jongleur Gautier le Leu: Etude sur les fabliaux*. Cambridge: Harvard University Press.

Loos, Milan (1974). *Dualist Heresy in the Middle Ages*. Prague: Academia.

Lucas, Ian (this volume). "The Color of His Eyes: Polari and the Sisters of Perpetual Indulgence."

Maiorino, Giancarlo (1990). *The Cornucopian Mind and the Baroque Unity of the Arts*. University Park: Pennsylvania State University Press.

Markale, Jean (1983). *Mélusine ou l'androgyne*. Paris: Editions Retz.

Marnix de Sainte-Aldegonde, Philippe de (1857). *Tableau des différends de la religion*. Brussels: François van Meenen.

Ménage, M. Gilles (1750). *Dictionnaire etymologique de la langue françoise*. Paris: Chez Briasson.

Montaigne, Michel (1865). *Essais*, ed. M J.-V. LeClerc. Paris: Garnier Frères.

——— (1903). *The Journal of Montaigne's Travels in Italy by way of Switzerland and Germany*, ed. W. G. Waters. London: John Murray.

——— (1946). *Journal de voyage en Italie par la Suisse et l'Allemagne*, ed. Charles Dédéyan. Paris: Société des Belles Lettres.

——— (1991). *The Essays*, ed. M. A. Screech. London: Penguin.

Nelson, Ida (1976). *La Sottie sans souci: Essai d'interprétation homosexuelle*. Paris: Honoré-Champion.

Rabelais, Francis (1837). *Oeuvres*. Paris: Chez Ledentu.

——— (1858). *Oeuvres*, vol. II, ed. Mm. Burgaud des Marets et Rathery. Paris: Librairie de Firmin Didot Frères.

——— (1900). *Gargantua and Pantagruel*, vol. III, trans. Sir Thomas Urquhart and Peter Le Motteaux, ed. Charles Whibley. London: David Nutt.

——— (1981). *Gargantua and Pantagruel*, trans. J. M. Cohen. New York: Penguin.

Ranconet, Aimar de and Nicot, Jean (1960). *Thrèsor de la langue françoise tant ancienne que moderne*. Paris: Editions A. et J. Picard et Cie.

Rodgers, Bruce (1972). *The Queen's Vernacular: A Gay Lexicon*. San Francisco: Straight Arrow Books. (Reprinted [1979] as *Gay Talk*, New York: Paragon Books.)

Sainéan, Lazar (1922–1923). *La Langue de Rabelais*. Paris: E. de Boccard.

Sébillot, Paul (1968). *Le Folk-Lore de France*. Paris: Editions G.-P. Maisonneuve et Larose.

Sizaire, Pierre (1976). *Le Parler Matelot*. Paris: Editions Maritimes et D'Outre-Mer.

Smith, Pauline M. (1966). *The Anti-Courtier Trend in Sixteenth-Century French Literature*. Geneva: Librairie Droz.

Thevet, André (1575). *La Cosmographie universelle d'André Thevet cosmographe du roy*. Paris: P. L'Huilier.

Watt, Diane (this volume). "Clipping and Kyssyng in the Early Sixteenth Century: What Lesbians Do in Romances."

8

$\mathcal{S}$appho, or the Importance of Culture in the Language of Love

Tribade, Lesbienne, Homosexuelle

MARIE-JO BONNET

Allons! lyre divine
parle-moi
deviens une voix

—Sappho[1]

Although we now recognize that love between women has always existed, the terms used to describe it have varied over the years. The word *lesbienne* gained its present meaning only in the second half of the nineteenth century, while *homosexuelle* was created at the end of the nineteenth century, appearing in a French dictionary for the first time in the 1904 supplement to the *Nouveau Larousse illustré*. Before this period, only one term was commonly used in French; this was *tribade*, a word of Greek origin, that was brought to France during the Renaissance by Latin writers and adopted into the French language in the middle of the sixteenth century.

What motivated these changes? Do they reflect an evolution in the image of women and their status in society? For no term is neutral. If giving a name to love between women is to recognize its existence, it is also to identify it and, by so doing, to inscribe it in a specific political and philosophical framework, a sexual economy inevitably determined by the social relations between the sexes. One question begs to be answered: Why did reference to Sappho of Lesbos occasion such resistance in former centuries when today it is completely accepted as a designation of lesbianism? For centuries the great poetess's lifestyle was passed over in complete silence in favor of a more acceptable image of the *mascula* Sappho,[2] the chaste Sapho,[3] or the woman who killed herself at the Rock of Leucadius, throwing herself into the sea because the young shepherd Phaon rejected her advances.[4] That it should have been unthinkable for the humanists of the Renaissance that

147

Sappho was both a great poetess and a woman who loved women is already problematic. Had the status of women regressed to such a point during the Renaissance that one could no longer conceive that a poetic genius of her calibre might also be a "genius" of the freedom to love? And that it might have been through this freedom that she was able to create erotic poetry and achieve such a capacity for lyrical evocation that her poems have become a kind of archetype for sexual desire?

Sappho was the founder of lesbian love in the Western world, the first woman we know of who recognized women as the subject of her desire, giving them a new erotic and poetic status. In a society that was preparing to lock Greek women up in the gyneceum, this was indeed a historic event, a moment when a woman could recognize the existence of another woman through her own sexual desire. This desire stemmed not only from the dart of Eros, as Sappho would say, but also from the cult of Aphrodite, providing a glimpse of a community of women who studied singing, music, and poetry together—of a life lived collectively, a sharp contrast to that of the men of the Greek city.

Sappho the subversive! That she should have embodied the role of the subversive in her own time, as well as in our own, is cause indeed to reflect on twenty-six centuries of Western history. Sappho's world was one in which the female couple had meaning, a meaning that was recognized even by Greek men, as is evidenced by the Corinthian goddess couples (Greece, 620 B.C.E) and the "whispering women" of Myrina (second century C.E.)[5], whose whispering designates "the conversation of lovers."[6]

Has the original link been lost? Have we been dispossessed of a cultural identity by a (patriarchal) language that could not bear to see in Sappho a woman of free morals? Or are we in the process of regaining the political strength of that world, thanks to the revolt of women who, over the course of two centuries, have made possible the return of the Two Women Friends to the city of men?

Tribade: *Reasons for a Choice*

First, a question: Why doesn't *gomorrhe*[7] appear in the the lexicon of pleasure, while *sodomie* is commonly used to refer to lust between men (and anal penetration)? There seems to be no specific term for women's sexual practice in the Middle Ages, except the very vague phrase *péché de luxure* (the sin of lewdness) (which refers to pleasure outside marriage in general and to adultery in particular) or *infamen*, a term that comes directly from Saint Paul's *Letter to the Corinthians* condemning les *infames amours romaines* (unspeakable Roman lusts). The almost complete lack of interest displayed by organized religion in this particular sin of the flesh is actually ;. rfectly in keeping with church doctrine: Two women could not commit a sin between them, for until the secret of conception was discovered, the seed was considered to be the only carrier of life and its bearer the one who gave sense to the sexual act.

Religion did not, for all that, turn a blind eye to the asocial behavior of women. In the case of women who dared to *porter l'habit d'homme* (wear men's clothing), *dissimuler l'état de femme* (conceal their feminine state), or *utiliser l'état d'homme* (benefit from masculine status), it did not hesitate to punish transgressors by putting them to death. During a trial for witchcraft, several women were condemned to death by the Inquisition for offenses such as these. In the thirteenth century, two women were burned at Péronne by Robert le Bougre for having *porté l'habit d'homme* (worn men's clothing).[8] One of the twelve charges against Jeanne d'Arc was that she wore *continuellement l'habit d'homme* (men's dress continually).[9] Evidently there were legal sanctions against relationships between women. But, in contrast to those against relationships between men, they were social in nature rather than sexual, for the separation between the sexes is the foundation of the social cohesion guaranteed by the religion of the Father, the Son, and the Holy Spirit. This cohesion was, moreover, so important to the continued existence of patriarchy that during the Renaissance, civil justice took over from religious justice, condemning several women to the stake with the same ferocity that it was to use toward sodomites.

If pleasure between women seemed so insignificant, why did the religious authorities condemn it? It harmed not God, nor the institution of marriage, nor indeed the system of patriarchal descent that controls the transmission of patrimony. Nor was it a sin against nature, since no seed is involved; theologians therefore do not mention it. But what of the men of the Renaissance, who discovered the writings of the Ancients in the middle of the sixteenth century? These texts were full of statements on the issue—an issue that was less likely to embarrass since it originated in a pagan tradition. Why, then, did these men keep silent? Their appetites were whetted all the more by the fact that the Greek and the Latin writers brought with them a real breath of fresh air, lending the question of pleasure a sense of novelty that religious discourse had lost in its attempts to mould people's consciences and sexual behavior. Language too was in the process of being turned upside down. Clerics and cultivated people were abandoning Latin and writing in their native tongues. Was this not the moment to take on new subjects of wonder?

The word *tribade* first appeared under the pen of the famous humanist printer Henri Estienne. The context in which it appeared was far from neutral, as is shown by this extract from his *Apologie pour Hérodote:*

> A girl from Fontaines, which is between Blois and Romorantin, having disguised herself as a man, worked as a stable boy for about seven years in a hostelry in the faubourg of Foye. She then married a local girl, with whom she remained for about two years, and worked in a vineyard. After which time, the vileness she used to counterfeit the role of husband was discovered and she was arrested and, having made her confession, was burned alive. Thus our century may boast that as well as all the wicked acts of previous centuries, it has some which are unique to it. For this act has nothing in common with that of certain shameful creatures who used to be called tribads. (Estienne 1879: v. I, ch. 13, 177–178)

We stand forewarned! Wickedness should not be confused with shamefulness, marriage with sexual pleasure, the man's role with that of the woman. Henri Estienne may have been well informed about the customs of the ancients, but he neglects to state his sources. What exactly did the word *tribade* mean during the Renaissance?

It is not until Pierre Richelet published his *Dictionnaire françois tiré de l'usage et des meilleurs auteurs de la langue* almost a century later, in 1680, that we find an answer to this question, which goes to show how much time it took to create some order in a language that was evolving at such a rapid rate:

> *Tribad*: a word which comes from the Greek. She who couples with a person of her own sex and simulates the man (*sa contrefaçon*). See Martial, 91. "*C'est une tribade*" (She's a tribad).

Who is this Martial who writes about tribads? None other than the Latin author who lived in the first century C.E. Number 91 of Martial's epigrams, dedicated to a famous Roman courtesan by the name of Philaenis, does indeed feature the word *tribad*.

> Ipsarum tribadum tribas, Philaeni
> recte, quam futuis, vocas amicam . . .
>
> (Famous amongst all tribads, Philaenis,
> with reason do you call "your friend," she whom you plow.)
> (Martial 1969: vol.1)

Thus, although derived from the Greek *tribein*, meaning *to rub, to rub each other*, the word *tribad* itself is a pure product of the Latin culture of the first century C.E, communicated to the French humanists on Martial's authority.

Nevertheless, one wonders why Richelet chose Martial rather than Phaedrus, the Latin fabulist, for example, who uses the word *tribad* in his fable of Prometheus, in which he explains, following Plato, the origin of the tribads and the effeminate "*tribades et molles*" (1969: 16; see also Randy Conner this volume). Men of the Renaissance could not place love among women within the mythical perspective of the *androgyne*, for to do so would be to provide a theoretical foundation in which equality between the sexes would be possible. If one posits men and women as equivalent, there is then equality in "nature," which is in itself unthinkable. With the concept of *contrefaçon* (false imitation/counterfeit), however, man casts himself as the model for woman, as the norm of sexual behavior, the mirror of excellence. From this perspective, in which man is central, woman can be seen only as a simulacrum, or imitation. Even Sappho, despite being recognized by men for her poetic genius, in the role of lover only *simulated* the male role because she could not penetrate her lover without an imitation of the penis—a dildo. This explains why, in the sixteenth century, Sappho was discarded as a possible role model of love between women by Estienne himself—not from ignorance about her life and practice, since he was the first editor of her work, but by political choice.[10] A woman is not equal to a man, be it in love, politics, or society. In the sixteenth century, in this space from which man is absent, his *contrefaçon* remains. For this reason, men refer only to each other: Martial, Estienne, Brantôme, Baudelaire, Freud. . . .

One thing is certain, in any case: Not all of antiquity was resuscitated by the men of the Renaissance, but only part of it, the part that consolidated and legitimated their new power. The whole Greek tradition from the sixth century B.C.E., which witnessed the birth of lyric poetry with Sappho, the poetry of feminine desire whose appeal was so powerful that it inspired Boileau to write a hyperbolic commentary, was "forgotten" in favor of the Roman tradition, which witnessed the birth of Christianity. *L'homoïos*, the attraction of one's like, was incompatible with the Renaissance idea of balance. How could the feminine couple be recognized as a bearer of meaning and culture? "There are only men," Brantôme was to comment in his *Vie des dames galantes* (Life of gay ladies), and yet it was he who was best able to translate the moment of hesitation that heralded the teetering over of a whole culture from one world to the next, from a glimpse of the Greek world to its rejection in favor of the Latin world, whose mental structure was closer to that of sixteenth-century France:

> They say that Sappho of Lesbos was a past mistress of this art, and even that, as they say, it was she who invented it, and that from her day onward lesbian ladies have imitated her and continued until the present; as Lucian[11] says: such women are the women of Lesbos, that they will not suffer any man, but approach other women just as men do. And that such women are called *tribads*, a Greek word derived, as I have learned from the Greeks, from *tribo, tribein*, which is to say *fricare, freyer*, or *friquer* (to rub) or *s'entrefrotter* (to rub up against each other) and a tribad is called a *fricatrice*, in French *fricatrices*, or those who perform the *fricarelle* in affairs of *donna con donna*, as is the case nowadays. (Brantôme 1962: 123)[12]

Brantôme goes on to tell several stories about women he knew, like the one who kept and serviced her friend *à pot et à feu* (by pot and by fire, i.e., in every way) or the women who loved each other so much they could not refrain from making loving gestures to each other even in public. "I have seen so many of these lesbians who, for all their rubbing and humping (*fricarelles et entrefrottements*), still run after men," he concludes. "Even Sapho, who was past mistress of the art, did she not fall in love with her great friend Phaon, after which she died? . . . For, in the end, there are only men" (Brantôme 1962: 123).

The sexual pleasure of tribads does not endanger patriarchal society. It is the pleasure of courtesans, a harmless sensual game, a sensation obtained by rubbing, not by penetration. It bears no comparison to adultery, which, for its part, endangers the patriarchal order of descendance that is at the core of the transmission of inheritance. The real danger comes from elsewhere—from those who live together in their own towns, as in Gomorrha; those who found universities for women, as on Lesbos; those who transgress the social order, like the young women who lived in Vitry le François in 1580, whose story is recounted in Montaigne's *Diary of a Journey to Italy*:

> Several years ago, seven or eight girls living near Chaumont in Bassigny plotted to dress in masculine clothes, and present themselves in the world thus attired. Of this group, one woman, bearing the name of Marie came to the town of Vitry, earning her living as a weaver, a young man of good condition and helpful disposition. In the said town of Vitry, he became engaged to a woman who is still living, but, because of some disagreement which occurred between them, things did not go any further. After this, he moved to Montirandet, still earning his living at the said occupation. He fell in love

with a woman whom he married and lived with for four or five months, with her consent, according to what people say. But, having been recognized by someone from Chaumont, and the affair brought before the courts, she was condemned to be hanged: which she said she preferred to endure rather than resume the status of a girl. And she was hanged for employing illicit inventions to compensate for the lack inherent in her sex. (Montaigne 1946: 87–88)

These were the foundations upon which the Renaissance was built. "She was condemned to be hanged: which she said she preferred to endure rather than resume the status of a girl," Montaigne tells us. Was she a witch, a tribad, a lesbian, a rebel, a feminist? Noone says, but the men of the sixteenth century knew what they were doing by continuing the repressive actions of the Middle Ages, while searching for references among the Ancients that would reinforce patriarchal mental attitudes. But they perverted the Greek message and revived a Greco-Latin tradition amputated from the best of itself—amputated from Phaedrus, from Plato, and, of course, from Sappho, who had nevertheless instilled in it the real power with which she is associated: the discovery of self-referential sentiments in the world of women.

Was it not this world that frightened them—this time of authentically feminine culture, a time when the creative woman had a recognized place in society? A time when a woman could construct an identity through her relationship with another woman, different from her, conceived on equal terms as her, and the subject of her own desire? If the Two Women Friends were swept away by the Renaissance perspective, which was built around a uniquely masculine point of view, it was because they potentially constituted a society and formed the basis for an oppositional force. Without culture, there could be no women's power. In the story Montaigne relates, both women are not hanged, only the one who played the man's role and who is therefore considered the guilty party. The other woman does not exist; she is responsible neither for her choices nor for her acts.

The choice of the word *tribade*, a choice made during the Renaissance, seals the defeat of women. It names a cultural defeat, since this term reduces the notion of love between women to a technical question of sexual pleasure. How do they manage without men? They rub themselves, rub against each other; they are tribads. The whole cultural perspective is eliminated. This development is paralleled by a decline in the political status of women, officially instigated by the Loi Salique[13], which prevented women from succeeding to the French throne. After this law was passed, women could no longer reign in France. And Martial gained authority over Sappho to speak of what concerns them.

Although for three centuries the word to describe women who love one another remained the same, the definitions were to change during the Enlightenment. What then did *tribade* mean to an educated man of the eighteenth century, faced with the task of defining words in his own language? For members of the Academy, who bore the responsibility of "legislating on linguistic matters" (in Vaugelas's terms[14]), it meant revising the *Dictionnaire de l'Académie* (Dictionary of the Academy). The word *tribade* does not appear in the *Dictionnaire* until its fourth edition, published in 1762, where it is defined as follows:

Tribad: woman who abuses another woman.

What exactly is the significance of the word *abuse*? According to the *Dictionnaire*, "*on dit abuser d'une fille pour dire jouir d'une fille sans l'avoir épousée*" (one uses the phrase *to abuse a girl* to mean obtaining sexual pleasure from her without having married her). Between rape and mutual consent, as we see, the dividing line was pretty narrow. But what else could we expect from writers whose job was to define for the monarchy the *bon usage* (correct use) of the language? It was the philosophers of the Enlightenment who provided a glimmer of hope, and it is in *l'Encyclopédie* that we see the emergence of a completely new definition of the word *tribade*, in which pleasure regains its philosophical value:

> *Tribad*: woman who feels passion for another women. A particular kind of depravity as inexplicable as that which excites a man for another man.

Two new elements are introduced in this definition, which has at least the benefit of not attempting to explain everything: the idea of passion, which invokes feeling but also passivity, and that of *dépravation* which refers to pathology and to a particular medical discourse about passions considered to be *affectations de l'âme* (afflictions of the spirit).

The definitions of these words offered by the *Encyclopédie* clearly reveal that the exact meaning of the word *tribade* was among the hot topics of philosophical debate in the eighteenth century! It was a burning subject for the Encyclopédistes, who blended medicine, metaphysics, and the philosophy of the Enlightenment. Previous medical knowledge, which had explained "the abuse of a woman by another" based on anatomy (a clitoris the size of a penis),[15] was no longer applied to physical love between women. Instead, this activity was attributed to another factor, the ambiguity of which Diderot explores in detail in *La Religieuse* (1768) in his portrait of the Abbesse d'Arpajon, whose passion for Sister Suzanne would lead to "depravity," that is, to insanity and "damnation." Contemporary critics such as George May have seen Diderot as an ancestor of sexology who conceived of the term *homosexuality* a century before psychiatrists (May 1954: 114)[16]. However, this interpretation takes no account of the liberatory side of Diderot's philosophical premise, which broke through a formidable religious deadlock, "Everything that is can be neither against, nor beyond nature" (1956: 379–380). Pleasure, a source of sin according to Catholic moral standards, is in this way freed from its status as infamous, criminal, abusive, or useless.

Another event that would lay the groundwork for the cultural affirmation of lesbians was the presence of women on the social and artistic scene who openly expressed their passions for women: Françoise Raucourt, an actress at the Théâtre Français, nicknamed the Great Priestess of Lesbos by the underground chroniclers; the singer Sophie Arnould; Madame Démailly, whose liaison with Françoise Raucourt was public knowledge; the Duchess of Villeroy; Mistress Clairon; Mistress Julie; not forgetting Madame, Countess of Provence, the sister-in-law of Louis XVI, who fought to keep the woman she loved, Madame de Gourbillon, at her side, nor Marie-Antoinette, of course, whose "excessive friendship" for the

Countess of Polignac was the news of the day. All these women participated in the wave of freedom that rocked prerevolutionary France, a freedom that the libertines put to good use in works such as the *Apologie de la secte anandryne*,[17] their poetry and stories rekindling the *mystère* surrounding the "priestesses of Lesbos."

However, the French Revolution did not accord this same freedom to women. Although in principle women were granted basic human rights by the "Droits de l'homme et du citoyen" (1789), in reality they were sent back to the gynaeceum from 1793 on—that is to say, to maternity and to the family—and excluded from the freedom of the city. Strangely enough, the story of Sappho's suicide on the rocks of Leucadius came back to haunt the collective unconscious, creating a passionate interest among writers and artists. Constance Pipelet was, it seems, the first to introduce to a readership highly receptive to the heroes of Antiquity this new figure of Greek womanhood, who was the embodiment of both Poetry and the lovelorn despair that leads to suicide. Pipelet's lyric tragedy, titled *Sapho*, appeared in 1794. The following year, six artists presented works inspired by Sappho at the Salon du Louvre, each work based either on Sappho's (heterosexual) love affairs or on her suicide. Was this renewed interest in the poetess caused by women's defeat during the Revolution, a defeat that some celebrated as the revenge of men against an exceptional woman who hoped to gain her freedom and was punished by death? It was also a defeat that inspired revolt against the exclusion of women (of genius) from the political arena. The painters A. J. Gros, Michel Grandin, David, Elise Bruyère, Chasseriau, the sculptor Pradier in 1852, the poet Baudelaire, the painter Courbet in 1860, and Rodin at the end of the nineteenth century all addressed the question. Their responses were starkly polarized between the lesbian as model for the sexually liberated and socially emancipated woman and the lesbian as the image the damned woman.

Rupture of the Renaissance Point of View

The revolution that turned France upside down so transformed the social consciousness that it seemed as though the culture of the *ancien régime* had been decapitated along with its king. Though the Restoration brought back not only royalty but also something of the climate of former times, the revolution of July 1830 ended all hope of continuity with the past. New ideas sprang up, released from the Greco-Roman tradition. New figures appeared, among them George Sand whose novel *Lélia*, published in 1833, would have a considerable impact on the period. "A cry of pain," George Sand would declare; "a burst of anger," the critic and author Charles-Augustin Sainte-Beuve would affirm, "which breathed a spirit of revolt against society" (*Le National*, 29 September 1833, quoted in Sand 1960: 590). *Lélia* was written in a very specific political context: the failure of the July revolution, the failure of the Saint-Simonist doctrine of social and sexual emancipation ("which was unable to resolve the great question of love" [Sand 1971]), and the attacks on romanticism.

The passage of interest to us comes at the end of the first section of the novel. After several years of separation, Lélia meets up with her sister, Pulchérie, who has become a courtesan. Her sister decides to tell Lélia about a formative event from their youth, when, after a walk in the countryside, they had stretched out on the grass next to a stream. "We fell into a deep sleep. We awoke in each other's arms, without feeling that we had ever been asleep" (Sand 1960: 154). It was during this sleep that Pulchérie had a revelation of something essential for her life to come, which she decribes to her sister in these words: "It was in your innocent arms, on your virginal breast, that for the first time God revealed to me the force of life. Do not move away like that. Listen to me without prejudice."

Before following this story further, I should describe the two sisters. The most salient point is that they do not resemble each other, which obviates the question of narcissism. "Wiser and happier than I, you lived only for pleasure," Lélia declares to Pulchérie. "More ambitious and less obedient to God, perhaps, I lived only for desire." Thus we have two opposites juxtaposed, ripe for philosophical reflexion. One embodies pleasure, the other desire, forces that bring to mind the two most prominent divinities in the Sapphic pantheon: Eros and Aphrodite.

What was so extraordinary in what happened between the two women to cause the novel to become such a hot item and place George Sand firmly in the Sapphic camp? I will let Pulchérie explain as she relates what happened while she slept.

> A strange, frenzied dream, unparalleled, revealed to me the mystery which had been impenetrable until then, and, until then, obediently respected. Oh my sister! Deny the influence of heaven. Deny the saintliness of pleasure! You would have said, if this extasy had been accorded you, that an angel, sent to you from the breast of God, was charged with initiating you into the sacred trials of human life. I dreamed, quite simply, of a man with dark hair who bent toward me to brush my lips with his warm, red ones; and I awoke feeling weighed down, thrilled, happier than I had ever imagined I could be. I looked around me: glints of sunlight were strewn over the depths of the wood. (Sand 1960: 155)

Notice that the erotic symbolism of the kiss resembles more closely the union of two women than a man and a woman: lips against lips, not tongue in mouth. Was this the source of the "strangeness" and the excitement that makes her open her eyes? What does she see then? Her sister asleep beside her.

> I looked at you then. Oh my sister, how beautiful you were! . . . At that moment the meaning of beauty was revealed to me in another creature. I no longer loved myself alone; I needed to find an object of admiration and love outside myself. (Sand 1960: 157)

When she gazes at Lélia, she becomes troubled, and the image of her dream is superimposed on that of her sister, until she finds a resemblance to the "beautiful child with dark hair" of her dream:

> and, trembling, I kissed your arm. Then you opened your eyes, and your gaze penetrated me with an unknown shame; I turned away as though I had done something wrong. And yet, Lélia, no impure thought had even come into my mind. How could

this have happened? I had no idea. I had received from nature and from God, my creator and my master, my first lesson in love, my first sensation of desire. (Sand 1960: 158)

Pulchérie then asks her to bend over the water. "You look like a man," she says to Lélia. "And that makes you shrug with scorn."

This, then, was one of the scenes that caused such scandal that "it was even interpreted as obscene and depraved," as George Sand reports (1971: 197). What exactly is scandalous about the passage? That Pulchérie should receive her first lesson in love "from nature and from God," rather than from a man? That Lélia occupies the position of a man during this event, later to supplant him? For it is the fantasized image of a man created by society that leads Pulchérie to see her sister differently and to discover another reality buried inside her, her desire for a woman. She who lived only for pleasure discovers within her desire, and through it the existence of the "other" who becomes "an object of admiration and of love" in her eyes, which are now opened to the world. Is this experience not fundamental to the construction of the self: the passage from narcissism (she remarks that she found herself so beautiful that she would sometimes kiss herself in the mirror) to real human relations? This passage is accomplished through the recognition of her desire for a woman experienced as "different," even though she is familiar to her. By desiring her sister, Pulchérie integrates another dimension of her self (an experience which she calls "an initiation") transforming this event into a veritable advent. Desire plays the role of catalyst, infusing new values (human, esthetic, moral), and arousing the need to admire and to love in the new initiate.

One can well understand why this passage might have shocked Sand's contemporaries! Not all cried scandal, however, and some, like Saint-Beuve, lucidly analyzed its political import.

> One cannot but be struck by the remarkable moral and literary movement which has sprung up among the women of France. They too have been roused by the spirit of emancipation, and large numbers of them are speaking out, in newspapers, in books of short stories, in long novels, they are all voicing their ills, denouncing society and demanding a more equal share in their own destiny. (*Le National*, 29 September 1833, quoted in Sand 1960: 590)

George Sand's subversive power lay in the absence of labels. The women are neither tribads nor lesbians but women without taboos who discover in an unexpected way "the forces of life," as Pulchérie puts it.

There are strong indications that Lélia was based to some extent on Sand's "friendship" with Marie Dorval, whom Sand met in 1832, a few months before she began the novel. Indeed, André Maurois remarks that the dialogues between Lélia and the wise courtisan Pulchérie were taken from conversations between George and Marie (1953: 170), although he does not specify whether that includes the passage just quoted. Several letters dating from 1833 are reminiscent of the highly charged atmosphere of the novel, including the following from George to Marie, for example: "I cannot see you today, my darling. I am not to be so lucky.

Monday, morning or evening, at the theater or in your bed, I shall have to come and embrace you, my lady, or I shall commit some folly" (Simone André-Maurois 1952: 212). The letter that best supports my argument dates from 18th July 1833, in which George writes, "If you reply swiftly, saying only: come! I will set forth, had I cholera or a lover. Yours forever." This letter would have been no more compromising than the other if the poet Alfred de Vigny, who was Marie's lover, had not written on it in pencil: "I have forbidden Marie to reply to this Sapho who keeps importuning her" (Simone André-Maurois 1953: 199). Clearly, Vigny was not thinking of the "chaste Sapho" when he wrote these lines. In calling George Sand "Sapho," Vigny shows her much more respect than if he had called her a tribad. By choosing this epithet, he is giving recognition to a whole culture, a culture of women, and a liberatory voice to which Victor Hugo was to pay homage in his funeral oration, saying, "the lyre was within her" (Hugo 1954: 420).

How different *Lélia* is from another novel that appeared at the same time under the title *Gamiani ou deux nuits d'excès* (Gamiani or two nights of excess). It was signed Alicide, Baron de M^{XXX}, and attributed to the poet Alfred de Musset. It became a best-seller among the erotic literature of the nineteenth century. This is what Musset has to say about tribads: "A tribad! Oh, how strangely the word reverberates in the ear, stirring up inside one confused images of unknown pleasures, lascivious in the extreme. A paroxysm of lust, frenzied lubriciousness, and appalling pleasure never to be fulfilled (Alcide, Baron de M^{XXX}, ou Alfred de Musset 1974: 10).

The Arrival of the Lesbians

Lélia was an important event in the culture of women. Not only was it the first novel in the French language in which a woman tackled the question of love in the feminine, but, through George Sand's own personality, it announced and paved the way for the return of the Two Women Friends to the city of men.[18] George Sand embodied a new role for women in society, that of the free-living woman writer. Constance Pipelet and Madame de Stael certainly appealed to Sappho in their demand to be accorded the status of a writer,[19] but they had left in the shadows "the great question of love." George Sand combined the two, an important feat in a century in which Baudelaire would play exactly the opposite role.

The emergence of a new meaning for the word *lesbienne* is usually believed to date from the publication of Charles Baudelaire's *Les Fleurs du mal* because of the poet's trial for obscenity in 1857 and the publicity that followed the condemnation of some of the poems, including "Lesbos" and "Femmes damnées." This belief is supported by the fact that in 1847 Baudelaire had considered calling his future collection of *Les Fleurs du mal* "Les Lesbiennes." By this time, Sappho could hardly be considered an unknown, either to the artists who had been painting her portrait for half a century or to the hellenists who had discovered new fragments of her poems. Indeed, Baudelaire commented on Dugasseau's *Sappho Making the Leap at Leucadio* at the Salon of 1845, calling it a a "pretty composition" (Baudelaire 1992: 27). In 1847 Emile Deschanel published a study of antiquity titled

"Sappho et les lesbiennes" in the *Revue des deux mondes*, followed by a translation and commentary on seventy-nine fragments. If the publication of this article is memorable for the number of fragments assembled in one place, it also reverses a taboo of the same magnitude, that of speaking openly about the poetess's lifestyle. Moving from the ethnic designation to the sexual label, Deschanel remarks:

> Sappho was lesbian in every sense of the word. "It is not men who are beloved of lesbians" Lucian writes. And indeed, the name *lesbian* and the verb *to love as a lesbian* have remained in the Greek language as incontrovertible evidence of this dreadful dissoluteness. Certainly we would like to be able to think that our Sapho, that great poet, was exempt from these defilements, but since we love the truth even more than the ideal, we must, regretfully, incline to the opposite opinion. (Deschanel 1847: 343)

When, ten years later, the trial of *Les Fleurs du mal* attracted public attention to the "Lesbos" poems, the name *lesbienne* was already widely known to the educated public. Widely known, yes, but not widely used, and it could well be that this next step was achieved thanks to the help of the "Femmes damnées." Consider what Baudelaire's lawyer, Master Gustave Chaix d'Est-Ange, says in his speech for the defense: "As for the *Femmes damnées* (Damned women) whom Monsieur le Substitut has called the two tribads!!!—pretty strong language, we would certainly not have allowed ourselves to use such language in court—as for the damned women, for I beg permission to prefer my client's expression to that of the Public Prosecutor" (Crépet 1968: 442).

As for the "femmes damnées," why would they be more acceptable than the tribads? Precisely because they are damned, that is to say, excluded from the city of men and from the city of God. Damnation is complete exclusion, which is morally more acceptable than an attitude of tolerance toward tribadic pleasure— a pleasure, let us say in passing, marked by sterility, as Baudelaire remarks several times, invoking *l'âpre stérilité de votre jouissance* (the bitter sterility of your pleasure). To describe the pleasure of women, the poet refers to their reproductive functions, just as religious discourse has done for centuries.

Is there any difference between the lesbian and the damned woman? A priori yes, since for Baudelaire Lesbos is *la mère des jeux latins et des voluptés grecs* (the mother of Latin games and Greek pleasures), in other words, an erotic play familiar to the ancients. As for Greece, he makes no further mention of it, as Edith Mora points out (1966: 193). He uses the phrase *la mâle Sapho* (the masculine Sappho), which comes directly from the Latin poet Horace, as we have seen. When he writes, *De Sapho qui mourut le jour de son blasphème* (Of Sapho who died the day of her blasphemy), he is referring to the legend invented by Ovid of the death of Sappho at the rock of Leucadius, a legend that had become a nineteenth-century commonplace. Clearly Baudelaire had not read Sappho! He tries to measure himself against her as a poet, and perhaps as a lover, but as a man he reproduces all the hackneyed conventions of his century by associating sexual pleasure with religious pontification about blasphemy, sin, and guilt. In "Lesbos" he superimposes on the Latin tradition, which formed the foundation of his culture as a nineteenth-century man, his own vision of woman as an exciting, arousing, languid, volcanic, fresh, perfumed being who entices one away on distant voyages. In a word, he reifies her, he makes of her an object, a slave even, a way of attaining the infinite, which she carries within her. Perhaps he drew inspiration from the female friendships of Jeanne Duval, his mistress. Above all, he projects onto lesbians a masculine erotic of damnation in which the arousal born of guilt is reinforced by a deep disdain for women. He even goes so far as to call *la brûlante Sapho* (the enflamed Sappho) *patronne des hystériques* (the patroness of hysterical females) (Baudelaire 1992: 68).

The impulse of Baudelaire's poetic genius to find in "Lesbos" something of the new and the unknown is violently aborted by his own limitations as a man of the nineteenth century. Once again, Sappho is deprived of the cultural dimension in favor of the sulphurous "flower of evil," which was apparently necessary to his own sexual pleasure. As for Lesbos, it was completely misrepresented by this man who turned it into an item of consumption for a patriarchal society that needed to restructure itself after the blows it had received from women during the revolution of 1848.[20] As Théophile de Banville wrote in his review of a novel about Sappho that appeared at the same time, "Why does the name of Sappho play on all our lips? Why is it like a reproach, like a threat in the depths of all uneasy hearts? . . . The novel of Sapho is our own story, her madness is the raging madness of the women around us" (*Le Pouvoir*, 18 November, 1850, quoted in Mora 1966: 191). There was certainly reason for women to be raging mad after men had refused them the right to vote in 1848.

The poetry of Baudelaire might have delivered sexuality from the crushing weight of bourgeois morality, but in fact it relegitimated the power of men over women. Instead of a recognition of lesbianism, there was merely a substitution of one term for another. In half a century the word *tribade* became synonymous with *lesbienne* (entering the *Dictionnaire du nouveau larousse illustré* in 1904), and in another half century it fell into disuse under the dual pressure of the women's liberation movement and the development of psychiatry.

Under the veil of poetry, Baudelaire was allowed to redefine the term because he did not call into question men's sexual fantasies about lesbians. Although this redefinition was not accepted without difficulty, as Larousse shows at the end of its article on Sappho in the edition of 1875 (*Dictionnaire universel du XIXème siècle*):

> It is hard to know what is well-founded in the allegations made by the Ancients about Sappho's loose morals, and particularly as concerns the specific depravity of lesbianism, of which she is vehemently accused. Modern criticism, embarrassed to find reunited in one person so much talent for poetry and a freedom of morals which is no longer deemed appropriate in contemporary society, found an excellent way out in the last century: that of splitting the figure in two.

It would take another century to reunite the two facets of Sappho's persona without any sense of reticence. It was as a result of pressure from the women's liberation movement that in an article in 1976, the *Robert: Dictionnaire universel des noms propres*, finally recognized Sappho's lifestyle:

Her affinities for some of her pupils are evident in her poetry and have caused a scandal from Antiquity onward. Comprehensible and tolerable in the context of the emancipation of the Eolian woman, they were ridiculed by the Attic dramatists who wanted to put a stop to the feminist movement of Athenian women (hence the name *lesbienne* to designate a homosexual woman).

Certainly Sappho had achieved recognition—but one could not imagine a better guarantee against a positive projection than this *femme homosexuelle* (homosexual woman) who sprang from the lunatic asylum at the beginning of the century.

The Tribad's New Clothes

Conceived in Germany at the end of the nineteenth century, in the context of a struggle against the penal code, which made sodomy illegal, the theory of homosexuality had its roots in the dim reaches of the medical knowledge of the classical age. With little influence until the nineteenth century, the science of sexuality, based on anatomy, began to develop in leaps and bounds toward the middle of the century, becoming so important that the *Larousse universel du dix-neuvième siècle* (Universal Larousse of the nineteenth century) included in its new definition a description derived from the sexologists:

> *Tribad*: woman whose clitoris shows exaggerated development and who abuses her own sex.

Thirty years later (in the edition of 1904, to be exact) the word *homosexuel/ homosexuelle* made its offical entry into the supplement of the *Nouveau Larousse illustré*, with the following definition:

> *Homosexuel/le*: Pathology: A male or female individual who feels no sexual affinity save for persons of their own sex.

This definition constituted undeniable progress since it recognized the existence of gender difference. The whole vision of sexuality changed, or at least shifted from one norm to another. Before, the major distinction had been between the sexual act conceived with the aim of procreation and that embarked upon for pleasure alone, as in adultery, sodomy, masturbation, tribadism, and so on. Now the major distinction was that between the same and the other, whatever the sex, bringing with it an inevitable mirror effect in which women were once again made to disappear. From this homosexual perspective, man continued to be the model for a woman's sexual relationship. The norm simply shifted from man as "provider of seed," and thus of meaning, to the heterosexual couple in which the man has the active role while the woman remains, in the blinkered eyes of men of science, a "dark continent."

A double displacement was now at work. The first was from the physical to the mental. In the anatomy books of the seventeenth and eighteenth centuries, the pathology of the clitoris (described as "enormous") provided an explanation for the fact that a woman could physically "abuse" another woman; for Freud, she suffered from penis envy. The second displacement was from the social to the psychological. This time the homosexual woman identified as a man. As if by chance, the first case of homosexuality studied by the German psychiatrist Carl Von Westphal was that of a young woman who liked to wear men's clothes and was attracted only to women. In the sixteenth century this was called *contrefaire le métier de l'homme* (counterfeiting the man's role); in the nineteenth century it became the *sentiment sexuel contraire* (contrary sexual feeling), and then *homosexualité*. A defensive weapon in a repressive Germany, this theory annexed "woman" to male objectives. Once again, women were to be trapped by the male norm. The female homosexual was seen as one who feels like a man, before becoming a (symbolically) castrated man. "As far as we are concerned," wrote the Lacanian Moustapha Safouan, "female homosexuality represents a retarded stage in the assumption of symbolic castration" (1976: 127).

The theory of female homosexuality remodels and systematizes the patriarchal history of the tribad, claiming authority—scientific authority this time—over women's discourse. For the crucial distinction between the sixteenth century and the present resides not in this so-called new knowledge but in the existence in France of a feminist and lesbian cultural movement of unprecedented vitality. While psychiatrists studied cases of female inversion in mental hospitals or in their own consulting rooms, women were obtaining new rights and a new place in society. Rosa Bonheur (1822–1899) and Louise Breslau (1856–1927) led the way. In Paris, the 1920s was the period of the *garçonne* (tomboy), of the literary salons like those of Natalie Barney and Gertrude Stein, and of Franco-American solidarity between women artists, initiated most notably by Janet Scudder and Jane Poupelet. Artists came from all over the world to breathe the fresh air of freedom, which was so scarce elsewhere. Tamara de Lempicka (Bonnet 1994c), Romaine Brooks, Mariette Lydis, Louise Janin, Marie Laurencin painted a new picture of women, flouting the prohibition on nudity and, by way of healthy provocation, taking up the theme of the Two Women Friends—as did Rodin, Bourdelle, Matisse, Foujita, and Pascin, who made their own contribution to the acceptance of women's reality as a political and cultural fact which must be taken into account. But to do this seriously would have entailed granting women the vote, contraception, and access to education and opening up the professions, the university, and the sciences. There was a solution to this new problem: psychiatry, the new rampart against feminism.

In the course of this historical overview, one is struck by the poverty of the lexicon used to describe love between women as compared to that of heterosexual love: a single term in use for three centuries, with varying definitions, the (ambiguous) appearance of the term *lesbienne* in the middle of the eighteenth century and of *homosexuelle* in 1904, the only "innovation" the introduction of the word *gouine* in the middle of the twentieth century. This last word is particularly derogatory and constitutes a real cultural regression, since it once meant "a loose woman, a woman of ill repute" (*Dictionnaire de l'Académie*, 1694) and "a prostitute who frequents places of debauchery" (*Dictionnaire de Trévoux*, 1721). It is not entirely clear how the meaning of *gouine* changed from "prostitute" to "homosexual woman," but this association is less surprising when we consider that it was in the first century C.E. that the Roman Martial met Philaenis, the courtesan, and described her as a *tribade*.

In the 1970s, lesbians in the *mouvement de libération des femmes* (women's liberation movement) reappropriated the word *gouine* and added the word *rouge* (red) to form the group *Gouines rouge* (Red Dykes, of which Monique Wittig, Christine Delphy, and I were members). This attempt to change the insulting character of the term *gouine* by adding the qualifier *rouge*, signifying *revolutionary*, was quickly abandoned, because it did not create a social identity that could be readily assumed. Another term, *goudous*, is used more frequently by lesbians to refer to themselves and each other, but since it serves mostly as an ingroup expression, rarely used by outsiders, it is not discussed further here.

If feminist debate over the choice between *lesbian* and *homosexual* has been less animated in France than in the United States, this may be due to the weight of patriarchal history, which, in its pretended tolerance of love between women, has scarcely been able to hide its contempt in its effort to diffuse any potential threat by reducing "lesbianism" to the mere pursuit of pleasure. It is also striking that since the nineteenth century French lesbians have seldom used the word *lesbiennes* to refer to themselves, preferring the term *amitié* (friendship). The painter Rosa Bonheur christened her residence at Thomery (close to Fontainebleau), where she lived with Nathalie Micas for forty years, "Le Domaine de la parfaite amitié"[21] (the domain of perfect friendship) (Klumpke 1908; Bonnet 1994b); Louise Breslau titled her portrait of Madelaine Zillhardt, with whom she spent thirty years, *Portrait des amies* (Portrait of women friends) (Breslau 1881, 1889; Bonnet 1994a). As for Natalie Clifford Barney, the temple in her garden in the rue Jacob in Paris was christened "Temple à l'Amitié." The social relationship among women who share this choice of lifestyle was conceived of as *friendship*.

This leads us to question the social status of lesbians. All the terms we have studied refer either to a sexual status or a cultural status, but they never define social status, as though women could choose only between the status of *femme mariée* (married woman) and *célibataire* (single). The only attempt to find another way of conceptualizing the lesbian was made in the eighteenth century with the introduction of the term *anandryne*, but the word was not taken up. This word is much more interesting than it first appears. *L'espion anglais* (1778) defines it as *anti-homme* (anti-man) (de Mairobert 1977: 70), but Mirabeau, who appears to have created it, devotes an entire chapter to it in his *Erotika Bilblion*, defining it as a word "which comes from the Greek *anandros*, feminine *anandré*. For a man: lacking in virility. For a woman: lacking a husband" (1984: 523).

The woman "lacking a husband" is rooted in a tradition as old as the *tribade*, if not older. In Rome, she was a "virgin," whom Georges Devereux has defined as "a sexually active woman who was not subject to a man." Such an "untamed" woman (*admêtis*) was formerly called *parthénos*, a word that did not acquire the meaning of *virgin* until much later" (1982: 16).

If the wife is statutorily "the woman belonging to the man," we need to find another word besides *célibataire* (single) to designate "she who belongs to herself" and who loves women. This is perhaps the direction in which we need to turn in our search for lesbian visibility, since lesbian life choices go far beyond the domain of the sexual to which the patriarchy would like to restrict it in order to disarm its revolutionary potential. Love between women is a conquest, a gratuitous act that creates an individual identity with no social meaning. If we want it to be recognized, we need to invest it with social significance by according it a real social status.

NOTES

This chapter was translated from the French by Anna Livia with input from Diane Long.

1. Translation by Edith Mora, 1966. *Sappho* is written with either one *p* or two. Following Mora's suggestion, I write *Sappho* when referring to the historical figure and *Sapho* when referring to the social discourse.

2. A phrase that appears in the work of the Latin poet Horace, first century B.C.E. "La mâle Sapho règle le pas de sa muse sur la marche d'Archiloque" (The masculine Sapho measures the rhythm of her muse to the steps of Achiloquus) (Horace, *Epistle* 1:19). Horace is expressing a literary judgment about Sappho's mastery of prosody. In the seventeenth century, the term *mâle* was understood in terms of the heroic female who had the courage to jump from the rock at Leucadius.

3. The chaste Sappho comes from Ovid, the Latin poet who invented the myth of her suicide at Leucadius, caused by her despair at having been rejected by Phaon, with whom she had fallen in love in her old age. In the seventeenth century, in reaction to this myth, her biography was rewritten as heterosexual, and Sappho became the model of the woman writer. The entire story of her love for women was erased. This phenomenon had such a wide-reaching effect that the term *Sapho* replaced that of *Précieuse* or *Femme savante* to refer to a woman writer. Madeleine de Scudéry became the Sapho of the Hôtel de Rambouillet (a salon), Julie de Lespinasse the Sapho of the eighteenth century, and so on. See Joan Dejean 1989 for *The Fictions of Sappho*.

4. A legend that originated in Ovid's fifteenth Heroid. See also Mora 1966.

5. I thank Michèle Brun for drawing my attention to the existence of these statues. Excavations in the necropolis of Tanagra, a Greek city in Boetia, have recovered numerous earthenware statues that date from the third century B.C.E. and portray scenes of daily life. These include representations of women such as "Girls playing knucklebones" and "Young girl carrying another girl on her back," while others portray "Young girls pressed tenderly against one another," a theme that archeologists have connected to two Corinthian godesses found in Thèbes. It was at Myrina also that a figurine representing Sappho seated was found. See the reproductions in Higgins 1969, plates A and D: 6, and Loraux 1981 for Athenian concepts of citizenship and the division of the sexes.

7. Gomorrha is one of the five biblical cities destroyed by Jehova to punish its inhabitants for their immorality. Lot and his two daughters were saved, but his wife was transformed into a pillar of salt for having turned back to view the destruction (Gen. 19: 1–29).

8. These events occurred between 1235 and 1238, notes Michèle Bordeaux, Professeur de Droit at the University of Nantes, to whom I am endebted for providing me with this information.

9. Information taken from *Mémoires pour servir à l'histoire de France*, an analysis of the documents pertaining to the case of Joan of Arc and her trial. 1st series, LIII: 167.

10. Estienne edited two of Sappho's poems, to be precise: "La Lune a fui" (The moon

has fled) and "A Aphrodite" (To Aphrodite), published in Greek in 1550, following the *Odes* of Anacreon.

11. See the *Dialogue des courtisanes* (Dialogue of the courtesans), which I have not quoted here due to space restrictions.

12. This text was not published in his lifetime. Written in 1587, it was "forgotten" by his heirs and did not reappear until 1666, when it achieved great success.

13. Salic law. This collection of laws of the Salien Franks dates back to the Middle Ages and includes an interdiction preventing women from inheriting land. It was reinstated in the sixteenth century by the Valois after Henri III had succeeded to the throne only to be assassinated in 1589, leaving no male heir. The Guises, heirs through the female line, wanted to do away with Salic law, but Henri de Navarre, soon to be Henri IV, converted to Catholicism and after four troubled years was annointed king in 1594. Unlike in Russia and England, no woman was to sit on the French throne under the *ancien regime*.

14. An eighteenth-century grammarian and member of the French Academy, Vaugelas defined the rules of "bon usage" (correct use) in his *Remarques sur la langue française utiles à ceux qui veulent parler et bien écrire.*

15. Clitoris: "Colombe calls it the sweetness of love and the spur of venus because this part of the body is the primary source of pleasure during copulation. The Greeks call it Clitoris and others the penis or the woman's member . . . because it grows in some women to the size of the male member, so that women abuse with the clitoris rather than the male member, and copulate with each other, whom the Greeks call Tribads" (Bartholin 1647: 1, 205).

16. See especially Georges May 1954, in the chapter entitled "Diderot sexologue." "Diderot's originality comes from his having rejected an explanation of sapphism based on the abnormal formation of the sexual organs, and having classified it not as a physical vice but a spiritual one" (114). This is a highly debatable statement based on the belief that sapphism is a vice. An attentive reading reveals that Diderot provides no rational explanation but describes only passionate acts.

17. *Anandryne* is a Greek word meaning "without a man." The extraordinary *Apologie de la secte Anandryne ou Exhortation d'une jeune tribade* (Mademoiselle Sapho), a speech delivered by Mademoiselle Raucourt on 28 March 1778, was published in vol. 10 of the *Espion anglais* in 1784. The *Espion anglais* is an anonymous chronicle of the customs of the period.

18. Unfortunately, we do not have space here to discuss Courbet, whose painting *Les Demoiselles des bords de la Seine* (The young ladies on the banks of the Seine, Paris: Musée du Petit Palais) was clearly inspired by *Lélia* , as Michèle Haddad has pointed out (1989: 159–167).

19. As may be seen in these lines from Pipelet:
O femmes, c'est pour vous que j'accorde ma lyre,
O femmes, reprenez la plume et le pinceau. . . .

(O women, it is for you that I tune my lyre,
O women, take up again the quill and brush. . . .)
Constance Pipelet, Epître aux femmes, 1797

20. The women's revolt during the revolution of 1848 was surprising for its radicalism and its collective nature. Men fear groups of rebellious women. For the first time women claimed political and economic rights such as the right to vote, divorce, and work; they created newspapers like *La Voix des femmes* (The voice of women) and *La Politique des femmes* (Women's politics) and formed clubs and regiments of Amazons.

21. The "domain of perfect friendship" was transformed into the Musée-Atelier Rosa Bonheur, which is open to the public two days a week.

REFERENCES

Alcide (Alfred de Musset) (1953). *George Sand–Marie Dorval: Correspondances inédites.* Paris: Gallimard.

——— (1974). *Gamiani ou deux nuits d'excès.* Paris: Filipacchi.

André-Maurois, Simone (1952). *Lélia ou la vie de George Sand.* Paris: Hachette.

Badinter, Elisabeth (1983). *Emilie, Emilie.* Paris: Livre de Poche.

Bartholin, Gaspar, and Thomas Bartholin (1647). *Institutions anatomiques.* Paris.

Baudelaire, Charles (1964). "L'Ecole païenne." In *L'Art romantique*, ed. Lloyd James Austin. Paris: Julliard Littérature.

——— (1968). *Procès des Fleurs du mal.* Edition critique, J. Crépet. Paris: J. Corti.

——— (1992). *Ecrits sur l'art.* Paris: Livre de Poche Classique.

Bonnet, Marie-Jo (1981). *Un Choix sans équivoque.* Paris: Denoël-Gonthier.

——— (1994a). "Louise Breslau." *Lesbia Magazine* (June).

——— (1994b). "Le Musée de l'atelier de Rosa Bonheur." *Lesbia Magazin* 129 (July–August). 31–32.

——— (1994c). "Tamara de Lempicka." *Lesbia Magazine* 130 (September), 35.

——— (1995). *Un Choix sans équivoque: Les Relations amoureuses entre les femmes du XVI au XX siècle.* Paris: Denoël Gonthier.

Brantôme (1962). *Les Dames galantes.* Texte établi et annoté par M. Rat. Paris: Livre de Poche.

Breslau, Louise (1881). *Le Portrait des amies* (painting). Musée de Genève.

——— (1889). *Contrejour* (painting). Musée de Berne.

Conner, Randy (this volume). "*Les Molles et les chausses*: Mapping the Isle of Hermaphrodites in Premodern France."

Dejean, Joan (1989). *Fictions of Sappho, 1546–1937.* Chicago: University of Chicago Press.

Deschanel, E. (1847). *Etudes sur l'antiquité: Sapho et les lesbiennes.* Revue des Deux Mondes 18 (15 June), 340–351.

Devereux, Georges (1982). *Femme et mythe.* Paris: Flammarion.

Diderot, Denis (1968). *La Religieuse.* Paris: Classique Garnier.

Estienne, Henri (1879). *Apologie pour Herodote*, ed. P. Ristelhuber. Paris: Isidore Lisieux. vol. 1, ch. Xiii: "Du pécé de Sodomie et du péché conte nature en nostre temps." Geneva:

Fourier, Charles (1967). *Le Nouveau monde amoureux.* Paris: J. J. Pauvert.

Haddad, Michèle (1989). "Des Origines littéraires pour des 'demoiselles' bien réalistes, Courbet et George Sand." *Bulletin de la Société de l'Histoire de l'Art Français* (Paris). November-4, pp. 159–167.

Higgins, R. A. (1969). *Greek Terracotta Figures.* London: British Museum.

Hugo, Victor (1954). "Depuis l'exil." *Oeuvres complètes: Actes et paroles.* Paris: Martel.

Klumpke, Anna (1908) *Rosa Bonheur, sa vie et son oeuvre.* Paris: Flammarion.

Loraux, Nicole (1981). *Les Enfants d'Athéna.* Paris: Librairie François Maspéro.

Martial (1969). *Epigrammes*, vol. 1 (édition bilingue). Paris: Les Belles Lettres.

Maurois, André (1953). *George Sand–Marie Dorval: Correspondances inédites.* Paris: Gallimard.

May, Georges (1954). *Diderot et la religieuse.* Paris: Presses Universitaires de France.

Michaud, A., and E. Poujolat (1837). *Nouvelle collection des mémoires pour servir à l'histoire de France depuis le XIIIème siècle jusqu'à la fin du XVIème siècle: Indications analytiques des documents pour servir à l'histoire de Jeanne d'Arc sur le procès*, series 1, vol. 3. Paris: Editeur du Commentaire du Code Civil.

Mirabeau, Comte de (1983). "*Erotika Biblion*: ch. vii, 'L'Anandryne ou les vestiges de l'androgynat primitif d'Adam et notamment le saphisme." In *Oeuvres Erotiques*. Paris: Fayard.

de Mairobert, Pidansat (1977). *Confession de Melle Sapho*. Paris: Aphrodite Classique.

Montaigne, Michel de (1946). *Journal de voyage en Italie par La Suisse et l'Allemagne*, ed. Charles Dédéyan. Paris: Société des Belles Lettres, pp. 87–88.

Mora, Edith (1966). *Sappho: Histoire d'un poète et traduction intégrale de l'oeuvre*. Paris: Flammarion.

Pipelet, Constance (1978). "Epître aux femmes." In *Le Grief des femmes, anthologie de textes féministes*, ed. M. Albistur and D. Armogathe. Paris: Editions Hier et Demain, vol. 1.

Planté, Christine (1990) "Constance Pipelet; La Muse de la raison et les despotes du Parnasse." In Citoyennes: *Les Femmes et la révolution française*, ed. Rosa Annette, vol. 1. Toulouse: Presses Universitaires du Mirail, pp. 285–294.

Safouan, M. (1976). *La Sexualité féminine dans la doctrine Freudienne*. Paris: Seuil.

Sand, George (1960). *Lélia*. Paris: Classiques Garnier.

———— (1971). *Histoire de ma vie. Oeuvres autobiographiques*, vol. 2. Paris: Gallimard, Bibliothèque de la Pleiade.

Vaugelas (1647). *Remarques sur la langue française utiles à ceux qui veulent parler et bien écrire*. Paris: Collection of the Widow J. Camusat and P. Le Petit.

9

*R*ead My Lips

Clippyng and Kyssyng in the Early Sixteenth Century

DIANE WATT

The following passage comes from the legend of Ide, which appears in the early-sixteenth-century English *The Boke of Duke Huon of Bordeux* (691–737),[1] the whole of which was translated by Sir John Bourchier, Lord Berners, from a French prose version of the legend of Huon of Bordeaux.

> Than themperour made hym to be taken & kept, to the entent to proue the trouthe, for he thought the matter straunge to byleue [believe]. . . . Than the emperour, who was right pensyfe, sware and made promyse that if he found the mater in that case he wolde cause both his doughter and Yde to be brent, bycause of hydynge of that straunge cas. . . . Than he commaunded a bayne [bath] to be made redy in his owne chambre, whearin he wolde haue Yde to be bayned [bathed], to the entent that he myght know the trouth or she scaped away, for he sayd he wold not suffre suche boggery to be vsed. The baynge was made redy, and Yde was sent for, who knewe nothynge of that matter. Than themperour says to him, "Yde, do of [take off] your clothes, for ye shal bayne you with me." (Bourchier 1882–1887: 726–727)[2]

The adventures of Ide are descended from the medieval *Chanson d'Ide et d'Olive.* The story goes that Huon's granddaughter, the beautiful princess Ide, is forced to flee the incestuous desires of her father Florence, the King of Aragon. Disguised as a man, Ide escapes to Lombardy and from thence to Germany; finally, after various adventures, she arrives in Rome. Once there, she enters the service of the Emperor and, having been dubbed by her new lord, performs great feats of chivalry against an invading army of Spaniards. The Emperor, ignorant of Ide's true identity, rewards her with the hand of his daughter Olive, who has for some time nurtured feelings of love for the valorous knight. Initially Ide resists the Emperor's wishes, but eventually she is forced to submit to his command to marry. After the wedding the couple "clyppe"[embrace] and "kysse" (Bourchier 1882–1887: 725), but eventually Olive proves so insistent in her desire for Ide that Ide feels compelled to reveal to Olive her sex.

Rather than reacting with horror, Olive is sympathetic to Ide's predicament and vows to remain true to her and keep her secret:

> My right swete louer, discomforte not yourselfe [do not fear] for ye shall not be dewrayed [betrayed] for me nother to no man nor woman lyuynge. We are wedded together. I wyl be good and trewe to you syn ye haue kept youre selfe so trewly. With you I wyll vse my tyme and pass my destany syn it is thus, for I se wel it is the pleasure of our lorde godde. (Bourchier 1882–1887: 726)

Unfortunately, a page overhears their conversation and reveals the truth to the Emperor, who immediately sentences the women to death at the stake. Their lives are only saved after the Blessed Virgin intercedes and transforms Ide into a man. Subsequently Ide is himself crowned Emperor, and eventually he returns to Aragon, where he is welcomed by his father, whom he helps to rule the kingdom.

What significance ought to be placed on the adventures of this female knight, and in what terms should we attempt to understand the marriage of Ide and Olive? It was certainly not unheard of in the literature of the later Middle Ages and of the early modern period for women to dress as men; in the saints' lives, described in the extremely popular *Golden Legend* and elsewhere, as well as in medieval and Renaissance romances, female transvestites were not uncommon figures, and it has been argued that they have their origins in Classical mythology.[3] In such works the adoption of a male guise was for the woman, as for Ide, a means to an end. Ide is not untypical in deciding to dress as a man to escape forced marriage and defilement, although the threat of incest is an unusual detail, which, rather surprisingly, seems to anticipate modern attempts to explain away lesbianism as the result of child sexual abuse and a dysfunctional family background. There is also in the Middle Ages a distinct tradition of abandoned wives who put on masculine clothes in order to search for their husbands. Yet in both saints' lives and romances such cross-dressing was sometimes more than simply a temporary measure taken to enable flight; it could also signify a complete rupture with the past. Disguised as a man, the heroine no longer needed to be "feminine," in other words, emotional, passive and powerless, but could take upon herself a "masculine" role, becoming rational, authoritative, active, and strong, and to such an extent that s/he now surpassed all other men in virtue and ability. In real life, too, the masculine dress of a woman like Joan of Arc (who unlike many other historical cross-dressers did not actually pretend to be a man) not only served a clear practical purpose but may also have enabled her to *feel* like a soldier and to be perceived as such by her supporters and troops.[4] In the literature of the Renaissance the transvestite knight continued to play a central role, and like the Princess Ide and a number of their saintly predecessors, she was sometimes such a convincing figure that she became the object of (unknowing) female desire: one need only think of Spenser's *The Fairie Queene*, III.i, in which the Amazonian Britomart is pursued by the lustful Malecasta. It is, however, my contention that the story of Ide is exceptional among the English religious and secular legends and tales in that both the unfolding of the plot and the language of the text (in particular the references to "clippyng and kyssyng" and to "boggery") reveal it to be clearly addressing the matter of female homoeroticism.

The late-Victorian scholar Sidney Lee, in his introduction to the Early English Text Society edition of Bourchier's translation (1882–1887), says of the story that "here the imagination of the author assumes very repulsive features" (xxxiv–xxxv). Although Lee does not specify what it is that so shocks him about the tale, it seems likely that it is the possibility of two women enjoying a close physical as well as emotional relationship that disgusts him most. While in many ways the adventures of Ide conform to accepted literary conventions, in other respects they are far from typical. We might note, for example, that Olive, unlike Malecasta, is represented not as an evil seductress but as a loyal and loving wife who refuses to betray her spouse. That Olive should choose to continue their marriage even after Ide has confessed to her that she is a woman indicates the extent to which she values their relationship. In other words, in this story female homoerotic desire (if not actual sexual relations between women) seems to be validated as a possible way of life. Furthermore, whereas the transvestite saint often completely renounces her sexuality and the traditional woman-warrior is certainly not portrayed as experiencing same-sex desire herself even if she inspires it in another, Ide not only arouses Olive but also appears to reciprocate her feelings.

There can then be no question about whether this tale is addressing the issues of female homoerotic relations. By presenting Ide as restrained in her behavior towards her wife (for fifteen nights "Yde touched her not but with clippyng and kyssyng" (Bourchier 1882–1887: 725)), the narrator implicitly reveals his awareness of the *possibility* that as a woman Ide could have behaved toward Olive in a manner that would have compromised both of them. The phrases "clippen and kissen" and "clippinge and kissing(e)" are common enough in Middle English and are defined in the *Middle English Dictionary* (*MED*) as "to hug and embrace" and "embracing and kissing."[5] They denote a wide range of expressions of affection and reconciliation and are used equally for both sexes. Although not its dominant meaning, "clippen," like "kissen," can have an overtly sexual connotations and is sometimes used, apparently euphemistically, to refer to (heterosexual) sexual intercourse.

In the story of Ide, such a meaning, if it is present at all, remains under the surface. The narrator rather pointedly refrains from making any judgments on the situation, and this would seem to suggest that he sympathizes with Ide's predicament. In contrast, the account of the Emperor's reaction to the page's revelations—"he wold not suche boggery to be vsed"—makes it clear that he perceives the couple's relationship to be immoral. In using the word *boggery*, the Emperor is actually using one of the few terms available to him to express what he understands to have happened. The *MED* defines *buggery* [*bugerie*] as "unfaithfulness towards God, heresy."[6] *Bugger* [ME *bougre*] derives from the French word *bougres*, meaning "Bulgars" or "heretics" and referring to the Albigensians whose heterodox beliefs were thought to have spread from Bulgaria; it was widely believed that the Albigensians actively encouraged homosexual sex (an accusation that was also made against many other heretical sects).[7] Thus, according to the *Oxford English Dictionary* (*OED*), by the early sixteenth century *buggery* had also acquired the dominant modern sense of "unnatural intercourse of a human being with a beast, or of men with one another, sodomy" as well as being "used of unnatural intercourse of man with a man."[8] Neither of these senses seems accurately to reflect the meaning in this case, where it certainly has implications of not only intercourse between men but also intercourse between women. The legend of Ide is then of crucial importance, because it provides us with one of the earliest explicit references to sexual relations between women in the English language.

The question of terminology is a crucial one because it appears that the entire history of lesbianism depends on it. Eve Kosofsky Sedgwick succinctly sums up one of the principal academic justifications for ignoring our homosexual past when she says: "Same-sex genital relations may have been perfectly common during the period under discussion—but since there was no language about them, they must have been completely meaningless" (1991: 52). In other words, if there were no words to describe lesbians or lesbian acts, then there were no lesbians. The historian Judith C. Brown, in her important study of the life of a nun whom we would now describe as lesbian and who was tried for heresy in Renaissance Italy, uses this very argument when she claims that "the conceptual difficulties contemporaries had with lesbian sexuality is reflected in the lack of an adequate terminology" (1986: 17), and she goes on to assert that in the early modern period "lesbian sexuality did not exist. Neither, for that matter did *lesbians*."

The *OED* appears to confirm Brown's position. The earliest cited examples of the words *lesbian* and *lesbianism* date to the late nineteenth and early twentieth centuries, and a similar pattern emerges with the words *sapphism* and *sapphist*.[9] The first recorded use of the word *tribade*, meaning "a woman who engages in sexual activity with other women" (or, more literally, "one who rubs"), is attributed to Ben Jonson in 1601.[10] However, Emma Donoghue has recently set out to correct the erroneous impression conveyed by the *OED* that "only after the publications of late-nineteenth-century male sexologists such as Havelock Ellis did words for eroticism between women enter the English language" (1993b: 2). Donoghue reveals that by the seventeenth and eighteenth centuries not only were the terms *lesbian*, *sapphic*, and *tribade* being used, but there also existed a veritable treasure-trove of euphemisms, synonyms, foreign phrases, and slang to describe both the women and their acts, reflecting perhaps something of the "cornucopian" quality of the language of premodern France described in Randy Conner's article in this volume.

The same wealth of material that Donoghue has uncovered from the later period does not appear to have survived from the early sixteenth century, if it ever existed.[11] Clearly, however, the climax of the legend of Ide does reveal that, while it is the case that there is no evidence for the use of the word *lesbian* or a gender-specific equivalent in the Middle Ages or the Renaissance, this does not mean that the concepts of female homoerotic relationships and same-sex intercourse did not exist. In Middle English the general terms for homosexual and homosexual activity were *sodomite* and *sodomy*, which are respectively defined in the *OED* as "one who practises or commits sodomy" (with a first citation dating to c. 1380) and "an unnatural form of sexual intercourse, especially that of one male with another" (1297).[12] In the Middle Ages *sodomy* also shared with *buggery* the connotations of heresy: There was a close correlation between homosexual acts and heterodox belief. The *OED* also gives one example of *sodomitess*, meaning "a woman sodomite": this occurs as a marginal gloss in the 1611 Bible on Deuteronomy 23.17, "There shall be no whore of the daughters of Israel."[13] In this context it seems that *sodomitess* has a general sense of an immoral woman or prostitute. Yet the definition of *sodomy* as "an unnatural form of sexual intercourse" is broad enough to include lesbian activity and may have been frequently understood in this way in the Middle Ages. Indeed, St. Thomas Aquinas, one of the most influential of the medieval theologians, interpreted sodomy as "copulation with an undue sex, male with male, or female with female," explaining that it is like bestiality or masturbation insofar as it is a "crime against nature" performed only for pleasure rather than procreation, and unlike other forms of lust such as rape, which might result in impregnation and therefore do not subvert the "natural" order (Crompton 1980–1981: 15). The word *sodomy*, like *buggery* included the acts of women as well as those of men. What is more, as Brown points out, a number of other more general terms might have been used to describe what we would now think of as lesbian acts, including *fornication, corruption, pollution, mutual masturbation, coitus, copulation, vice, defilement,* and *impurity* (1986: 17). Almost all of these words and phrases indicate immoral activity, and it is unlikely that many women would use them in relation to themselves. The implications of the absence of exclusive language and specific terminology to describe lesbianism are self-evident: Lesbians and lesbian acts are all too often hidden from sight.

THE MYTH THAT LESBIANS did not exist before the Victorian age is often reinforced by the assertion that the law itself did not recognize or condemn sexual activity between women. To adapt Sedgwick's words: "Prohibitions against lesbianism didn't exist back then . . . so if people did do anything, it was completely meaningless" (1991: 52). As Donoghue notes, "The more obvious persecution of male 'mollies' and 'sodomites' has led many historians to assume that lesbians avoided attack" (1993a: 213, n.2). Yet, if the story reflects any sort of social reality, the Princess Ide episode illustrates that this was certainly not the case. On discovering Ide's sex, the Emperor refuses to have mercy on her, insisting that "he must nedes se Iustyce to be done vpon Yde," and the death sentence is immediately confirmed "by the peers and lordes of Rome" (Bourchier 1882–1887: 728). Over a decade ago Louis Crompton challenged the notion that civil and canon law in the Middle Ages and in later periods did not make sex between women a punishable offence (1980–1981). Central to Crompton's argument is St. Paul's teaching in Romans 1.26: "For this cause God gave them up unto vile affections: for even their women did change the natural use into that which is against nature." Crompton explains that these verses, written in condemnation of pagans who had turned away from God, were interpreted in terms of what we would now perceive to be lesbian acts by medieval commentators such as St. John Chrysostom, St. Ambrose, St. Anselm of Canterbury, and Peter Abelard, as well as St. Thomas Aquinas (1980–1981: 12–15).

The fact that Thomastic theologians equated sexual activity between women with sodomy almost certainly had its impact on the development of civil law. By 1400 an edict of Roman law, the *lex foedissimam*, was reinterpreted to justify imposition of the death penalty for women found guilty of committing sodomy with one another; records survive from the late fifteenth century that tell of women in Europe being executed for having sex with other women (Crompton 1980–1981: 15–22). Of course, not all women who were tried were sentenced to death, but their punishments could still be extremely severe: One European statute suggests that mutilation is appropriate for the first two offences but a third conviction should result in burning (Bailey 1955: 142); the subject of Brown's study, Sister Benedetta Carlini of Pescia, was imprisoned for thirty-five years. If, in the legend of Ide, the Emperor seems to be overreacting somewhat (as the narrator has implicitly assured us that Ide and Olive have not committed buggery), it seems that, in Europe at least, even kissing and embracing would have been viewed censoriously by the Inquisition. In the fourteenth century a group of religious women in Silesia were investigated, and during the examination a novice testified that she had heard that sisters indulged in mutual petting and put their tongues in each other's mouths (Goodich 1976: 296).

Yet the situation on the continent was rather different from that in England. The English legal system is not, of course, based on Roman law, nor was there an English Inquisition, and there is no evidence in the records of medieval and early modern England of women being charged with the offense of sodomy or examined about other forms of sexual misconduct with women. Nonetheless, the linguistic evidence that I have already put forward, limited although it is, places in doubt the prevailing notion that women who had sexual relations with women were invisible in England in the Middle Ages and the Renaissance, and it seems extremely likely that in England, as elsewhere, such women would not have been exempt from moral censure.

FINALLY, I WOULD LIKE to consider the ending of the story of Ide (an ending that will almost certainly seem unsatisfactory from our point of view)—her transformation into a man. Valerie Hotchkiss notes that medieval romance tales of abandoned wives who dress as men usually end with the status quo being restored and the women returning to their female roles. As Hotchkiss explains:

> As the clever rescuer, faithful servant, or influential male figure, she conflates gender-specific behaviour, functioning as a male, but striving to achieve a female identity. Male disguise, therefore, does not countermand traditional aspects of women's roles. Though there is a certain sensationalism in the concept of the transvestite wife, the image is far from radical. The sexual dichotomy of disguise rarely defeminizes female characters, but it often endows them with the power to act in their own behalf and

with an individualism unheard of for other female characters in medieval literature. (1994: 218)

I have already suggested that the legend of Ide does not fit into the expected pattern. In the case of Ide, cross-dressing has no associations with uxorial service, nor is it a temporary measure, so even when faced with the prospect of marriage Ide does not reveal herself to the Emperor because it appears that she does not want to have her new-found freedom curtailed. Even in the bedroom, Ide is unwilling to abandon her male identity. Like Olive, she soon begins to value their marital relationship. Ide's male disguise is also taken so seriously by the narrator that from her marriage right up until the moment at which Ide is forced to reveal her sex to the Emperor, she is referred to by the masculine third-person pronouns. Ide, then, is exceptional in the extent to which she transgresses gender boundaries.

Why exactly was it that transvestism and lesbianism were so unacceptable in the Middle Ages and the early modern period? Vern Bullough has suggested that what was really objectionable about female transvestism was not that women dressed as men but that they might compete with men (1974: 1390). Traub argues that in the Renaissance, female sodomy was likewise perceived to be monstrous because it was nonreproductive and also imitated the "male" role in sexual intercourse, but she believes that female same-sex desire was not an issue in itself (1992: 163). Traub concludes, "[T]he absence of outcry against 'feminine' homoeroticism suggests that it posed very little gender trouble at all" (164). The real issue was the usurpation of male prerogative, which could not be tolerated on any terms. In the legend of Ide it is the fact that a woman plays the masculine part, as knight and then as husband, that is problematic for the Emperor. The slightly odd expression "he wold not suche boggery to be vsed" could even suggest that he feared that a dildo or other instrument had been used as a "substitute penis" in the women's lovemaking. In the legend of Ide, the solution that is offered at the end still restores "normal" male-female relations: Not only does Ide's miraculous sex change enable the marriage to be consummated and a child to be immediately conceived, but Ide is now able rightfully to inherit the Emperor's title and lands, and he is also finally able to return to his father, whom he helps to rule the kingdom of Aragon. Yet the fact remains that Ide was a woman who dressed as a man and who responded to the desire of another woman. By not returning Ide to her previous feminine state, the narrative does not totally curtail the subversive possibilities of the story, and the woman-turned-man ultimately succeeds in getting what she wants in sexual, economic, and political terms.

Perhaps, then, it is not really remarkable that Ide, who took upon herself a masculine role when she was still a woman, should eventually undergo a full sex change. If the status quo is to be restored in a society that classifies sexual relations between women as crimes against nature, Ide must either die as the Emperor decrees or become a man. In any case, according to premodern theories of medicine, the transformation from female to male was not in itself contrary to nature (Jones & Stallybrass 1991: 81–84). The Galenic tradition asserts that women's sexual organs are identical to men's except that they are inverted (in other words, the vagina is an inverted penis). The only difference between men and women is in terms of *heat*: If a woman becomes too hot, she can, in theory, become a man. Because women are perceived to be inferior to men, such a transformation can be seen only as an improvement, a change from an imperfect state to a perfect one. Sex, if not gender and sexuality, was fluid, rather than fixed. Certainly no one seems remotely perturbed by Ide's sex change: Indeed, as we have just seen, at the end of the story Ide is reconciled with the Emperor and welcomed back like the prodigal son by the King of Aragon.

The role played by the Blessed Virgin Mary in the final resolution of the story of Ide can be explained in part by a classical analogue of the story: the legend of Iphis and Ianthe, which appears in Ovid's Metamorphoses IX.666–797 and which was retold in the late fourteenth century by the English writer John Gower. Like Ide, Iphis is thought to be a man by her lover, and again like Ide she is eventually transformed into one by divine intervention (in Ovid, by the goddess Isis, who, as scholars have noted, bears some striking similarities to the Virgin Mary) (Warner 1985: 193, 195, 208–209, 256, 266, 323). It is appropriate that Ide, who seeks to have her own "unnatural" love made "natural," should choose to pray to the Mother of God because, under Christ himself, the Virgin is the most powerful intercessor for sinners. Furthermore, the Virgin Mary represents perfect purity and has particular associations with the abject and the marginal in medieval society—Jews, lepers, heretics, and, of course, homosexuals. On the continent there were confraternities dedicated to the Blessed Virgin Mary, which were entrusted with the responsibility of seeking out those who indulged in homosexual acts and bringing them to the attention of the Inquisition (Goodich 1976: 297–298). The Virgin Mary was connected, then, both with integrating outsiders and with the rooting out of "unnatural" activities. In order to give this story a happy ending, the Blessed Virgin Mary uses her miraculous powers to provide another solution for the problem of (in the words of the Emperor) a "matter straunge to byleue."

In conclusion, evidence of women having sex with women will always prove difficult to uncover. The lack of specific language to describe such women and their activities is central to the problem, but even more important, women who had sex with women in England in the Middle Ages and the Renaissance were forced to try to become invisible because, despite the fact that the law seemed to ignore them, they were nonetheless vulnerable to moral persecution. Referring to the seventeenth and eighteenth centuries, Donoghue contends that "the lack of explicit acknowledgement in surviving personal papers is no proof of a lack of perception; the women's own discretion and desire for privacy, as well as the censoring actions of families and scholars, would have ensured that most passions between women were presented in letters and memoirs as harmless and innocent" (Donoghue 1993b: 3). How much more is this likely to be true in the Middle Ages and the Renaissance, when so many texts of the period have been lost; when much of the literature that has survived and that belongs to the earliest centuries is anonymous; when few but the most privileged women were able to write at all; and when, even in collections like the fifteenth-century Paston letters, no correspondence between the women of the family has been preserved?

But perhaps the prejudices of modern academics construct a barrier between ourselves and our past that is just as great as any of those that I have just listed. This point is illustrated by the case of both historical and literary female transvestites. It is generally assumed that such women put on men's clothes in order to achieve economic independence or greater freedom of action, but can we be sure that cross-dressing was not equally motivated by same-sex desire? In their separate studies both Marie-Jo Bonnet (this volume) and Randy Conner (this volume) cite examples of women in early modern France who cross-dressed and married other women. If women who had sex with women in medieval and Renaissance England really did lack a conceptual framework within which they might define themselves on their own terms, but still remained vulnerable to accusations of heresy and immorality, then it seems only logical that some might have assumed a masculine identity in order to protect themselves and their lovers. Thus, so long as they were not discovered, they could live their lives as they wanted without overtly challenging the social order.

In this chapter, I have suggested that the legend of Ide provides us not only with a story of a woman cross-dresser who, contrary to literary tradition, does not return to her female role but also with an early example of a "lesbian" romance. By concentrating on linguistic rather than legal evidence, one can question the prevailing notion of the "invisibility" of lesbianism in the Middle Ages and the early modern period. The text I have looked at here is an important one because there is so little other evidence of lesbians in medieval and early Renaissance English literature and history. In the light of the story of Ide, it might prove worthwhile to re-read other stories of women who dress as men. While not all such women were "lesbians," the story of Ide suggests that notions of cross-dressing and sexual transformation nevertheless offered ways of conceiving sexual relations between women. If female transvestites pose a problem for analysis, they also provide a point of entry into lesbian history.

NOTES

1. All subsequent references are to this edition. I have kept the original spelling but modernized the punctuation.

2. Lee suggests that Bourchier's translation was originally published around 1534, but a date of 1515 for the first edition is proposed by the *Short Title Catalogue, 1475–1640*, compiled A. W. Pollard and G. R. Redgrave, rev. W. A. Jackson and F. S. Ferguson, completed K. Panzer (London: London Bibliographical Society, 2d ed. rev., 1976–1986), 2 vols.: STC 13998.5.

3. On the female transvestite in saint's lives and legends, see Anson (1974: 1–32); Bullough (1974: 1381–1394); Delcourt (1976: 84–102); Delehaye (1962: 150–156). A recent essay on the female transvestite in medieval romance is that by Valerie R. Hotchkiss (1994: 207–218). Women's cross-dressing in early modern history and literature is discussed in a considerable number of studies, for example, Valerie Traub (1992: 150–169).

4. On Joan of Arc, see Marie Delcourt (1976: 84–102); Marina Warner (1981). On other historical female transvestites, see Caroline Walker Bynum (1984: 105–125, 111–112).

5. *MED*, sv *kissen* and *kissing(e)*.

6. *MED*, sv *bugerie*.

7. *MED*, sv *bougre*. See Derrick S. Bailey (1955:135–144); and Michael Goodich (1976: 295–302).

8. *OED*, sv buggery.

9. *OED*, sv *lesbian* and *sapphism*. Certainly, it has been argued that for the first century after Sappho's poetry was rediscovered in 1546, the poet was not associated with female homoerotic desire: Joan DeJean (1989: 4); but see also Marie-Jo Bonnet (this volume).

10. *OED*, sv *tribade*.

11. For two examples of medieval European Latin poetry about lesbianism, see John Boswell (1980: 185 and 220–221). For a solitary example of a vernacular European love poem addressed to a woman that was possibly also written by a woman, see Meg Bogin (1976: 132–133 and 176–177). For a Renaissance Scottish poem, see Jane Farnsworth (1996: 57–72). Of course, some of the many anonymous medieval love poems addressed to women may also have been written by women. Although no evidence of medieval lesbian subcultures has yet been uncovered, there is evidence of male homosexual subcultures, which had their own coded languages or slang: see, for example, Jeffrey Richards (1990: 137).

12. *OED*, sv *sodomite* and *sodomy*.

13. *OED*, sv *sodomitess*.

REFERENCES

Anson, John (1974). "The Female Transvestite in Early Monasticism." *Viator* 5: 1–32.

Bailey, Derrick S. (1955). *Homosexuality and the Western Christian Tradition*. London: Longmans.

Bogin, Meg (1976). *The Women Troubadours*. New York: Paddington Press.

Bonnet, Marie-Jo (this volume). "Sappho, or the Importance of Culture in the Language of Love: *Tribade, Lesbienne, Homosexuelle*."

Boswell, John (1980). *Christianity, Social Tolerance, and Homosexuality: Gay People in Western Europe from the Beginning of the Christian Era to the Fourteenth Century*. Chicago: University of Chicago Press.

Bourchier, Sir John, Lord Berners (1882–1887). *The Boke of Duke Huon of Burdeux*, intro. S. L. Lee. London: Early English Text Society, Early Series 40, 41, 43, 50, parts 1–4.

Brown, Judith C. (1986). *Immodest Acts: The Life of a Lesbian Nun in Renaissance Italy*. Oxford: Oxford University Press.

Bullough, Vern L. (1974). "Transvestites in the Middle Ages." *American Journal of Sociology* 79: 1381–94.

Bynum, Caroline Walker (1984). "Women's Stories, Women's Symbols: A Critique of Victor Turner's Theory of Liminality." In Robert L. Moore and Frank E. Reynolds (eds.), *Anthropology and the Study of Religions*. Chicago: Center for the Scientific Study of Religion, pp. 105–125.

Conner, Randy (this volume). "*Les Molles et les chausses*: Mapping the Isle of Hermaphrodites in Premodern France."

Crompton, Louis (1980–1981). "The Myth of Lesbian Impunity: Capital Laws from 1270 to 1791." *Journal of Homosexuality* 6: 11–25.

DeJean, Joan (1989). *Fictions of Sappho 1546–1937*. Chicago: University of Chicago Press.

Delcourt, Marie (1976). *Hermaphrodite: Myths and Rites of the Bisexual Figure of Classical Antiquity*, trans. Jennifer Nicholson. London: Studio Books.

Delehaye, Hippolyte (1962). *The Legends of the Saints*, trans. Donald Attwater. London: Geoffrey Chapman.

Donoghue, Emma (1993a). "Imagined More than Women: Lesbians as Hermaphrodites, 1671–1766." *Women's History Review* 2: 199–216.

——— (1993b). *Passions between Women: British Lesbian Culture 1688–1801*. London: Scarlet Press.

Farnsworth, Jane (1996). "Voicing Female Desire in 'Poem XLIX.' " *Studies in English Literature* 36: 57–72.

Goodich, Michael (1976). "Sodomy in Medieval Secular Law." *Journal of Homosexuality* 1: 295–302.

Hotchkiss, Valerie R. (1994). "Gender Transgression and the Abandoned Wife in Medieval Literature." In Richard C. Trexler (ed.), *Gender Rhetorics: Postures of Dominance and Submission in History*. Binghamton, NY: Medieval and Renaissance Texts and Studies 113, pp. 207–218.

Jones, Ann Rosalind, and Peter Stallybrass (1991). "Fetishizing Gender: Constructing the Hermaphrodite in Renaissance Europe." In Julia Epstein and Kristina Straub (eds.), *Body Guards: The Cultural Politics of Gender Ambiguity*. London: Routledge, pp. 80–111.

Richards, Jeffrey (1990). *Sex, Dissidence and Damnation: Minority Groups in the Middle Ages*. London: Routledge.

Sedgwick, Eve Kosofsky (1991). *Epistemology of the Closet*. Hemel Hempstead, Eng.: Harvester Wheatsheaf.

Traub, Valerie (1992). "The (In)significance of 'Lesbian' Desire in Early Modern England." In Susan Zimmerman (ed.), *Erotic Politics: Desire on the Renaissance Stage*. London: Routledge, pp. 150–169.

Warner, Marina (1981). *Joan of Arc: The Image of Female Heroism*. New York: Vintage.

——— (1985). *Alone of All Her Sex: The Myth and the Cult of the Virgin Mary*. London: Picador.

II

QUEERSPEAK

10

${\cal T}$he "Homo-genius" Speech Community

RUSTY BARRETT

The uniformity of the code, "sensibly the same" for all members of a speech community, posited by the *Cours* and still recalled from time to time, is but a delusive fiction; as a rule, everyone belongs simultaneously to several speech communities of different radius and capacity; any overall code is multiform and comprises a hierarchy of diverse subcodes freely chosen by the speaker with regard to the variable function of the message.

—Roman Jakobson (1971), "Retrospect"

The notion of the speech community is a basic component of linguistic theory. Speech communities are usually constructed through abstract notions of ideal speakers living in communities that display homogeneous use of language. In this chapter, I reconsider the notion of a speech community from a queer perspective. Building on Mary Louise Pratt's (1987) critique of what she calls a "linguistics of community" (i.e., a linguistics centered around the notion of the speech community), I examine the ways in which traditional notions of a homogeneous speech community do not adequately relate to the notion of a "homo-genius" speech community (a community that is essentially and crucially "homo" or queer[1]). In considering a truly queer community, the notion of community itself is called into question. Indeed, the variety of articles found in this volume suggests that no overall external definition of what constitutes membership in a queer community will adequately allow for the variety of social realities that might be seen as queer.

In considering the ways in which one might begin to develop a queer linguistics, I argue that linguistics founded on the notion of community cannot adequately handle queer uses of language. Instead, I propose that queer linguistics take the form of what Pratt calls a "linguistics of contact" in which the notions of community and identity are not held to be externally definable categories. As an example of the directions such a linguistics might take, I draw on personal experience and previous research (Barrett ms.) to discuss briefly the language of gay men (more specifically, "bar queens") in Texas. The perspective offered here is from the viewpoint of a gay male. I assume that lesbian, bisexual, and transgender issues of language use may be quite different from the issues relevant to gay men. Thus, rather than attempt to provide an all-encompassing perspective, I provide one form of a gay male perspective with the hope that other queer approaches will contribute to the evolution of a better understanding of queer uses of language.

The Homogeneous Speech Community

Following the work of Ferdinand de Saussure and Noam Chomsky, the majority of contemporary linguists in Western societies have focused on the formal properties of linguistic structure. Saussure (1986) argued that the "primary concern" of linguistics must be the study of the "independently definable" linguistic structure found in a given society (9). Saussure saw this linguistic structure (*langue*) as part of a social bond that may differ across individuals but that exists in its *purest* form "only in the collectivity" of all members of a given society (1986:13). Chomsky (1957, 1965) moved this "perfect" linguistic structure into the mind of a single ideal speaker who reflects the uniformly homogeneous linguistic structure found in her or his society:

> Linguistic theory is concerned primarily with an ideal speaker-listener, in a completely homogeneous speech-community, who knows its language perfectly and is unaffected by such grammatically irrelevant conditions as memory limitations, distractions, shifts of attention and interest, and errors (random or characteristic) in applying his knowledge of the language in actual performance. (Chomsky 1965: 3)

Given the assumption of an entirely homogeneous community of speakers, it seems natural to allow one "ideal" speaker to stand in place of the entire community. As Pratt (1987: 51) has noted, however, abstract ideal speakers cannot be constructed in a socially neutral fashion. In practice, these "ideal speaker-listeners" are typically linguists themselves, using intuitions to uncover their own linguistic "competence." In other cases, a native speaker consultant may convey knowledge of her or his language to a linguist as a means of uncovering the linguistic structure found through a homogeneous community. In either case, little consideration is given to the amount of socialization that has gone into the construction of the linguistic competence of a given speaker.

In theory, the "grammar" generated by the Chomskian framework is thought to reflect the formal system of the language found throughout any given society. V. N. Voloshinov has argued that this formal system exists only "from the point of view of the subjective consciousness of an individual speaker belonging to some particular language group at some particular moment of historical time" (1973: 66). By discounting the subjective nature of positing an abstract "objective" formal system of language, linguists have typically ignored the fact that the "grammar" they propose is (in actual practice) usually the elaboration of the abstract conception of "Standard" English. By removing social variation from the system of language, formal linguists have reencoded the very prescriptive norms they claim to reject.

Recent studies in the political economy of language (e.g., Bordieu 1991; Woolard 1985; Gal 1989) have demonstrated that the concept of a "Standard" language has a crucial role in upholding and enforcing the power structure in a given society. By claiming that a language, for example "English," can be reduced to a formal system that is shared by all members of a society and then equating that shared language with the "Standard," linguists have equated the "grammar" of society at large with an abstract conception of language that is a means by which the ruling class maintains power. As Pratt notes, this "shared grammar" corresponds to a "shared patrimony" (1987: 50); it assumes that "English" is equivalent to the intuitions of white, northern, middle-class men (and some women). The problem does not stop with studies of English. Paradigms such as Government and Binding (GB) theory (Chomsky 1981), which are based on "Standard" English, are then applied to other languages throughout the world, often with the effect of forcing the structure of those languages to conform to the structures proposed for English. Van Valin, for example, has pointed out that most linguistic frameworks, and in particular Government and Binding theory, force linguists to ensure that the linguistic structures of a given language "can be accommodated within some antecedently given theoretical perspective" (1987: 394). Thus, "exotic" languages are forced into a theoretical framework based on English, even if the actual structures of those languages are not particularly well suited for descriptions in this English-based framework. The version of Universal Grammar produced by most accounts of generative syntax typically forces all of the world's languages to conform to a set of subjectively derived concepts of language structure based on intuitions reflecting the "grammar" of the ruling class in the United States. Contrary to being devoid of social meaning, the program of formal linguistics serves as a means of legitimizing the domination of the American ruling class by forcing the study of any language to conform to an idealization derived from "Standard" English. It is a means of "manufacturing consent" for the power structure of white colonialist patriarchy.

In attempting to overcome such problems, sociolinguists have focused on variation in the formal character of language and have moved the homogeneous nature of language from the "system" itself to the set of "norms" held within a speech community. Gumperz (1972) and Labov (1972b) have both argued that a speech community is defined by shared rules and norms for language use. Gumperz writes that membership in a speech community is based on shared knowledge of "communicative constraints and options governing a significant number of social situations" (1972: 16). Gumperz sees this shared knowledge as an understanding of how language encodes social meaning:

> [M]embers of the same speech community need not all speak the same language nor use the same linguistic forms on similar occasions. All that is required is that there be at least one language in common and that rules governing basic communicative strategies be shared so that speakers can decode the social meanings carried by alternative modes of communication. (1972: 16)

In theory, the makeup of a speech community need not reflect any community defined in external terms such as ethnicity, religion, nationality, gender, sexual orientation, and so on, although Gumperz notes that the boundaries of a speech community "tend to coincide with wider social units" (1972: 16). In actual practice, however, these shared boundaries have often been assumed. Even where they are not assumed, the boundaries of speech communities often end up delineating a certain social group within society. The membership of such communities often tends to reify stereotypes of a community defined by language-external factors.

This is the case with Labov's (1972a) ground-breaking study of African American Vernacular English (hereafter AAVE). Labov's definition of a speech community differs slightly from that of Gumperz in that Labov finds shared knowledge in behavioral patterns, rather than in understanding of the language/ society relationship. Nevertheless, both definitions assume that it is shared norms for usage that define a given speech community. Labov (1972b) defines the speech community as follows:

> The speech community is not defined by any marked agreement in the use of language elements, so much as by participation in a set of shared norms; these norms may be observed in overt types of evaluative behavior, and by the uniformity of abstract patterns of variation which are invariant in respect to particular levels of usage. (1972b: 120–121)

In Labov's framework, a speech community's linguistic system contains linguistic variables (such as the presence or absence of word-final /r/), but the appearance of such variables displays statistical patterns related both to social class and "attention paid to speech."

If one bases the definition of a speech community on norms (or the statistical patterns thought to reflect those norms), one would expect community membership to mirror actual behavior. In actual practice, however, the use of statistical measures has sometimes reified external stereotypes of community membership. In Labov's (1972a) work, for example, the "members" of the "African American speech community" were primarily heterosexual males between the ages of nine and eighteen who belonged to gangs and hung out on the street in Harlem. Morgan (1994) has argued that Labov's study of *lames* has perpetuated a stereotyped image of unemployed adolescent males as representative of the African American community as a whole. In Labov's study, speakers who did not fit the statistical patterning that "defined" the African American speech community were classified as *lames* that were peripheral to the *vernacular culture*. The term *lame* was used by the young men in the study to refer to those who "are not *hip*, since they do not hang out" (Labov 1972a: 258). Labov offers several reasons for one's being a *lame*:

> There are many reasons for someone to be lame. Separation from the peer group may take place under the influence of parents, or of school, or of the individual's own perception of the advantages of the dominant culture for him; on the other hand, he may be too sick or too weak to

participate in the peer-group vernacular activities, or he may be rejected by the peer-groups as mentally or morally defective (a *punk*).
(1972a: 259)

In African American Vernacular English (AAVE), the term *punk* is generally used
to refer to homosexuals (e.g., Smitherman 1976: 254; Folb 1980: 250). Thus, gay
African Americans (the "morally defective") do not constitute "real" members of
the speech community. Similarly, the majority of research on AAVE has ignored
women (see Morgan 1994; Stanback 1985). The process of limiting the participants in the study to a specific subset of possible members in the African American speech community creates a circular experimental framework in which the
choice of participants limits the range of language usage so that the homogeneity
of the speech community has been predetermined. In the case of Labov's study of
the African American speech community, the supposedly scientific approach of
using statistical patterning as the basis for determining community membership
has served to reestablish a white stereotype of what constitutes "typical" members
of the African American community.

Like Labov's study of the African American speech community, attempts to
study the speech of gay men have generally restricted the membership of the
"speech community" in some way. Studies of gay male language have focused almost exclusively on middle-class European Americans.[2] In attempting to define
the "gay community," many linguists (e.g., Leap 1993; Gaudio 1994; Moran 1991)
have focused on their own personal conceptions of their "community." Due to the
power structure of American society, most academics are white and middle class.
While the study of white middle-class gay men is certainly as valid as the study of
any other segment of society, it is important that white middle-class men do not
"stand in" for the gay community as a whole. Representations of the gay community as a "white" community, combined with representations of minority communities as "straight" communities (such as Labov's African American speech community), serve to maintain stereotyped exclusive identity categories that place
many gays and lesbians outside both queer communities and communities constructed on the basis of ethnicity. A number of gays and lesbians of color have expressed feelings of being torn between a queer identity and an ethnic identity (e.g.,
Icard 1985; Tinney 1986, Smith 1988; Peterson 1992; Almaguer 1993). The social
stereotypes that create such dichotomies between ethnic and queer identities
might be a valid area for linguistic study. However, reproducing these dichotomies
through a theoretical paradigm that assumes externally definable "communities"
based on identity categories not only reproduces potentially harmful stereotypes; it
fails to accurately depict a social reality in which people may have multiple overlapping identities that may not easily fall into category-based "communities."

Although placing homogeneity at the level of "norms of usage" may help resolve some of the problems arising from ignoring social variation in language, it
may result in stereotyped representations that are perhaps no better than those
provided by formal linguistic descriptions of "homogeneous" linguistic systems.
Voloshinov has argued that "community norms" occupy an "analogous position" to
a homogeneous linguistic system, in that both "exist only with respect to the sub-

jective consciousness of members of some particular community" (1973: 66). The "norms" for using language are thus a subjective set of concepts concerning what form of language is appropriate for a given speaker in a given setting. Attempts to "objectify" such norms of behavior (through quantitative studies focusing on variable rules) do not necessarily produce accurate representations of language use in a given community but may simply reflect stereotypes held (consciously or not) by researchers.

Both formal linguists and sociolinguists have typically defined a speech community through some objectifiable criteria that allow for homogeneity at some level (either in the linguistic system itself or in the norms of language use). This process, however, may produce a false conception of what constitutes membership in a given speech community. Such conceptions may serve to reinforce negative stereotypes and misrepresentations by offering supposed "scientific validation" for prevelant stereotypes and misrepresentations.

There are, however, more subjective approaches to the notion of speech community. Studies of language death (e.g., Dorian 1982; Guion 1993) have suggested that speech communities need not display homogeneous knowledge of language or even the full range of usage norms. Dorian suggests that, at least in situations of language death, the definitions of speech community proposed by Dell Hymes (1972) and Pit Corder (1973) might be more appropriate than those of Gumperz and Labov. Hymes suggests studying the organization of language uses within specific social groups, rather than defining a speech community on the basis of linguistic criteria. Corder sees the speech community as consisting of those who perceive themselves as speakers of the same language. By allowing for language-external definitions of the speech community, these approaches may allow for more subjective understandings of linguistic structure and norms of language use compared with the understanding offered by analyses based on objectified aspects of linguistic structure. In the following section, I consider the ways in which queer communities have attempted to define themselves as a means of considering the form that a self-defined queer speech community might take.

The Homo-genius Speech Community

Any attempt to define a gay, lesbian, or transgender speech community using "objectifiable" criteria based on language usage would likely, at least in the United States, exclude many people who see themselves as members of such a community. It is highly unlikely, for example, that the speech of gay men who are African American, Latino, Asian American, Native American, or European American could all be unified through homogeneous norms in the usage of any given variable rule. It might be possible to overcome such problems by using a more subjective approach that defines queer speech communities on their own terms. In other words, would it be possible to replace the notion of a homogeneous speech community (with shared norms of language usage) with that of a "homo-genius" speech community (one that has an essential spirit that is fundamentally "homo," or queer)? The question of defining a queer speech community then becomes one of simply defining a queer community itself. The notion that a community has some essential spirit is related to Sapir's conception of genuine culture:

> Culture thus becomes nearly synonymous with the "spirit" or "genius" of a people, yet not altogether, for whereas these loosely used terms refer rather to a psychological, or pseudo-psychological background of national civilization, culture includes with this background a series of concrete manifestations which are believed to be peculiarly symptomatic of it. (1949: 84)

Some gay scholars have used Sapir's notion of authentic or genuine culture as a starting point for examining such "concrete manifestations" of gay culture. A particular school of gay male studies led by the anthropologist Gilbert Herdt argues for an approach to the gay community that centers around the examination of "authenticity" as gay culture:

> We shall argue for the existence of a gay *cultural system*, with a distinct identity and distinct institutions and social supports in particular times and places. We see this as a major battleground for social change in America into the twenty-first century.
> "Authenticity" as a criterion of gay culture is meant to indicate here what is genuine as opposed to what is spurious in gay men's worldviews and relationships. Relevant to this issue is Edward Sapir's discussion of the anthropological problem of what makes a culture great or feeble, balanced or unstable, satisfying or frustrating to its natives. (Herdt and Boxer 1992: 3)

Frameworks based on the assumption that there is some "genuine" or "authentic" gay male culture usually define the gay male community as primarily consisting of those who are "out" (i.e., open about their sexuality) or those who are in the process of coming out. The process of coming out is thus seen as a rite of passage in which gay men become full members of the community and participate in "authentic" gay culture (e.g., Herdt and Boxer 1992; Leap 1994). Similarly, Valerie Jenness has argued that taking on a lesbian identity (and thereby joining the lesbian community) is a process of reanalyzing and personalizing "lesbian" as an identity category:

> [T]he adoption of a lesbian identity—the difference between "doing" and "being"—fundamentally hinges upon a process that I refer to as detypification. *Detypification is the process of redefining and subsequently reassessing the social category "lesbian" such that it acquires increasingly concrete and precise meanings, positive connotations, and personal applicability.* (Jenness 1992: 66)

The use of identity categories such as "lesbian," "gay," "bisexual," or "transgender" as a means of defining community membership is founded in identity politics and the desire for recognition of specific "communities" as legitimate minorities in American society. Considering the political reasoning behind such approaches to queer communities, it is not surprising that Herdt and Boxer state that their view of gay culture represents "a major battleground for social change in America into the twenty-first century."

Identity politics leads other queer theorists to find the essential nature of queer communities rooted in biology. In this view of community, one is born gay or lesbian and has no choice but to belong to the gay and lesbian community (even if denying membership in the community). Richard Mohr (1992), for example, argues that one cannot "decide" to enter into the gay community, for one is born into the community:

> The gay community cannot be thought of as an artifice like, say, a stamp collectors' club or Alcoholics Anonymous. In such social groupings, as a condition of membership, one agrees to abide by the club's bylaws, and if one doesn't like the club's rules, one can set up one's own competing club. Rather, the gay community is a natural community in the way that English is a natural language but the computer languages Fortran and Cobol are not. If one is born in England of English parents, it is not an option to decide not to speak English as one's mother tongue but to set up linguistic shop instead in some artificial language, in the way one can, if one does not like some computer language, simply make up one's own. Gays simply find themselves immersed in the presumption of protecting each other's closets. Individual consent has nothing to do with it. (Mohr, 1992: 27)

Although Mohr and Herdt and Boxer ground their definitions of the gay community in terms of identity politics, the resulting "communities" have highly divergent memberships. For Mohr, those who are not "out" are community members in denial, while for Herdt the community contains only those who openly define themselves as members of the gay community.

The problem of how to deal with those who have not come out of the closet often falls at the center of discussions of how to define queer communities. Most gays and lesbians are familiar with the problem of determining who is actually part of the "family." Many of us have encountered those whom we thought were gay but who claimed otherwise. Similarly, we have encountered those we thought to be straight but who turned out to be gay. Because our "gaydar" is not infallible, we must constantly question who is actually a member of a gay or lesbian community, no matter how that community is defined. In addition, sexualities are fluid, and communities based on definitions of sexual practice may not adequately reflect any real concept of how people define their own identities. There are those who go through periods of questioning their sexuality without ever actually defining themselves as gay. There are those, such as "fag-hags," who are clearly part of some queer community but who may be entirely heterosexual in terms of behavior.

For reasons such as these, many queer theorists have argued that the entire notion of identity categories (and the communities based upon such categories) are ill suited for attempting to understand the reality of queerness. Judith Butler (1993a, 1993b), for example, has continually attempted to call into question the meaning of identity categories. Although critics have claimed that this depoliticizes theory (by questioning identity politics), Butler has argued that by leaving the determinant of "community membership" purposely vague, the community itself is defined in a more open and approachable way:

Those of us who have questioned the presentist assumptions in contemporary identity categories are . . . sometimes charged with depoliticizing theory. . . . [T]he critique of the queer subject is crucial to the continuing *democratization* of queer politics. As much as identity terms must be used, as much as "outness" is to be affirmed, these same notions must become subject to a critique of the exclusionary operations of their own production: For whom is outness a historically available and affordable option? Is there an unmarked class character to the demand for universal "outness"? Who is represented by *which* use of the term, and who is excluded? For whom does the term present an impossible conflict between racial, ethnic, or religious affiliation and sexual polities? (1993a: 227)

In a similar vein, Michael Warner (1993) has argued that the notion of "community" will always be problematic for queer studies:

Although it has had importance in organizational efforts (where in circular fashion it receives concretization), the notion of a community has remained problematic if only because nearly every lesbian or gay remembers being such before entering a collectively identified space, because much of lesbian and gay history has to do with noncommunity, and because dispersal rather than localization continues to be definitive of queer self-understanding ("We Are Everywhere"). (1993: xxv)

Rather than providing a clear consensus on what constitutes a gay and lesbian community, work in queer theory suggests that gays and lesbians view such communities in a wide variety of ways, ranging from biologically determined to virtually nonexistent. Anderson has argued that "all communities larger than primordial villages of face-to-face contact (and perhaps even these) are imagined," asserting that communities "are to be distinguished not by their falsity/genuineness, but by the style in which they are imagined" (1991: 6).

What, then, is the style in which queer communities are imagined? One unifying principle to all discussions of what constitutes a queer community has been the focus on the problem of knowing who is "family" and who is not. While many communities are imagined in ways that focus on what constitutes a "good" or "typical" community member (without a great deal of doubt about who those members might be), queer communities seem to focus extensively on what (if anything) constitutes a community member. Even essentialists who may offer ways of defining community members (such as by their genes) seem to recognize that the question of determining who "belongs" is the central question in the construction of a queer community. Thus, one style in which queer communities are imagined is a style in which the boundaries of community membership are consciously vague and uncertain. While all communities are imagined in some sense, queer communities recognize that they are imagined and knowingly and openly question the membership status of a variety of potential members. Thus, a "homo-genius" community is one in which the very notion of community cannot be taken for granted. The essential nature of a queer community can be seen as the self-recognition that it is socially constructed. Although the degree and importance of such construction may be called into question (e.g., Mohr 1992), the fact that community membership may not always be accurately determined is rarely denied. By imagining itself in such an ambiguous and uncertain style, a queer community calls the very notion of community into question. In terms of linguistics, issues of sexual orientation and gender identification do not easily lend themselves to studies in what Pratt (1987) calls the "linguistics of community."

Linguistics of Community

In offering a critique of "linguistics of community," Pratt notes that the prototypical case of language examined in linguistics is taken to be "the speech of adult native speakers face to face (as in Saussure's diagram) in monolingual, even monodialectal situations—in short, the maximally homogeneous case linguistically and socially" (1987: 50). This focus on homogeneous communities and the assumption of shared systems or norms of usage is embedded in the tradition (within historical linguistics) of "genetic" linguistics. The genetic tradition focuses on language as it changes over time, as a "mother" language divides into various "daughter" languages. Although a language is assumed to be a homogeneous linguistic system at any given moment, it changes over time, primarily through "imperfect" learning as language is passed from parents to children. Within the theoretical framework of traditional genetic linguistics, language change is primarily a language-internal process in which contact between languages and dialects is often seen as secondary (or entirely uninteresting). Within the genetic framework, the assumption of a homogeneous speech community and the focus on language as "inheritance" go hand in hand. Saussure, for example, argued that "no society has ever known its language to be anything other than something inherited from previous generations, which it has no choice but to accept" (1986: 72).

This genetic/community framework assumes that language is a social inheritance, a part of one's identity from early childhood that marks one as belonging to a specific community throughout one's life. As LePage and Tabouret-Keller have pointed out, "language" in the sense of one's native language or mother tongue remains "an important hypothetical base for many linguists and educationists" (1985: 190). The theoretical frameworks of genetic linguistics and its descendant, generative grammar, continue to treat the language one learns in childhood as a basic marker of social identity that is relatively constant across situational settings and the time of one's lifespan. Although linguists have (from the time of Boas, at least) adamantly argued that there is no direct relationship between language and race, the formal frameworks of genetic/generative linguistics continue to reify widely held assumptions about the association between language and race by placing speakers in isolated static homogeneous communities that often reflect common stereotypes of identity categories. In addition, the genetic framework thus fails to acknowledge the role of contact in the historical development of languages and the great deal of cultural history that can be extracted from considering the history of languages as a contact or areal phenomenon (Bauman and Sherzer 1972).

In the sense that genetic and generative linguistics focus on a static formal system that is inherited from one's parents, these theoretical frameworks are centered exclusively on what Warner (1993) has called "heteronormative behavior." That is, the basic assumptions of normative heterosexuality (including the processes of socialization associated with child-rearing) become the basis for linguistics as a field of study. This acceptance of heteronormative behavior is an example of how the community-based framework limits itself in ways that are difficult to acknowledge (Pratt 1987: 52). As Warner (1993) argues, the theoretical frameworks in many academic disciplines (re)produce the ideology of heterosexual society, even when allowing for the existence of sexual minorities. Studies of gay and lesbian language that are situated in a linguistics of community, for example, may produce descriptions of the linguistic behavior of a small subset of some assumed queer community. In doing so, they produce hypothetical (though unrealistic) communities of typical speakers who share some common language or norms of usage. Studying such communities in isolation does not actually convey the complexity of the relationship between language and queerness.

A framework that isolates fairly homogeneous queer communities fails fully to acknowledge the uncertainty involved in establishing concepts of community membership. In addition, such a framework fails to account for the fact that gay and lesbian language, or at least those things that make gay and lesbian language distinctive, do not originate in traditional (heterosexual-dominated) communities. Generally, people do not raise their children to talk like homosexuals. Quite to the contrary, language associated with gayness is probably discouraged by parents. Considering the fact that queer language is probably highly divergent from the language we are socialized into using, why should we base queer linguistics on a framework that assumes that language is a homogeneous system (of rules or norms) accepted throughout the community in which we are born?

The concept of isolated communities fails to recognize the ways in which contact influences the construction of gay and lesbian uses of language. Gays and lesbians are not isolated from straight society, and assuming that queer communities can be isolated does not convey the realities of living in an (often homophobic) heterosexist society. Gay and lesbian language may occur entirely within a context of straight society, where language may convey social information about sexual orientation that is not detected or understood by straights present during the interaction. In addition, the linguistics of community fails to acknowledge that gay and lesbian uses of language often occur *across* "community" boundaries. Language within a queer community is often simultaneously language across communities defined in terms of ethnicity, class, age, or regional background. For these reasons, a linguistics of community does not adequately deal with the realities of the relationship between language and queerness.

In her critique of the linguistics of community, Pratt proposes a different view of linguistics, one that she calls a *linguistics of contact*:

> Imagine, then, a linguistics that decentered community, that placed at its centre the operation of language *across* lines of social differentiation, a linguistics that focused on modes and zones of contact between dominant and dominated groups, between persons of different and multiple identities, speakers of different languages, that focused

on how such speakers constitute each other relationally and in difference, how they enact difference in language. Let us call this enterprise a *linguistics of contact*, a term related to Jakobson's notion of contact as a component of speech events, and to the phenomenon of contact languages, one of the best recognised challenges to the systematising linguistics of code. (1987: 60)

Taking Pratt's notion of a linguistics of contact as a starting point, I would like to suggest that queer uses of language can be studied without the tradition of a linguistics of community and the social (heteronormative) trappings that it carries. A linguistics of contact offers a starting point for the formation of a queer linguistics, that is, a linguistics that takes queerness as its center rather than forcing gay and lesbian language to conform to a heterosexual model of language production and learning.

As a starting point for examining the issues related to gay uses of language, I refer to the use of language among bar queens in Texas. Bar queens are gay men with dense social networks centered on gay bars and for whom being gay is a self-categorization of primary importance. This discussion is based partly on research conducted on the speech of African American drag queens (Barrett ms.) and partly on personal experience and casual observations in gay bars. This consideration of bar queen speech is not meant to be a detailed study of specific examples of recorded speech but is rather a broad discussion of the form and use of bar queen speech intended to raise issues relevant to the way in which gay male speech might be studied.

Structural Aspects of Bar Queen Speech

In their work on the role of language in the construction of social identity, LePage and Tabouret-Keller examine the ways in which people recognize and imitate forms of language that reflect the social identity of a group with whom they wish to be associated. LePage and Tabouret-Keller argue that "what they recognize and imitate are stereotypes they have constructed for themselves" (1985:142). For speakers who wish to use language in a way that will index a gay identity (see Ochs 1992), the form of language often reflects a stereotype of gay men's speech. As such, it may contain one or more of the components attributed to gay male speech by various linguists, such as the following features:

- The use of lexical items included as part of Lakoff's woman's language (Walters ms.; Moran 1991), including specific color terms and the so-called empty adjectives (e.g., "marvelous," "adorable"), as well as hedges and boosters (such as "like")
- The use of a wider pitch range for intonational contours (compared to the speech of straight men) (Walters ms.; Goodwin 1989; Moran 1991; Gaudio 1994)
- Hypercorrect pronunciation; the presence of phonologically nonreduced forms (Walters ms.) and the use of hyperextended vowels

- The use of lexical items specific to gay language (Walters ms.; Moran 1991; Farrell 1972; Rodgers 1979)
- The use of a H*L intonational contour (often co-occurring with extended vowels, as in "FAABulous") (Barrett ms.)

These features may (in a given context) index a gay identity. Thus, studies in which these features are considered out of context (e.g., Gaudio 1994) might not capture the relationship between the structural features and gay identity. In isolation, most of these features can also index some other identity in a different context. Specific color terms and empty adjectives, for example, may index a stereotype of female identity, while the use of hypercorrect pronunciation and phonologically nonreduced, hyperenunciated forms may index the "schoolteacher" speech of some older African American women. Thus, the indexical power of these structural elements often overlaps between gay male speech and the speech of some other social group. The linguistics of community cannot easily acknowledge this overlap, except where it might be seen as "dialect borrowing" or "accommodation." Within a linguistics of contact, however, such elements need not be viewed as the sole property of a single social group.

Consider, for example, the overlap between gay male speech and African American Vernacular English. In addition to hypercorrect pronunciation, speech events involving ritual insults can be found both among African American straight men (e.g., Labov 1972a) and among gay men (e.g., Murray 1979). Also, there are a number of lexical items that may index either gay or African American identity, depending on the speaker and the context. A few (but certainly not all) examples include the following:

> *fish:* a pejorative term for women (a reference to myths concerning the fragrance of female genitalia) (Folb 1980: 237, Major 1970: 54 and Smitherman 1994:110, for AAVE; Rodgers 1979: 81 and Farrell 1972: 102 for gay male speech).

> *work,* often *"work it":* to strut or show off; to try to draw attention to one's self in the bar. In AAVE "work" has historical roots as a jazz term for playing with great energy (Major 1970: 123, Smitherman 1994: 240–241). In gay male speech it has traditionally meant to put great effort into cruising, occurring in phrases such as "work the toilets" (Rodgers 1979: 215). The term *work* became quite common in bars in Texas in 1993 after the release of RuPaul's dance song "Supermodel (You Better Work)."

> *girl; girlfriend:* Used as a term of address or solidarity between African American women (Smitherman 1994:122) or between gay men (of any ethnic background).

> *Miss Thang (or Mizz Thang):* Used by both African American women and gay men to refer to someone who thinks highly of her- or himself or who may behave in a way that draws attention to himself or herself (Smitherman 1994: 161).

read: a specific speech event in which the speaker "tells someone off" (Smitherman 1976: 259; Smitherman 1994: 192) for AAVE; Rodgers 1979: 169 and Farrell 1972: 106 for gay male speech). Among African Americans, the term *reading* is sometimes associated with women (Morgan 1994). Among gay men it also has an older form (still in use among older gays) of "read his beads." It may also refer to the act of recognizing another homosexual.

Within a community-based framework, the elements that overlap between AAVE and gay male speech would probably be interpreted as borrowings from one community by another. As such, they might be seen as cultural appropriations. While some of these examples might be the result of appropriation, such an analysis does not fully account for situations such as that in which white gay men (even those who have little contact with African Americans) use linguistic markers of gay solidarity that are identical at the level of form to those used by African American women to mark their solidarity with other African American women.

A linguistics of contact, in which community boundaries are not assumed to be static and rigid, allows for an analysis in which bar queen speech may be constructed from the speech of a variety of individuals (or groups of individuals) with different linguistic backgrounds who participate in mutual acts of identity (Le-Page and Tabouret-Keller 1985) to create shared linguistic markers of social identity. As such, bar queen speech can be viewed as an abrupt creolization (Thomason and Kaufman 1988) at the level of language style, in which the linguistic elements that index gay identity are brought together from a wide variety of sources. As Moran (1991) argues, the use of "feminine" linguistic elements in the speech of gay men may be seen as a reclaiming of stereotypes of the extent to which gay men behave like women. In a situation where gay men from various ethnic backgrounds come together in the setting of a bar, stereotypes of effeminate linguistic behavior from white English and African American English, as well as from other ethnic and regional varieties, come together to create a unified stereotype of what constitutes gay English.

Another important aspect of these structural elements is the fact that almost all of them are markers of what Brown and Levinson (1987) have termed "positive politeness." Markers of positive politeness serve as a means of conveying common ground between speakers. Exaggeration (including exaggerated intonation), the use of ingroup lexical items and slang, the use of hedges, and a tendency toward standard varieties are all considered markers of positive politeness. Brown and Levinson suggest that the use of positive politeness markers might be more prevalent in the speech of dominated groups:

> In general we have a hunch that all over the world, in complex societies, dominated groups (and sometimes also majority groups) have positive-politeness cultures; dominating groups have negative-politeness cultures. That is, the world of the upper and middle groups is constructed in a stern and cold architecture of social distance, assymetry, and resentment of impositions, while the world of the lower groups is built on social closeness, symmetrical solidarity, and reciprocity. (1987: 245)

Similar (independent) evidence for Brown and Levinson's "hunch" comes from studies of social identity (within the framework of self-categorization theory) by Willem Doise and Fabio Lorenzi-Cioldi. Doise and Lorenzi-Cioldi argue that members of dominating groups (or groups with higher social status) "perceive themselves as unique individuals and do not seek self definition in terms of group membership. On the other hand, members of dominated groups define them-selves, and are also defined by others, more in terms of social categorizations im-posed on them" (1989: 55). Thus, members of lower status groups, which define themselves according to group memberships, would be expected to display less so-cial distance among ingroup members, since social distance is a function of the de-gree to which one views others as sharing similar social identity.

The presence of a variety of positive politeness strategies as the main indexi-cal markers of bar queen speech suggests that language may serve as a means of producing a unified social identity among gay men from divergent backgrounds. Many of these positive politeness strategies can be found in stereotypically "femi-nine" language (e.g., Lakoff 1975). In bar queen speech, the manipulation of stereotypes about the effeminate behavior of gay men is combined with the use of positive politeness strategies that forge solidarity within a given social network centered around the bar. Thus, in order to study gay male speech adequately, con-sideration must be given to the unique role of language in both gender construc-tion and the formation of solidarity.

The Uses of Gay Male Speech

The study of gay male speech as a behavioral characteristic of a homogeneous speech community cannot easily account for the wide range of competences found among gay men with different backgrounds who participate in various social net-works. In discussing ritual insults among gay men, for example, Murray is careful to state that "very few gay men and seemingly fewer lesbians spend an appreciable amount of time verbal dueling" (1979: 217–218). Thus, a genre that indexes a gay identity may in actual practice occur only among a small subset of gay men. Al-though competence in bar queen speech may vary a great deal, most gay men (and many straights) recognize bar queen speech as indexing a gay identity. As Pratt notes, "for a linguistics of contact, it is of great interest that people can generally understand many more varieties of discourse or even languages than they can pro-duce, or understand them better than they can produce them" (1987: 62). The range of competence in bar queen speech may vary according to participation in the social networks of the bars or the degree to which one desires to be seen as a member of the bar crowd. Because of the gradient nature of language style, the degree to which bar queen speech actually indexes gay identity may vary a great deal. De-pending on the context, for example, the use of *mauve* may not index a gay identity as much as the use of *Miss Thang*. Similarly, greater frequency and variety in the el-ements of bar queen speech used might convey a stronger sense of gay identity. Be-cause the indexical value of any element of gay male speech (or any speech, for that matter) is highly dependent on context, sociolinguists need to be aware of the ways in which language may convey intertextuality (Kristeva 1980), as in studies of linguistic genre in the field of folklore (e.g. Briggs and Bauman 1992).

The categories of language variety proposed by Charles Ferguson are extremely useful in considering the relationship between the indexical value of language and context. Ferguson (1994) proposes three basic types of language variety: dialect, register, and genre. Basically, in Ferguson's terms, dialect is language that indexes the identity of a specific social group, register is language that indexes social context, and genre is language that indexes a particular speech act. For some speakers, bar queen speech may be a dialect in that it is practically the only form of English that they use. Although such speakers may have spoken in a stereotypically gay style for most or all of their lives, the details (mostly lexical items) that differentiate bar queen speech from other gay-sounding styles would have been acquired after the speaker came out and joined the social networks surrounding the bar(s). For other speakers, bar queen speech is a specific register in that its use is reserved for the bar setting. For these speakers, the overt display of gay identity is restricted to certain times, places, and interlocutors. Speakers for whom bar queen speech is a register may not be out in their lives outside the bar and are thus forced to restrict their speech to settings in which straights are absent. They may also be completely open about their sexuality outside the bar but reserve behavior that is overtly gay for the bar setting. Because of the gradient nature of language style as an indexical marker of identity, these two groups are not always clearly differentiated but exist along a continuum. A better understanding of how these differences in usage occur across gay communities would likely offer a better understanding of variation in the display of overtly gay behavior, as well as of the relationship between dialect and register. The distinction between register and dialect offers a way of beginning to understand how language as a site of contact between gay and straight settings might act differently for different speakers.

As Ferguson notes, in actual practice the distinctions between dialect, register, and genre are not necessarily absolute. In cases where bar queen speech is a register, for example, it is still a marker of social identity. In addition, language style that falls under genre (i.e., that indexes a particular speech event) may also index identity or context. A genre such as "reading" (telling someone off through ritual insults) is an example of a speech event that may also serve as a register (in that it may only occur in gay settings) or as part of a dialect (in that it indexes a gay identity). Because the distinctions among dialect, register, and genre are not absolute, gay speech must be considered in relation to the context in which it occurs.

One means of relating language and context is to consider the use of gay male speech in terms of code-switching or style-switching. Myers-Scotton's (1993) Markedness Model provides a means of analyzing style-switching in terms of the indexical meaning conveyed by any particular switch. In Myers-Scotton's model, speakers choose the linguistic form of an utterance so that it indexes the set of social relationships (a "rights and obligations set" or "RO set") the speaker wishes to have in place for a given interaction. The model analyzes switches in terms of whether or not the linguistic form of an utterance is expected for a given interaction. Myers-Scotton offers four specific types of code-switching:

1. Sequential unmarked code-switching. "When one or more of the situational factors change *within the course of a conversation*, the unmarked RO set may change. . . . Whenever the unmarked RO set is altered by such factors, the speaker will switch codes if he or she wished to index the new unmarked RO set" (1993: 114).

2. Code-switching as the unmarked norm: "Speaking two languages in the same conversation [as the unmarked norm between bilingual peers] . . . *each* switch . . . does not necessarily have a special indexicality; rather, it is the *overall pattern* which carries the communicative force" (1993: 117).

3. Code-switching as a marked choice: "A marked choice derives its meaning from two sources: first, since it is *not* the unmarked choice, it is a negotiation against the unmarked RO set; and second, as 'something else,' the marked choice is a call for *another* RO set in its place, that for which the speaker's choice is the unmarked index" (1993: 131).

4. Code-switching as an exploratory choice: "When an unmarked choice is not clear, [speakers] use code switching to make alternate exploratory choices as candidates for an unmarked choice and thereby as an index of an RO set which [they] favor" (1993: 142).

One way of examining the social relevance of gay speech is to use the markedness model to analyze the ways in which switches between gay speech and other varieties of English serve to convey specific social relationships. In cases where gay male speech may act as a register, for example, code-switching as an unmarked choice will most likely occur. Instances of code-switching as a marked choice could provide insight into where and why the foregrounding of gay identity is important for various speakers. The distinctions between code-switching as the unmarked norm and code-switching as an unmarked/marked choice may serve as a starting point for studying the ways in which gay male speech relates to other types of speech that index different aspects of one's personal identity. In another work (Barrett 1995), I have used the model to consider the ways in which African American drag queens use language style to negotiate their overlapping identities as gay men, as African Americans, and as drag queens.

The case of code-switching as an exploratory choice is of great importance in the understanding of gay male speech. Although Myers-Scotton (1993: 142) suggests that exploratory switching is probably quite rare in most situations, it is actually quite common in gay male speech. Indeed, one important focus of research on gay male speech has been this very issue (e.g., Hayes 1981; Leap 1993). In encounters outside a specifically gay setting, exploratory switching may be used as a means of determining the sexual orientation of one's interlocutor. One may, for example, use linguistic forms that index gay identity to see if a listener recognizes the indexical power of the forms and uses more elements of gay speech in return. In such cases, the elements of gay speech may not be extremely salient markers of gay identity, so straight overhearers might never recognize the actual importance of the exchange. Exploratory switching thus represents an important site of contact between gay and straight settings, as it may be used covertly to establish gay solidarity even in entirely straight settings.

Conclusion

The study of the actual use of gay male speech provides a means of examining the fluidity of gay identity—how it is constructed and used in a variety of settings for a variety of purposes. Studies of both the structure and the use of gay speech may provide insight into the ways in which gay identity is constructed and maintained across different contexts. As such, it provides a powerful tool for understanding the style in which gay communities are imagined.

Because of the unique social realities of gay, lesbian, bisexual and transgender persons, the study of queer forms of speech has much to offer the field of linguistics as a whole. Queer linguistics may provide a start towards overcoming the problems produced by a linguistics of community. It may also produce valuable insight into understanding commonly used terms such as *dialect* and *register*. In addition, queer linguistics has much to offer queer studies. It provides a means for beginning to understand the ways in which people actually construct and produce markers of queer identities and deal with the ambiguity of identity categories and communities that are imagined differently by different community members. Beginning to understand the various ways in which gays, lesbians, bisexuals and transgenders imagine their own communities, we can begin to try and understand what exactly constitutes a "homo-genius" community.

NOTES

1. The use of *queer* here is intended to convey any variety of lesbian, bisexual, transgender, or gay culture/society and is otherwise purposely left vague in terms of who actually claims membership in or is considered to belong to such a culture/society.

2. Gaudio (1994) includes one African American in his study of gay intonation but does not include ethnicity as a factor in his final analysis.

REFERENCES

Almaguer, Tomás (1993). "Chicano Men: A Cartography of Homosexual Identity and Behavior." In Henry Abelove, Michèle Aina Barale, and David M. Halperin (eds.), *The Lesbian and Gay Studies Reader*. New York: Routledge, pp. 255–273.

Anderson, Benedict (1991). *Imagined Communities: Reflections on the Origin and Spread of Nationalism*. London: Verso.

Barrett, Rusty (1993). "Queen's English: Language and Polyphonous Identity among African American Drag Queens." University of Texas at Austin. Unpublished manuscript.

———— (1995). "The Markedness Model and Style Switching: Evidence from African American Drag Queens." In Pamela Silberman and Jonathan Loftin (eds.), *SALSA II: Proceedings of the Second Annual Symposium about Language and Society —Austin*, pp. 40–52.

Bauman, Richard, and Joel Sherzer (1972). "Areal Studies and Culture History: Language as a Key to the Historical Study of Culture Contact." *Southwestern Journal of Anthropology* 28: 131–152.

Bourdieu, Pierre (1991). *Language and Symbolic Power*, ed. John B. Thompson, trans. Gino Raymond and Matthew Adamson. Cambridge, MA: Harvard University Press.

Briggs, Charles, and Richard Bauman (1992). "Genre, Intertextuality, and Social Power." *Journal of Linguistic Anthropology* 2, no. 2: 131–172.

Brown, Penelope and Stephen Levinson (1987). *Politeness Theory: Some Universals in Language Use.* Cambridge: Cambridge University Press.

Butler, Judith (1993a). *Bodies that Matter: On the Discursive Limits of "Sex."* New York: Routledge.

—— (1993b). "Imitation and Gender Insubordination." In Henry Abelove, Michèle Aina Barale, and David M. Halperin (eds.), *The Lesbian and Gay Studies Reader.* New York: Routledge, pp. 307–320.

Chomsky, Noam (1957). *Syntactic Structures.* The Hague: Mouton.

—— (1965). *Aspects of the Theory of Syntax.* Cambridge, MA: Massachusetts Institute of Technology Press.

—— (1981). *Lectures on Government and Binding.* Dordrecht: Foris.

Corder, Pit S. (1973). *Introducing Applied Linguistics.* New York: Penguin.

Doise, Willem, and Fabio Lorenzi-Cioldi (1989). "Patterns of Differentiation within and between Groups." In Jan Pieter van Oudenhoven and Tineke M. Willemsen (eds.), *Ethnic Minorities.* Amsterdam: Swets and Zeitlinger, pp. 43–59.

Dorian, Nancy C. (1982). "Defining the Speech Community to Include its Working Margins." In Suzanne Romaine (ed.), *Sociolinguistic Variation in Speech Communities.* London: Edward Arnold, pp. 25–34.

Farrell, Ronald A. (1972). "The Argot of the Homosexual Subculture." *Anthropological Linguistics* 14, no. 3: 97–109.

Ferguson, Charles (1994). "Dialect, Register, and Genre: Working Assumptions about Conventionalization." In Douglas Biber and Edward Finegan (eds.), *Sociolinguistic Perspectives on Register.* New York: Oxford University Press, pp. 15–30.

Folb, Edith A. (1980). *Runnin' Down Some Lines: The Language and Culture of Black Teenagers.* Cambridge, MA: Harvard University Press.

Gal, Susan (1989). "Language and Political Economy." *Annual Review of Anthropology* 18: 345–367.

Gaudio, Rudolf P. (1994). "Sounding Gay: Pitch Properties in the Speech of Gay and Straight Men." *American Speech* 69, no. 1: 30–37.

Goodwin, Joseph P. (1989). *More Man than You'll Ever Be: Gay Folklore and Acculturation in Middle America.* Bloomington: Indiana University Press.

Guion, Susan (1993). "The Death of Texas German in Gillespie County." Paper presented at the Annual Meeting of the Linguistic Society of America, Los Angeles, January 8.

Gumperz, John J. (1972). "Introduction." In John J. Gumperz and Dell Hymes (eds.), *Directions in Sociolinguistics.* New York: Holt, Rinehart & Winston, pp. 1–25.

Hayes, Joseph J. (1981). "Gayspeak." In James W. Chesebro (ed.), *Gayspeak: Gay Male and Lesbian Communication.* New York: Pilgrim Press, pp. 45–57.

Herdt, Gilbert, and Andrew Boxer (1992). "Introduction: Culture, History, and Life Course of Gay Men." In Gilbert Herdt (ed.), *Gay Culture in America: Essays from the Field,* pp. 1–28.

Hymes, Dell (1972). "Models of the Interaction of Language and Social Life." In John J. Gumperz and Dell Hymes (eds.), *Directions in Sociolinguistics: The Ethnography of Communication.* New York: Holt, Rinehart & Winston, pp. 35–71.

Icard, Larry (1985). "Black Gay Men and Conflicting Social Identities: Sexual Orientation versus Racial Identity." *Journal of Social Work and Human Sexuality* 4, no. 1–2:83–93.

Jakobson, Roman (1971). "Retrospect." *Selected Writings, vol. 2.* The Hague: Mouton.

Jenness, Valerie (1992). "Coming Out: Lesbian Identities and the Categorization Problem." In Ken Plummer (ed.), *Modern Homosexualities: Fragments of Lesbian and Gay Experience.* New York: Routledge, pp. 65–74.

Kristeva, Julia (1980). *Desire in Language: A Semiotic Approach to Literature and Art,* ed.

Leon S. Roudiez, trans. Thomas Gora, Alice Jardine, and Leon S. Roudiez. New York: Columbia University Press.

Labov, William (1972a). *Language in the Inner City: Studies in the Black English Vernacular.* Philadelphia: University of Pennsylvania Press.

——— (1972b). *Sociolinguistic Patterns.* Phildelphia: University of Pennsylvania Press.

Lakoff, Robin (1975). *Language and Woman's Place.* New York: Harper & Row.

Le Page, R. B., and Andrée Tabouret-Keller (1985). *Acts of Identity: Creole-Based Approaches to Language and Ethnicity.* Cambridge: Cambridge University Press.

Leap, William L. (1993). "Gay Men's English: Cooperative Discourse in a Language of Risk." *New York Folklore* 19, no. 1–2: 45–70.

——— (1994). "Can There Be Gay Discourse without Gay Language?" Paper presented at the Third Berkeley Women and Language Conference, Berkeley, CA, April 10.

Major, Clarence (1970). *Dictionary of Afro-American Slang.* New York: International Publishers.

Mohr, Richard D. (1992). *Gay Ideas: Outing and Other Controversies.* Boston: Beacon Press.

Moran, John (1991). "Language Use and Social Function in the Gay Community." Paper presented at NWAVE 20.

Morgan, Marcyliena (1994). "No Woman No Cry: The Linguistic Representation of African American Women." In Mary Bucholtz, A. C. Liang, Laurel Sutton, and Caitlin Hines (eds.), *Cultural Performances: Proceedings of the Third Berkeley Women and Language Conference.* Berkeley: Berkeley Women and Language Group, pp. 525–541.

Murray, Stephen O. (1979). "The Art of Gay Insulting." *Anthropological Linguistics.* 21, no. 5: 211–223.

Myers-Scotton, Carol (1993). *Social Motivations for Codeswitching: Evidence from Africa.* Oxford: Oxford University Press.

Ochs, Elinor (1992). "Indexing Gender." In A. Duranti and C. Goodwin (ed.), *Rethinking Context.* Cambridge: Cambridge University Press, pp. 335–358.

Peterson, John L. (1992). "Black Men and Their Same-Sex Desires and Behaviors." In Gilbert Herdt (ed.), *Gay Culture in America: Essays from the Field.* Boston: Beacon Press, pp. 87–106.

Pratt, Mary Louise (1987). "Linguistic Utopias." In Nigel Fabb, Derek Attridge, Alan Durant, and Colin MacCabe (eds.), *The Linguistics of Writing: Arguments between Language and Literature.* Manchester, UK: Manchester University Press, pp. 48–66.

Rodgers, Bruce (1979). *Gay Talk: A (Sometimes Outrageous) Dictionary of Gay Slang (formerly entitled* The Queen's Vernacular*).* New York: Paragon Books.

Sapir, Edward (1949). *Culture, Language and Personality,* ed. David G. Mandelbaum. Berkeley: University of California Press.

de Saussure, Ferdinand (1986). *Course in General Linguistics,* ed. Charles Bally and Albert Sechehaye, trans. Roy Harris. London: Duckworth.

Smith, Max C. (1988). "By the Year 2000." In Joseph Beam (ed.), *In the Life: A Black Gay Anthology.* Boston: Alyson, pp. 224–229.

Smitherman, Geneva (1976). *Talkin and Testifyin: The Language of Black America.* Detroit, MI: Wayne State University Press.

Stanback, Marsha Houston (1985). "Language and Black Woman's Place: Evidence from the Black Middle Class." In Paula A. Treichler, Cheris Kramarae, and Beth Stafford (eds.), *For Alma Mater: Theory and Practice in Feminist Scholarship.* Urbana: University of Illinois Press, pp. 177–196.

——— (1994). *Black Talk: Words and Phrases from the Hood to Amen Corner.* New York: Houghten Mifflin.

Thomason, Sarah G., and Terrence Kaufman (1988). *Language Contact, Creolization and Genetic Linguistics.* Berkeley: University of California Press.

Tinney, James S. (1986). "Why a Gay Black Church?" In Joseph Beam (ed.), *In the Life: A Black Gay Anthology.* Boston: Alyson, pp. 70–86.

Van Valin, Robert D., Jr. (1987). "The Role of Government in the Grammar of Head-Marking Languages." *International Journal of American Linguistics* 53, no. 4: 371–397.

Voloshinov, V. N. (1973). *Marxism and the Philosophy of Language,* trans. Ladislav Matejka and I. R. Titunik. Cambridge, MA: Harvard University Press.

Walters, Keith (ms.). "A Proposal for Studying the Language of Homosexual Males." University of Texas at Austin, 1981.

Warner, Michael (1993). "Introduction." In Michael Warner (ed.), *Fear of a Queer Planet: Queer Politics and Social Theory.* Minneapolis: Minnesota University Press, pp. vii–xxxi.

Woolard, Kathryn A. (1985). "Language Variation and Cultural Hegemony: Toward an Integration of Sociolinguistic and Social Theory." *American Ethnologist* 12, no. 4: 738–748.

11

Toward a Study of Lesbian Speech

BIRCH MOONWOMON-BAIRD

This paper is a decade old. I have gone somewhere else in my work on lesbian language use, but one thing I like about this conference paper is that in it I observe that lesbian practice is regarded as marked behavior but goes unremarked much more than is true of gay male practice, even in this era of both friendly and hostile societal discourses on queers. Lesbian language behavior in particular goes unremarked. I ask why the dominant society's negative sanction on lesbian revelation and its general refusal to acknowledge lesbian existence, a state of affairs referred to as "enforced invisibility," manifests especially as, in fact, "inaudibility." Why are we not heard as lesbians, apparently even by ourselves?

It may be the case that careful, quantitative study of lesbian speech will show that some phonological or other linguistic forms have a greater probability of showing up in lesbian talk than in heterosexual women's talk, and if this is the case, it will be good for us to know it. A decade ago I expected that it would be shown to be so. But I have come to think that language use among lesbians, at least across ethnicities and social classes of English-speaking American lesbians, is peculiarly lesbian in that interlocutors assume shared knowledge about many extradiscoursal matters touching on both gender and social-sexual orientation. These areas of knowledge partly inform and are partly constituted by societal discourses (not confined to any set of situated linguistic discourses), such as those on gay civil rights, lesbian motherhood, body piercing, and dental dams. Specifying the societal discourses that background lesbian talk allows the construction of lesbian cultural knowledge, including ideological knowledge. We are heard as lesbians, at least by ourselves; the authentic lesbian voice is characterized not by intonational peculiarities or, for the most part, by use of special lexicon but by implication, inference, and presupposition that reveal a speaker's stance within the territories of various societal discourses. It is qualitative analysis of the structures of situated lesbian discourses and the social practices in which they are embedded that will teach us the most about the lesbianness of lesbian language use.

This is a paper of three parts. I begin with some theoretical and political thoughts on women and language study and lesbian speech. I then report on two studies I have done, one a test for stereotyping of lesbian speech, the other a small intonation study comparing lesbians' pitch pattern with heterosexual women's pitch patterns. I am trying to find my way toward theory and methodology for the study of lesbian use of language.

A Different View of Women and Language

You can't win, you can't break even, and you can't get out of the Game. Women's attempts to do any of these three things are strategies that reflect our gender identification (or aspiration), gender orientation, and gender role assumption. The attempts fail because all space is George's space. "It's all George's space" is a line from the Cinderella Piece of the Woman Rite Theater, as performed in 1974 in Woodstock, New York. The idea is that all the territory is claimed and controlled by men in power. A woman may identify with other women or with men; very likely she will sometimes identify with other women and sometimes aspire to be manly. One strategy—an attempt at winning—is to be an "exceptional woman," for instance, to think like a man, write like a man, run the office like a man. A woman may orient herself toward other women or toward men. The orientation issue is: Who is central, who is in focus? A woman may identify with women and still be oriented toward men; this is in fact what's expected of us. A second strategy —an attempt at breaking even—is to be male oriented, for instance, to pacify a husband rather than to stick up for a daughter; this strategy involves making one's own interests and the interests of other women of lower priority than the interests of men, in the hopes of being treated benevolently. This is submission. A woman may assume a role which is defined by the gender behavior dichotomy, that is, a role toward a pole of that dichotomy or somewhere in between. A third strategy— an attempt at getting out of the Game—is to be a gender-roleless woman, for instance, to fix the car and later crochet the baby booties. This is the strategy of the would-be escapee, the refugee running for the border. I bet it is the one that will take us women the furthest within the Game. However, all space is George's space. There is no escape, although there may be respite within one's own psyche or immediate social circle. In the world, all behavior is liable to interpretation as in conformity with or defiance of ascribed gender roles.

Linguistic behavior is interpreted in these terms. Non-dominant people must learn and be good at controlling more than one code. In our code switching women play to or against expectations for gender identification, orientation, and role playing. Male mimicry of women, too, takes advantage of extreme values for some stereotyped feature. Examples are the use of hedges or of high pitch. The mimic is understood to be making a female presence. He is not heard simply as a man speaking in a high voice.

Women's actual linguistic behavior is both marked and unremarked. I mean that it isn't observed *well* by women or men. What we do is largely unnoticed because of interference from notions of what we do. Often our behavior is lost, and caricature is put in its place. When it is noticed, our behavior is judged inferior, if it is different from male behavior, and aberrant and a display of hubris, if it is like male behavior. Some of us may declare women's use of language unmarked to us—and I think this is a good idea—but to the larger society it is marked in contrast to unmarked men's use of language. There exists a paradigm in which actual and imagined female speech is a structural contrast to "ordinary" male speech. The structure of the paradigm depends on androcentrism. From an androcentric point of view, women's speech is a conditioned variant, men's speech the "elsewhere" variant, the basic one.

Lesbian behavior, linguistic and other, is particularly marked and particularly unremarked. It is caricatured and so largely not observed, and when observed, devalued. From a homophobic point of view, lesbians are not seen simply as strange, we are not allowed; we aren't supposed to exist at all.

However, some of us do. The least we could do is keep quiet about it— quiet as women, quiet as queers. I have just said that our linguistic behavior is caricatured. This is clearly much less true than that gay male linguistic behavior is caricatured. Also, lesbian non-linguistic behavior is stereotyped much more than linguistic behavior. Why is there so little idea about what lesbians sound like? I believe it's because the development of stereotypes in this area is counteracted by what I call "enforced invisibility," an aspect of the oppression of gays: We are strongly discouraged from making ourselves noticeable as homosexuals. This pressure naturally pushes hardest and works best against women, who are already peripheral humans. I mean for the term "enforced invisibility" to cover invisibility, inaudibility, and so on—the state of not being perceived, not acknowledged.

But why especially inaudibility? In order for lesbians to be heard or even misheard, as lesbians, we have to speak, as lesbians. I assume that community is always, somehow, speech community. There are at some times and in some places undeniably lesbian communities. In other situations there seem to be just some lesbians, with fragile, limited networks. Even when lesbian community clearly exists, not every lesbian in its vicinity is part of it. We live our lives in many different ways. Two things that are characteristic of our ways of living are diversity and, sadly, isolation. What are the communicative needs of lesbians, as lesbians? Among ourselves there are the ordinary group needs to share and compare experiences, create and express values, exchange and verify information pertinent to members of the group, check out assumptions. There are also particular group needs, to be taken care of among ourselves and in relations with others; these two situations will sometimes require different behaviors. Lesbians maintain primary sexual and friendship bonds that are permanently outside the positive sanctions on marriage and family. We need to reassure one another and reinforce these relationships. On the other hand, our most important bondings often have to be kept secret in the situations in which we spend most of our daily lives, like work, and in circles which, for heterosexuals, serve to strengthen and encompass alliances of affections, like family. Lesbians do all this as members of the gender caste that is marked [+ peripheral] and [- powerful]. We are in a different place than gay men. Isolation and otherness make solidarity hard to maintain, and make something as simple as the establishment of common linguistic markers of identity difficult to accomplish and, I think, dangerous to display.

As I begin investigation of lesbian language use, I keep in mind women's strategies in the Game in relation to gender identity, orientation, and role. I need to note what verbal behavior is expected of women in general and to try to elicit what verbal behavior, if any, is expected of lesbians. I expect enforced invisibility to work against easy discernment of lesbian speech in contrast to the speech of heterosexual women.

I speculate that a descriptive, bottom-up approach to women and language study will continue to reveal a great range in women's linguistic behavior. I suppose our behavior just about encompasses the range of human linguistic behavior. There are, after all, more female than male language users; and women's role in child language acquisition is very important; and women of different classes and races must be able to gender code switch in different ways. So I consider women's speech ordinary. Suppose a center, characterized by certain traits, can be found for the speech of women of a given class in a given geographic setting. Because of enforced invisibility, in part, I expect lesbian speech to deviate from this center toward a male language use extreme much less than gay men's speech deviates from the male extreme toward the female center (or toward a separate area of caricature). Because of group communicative needs, however, I expect comparisons of lesbian conversations and heterosexual women's conversations, of women otherwise socially similar, to show differences in discourse that include at least: the subjects discussed and alluded to—lexicon presuming knowledge from various kinds of women's experience; intonation patterns functioning to maintain conversational turn; and the degree of tolerance for silence. I expect that differences between lesbian and heterosexual women's language use, if interpreted in terms of strategies for winning, breaking even, or getting out of the Game, will pattern this way: about as often as heterosexual women, lesbians try to win; less often than heterosexual women, lesbians try to break even; more often than heterosexual women, lesbians try to get out of the Game. Importantly, though, most women try to break even most of the time. In so far as lesbians do not *make* ourselves heard as lesbians, I say we are trying to break even. We cooperate in the enforcement of inaudibility. Therefore, we are hard to hear, as lesbians.

A Test for Stereotyping

In the fall of 1983, I conducted an experiment (1) testing for a correlation between the judgment that a speaker was a lesbian and the judgment that a speaker had certain other social characteristics or had certain voice traits, or both. I was not concerned with accuracy but with relationships among listeners' perceptions. I was probing for sterotyping and trying to counteract enforced inaudibility. I expected that, when pushed, listeners would associate speech traits marking some kind of otherness with lesbians. The two-part hypothesis was: If the question of lesbianism is introduced, listeners will be willing to call some female speakers lesbian; and selection for "lesbian" will correlate positively with selection for membership in other little valued social categories and with selection for voice characteristics associated with unladylike speech.

I used 30-second stretches of the recorded speech of six heterosexual women and six lesbians, segments taken from much longer stretches of natural speech recorded in relaxed settings. These women were all white, native speakers of American English, including working-class and middle-class individuals of various ages and educational backgrounds who grew up in several different parts of the country. Three were Jewish. The 21 listeners were students from lower division social science courses at U.C. Berkeley. The average listener age was 23. All were native American English speakers. The listeners heard the taped segments and answered a questionnaire designed to elicit judgments about the speakers' social identities and voice characteristics. Social characteristics were class, age, educational background, region of upbringing, ethnicity (in a limited way), and sexual preference. The ethnicity question gave listeners the option of answering "Jewish" or "non-Jewish." I placed the question eliciting judgment about sexual preference in the middle of the questionnaire, embedding it in a matrix of other social and voice characteristic questions. I was trying to make it easy for listeners to judge a woman speaker as lesbian. The voice traits I asked about were rate of speech, pitch, amplitude, and "forcefulness."

In analyzing the results I looked for correlations between selections for lesbian and selections for other traits. Accuracy played very little part in determining the results. Of the selections made for lesbian, about half were right. Of the selections made for Jewish, about half were right. Analysis of the results revealed three things. First, listeners were willing to select some traits more than others. For instance, listeners often (53.6% of the time) picked "middle class" rather than "working class" or "upper class," and often (30.9% of the time) picked "grew up in the West" rather than any of the other five regional choices (Table 11-1). From the selection preference results I made a markedness scale (Table 11-2). The young Berkeley students tended to hear speakers as young, middle class, heterosexual, West Coasters. Second, although no single relationship between selection for lesbian and selection for other marked traits is very strong, overall there is greater correlation between selection for "lesbian" and some other characteristics than for "heterosexual" and those other characteristics. Table 11-1 shows that listeners favored the selection for "lesbian" and "grew up in the West," for instance; and they

Table 11.1. Correlations between sexuality and other selections.

% of Speakers Selected for:	(1) Trait	(2) Lesbian and Other Trait	(3) Heterosexual and Other Trait	Degree (2) Deviates from (1)	Degree (3) Deviates from (1)
		Social Characteristics			
class					
working	28.2	26.7	28.4	1.5	0.2
middle	53.6	56.7	53.2	3.1	0.4
upper	18.2	16.7	18.1	1.5	0.1
age					
under 40	73.0	73.3	73.0	0.3	0
over 40	26.9	27	26.1	0.1	0.8
educational level					
college grad	44.4	40.0	45.0	4.4	0.6
not grad	55.2	56.6	54.9	1.4	0.3
region					
SE	7.1	0	8.1	7.1	1.0
MA	20.2	16.6	20.7	3.6	0.5
NE	9.9	10.0	9.9	0.1	0
MW	19.4	26.6	18.5	7.2	0.9
SW	12.3	3.3	13.5	9.0	1.2
W	30.9	43.3	29.3	12.4	1.6
ethnicity					
Jewish	12.7	23.3	11.3	10.6	1.4
not Jewish	87.3	76.6	88.7	10.7	1.4
		Voice Characteristics			
speed					
fast	30.2	23.3	31.0	6.9	0.8
ordinary	55.5	40.0	57.6	15.5	2.1
slow	14.3	36.6	11.5	22.3	2.8
pitch					
low	30.5	26.6	31.1	6.9	0.8
mid-range	63.5	63.3	63.5	0.2	0
high	5.9	10.0	5.4	0.5	0.9
loudness					
loud	17.7	13.3	18.5	4.5	0.7
moderate	82.3	70.0	69.4	0.6	0
force					
gentle	24.2	36.6	22.5	12.4	1.7
ordinary	62.7	46.6	64.9	16.1	2.2
harsh	13.0	16.6	12.6	3.6	0.4

Average deviation of (2) from (1):	5.63
Average deviation of (3) from (1):	0.08
Difference between averages:	5.55

Table 11-2. Percentages of an "even distribution" figure of traits that were selected.

Social Characteristics		Voice Characteristics	
lesbian	23.8	high	17.7
Jewish	25.4	soft	38.1
Southeast	42.8	harsh	39.0
over 40	54.0	slow	42.9
upper class	54.7	loud	53.4
New England	59.5	gentle	72.6
Southwest	73.8	fast	90.6
working class	84.5	low	91.5
college graduate	88.8	ordinary speed	166.6
not a graduate	110.2	ordinary force	188.8
Midwest	116.4	mid range	190.5
Middle Atlantic	121.4	moderate (loudness)	208.2
under 40	146.0		
middle class	160.7		
not Jewish	174.6		
heterosexual	176.1		
West	185.7		

seemed to think that lesbians could not be speaking with Southern accents, since they never judged either of the two Southern speakers as lesbian. (One is). Third, there is a stronger correlation between selection for "lesbian" and selection for "Jewish" than anything else. "Lesbian" and "Jewish" are the most marked traits in the markedness scale; that is, listeners were extremely reluctant to choose either of these: There were 32 (out of 252 possible) selections for Jewish, and 30 (out of 252 possible) selections for lesbian. Since these were the least popular choices, chances against their being picked together were very high. In spite of this they were selected together about one-fourth of the time (23.7% of the time).

The markedness scale only shows relative selection favoring. It does not indicate that less selected traits were less valued. "Upper class," for instance, is marked: That is, it was selected very little. It seems reasonable, however, to interpret the great reluctance on the part of listeners to choose either "lesbian" or "Jewish"—the two traits that are the most marked choices for their own categories and the most marked of all social selections—as an indication that the listeners value these traits little. The traits are stigmatized.

The first part of the hypothesis was not strongly validated. Listeners were reluctant to call female speakers lesbians. The experimental attempt at undercutting enforced inaudibility was not successful. The second part of the hypothesis was more strongly validated, especially since I found a positive correlation between selection for lesbian and selection for Jewish which is not explained by accurate judgment and does not itself correlate with selection for unladylike voice characteristics like loud, harsh, or low-pitched (or high-pitched, for that matter; that is, "shrill"). Something not directly reflected in the answers to the questionnaire prompted selection for lesbian and Jewish together. A study probing the reasons for these correlated selections would be a very good idea.

The pilot experiment was conducted on too small a scale for the results to be statistically meaningful. The study shows me, however, that enforced invisibility is hard to counteract. It's possible that the youth of the listeners, and therefore lack of exposure to different groups of people, was a factor here, assuming that the listeners were mostly heterosexual. Perhaps these listeners were less willing than some others would have been to decide they were hearing lesbians. Or it may be that expectation of—the prescription—of heterosexuality is even stronger than I thought. There is no lack in the world of general stereotyping of lesbians, but the experimental elicitation of stereotypes for lesbian speech elicited little stereotyping and much avoidance. The real problem, I believe, is unwillingness to acknowledge lesbian presence. More than a third of the comments written on the backs of the questionnaires concern the difficulty of making a sexual preference question selection for lesbians. One comment reads, "It's hard to determine for lesbians. Lesbians may lower their voices." This comment shows that the listener did have some idea of what lesbians may sound like. The listener did not want, however, to make a determination. Selection for lesbian would be acknowledgment that "lesbian" is not an empty set. The default category, that is the unmarked one, is "heterosexual." The listener was willing "to determine for" heterosexuality. No listener complained the class, age, or educational level was hard to determine from 30 seconds of speech. Sexual preference was more troublesome. Why? One possible answer is that to pick the deviant choice in the category is to go against enforced invisibility. Another questionnaire comment reads, "I, basically, could not tell whether a speaker was lesbian/heterosexual. Jewish/non-Jewish. I just marked it if it *possibly* could be." I understand the antecedent of "it" to be "lesbian" and "Jewish." The comment is itself a comment of markedness. What possibly can be?

A Study of Women's Intonation

What *is* is often a larger package than what one is willing to imagine *can* be. I am interested in how women—lesbians and heterosexual women—talk with each other. In 1984 I conducted a small, exploratory, comparative study of lesbian and heterosexual conversation management styles, focusing on intonation.[1] As a framework I used Sally McConnell-Ginet's seven-point theoretical perspective on sex differences in intonation. She believes that "intonation . . . may well prove to be the chief linguistic expression in American English of (relative) femininity and masculinity" (1978: 542).[2] McConnell-Ginet's seven points tell me this: Speech melodies, learned early and unconsciously, include patterns that the speech community associates with women's speech, so these intonational patterns have social meaning and can be exploited; they are cues to speaker sex; the extreme values of their features can be targets in the displays femininity and masculinity; their use involves strategies of speech action for which an understanding of dominance and submission behaviors is relevant. McConnell-Ginet further suggests examining behavior of women and men "in similar . . . communicative situations" (546).

I set out to compare not women and men but lesbian women and heterosexual women. What is a similar communicative situation? Participants partly define a situation; they don't simply come into it. How conversants think of themselves and of each other, in gender terms, may be somewhat different for lesbians than for heterosexual women, on the whole. Identity, orientation, role. Would speech action strategies, as seen in intonation patterns, be different for lesbians speaking together than for heterosexual women?

I taped the conversations of two pairs of women, a lesbian pair, J and G, and a heterosexual pair, H and S. The women in each pair are acquaintances. I selected about 2½ minutes of the conversation of each couple for analysis. Oscillomink prints of four sample exchanges showed me contours in which I imposed an artificial stratigraphy; each level measured a depth of 60 Hz. I looked at direction of pitch, steepness of rises and falls, height of peaks, utterance position of peaks, low points, and glides. I looked at management of the conversations. I compared patterns within and between dyads.

An experiment conducted by Elizabeth Udall (1964) uncovered several dimensions of salient non-referential meanings for listeners in pitch contours, for instance, pleasant/unpleasant, submissive/authoritative, and strong feeling/weak feeling. These are associated by informants with certain contour traits: pleasant and submissive with terminal rises; strong feeling with wide pitch range and change in contour direction. Women, we know, are said to speak more pleasantly than men. And women are said to be submissive by nature or conditioning. Women's speech is said to be characterized by frequent use of sentence or utterance final rises. Also, women are supposedly more emotional, or emotionally expressive, than men. Women's speech is supposedly marked by pitch range greater than men's and by quick, steep glides. Ruth Brend claims (1971: 84–85) that women and men use and avoid certain contours. In American English, women use but men avoid: high pitch levels in their range, and wider range in general; terminals other than falling ones; incomplete or "question" rises that are other than slight upglides; and large glides on monosyllables.

In my examination of the intonation of the taped couples I assumed that women exhibit gender role behavior in relation to each other. I asked if the pattern of pitches—rises, falls, and glides—would tell me anything about whether lesbians speak differently than heterosexual women. I found: there is a great deal of individual variation; and there is also a suggestive pattern with J and G, the lesbians, toward one side of things and H and S, the heterosexuals, toward the other. Overall, H and S's behavior validates the claims of Brend better than J and G's behavior (See Table 11-3). H and S are fond of using their highest pitch levels; they use a greater intonation range than J and G do; S uses particularly steep glides.

The average height of peak pitch syllables for J and G is lower than for H and S. H and S have higher ranges than J and G, which is not important in itself: but they explore them more. They seem comfortable in the high pitch levels in their ranges. Also H and S use greater range overall. J has the lowest and narrowest pitch ranges. G also has a tight range. Of the four speakers, J has the levelest pitch and S has the most undulating. J's range amounts to something over 60 Hz; S's amounts to about 90 Hz. G and H both make use of substantial glides. The steepness of S's glides is truly impressive. On the whole, all four women have falling contours. If she is not asking a question and if she is finished speaking, each speaker avoids terminals that are other than falling. It interests me that in spite of

Table 11-3. Comparison of speaker contours.

Speaker	Contour Range		Contour Mean		Difference		Initiation	Termination	No. of Peaks	No. of Utterances	No. of Glides
	act.	aver.	act.	aver.	act.	aver.					
J	1.5 - 5.0	2.0 - 3.1	3.3	2.5	3.5	1.0	2.8	2.1	3.1	26	6.0
G	1.7-4.8	1.9-3.0	3.3	2.5	3.1	1.1	2.7	2.2	3.1	38	14
H	1.8-5.0	2.9-3.4	3.6	2.8	3.2	1.2	2.1	2.4	3.8	31	5
S	1.8-5.0	2.3-3.8	3.4	3.1	3.2	1.4	3.3	2.6	3.8	45	10

the overall evenness of her pattern, J's contours fall the farthest. It interests me that, while all four speakers will use "incompletive" rises to maintain conversational turn, J does this least and S does it the most. H is a close second.

H and S behave more "like women," in Brend's terms. I would like to know what women's use of intonation, however it manifests, is doing in various situations. McConnell-Ginet emphasizes the importance of speech strategy. Strategy depends on situational needs, communicative expectations in general, and internalized gender identity and role assumption. The patternings for the speech of women in my sample suggest not only that the individuals differ as to strategies but that some differences between the pairs may have to do with different communicative expectations about things like turn negotiations. Different expectations about turn-taking may reflect different role assumptions.

Concluding Remarks

The late lesbian writer Barbara Deming, my good friend for eighteen years, once (or twice, or maybe three times) told me this story. When she was a woman in her early thirties, visiting an old friend, her friend said, "I think of lesbians as something like brownies. I've never seen one and I don't quite believe in them." The friend had seen Barbara very often and for a long time and yet had never allowed herself to truly see her. My test for stereotyping suggests that even now, when lesbians in great numbers have been insisting for the past decade and a half on being as visible as possible, lesbian presence can be refused acknowledgment. This doesn't mean that listeners have no expectations about what lesbians do. Lesbians "may lower their voices." Lesbians and Jews do some of the same things. (But what are these things?)

In her proposals about women's intonation Brend uses women's stereotypical intonation as a starting point and asks how men deviate from it. She does not ask

how much women actually exhibit the behavior themselves. I find a range of behavior in my sample, although the heterosexual women speakers validate Brend's
claims better than the lesbians. McConnell-Ginet deals not only with behavior
but with purpose. She looks to the importance of strategy in a communicative situation. A hypothesis to test by a much larger comparative study than the one I
have done would be that lesbians and heterosexual conversation dyads use different intonation patterns in order to manage conversation differently.

NOTES

Reprinted from Sue Bremner, Noelle Caskey and Birch Moonwomon (eds). *Proceedings of
the First Berkeley Women and Language Conference.* Berkeley, CA: Berkeley Women and
Language Group, pp. 96–107.

1. Janice Gould, now in the English Department at U.C.B., conducted this experiment with me. We did not collaborate on the analysis.

2. a. Speech melodies (pitch and amplitude) are the primary cues of speaker sex in
oral communication.
   b. The speech community associates some patterns with women's speech.
   c. Certain global features in intonation correlate with sex, so in order to present
oneself as feminine or masculine, one shifts to the extreme values for these features.
   d. Our culture deems learned behaviors androgynous and so considers differences
within these behaviors to be biologically determined.
   e. Intonational habits are established early and without conscious consideration of
options.
   f. Female intonational habits may be strategies used by members of a non-dominant group to get and keep the attention of those who do not have to listen to
them.
   g. Women and men will typically use different patterns for equivalent situations because they have different strategies for speech action. (McConnell-Ginet 1978:
556–558)

REFERENCES

Bolinger, Dwight (1958). "A Theory of Pitch Accent." *Word* 14: 109.
———— (1969). "Around the Edge of Language: Intonation." In Dwight Bolinger (ed.), *Intonation.* Harmondsworth: Penguin.
Brend, Ruth (1972). "Male-Female Intonation Patterns in American English." *Proceedings
of the 7th International Congress of Phonetic Sciences,* pp.866–870. The Hague: Mouton.
Crystal, David (1969). "The Intonation System of English." In Dwight Bolinger (ed.), *In-
tonation.* Harmondsworth: Penguin.
Edelsky, Carole (1979). "Question Intonation and Sex Roles." *Language and Society* 8:
15–31.
Key, Mary Richie (1972). "Linguistic Behavior of Male and Female." *Linguistics* 88: 15–31.
Ladd, D. Robert (1980). *The Structure of Intonational Meaning,* ch. 5, "Paralanguage and
Gradience." Bloomington: Indiana University Press.
Lakoff, Robin (1975). *Language and Woman's Place.* New York: Harper & Row.

Moonwomon, Birch (1985). "Toward the Study of Lesbian Speech." In Sue Bremner, Noelle Caskey, and Birch Moonwomon (eds.), *Proceedings of the First Berkeley Women and Language Conference.* Berkeley, CA: Berkeley Women and Language Group, pp. 96–107.

McConnell-Ginet, Sally (1978). "Intonation in a Man's World." *Signs* 3: 541–559.

Pike, Kenneth (1945). "General Characteristics of Intonation. From the Intonation of American English." In Dwight Bolinger (ed.), *Intonation.* Harmondsworth: Penguin.

Trager, George (1964). "The Intonation System of American English." In Dwight Bolinger (ed.), *Intonation.* Harmondsworth: Penguin.

Udall, Elizabeth (1964). "Dimensions of Meaning in Intonation." In Dwight Bolinger (ed.), *Intonation.* Harmondsworth, Middlesex, England: Penguin Books.

Wells, Rulon (1945). "The Pitch Phonemes of English." *Language* 21: 27–39.

12

Que(e)rying Friendship

Discourses of Resistance and the Construction of Gendered Subjectivity

JENNIFER COATES AND MARY ELLEN JORDAN

Talk is central to female friendship, but the discursive practices of female friends have been largely ignored by linguists. This chapter analyzes the talk of young women to explore these discursive practices and to show how they construct and maintain particular versions of the feminine subject. We take the position that "discourses ... [are] ... practices that systematically form the objects of which they speak" (Foucault 1972: 49). We use as data the spontaneously occurring conversations of several overlapping groups of young women, some lesbian, some heterosexual, recorded in Melbourne, Australia, in 1994.

The young women's sense of their femininity is at times contradictory and precarious, and they draw on a range of discourses. What interests us is the way certain discourses seem to dominate, in particular a feminist discourse that enables these young women to establish a nonpassive sense of themselves as women living under heteropatriarchy. This discourse functions to bond the friends and overrides other potentially conflicting discourses arising from the noncongruent sexual orientation of these women. Linguistically, the women draw on collaborative strategies typical of all-female talk (see Coates 1996). Given that talk is social action, it is through their talk that these women maintain their close relationships with each other. In their talk, these women are both doing friendship and doing femininity.

Women, Friendship, and Sexual Orientation

It is now acknowledged that women are not one homogeneous group, and research focusing on women's linguistic usage has begun to be more sensitive to differences of age, class, and ethnicity among women speakers. But the variable of sexual orientation seems to have been largely ignored in work on women's talk (but see a number of papers presented at the Third Berkeley Women and Language Conference, available in Bucholtz, Liang, Sutton, and Hines 1995). We began thinking about this chapter because we wanted to explore the question Does sexual orientation matter? In other words, does being lesbian or nonlesbian make a difference to how women talk? In particular, we wanted to focus on women as friends and to ask the question, Is friendship possible across the potential divide of sexual orientation?

This question seemed important to us because it has been claimed that heterosexual women and lesbian women cannot truly be friends and that "bonding between heterosexual women acts to shore up heteropatriarchy" (Wilton 1992: 507). Wilton argues that heterosexual woman-bonding has been wrongly construed as subversive. She disagrees with Adrienne Rich's idea of a "lesbian continuum" (Rich, 1980), arguing instead for a clear divide between women in heterosexual relationships and women in lesbian relationships. Certainly, current theorizing about heterosexuality has made far clearer the ways in which "the gender scripts found in heterosexuality prescribe male dominance and female subordination" (Schact and Atchison 1993: 121). Those who, like Wilton, argue that female friendship is a conservative force see friendship as an emotional outlet for women who are frustrated in their marriages or relationships with men. In other words, by taking up the slack in male-female relationships, female friendship helps to prop up the institution of marriage and thus helps to perpetuate male domination of women.

We argue, with Rich (1980), however, that, far from being a relationship that perpetuates the status quo, friendship between women is potentially liberating. As Janice Raymond puts it: "[T]he empowering of female friendship can create the conditions for a new feminist politics in which the personal is most passionately political" (Raymond 1986: 9–10). In our view, this can be the case regardless of the sexual orientation of the women involved.

Certainly, the group of young women whose talk is the focus of this chapter have established a friendship that can be described as subversive; that is, their friendship promotes a sense of themselves as antipatriarchal women. The friends share a value system that has strong links with the feminist community centered on the Melbourne University Women's Department (a subsection of the student union). These women are political activists, especially around feminist issues but also around green and general left issues; they assume a norm of lesbianism rather than of heterosexuality (even though several of them are not lesbian); their social lives are largely women-only; they take responsibility for keeping up to date with contemporary debates on class, ethnicity and sexuality and their intersection with gender. Given the similarities in values shared by these women, our initial research questions began to look a little strange: There was no hint of a divide in terms of sexuality in the group, much less a pattern of friendship being possible only among women of the same sexual identification.

Thus our research changed its focus and became an exploration of *why* there is no division in this group, given that sexual orientation is an important and controversial aspect of a person's identity in so many facets of life. We have concluded that what is interesting about this group and the way it talks is that new subject positions are made available to members of the group through the subversive discourse it fosters and that the feminist identity it supports is superordinate to identities defined in terms of sexuality.

However, we recognize that this would not be the case for all women in all situations. We can imagine many instances where sexuality would be a divisive issue among women (perhaps most particularly in a group that was less homogenous, especially in terms of privilege—our group is overwhelmingly white, middle-class, and tertiary educated). And while sexuality could not be identified as an issue in this network of friends, it can be an issue in other areas of their lives, particularly in the context of the family or in the workplace. In fact, it seems that the privilege and the homogeneity that mark this group are the two factors that enable this subversive discourse to function. University is a time when people can live relatively independent of the social structures that confine us to a greater extent when we move more in the worlds of work and family. The social structures that regulate these domains rely on difference, particularly differences in sexuality. The fact that this group of women is in a position to ignore such structures shows the extent to which sexual identity is constructed by patriarchal discourses. In exploring their discourse and the subject positions it makes available to these women, we see that the patriarchal constructions of subjectivity, which include sexuality as a pivotal factor, can be subverted.

How friendship is viewed by individual women, and how it is "done" in our lives, depends very much on the discourses available to us. "Discourses do not just reflect or represent social entities and relations, they construct or 'constitute' them; different discourses constitute key entities [such as friendship] . . . in different ways, and position people in different ways as social subjects" (Fairclough 1992: 3–4). The women in this group resist patriarchal discourses, and although they must operate under dominant discourses for much of their lives, one of the spaces in which a feminist discourse can be invoked is in their shared conversation as friends. Consequently, the two main (and conflicting) discourses that concern us in this chapter are a patriarchal, or androcentric, discourse and a more radical or feminist discourse. We want to focus in particular on this second discourse, to try to describe it accurately and to ask where it comes from.

Our data in this chapter comes from a series of recordings made by one of the coauthors (MEJ) of conversations among members of a friendship group to which she belongs. Conversations involved groups of two, three, or four speakers and covered all permutations: lesbian-lesbian, straight-straight, and mixed. Our main research focus is on how the subversive antipatriarchal discourse characteristic of these friends operates in their conversations and how it intersects with other, more mainstream discourse. We also investigate the linguistic characteristics of this discourse, since in our view *how* we talk is as important as *what* we say in the construction of subjectivity.

A Discourse of Resistance

So how does the discourse evolved by this group of friends operate in their everyday lives? As we see it, the existence of such a discourse is not a trivial matter. Given that discourses are in competition and that they provide different ways of understanding the world, then language is inevitably a site of political struggle. As Chris Weedon puts it: "The site of this battle for power is the subjectivity of the individual" (Weedon 1987: 41). By examining the discursive practices of this group of women friends, we hope to illuminate the workings of this "battle for power". In their conversations, these young women draw on a discourse that we describe as subversive and antipatriarchal. This discourse makes available to members of the friendship network powerful and resistant subject positions.

Initially, we focus on one brief extract from a conversation among three of these friends (one lesbian, two straight) to demonstrate what this discourse is like. The full extract can be found in the Appendix, p. 226. At the point in conversation from which this extract is taken, A tells her two friends that the mother of a friend of theirs is proposing to marry the man she has been having an affair with for a month.

```
-------------------------------------------------------------
A: oh I got a postcard from Dave today/ and apparently Ros
B:
-------------------------------------------------------------
A: is MARrying the |guy/
B:                 |oh my god WHAT?
-------------------------------------------------------------
```

We focus here on three aspects of the discourse: its critical view of heterosexual marriage, its critical view of the particular man talked about and, by implication, men in general, and its positioning of heterosexual sex as "Other."

The group's main reaction to A's news is horror, horror that is expressed in a discourse that is explicitly skeptical about marriage. They are horrified that an apparently sane woman who they like and respect could contemplate marriage. This reaction is expressed through a series of utterances that echo B's initial response *oh my god what?*:

oh my god TWO WEEKS (B, 3–4)

oh my god that is sick (B, 6)

that's aww- (C, 7)

that is awful (C, 13)

that is terrible (B, 13)

that is horrible (B, 14)

that is foul (B, 14)

that is really foul (B, 15)

I just thought "oh god how shit" (A, 22)

it's awful horrible horrible (C, 22–23)

oh yuk that's gross (B, 23)

These utterances function as a commentary on the main text. The main text consists of two main strands: a factual one involving further details, for example, *this is the guy that just moved in* (C, 3-4) and clarification, for example, *it was just a postcard and it just said. . . .* (A, 8), and a more explicitly antimarriage strand: *but I was like ma- ma- the M-word "marry"* (A, 12–13).

This latter strand is developed after some discussion of the two main protagonists, who are summed up as *a dickhead* (the man) and *a groover* (the woman). This analysis of the two leads to the logical conclusion *she doesn't want to be living with a dickhead.* But since the evidence of Dave's postcard is that that is precisely what the woman is choosing to do, the friends are left asking the question *why would you marry someone after a month?* This question is phrased so that it presupposes that no one in their right mind would marry anyone after just a month, even if the two people were OK and marriage weren't a questionable institution. A sums up this strand of their discussion with her utterance: *so you know fling, affair, relationship, these things I can deal with, marriage I can't* (69–70).

What we see accomplished in this extract is an overturning of the hegemonic discourse that represents marriage as the be-all-and-end-all of women's lives. These young women talk about marriage in negative terms—*the M-word*—and place it as one of a set of alternatives—fling, affair, relationship, marriage—of which marriage can be construed in many cases as the least good option. A's opening utterance, with its heavy stress on the word *marrying*, constructs marriage as the marked—and undesirable—option from the very beginning of the discussion. B's remark *I thought at least she could have come to her senses after a few weeks. . . .* (lines 23–25) assumes that the state the woman is in is one where she has lost control, and implies that to get married would be to continue to take leave of your senses. This antimarriage discourse stems in part from the specific case being discussed, where the shortness of the relationship and the man himself are both significant factors. But this raises another aspect of the discourse: the male-as-norm value intrinsic to hegemonic discourses is completely undermined. Since "man" is no longer at the center and may easily incur a negative value, then any talk of the union of a woman and a man can be seen as problematic rather than inherently beneficial for the woman involved. In this feminist discourse, marriage is a questionable rather than a necessary or desirable facet of life.

The construction of the male protagonist in negative terms rests partly on the group's existing slight knowledge of the man in question, combined with a feminist ideology that subverts male-as-norm, reversing the hegemonic heteropatriarchal order. Most important, however, it rests on the women's wider political values and is an important indication of the nature of this discourse. They see him as racist, oppressively capitalist and privileged, and offensively ignorant about issues of gender and sexuality. He seems to embody the dominant ideology, which they position themselves in opposition to, and consequently they assess Dave's view of the man as *all right* as *false consciousness* and label him unequivocally as *a dickhead.* Later (lines 60ff) the three make a series of moves that in effect works to justify this label. Again, there is a series of parallel utterances that starts reasonably innocuously (though all references to mobile phones are suspect, given B's earlier joke) but soon becomes completely negative:

the man has a mobile phone (A, 60-61)

he's an architect (B, 61)

he's got a spa in his office on the roof of his building (B, 61–62)

he's revolting, he's really foul (B, 62)

and he reckons that the main problem with Aborigines is that they've got a victim mentality (B, 63–64)

The climax of their negative evaluation of the man is achieved in an (incomplete) sequence of highly cohesive questions initiated by B:

would you want to marry this man? (B)

would you want to be in the same room as this man? (B)

would you want to bloody use this man's mobile phone? (A)

would you want to bloody use this ma- (C) [interrupted by A]

The final section of the discussion is devoted to an analysis of the man's behavior in driving to Bondi to buy strudels. This seemingly innocuous act is evaluated as "ridiculous" and as totally over the top. Discussion of this particular man all the time draws on an ideology where aspects of patriarchy and capitalism are constantly critiqued: This means that even superficially neutral statements like *he's an architect* have negative connotations, as the picture built up of this man epitomizes much of what they are opposed to—the status and power accorded to privileged white men. The friends are able so easily to put themselves in the powerful position of labeling this man as "foul" because they draw on their shared feminist worldview and on their habitual antipatriarchal discourse.

In order to try to understand the couple (who are constructed as deviant in the subversive discourse of the group), A suggests that the reason must be sex, or rather she says that a friend of theirs, Clare Keaney, thinks the reason is sex: *Clare Keaney says it must be really good sex* (50).

The subject of sex has already come up earlier in discussion, at the end of the initial section when they are voicing their horror at Dave's news, after B makes her remark about the woman "coming to her senses":

```
--------------------------------------------------------------
B: I thought at least she could have come to her senses after a few
--------------------------------------------------------------
A:                                  =mhm=
B: weeks of whatever they do together=     =I hate to think=
C:                                    <LAUGHING> =Jody!=
--------------------------------------------------------------
A: =probably heterosexual for one thing/
--------------------------------------------------------------
```

This is an interesting passage. B's *whatever they do together* is initially received with only a minimal response from A; at this point the idea of the woman coming to her senses is the focal point. But B chooses to refocus attention on the idea of "whatever they do together" by adding *I hate to think*. This sexualizes the reference, provoking C into a laughing protest and A into the comment *it's probably hetero-sexual*. This latter utterance is on the face of it tautologous: All three speakers know that a man and a woman are involved, and so if B's remark about "whatever they do together" is understood sexually, it can only refer to heterosexual sex. In other words, this utterance of A's breaks the Gricean maxim of quantity. But as competent speakers, the three young women here recognize this remark as an in-joke. They make the relevant conversational inferences, drawing on their dis-course, which challenges the heteropatriarchal norms, to understand that A is foregrounding the heterosexual aspect of this couple's sexual relationship in a de-liberate and ironic inversion of the normal pattern, where lesbian or gay sex is viewed as marked and thus worthy of mention. Her comment also implies "het-erosexual and therefore (probably) disgusting," again in an ironic parody of hege-monic discourses around homosexual practices.

A's joke is picked up with relish by the other two speakers. B launches into a series of utterances that talk about the man's mobile phone, with heavy sexual in-nuendo. C cleverly responds to both A and B. Her utterance *well we KNOW what they do then DON'T we* can be read as a mock-patronizing reference to the (het-erosexual) act of sexual penetration. At the same time, she cohesively ties in B's reference to mobile phones by saying, in effect, that what we imagine them doing involves a mobile phone in some unspeakable way. This reading is confirmed by A's subsequent teasing remark to C: *you're the techno-sex guru Clare/ you can hardly talk/*, in which the reference to "techno-sex" can be understood only if C's utter-ance is interpreted as having some meaning that can be explained in terms of techno-sex.

The mobile phone joke recurs throughout the extract, with the young women constantly sending up the normative discourse of Romantic Love. The following example comes at line 57ff:

```
-------------------------------------------------------------------
A: I think it might be one of those things where the man is incredibly
   charming and sweet/ and sweeps the woman off her feet/ and marries
   her/ and puts her signature onto all of his tax dodges/ <LAUGHTER> I
   mean the man has a mobile phone/ so one thing leads to another [...]
-------------------------------------------------------------------
B: would you want to marry this man?  would you want to be in
C:                                     no/
-------------------------------------------------------------------
A:                              =would you want to bloody .
B: the same room as this man?=
C:                              =no/
-------------------------------------------------------------------
A: |USE THIS MAN'S MOBILE PHONE? <LAUGHS>
B: <LAUGHS---------------------------->
C: |yeah/ <LAUGHS---------------------->
-------------------------------------------------------------------
```

During the brief digression in lines 29–38, where A and C get involved in a jok-ing sequence about C and computers and sex, B teases them with these words: *you heterosexual girls/ I don't know/ you can't keep your mind off it/* to which A accedes with *absolutely*. This joke works only when understood as heavily ironic: B's utter-ance draws on the dominant ideology where sex (for men in particular) can be construed as an overwhelming force; it also inverts the homophobic discourse that constructs gay and lesbian identity entirely in sexual terms. The use of the word *girls* marks the utterance as nonserious, as for these feminists (as for most feminists) the use of the word *girl* to refer to adult, sexually mature women is politically unacceptable. In other words, B's joking taunt here contributes to the overall subversion of the normal patterns, with heterosexual being positioned as other.

Conflicting Discourses

While the previous section has demonstrated the alternative discourse used by these women friends to position themselves as powerful feminist subjects in relation to their world, we are certainly not claiming that they do not use other discourses. We are certain that, like other young women in contemporary Australia, they are positioned as feminine subjects of various—sometimes incompatible— kinds. However, it is difficult to locate more mainstream subjectivities in our data except when invoked as a source of humor. As we saw in the previous section, they joke among themselves continually, and their jokes rely on their awareness of other, more mainstream discourses, for example, a discourse we could label "Romantic Love" and a dominant discourse of heterosociality and marriage. The following extract, most of it spoken in a heavily ironic tone, demonstrates this:

```
[C is going to a party given by a single male friend]
---------------------------------------------------------------------
A: what time are you going to John's?
B:                              eight o'clock/ <MOCK TENSION>
C:                        um-              when I've decided
---------------------------------------------------------------------
A:            oh I understand/
B:                    we- we've been trying on our outfits/
C: what to wear/                      it's taken an hour so far/
---------------------------------------------------------------------
```

The talk here is a framed in a discourse where worrying about one's appearance and spending hours trying on different clothes before going out constitute a normative femininity. But these friends can adopt such a discourse only ironically, as a joke. The same ironic use of a conflicting discourse was shown in B's joke *you heterosexual girls/ I don't know/ can't keep your minds off it/*, discussed in the preceding section, where the humor works because the words are understood to be part of another discourse in which sexuality is a primary aspect of subjectivity.

Another discourse that emerges in the talk of these friends, and that we think needs to be viewed as separate from the subversive, antipatriarchal discourse discussed in the preceding section, is a discourse that constructs them all as competent and confident intellectual women. It seems to us that, though less overtly subversive, this discourse is a very powerful item in the friends' armory of discursive practices. It positions them as powerful, even formidable, feminine subjects, and unlike the resistant feminist discourse we've discussed, it takes as given that women are intellectually active and successful, both on their own terms and in traditional academic structures. It is constructed partly through lexicon: phrases like *techno-sex guru* and *false consciousness* and the vocabulary of poststructuralism (*sign, signifier*, and *rubric*) occur throughout the data, side by side with more vernacular terms like *dickhead* and *shit*. It is also constructed through the management of the conversational floor, since this group of friends demonstrates an impressive ability to move between an adversarial, intellectual debating style and a collaborative, sisterly, all-in-together style. Many of the friends' utterances draw on this shared intellectual world, a world where familiarity with feminist theory, psychoanalytic theory, and postmodernism, for example, is taken for granted. This shared knowledge of ideas and theories is often discussed seriously but is also used as a frequent source of humor, as the following extract illustrates:

```
---------------------------------------------------------------------
A: it's scary with the fridge off/
B:                           mhm/ it is/
C:                                   it is/ I know/ you turned it
---------------------------------------------------------------------
A:                           mhm/ it's not just the vibe
B:          yeah/ |it's quiet for once/
C: off and I went       |woooow!/
---------------------------------------------------------------------
A: in the |house/                  fridge as lack/ <LAUGHS>
B:                                              <LAUGHS>
C:       |it is really like a . lack/            <LAUGHS>
---------------------------------------------------------------------
A: if we get a new fridge that's quiet it'll just be really weird/
---------------------------------------------------------------------
A:                         <LAUGHS----------->
B:                         <LAUGHS--------->
C: no/ the lack will become the norm/ <LAUGHS>
---------------------------------------------------------------------
```

The following example is similar to the previous extract in its assumption of theoretical knowledge, but in contrast it is a relatively serious discussion. The discussion begins with A's joking question *how can I put "rubric" into this sentence?* but is focused by B's information-seeking question *what does "rubric" mean?*

```
---------------------------------------------------------------------
A: like as a signifier or as a sign or as a title=      =a heading
C:                                     =a heading=
---------------------------------------------------------------------
A: yeah/
B:     but what's the difference between that and say under the
C:
---------------------------------------------------------------------
A:         under the name of/ sort of/ you do it all in the name of-
B: you know-
C:                                        under   the   front=
---------------------------------------------------------------------
A: =like a front/ yeah/ like it stands for lots of things=   =but you
B:
C:                                      =yeah=
---------------------------------------------------------------------
A: call it politics=
B:             =and you could call any of those things politics?
C:
---------------------------------------------------------------------
A: under the rubric of door/ <LAUGH> no/ under the-
B:
C:                 no/
---------------------------------------------------------------------
A:                     yeah/ like classifier/
B:                                         uh-huh/
C: classifier or something/
---------------------------------------------------------------------
```

In this extract the speakers are working together to define a term that none of them is certain about. They all make contributions, including B, despite the fact that she asked the question initially. In suggesting various words that might help them understand the term, there is an assumed familiarity with the ideas being explored, if not with the precise words that are used, so that the correct alternative will be recognized when it is spoken. Both the style of speaking collaboratively (and humorously) and the lexicon used by the speakers demonstrate how comfortable they are with this kind of intellectual discussion.

Conflicting discourses can construct very different subjectivities. These differences can be irreconcilable, for example, as patriarchal and feminist ideologies conflict within an individual. However, they can also enhance each other, as the academic discourse just discussed strengthens and informs the resistant feminist discourse that dominates when these women are talking together.

Conversational Style

Little attention has been paid to the *how* of discursive practice (but see Coates 1994). Discourses are not randomly constructed; the linguistic practices in which particular discourses are embedded are an essential aspect of their formative power. The resistant discourse that is the focus of this chapter has particular lexical, syntactic, and floor-constructional patterns that are an intrinsic part of it. They are linguistic strategies that have been identified as characteristic of women friends (Coates 1996) and include particular uses of epistemic modality, interrogative structures, and repetition. While there isn't space to fully explore these here, we look very briefly at floor construction.

For many kinds of talk, the floor, that is, the conversational space available to speakers, is handled on a one-at-a-time basis. This is known as a single or singly developed floor (Edelsky 1981). In contrast, in certain contexts, particularly where speakers know each other well and want to mark connectedness rather than separateness, conversational participants use a collaborative floor. Collaborative floors, in Edelsky's account, typically involve shorter turns than single floors, much more overlapping speech, more repetition, and more joking and teasing. But this summary implies that the collaborative floor simply involves more or less of something that is regularly found in a single floor. In fact, the collaborative floor is radically different from the singly developed floor, since it is qualitatively as well as quantitatively different from one-at-a-time turn-taking. This is precisely because the collaborative floor is a shared space, and therefore what is said is construed as being the voice of the group rather than of the individual. In other words, the collaborative floor in itself can be a subversive instrument, since it challenges the liberal-humanist idea of the supremacy of the individual.

The resistant feminist discourse of the group of women friends that is the subject of this chapter is typically associated with a collaborative floor. To illustrate how a collaborative floor works, we give examples of two collaborative strategies, jointly constructed utterances and overlapping speech. These are both classic components of a collaborative floor.

The first example of a jointly constructed utterance comes from a conversation between two of the friends (both lesbian) about a crush one of them had had on someone in Student Council.

```
------------------------------------------------------------------------
A: I decided to get drunk=
B:                         =and seduce her/
------------------------------------------------------------------------
```

The following, more complex example comes from the Marriage text:

[topic = buying strudels in Bondi]
```
------------------------------------------------------------------------
B: like you wouldn't drive from Lane Cove to Bondi to buy a strudel/
------------------------------------------------------------------------
A:             |it'd be like driving from-
B: like you know |even if you were trying to impress her kids like=
------------------------------------------------------------------------
A: =yeah=                                          =it's ridiculous/
C:        =Melton to North Melbourne/ <LAUGH> no=
------------------------------------------------------------------------
```

What is striking about both these examples is that linguistic structures are shared between speakers: All participants share in the construction of talk in the strong sense that they don't function as individual speakers; the group takes priority over the individual. In the first example, B completes A's utterance. In the second example, A's incomplete utterance *it'd be like driving from-* is completed by C: *Melton to North Melbourne*, at the same time as B's utterance *even if you were trying to impress her kids like* is acknowledged by A: *yeah*. This fragment is rounded off with C and B collaborating in summarizing their position: C says *no*, and B says *it's ridiculous*.

This second example also illustrates the way in which speakers overlap in talk, that is, more than one voice may contribute to talk at the same time. This kind of overlapping speech is not seen as competitive, as a way of grabbing a turn, because the various contributions to talk are on the same theme. Here are some more examples:

[topic = anonymity on tape]
```
------------------------------------------------------------------------
A:        |we could speak in code and that would really PISS Mary Ellen
B: well |I know/ I could disguise    .           the name of the person
------------------------------------------------------------------------
A: off/
B: who it is/
------------------------------------------------------------------------
```

[topic = marriage]
```
------------------------------------------------------------------------
B: what did we have? vanilla slices- what are they called/ oh strudels=
------------------------------------------------------------------------
A: =oh yeah/ and ranted on about how it was |the best strudel shop/
B:                                           |how wonderful they were/
------------------------------------------------------------------------
```

[topic - marriage]
```
------------------------------------------------------------------------
A: I mean the man has a mobile phone so- |one thing leads to another/
B:                                        |he's an architect/
------------------------------------------------------------------------
```

[topic = marriage]
```
------------------------------------------------------------------------
A: Sue is a groover/ she doesn't want |to be living with a dickhead/
B:                                     |yeah she's a filthy groover/
------------------------------------------------------------------------
```

This has been a necessarily brief overview of the conversational style associated with the resistant discourse that is the subject of this chapter. We have suggested that the way these women interact is an important component in the constitution of their identity. This way of talking can be as subversive as the ideology it embodies: Combined with a feminist discourse in the talk of these women, it works to undermine the traditional liberal-humanist subject and promotes the group rather than the individual, collaboration rather than competition.

Conclusions

Good sociolinguists are urged to "think practically and look locally" in work dealing with language and gender (Eckert and McConnell-Ginet 1992). This is what we have tried to do in this chapter by grounding our theorizing in the everyday social practices of a particular local group. While this may limit the generalizability of our claims, it strengthens our understanding of the intersection of language, gender, sexuality, and power in this particular social context at this particular moment in time. By analyzing the discursive practices of a group of young women friends in Melbourne in 1994, we have aimed to clarify the ways in which discourses construct and maintain subjectivity. In particular, we have aimed to demonstrate how, through communities of friendship, women speakers create and sustain resistant antipatriarchal discourses that constitute them, whatever their sexual orientation, as powerful feminine subjects.

MELBOURNE DATA

```
     ----------------------------------------------------------------
     A: oh I got a postcard from Dave today/ and apparently Ros
     B:
     C:
     ----------------------------------------------------------------
     A: is MARrying the gu|y/                have you heard about
  2  B:                    |oh my god WHAT?
     C:
     ----------------------------------------------------------------
     A: this?  Dave and Miriam's mum/
     B:                                             oh my god
     C:     no/                        yeah/ this is the guy
     ----------------------------------------------------------------
     A:                       yeah/                        oh a
  4  B: TWO WEEKS/             like how long's it been?
     C: that just moved in an-
     ----------------------------------------------------------------
     A: month may- er when were |you in Sydney?
     B:                         |a month/ must have been/ . oh
     C:
     ----------------------------------------------------------------
     A:                       I know/
  6  B: my god this is sick/        I better write a commiserations
     C:
     ----------------------------------------------------------------
     A:      |th a t's  wh a t    I was thinking/
     B: card |to Miriam/                    what was Dave
     C:               that's aww-
     ----------------------------------------------------------------
     A:                     well it was just a postcard/ and it just
  8  B: saying about it?
     C:
     ----------------------------------------------------------------
     A: said "hi/ how are things in Melbourne/ you've probably
     B:
     C:
     ----------------------------------------------------------------
     A: heard m- mum's marrying Steven/ and um yeah I'm going
 10  B:
     C:                                    <LAUGHS>
     ----------------------------------------------------------------
     A: overseas on the 26th of December/ love Dave"/      it's
     B:
     C:                                         <LAUGHS>
     ----------------------------------------------------------------
     A: like very informative Dave/ . um but I was like ma- ma-
 12  B:
     C:
     ----------------------------------------------------------------
     A: the M-word 'ma-arry'/              ((ma- a-
     B:                                    that is terrible/
     C:                   that is awful/
     ----------------------------------------------------------------
```

```
      ----------------------------------------------------------------
   A: -arriage/))                       mhm/
14 B:             that is horrible/    that is foul/ that is
   C:
      ----------------------------------------------------------------
   A:
   B: really foul/ like you really wouldn't want to marry
   C:                          %I'll just put the oven on%
      ----------------------------------------------------------------
   A:      but I can't write back with a postcard/ Ros will
16 B: him/                                          no you
   C: <LAUGH> darlings/
      ----------------------------------------------------------------
   A: probably read it and say "oh my gahhdd"/ so I- I'm gonna
   B: can't/
   C:                                                    no/
      ----------------------------------------------------------------
   A: |have to enclose something in an envelope/           mhm/
18 B:         ((you'll have to))
   C: |you'll have to write it-    a postcard in an envelope/
      ----------------------------------------------------------------
   A: you can't ((xxxx))
   B:
   C:      you can't light the oven with tea can you? <LAUGHS---
      ----------------------------------------------------------------
   A: oh it has been known/ <LAUGH> you light the teabag and
20 B:
   C: -------------------------------------------------------
      ----------------------------------------------------------------
   A: sort of wave it in the general direction-       yeah I
   B:
   C: -----------------> in the oven/ <LAUGHS--->
      ----------------------------------------------------------------
   A: just thought "oh god/ how shit"/
22 B:
   C:                   mhm/         it's awful/ horrible/
      ----------------------------------------------------------------
   A:
   B:          oh yuk that's gross/ I thought at least she
   C: horrible/ .
      ----------------------------------------------------------------
   A:
24 B: could have come to her senses after a few weeks of
   C:
      ----------------------------------------------------------------
   A:                          =mhm=
   B: whatever they do together=   =I hate to think=
   C:                          <LAUGHING>    =Jody!=
      ----------------------------------------------------------------
   A: =probably heterosexual for one thing/
26 B:                                       he's got a bloody
   C:
      ----------------------------------------------------------------
   A:              mhm/
   B: mobile phone/  he wears it around his waist/
   C:              <LAUGH> well we KNOW what they do then DON'T
      ----------------------------------------------------------------
```

```
       ------------------------------------------------------------------
       A:                                                     you're the
28     B:      in his little pocket/ . little leather pouch for his
       C: we?/
       ------------------------------------------------------------------
       A: techno-sex guru Clare/ you can hardly talk/  <LAUGHS----->
       B: mobile phone/                                WHAT!? <LAUGHS>
       C: <LAUGHS------------------------------------------------------>
       ------------------------------------------------------------------
       A:                                                     <LAUGHS>
30     B: um this side of Clare hasn't come out yet/ <LAUGHS>
       C:                                                   <LAUGHS>
       ------------------------------------------------------------------
       A: cyber|sex/         there's nothing virtual about it let
       B:      |virtual sex?
       C:                    yeah/ <LAUGHS> no/
       ------------------------------------------------------------------
       A: me tell you/ <LAUGHS>
32     B:            <LAUGHS> would you like to explain or..?
       C:            <LAUGHS HYSTERICALLY-----------------> we're
       ------------------------------------------------------------------
       A:                    I can't even remember/ . where that came
       B:            oh/
       C: making it up/
       ------------------------------------------------------------------
       A: from/ Clare was coming over to use the computer/ and I
34     B:
       C:
       ------------------------------------------------------------------
       A: must have said "oh yeah USE the computer"/
       B:
       C:                                             that's right/
       ------------------------------------------------------------------
       A:                              sex on the computer/
36     B:
       C: sex on the computer/ that was it/
       ------------------------------------------------------------------
       A: something about on the computer/   oh I don't know what
       B:
       C:                        ((oh well xxxxxxxxxxxxx
       ------------------------------------------------------------------
       A: brought sex into it/
38     B:                 you heterosexual girls/ I don't
       C: xxxxxxxxxxxxxxxx))
       ------------------------------------------------------------------
       A:                                 absolutely/ . er um
       B: know/ you can't keep your mind off it/
       C:                                     <LAUGH>
       ------------------------------------------------------------------
       A: yeah so I thought that was a bit of a worry/
40     B:                                         yeah it's
       C:
       ------------------------------------------------------------------
       A:       and I sort of thought I wonder if there's a cause
       B: gross/
       C:
       ------------------------------------------------------------------
```

228

```
      ------------------------------------------------------------
      A: and effect relationship between Dave's plans for going
42    B:
      C:
      ------------------------------------------------------------
      A: overseas taking place and his mum marrying Steven/
      B:                                          oh I don't
      C:
      ------------------------------------------------------------
      A:                                                  yeah/
44    B: think so/ like he seemed to think he was alright/
      C:
      ------------------------------------------------------------
      A: but that was sort of funny/
      B:         ((some sort of)) false consciousness/
      C:                                          yes I was
      ------------------------------------------------------------
      A:                              the man IS a dickhead even
46    B:                                          yeah/
      C: gonna say/ he's got it wrong/
      ------------------------------------------------------------
      A: if you don't think so/ . and Ros is a groover/ she
      B:                         yeah/
      C:
      ------------------------------------------------------------
      A: doesn't want to be living with a dickhead/
48    B:              yeah/ she's a filthy groover/ no she
      C:
      ------------------------------------------------------------
      A:
      B: certainly doesn't=
      C:              =why would you marry someone after a
      ------------------------------------------------------------
      A:                              Clare Keaney says it must be
50    B:
      C: month? I mean really sss-
      ------------------------------------------------------------
      A: really good sex/ but I was thinking about that/     I
      B:
      C:                        but you wouldn't MARRY someone
      ------------------------------------------------------------
      A: know/
52    B:               eeeerrrgh!
      C: for good sex/            how does Clare Keaney know?
      ------------------------------------------------------------
      A:         bacause Jody said Ros was looking . radiant/
      B:
      C: about Dave/ <LAUGHING>
      ------------------------------------------------------------
      A:      um
54    B: mhm/  I mean I think it is/ like it was a fairly sexual
      C:
      ------------------------------------------------------------
      A:                         mhm/
      B: kind of relationship/  you could TELL/ they were kind of
      C:
      ------------------------------------------------------------
```

```
    -----------------------------------------------------------------
    A:                              I'm a bit worried about it/
 56 B: all over each other/ really/
    C:
    -----------------------------------------------------------------
    A: I think it might be one of those things where the man is
    B:
    C:
    -----------------------------------------------------------------
    A: incredibly charming and sweet/ and sweeps the woman off her
 58 B:
    C:
    -----------------------------------------------------------------
    A: feet/ and marries her/ and   . puts her signature onto all
    B:
    C:
    -----------------------------------------------------------------
    A: of his tax dodges/         I mean the man has a mobile phone so-
 60 B:
    C:                 <LAUGHS>                                  <LAUGHS-
    -----------------------------------------------------------------
    A: |one thing leads to another/
    B: |he's an architect/ he's got a spa in his office/ on the roof
    C: ----->
    -----------------------------------------------------------------
    A:
 62 B: of his building/        he's revolting/ he's really foul/
    C:              wwwwwwhat?
    -----------------------------------------------------------------
    A:                       mhm/
    B:                       and he reckons that the main problem
    C: <COUGHS> that's awful/
    -----------------------------------------------------------------
    A:
 64 B:  with Aborigines is they've got a victim mentality/
    C:
    -----------------------------------------------------------------
    A:                                   <LOW LAUGH>
    B: I mean you know/     would you want to marry this man?
    C:                 oh yeah/                          no/
    -----------------------------------------------------------------
    A:                                           =would you want
 66 B: would you want to be in the same room as this man?=
    C:                                           =no/
    -----------------------------------------------------------------
    A: to bloody . |USE THIS MAN'S MOBILE PHONE? <LAUGHS>
    B:             <LAUGHS---------------------------->
    C:             |yeah/ <LAUGHS----------------------> would you want
    -----------------------------------------------------------------
    A:                               mhm/
 68 B:    to bloody use . |and he's fat and ugly and . |foul/
    C:                    |use this ma-                 |oh yuk/
    -----------------------------------------------------------------
    A:                            so you know  . fling/  .       affair/
    B: he's revolting/ . picky/ .     pedantic/    .    arrogant/
    C:
    -----------------------------------------------------------------
    A: relationship/ these things I can deal with/ marriage I can't/
 70 B:
    C:
    -----------------------------------------------------------------
```

```
    ------------------------------------------------------------
    A:
    B: he's got a yacht/ . he goes yachting/
    C:
    ------------------------------------------------------------
    A:                              maybe it's just-
 72 B: . on the harbour/ .
    C:                         well maybe she's just got a
    ------------------------------------------------------------
    A:          yeah/
    B:
    C: good deal/ .   well maybe she just wants to screw him
    ------------------------------------------------------------
    A:               =so to speak/
 74 B:                       he goes all the way to Bondi
    C: for his money=
    ------------------------------------------------------------
    A:
    B: to buy- um what did we have? vanilla slices/ what are
    C:
    ------------------------------------------------------------
    A:                         oh yeah/ and ranted on about |how
 76 B: they called? oh strudels/                            |how
    C:
    ------------------------------------------------------------
    A: it was the best strudel shop/
    B: wonderful they were/ and that was the only strudel shop/
    C:
    ------------------------------------------------------------
    A:
 78 B: and           you know like you wouldn't drive
    C:     you'd drive/
    ------------------------------------------------------------
    A:
    B: from Palm Cove to Bondi to buy a strudel/ like you know/
    C:
    ------------------------------------------------------------
    A: ((it'd be like driving from-))               yeah/
 80 B: even if you were trying to impress her kids like/
    C:
    ------------------------------------------------------------
    A:
    B:                                   it's ridiculous/
    C: Melton to North Melbourne/ <LAUGH> no/
    ------------------------------------------------------------
    A:                     it's sort of like Camberwell to
 82 B: it's extraordinary/
    C:
    ------------------------------------------------------------
    A: Williamstown really/      for a strudel/
    B:                     yep/             I don't know/ call
    C:
    ------------------------------------------------------------
    A:
 84 B: me crazy <FUNNY VOICE>_
    C: yeah/ think about it/ shit/ it's not quite that far/
    ------------------------------------------------------------
    A:
    B: it would be/ Palm Cove's twenty minutes from the city/
    C:
    ------------------------------------------------------------
```

```
        ----------------------------------------------------------------
     A: and Bondi's not-
86   B: ((twenty-five minutes)) Bondi- well depending on what time of
     C:
        ----------------------------------------------------------------
     A:
     B: day/ well we got there at seven so- mhm/ I don't know what time
     C:
        ----------------------------------------------------------------
     A:
88   B: he did it but       probably peak hour/
     C:              god/                      from five to seven
        ----------------------------------------------------------------
     A:                                     I hope it was good
     B:
     C: ah he was just picking up the strudel/
        ----------------------------------------------------------------
     A: strudel/ . was it good strudel?
90   B:                   it was nice/ you know . strudel/
     C:
        ----------------------------------------------------------------
     A:                     oh god it's a worry/
     B: like/ strudel/
     C:                            hey um should I put
        ----------------------------------------------------------------
     A:                           yeah/
92   B:
     C: the surprises in the oven?
        ----------------------------------------------------------------
```

REFERENCES

Bucholtz, Mary, Anita Liang, Laurel Sutton, and Caitlin Hines (1995). *Cultural Performances: Proceedings of the 1994 Berkeley Women and Language Conference.* Berkeley, CA: Berkeley Women and Language Group.

Coates, Jennifer (1994). "Gender, Discourse, and Subjectivity: The Talk of Teenage Girls." In Mary Bucholtz, Anita Liang, Laurel Sutton, and Caitlin Hines (eds.), *Cultural Performances: Proceedings of the 1994 Berkeley Women and Language Conference.* Berkeley, CA: Berkeley Women and Language Group.

Coates, Jennifer (1996). *Women Talk — Conversation between Women Friends.* Oxford: Basil Blackwell.

Eckert, Penelope, and Sally McConnell-Ginet (1992). "Think Practically and Look Locally: Language and Gender as Community-Based Practice." *Annual Review of Anthropology* 21: 461–490.

Edelsky, Carole (1981). "Who's Got the Floor?" *Language in Society* 10, no. 3: 383–421.

Fairclough, Norman (1992). *Discourse and Social Change.* Cambridge: Polity Press.

Foucault, Michel (1972). *The Archaeology of Knowledge and the Discourse on Language.* New York: Pantheon.

Raymond, J. (1986). *A Passion for Friends.* London: Women's Press.

Rich, Adrienne (1980). "It Is the Lesbian in Us . . . ." In A. Rich, *On Lies, Secrets and Silence.* London: Virago, pp. 199–201.

Schact, S. P., and Patricia Atchison (1993). "Heterosexual Instrumentalism: Past and Future Directions." In Sue Wilkinson and Celia Kitzinger (eds.), *Heterosexuality.* London: Sage, pp. 120–135.

Weedon, Chris (1987). *Feminist Practice and Poststructuralist Theory.* Oxford: Basil Blackwell.

Wilton, Tamsin (1992). "Sisterhood in the Service of Patriarchy: Heterosexual Women's Friendships and Male Power." *Feminism and Psychology* 2, no. 3: 506–509.

13

"*I* Don't Speak Spritch"

Locating Lesbian Language

ROBIN M. QUEEN

The few studies that exist on lesbian language either center on lexical and topical issues (Painter 1978, 1981; Gever and Magnan 1991; Day and Morse 1981) or come to the conclusion that there are no unique linguistic features used by lesbians (Moonwomon 1985, reprinted in this volume). Both of these analyses result from the assumption that there is a lesbian speech community that can be identified and that, once identified, exhibits a specific set of linguistic features. In this chapter, I question the nature of the speech community and find it inadequate for accommodating the unique form of lesbian language. I propose instead the use of a contact-based model for accounting for lesbian language. Through the example of lesbian comic-book characters, I demonstrate how lesbian language consists of the interaction between several stylistic tropes and their conventionalized social meanings.

Lesbian comic-book characters are useful sources of data for a study of lesbian language because they play on commonly held stereotypes accessible to queers in general and lesbians specifically. Furthermore, they draw on stereotypes from both within and outside the queer community, stereotypes that include specific linguistic forms and patterns. While lesbian comic-book characters' speech is not an example of the naturally occurring speech of lesbians, it is a representation of the ways in which lesbians are assumed to speak. The characters are all created by lesbians for a predominantly lesbian audience, and thus the characters' believability relies on social knowledge that is assumed to be shared. They are characters who are politically and socially positioned within a larger context that includes elements specific to lesbians, specific to women, specific to queers, and specific to a full range of groups marginalized on the basis of their ethnicity, their socioeconomic status, and/or their political beliefs. The use of unique linguistic patterns and tropes is one method by which the creators of lesbian characters can project identities that are unquestionably lesbian.

The data are drawn from the following sources: *Hothead Paisan: Homicidal Lesbian Terrorist* (DiMassa), *Dykes to Watch Out For* (Bechdel), and *Rude Girls and Dangerous Women* (Camper). Dana Heller (1993) writes that Hothead Paisan is especially effective as a lesbian comic-book character because "she keeps alive many of the myths and symbols around which lesbian communities have constructed a culture and an identity" (28). Thus, she is a representation of a uniquely lesbian image that embodies the intersection of a number of distinct, yet overlapping, identities. A popular bumper sticker reads, "I read Hothead to stay out of jail." Readers write in with statements such as, "I just want you to know that Hothead Paisan is one of my biggest heroes and sources of inspiration"; "Your spirit possessed me the other night"; "Just wanted to let you know that Hothead saved my sanity the other night." Additional responses include, "I don't agree with all that she (HH) has to say, but . . ."; "You two are totally psycho, but I love it"; "Personally, my struggle is a cross between Hothead and Roz."[1] These responses to Hothead Paisan show that readers share the social knowledge required to understand why Hothead reacts to the world the way that she does and that readers either identify with the character themselves or see an "Other" with whom they may not identify but whom they can nonetheless appreciate (see also Painter 1978).

Dykes to Watch Out For provides an additional example of lesbian humor that relies on the representation of characters who exemplify stereotypes commonly held among lesbians. The characters in this comic strip exhibit a diverse set of individual identities, all of which have unique, yet recognizable, attributes. These attributes include particular linguistic traits. The queer activist Lois, for instance, tends to use more nonstandard phonological forms, as well as curse words like *fuck* and *shit*. The diversity in the representation of the characters provides the audience with an opportunity to identify with the characters; more critically, the diversity itself calls into question monolithic definitions of lesbians and lesbian communities.

Lesbians and Lesbian Communities

One of the primary issues for defining the lesbian community typically revolves around trying to specify who might or might not belong to such a community. While most of the discussions concerning the category *lesbian* refer to both one's biological sex and one's sexual orientation, all definitions based on such criteria remain problematic. As Celia Kitzinger points out, externally imposed definitions of lesbians tend to rely on sexual orientation or sexual activity:[2]

> To qualify as a 'real' ('true', 'fixed', 'obligatory') lesbian, a woman must be able to demonstrate that her 'sexual orientation' is a stable part of her adult personality. The

'real' lesbian is required to be over a certain age (Saghir and Robins 1969; Kaye 1967), not sexually attracted to men (Dilis 1969), sexually attracted to women (Gagnon and Simon, 1973; Poole, 1972) and to have 'repetitive' or 'regular' genital sexual activity with women (Bieber 1969; Saghir and Robins, 1969; Kaye, 1967) under conditions in which male sexual partners are seen to be accessible to her (Ward and Kassebaum 1964) and in which ideological reasons for being lesbian are absent (Defries 1976). (1987: 67)

A further criterion tends to include the specification that only women who were born female may qualify as lesbians.[3] Such definitions may exclude many women who consider themselves to be lesbians and may include women who do not consider themselves lesbians but whose activities correspond with the definition of lesbians. Sarah Lucia Hoagland (1989) notes further that even group-internal definitions may be problematic because they tend to emphasize criteria for "realness" rather than considering the diversity of life experiences found among women who consider themselves lesbians. Nonetheless, even self-identified lesbians may be rejected as "true" lesbians by others (Hoagland 1989; Bland 1995).

The basic dichotomy between relative (and continued) invisibility and generally negative stereotypes that come from external sources adds to the difficulty of defining *lesbian* and the *lesbian community*. As Martha Gever and Nathalie Magnan explain: "An enormous rift exists between how we are portrayed and portray ourselves as deviant women in patriarchal, heterosexist societies and how we function and represent ourselves within our own subculture. Not that these are independent social systems, nor are lesbian identities free from gender-based definitions and descriptions" (1991: 67). Because lesbians have identities not defined by a single characteristic (such as lesbianism) but by multilayered membership in any number of groups and subgroups, it is futile to try and define either *lesbian* or the *lesbian community* using externally imposed criteria. Nonetheless, the notion of the "lesbian community" may be useful as a tool for constructing an identity that includes, or even projects, a woman's identity as a lesbian.

Benedict Anderson (1991) points out that communities are typified by the way in which they are imagined rather than by their genuineness or falsity. As Figures 13-1 and 13-2 show, individuals may have shifting ideas about the lesbian community and their position within that community. This sort of fluctuation exemplifies the problem with trying to use externally based (or academically imposed) criteria for specifying communities and demonstrates the utility of considering communities to be particular constructions based on the ways in which individuals imagine them rather than tangibly identifiable entities.

If we accept Anderson's (1991) claim that "all communities are imagined," then defining communities through any set of external criteria becomes both irrelevant and effectively impossible. Similarly, any discussion of language that involves the notion of a speech community or members of a speech community (Gumperz 1971; Labov 1972; Ferguson 1971) may be of doubtful value. In other words, the problem is not with contriving the proper semantics for defining membership into a given speech community but rather with the very nature of the categorization. Valerie Jennes writes:

Figure 13-1.   A. Bechdel (1992: 16–17), copyright Firebrand Books. Reprinted with permission.

We are active in the establishment of our identities as we undergo changes in our knowledge base, including our understanding and interpretations of social categories and ourselves as an instance of them. As our understandings of the meanings associated with the kinds of people it is possible to be in society undergo substantive changes, we continually reassess the personal applicability of any given category. (1992: 69)

Figure 13-2. DiMassa (1993: 42), copyright DiMassa and Giant Ass Publishing. Reprinted with permission.

Rusty Barrett (this volume) recognizes this issue for queer communities in particular and addresses it by noting that "queer communities are imagined in a style in which the boundaries are consciously vague and uncertain.... Queer communities also know that they are imagined in some sense and knowingly and openly question the membership status of a variety of potential members." Furthermore, as Keith Walters (1995) points out, communities are imagined on a number of levels, including the ways in which researchers themselves imagine the communities which they study. One of the problems with previous research on the language of lesbians may have been the result of the ways in which the researchers imagined the lesbian speech community—even researchers who consider themselves to be members of that community.

Because of the complexities of trying to accommodate diversity in a generalized category, particularly one in which the variables are essentially infinite, the category itself must either be so very narrowly defined that it excludes many, regardless of whether they believe themselves to be members, or so broadly defined that it ceases to have concrete boundaries. A third option, of course, is to question the need for a categorical distinction in the first place. Such a questioning allows for fluctuation in the personal applicability of a given category, while still recognizing the social relevance of the characteristics associated with that category and the ways in which behavior may reflect or even construct concepts of it.

Linguistics of contact

In a discussion of gay male speech, Keith Walters and Rusty Barrett (1994) note that there is nothing specific to gay male speech in terms of its grammar or linguistic system but that there is a unique, conventionalized set of meanings attached to some of the linguistic resources used by gay men. It is the exploitation of these conventionalized meanings that becomes indexical of "gay male." While Walters and Barrett state explicitly that they are dealing with gay men only, they also predict that their model will account for the speech patterns of lesbians as well. Their model examines language from a position that takes into consideration axes of social difference and as such predicts that it is specifically the ways in which linguistic resources are used, rather than a set of linguistic tokens that are unique to a speech community, that index a given identity.

They ground their work, as I ground this work, in what Mary Louise Pratt (1987) has called a *linguistics of contact*. In her critique of community-based approaches to linguistic analysis, Pratt points out the utopian nature of the ways in which communities are generally imagined, that is, as homogeneous, both linguistically and socially. As an alternative, she offers a framework for acknowledging diversity among speakers:

> Imagine, then, a linguistics that decentered community, that placed at its center the operations of language across lines of social differentiation, a linguistics that focused on modes and zones of contact between dominant and dominated groups, between persons of different and multiple identities, speakers of different languages, that focused on how speakers constitute each other relationally and in difference, how they enact differences in language. Let us call this enterprise a linguistics of contact, a term linked to Jakobson's notion of contact as a component of speech events, and to the phenomenon of contact languages, one of the best challenges to the systematizing linguistics of code. (Pratt 1987: 60)

It is through such a framework that we can begin to understand how the linguistic choices that a speaker makes may in fact index membership in some "imagined" group.

Dorothy Painter (1981) notes that lesbians can identify each other in a variety of settings but that they cannot always explain how the identification takes place. I propose that one of the primary ways in which lesbians may index themselves (and thus are able to identify one another) is through the decidedly marked combination of a number of linguistic styles. In other words, it is not membership (assumed or imposed) in the abstract conception of the lesbian community that makes the language of lesbians unique but rather the fluid contact between a number of styles to which lesbians have access and that carry various "conventionalized" meanings that can be exploited in uniquely "lesbian" ways.

Lesbian Language

While there are several styles from which lesbians appear to draw when using "lesbian" language, it is important to note that "styles" refers to a set of stereotyped assumptions about a set of linguistic features and their associated social connotations, rather than actual linguistic practice. For example, women do not consistently speak in the ways Robin Lakoff outlined in her pioneering work *Language and Woman's Place* (1975). Mary Bucholtz and Kira Hall (1995) note, however, that there is nonetheless a stereotype concerning the ways in which women speak, and it is this stereotype that women either aspire to or reject (and sometimes both simultaneously). Thus, the stereotype has taken on a conventionalized social meaning that is recognized by a large number of speakers. As Barrett (this volume; 1995) points out, African American drag queens draw on the stereotype of a particular group of women rather than actually trying to sound like "real" women.[4] Similarly, lesbians draw on several stereotyped styles when using lesbian language.

I consider the use of these styles to be linguistic tropes because the features carry conventionalized social meanings. As Paul Friedrich (1991) writes:

> [A] trope means anything. . . . Everyman uses to create poetic texture and effect, poetic meanings, and poetic integration. . . . The full multitude of tropes and the feedback between them should be recognized, as should their partial independence and their partial interdependence. By thinking in terms of the whole field of tropes we are closer to being Everyman; that is, someone using language in a fairly natural, familiar way. (1991: 26)

Through the interaction of tropes, we have the classic poetic projection of the paradigmatic onto the syntagmatic (Jakobson 1960). Linguistic features may be combined to simultaneously create and enact a uniquely lesbian language. Thus, various paradigms of social meaning, indexed through linguistic forms, are brought together to form a new set of conventionalized associations. By combining the stereotypes of nonlesbian communities with the stereotypes that lesbians hold about themselves, lesbians create an indexical relationship between language use and a lesbian "identity."

Interaction of tropes

On the basis of both personal observation and analysis of cartoon characters, I propose four stylistic tropes that lesbians use to construct lesbian language:

1. *Stereotyped women's language* (see Lakoff 1975: 53–56)

   A large stock of words related to specific interests, generally relegated to "woman's work": *dart* (in sewing) and specific color terms

   Empty adjectives like *divine, charming, cute*

   "Question" intonation where we might expect declaratives: for instance, tag questions (it's hot, isn't it) and rising intonation in statement contexts

   Use of hedges of various kinds. Women's speech seems in general to contain more instances of *well, y'know, kinda* and so forth

   Related to this, is intensive use of *so*; again, this is more frequent in women's speech than men's

   Hypercorrect grammar (women are not supposed to talk rough)

   Superpolite forms (women don't use off-color or indelicate expressions; ' women are the experts at euphemism)

   Lack of humor (women don't tell jokes)

2. *Stereotyped nonstandard varieties, often associated with working-class, urban males* (see Labov 1972)

   Cursing

   in' vs. *ing*

   postvocalic /r /deletion (may be regionally marked as well)

   Nonnormative consonant cluster simplification

   Contracted forms, for instance *gonna, oughta, I dunno*

   Ethnically marked linguistic forms, *kapeesh, yo' mama*

   Some vowel quality changes depending on region

3. *Stereotyped gay male language* (see Barrett, this volume)

   Use of wider pitch range for intonational contours

   Hypercorrection: the presence of phonologically nonreduced forms and the use of hyperextended vowels

   Use of lexical items specific to gay language

   Use of a H*L intonational contour (often co-occurring with extended vowels like FAABulous)

4. *Stereotyped lesbian language*[5]

   Use of narrow pitch range and generally "flat" intonation patterns

   Cursing

   Use of expressions such as *bite me* and *suck my dick*, which are normally associated with men and their anatomy

   Lack of humor and joking, especially in terms of sarcasm and irony

While all four tropes are integral to a discussion of lesbian language, stereo-typed women's speech deserves particular discussion because it can be used both positively and negatively. Lesbians can appropriate the stylistic features associated with stereotyped women's language, or they can consciously reject those features. One of the most salient stereotypes about lesbians' speech patterns, for instance, concerns the use of "flat intonation."[6] By the same token, one of the most salient aspects of stereotypical women's language is the use of extreme fluctuations in in-tonation. Thus, when a women does not intonate in the "normative" way, she may be trying to distinguish herself from the stereotyped, heterosexual woman. As R. B. LePage and André Tabouret-Keller (1985) point out, a speaker marks his or her speech so as to be like the speech of those he or she wants to be identified with or to be different from the speech of those from whom he or she wishes to be dis-tinguished. Lesbians may use structural elements that do not conform to stereo-typed women's speech in order to distinguish themselves from the stereotyped woman, or they may use particular aspects of stereotyped women's language in order to index their identity as women.

The use of stereotypical women's language points to a further dynamic that in-forms lesbian identities as well as lesbian speech: the butch/femme dichotomy. Lillian Faderman (1991) points out that the butch/femme dynamic served as a sign of "membership" during the 1950s when lesbian subcultures were being fully established in the United States. Although the butch/femme dichotomy was disdained with the advent of the lesbian-feminist movement in the early 1960s, it has nonetheless main-tained a defining position among lesbians. As Lisa Bland (1995) states in a discussion of the humorous use of the butch/femme dynamic, "the butch/femme dichotomy plays a particular ideological role in the construction of lesbian identity. . . . Each les-bian has to deal with the butch/femme stereotype in some way, accepting it some-times, rejecting it other, and co-opting it in still other cases." While this chapter is not about the butch/femme dynamic, the emergent and conventionalized meaning at-tached to it is an important source of social knowledge that lesbians share.

Anna Livia (1995) notes in her discussion of butch/femme language in fiction that the portrayal of butches and femmes draws on particular stereotypes but does not conform to all of the features of stereotyped language. In particular, she points out that the stereotypical "butch grunt syndrome," which is indicative of the silent butch, is actually antithetical to stereotyped male language, in which males assume a larger amount of the discourse space. Thus, it is the case not that butches "talk like men" and femmes "talk like women" but that butches and femmes (and the representations of "butch" and "femme") appropriate particular elements of those stereotyped styles and then construct their butch or femme identities through the dynamic (and unique) interaction of some (but not all) stylistic elements. I con-tend that all lesbian speech is constructed through such stylistic interaction.

In using a linguistics of contact as a model for discussing lesbian language, we have a research mechanism that can account for the fact that most lesbians make linguistic choices on the basis of any number of individual and/or contextual fac-tors that may or may not overlap. When a speaker chooses to index the "lesbian" aspect of her identity, the linguistic choices she makes reflect the construction of that lesbian identity. The point, then, is not to predict when a lesbian will use "lesbian language" or to offer a diagnostic tool for identifying lesbians but rather to understand that lesbians (like all speakers) have access to a number of speech styles, as well as the conventionalized meanings associated with the use of those styles. It is through the recontextualization and reappropriation of particular features found in various styles that lesbians create new conventionalized meanings and associations and, thus, a uniquely lesbian language.

Hothead Paisan and Others

Having identified the linguistic tropes that appear to be the predominant source of lesbian language, I now turn to an examination of comic-book characters in order to demonstrate the points of contact between the different styles and the ways in which the larger tropes are used to portray lesbian language. I examine Hothead Paisan in particular detail since she "keeps alive many of the myths and symbols around which lesbian communities have constructed a culture and identity" (Heller 1993: 27). I begin, however, by examining a strip that demonstrates the important role of language for lesbians and lesbian identities.

In Figure 13-3, there is explicit reference made to the assumptions about how women should talk and to the fact that lesbians typically do not talk in such a way. Note that the lesbian character uses full progressive forms throughout except in the final frame, where she says *fuckin'*. Interestingly, her mother ignores all the other signs of the woman's lesbianism and says only that nice girls shouldn't curse (cf. Lakoff's distinctions).

Figure 13.3.   Camper (1994: 87), copyright Bala Cynwyd Press. Reprinted with permission.

Figure 13-4. DiMassa (vol. 13: 8–9), copyright DiMassa and Giant Ass Publishing. Reprinted with permission.

The next example shows another explicit reference to the expectations for women's speech. In this comic, however, Hothead Paisan openly rejects that type of language. Note that the mother and the sister exhibit most of the stereotypical women's language features. The print used to portray their speech is smaller and lighter than Hothead's print, thus indicating "smaller" voices—they use higher pitches with less amplitude, and the mother uses marked forms such as *panties*. Hothead ends the encounter by identifying stereotyped women's language as Spritch and saying that she does not speak it.[7]

Figure 13-5 shows the inside cover of volume 17, where we again find a blend of standard and nonstandard linguistic features, in particular regionally and ethnically marked phonological forms and lexical items. Although the cover is generally in standard orthography, we find postvocalic /r/ deletion (*publisha*) and initial vowel deletion (*sistant*), as well as the use of taboo words such as *fuck* and *shit*. We also find some stereotypical "women" features with items such as *love support staff* and, in the note from the publisher, terms like *whoopsie*, *LOVE*, and *feel kisses now and now and now*. There are also references to stereotypical lesbian characteristics, such as naming the cats as the love support staff and referring to Hothead's astrological sign. Again, these references point out the fuzziness of the boundaries between styles, as well as the ways in which styles can be dynamically combined to create lesbian language.

In Figure 13-6, there are several additional "nonstandard" elements to Hothead's speech. Notably, there are the contracted forms *needa* and *sorta*. These examples are particularly interesting because they violate the constituency of the syntactic phrases *need to find* and *sort of freak*. According to most generative theories of syntax, such contractions should be ill formed; however, as these examples demonstrate, the representation of nonstandard speech relies on phonetic representations that may conflict with standard conventions for marking syntactic constituency. Thus, DiMassa is essentially representing spoken language.

Figures 13-7 and 13-8 offer an interesting comparison between the representation of lesbians' use of nonstandard features typically associated with working-class men (Labov 1972; Trudgill 1983) and the representation of actual working-class men. In Figure 13-7, we have instances of *in'* (*spendin'*, *datin'*); use of /d/ (*da*) instead of /ð/; nonstandard syntactic forms, *shoot them bones*, *so's*, *hafta*; nonstandard vowel qualities (*yer*); and remarks that use taboo words (*Fuck you, shit.*) All of these examples are marked in terms of their nonstandardness, as well as their general association with urban working-class men (and disassociation with women).

However, it is not the case that the lesbians in Figure 13-7 are trying to imitate "real" men in terms of their language. When we compare Figure 13-7 to Figure 13-8, we find several additional nonstandard features that differentiate the lesbians from the men. The male characters exhibit vowels shifts (*fooken* 'fucking', *yiz* 'you (pl.)') and postvocalic /r/ deletion (*kweehs* 'queers', *nawmul* 'normal') not found among the lesbians in Figure 13-7. Furthermore, /ð/ is consistently represented as /d/, whereas when the lesbians speak, it is variable (see also Figure 13-9). In addition, the men use *in'* instead of *ing* (*fooken'*, *disgustin'*) consistently. The les-

GIANT ASS
PUBLISHING

Giant Ass Publishing

PRESENTS

HOTHEAD
PAISAN
HOMICIDAL LESBIAN TERRORIST

#17

WRITTEN, ILLUSTRATED & PURGED BY: DIANE DiMASSA
PUBLISHA & HEAD OF BOO BOO'S: STACY A. SHEEHAN
BACK COVER PHOTOS: STACY A SHEEHAN
SISTANT TO DA PUBLISHA: CARRIE FOLEY
CAT-A-LOG LAYOUT: SUE CZARK
COVER COLOR SEPARATION: GEORGINE HOWE
PRINTED AT AND BY: THE ADVOCATE PRESS
LOVE SUPPORT STAFF: GOALIE J. WILSON (AKA CHICKEN),
FRANK (AKA BOOGUMS), ROULETTE AND IGGY (AKA HENRY)
SPECIAL THANKS FOR TECHNICAL SUPPORT TO: ELISE WRIGHT
AND SUSAN CALDWELL

Hothead Paisan is published 4 times per year: February, May, August and November.
Subscriptions $15.00 per year, $16.00 Canada, $20.00 Overseas
Payment must be payable in U.S. currency. Send checks or money orders to:
Giant Ass Publishing P.O.Box 214 New Haven CT 06502
Need another cat-a-log? Call the Hotline: 203/865-6113
or Email us: giantass.aol.com

Note from Head of Boo Boo's,
It is appropriate that I am writing this today 2/14/95 as it is the official birthday of Giant Ass Publishing and Hothead Paisan (though, no she is not an aquarian). Today we are all 4 years old. That feels more accurate than you can imagine. I made a mithtake on #16's inside front cover when I wrote "the 3d year end, love will set you free, ishoo." I still testify that "love will set you free" but it was our 4th year end ...whoops! whoops! whoopsie! NO I Can't coUnT! -doesn't anyone proof read this shit! You may notice this issue is a wopping 8 pages bigger than usual. We're really trying not to raise the cover price though paper, envelopes, printing, postage, shipping, coffee, litter, essential oils and everything under the sun has and is going up .We'll hold off as long as we can. We LOVE your partaking in the purchasing of our crapola and your spreading us around to your people. We invite you to stay with us. You're the best company we ever had!
As always, we wish you love. Feel kisses now and now and now and now... ✕✕✕

Figure 13-5. DiMassa (vol. 17: cover), copyright DiMassa and Giant Ass Publishing. Reprinted with permission.

Figure 13-6. DiMassa (vol. 15: 2), copyright DiMassa and Giant Ass Publishing. Reprinted with permission.

bians, however, show some variation (again compare with Figure 13-9, where nonreduced *something, thinking* occur).

Although Figure 13-9 shows that the use of nonstandard features is not an essential part of the portrayal of lesbians, there are nonetheless a number of nonstandard features that either violate the stereotypical norms for women or appropriate those nonstandard, covert prestige items from stereotyped male speech. For instance, in frame 1, Hothead asks her soon-to-be lover about her anatomy, using vocabulary terms that are markedly nonstandard as well as not "lady-like."[8] Then, in frame 2, DiMassa (the creator) appears as a character in the comic strip. She shows variation between the use of /ð/ (*that*) and /d/ (*da*). In frame 3, we have the contracted forms *resta, wanna,* and *gotta,* as well as vowel shifts in *ya* and *yer.* Finally, in frame 4, we find no markedly nonstandard linguistic features; thus demonstrating the variable nature of the contact between the different tropes.

Figures 13-3–13-9 center on the use of nonstandard linguistic forms. Lesbian language, however, is not simply made up of movement along a linguistic scale where "standard" (stereotypical white, middle-class female) is on one end and

Figure 13-7. DiMassa (vol. 14: 1), copyright DiMassa and Giant Ass Publishing. Reprinted with permission.

"nonstandard" (stereotypical white, working-class male) is on the other. In figures 13-10 and 13-11, for instance, we find examples of lexical items that tend to be marked as stereotypical gay male (see Barrett, this volume). In Figure 13-10, Chicken, the cat, talks about the fez being *fabulous*. Furthermore, the print is somewhat lighter, and each sentence ends in an exclamation point. Taken together, these facts indicate different phrase final intonational contours (most likely high rising contours rather than the more normative fall of a declarative). The lex-

Figure 13-8.   DiMassa (1993: 102), copyright DiMassa and Giant Ass Publishing. Reprinted with permission.

ical item *cute* in frame 13-4 appears to be one of the empty adjectives noted by Lakoff, which may coincide with both stereotypical gay male and stereotypical women's speech. In Figure 13-11, we also see a stereotypical gay male speech with lexical items such as *exquisite*, as well as marked stress on function words such as *so* and *too*. The outlined word *far* may also indicate the H*L contour noted by Barrett (this volume).

In Figure 13-12, we have the use of stereotypical "women's" speech with phrases like *o my God* where the *o* is shortened and *God* stressed, which may indi-

Figure 13-9. DiMassa (vol. 19: 10), copyright DiMassa and Giant Ass Publishing. Reprinted with permission.

cate one of the more stereotypical phrases conventionally associated with "Valley Girls." In Figure 13-13, we have a similar phrase, except for the fact that we do not have a clipped form of "oh" and there is the insertion of the lexical item *fuckin'*. Here, *fuckin'* may be an example of the infixed morpheme *fuckin-'* found commonly in nonstandard uses such as *fan-fuckin'-tastic* or *abso-fuckin-lutely*. In this case, the *fuckin'* is inserted into the phrase as if the phrase were a phonological word. Note also, the nonstandard spelling of *fukin'*. Again, examples such as figure 13-13 demonstrate the blending of stylistic tropes in unique ways. Figure 13-13 gives neither a representation of stereotypical women's speech nor a representation of wholly nonstandard speech but is rather a combination of both. The primary point for lesbian language is that examples such as 13-12 and 13-13 show that lesbians do use features of stereotypical women's speech as a part of the construction of lesbian language.

Finally, Figures 13-14 and 13-15 give examples of the use of stereotyped les-

Figure 13-10. DiMassa (vol. 14: 15), copyright DiMassa and Giant Ass Publishing. Reprinted with permission.

Figure 13-11. DiMassa (vol. 13: 13), copyright DiMassa and Giant Ass Publishing. Reprinted with permission.

Figure 13-12. DiMassa (vol. 19: 9), copyright DiMassa and Giant Ass Publishing. Reprinted with permission.

Figure 13-13. DiMassa (1993: 32), copyright DiMassa and Giant Ass Publishing. Reprinted with permission.

bian ways of speaking. In these cases, there is no use of either stereotypical non-standard "working-class" male forms or stereotypical women's forms. Instead, there is a hyperarticulation, with little pitch modulation or apparent language play. In both examples, there is little or no nonstandard phonology. Particularly in Figure 13-14, note Hothead's speech with its consonant cluster simplification (*an'*), non-standard contractions (*sorta*), use of *in'* rather than *ing* (*helpin'*, *fuckin'*), and inclusion of taboo words (*fuckin'* and *motherfuckers*). Alice, on the other hand, exhibits few such features. In frame 4, she says *Shall I respond*—an interrogative form marked as typically female as well as formal. In frames 5 and 6, she uses very formal constructions such as *Do you dare* and full forms rather than contractions in

Figure 13-14. DiMassa (1993: 169–170), copyright DiMassa and Giant Ass Publishing. Reprinted with permission.

Figure 13-15. DiMassa (vol. 12: 11), copyright DiMassa and Giant Ass Publishing. Reprinted with permission.

examples like *I have* (although she also uses standard contractions like *can't* and *don't*).

Similarly, in Figure 13-15, we see the portrayal of stereotypical "earth mother" language actually being used by the mother earth and the moon goddess.[9] Note the stylistic change between frames 2/3 and 4/5, where ritualized speech is being used to cause women all over the earth to start menstruating. Again, we see no phonologically reduced forms, no contracted forms, and no signs of any nonstandard speech. At the same time, the speech is not marked as "female" in the Lakoff sense, either, although it is clearly being spoken by women (compare with Figures 13-7 and 13-8).

Conclusion

As the examples have demonstrated, the creators of comic-book characters not only draw on linguistic stereotypes in molding their characters but also combine

various linguistic features associated with different stereotypes. The characterization of lesbian language does not revolve around a simple binary choice: Either we
speak like women or we speak like men. Instead, lesbians have a rather broad range
from which to draw their linguistic choices. Elements of those choices incorporate
the construction and enactment of a lesbian identity, a queer identity, a female identity, an ethnic identity, and a class identity, in addition to a variety of other kinds of
identities. There may be times when a lesbian privileges one aspect of her identity
over the others or when she simultaneously represents several or all aspects.

Although this study is limited in that it is based on fictional, humorous representations of lesbians' speech rather than on naturally occurring discourse, it may
nonetheless serve as a new starting point for thinking about how lesbians may use
language in ways that are specifically lesbian. If we accept the assertion that lesbian
comic-book characters present representations of lesbians and the ways in which
lesbians speak, then the examination of their speech demonstrates many of the
ways in which the social meanings associated with various linguistic styles become
reconventionalized and thus index a uniquely lesbian language. Consequently, I
propose that it is through the combination of the linguistic resources available
from each of the "imagined" communities to which lesbians "belong" that we get
a lesbian speech style. Through taking such a contact-based perspective, we may
begin to accommodate the vast social and individual diversity found among lesbians as well as understand the complex and unique ways that lesbians use language as indexical markers of identity.

NOTES

An earlier version of this chapter was presented at the third annual conference on Lavender Languages and Linguistics, American University, September 1995. I would like to
thank Rusty Barrett, Susan Garrett, Kira Hall, Keith Walters, and Kathy Wood for their
helpful comments on various drafts of this chapter. All errors in fact or interpretation remain entirely my own.

1. Roz is a friend of Hothead's, who generally tries to tone down Hothead's violent
tendencies. She is the other character in Figure 2.

2. I would like to thank Lisa Bland for pointing out this quote to me.

3. This criterion is especially identified with the ongoing debates surrounding the inclusion of male-to-female transsexuals at women's music festivals, especially the Michigan
Womyn's Music Festival.

4. An interesting distinction may be drawn between the drag queens described by Barrett and their appropriation of stereotyped speech and the portrayal of drag queens in the
film *To Wong Foo, Thanks for Everything, Julie Newmar,* where the actors appear to be trying to sound like women rather than like drag queens.

5. Stereotypes of lesbians' speech are based on personal discussions with lesbians as
well as informal elicitations in three introductory courses in linguistics at the University of
Texas at Austin.

6. "Flat" intonation refers to a lack of peaks and troughs in the fundamental frequency.

7. Spritch refers to the term *spritzhead,* a term that Hothead uses to identify stereotypical heterosexual women, particularly those who happily let men treat them poorly and
who spend inordinate amounts of time doing their hair and applying makeup. The comic

book character Cathy offers a canonical example of the women to whom Hothead is referring when using the term *spritzhead*.

8. Daphne has had an ambiguous biological sex from the beginning. In Volume 15, she makes indirect reference to a "major transition" going on in her life, which brings into question whether or not she is a transsexual. No resolution of this issue is offered (most likely a deliberate ommision); however, Daphne is presented as anatomically female in Volume 19.

9. Quote from Heller (1993); both figures are stereotyped figures found among lesbians.

REFERENCES

Andersen, Benedict (1991). *Imagined Communities: Reflections on the Origin and Spread of Nationalism.* London: Verso.

Barrett, Rusty (1995). "The Markedness Model and Style Switching: Evidence from African American Drag Queens." In Pamela Silberman and Jonathan Loftin (eds.), *SALSA II. Proceedings of the Second Annual Symposium about Language and Society—Austin.* Austin: Department of Linguistics, University of Texas at Austin, pp. 40–52.

——— (this volume). "The 'Homo-genius' Speech Community."

Bechdel, Alison (1992). *Dykes to Watch Out For: The Sequel.* Ithaca, NY: Firebrand.

Bieber, Irving (1969). "Homosexuality." *American Journal of Nursing* 69: 2637–2641.

Bland, Lisa (ms.). "The Humorous Side of Butch and Femme." University of Texas at Austin, 1995.

Bucholtz, Mary, and Kira Hall (1995). "Introduction: Twenty years after *Language and Woman's Place.*" In Kira Hall and Mary Bucholtz (eds.), *Gender Articulated: Language and the Socially Constructed Self.* New York: Oxford University Press.

Camper, Jennifer (1994). *Rude Girls and Dangerous Women.* Bala Cynwyd, PA: Laugh Lines.

Day, Connie L., and Ben Morse (1981). "Communication Patterns in Established Lesbian Relationships." In James W. Chesebro (ed.), *Gayspeak: Gay Male and Lesbian Communication.* New York: Pilgrim Press, pp. 80–86.

DiMassa, Diane (1993–1995). *Hothead Paisan: Homicidal Lesbian Terrorist,* vols. 10–19. New Haven: Giant Ass.

——— (1993). *Hothead Paisan: Homicidal Lesbian Terrorist.* San Francisco: Cleis.

Ellis, Albert (1969). "The Use of Sex in Human Life." *Journal of Sex Research* 5: 41–49.

Faderman, Lillian (1991). *Odd Girls and Twilight Lovers: A History of Lesbian Life in the Twentieth Century.* New York: Penguin.

Ferguson, Charles (1971). "Diglossia." In Pier Paolo Giglioli (ed.), *Language and Social Context.* New York: Penguin, pp. 232–282.

Friedrich, Paul (1991). "Polytropy." In James W. Fernandez (ed.), *Beyond Metaphor: The Theory of Tropes in Anthropology.* Stanford, CA: Stanford University Press, pp. 17–55.

Gagnon, J. H., and W. Simon (1973). *Sexual Conduct: The Social Sources of Human Sexuality.* Chicago: Aldine.

Gever, Martha, and Nathalie Magnan (1991). "The Same Difference: On Lesbian Representation." In Tessa Boffin and Jean Fraser (eds.), *Stolen Glances.* London: Pandora, pp. 67–75.

Gumperz, John (1971). "Speech Communities." In Pier Paolo Giglioli (ed.), *Language and Social Context.* New York: Penguin, pp. 219–231.

Heller, Dana (1993). "Hothead Paisan: Clearing a Space for a Llesbian Feminist Folklore." *New York Folklore* 19, no. 1–2: 27–44.

Hoagland, Sarah Lucia (1989). *Lesbian Ethics*. Palo Alto, CA: Institute of Lesbian Studies, pp. 206–207, 294–295.

Jakobson, Roman (1960). "Closing Statement: Linguistics and Poetics." In Thomas Seboek (ed.), *Style and Language*. Cambridge: MIT Press, pp. 350–377.

Jenness, Valerie (1992). "Coming Out: Lesbian Identities and the Categorization Problem." In Kenneth Plummer (ed.), *Modern Homosexualities: Fragments of Lesbian and Gay Experience*. London: Routledge, pp. 65–74.

Kitzinger, Celia (1987). *The Social Construction of Lesbianism*. London: Sage.

Labov, William (1972). *Sociolinguistic Patterns*. Oxford: Basil Blackwell.

Lakoff, Robin (1975). *Language and Woman's Place*. New York: Harper & Row.

Livia, Anna (1995). "'I Ought to Throw a Buick at You': Fictional Representations of Butch/Femme Speech." In Kira Hall and Mary Bucholtz (eds.), *Gender Articulated: Language and the Socially Constructed Self*. New York: Routledge.

Moonwomon, Birch (1985). "Toward the Study of Lesbian Speech." In Sue Bremner, Noelle Caskey, and Birch Moonwomon (eds.), *Proceedings of the First Berkeley Women and Language Conference*. Berkeley, CA: Berkeley Women and Language Group and Department of Linguistics, pp. 96–107 (reprinted in this volume).

Painter, Dorothy (1978). "Lesbian Humor as a Normalization Device." In Cynthia L. Berryman and Virginia A. Eman (eds.), *Communication, Language, and Sex: Proceedings of the First Annual Conference*. Rowley, MA: Newbury, pp. 132–148.

———— (1981). "Recognition among Lesbians in Straight Settings." In James W. Chesebro (ed.), *Gayspeak: Gay Male and Lesbian Communication*. New York: Pilgrim Press, pp. 68–79.

Poole, Kenneth (1972). "The Etiology of Gender Identity and the Lesbian." *Journal of Social Psychology* 87: 51–57.

Pratt, Mary Louise (1987). "Linguistic Utopias." In Nigel Fabb et al. (eds.), *The Linguistics of Writing: Arguments between Writing and Literature*. Manchester: Manchester University Press, pp. 48–66.

Saghir, Marcel, and Eli Robins (1969). "Female Homosexuality." *Archives of General Psychiatry* 20: 192–199.

Walters, Keith (1995). "Closing Remarks: Sociolinguistics and Linguistic Anthropology." In Pamela Silberman and Jonathan Loftin (eds.), *SALSA II. Proceedings of the Second Annual Symposium about Language and Society—Austin*. Austin: Department of Linguistics, University of Texas at Austin, pp. 266–273.

Walters, Keith, and Rusty Barrett (1994). "Imagining Gay Communities: Gay Language and Acts of Identity." Paper presented at the Second Lavender Languages and Linguistics Conference, American University, Washington D.C.

Ward, David A., and Gene G. Kassebaum (1964). "Homosexuality: A Mode of Adaptation in a Prison for Women." *Social Problems* 12: 159–177.

14

$\mathcal{N}$arrative Iconicity in Electronic-Mail Lesbian Coming-Out Stories

KATHLEEN M. WOOD

Because mainstream heterosexist society would have it that everyone be heterosexual until proven otherwise, gay men and lesbians have, throughout the course of a lifetime, an infinite number of situations in which we must experience and reveal ourselves as "other." Although not every gay man or lesbian makes a conscious decision to "come out of the closet" and declare his or her homosexuality, those who do often recount these experiences in coming-out stories. Penelope and Wolfe (1989:10) explain that coming-out stories often describe a process of self-recognition and acceptance that extends over years, even decades.

Coming out involves revealing one's identity to oneself, family members, colleagues, and communities. Coming-out stories characterize the journey's two levels: the external events of becoming a lesbian and the internal processes that accompany these events.

A common ritualized conversation starter in white, middle-class, self-identified lesbian communities is, "So, what is your coming-out story?" To answer this question, lesbians in these communities must do what all people do when they tell a life story: choose which parts of their lives they will narrate, while respecting the social and linguistic constraints of the telling.

Cross-disciplinary studies in anthropology, literary criticism, and linguistics (Gee 1991; Ginsburg 1987; Riessman 1991) suggest that all stories of the life-story genre exhibit a there-is-more-but-I'll-end-it-here quality. That is, people do not have one fixed and rigid understanding of their lives. Instead, as Linde (1993) points out, when people tell their life stories and personal-change stories, they tell different versions of their experiences, transforming the past and creating new meanings for themselves. Stromberg (1993), in his work on religious conversion stories, demonstrates that transformation life stories are ways of labeling experiences and giving them coherence, ways that shape and form the past as well as represent it.

What makes coming-out stories unique, however, is that the coming out cannot be represented as a single event, like the day someone accepted religion into her life, but must be represented as a series of life-long experiences. That is, gay men and lesbians must narrate a life that is not over and characterize, as Liang (this volume) calls it, the "processual" nature of coming out.

In this chapter, I examine four electronic-mail lesbian coming-out stories to show that the ends of these stories have an iconic relationship to the interpersonal contextual function; that is, their narrative configurations indicate the real-world "processual" nature of coming out.

Traditional discourse analysis approaches to narrative analysis frequently begin with Labov's framework (Labov and Waletzky 1967; Labov 1972), in which he describes the prototypical or "well-formed narrative," which has an abstract, orientation, complicating action, evaluation, result or resolution, and coda. Labov (1972: 369) explains: "A complete narrative begins with an orientation, proceeds to the complicating action, is suspended at the focus of evaluation before the resolution, concludes with the resolution, and returns the listener to the present time with the coda." He explains that resolutions and codas of narratives answer the question "What finally happened?" and give closure to the narrative. Although this framework is useful for characterizing life-story narratives structurally, it does not characterize them functionally. How is this prototypical narrative structure, which is generally associated with conversational narratives, especially the resolution/coda sequence, manifest in these electronic-mail data, and how is the "processual" nature of coming out displayed?

Ishikawa (1991) suggests that meaning does not arise from the semantic content of form alone—that linguistic forms may signal interactive meaning beyond what the structure indicates. I focus on two forms at the end of coming-out stories, the narrative resolution/coda sequence and the telling-frame coda. I suggest that these endings are not intended to lead the listener/readers to a feeling of completeness but rather function to portray coming out as the life-long process that it is.

The Data

After taping and transcribing a friend's coming-out story, I noticed that at the point where the story seemed to be winding down to a final resolution/coda, she had a series of resolutions and codas and even told a few more narratives. What is more, when she did finally end the story, she called it the "short" version. Keeping in mind that this processual resolution/coda sequence occurred in a spoken, conversational coming-out story, I decided to examine lesbian coming-out stories told in various settings. In this section I discuss four stories that I elicited from a thirty-five-member electronic-mail, all-lesbian distribution list by sending out a request to "send me your coming-out stories."[1]

Tess's coming-out story

Tess, a white, full-time professional and part-time student, sent me the first and the shortest of the four stories I got. Although Tess is Deaf and we might expect her story to contain evidence of "Deaf-lesbian" identities (see Neumann, this volume), there is nothing that overtly marks this coming-out story as different from hearing-women's stories. We can see that she narrates some events and, in lines 15–17, evaluates them. After describing her coming out to family members, she says:

15 I don't have much of a coming out story to tell because it hasn't been that
16 dramatic for me or anyone else. I guess it would be different if I had a long-
17 term relationship.

After this resolution/coda in lines 15–17, she goes back to the story world of the past and begins to narrate another part of her "coming-out" experience (lines 19–22).

19 When I attended my (nice) sister's wedding, I felt very out of place, as if I
20 was celebrating values that weren't mine, among people I didn't even know very
21 well, and who were living in totally different worlds than I was experiencing.
22 That event was the last time I remember being asked when I would get
       Married.

In line 19, "When I attended my (nice) sister's wedding I felt very out of place," she is actually telling another story, and in line 22, "That event was the last time I remember being asked when I would get married," she evaluates it and brings the reader out of the story world.

Tess's coming-out story is a combination of two shorter narratives: (1) coming out to immediate family and (2) attending the nice sister's wedding. Although she ends the second story with a narrative resolution/coda in line 22, "That event was the last time I remember being asked when I would get married," she provides no closure to the overall telling of the coming-out story.[2]

Schiffrin (1993: 249–250) describes this story-telling frame as a "social occasion" and suggests that it provides story tellers with a "dominant frame within which what is said is understood." Although Tess addresses this "telling-of-the-coming-out-story" frame in line 15, "I don't have much of a coming out story to tell," she does not close the telling frame at the end of her coming-out story ("so that's my coming-out story"). Instead, the narrative resolution/coda to her second and final narrative necessarily functions as the end to her entire story.

Kelly's coming-out story

Unlike Tess, who refers to the story-telling frame in the middle of the story, Kelly directly addresses it at the beginning of her story in line 10, "I'm 41 years old so it could be a long story <grin>," and closes this telling frame at the end, as I will discuss.

Kelly's coming-out story begins with her adolescence in a small town in southern Maryland. In the second to last paragraph, lines 83–90, Kelly describes coming out to her parents, focusing on her mother's reaction:

83   At 25, I entered into what was to become the longest relationship I've ever
84   had. It lasted nearly 13 years—until I was 38. I've been single the last
85   three years. During the time of the break-up, I was such a basketcase,
86   that I finally came out to my parents because I felt that they deserved an
87   explanation for my unusually depressed behavior. My mother cried for about
88   15 minutes . . . I thought she was concerned about my heartbreak . . . but she
        was
89   more worried about my "hereafter" . . . convinced that I would be spending
90   eternity in hell. I ended up comforting her.

In line 90, she resolves it with the narrative resolution, "I ended up comforting her." After that, she provides what functions as the story-final coda, in lines 90–93.

90   eternity in hell. I ended up comforting her. <u>Since that time, my parents</u>
91   <u>have been very supportive of me . . . and I'm grateful for that. I've tried</u>
92   <u>very hard to convince them that I'm happy with my life and there's nothing</u>
93   <u>they did to "cause" me to be this way.</u> Whenever I go to Florida for a

"Since that time" signals the coda of this story, the prototypical end. But after this end, she continues to tell another story in lines 93–95.

93   they did to "cause" me to be this way. <u>Whenever I go to Florida for a</u>
94   <u>visit, my mother always takes me by the arm so she can introduce me to all</u>
95   <u>of her friends</u> . . . she's obviously proud of me and wants folks to know who I
96   am. That's a good thing.

This story, which came after what could be considered a coda, effectively postpones closure. And she resolves it with line 95.

95   of her friends . . . <u>she's obviously proud of me and wants folks to know who I</u>
96   <u>am. That's a good thing.</u>

In line 96, "That's a good thing," she provides another story-final coda, bringing the reader up to the present and out of the story world. After this, in lines 98–102, she provides telling-frame closure, in order to end the telling of the narrative, as we see in lines 101–102: "Hope this story will be a help to you . . . good luck on your paper."

    98   So I guess that's my "lifestory as a lezzie" . . . not to[o] exciting or
    99   unusual, I think. I'm happy and confident and pleased about how I've
    100 turned out. My life so far has been a good one . . . and I hope it continues to
    101 be that way. Hope this story will be a help to you . . . good luck on your
    102 paper.

In addition to this stop-start-stop narrative sequence Kelly portrays the processual nature of coming out in lines 98–102 with syntactic indications of the process-nature of coming out. Specifically, lines 99–100 contain the present perfect form of the verb "I've turned out," indicating a process that was begun in the past and has continued into the present.

    99   unusual, I think. I'm happy and confident and pleased about how <u>I've</u>
    100 <u>turned out</u>. My life so far has been a good one . . . and I hope it continues to

Likewise, in line 100 she uses the adverbial marker "so far" and the present per-fective form "has been," both of which specify an ongoing, up-to-the-present event. In lines 100–101 she actually uses the structure "continues to be":

    100 turned out. My life so far has been a good one . . . and I hope it <u>continues to</u>
    101 <u>be</u> that way. Hope this story will be a help to you . . . good luck on your

These lines contain process-oriented lexical and syntactic structures that display the processual nature of coming out.

Heidi's coming-out story

Like Kelly's story, Heidi's coming-out story is framed within the telling-of-a-story frame.[3] Heidi begins with line 5, "Hmmm, ok, coming-out stories, huh?," opening the telling frame. In her sixty-six line narrative, she tells a series of stories about coming out to her family members and of how she met her life-partner, Gina. At the end of the story of coming out to her mother and stepfather, lines 41–50, she goes on:

    41   The next week, I ended up at my mother and step-father's house for a week, with
    42   most of my relatives, while we grieved for my brother immediately after his
    43   death. During that week, I came out to most of the rest of my family,
    44   including my mother, who has many lesbian friends and often talks about her
    45   sexuality in terms of "if I had been born in a different era. . . ." She was
    46   elated. After years of seeing me try to be someone I wasn't in order not to
    47   threaten the men I dated, she was really pleased to see me accept myself. As
    48   she now puts it, it was very special for her that while we grieved for my

49   brother who never felt he could discover who he was, I was announcing that I
50   HAD found my niche.

Heidi resolves the story, signaling the wind-down and a shift from the story world
by switching to the present tense in line 48:

47   threaten the men I dated, she was really pleased to see me accept myself. As
48   she <u>now puts it,</u> it was very special for her that while we grieved for my
49   brother who never felt he could discover who he was, I was announcing that I
50   HAD found my niche.

This present tense "puts it" in line 48 signals her evaluation and a pulling-away
from the story world. In lines 49-50 she also sets up an opposition between what
her brother never could do and what she did do.

49   brother who never felt he could discover who he was, I was announcing that I
50   <u>HAD</u> found my niche.

She emphasizes this opposition by capitalizing the entire HAD in line 50, marking it as a resolution to her story. This perfective form of the verb "had found" also
indicates action that began in the past and continued for some time. Her telling-
frame coda begins in the last paragraph in lines 52–53.

52   <u>Basically, the rest of the story is the same. Almost uniform and glowing</u>
53   <u>support</u> from all my family (YAY family!). The few people who were stumbling

In this coda in line 52, she has left the story world, and is getting ready to wrap up
her telling frame. But in the middle of this paragraph (lines 55–58), Heidi begins
narrating another story and tells of another coming out, first signaling her intention with "in one instance . . ."

55   <u>In one instance,</u> my other brother, Steve, was lamenting that he hadn't "been
56   there" for David, and that he hadn't known him very deeply. I took that
57   opportunity to say "well look, Steve, let's not let that happen with us; let me
58   tell you who I am. . . . " <u>I think it went down easier that way.</u>

She resolves this story with the evaluative comment "I think it went down easier
that way" in line 58. After this, she closes the entire telling with a telling-frame
coda, lines 61–64.

61   <u>There's more,</u> but I've probably given you way more than you wanted anyway.
62   Thanks Kathy for letting us tell our stories! I'd love a copy of what you come
63   up with. By the way, I don't need to be anonymous, in case that makes any
64   difference to you.

In line 61, "there's more," Heidi alludes to the presence of a pool of stories, prior
"texts" that constitute her coming-out experience, indicating that the story told

here is not her full story. In this reference she suggests that her story is not complete but that, for now, its narration is over. Like Tess and Kelly, Heidi has linguistically displayed the processual nature of coming out.

Helen's coming-out story

Like Heidi, Helen provided and made reference to the telling frame at the beginning of her story in line 6, "Okay . . . to help out a fellow (reference to electronic-mail list title), here is my story." Within this frame, Helen tells the 107-line version of her experience growing up in a rural setting and discovering that she was "different" while she was in junior high. Later in the story, Helen describes college life, where she, as a Deaf lesbian, dealt with dual identities. At the end of her narrative, in the third-to-last paragraph, lines 84–92, she signals the end of the story with a narrative coda beginning with "At this point" in line 86.

> 86 openly. <u>At this point, it is common knowledge in my family. My</u>
> 87 <u>aunts, uncles, cousins, sisters and grandparents all know about my</u>
> 88 <u>sexual orientation.</u> Whenever my sisters and I get together, they always

But by line 88, Helen has begun another story, one that occurred in the recent past.

> 88 sexual orientation. <u>Whenever my sisters and I get together, they always</u>

She proceeds with more narrative in lines 88–92.

> 88 sexual orientation. Whenever my sisters and I get together, they always
> 89 ask, "Have you found a partner yet?" This past Thanksgiving, we discussed
> 90 artificial insemmination (sp?) and approaching my nephews about my
> 91 gayness. I have five nephews (ages 8 to 18 months) and a neice who is
> 92 now 5 months old.

She does not cap this story with a coda but instead proceeds immediately to another story about being harassed, in lines 94–102. In this story, the setting is a dormitory for students who are Deaf. Each room is wired with a light doorbell so that the occupants can see when someone is calling at the door.

> 94 during my undergrad years here at (school), I have been involved in
>   activities
> 95 and issues related to homosexuality. I was openly gay. I told a few
> 96 friends and the word kinda spread around. I did not care one whit how
> 97 others thought/felt about me. However, in my freshman year, I did
> 98 encounter some harrasment. One Thanksgiving, prior to my upcoming trip,
> 99 someone kept flicking my light and disappeared. Knowing (gut instinct)
> 100 the culprit, I went over to the other wing and flicked his light. I
> 101 said in no uncertain terms that if he was to harrass me further, I would
> 102 report him. It had the intended effect. Harrassment stopped there forever!

She ends this story with a resolution/coda in line 102, "Harrassment stopped there forever."

    105   Boy, wasn't this a bit long?????? (alot better than doing it in some
    106   dark bar!)

Although Helen ends her story abruptly, she provides an ending in which she acknowledges the telling of a story, in her telling-frame closure in lines 105–106, and suggests that her coming-out story was "long."

Summary

In the four coming-out stories I have presented, the ongoing nature of the coming-out process is reflected in the linguistic forms and the configuration of the final resolution/coda sequence. The narrative structures at the end of these stories are summarized in Table 14-1.

In each of these lesbian coming-out stories, the final resolution/coda sequence is iconic, relating the never-ending, processual nature of coming out to the linguistic forms of the ends of these stories. In the shortest story, Tess resolves the story she tells, provides a telling-frame coda in line 15, "I don't have much of a coming out story," but then goes on to tell another story beginning in line 19, "When I attended my (nice) sister's wedding, I felt very out of place," after which she provides a narrative resolution/coda in line 22, "That event was the last time I remember being asked when I would get Married." Tess eliminates an overall telling-frame coda, one that would have effectively acknowledged the telling, indicating that there was more to tell.

In Kelly's story, she resolves a narrative and provides a coda in lines 90–91: "Since that time my parents have been very supportive of me." Yet she tells another story and closes that off with another resolution/coda in line 98, "So I guess that's my 'lifestory as a lezzie.'" At the very end she also provides a telling-frame coda where she closes the "telling-of-the-story" frame in lines 101–102, "Hope this story will be a help to you . . . good luck on your paper."

Heidi resolves a story and provides a coda in line 52, "Basically, the rest of the story is the same." But like Tess and Kelly, she begins another story, in line 55, "In

Table 14-1. Coming-out-as-process ends of stories.

Lesbian Coming-Out Story	Coming-Out Story Ends
Tess	telling-frame coda + narrative + narrative-resolution/coda
Kelly	narrative + narrative resolution/coda + narrative + narrative resolution/coda + telling-frame coda
Heidi	narrative + narrative resolution/coda + telling-frame coda + narrative + narrative resolution/coda + telling-frame coda
Helen	narrative + narrative resolution/coda + narrative + narrative + narrative resolution/coda + telling-frame coda

one instance, my other brother, Steve, was lamenting . . ." After this story, she resolves the narrative about Steve and provides a narrative resolution/coda, and in line 61 she gives a telling-frame coda, "There's more, but I've probably given you way more than you wanted anyway." In this coda, like Kelly and Helen, she closes the telling frame.

Conforming to this pattern of stopping and starting at the end of the narrative, Helen resolves one narrative and provides her first coda in line 86, "At this point, it is common knowledge in my family." After this, she tells another story, resolves it, and provides a telling-frame coda in line 105, "Boy, wasn't this a bit long??????"

In addition to having this stop-start-stop narrative structure at the ends of their coming-out stories, Kelly and Heidi make direct comments about the processual-nature of coming out by using lexical and syntactic forms like Heidi's line 61, "There's more," and Kelly's line 100, "My life so far has been . . ." These lexical/syntactic markers and the structure of the ends of the narratives are iconic portrayals of the processual nature of coming out.

Discussion and Conclusion

Lesbian coming-out stories are the linguistic setting in which the tellers narrate events and perceptions, create coherent identities (sometimes simultaneous identities, as in the case of Deaf lesbians), and characterize the process of coming out. Although there is a lack of research related to the telling of stories via electronic mail, Kiesler et al. (1984) suggest that social psychological factors (time and information-processing pressures; absence of regulating feedback; few status and position cues; social anonymity; and computing norms and immature etiquette) influence these transmissions, further challenging what we understand about the nature of spoken and written stories. Although the scope of this paper prevents discussion of these computer-mediated communication characteristics, the stories display the same iconic relationship between the forms of the narratives and the processual nature of coming out that I have observed in orally narrated coming-out stories. In addition to the differences among spoken, written, and electronic stories, there is much to be learned about the task of managing several linguistic frames (e.g., the telling frame and the narrative endings), multiple identities (e.g., Deaf/lesbian), and the incomplete, processual-nature of coming out.

Although I suggest similarities between coming-out stories and other life stories, this study points to the fact that coming-out stories not only construct and portray a life but constitute the performative act of coming out itself. While narrating heterosexual life stories may strongly influence the way the narrator perceives his or her life, as personal change stories, lesbian coming-out narratives not only reflect but create that change of state. The ends of these stories are iconic and look processual because the lesbians telling them are indeed coming out in their telling.

Appendix A
Tess's Coming-Out Story

1 From: Gallua: : TESS
2 To: Gallua: : KMWOOD
3 CC:
4 Subj: RE: coming-out stories . . . send them my way . . .
5
6 Date sent: 2-DEC-1993 08:30:24
7 I told my dad that I was lesbian because my youngest sister threatened to
8 blackmail me with it. My matter-of-fact announcement plus explanation of
   why i
9 was telling him that seemed to take him by surprise so that he didn't really
10 have much chance to react to my news.
11
12 After I told my mom, she began to act uncomfortable around me, but I think
   she
13 is getting better with time.
14
15 I don't have much of a coming out story to tell, because it hasn't been that
16 dramatic for me or anyone else. I guess it would be different if I had a long-
17 term relationship.
18
19 When I attended my (nice) sisters's wedding, I felt very out of place, as if I
20 was celebrating values that weren't mine, among people I didn't even know
   very
21 well, and who were living in totally different worlds than I was experiencing.
22 That event was the last time I remember being asked when I would get
   Married.
23
24 Tess

Appendix B
Kelly's Coming-Out Story

1 From: GALLUA: : Kelly
2 To: GALLUA: : KMWOOD
3 CC:
4 Subj: a higher place in heaven . . .
5
6 Kathy,
7
8 I've got a soft spot in my heart for last minute appeals . . . and I love
9 stories . . . so I thought I'd send you mine . . . anything to help a "sistah"
10 excel academically. I'm 41 years old . . . so it could be a long story. <grin>
11 As far back as I can remember, I have always been attracted to women.
12 I've often thought that I was "born that way." I was born and raised up in
13 a small town in Southern Maryland . . . both my parents were southern

14 "immigrants" . . . their families had travelled North in search of jobs
      during
15 WWII. Mother is from the (name of the) area of (state), and Daddy is from
      the
16 farmlands of (state). A large part of my childhood was spent in the
17 local Baptist Church . . . not quite like Holy Rollers . . . barely one step
18 removed. (Just for the record, I *do* have an Uncle who's a (church)
19 preacher . . . those are the folks who bang on pot lids and roll on the floor
20 speakin' in tongues.) Baptised at 12 I understood the language of hellfire
21 and damnation, but deep in my heart doubted it could be possible . . . (if God
22 really loved us, why would he do that?)
23
24 Spent an idyllic tomboy childhood growing up in the country . . . lots of open
25 spaces and freedom. I rode my bicycle everywhere, had lots of friends,
26 felt pretty good about myself.
27
28 With the onset of adolescence, my orientation toward women became very
29 strong. Oh, I did the regular thing in high school . . . dated lots of boys
30 (they never got very far) and then on the way home would ask them to drop
31 me off at my girlfriend's house . . . (a totally different story there). I
32 thought boys were okay . . . (actually I thought they were pretty borderline and
33 could never figure out what girls saw in them . . . I thought they must be
34 fakin' it, too) . . . but girls were the icing on the cake. Much better than
35 boys . . . they smelled better, their skin was soft, their mouths were smaller,
36 their hands more delicate . . . they just seemed to be a more natural choice
37 for me than boys. I remember one time in High School I overheard a
38 conversation in the girls' locker room about "lezzies". . . I was really
39 curious so I stayed real still and slowly buttoned up my dorky uniform so I
40 could hear the whole thing. One girl was telling the other what "lezzies"
41 were . . . I bought the part about them likin' other girls but I didn't buy the
      other
42 part, but I figured that neither of those girls knew what they were talking
43 about because I liked girls and I *wasn't* a pervert. So I dumped that
44 theory real quick. It never bothered me again.
45
46 At 16, I finally met a woman that I had been incredibly attracted to when I
47 was 12 years old . . . tell me about early sexual development. The very first
48 time I saw her, I was sitting in the school bus swinging my feet when she
49 stepped up into the doorway. She was a Senior and the bus driver picked up
50 her and her sister as a courtesy . . . upperclassmen almost never rode with us
51 "little kids". Anyhow, I stopped swinging my feet, leaned forward on the
52 seat and just stared at this woman who stood at the front of the bus with
53 the morning sun thru the window making a halo around her head. I felt
54 real weird inside . . . kinda squishy and faint . . . but didn't want the feeling to
55 stop . . . I asked the other kids who she was, and was told her name. The next
56 time I saw her, I was 16 years old looking for a job at the local swimming
57 pool where she was the manager. I couldn't believe it. All those old
58 feelings came flooding back again and I thought I would faint dead away.
59
60 She was 21 at the time and teaching elementary phys. ed. in the community.

61 I was absolutely nuts about her and pursued her with the enthusiasm that
62 only a 16 year old has . . . I knew exactly what I wanted from her and if she
63 could've been able to give that back to me, I imagine that I would still be
64 there in my old hometown. We had an "on again, off again" kind of
65 relationship that lasted until I was 21 and went away to college.
66
67 In college, I met lots of girls like me and felt at last that I had found a
68 community of friends that suited me. I was so relieved to discover that I
69 was not the only one! Got involved with the women's center and made lots
70 of friends . . . some straight and most of them gay. It was a heady time for
71 me . . . my orientation was constantly affirmed by the presence of all of my
72 friends and lovers. (my mother still maintains that my "going away to
73 school and getting educated" is what caused me to be a lesbian.) I 'spose
74 that in that case, a little education *can* be a dangerous thing. <grin>
75 All that time, I was never overtly "out" to my family . . . but they had to
76 notice that I only brought girls home with me from school . . . I lived with
77 girls, travelled with girls and all my stories were about me and my
78 girlfriends. Daddy seemed to like some of the girls I brought home . . . poor
79 Momma didn't quite know what to make of it. My family was never rude to
80 anyone who came home with me . . . even today, they still know all my friends
81 and often ask me how they are doing.
82
83 At 25, I entered into what was to become the longest relationship I've ever
84 had. It lasted nearly 13 years—until I was 38. I've been single the last
85 three years. During the time of the break-up, I was such a basketcase,
86 that I finally came out to my parents because I felt that they deserved an
87 explanation for my unusually depressed behavior. My mother cried for about
88 15 minutes . . . I thought she was concerned about my heartbreak . . . but
        she was
89 more worried about my "hereafter" . . . convinced that I would be spending
90 eternity in hell. I ended up comforting her. Since that time, my parents
91 have been very supportive of me . . . and I'm grateful for that. I've tried
92 very hard to convince them that I'm happy with my life and there's nothing
93 they did to "cause" me to be this way. Whenever I go to Florida for a
94 visit, my mother always takes me by the arm so she can introduce me to all
95 of her friends . . . she's obviously proud of me and wants folks to know who I
96 am. That's a good thing.
97
98 So, I guess that's my "lifestory as a lezzie". . . not to[o] exciting or
99 unusual, I think. I'm happy and confident and pleased about how I've
100 turned out. My life so far has been a good one . . . and I hope it continues to
101 be that way. Hope this story will be a help to you . . . good luck on your
102 paper.
103
104 Kelly

Appendix C
Heidi's Coming-Out Story

1 From: GALLUA: : "Heidi"
2 To: GALLUA::KMWOOD
3 CC:
4 Subj: RE: coming out stories . . . send them my way . . .
5
6 Hmmm, ok, coming out stories, huh?
7
8 Well, for me, I went through 26 years of life as a straight person. Broke up
9 with the last serious relationship guy, and moved out on my own. Spent a few
10 months letting the idea of lesbianism creep closer and closer to my
11 consciousness. I started participating a little bit in gay activities, mostly
12 lesbian rap group sessions at the (now defunct) gay community center in DC.
     I dated
13 a little bit, but didn't get into anything serious. Finally I was ready
14 to tell my family.
15
16 I told one of my older brothers over the phone, and he was pretty weirded out,
17 mostly from my delivery (I vowed to do the rest face to face). Next my younger
18 brother, Dave, and my father and step-mother came to DC for a 5 day visit. I
19 told my brother that I was BI (that's how I thought of myself at the time), and
20 he said "that's GREAT!" This ended up being extremely important to me,
     because
21 several years earlier when he was a freshman in college, Dave shared with me
22 that he had a few encounters with gay men. I was pretty sure it was a
23 passing thing that hadn't re-emerged again, and after I came out to him, he
24 confirmed this. It all became important later because (name) committed
     suicide
25 the next week. I know that if I had not been able to share my sexuality with
26 him and have that discussion, I would have been plagued forever with the
27 suspicion that Dave had been gay, and had killed himself out of some sense of
     isolation. But this
28 emotion does not have to complicate my feelings about his death, since I know
29 he supported me fully.
30
31 It was Dave who strongly urged me to take off a weekend from law school and
32 travel down to Atlanta for the Lavendar Law II conference where I ultimately
     met
33 Gina.
34
35 During the same visit, I came out to my father and step-mother. My father
36 turned and looked me in the eyes and said in a very steady voice "NO
     problem"
37 We went on to discuss some of their misconceptions and fears, involving safe
38 sex and the idea that this foreclosed my becoming a mother. They've never
39 ceased to be great.
40

41 The next week, I ended up at my mother and step-father's house for a week, with
42 most of my relatives, while we grieved for my brother immediately after his
43 death. During that week, I came out to most of the rest of my family,
44 including my mother, who has many lesbian friends and often talks about her
45 sexuality in terms of "if I had been born in a different era. . . . " She was
46 elated. After years of seeing me try to be someone I wasn't in order not to
47 threaten the men I dated, she was really pleased to see me accept myself. As
48 she now puts it, it was very special for her that while we grieved for my
49 brother who never felt he could discover who he was, I was announcing that I
50 HAD found my niche.
51
52 Basically, the rest of the story is the same. Almost uniform and glowing
53 support from all my family (YAY family!). The few people who were stumbling
54 blocks, because of religious convictions, I plowed ahead and told them anyway.
55 In one instance, my other brother, Steve, was lamenting that he hadn't "been
56 there" for Dave, and that he hadn't known him very deeply. I took that
57 opportunity to say "well look, Steve, let's not let that happen with us; let me
58 tell you who I am. . . ." I think it went down easier that way.
59
60
61 There's more, but I've probably given you way more than you wanted anyway.
62 Thanks Kathy for letting us tell our stories! I'd love a copy of what you come
63 up with. By the way, I don't need to be anonymous, in case that makes any
64 difference to you.
65
66 Heidi

Appendix D
Helen's Coming-Out Story

1 From: Helen
2 To: KMWOOD
3 CC:
4 Subj: ahhh . . . weepy stories . . . ??
5
6 Okay . . . to help out a fellow (name of distribution list), here is my story.
7
8 Background information: My parents were divorced when I was two. Both
9 are now re-married. I was raised primarily by my father and step-mom.
10 I have four sisters (by different papas).
11
12 Helen: The True Story
13
14 Growing up, I was always, always attracted to girls and women who had
15 blond hair (which explains why I tend to date women who have blond hair).
16 Coming from a straight union (no kidding!!??) and raised in a heterosexual

17　environment, I tried to date boys in junior and high school. I was
18　absolutely not interested in them sexually, emotionally, or
19　spiritually (I was in a physcial and mental sense—liked smart guys who
20　had pretty good bods).
21
22　The first inkling that I was somehow "different" occurred while I was in
23　junior high. All of the girls who I grew up suddenly became totally
24　absorbed in boys—gabbed alllll the silly day about them. I thought it
25　was odd and stupid to talk just about boys. I thought "Gee, what is
26　so fascinating about them??? I don't swoon over them like my friends do."
27　For a while, I played a charade that I was indeed interested in boys and
28　even went out on dates with them (other girls got jealous cuz I went out
29　with the cutest of the crop). That in itself did not _feel_quite right
30　to me. I was always slobbering over girls who had curves and next door
31　girl personality types.
32
33　Because of my libido over girls/women, I went to my father when I was in
34　8th grade (probably about 12/13 yrs old) and said "I think I am gay
35　because I am always looking at (name) (a smashing looking gal!)" Dad
36　tells me in his fatherly manner, "Oh no, you are not. It is normal
37　to look at girls and say 'Wow, she looks real good.'" Doubtful, I
38　asked him if it was alright to desire them in a sexual way—wanting
39　to touch their bodies and dreaming about them. Dad says,
40　"that is normal. That is a stage that all teenagers like you go through."
41　I let it go at that. End of conversation.
42
43　In a hallowed hallway in a huge high school, I am now a freshman. My
44　attraction for girls did not abide on[e] iota. (Bring in those straight-
45　jackets!!!) I became totally convinced that I am gay and eventually
46　linked up with a girl who was also gay (gorgeous blonde!). My first
47　budding gay romance with a track star. Ohhhh . . . nice and pretty. Dad
48　first thought we were just real good friends. It was mid-way through
49　my freshman year that I decided I would "tell" my father that I am
50　definitely gay!
51
52　Enter living room: I told my father in no uncertain terms that I am
53　indeed gay. (Thank god for my step-mom!!!) His reaction??? He grabbed
54　at my shirt collar by the throat area and pushed me back to the wall
55　and screamed "NO, YOU ARE NOT GAY!" My stepmother (name) said,
56　"calm down and let's all sit and talk about this." So we did. For
57　three long hours. They asked me some sexual questions and I refused
58　to answer them (none of their buziness!). But it was at that point
59　that they *knew/got it* that I am gay to the bone.
60
61　The issue wasn't brought up for some time. Shift to Texas (the above
62　scenes were played out in Indiana) where my mother [(name)] and my
63　three sisters lived. I moved there when I was 17. After settling in
64　a bit . . . I called my mother into my bedroom and said "I am gay." Here
65　reaction was the [THE] total opposite of my dad's. "So what?"
66　Thinking she did not understand me or did not quite go through her

67   head, I repeated my statement. Same reaction. We had a discussion . . .

68   turned out that (name of step mother) and (name of mother) had been in
          touch over the phone on

69   this issue. Oh . . . okay.

70

71   My sisters . . . varying reactions. My two oldest ones ([sister's name] and
          [sister's name])

72   were great and took it in stride. Probably cuz they were on their

73   own. My youngest sister, (name), was another issue. Since we both

74   attended the same school, it had an effect on (sister's name). She was a

75   cheerleader with model looks whose reputation mattered a great deal

76   to her. When word got around the school that I was gay, she confronted

77   me at school (in between classes) and said, "There are rumors going

78   around that you are gay!" "Well, I am gay. It is not a rumor!" I

79   did not care who knew because I was a stranger to these people and

80   did not grow up with them. (I think it was a major factor in my

81   coming out earlier than expected) Until I left for college, (youngest sister's
          name)

82   would not kiss me (on the lips) or hug me for a while.

83

84   It was not until I entered college that (youngest sister's name) and my Indiana
          parents

85   came around to accept my gayness. We talked about it more and more

86   openly. At this point, it is common knowledge in my family. My

87   aunts, uncles, cousins, sisters and grandparents all know about my

88   sexual orientation. Whenever my sisters and I get together, they always

89   ask, "Have you found a partner yet?" This past Thanksgiving, we discussed

90   artificial insemmination (sp?) and approaching my nephews about my

91   gayness. I have five nephews (ages 8 to 18 months) and a neice who is

92   now 5 months old.

93

94   During my undergrad years here at (school), I have been involved in activities

95   and issues related to homosexuality. I was openly gay. I told a few

96   friends and the word kinda spread around. I did not care one whit how

97   others thought/felt about me. However, in my freshman year, I did

98   encounter some harrasment. One Thanksgiving, prior to my upcoming trip,

99   someone kept flicking my light and disappeared. Knowing (gut instinct)

100   the culprit, I went over to the other wing and flicked his light. I

101   said in no uncertain terms that if he was to harras me further, I would

102   report him. It had the intended effect. Harrassment stopped there forever!

103

104

105   Boy, wasn't this a bit long?????? (alot better than doing it in some

106   dark bar!)

107

108   Helen

ACKNOWLEDGMENTS   I would like to thank Anna Livia, Kira Hall, and Deborah Tannen for feedback on early drafts and the Berkeley Women and Language Group for permitting me to submit this revised version of my coming-out paper that appeared in *Cultural Performances: Proceedings of the Third Berkeley Women and Language Conference.*

NOTES

1. These data represent all of the responses I received from my request. The distribution list comprises both deaf and hearing women. Two of the respondents, Tess and Helen, are deaf and use English as their first language.

2. Because Tess's ending felt abrupt to me, I discussed it with her later; she told me that she just didn't know how to end it, so she pushed the "control Z" key to exit and send the message.

3. I have used Heidi Norton's real name here, as well as the name of her partner, Gina Smith. They wanted to come out in this chapter in this way.

REFERENCES

Gee, James P. (1991). "A Linguistic Approach to Narrative." *Journal of Narrative and Life History* 1, no. 1: 15–39.

Ginsburg, Faye (1987). "Procreation Stories: Reproduction, Nurturance, and Procreation in Life Narratives of Abortion Activists." *American Ethnologist* 14: 623–636.

Ishikawa, Minako (1991). "Iconicity in Discourse: The Case of Repetition." *Text* 11, no. 4: 553–580.

Kiesler, Sara, Jane Siegel, and Timothy W. McGuire (1984). "Social Psychological Aspects of Computer-Mediated Communication." *American Psychologist* 39, no. 10: 1123–1134.

Labov, William (1972). "The Transformation of Experience in Narrative Syntax." In *Language in the Inner City.* Philadelphia: University of Pennsylvania Press, pp. 354–396.

Labov, William, and Joshua Waletzky (1967). "Narrative Analysis: Oral Versions of Personal Experience." In June Helm (ed.), *Essays on the Verbal and Visual Arts.* Seattle: University of Washington Press, pp. 12–44.

Liang, A. C. (this volume). "The Creation of Coherence in Coming-Out Stories."

Linde, Charlotte (1993). *Life Stories: The Creation of Coherence.* New York: Oxford University Press.

Neumann, Tina M. (this volume). "Deaf Identity, Lesbian Identity: Intersections in a Life Narrative."

Penelope, Julia, and Susan Wolfe (1989). *The Original Coming-Out Stories.* Freedom, CA: Crossing Press.

Riessman, Catherine Kohler (1991). "Beyond Reductionism: Narrative Genres in Divorce Accounts." *Journal of Narrative and Life History* 1, no. 1: 41–68.

Schiffrin, Deborah (1993). "'Speaking for Another' in Sociolinguistic Interviews: Alignments, Identities, and Frames." In Deborah Tannen (ed.), *Framing in Discourse.* New York: Oxford University Press.

Stromberg, Peter G. (1993). *Language and Self-Transformation: A Study of the Christian Conversion Narrative.* Cambridge: Cambridge University Press.

15

Deaf Identity, Lesbian Identity

Intersections in a Life Narrative

TINA M. NEUMANN

Two questions arise in the study of queer language, especially as concerns Deaf lesbian and gay language. How is identity constructed for a Deaf person and for a lesbian? What role do culture and community play within that identity construction? When studying Deaf[1] lesbian language, I emphasize the need for understanding and defining Deaf culture and lesbian culture as two research considerations, as well as understanding where these cultures and perhaps others intersect within the framework of life stories or coming-out narratives. There is a scarcity of study in American Sign Language related to gay and lesbian languages. To my knowledge, no discourse-level analysis of Deaf lesbian and gay language or culture has been published. This research is being done but has not yet reached a wider audience.

Padden and Humphries (1988) attempt to give a broader definition of Deaf culture by acknowledging the diverse origins of the people who constitute the community itself. Deaf people from Deaf families (about 10 percent of all Deaf people) enjoy a respected status within the Deaf community (48). However, many Deaf children have their first exposure to ASL when they enter a residential school, where they interact with the Deaf children of Deaf families and any Deaf adults who may work at the school (6). At the residential school, in the dormitories, these children not only learn ASL but become acculturated into the Deaf community. Yet many Deaf children do not attend residential schools but rather attend public schools with hearing children. Some of these children enter the Deaf community at a later point in life, at which time they learn ASL and meet other Deaf adults. Thus, some Deaf people use ASL as a first language; others begin to learn it at the age of four or five, while still others are not introduced to it until adulthood.

Because of this diversity of backgrounds within the Deaf community, the face of the culture is changing. Identity construction within Deaf culture is not something that occurs in a vacuum; it is shaped by the community in relation to others. Maxwell and Kraemer (1990) examined the link between speech and identity in deaf narratives. The conclusion they drew was that identity is not of singular form but is plural in nature, "as each deaf individual can incorporate his or her own experiences into . . . a narrative and become the hero" (359).

There are several issues related to the concept of lesbian culture as a whole and to the problematic definitions of lesbianism and culture. Two views of culture, objective and subjective, are discussed by Ferguson (1991) with regard to lesbianism. The objective view of culture is more traditional, defining it in terms of common social attributes held by members, who constitute a distinctive social group. Ferguson takes the subjective viewpoint, that culture is a consciously accepted definition of the self and others as members of a distinctive group, a social category; individuals have to consciously accept the cultural characterization themselves. Within this perspective, she offers her theory of lesbian cultures as being cultures of resistance.

Ferguson does not believe in the potential existence of an international lesbian culture; she defends the view that lesbian cultures are cultures of resistance within individual patriarchal cultures. Her historical and dialectical approach allows for the recognition of a variety of lesbian cultures, rather than imposing the concept of Western lesbianism onto others. What constitutes "lesbian" for one culture as a form of resistance may not do so for another.

Lesbians construct their community and their culture. They also construct and redefine themselves and their identities, as well as forming alternate bonds of kinship and family associations. Weston (1991) theorizes that the revelation that one is gay or lesbian provides a challenge to social ties, and often to kinship ties. As Wood (this volume) states, because lesbianism is embedded in a heteropatriarchy, coming out is a recursive, never-ending process of self-discovery and self-disclosure. Within "coming-out" stories, both spoken and written, there is often a dominant theme of long self-discovery culminating in identification as lesbian or gay and the subsequent struggle toward understanding and acceptance from family, either biological or adopted (Weston 1991: 77–102).

Community as a concept has undergone a change, from being seen as a "whole," thereby perpetuating some of the invisibility of lesbians' and gays' other identities, to being seen as a "population" that recognizes the diversity of identities within the community itself. Padden and Humphries (1988) relate this view to the Deaf community. There is a growing recognition that there is no one Deaf culture. Although Deaf communities share many things, there is a new recognition of the diversity of those communities and their cultures. Padden and Humphries mention this awareness but do not address the issues related to this diversity. There is, for example, no in-depth discussion of the African American Deaf or of the Deaf lesbian and gay communities in their work.

The construction of a lesbian feminist collective identity in social movements has been examined by Taylor and Whittier (1992: 104–129), who established a framework for that construction. They proposed three apparently separate, but interacting, perspectives for analysis: *boundaries, consciousness,* and *negotiation.* Taylor and Whittier also listed three factors that contribute to the formation of a collective identity: boundaries that separate and distinguish a group of people from the majority of society; a consciousness that arises from the assumption of the existence of socially constituted criteria that are the rationale for a group's position; and the recognition of the everyday life of the group members as a political issue, their differences becoming a source of pride (Taylor and Whittier 1992: 122). This approach attempts to be broad enough to apply to what Taylor and Whittier call "oppositional identities" (122) based on issues of class, gender, race, ethnicity, sexuality, "and other persistent social cleavages" (122), which I take to include the Deaf-hearing dichotomy that exists within these communities.

In order to study the connections between the linguistic construction of Deaf identity and that of lesbian identity, I interviewed a Deaf informant, recorded her narrative on videotape, and transcribed and then analyzed the ASL signs used. (A transcription of the glosses and a translation are provided in the appendix to this chapter.) The informant (BB) is a Deaf woman in her late twenties and an ASL user since the age of four when she entered the Louisiana School for the Deaf. For the elicited life story, she was videotaped alone, and I was present behind the camera.

I began by asking BB to tell me about her life, suggesting that she begin her narrative by introducing herself. BB followed a formula used within the Deaf community by first stating her name, her name sign, and where she attended school. The mention of her school is an important cultural marker because, as we shall see further on, entry into a residential school for the Deaf often constitutes the first stage of the creation of a Deaf identity for children who do not have Deaf parents. Information about which residential school one attended also allows Deaf addressees to place one in a specific linguistic and cultural context.

BB's life story spans several topics. Two recurring main themes are related to her identity as a Deaf woman and as a lesbian. The first mention of conflict over her Deaf identity occurs in lines 10–13, where she explains that she knew she wanted to go to the residential school, in opposition to her mother's insistence that she attend public school.

    10   PRO1 DON'T^WANT
    11   *PRO1 KNOW
    12   *PRO1 DEAF^INSTITUTE

BB's refusal echoes Ferguson's concept of identity as resistance, which Ferguson related to lesbianism. However, it can be seen that identification as a Deaf person is also resistance; not only does BB repeat the first-person pronoun (PRO1) several times for emphasis in this string of utterances; she marks it by signing emphatically. In ASL, use of the first person singular pronoun is marked. It is unnecessary as a simple deictic, since all verbs are assumed to take the speaker as subject unless otherwise specified. Even as a child, BB's resistance was tied in with the fact that she knew that her identity was linked with the residential school.

This sense of agency is repeated further along in her narrative. BB recounts the time she first realized she was Deaf, upon her arrival at the residential school. She had come to the knowledge of herself as "other" in her family, but the knowledge of herself as "Deaf" came when she attended the school and found her community (cf. Padden and Humphries 1988: 6).

Agency is marked again, in lines 33–45:

```
33   PRO1 REMEMBER PRO1 FIRST REMEMBER
34   [PRO1 DEAF]
35   (2h)PRO1
36   [PRO1 DON'T^KNOW]
37   GROW-UP FAMILY HEARING
38   [#ALL HEARING]
39   PRO1 ONLY-ONE DEAF
40   PRO1 KNOW^THAT PRO1 DIFFERENT
41   BUT #WHAT
42   THAT
43   UNTIL ARRIVE DEAF^INSTITUTE
44   OH THAT
45   [PRO1 DEAF]
```

These utterances set the stage for what Taylor and Whittier (1992) would term "persistent social cleavages" (122) between BB and her family. The first social cleavage takes place within the Deaf-hearing dichotomy, through BB's recognition of the new ties to the Deaf community she has developed via the school and her friend's Deaf family. Her encounter with her friend's family (see the transcription in the appendix, lines 48–89) and the exposure it provided to Deaf culture and community (ease of communication through ASL; introduction to the Deaf club) contrasts with her experience in her hearing family.

Expressions of resistance to her family, of wanting to stay with the Deaf family, occur in lines 59–62:

```
59   PRO1 ARRIVE HOME GET-ATTENTION-OF MOTHER
60   PRO1 LIKE
61   WANT STAY WITH DEAF FAMILY
62   MOTHER LOOK-AT-ME SAY NO
```

The concept of the "chosen family" as opposed to the "biological family" is important (cf. Weston 1991). Her mother does not allow her to stay with her friend's family, but BB finds a way to visit often:

74 MANY TIME PRO1
75 PRO1 GO-TO WEEKEND
76 FINE #OK
77 GET-ATTENTION-OF MOTHER PRO1 GO-TO FRIEND
78 MOTHER #OK

BB lies to her mother about being invited to her friend's home. In lines 74–76 BB tells her friend that she will stay the weekend with her friend's Deaf family; in lines 77–78 BB tells her mother that she was invited. This amounts to resistance to the point of lying and represents another example of social schism. This schism not only is based on pathological deafness but also represents a cultural schism between the hearing world on one hand and BB's new bonds with Deaf peers and her new-found Deaf culture on the other. The Deaf culture here is represented by the deaf residential school where BB went to school, the Deaf family she joins on weekends, and her exposure to the Deaf club (lines 81–89).

81 ALSO GO-TO DEAF #CLUB
82 PRO3 FAMILY GO-TO FRIDAY NIGHT #CLUB SOMETIMES
83 LOOK
84 MANY+++ DEAF
85 YES OF-COURSE
86 PRO1 NOT-KNOW RIGHT
87 [PRO3 HEARING]
88 MINGLE LOOK FINE
89 EVER-SINCE KISS-FIST DEAF . . .

These lines are significant in terms of Weston's (1991) analysis of the realization of the self as gay and as part of a gay community: "Such a discovery need not entail meeting other gay people, but rather becoming convinced of their existence" (Weston 1991: 123). Thus, BB comes to a realization of herself as Deaf and as a member of a Deaf community.

The process of self-identification as Deaf is similar to BB's realization of herself as lesbian and her knowledge of the existence of a lesbian community:

98   KNOW^THAT GROW-UP
99   KNOW^THAT BORN LESBIAN
100 BUT KNOW UNDERSTAND LESBIAN
101 NOT-KNOW UNTIL PRO1 AGE-NINETEEN
102 PRO1 THAT
103 MY FRIEND HEARING
104 TOOK-ME B-A-R BAR
105 LOOK
106 KNOW^THAT MY HOME

This sets up another social schism, or opposition, in Taylor and Whittier's terms. It also begins to establish another form of resistance and another way of being viewed by her family as the "other," as BB recounts coming out to her family:

125 MOTHER FAMILY HATE PRO2
126 THOUGHT PRO2 INFLUENCE-ME
127 REALLY PRO1 START ALL MOVE
128 BECAUSE PRO1 CURIOUS
129 TOUCH THAT+++
130 LESBIAN THAT

Weston (1991: 94) quotes a common heterosexual belief that a young lesbian cannot know her own mind because she has been influenced by gay friends. This belief is often articulated when the lesbian comes out to her parents. There are several factors to be considered here. An adult should be capable of knowing her own mind and making her own decisions about her life. The family's resistance and doubts about BB's abilities alters the family relationship, for her parents are effectively saying that BB is not capable of knowing her own mind or her own sexuality. For BB, the problem is not only the explicit statement that her family hated her girlfriend because they thought she influenced BB to become a lesbian but also the implicit issue of her parents' control (or lack of control) over her life and her sexuality. Her own agency in this prevails, as BB asserts her right to decide for herself.

In the beginning of her life narrative BB sets up the Deaf-hearing dichotomy fairly clearly. Her family are hearing; they do not know anything about the importance of the deaf residential school, ASL, the Deaf club. In the lesbian coming-out passage, they do not know anything about BB's sexuality, since BB was the instigator in the relationship (lines 127–130). This section of the narrative emphasizes her family's ignorance of BB's parallel/intersecting identities: Deaf and lesbian. The social cleavages occur twice in this narrative, once related to the Deaf-hearing divide, the second time related to the lesbian-heterosexual divide. These two areas are equally important to BB's identity. Linguistically, they parallel each other in their discourse structure, as I have shown.

The realization of one's identities may seem to develop in a pattern that parallels several cultural/social theories of identity construction, but in the case of this narrative, the identities of Deaf and lesbian actually can be seen to intersect. This intersection may not be obvious at first glance; it occurs in the narrative when BB relates her family's resistance to her coming out as lesbian and their reasons for "hating" her girlfriend. At first, it seems that their resistance is due to their belief that the woman had led BB into lesbianism; on a deeper level, however, their resistance goes back to BB's childhood and their objection to her persistence in her Deaf identity: They were hearing and therefore (supposedly) knew what was best for her. The identity intersection does not occur earlier, apparently because one essential identity had to be established before the next could be explored.

Identity construction in ASL narratives is still very new to discourse analysis and even to anthropological/ethnographic analysis. I hope that, in time, a larger body of work will be established, providing a richer theoretical base for life-story analysis.

Identity does not occur in a cultural vacuum and so cannot be analyzed in merely linguistic terms; it is created in relation to the communities and cultures of which the speaker feels herself to be a part, how she sees her place within the world, and how she perceives the world's place within her life. An interdisciplinary approach that combines linguistics, anthropology, and sociology is therefore necessary to any analysis of identity construction in narrative.

Appendix

Glossing Conventions

(Adapted from Baker and Cokely 1980.)

KNOW	An English word, capitalized, represents the gloss for an American Sign Language (ASL) sign
#ALL	The symbol (#) represents a fingerspelled loan sign
G-R-A-D-E	The hyphen between letters is used when an English word is fingerspelled
KNOW^THAT	Two glosses linked by (^) represent a compound sign
NO+++	A (+) symbol following a gloss indicate that the sign is repeated; the number indicates the number of repetitions; in this example, NO is repeated three times
*#ALL	The asterisk (*) indicates that the sign is stressed
(2h)#ALL	(2h) indicates that the sign is produced with both hands
[PRO1 DEAF]	Underlining is used when two signs are produced simultaneously. The underlined gloss indicates that the sign is produced by the nondominant hand, while the other gloss indicates that the sign is produced by the dominant hand

Transcription

```
 1   MY NAME B - - - - - - B - - - - - -
 2   SIGN NAME B-B PRO1
 3   PRO1 GROW-UP DEAF^INSTITUTE L-A
 4   LOUISIANA DEAF^INSTITUTE . . .
 5   GROW-UP NO
 6   PRO1 UP-TO FOURTH G-R-A-D-E
 7   PRO1 MOVE-TO HEARING SCHOOL ONE-YEAR
 8   NUDGE MOTHER PRO1 WANT DEAF++ SCHOOL
 9   MOTHER NO+++ TRY SEE IF LIKE HEARING
10   PRO1 DON'T^WANT
11   *PRO1 KNOW
12   *PRO1 DEAF^INSTITUTE
13   MOTHER NO+++
14   PRO1 [ ] ONE-YEAR
```

15 TRUE^ENOUGH PRO1 LAIDBACK
16 DECIDE #BACK DEAF^INSTITUTE
17 EXCITED #BACK DEAF^INSTITUTE
18 FEEL^LIKE BEHIND E-D
19 MOTHER SAY NO+++
20 FEEL++ GOOD G-R-A-D-E IN DEAF^INST (incomplete utterance)
21 HEARING SCHOOL
22 GOOD G-R-A-D-E FOURTH G-R-A-D-E
23 RESIST MOTHER
24 BUT ANYWAY
25 PRO1 GRADUATE DEAF^INSTITUTE
26 WENT-TO PRO1 GRADUATE GALLAUDET FINISH
27 NOW WORK ON MY GRADUATE
28 [THERE #WMC]
29 DEAF E-D
30 GRADUATE FINISH #WMC
31 #BACK HOME LOUISIANA
32 PRO1 PREFER SETTLE-DOWN . . .
33 PRO1 REMEMBER PRO1 FIRST REMEMBER
34 [PRO1 DEAF]
35 (2h)PRO1
36 [PRO1 DON'T^KNOW]
37 GROW-UP FAMILY HEARING
38 [#ALL HEARING]
39 PRO1 ONLY-ONE DEAF
40 PRO1 KNOW^THAT PRO1 DIFFERENT
41 BUT #WHAT
42 THAT
43 UNTIL ARRIVE DEAF^INSTITUTE
44 OH THAT
45 [PRO1 DEAF]
46 OH
47 GROW-UP [PRO1 AGE-TEN ELEVEN]
48 FIRST^TIME
49 JOIN DEAF FAMILY SEE
50 DEAF PARENTS SIGN-FLUENTLY
51 PRO1 WATCH
52 EAT+++ CL: PEOPLE-SIT-AROUND-TABLE
53 SIGN-FLUENTLY
54 PRO1 WATCH
55 ENVIOUS
56 PRO1 COMFORTABLE
57 STORIES
58 EASIER
59 PRO1 ARRIVE HOME GET-ATTENTION-OF MOTHER
60 PRO1 LIKE
61 WANT STAY WITH DEAF FAMILY
62 MOTHER LOOK-AT-ME SAY NO
63 SORRY
64 LEARN SIGN

65 MOTHER CAN SIGN
66 MY TWO SISTER SIGN
67 SIGN-FLUENTLY NO++
68 RIGHT+++
69 MY TWO BROTHER FATHER
70 INCOMPETENT SIGN
71 FINGERSPELL GESTURE
72 G-E-S-T-U-R-E GESTURE KIND-OF
73 PRO3 DEAF FAMILY PRO1 KISS-FIST
74 MANY TIMES PRO1
75 PRO1 GO-TO WEEKEND
76 FINE #OK
77 GET-ATTENTION-OF MOTHER PROS GO-TO FRIEND
78 MOTHER #OK
79 PRO1 GO-TO OCCASIONALLY
80 MANY TIMES REALLY LIKE
81 ALSO GO-TO DEAF #CLUB
82 PRO3 FAMILY GO-TO FRIDAY NIGHT #CLUB SOMETIMES
83 LOOK
84 MANY+++ DEAF
85 YES OF-COURSE
86 PRO1 NOT-KNOW RIGHT
87 [PRO3 HEARING]
88 MINGLE LOOK FINE
89 EVER-SINCE KISS-FIST DEAF . . .
90 KNOW^THAT IDENTITY
91 (2h)PRO1
92 AS DEAF PERSON . . .
93 REALLY . . .
94 FEEL^LIKE
95 PRO1 COMPLETE (unfinished utterance) . . .
96 NOW KNOW ABOUT LESBIAN
97 (2h)PRO1
98 KNOW^THAT GROW-UP
99 KNOW^THAT BORN LESBIAN
100 BUT KNOW UNDERSTAND LESBIAN
101 NOT-KNOW UNTIL PRO1 AGE-NINETEEN
102 PRO1 THAT
103 MY FRIEND HEARING
104 TOOK-ME B-A-R BAR
105 LOOK
106 KNOW^THAT MY HOME
107 AWF
108 PRO1 UNDERSTAND LESBIAN
109 NO
110 MINGLE MEET WOMAN
111 SELF SUPERVISOR MY DEAF^INSTITUTE
112 LONG-TIME-AGO CL: SHE-CAME-UP-TO-ME
113 [HER] FIRST^TIME
114 [MY] FIRST^TIME

115	MEET
116	TWO-OF-US SLEEP-TOGETHER
117	TWO-OF-US SWEETHEARTS
118	BUT UNDERSTAND WHAT MEAN
119	TWO-OF-US FIRST^TIME
120	[PRO2 NEVER] EXPERIENCE BEFORE
121	FIRST^TIME
122	PRO1 NEVER EXPERIENCE BEFORE
123	AWKWARD
124	AWF
125	MOTHER FAMILY HATE PRO2
126	THOUGHT PRO2 INFLUENCE-ME
127	REALLY PRO1 START ALL MOVE
128	BECAUSE PRO1 CURIOUS
129	TOUCH THAT+++
130	LESBIAN THAT
131	ARRIVE GALLAUDET PROS DATE FEW
132	BUT THEN-ON THROUGH-COLLEGE DATE
133	WHY
134	DON'T^KNOW
135	FOCUS BASKETBALL BLAME SELF
136	MY FAULT . . .
137	FAULT PRO1
138	ENJOY FOCUS BASKETBALL
139	NOW PRO1 FEEL TIME FOR PRO1 FOCUS WITH WOMAN ..
140	KNOW^THAT LESBIAN DEAF
141	BITTER NO
142	IMPOSSIBLE PRO1 BECOME STRAIGHT IMPOSSIBLE
143	AWF
144	NO+++ STAY LESBIAN AND DEAF
145	SOME PEOPLE ASK
146	WHY^NOT COCHLEAR-IMPLANT
147	C-O-C-H-L-E-A-R I-M-P-L-A-N-T SO-FORTH
148	PRO1 AGAINST
149	AWF
150	MAINSTREAM
151	PRO1 AGAINST
152	MAYBE MAINSTREAM #OK
153	GROW-UP WITH MOMMY DADDY
154	WITH +++
155	PRO1 UNDERSTAND++
156	BUT GROW-UP J-R #HS #HS
157	SHOULD SEND-TO DEAF^INSTITUTE
158	BECAUSE START
159	1 LEADERSHIP
160	[2 <u>DEAF #CLUB</u>]
161	[3 <u>S-P-O-R-T-S</u>]
162	KEY
163	SEND-TO
164	GROW-UP

165   ADMIT PARENTS WITH ELEMENTARY MAINSTREAM
166   DON'T^MIND BUT GROW-UP
167   N-O
168   ESTABLISH
169   MUST CONTINUE DEAF^INSTITUTE
170   MY DEAF^INSTITUTE
171   ANY TIME COLLAPSE
172   TRUE FEW TIMES TRY
173   ESTABLISH-NOT
174   BUT DEAF PEOPLE
175   THEY NO+++
176   NOW NEW SUPERINTENDENT
177   PRO3 B-I-L-L- P-R-I-C-K-E-T-T (?)
178   HOPE PRO3 CONTINUE
179   MY DEAF^INSTITUTE BIG INSTIIU1E
180   CAN HOLD UP-TO FIVE-HUNDRED PEOPLE
181   DEAF^INSTITUTE UP-TO FIVE-HUNDRED
182   NEW WITH NEW DESIGN BUILDING
183   COLLAPSE DO+++
184   WASTE++
185   M-S-S-D COLLAPSE MOVE-TO LOUISIANA DEAF^INSTITUTE
186   WHY^NOT
187   WRONG+++
188   MOVE MORE EXPAND STAY ALL ALONG
189   NO
190   BAD IDEA WHY
191   FOR^SURE M-S-S-D PARTY HEAD
192   REALLY LOUISIANA PEOPLE PARTY HEAD
193   WORTHLESS
194   WHAT ELSE SHOULD SAY

Translation

This written English translation is based upon the original videotaped text and is not to be taken for an exact translation of the ASL glosses or the ASL signs.

Lines 1–32:

My name is B - B -. My name sign is [ASL sign]. I grew up attending a school for the deaf in Louisiana, Louisiana School for the Deaf . . . well, actually, no, I went there up until the fourth grade, and then I was transferred to a public school for a year. I told my mother I wanted to go to the residential school, but my mother insisted that I try and see if I liked the public school. I didn't want that—I *knew* I wanted to be at the residential school, but Mom disagreed. I [intelligible] one year, sure enough, I didn't learn anything, it was a waste of time. So, Mom decided that I should go back to the residential school, and I was excited to be back. I felt as if I were educationally behind, but my mother disagreed—she felt that I got good grades that year in public school. Good grades? I still disagree with Mom over that point. Anyway, I graduated from deaf school, and I went on to graduate from Gallaudet. Now, I'm working on my MA at WMC in Deaf education. When I graduate from there, I plan to go back home to Louisiana, where I want to settle down.

Lines 33–89:

I remember when I first realized I was deaf. I didn't know what that meant, I was born to a hearing family; they're all hearing. I'm the only deaf person. I knew that I was different, but I didn't know in what way, until I arrived at the residential school, and I learned what "deaf" meant. I'm *deaf*, oh, that!

Growing up, I was about ten or eleven when I went home with a Deaf classmate, who had a Deaf family. For the first time I saw Deaf parents signing fluently with family members. I would watch as around the dinner table everyone was communicating fluently with each other. I was envious of that; I felt so comfortable there, and it was so much easier to converse. I would arrive home and tell my mother that I liked that family, I wanted to stay with them. Mom would look sadly at me and say no.

Signing? My mother can sign, and so can my two sisters—not fluently, though. My two brothers and my father can't sign; they can just barely fingerspell and kind of gesture.

I loved that Deaf family. Often I would tell my friend that I'd be going home with her for the weekend and then tell my mother that I was invited—and of course Mom would let me go. I'd stay with them occasionally. I really enjoyed it.

Friday nights, my friend's family and I would go to the Deaf club. My first time there, I just looked and looked; my jaw dropped to the floor. There were so many Deaf people! My friend took it as a matter of course. I hadn't known that so many Deaf people existed—my family is all hearing, remember. I would hang out with these people at the club, participate in conversations, have a good time. Ever since those days, I've cherished my Deaf community. . . .

Lines 90–144:

I am confident of my identity as a Deaf person . . . really . . . I feel like I'm complete [unfinished utterance]. Now, about lesbians—I knew as I was growing up, I knew that I was a born lesbian . . . but did I know or understand what being a lesbian meant? I didn't realize until I was nineteen that I was a lesbian. My hearing friend took me to a bar. I looked around and I knew that I was home. Did I understand anything about lesbianism? No! I would hang out with these women, and I met someone who was a dorm supervisor at my residential school a long time ago. She came up to me, and it was the first time for both of us. We slept together and were sweethearts. It was really awkward, since it was the first time in a lesbian relationship for both of us.

My mother and family hated her, because they thought that she influenced me to be a lesbian. Actually, I was the one who made the first move! I was curious about what lesbians did, so . . . When I came to Gallaudet, I dated a few women, but as I went through college, I didn't date anyone . . . I'm not really sure why. Because I was so engrossed with basketball? My own fault. Yeah, I enjoyed basketball, but now I feel it's time for me to start concentrating on women again!

I know I'm lesbian and Deaf. Does that make me bitter? No . . . it's impossible for me to become straight, impossible! No, I think I'll stay lesbian and Deaf!

Lines 145–194:

Some people have asked me why I don't have a cochlear implant. I'm totally against that! I'm also against mainstreaming and all that . . . well, maybe mainstreaming is ok for kids to stay with their parents, I understand that, but when they get to be in junior high school, high school, they should go to a residential school. That's where they can learn about leadership, deaf clubs, participate in sports—these are crucial. They should go there. I guess it's ok if they are mainstreamed in elementary school, to be with their parents, but after that, no. . . . Once residential schools are established, they must remain open.

Several times, there's been threats to close my residential school, but the Deaf community protested, so they kept it open. Now there's a new superintendent, Bill Prickett [fingerspelling not clear], and I hope he keeps it open.

My residential school is large, it has about 500 students; the buildings are new with modern architecture. If they closed it, what would they do with it? That would be a waste! Maybe they should close MSSD and move them to Louisiana School for the Deaf. Why not? What's wrong with that? If they moved there, it would become larger and remain open! Nah, that may be a bad idea, because the MSSD students would become party-heads! Really, it's the people in Louisiana who are party-heads! It's a worthless idea. . . .

What else should I talk about?

NOTES

1. Following the convention of Woodward (1972), a capitalized "D" in "Deaf" denotes one who uses ASL and considers herself to be culturally affiliated with the Deaf community. The lower case *d* in *deaf* denotes a pathological/medical condition of hearing loss, with no linguistic or cultural affiliates.

REFERENCES

Baker, Charlotte, and Dennis Cokely (1980). *American Sign Language: A Teacher's Resource Text on Grammar and Culture*. Silver Spring, MD: T.J. Publishers.

Ferguson, Ann (1991). "Is There a Lesbian Culture?" In Jeffner Allen (ed.), *Lesbian Philosophies and Cultures*. New York: State University Press, pp. 63–88.

Maxwell, Madeline M., and Pam Kraemer (1990). "Speech and Identity in the Deaf Narrative." *Text* 10: 339–363.

Padden, Carol, and Tom Humphries (1988). *Deaf in America: Voices from a Culture*. Cambridge, MA: Harvard University Press.

Taylor, Verta, and Nancy E. Whittier (1992). "Collective Identity in Social Movement Theories: Lesbian Feminist Mobilization." In Aldon Morris and Carol McClurg Mueller (eds.), *Frontiers in Social Movement Theory*. New Haven: Yale University Press.

Weston, Kath (1991). *Families We Choose: Lesbians, Gays, Kinship*. New York: Columbia University Press.

Wood, Kathleen M. (this volume). "Narrative Iconicity in Electronic-Mail Lesbian Coming-out Stories."

Woodward, J. (1972). "Implications for Sociolinguistics Research among the Deaf." *Sign Language Studies* 1: 1–7.

16

*The Creation of Coherence in Coming-Out Stories

A. C. LIANG

I've realized now that I can tell all my friends about the kind of guys I like to date. . . . I can write to some 30,000 Cal students a week on the importance of (and secrets to) drag makeup. And, honey, I don't care if the whole world knows that I can't take it as a bottom. But I can't show these clippings of my newspaper columns to my dad. I can't tell my grandma that the "ugliest" baby she has ever seen took first runner-up in a beauty pageant and has serious hopes of becoming a future Miss Gay Universe. I can't tell my mom about my love life (or lack of it). I haven't come out. At least not where it counts: to my family.

Eddie Jen, "It's Snowing in Berkeley," *Daily Californian* (October 9, 1996)

The 1996 reelection of Bill Clinton, the first gay-friendly U.S. president to engage in public discussion of homosexuality, marked a begrudging public recognition, if not acceptance, of homosexual ways of being. As columnist Deb Price of the Detroit *News* put it, "Anyone doubting [the significance of Clinton's reelection] should take a moment to ponder how a Clinton defeat would have been interpreted: Every newspaper in America would have at least partially blamed his gay-rights advocacy" (November 8, 1996). Historically momentous for gay visibility and equality, Clinton's reelection overlays a plethora of less dramatic though no less consequential instantiations of the changing status of lesbians and gays in the United States today. Each week, one hears of one or two more municipalities adding sexual orientation to its antidiscrimination clause; of another corporation expanding its employee benefits package to include domestic partners; of a city instituting a domestic partners registry. In mainstream popular culture, lesbian and gay characters are no longer exclusively and simplistically portrayed as criminals or deviants. They now appear in recurring roles on TV shows like *Roseanne* and *Melrose Place*, and their relationships are common themes in films and theater. Since the late 1960s, the number of books on the subject of homosexuality has proliferated from 500 or so to roughly 9,000 in the late 1980s, an increase of nearly two orders of magnitude (Gough and Greenblatt, 1990: xxi, cited in Plummer 1992:

287

xiv). But the mainstay of this cultural transformation is the sheer number of individuals who accept and define themselves, at least in part, by their homosexuality, and this increasing number is itself reinforced by the admittance of the topic of homosexuality into public discourse. Homosexuality in the United States has come out of the closet.

Even so, homosexuality as a personal characteristic is still highly negatively valued, and there is vehement resistance to granting it legitimacy within the fabric of U.S. society and politics. National polls continue to indicate that a majority of Americans disapprove of homosexuality, and over a third would not vote for a political candidate because of his or her sexual orientation. As of late 1996, in only nine states of the Union and in the District of Columbia was discrimination based on sexual orientation in housing, employment, and public accommodations illegal. And in no state are homosexual relationships legally protected.[1] Violence against lesbians and gays is a major component of hate crimes, and it is rising in frequency (28 percent in five major cities between 1994 and 1996) with the increase in gay visibility. In custody battles, a homosexual parent is typically denied custody or visitation rights of his or her own children, even when the competence and sanity of the other parent is in doubt. Teachers still get fired for being gay or lesbian; lesbian and gay youths are subject to antigay harassment. And children who are active in their community promoting lesbian and gay rights still do not talk to their parents about their personal lives.

Thus, cultural norms are in a state of flux as far as social approbation of homosexuality is concerned. It is therefore interesting to study the ways in which individuals incorporate their gayness into their personal narratives. Any decision to define one's self as lesbian or gay is necessarily one which requires explanation. Indeed, it is the explanation, or to use Mills's words, "the ultimates of discourse" (1940 [1984]: 19), through which an individual's narrative can be understood by and thus shared with others. So common and necessary is this personal and social process of making sense of a lesbian or gay identity via the personal narrative that it has been termed the "coming-out story." Before going into the details of the forms and functions of the coming-out story, I want to consider those properties of identity which are established and expressed through language.

Language and Self

The central role of language in the constitution of self is alluded to by Linde's definitive statement of the personal narrative: "Narrative is among the most important social resources for creating and maintaining personal identity" (1993: 98). The presentation and construction of the self is a social process conducted through the telling of a personal narrative. In order for one individual to express herself to another, not only must she be able to tell a life story which is intelligible, but both she and the audience must reach more or less the same understanding of the point of the story.

Linde (1993: 100) identifies three characteristics of the self which are maintained and expressed through language:

- continuity of the self
- the self's separateness from and relatedness to others
- the reflexivity of the self

Continuity of the self refers to the sense that one's previous experiences are related to one's later experiences and that the past bears on who one is at the moment. In western cultures, continuity of the self is constructed linguistically through the *narrative presupposition* (Labov 1972), whereby the events in a narrative are assumed to occur in a temporal sequence analogous to that in which they are reported. Further implicit in the narrative presupposition is the relationship of causality. Events which are temporally ordered permit the inference that those events are causally related to each other. Since, according to Linde, "The ability to perceive or create a sense of historical continuity is an achievement of a normal personality" (1993: 101), the narrative presupposition itself is fundamental to the creation of a coherent self-presentation.

The second property of the self that may be established and maintained linguistically is the *self's relationship to others*. The ability to reconcile the self's separation from and relatedness to others is the basis for what R. D. Laing (1969) terms *ontological security*, the feeling of being in possession of a whole, integrated person, whether coping with the stresses of social interaction or those of isolation. According to Linde, all languages appear to have a way of distinguishing the speaker (first person) of an utterance, the addressee (second person) to whom the speaker is directing the utterance, and the nonparticipants (third person) of the speech event in which the utterance is being made; hence, all languages recognize the existence of distinct persons. Linde further points out that the "reuseability" of pronouns by any speaker to refer to the self, her addressee, and others who are neither the speaker nor the hearer establishes the self as related to others:

> *I* is not a name, like Susie or Jack, that refers to the same person, no matter who uses it. Rather, *I* changes its reference depending on who uses it. To understand this is not merely to understand an arbitrary fact about language use—like the fact that we do not say *childs*, but instead say *children*. To understand the shifter nature of *I* is to come to comprehend that others exist in one's world who have the same nature and who must be seen as separate but fellow beings. (Linde 1993: 112)

At a more abstract level of linguistic structure, the personal narrative (and other self-presentational genres) functions, on the one hand, to present the speaker's self as distinct from her addressee while, on the other hand, engaging in a social process in which the interpersonal relationship between speaker and addressee is evoked. For instance, the telling of the narrative may serve to demonstrate how the addressee herself should behave in similar circumstances. An individual may evidence her group membership by modeling the structure of her narratives after that of the group (cf. Silberstein 1982, cited in Linde 1993: 113); she may make reference to interests she shares with her interlocutors.

Finally, Linde (1993: 121) refers to the *reflexivity of the self* as the third property of the self that is displayed and maintained linguistically. All questions of

"How am I doing?," whether in relation to one's own standards or in relation to the standards of others if such a distinction can even be made, require the ability to make evaluations, and the evaluations cannot be done by the immediate liver of the life; the task requires a watcher and narrator who is related but not identical. It is through this feature that the self can change. The individual can look back on her life, even if it was just a moment ago, and put it into narrative form, to be revised and edited in accordance with the norms and values shared by herself and her audience. She can thereby present a self which is socially (and morally) agreeable. Tannen demonstrates the complexity of this relationship between the self and other through the concept of involvement. She invokes Chafe's tripartite schema (Chafe 1985, cited in Tannen 1992), whereby conversation consists of the speaker's self-involvement, the involvement between the speaker and her audience, and the speaker's involvement with what she is talking about. Tannen illustrates how the speaker's attempt to retrieve from memory extraneous details, on the surface, constitutes self-, and not other-involvement, since the details do not clarify or provide relevant information for the listener. Yet the interpersonal relationship between self and other is implicated in that such details enhance the imagery and make the narrative seem authentic, thereby drawing the listener into the speaker's narrative.

Language and Lesbian/Gay Identity

When an individual encounters in herself a characteristic, such as gayness, that is subject to cultural disapprobation, then, theoretically, within that culture, that aspect of self cannot be incorporated into a tellable narrative. From the perspective of cultural norms, a gay self is not recognized as valid (or as existing at all) and hence not worth justifying. Thus, some individuals undertake aversion therapy or commit suicide as a way of doing away with what is culturally disapproved and hence ego-alien. Yet, the existence of the coming-out story is evidence that individuals do manage to incorporate gayness into their identities.

This chapter examines the structure of the coming-out story in order to ascertain the coherence principles by which the individual makes sense of his or her gayness. Of particular interest are those aspects of the narrative that have to do with how the speaker deals with recognition of a gay self. The group whose stories are under examination consists of Asian American and European American male college students, aged 18–27. Coherence principles of the coming-out stories of the two groups are delineated. The stories were told in rounds and, with the permission of participants, tape-recorded during a ninety-minute Coming-Out Stories rap session held in celebration of Coming-Out Week on a university campus. The chapter is arranged as follows. First, the coming-out story is defined in terms of its content and form. Next follows a comparison of one component of the coming-out stories of Asian Americans and of European Americans: the self-recognition of gayness. Finally, the coherence principles by which self-recognition is achieved are extracted.

Defining the Coming-Out Story

Because homosexuality is a contested concept (Barrett, this volume)—that is, one for which no prototypical meaning exists—whether or not an individual is homosexual is a matter of personal decision rather than convention. While, as Sweetser (1987) notes, meanings of words generally depend on "simplified or prototypical schema of personal experience," the invisiblity of homosexuals does not lend itself to personal experience out of which a prototype notion of a homosexual can emerge. As a result, definition as homosexual begins with the individual and the self's internal and highly idiosyncratic experiences and with the verbalizing of those emotions, instead of with any external criteria based on a simplified schema of a range of complex experiences.

The term for the act of naming and accepting one's same-sex emotions is *coming out*, the shortened form of *coming out of the closet*. It is a metaphor for both the recognition to oneself and the act of disclosing to another one's homosexuality. As implied by the question "How out are you?," coming out is a matter of degree rather than of a binary opposition. Just as there is no prototypical meaning of homosexuality,[2] so too is there no central definition of coming out. I will attempt to demonstrate that coming out, and whether or not it has taken place, is also something that varies according to individual opinion. Nonetheless, in any instance of coming out, there appears to be at least one of three recognizable properties: self-definition as lesbian or gay to the self; self-presentation as lesbian and gay to others; membership in a series of ongoing acts of self-definition, and/or self-presentation as lesbian or gay.

Depending on one's perspective, coming out to self can be seen as necessarily instigated by external homosexual behavior or, more probably, as constituting a gradual process of self-acceptance as homosexual. On the one hand, the nonpsychological viewpoint might hold, for instance, that the first experience of having sex with a person of the same sex constitutes coming out (Barrett 1989: 48). But categorical denial or rejection of the label *homosexual* for such behavior may continue even during long-term same-sex relationships (e.g., Barrett 1989). On the other hand, the extent to which gayness can rely not on behavior but on self-recognition as such is exemplified by the following personal advertisement.

> I don't consider myself gay. I'm a regular guy who likes men who like only men. I'm tired of nonsense & insincerity. I'm 40, tall, bearded, good looking, healthy, caring, straight forward & very discreet. I like to work outdoors & walk. I like good music & art. If you feel as I do, are about my age, handsome & interested in a relationship [*sic*]. Write Dept. 3819 Gannett Newspapers, 14614. (Rochester *Democrat and Chronicle/Times-Union*, 28 December 1994)

As the ad demonstrates, self-naming works both ways in the absence of well-established social naming conventions for identities whose cultural status is in flux. An individual may retain the labels reflecting normative (i.e., culturally accepted) identities despite nonnormative (i.e., culturally disapproved) preferences and behaviors; or he[3] may readily adopt labels (e.g., drag queen) consonant with his nonconventional behaviors and preferences. Among some members of the lesbian and gay community, however, criteria for identifying lesbians and gays are sufficiently stable such that there are even terms for those who are, according to these criteria, lesbian or gay but who refuse or have yet to define themselves as such. Thus, individuals such as the above advertiser would be deemed *closet case* or *fag-to-be*, or in more generic psychoanalytic terms, in denial (about his sexuality). Nonetheless, variable and contested though its definition may be, for the purposes of this chapter, coming out to self is the ability to utter phrases synonymous with "I am gay."

The definition of self-disclosure to another is equally protean. It can be brought about with or without the individual's express intention but also depends on the addressee's understanding. The intention to come out can be signaled with nonverbal cues, such as wearing an earring only on the right earlobe or suppressing the urge to conceal gay newspapers, paraphernalia, and photographs when guests visit.[4] Verbal disclosures span a range of explicitness, from "I am gay" to an ambiguous statement about being "together" with a same-sex lover. Yet, in all instances, if the addressee does not recognize the intention, that is, if he does not apprehend the significance of the earring on the right earlobe, then it is questionable as to whether coming out has taken place. Similarly, if the addressee chooses not to recognize the intention, then the discloser's status as a gay individual, with respect to the addressee, is still unclear. If through the gay individual's own unintentional behavior the addressee discovers the secret, coming out may or may not be said to have taken place, depending on how the individual assesses his own behavior, that is, if he "really wanted" to come out or if it was accidental. In the latter case, the term *outing oneself* may be appropriate. If he announces his gayness for one day only and never does so again, allowing, for the rest of his life, the heterosexual presumption to stand, he may or may not be said to have come out. In spite of the difficulty of determining a set of conditions for whether or not self-disclosure to another has taken place, for the purposes of this chapter, coming out to other will be viewed straightforwardly as the successful and intentional communication by one individual of his gayness to another to whom such information has not previously been conveyed by the gay individual himself.

Coming out to self and to other can overlap. The experience of articulating one's gayness to another can simultaneously induce an internal acknowledgment (much as insight in the psychotherapeutic setting can be gained merely with the linguistic formulation of feelings never before verbalized). What is clear is that the act of coming out is fraught with ambivalence on the part of both the discloser and the recipient, rendering precise definition difficult, as explained earlier.

Finally, coming out is processual. The fundamental nature of reproduction and its implications for what constitutes a legitimate relationship in this culture, and the consequent pervasiveness of heterosexuality and the vigor with which it is sold, give rise to the default assumption of heterosexuality as the natural condition of all members of the culture. Consequently, gays have to continually recreate themselves through self-naming to ensure that they are heard and understood as individuals who define themselves as and therefore are gay. At the same time, they are faced with the burden of having to decide with every interaction whether or not to self-disclose. It is by virtue of being compelled to make this decision with every interaction that coming out is processual. Not everyone can know, and therefore not everyone does, and the default assumption of heterosexuality remains in place. Still, with every disclosure, that assumption becomes further dislodged.

Coming out is therefore a speech act that not only describes a state of affairs, namely the speaker's gayness, but also brings those affairs, a new gay self, into being. By presenting a gay self, an individual alters social reality by creating a community of listeners and thereby establishing the beginnings of a new gay-aware culture. Coming out is, in this respect, a performative utterance (Austin 1962) that can be seen as revolutionary.

The form and function of the coming-out story

In this section the structure of the personal narrative, as proposed by Labov (1972), is reviewed. Next, the coming-out story is defined in terms of a particular type of personal narrative, the life story. Finally, one story is examined to exhibit the characteristic structure of a coming-out story.

The personal narrative

Labov (1972b: 359) described the narrative as "one method of recapitulating past experience by matching a verbal sequence of clauses to the sequence of events which (it is inferred) actually occurred." The clauses in question are termed narrative clauses, whose change in sequence alters the meaning of the event sequence. The structure of the narrative can include the following: *abstract* (an encapsulation of the story and why it is being told), *orientation* (an identification of the situation, consisting often of past progressive verbs that describe what was happening before the first narrated event), *coda* (the signal that the narrative has ended and that returns the participants to the present), and *evaluation* (how the speaker makes his points with regard to telling the narrative). A minimal narrative consists of two ordered narrative clauses, which Labov termed the "complicating action."

The pertinence of Labov's conceptualization of the personal narrative to the present analysis rests on the fact that, like the narratives upon which his analysis is based, the coming-out stories examined herein were elicited. This is reflected in the discrete, fully developed, structure of the narratives. In actual conversation, however, narratives are considerably less distinguishable from the surrounding conversational context. Moreover, a speaker who produces a spontaneous narrative is under a social obligation to establish the reportability of the narrative, its relevance to the conversation up to that point, how it impinges on the relationships among the participants of the conversation, its connection to the activities in which they are engaged, and so on. A teller of an elicited narrative is not burdened to the same extent since some degree of relevance has been preestablished by the addressee who has elicited the narrative. While the reportability of an event can be established just by virtue of its being unusual, such as spotting a naked man walking down a busy street, it can also be indicated by an explicit evaluation, as in the following (to use Polanyi's 1976: 60 example),

and here's the funny part

The evaluation directs listeners as to how they should interpret what is to follow. In the first person narrative, evaluatives also position the speaker as one who shares the norms of the listener. They may also have suggestive force in demonstrating to the listener what he should or would do under similar circumstances.

In any case, since the telling of a story is socially situated, it must contain some linguistic or paralinguistic devices to guide the listener toward an interpretation of the story which matches more or less that intended by the speaker. These devices are the evaluations, which, at minimum, justify to the listener why the story is worth listening to. The life story is a particular type of first-person narrative inasmuch as it is a story that "makes a point about the speaker, not the way the world is" and "is tellable over the course of a long period of time" (Linde 1987: 344). Because coming out can be considered an event about the speaker which has extended reportability, a story about coming out is classifiable as a subtype of the life story.

One person's coming-out story

The coming-out story can be defined as one that describes the speaker's internal experience of recognizing and acknowledging his gayness and the external experience of revealing that information to others. It may consist of accounts of one or both forms of coming out. That coming-out stories exist at all and are recognized by members indicates their centrality in defining a gay identity as well as a gay culture. For the gay individual, telling a coming-out story presupposes self-acceptance and self-definition as homosexual.[5] This presupposition is one of the central evaluative components of the coming-out story. A coming-out story is not only an account of the reportable event of coming out but a source of social validation for the narrator. It is told to a receptive audience (e.g., other gays) who can affirm the gay identity of the narrator and reinforces bonds of mutual support among participants.

Another major evaluative aspect of the coming-out story involves the ways in which the narrator (and his interlocutors) cope with the recognition or disclosure of his sexuality. Fear of exposure has prompted gays to engage in deception and other forms of concealment, but they have also felt hypocritical for doing so. Consequently, in telling their coming-out stories, speakers often distance themselves from the protagonist's actions, indicating to the audience that they now know better than to engage in the deceptive behavior of their former selves.

The following story, broken down into parts (a), (b1), (b2), and (c), reflects the three characteristics of coming out: the internal coming out (a), the external coming out (b), and its processual nature (c).[6] In excerpt (a), although Mark reports no trouble coming out to himself and therefore does not offer a narrative account, he does supply an explanation for how he circumvented inner conflicts concerning his gayness.

Uh I'll go next. /?/ Um I's pretty lucky 'cause um, I didn't have to deal with what a lot of people said, that coming out to yourself is very hard. Um I knew I was attracted to men before I knew that was wrong, and I think that was very strange, 'cause I I was attracted to um, uh other guys when I was pretty young, still. Um so I guess the circumstances around me coming out was just uh, coming out to other people an' an' that has been hard um, uh, two years ago, not anymore. Mark [a], Asian American male, aged 20)

The rationale Mark employs is that his attraction for men preceded his awareness of cultural values concerning homosexuality. I discuss this further in the section on coherence principles. However, at this point it is reasonable to ask why the speaker feels the need to preface his narrative with an explanation of his coming out to himself rather than simply going on to tell his stories (b). First of all, as mentioned, self-definition as gay involves two dimensions, coming out to self and coming out to other. As a member of the gay culture, the speaker understands this and thus addresses both aspects. But more crucially, in the context of a culture where heterosexuality is the unmarked case, gayness is ego-alien, and hence its acceptance by the individual of gayness in himself bears explanation, either by way of narrative or the discourse unit of the explanation, as defined by Linde (1993), who points out that speakers use explanations to "establish the truth of propositions about which the speakers themselves are uncomfortable, or to defend propositions whose validity they feel their addressee has in some way challenged" (92). Particularly in the case of coming-out stories, speakers anticipate that the implausibility of a proposition, acceptance of one's own gayness, will raise doubts in the addressee's mind. Consequently, the speaker addresses the issue of coming out to self despite the fact that, in this case, the speaker's narrative principally involves coming out to other.

After settling this issue, Mark goes on to tell a few stories of coming out to other people. The following account (b1) in Table 16-1 exemplifies how a segment of a coming-out story may consist of all the components enumerated in Labov's analysis. The external evaluation given at the beginning of the narrative ("Um, ih-it was kinda funny") explicitly states the reasons for telling the story. An abstract then sums up the story as involving lying and deceitful behavior. Next are three orientation clauses that situate the narrative events, followed by a series of narrative clauses that describe the protagonist's thoughts and actions. The (failed) outcome of the coming-out attempt signals the end of the narrative.

In (b1) the protagonist does not actually come out, so the speaker goes on in excerpt (b2) (Table 16-2) to relate more instances of "lying and deceit" before ending with a story in which there was no question of his success in self-disclosing. Again, the structure of the accounts conform to Labov's analysis of the personal narrative. Although there are many more evaluative clauses in part (b2) of the speaker's story, all of the components that make up the personal narrative, with the exception of the abstract, are present. Since this stretch of speech falls within the scope of the abstract mentioned in (b1), there is no need for an abstract for (b2). Furthermore, (b2) consists of two stories, one about lying to a priest and the other about hedging with an acquaintance in spite of mutual suspicions of the other's gayness. Although the first story ends not with a clear-cut coda but with an evaluation ("I lied to a priest"), it directs the audience's interpretations of the events

Table 16-1. Mark (b1)

Clause	Structural Type
Um, ih- it was kinda funny	Evaluation
'cause there w- it involved a lot of lying and deceit?	Abstract
Um, 'cause when I first came out, I went to this Neuman, um the Neuman center?	Orientation clause
The Catholic church had a, a panel discussion on gays.	Orientation clause
And I was sittin' in the audience,	Orientation clause
And I'm all, well now, I'm here w- um, they'll probably think I'm gay by association.	Narrative clause
So I'm all, well how do I mitigate this?	Narrative clause
So I raised my hand	Narrative clause
and I said um, I said, isn't being gay, um, a psychological thing so that you can change it?	Narrative clause
So everybody looked at me	Narrative clause
and they started going, boo:!	Narrative clause
So I go, shit!	Narrative clause
So um, so then you know, I I left the meeting	Narrative clause
um not coming out to anybody really,	Coda
maybe I did but um.	Evaluation

just reported and alludes to the abstract mentioned earlier, namely, the lying involved in the protagonist's attempts to come out. The fact that the stretch of talk that follows is unrelated to the priest incident confirms (to both analyst and audience) that it was intended to finish another narrative without ending the current story.

Following this segment is part (c), which pertains to the processual nature of coming out, signaled, in particular, by the "it," which refers to the person-by-person disclosure that makes up the coming-out process. This processual aspect is also underscored by the use of the past progressive in "it has been going well."[7]

> And um it's been going well since then, I'm out to all four of my siblings, um I'll probably wait till uh till I get outta school before I tell my parents though. 'S been pretty good. (Mark [c])

This coming-out story, containing an explanation of coming out to self, three narratives of "lying and deceit," and a record of who has been and who has yet to be told, is structured in accordance with the definition given earlier. I now compare the structures of the stories of Asian American and European American males.

Asian American and European American Coming-Out Stories Compared

As mentioned, the stories under examination take place in a rap session. In a rap session, individuals assemble to discuss issues or problems unique to those sharing

Table 16-2. Mark (b2)

Clause	Structural Type
So like the following year, I went back uh, to another meeting	Narrative clause
and this time it was explicitly just gay people, a gay group meeting over there,	Evaluation
and I came late on purpose	Narrative clause/ evaluation
'cause uh, you don't wanna be the first one there.	Evaluation
And you know, I came late on purpose,	Narrative clause/ evaluation
and I didn't realize, you know, being late wasn't like being gay late	Evaluation
'cause gay late's very late.	Evaluation
So I get there,	Narrative clause
and there's nobody there.	Evaluation
And I'm all, Shit!	Narrative clause
So then one of the father, one of the priests at the /?/ came up to me,	Narrative clause
he goes, are you here for the: meeting?	Narrative clause
'Cause he didn't wanna say gay meeting,	Evaluation
'cause it was still very low key back then	Evaluation
and I'm I'm all, uh: no I'm not.	Narrative clause
So I lied to a priest.	Evaluation
[laughter]	
So I went next door,	Narrative clause
and I was giftwrapping presents for the homeless,	Orientation clause
and I'm all, Okay I'll time this now, I'll go back over there when they break for ah refreshments, you know.	Narrative clause
So I'm over there wrapping for a while,	Orientation clause
and I go back,	Narrative clause
and I bump into a friend of mine who works at the bank with me,	Narrative clause
and I think,	Evaluation
well, we sort of suspected each other,	Evaluation
he's been trying to tell me that he's gay,	
'cause we're we're uh working,	
he'll be telling me, oh I went to church in the Castro last Saturday,	
and I'd just say, oh okay, you know.	
He's all, you know, all kinds of hints,	
and I'm just ignoring it.	
But now I'm,	Narrative clause
he goes he goes,	Narrative clause
we're standing there at the meeting,	Orientation clause
and we're pouring drinks,	Orientation clause
and he's all, oh what are you doing here?	Narrative clause
I'm all, oh I don't know, what are you doing here?	Narrative clause
And so then we just came out to each other.	Coda

membership in the same oppressed or stigmatized group and for which there is no institution within which those issues can be managed. Discussion usually takes the form of the exchange of stories, which serve to give definition to participants' experiences and to provide different ways of handling them, particularly in the face of discrimination and silencing by the politically dominant. Participation in the rap session is thus governed primarily by common experiences resulting from group membership rather than by acquaintanceship among participants. Above all, participants assume that it is therapeutic both for the speaker to verbalize his difficult experiences to a receptive and supportive audience and for audience members who have had similar experiences to feel validated by hearing the experiences of others.

In the coming-out stories under examination, speakers evidence awareness of the rap session frame (cf. Tannen 1993) in the telling of their stories. Remarks such as "My name's Kevin," which preface stories, allude to the fact that the gathering is among individuals who have not previously met. Others, like "Okay, I'll go next," signal the nature of turn-taking in the rap session. Individuals have the option of volunteering a story or yielding their turn to the next person. When speakers are done, they indicate this with remarks such as "That's it." Less linguistically salient, though still manifest, is the awareness that turn length should be such that everyone is permitted the opportunity to decide whether or not he wants to speak. Speakers tell their stories without diverging from the subject under discussion or occupying the floor for too long, in order to leave enough time for as many potential speakers as want to volunteer a story. Given that there is the sense among participants of an "acceptable" turn length for discussion of an "acceptable" topic, speakers choose to emphasize different components of their stories in ways that correlate by ethnicity.

The general pattern that emerges from these data is that Asian Americans, in contrast to European Americans, focus on experiences of coming out to others much more than on those of coming out to self. This difference is reflected in the proportion of the turn allotted to speakers' feelings about their gayness and to the outcome of coming out to others. Asian Americans spend almost all of their turns telling about the experience of coming out to other and virtually no time on the experience of coming out to self. Unlike European Americans, Asian Americans do not present a self that is racked with inner conflicts. It is interesting to examine the selves that members of each group do present and how each accounts for acceptance or incorporation of his gay identity in his narrative.

Coming out to self

Whereas the coming-out-to-other component presupposes the speaker's acceptance of his gayness, it is concerned only with external social events and does not address the psychological issue of how the speaker worked out any possible threats to his identity posed by gayness. In a sense, the coming-out-to-self component is the most important part of the coming-out story, since it enables the individual to understand his life as both a moral person—that is, one who shares cultural norms with his listeners—and a gay person. A gay individual must necessarily construct a coming-out-to-self story prior to telling coming-out-to-other stories, since the reverse, telling a coming-out story prior to coming out to self, would be interpreted as schizoid behavior, or, at the very least, require an explanation.

The coming-out-to-self component in the stories of Asian Americans tend, in these data, not to occur in narrative form. Instead, speakers explain how they managed to avoid inner conflict and often omit any reference to their own feelings about their gayness at all. The coming-out-to-self component, part (a) of Mark's narrative, reproduced here, is structured as an explanation as defined by Linde (1993: 90–94).

> Uh I'll go next. /?/ Um I's pretty lucky 'cause um, I didn't have to deal with what a lot of people said, that coming out to yourself is very hard. Um I knew I was attracted to men before I knew that was wrong, and I think that was very strange, 'cause I I was attracted to um, uh other guys when I was pretty young, still. Um so I guess the circumstances around me coming out was just uh, coming out to other people an' an' that has been hard um, uh, two years ago, not anymore. (Mark [a])

As a discourse unit, the explanation consists of the position to be proved and the supporting arguments. In (a), the statement of the proposition to be proven is "I's pretty lucky 'cause um, I didn't have to deal with what a lot of people said, that coming out to yourself is very hard." Mark then shows why this statement should be believed. Because he learned of his attraction to men before he became aware of societal disapprobation, he was able to accept his homosexual feelings easily.

Speakers may even decide not to mention coming out to themselves and instead simply proceed to tell a story about coming out to someone else. Still, the justification takes the form of an explanation, X so Y.

> Well I'm Thomas and um, I'm I'm out to selected people but um, you know I find myself—I mean I find my coming-out story boring so I'm not gonna tell the whole thing. (Thomas [a])

Given that this statement is made just at the beginning of his turn, "the whole thing" can be said to include the coming-out-to-self component of the speaker's story and therefore one part of the coming-out story he declines to tell. According to the speaker, its omission is warranted because it is "boring." Thus, the speaker appears to be more concerned with the impression made upon his audience in the telling of his story than with the purpose of the telling in the rap session, adding to the repertoire of alternatives of how speakers came to be aware and accepting of their homosexuality.

European Americans portray protagonists whose self-acceptance is preceded by a sometimes lengthy internal struggle with their gay feelings. This struggle, or inner conflict, is transformed into words using metaphor, inner speech, expressive phonology, repetition, and detailed imagery, to name a few of the devices that appear in the data. Rather than adding to the propositional content of what is being expressed, these devices add to the emotional effect of the story. The following is

an excerpt from a longer narrative that describes the journey toward self-acceptance. Several of the devices mentioned are employed by the speaker to describe
the protagonist's attempt at, and the consequences of, denial of his homosexual
feelings.

> When I was fifteen, I started thinking to myself, you know, this probably isn't a phase,
> I'm gonna have to deal with this someday soon. But I said, I'll deal with this later.
> When I was sixteen, I had my first massive massive crush on this guy in my high
> school, and I'm like, I do not how- know how to deal with this. So I sort of just let it
> sit, and it sit, and it got bigger, and it got bigger, and it got bigger, and then w- finally
> when I was seventeen, I could not deal anymore, and so I went and told my mother.
> (Gil, European American male, aged 22)

In this excerpt, the distance with which the speaker refers to his feelings—as
evidenced, for example, by the use of impersonal pronouns ("it," "this")—reenacts
the denial he describes. Metaphor describes his feelings ("it got bigger"), inner
speech reports his growing realization of their reality ("I started thinking to myself, you know this probably isn't a phase . . ."; "But I said, I'll deal with this later";
"I'm like, I do not know how to deal with this"), and repetition conveys the intensity of his feelings as well as his own inability to control them ("I . . . just let it sit,
and it sit, and it got bigger, and it got bigger, and it got bigger").

Another speaker, John, makes extensive use of repetition to describe how
badly he wanted to be straight. (The transcription has been arranged to emphasize
the repetitions, which are underlined.)

> My focus shifted to now, the one thing, the one <u>goal</u> I had was to be <u>cool</u>.
> It- <u>I just wanted to fit in.</u>
> <u>I wanted to fit in.</u>
> All my friends you know, were like, hetero- er <u>heterosexual,</u>
> or at least they thought of themselves as <u>heterosexual.</u>
> They had <u>girlfriends</u> and all that kind of stuff.
> <u>I wanted to fit in.</u>
> <u>I wanted to be cool.</u>
> <u>I wanted to have a girlfriend.</u>
> <u>I wanted to um,</u>
> well I <u>I w- wanted to fit in.</u>
> That was my my <u>goal,</u> my life's <u>goal</u> now. (John, European American male, aged
> 22)

In describing the protagonist's plight, the speaker employs "I wanted to . . . ," the
paradigmatic structure upon which the excerpt is built. The speaker becomes so
involved with the repetition (and presumably the intensity of emotion that it exhibits) that he repeats the paradigm once again before realizing that he has run out
of new information with which to fill it ("I wanted to um, well I I w- wanted to fit
in"). Indeed, a few lines following this excerpt, the speaker confirms his involvement with the text by reporting "I was really confused, just like I am talking about
it right now." The evaluative effect of the list is that it communicates the strength

of the protagonist's sentiments about being gay and the associated desire to belong. The last line in the excerpt ("That was my goal, my life's goal now") enhances the rhythm of the sentence, by contrast, and hence the intensity of the feelings conveyed by the repetition.

Now that we have seen some typical examples of excerpts from the coming-out-to-self components of the stories of Asian and European Americans, we may consider one Asian American exception found in the data. As mentioned, most Asian Americans tended to discount coming-out-to-self experiences as uneventful by giving explanations. In contrast, Mike related a narrative of his coming out to self. The following is the coming-out-to-self component:

> Okay, my name is Mike? Let's see, I've been out for one year, exactly one year last April, and the rea- one reason why I came out was um, um, I've always known since I's like seven or eight years old, I guess. I don't know the first time you think about these, things, but the reason why I came out 'cause I was I I know a lot of people, I have a lot of friends but /?/ so lonely like, during the month of February, March, basically isolated myself from everybody, would um, never return calls, didn't call anybody noone, /people call me back/, and was doing really poorly in school, and um, and suddenly you know I was, it was really bad, you know, I was really feeling depressed. So then I deci- and then one time there was this movie showing on TV, channel two, and I forgot the name of it but it's from- about a family, a dysfunctional family, one was gay, one was alcoholic, and the and the girl uh, the- and the woman was- had a bad marriage. And one, during the movie, um the best line that I heard I still remember you know, was when well, when the son came out to his father and uh, and 'cause he had tried to commit suicide and uh, he tried smashing himself into a pole, and then what happened was, the father or the mother said, look you think we would rather visit you in the graveyard than you know, accept you who you are. And then just thinking about /?/, I said myself, /?/ my parents, would I want to see my parents visit me in the graveyard? They would just, it was it was unfair for me and it was unfair for them. So then I decided to go out there and just look for things. (Mike [a], Asian American male, aged 20)

Distinguishable in passage (a) is the overall narrative of how the speaker came to accept his homosexuality and the narrative embedded within it describing the TV program that prompted his acceptance. That his concern is simply to give a summary report of his emotions before proceeding with the other components of the story rather than focusing on the coming out to self is illustrated by several points. First, the apparent abruptness of the onset of his depression and its equally sudden departure is quite different from the stories of European Americans, who spend years fighting off their gay feelings. The impression is that the disturbance to the protagonist's self-image is not as extreme or persistent as it is for European Americans. Second, unlike the previous European American speakers, Mike summarizes rather than dramatizes his emotions. This is evident from the absence of any of the devices used by the white speakers. Instead, the speaker does no more than state in gross terms that he was "really depressed" and that "it was really bad." His perspective is oriented externally, that is, upon his self-imposed isolation from social intercourse and the suffering of his schoolwork, both of which were caused by his depression. Third, and crucially, his original intention regarding his account was that it serve only as a subnarrative or introduction to the longer, more detailed accounts of his coming out to other, as evidenced by the "So then I deci-," which presumably would have ended the coming-out-to-self component if he had not self-interrupted at that point and proceeded with the description of the film. The fact that his coming-out-to-self account does indeed end with "So then I decided to go out there and just look for things" supports this argument. Had he continued with his sentence, that is, not self-interrupted, the passage up to that point would have served as an orientation for the coming-out-to-other narrative rather than as a narrative in its own right, as does the coming-out-to-self constituent in the other Asian American speakers' stories. Finally, in comparison with the rest of his rather lengthy turn, the intended coming-out-to-self story and the actual one are both quite short. This forms quite a contrast to the urgency and duration of inner conflict that characterizes the coming-out-to-self component of European Americans. Thus, while from a structural point of view this speaker's coming-out-to-self component constitutes an exception to the other stories told by Asian Americans, particularly because of the problems he had in self-acceptance, nevertheless, the tendency to focus away from internal experiences and the comparatively easier time had by Asian Americans in accepting their gay selves is evident in the structure of this speaker's story as well.

By examining the structure and the linguistic devices employed in the telling of the coming-out-to-self constituents of coming-out stories, we have seen that Asian American speakers are less concerned with the emotions associated with their coming out to self than European Americans are. The former do not address the issue at all, explain it away, or summarize without delineating the events through the use of external evaluations, while the latter spend most of their turns dwelling on what went on in their minds before they came out to themselves.

Beyond cultural coherence systems

According to Linde (1993: 12), in order for a text to be recognized as coherent, two relations must hold:

> One is that its parts—whether on the word level, the phrase level, the sentence level, or the level of larger discourse units—can be seen as being in proper relation to one another and to the text as a whole. The other is that the text as a whole must be seen as being a recognizable and well-formed text of its type. Thus, a cowboy movie is understood both because its internal structure is understandable—that is, the shootout follows rather than precedes the explication of the problem over the ownership of the ranch—and because it stands in a tradition of prior texts recognizable as cowboy movies.

Implicit in this definition is the idea that textual coherence is a product of the interaction between speaker and hearer. The speaker is expected to create a text whose coherence is evident to or can be constructed by the listener, while the listener attempts to understand the speaker's text as coherent and to indicate that this is so. *Adequate causality*, one of the coherence principles in life stories recognized by Linde (1987, 1993), is an expectation that all members of the culture have for a coherent story, and speaker and listener negotiate as to whether or not it has been achieved. On the one hand, the fulfillment of adequate causality depends on social norms of what constitutes a reasonable sequence of events, a decent person, a proper life, and so on. On the other, it also depends on the speaker's own creativity in constructing an account whose causality will be acceptable to the listener. For instance, we saw that Mark's explanation of how he managed to accept his gayness arose from the general unlikelihood that a member of a homophobic culture would simply accept this aspect of himself. If he had not explained his assertion that he avoided the problems of self-acceptance, it would have lacked adequate causality. Thus, it was necessary to spell out the reasons for self-acceptance. In the case of the rap session, where talk tends toward monologue and stories are told in rounds, however, whether or not a speaker's stories have adhered to coherence principles is less overtly subject to negotiation.

As mentioned, part of what constitutes adequate causality is determined by what is culturally defined as proper. What is an expected or recognized cause or explanation forms part of what Linde calls *coherence systems*. Linde (1993: 164) defines a coherence system as a set of assumptions that provides "a means for understanding, evaluating, and constructing accounts of experience." Some of the coherence systems used by Americans employ concepts from expert systems that have undergone simplification once they have reached the general public. Among the ones she discusses are Freudian, astrological, feminist, and Catholic confessional systems of thought. When speakers construct life stories, they rely on these systems to provide a means for structuring events so that the criteria for coherence are fulfilled. Linde contrasts the following constructed exchanges to show how one but not the other meets the criteria for coherence:

3a. How did you come to be an accountant?

3b. Well, I guess I have a precise mind, and I enjoy getting all the little details right.

4a. How did you come to be an accountant?

4b. Well, my mother started toilet-training me when I was six months old. (Linde 1993: 18)

The response in example 3 invokes the white middle-class American commonsense coherence system, which holds that individual character traits and preferences supply adequate justification for one's professional choice. As for the response in example 4, unless the listener shares the Freudian coherence system whereby current personal circumstances can be ascribed to events in one's childhood, the justification supplied does not provide a satisfactory account for why the speaker became an accountant.

In previous work (Liang 1995), I have shown that in telling coming-out stories, European American males portray a protagonist who attempts to reject or deny his gayness and who does so until some facet of his survival is at risk.

Since a stigmatized self is by definition not justifiable, the only way it can be dealt with is to carry cultural assumptions of normality to their logical conclusion. At this point, individuals arrive at the dilemma of having to decide between continuing to deny their gayness at the cost of friendships, their sense of morality, and sometimes, their lives or accepting their gayness in the face of cultural disapprobation. As mentioned, European American males tend to emphasize the coming-out-to-self component at the expense of stories describing coming out to others. I now consider the structure of one narrative told by a European American speaker in order to discover the coherence principles employed therein.

The following narrative contains characteristics of what Polanyi (1985) refers to as *generic narrative*. Narrative clauses in generic narratives are signaled by modal verbs such as *would* and *used to*. But most striking about the story is the use of negation.

> Um, I'm one of those people who had a great deal of trouble coming out to myself. Uh, I didn't come out to anyone in high school and I didn't come out to anyone during my four and a half years at Cal. Uh I, you know, I would see the MBLGA table or something, and, you know, I would never even think of approaching it. Um, it wasn't really until um, late last year th- that I started coming out, and this was after a period where, you know, I could see that there were a lot of costs associated with being in the closet for an extended period of time. Uh, basically, I found myself just kinda retreating from the world in a lotta of different ways. Uh, I've always, you know, have valued my friendship with my parents, but it was just ver- much easier just not to have to deal with /?/ Or even you know, I would even avoid calling them on the telephone, they they live in Orange county. Uh, same thing with friends. I just didn't keep up with people 'cause e- the easiest way to live a lie is to not uh, have to deal with someone, or just not have the issue come up. (Don [a], European American male, 27 years)

In addition to using the modal verbs, Don employs negated simple past tense verbs to describe a state of affairs by negation, that is, in terms of what has not happened ("I didn't come out to anyone in high school," "It wasn't really until um, late last year that I started coming out," "I just didn't keep up with people"). Thus, as well as describing the past, he evaluates it. He denies an expectation, either explicit or implicit, of the positive. The statement "I'm one of those people who had a great deal of trouble coming out to myself" reveals the speaker's assumption that coming out to oneself is expected. Following this is a series of statements describing what the protagonist had failed to do, and how he therefore fell short of morally proper behavior. The fact that the speaker subsequently terms the protagonist's behavior as "living a lie" indicates that the positive proposition which he has been denying should have taken place. Thus, the speaker's attitude toward the protagonist is one of censure. The past is therefore, as Labov (1972) and Tannen (1979) have noted, reportable because it shows that the events described deviated from what the speaker now holds to be expected or proper. This latter point is crucial.

Don has described the protagonist's efforts at concealment and the way in which the hypocrisy he felt at doing so prompts him to self-disclose. He remarks

on the fact that he started coming out after he began to see that his secretive behavior came at the expense of his own sense of morality ("This was after a period where I could see that there were a lot of costs," "I just didn't keep up with
people cause the e- easiest way to live a lie is to not have to deal with someone or
just not have the issue come up"). The assessment of the protagonist's behavior
as "living a lie" is adduced as the reason which prompts him to self-disclose.
Thus, the moral stance taken by the speaker vis-à-vis his own previous behavior
is that of regret for his own cravenness and deceptiveness. The ways in which
speakers understand their acceptance of their homosexuality have to do with de-
picting a protagonist who pushes his false assumptions to the limit until he finds
that some aspect of his identity is at stake, such as his sense of moral self, as in
Don's case.

   We may now examine the coming-out-to-self constituents of the stories of
Asian Americans to discover the coherence principles, the ways in that they justify and make sense of the incorporation of a gay self, that prompt them toward
self-acceptance as gay. We saw in the previous section that speakers place a comparatively low emphasis on internal conflict. While European Americans recount
their desperation and the measures they took to try to be straight or produce detailed descriptions of their attempts at denial, Asian Americans tend not to mention any desire to be heterosexual, nor do they dwell on inner struggles. Instead,
speakers frame the absence of internal conflict in terms of circumvention of cultural valuations by having become aware of their attraction to members of the
same sex before acculturation of knowledge of negative valuations of same-sex
attraction. As seen earlier, Mark explained that he knew that he "was attracted to
men before [he] knew that it was wrong" and thus avoided the conflicts that he
might have experienced if he had been socialized into the belief that homosexuality was wrong. Thomas doesn't even address the issue of coming out to self at all
because it is "boring."

   The coherence principle invoked by Asian Americans is that they became
aware of their same-sex attraction prior to learning the homophobic values of the
culture. Ted, with whom I conducted an interview to elicit his coming-out stories,
employed the same reasoning as Mark regarding acceptance of his gay identity,
that is, he was attracted to men before he became aware of societal disapprobation.
When I queried him about later socialization in values having to do with homosexuality and how that might retroactively affect one's self-image, he acknowledged that feelings about one's homosexuality could thereby be affected. Furthermore, as seen in the excerpt, he admits to having been aware of the negative
valuation of same-sex attractions and the consequences of revealing it to others, in
spite of his previous assertion that he learned of his homosexuality *before* he knew
it was socially disapproved.

> I guess so, it's it's um, y- yah, um, I think that uh, y'could, but in my case there's never
> a factor of um, wanting to change myself? An' I an' I an' I sort of uh attribute that to
> the fact that I was sort of aw- self-aware as being gay from a very young age. I'd never
> really wanted y'know to cure myself or to change myself. Uh my primary concerns
> were, how do I be a gay person and not let anyone else know about it, right? So it's not

like um, I just wanted to fool everyone around me. I didn't want to change myself. Right? So um, like yeah, I do- you do learn, well I I did know that everyone else would think it was wrong, even at that age, but it's not something I n- I really kinda took for granted myself. It's just something um, I knew would make other people ostracize me and therefore, they couldn't know. (Ted, Asian American male, aged 26)

But his explanation does not satisfactorily account for his success and the failure of others who also realize their attractions early on in avoiding internal conflict. Seeing this, he must assert that he never internalized the assumption that homosexuality should be negatively valuated ("it's not something I n- I really kinda took for granted myself"). This implies that at least some Asian Americans do not sustain completely the values of Western culture, particularly in the arena of homosexuality.

Nonetheless, the ways in which Asian Americans make sense of having accepted their sexuality is similar to the way whites do. Just as European Americans claim to arrive at a point at which some aspect of their survival is no longer viable under the assumptions (i.e., the negative valuation of homosexuality) derived from the cultural common-sense system as defined by Linde (1993), so too do Asian Americans claim that their innocence regarding the same cultural values enables them to accept themselves as gay. Both groups justify gayness outside of any system of cultural norms, but one does so as an outsider of the culture, both maturationally and also, by implication, ethnically, and the other does so when it finds that cultural assumptions cannot accommodate its existence. The exception is the case of Mike, for whom the television portrayal of a boy who attempts to kill himself because of his gayness is vivid enough to enable him to imagine the same fate if he indeed continued to remain depressed. For him, self-acceptance is a question of survival as it is for the European Americans, which suggests that Mike may have internalized Western homophobic values.

Conclusion

Researchers in cross-cultural psychiatry have recognized the apparent somatization of emotions among members of Chinese culture[8] (Marsella, Kinzie, and Gordon in Draguns 1990: 260). Even third- and fourth-generation Chinese Americans in Hawaii have been found to experience depression as physical symptoms, in spite of their assimilation into American culture (246–247). One possible explanation, employed in psychotherapy textbooks that address crosscultural issues (cf., e.g., McGoldrick, Pearce, and Giordano 1982; Berman 1990), is that whereas the overt expression of emotions would interfere with personal relationships, thereby drawing attention to the individual at the expense of relationship, somatization of emotions into physical pain allows for the retention of some form of social structure (e.g., the role of caretaker and the one cared for).

According to Linda Wai Ling Young (1982), this attention to harmonious relations is also manifested in Chinese discourse strategies. Whereas Westerners, particularly Americans, prefer a discourse strategy in which a point of view is first presented and then followed by supporting arguments, the Chinese see the Western strategy as confrontational and disruptive of social harmony. In Chinese discourse, reasons are stated first so that listeners can be led gradually to the position held. But to the Westerner, this strategy is oblique, hence the stereotype of the "inscrutable" Chinese.

One can speculate that Asian American gays evidence some aspect of this orientation toward external (i.e., social) reality in their coming-out stories. As we have seen, in all of the stories told in the rap session in question (as well as in the stories collected by the researcher in interviews and in informal settings), the protagonist is portrayed as one whose attention is directed toward the external aspects of coming out. He may report the external consequences of his feelings (e.g., Mike's poor academic performance) or the social circumstances of his disclosure (e.g., the words uttered in coming out). But in all instances, Asian Americans downplay the inward-looking, coming-out-to-self component of the coming-out story.

That Asian Americans tell coming-out stories at all means that the coming-out story constitutes one discourse genre in their repertoires of linguistic behavior. That is, it marks them as communicatively competent members of an American gay community. They demonstrate understanding of its role in defining an American gay identity. But the fact that their stories do not reveal the inner conflicts to the same extent as those told by European Americans can be attributed to adherence to the values of Asian culture, whether as a cultural predisposition to withhold expression of emotions or as a bypassing of certain presuppositions of Western culture (such as the communication of emotions and the homophobia that are embedded therein). That their stories assume a distinct form, different from those of European Americans, reflects their tie to Asian culture and thus indexes their identity as Asian. In telling their coming-out stories, they reaffirm not only their own existence as gay Asian Americans but also that of the gay Asian Americans in the audience.

NOTES

1. Although its legal implications have yet to be assessed, the signing into law by Clinton of the federal Defense of Marriage Act defines marriage, as used in federal statutes, as an institution between a woman and a man, and is, if anything a symbolic gesture affirming the institution of heterosexual marriage and heterosexuality.

2. The Kinsey scale is a seven-point gradient scale of sexual orientation based on sexual behaviors and preferences, ranging from exclusively heterosexual to exclusively homosexual. Homosexual behavior comprises all but the exclusively heterosexual category.

3. Because the subjects of this study are male, the masculine generic prounouns will be employed hereinafter.

4. The term for this is "straightening up," a pun on the word *straight* used for heterosexuals.

5. It should be added that an account of recognition of homosexual tendencies does not in itself constitute a coming-out story. Coming out implies a commitment to a gay identity. Accounts related in aversion therapy or in the Catholic confession booth, or more recently, in Ex-gay Ministries (*SF Weekly*, 1 March 1995), are not coming out stories. Rather, the coming-out story is defined here as those stories told to receptive audiences for the purposes of creating solidarity and community with other lesbians and gays, and the reinforcement through (re)construction of the teller's lesbian or gay indentity.

6. Because all of the stories analyzed in this chapter can be divided into at least two of

the three constituents, the letters are used to designate the corresponding constituents for those stories as well. Where no letter appears in the line identifying the speaker of a passage, it can be assumed that it is excerpted from but does not itself form one of the constituents.

7. Wood (1995, this volume) suggests that the difficulty in bringing the reader back to the present, evidenced in the absence of codas, is reflective of its ongoing, incomplete process. The iconic representation of the coming-out process is also seen in the coming-out stories told by the participants in the rap session. The order in which the stories are told (beginning with coming out to self, followed by coming out to other, and concluding with the people still to be told) and the way they comprise a series of narratives rather than a single one, as exemplified by Mark, illustrate the processual nature of coming out.

8. The notion of somatization is seen by Dragus (1990: 246) as a possibly Western bias toward the psychological origin of emotional pain. He suggests that externally-oriented cultures, like that of the Chinese, may experience emotional correlates of depression but emphasize sensitivity to "actual bodily manifestations of depression".

REFERENCES

Austin, J. L. (1962). *How to Do Things With Words.* Oxford: Clarendon Press.
Barrett, Martha Barron (1989). *Invisible Lives: The Truth about Millions of Women-Loving Women.* New York: Morrow.
Barrett, Rusty (this volume). "The 'Homo-genius' Speech Community."
Berman, John J. (ed.) (1990). *Cross-Cultural Perspectives.* Lincoln: University of Nebraska Press.
Draguns, Juris G. (1990). "Normal and Abnormal Behavior in Cross-Cultural Perspective: Specifying the Nature of Their Relationship." In John J. Berman (ed.), *Cross-Cultural Perspectives.* Lincoln: University of Nebraska Press, pp. 235–277.
Gough, C., and E. Greenblatt (1990). *Gay and Lesbian Library Service.* Jefferson, NC: McFarland.
Jen, Eddie (1996). "It's Snowing in Berkeley." *Daily Californian* (October 9, 1996), p. 4.
Labov, William (1972a). *Sociolinguistic Patterns.* Philadelphia: University of Pennsylvania Press.
——— (1972b). "The Transformation of Experience in Narrative Syntax." In *Language in the Inner City.* Philadelphia: University of Pennsylvania Press, pp. 354–396.
Liang, A. C. (1995). "Transition and Transcendance of the Public and Private Dichotomy." In Mary Bucholtz, A. C. Liang, Laurel Sutton , and Caitlin Hines (eds.), *Cultural Performances. Proceedings of the Third Berkeley Women and Language Conference.* Berkeley: Berkeley Women and Language Conference.
Laing, R. D. (1969). *The Divided Self.* New York: Pantheon.
Linde, Charlotte (1987). "Explanatory Systems in Oral Life Stories." In D. Holland and N. Quinn (eds.), *Cultural Models in Language and Thought.* Cambridge: Cambridge University Press, pp. 342–366.
——— (1993). *Life Stories.* New York: Oxford University Press.
McGoldrick, Monica, John K. Pearce, and Joseph Giordano (1982). *Ethnicity and Family Therapy.* New York: Guilford Press.
Marsella, A. J., D. Kinzie, and P. Gordon (1973). "Ethnic Variations in the Expression of Depression." *Journal of Cross-Cultural Psychology* 4: 435–456.
Mills, C. Wright (1940 [1984]). "Situated Actions and Vocabularies of Motive." In Michael J. Shapiro (ed.), *Language and Politics.* New York: NYU Press, pp. 13–24.

Plummer, Ken, ed. (1992). *Modern Homosexualities*. London: Routledge.

Polanyi, Livia (1976). "Why the Whats Are When: Mutually Contextualized Realizations of the Narrative." In K. Whistler et al. (eds.), *Proceedings of the Annual Meeting of the Berkeley Linguistics Society* (February 14–16). Berkeley: Berkeley Linguistics Society, pp. 59–78.

———— (1985). *Telling the American Story: A Structural and Cultural Analysis of Conversational Storytelling*. Norwood, NJ: Ablex.

Robinson, John A., and Linda Hawpe (1986). "Narrative Thinking as a Heuristic Process." In Theodore Sarbin (ed.), *Narrative Psychology: The Storied Nature of Human Conduct*. New York: Praeger, pp. 111–125.

Silberstein, Sandra (1982). "Textbuilding and Personal Style in Oral Courtship Narrative." Ph.D. diss., Department of Linguistics, University of Michigan.

Sweetser, Eve (1987). "The Definition of Lie: An Examination of the Folk models Underlying a Semantic Prototype." In Dorothy Holland and Naomi Quinn (eds.), *Cultural Models in Language and Thought*. Cambridge: Cambridge University Press, pp. 43–66.

Tannen, Deborah. (1979). "Processes and Consequences of Conversational Style." Ph.D. diss., Department of Linguistics, University of California at Berkeley.

———— (1992). "How Is Conversation Like Literary Discourse?" In Pamela Downing, Susan D. Lima, and Michael Noonan (eds.), *The Linguistics of Literacy*. Philadelphia: John Benjamins, pp. 31–46.

———— (1993). "What's in a Frame? Surface Evidence for Underlying Expectations." In Deborah Tannen (ed.), *Framing in Discourse*. Oxford: Oxford University Press, pp. 14–56.

Wood, Kathleen M. (this volume). "Narrative Iconicity in Electronic-Mail Lesbian Coming-Out Stories."

Young, Linda Wai Ling. 1982. "Inscrutability Revisited." In John Gumperz (ed.), *Language and Social Identity*. Cambridge: Cambridge University Press, pp. 72–84.

17

Performative Effect in Three Gay English Texts

WILLIAM L. LEAP

To date, most of my work in queer linguistics has focused on conversations and narratives as sites for the construction of gay message. In this chapter, I focus on single sentences as sites for such constructions—specifically, sentences that do not contain explicit gay vocabulary or flamboyant linguistic details but convey gay message through suggestion, implication, or other indirect means.

The examples discussed here come from my ongoing observations of gay men's language use in public and private settings and from discussions of those observations with gay men in focus-group settings, one-on-one interviews, and informal conversations. My analysis of these examples displays close connections between *speaking* and *doing* that often occur in Gay English text-making, and it offers (at least, in a preliminary form) a linguistic critique of now-popular claims about gender and performativity.

Background

While text-centered Gay English research is a relatively recent concern in queer theory, studies of Gay English within the textual moment speak directly to issues of displacement, destabilization, impossible desire, and marginality, which have now become prominent themes in critical queerness. Murray (1979) explores the positive affirmations underlying the seemingly vicious "gay insulting" at an all-gay dinner party. Goodwin (1989) explores the double-subjectivity of joke-telling among patrons in a small-town gay bar. Moonwomon (1995) explores the assertions of power and agency that lesbians (re)claim as they share and exchange life-story narratives. Read (1980) describes the comfort that older gay men find in their neighborhood gay tavern. Weston (1991) describes the shifts in interpersonal discourse that accompany the creation of the "families we choose."

In all of these studies, language provides the framework for the speakers' recasting of heteronormative expectations and for the speakers' valorizing of their own conditions of "otherness." Less clear in these discussion is the extent to which details of textual form actually contribute to the emergence of queer meaning within a textual moment or merely convey into that moment meanings derived from (t)external queer sources. Certainly, if any text can be given a queer reading, as Doty claims (1993: xi, ff.) and Gaudio's (1994) study of pitch properties in gay men's speech certainly suggests, then the source of gay messages must lie in what Moonwomon terms "societal" rather than "linguistic" discourses. But this arrangement does not require that linguistic forms become categorically neutral in their representation of societal discourse within particular texts. Recent studies of Gay English conversation have certainly underscored this point— an in-flight conversation between a passenger and an airline steward (Leap 1993); "dykes on bykes" distinguishing themselves from "ladies of Harley" (Joans 1995); men pursuing erotic exchange through gay telephone switchboards (Miller 1995); drag queens displaying gender autonomy on the nightclub circuit (Barrett 1995); or transsexuals mutually safeguarding their privacy while talking to each other in public places (Cromwell 1995). The examples I present in this chapter offer additional support to this claim.

But You People Are More Fun

I begin with a sentence from a conversation that I observed in a bookstore/cafe in the Dupont Circle area (the local, self-styled "gay ghetto") of Washington, D.C. The bookstore and the cafe attract a gay clientele, especially on weekends, but the popularity of the facilities with heterosexuals makes it difficult to consider these facilities to be "gay space."

Speaker A, age 42, is inquiring about the availability of a table for a (gay and straight) group of five. Speaker B, age 25, is the maitre d' and has been responding to requests for table-space from large parties throughout the evening. I, also the spokesperson negotiating a table for a large party, was standing to the right of the maitre d's podium when the conversation began. Example 1 shows my on-paper transcription of that exchange:

(1) *But you people are more fun*

1 A: Table for five—how long do we wait ?
2 B: Table for five [pause, consults list] about one hour.

3 A: One hour. [consults with group] Nope, can't do it. That's too long.
4 B: Try the Mocha House. They might not be too crowded tonight.
5 A: Yeah, OK, we can go there. But you people are more fun.
6 B: Well, I don't know about that. [while he says this, moves head to side, drops
       voice level, gives trace of smile]
7 A: Yeah, you're right. [establishes direct eye contact]
8   Maybe the Mocha House is more fun, but I still like your dessert drinks
       here.
9 B: [not breaking eye contact] Well, you'll just have to come back and try us again
       sometime.

There was nothing unusual about the turn-taking in the opening lines (1–3)
of this exchange. The customer asked about the wait for a large table, the maitre
d' responded, and the customer declined the offer. Line 4 also appears to be unre-
markable, but there is more to this comment than good customer relations. The
Mocha House is one of several coffee bars in the Dupont Circle area. While it is
located some distance (about a ten-minute walk) from the bookstore, it is also
around the corner from two of DC's popular gay restaurants and half a block away
from two popular gay bars. It attracts a large gay clientele, especially during the
later hours of the evening, and it can be just as difficult to get a table there as at
the bookstore's coffee bar. By recommending that the group go to the Mocha
House, the maitre d' was not actually helping speaker A and his party reduce their
waiting time; he was suggesting that speaker A and his party would be happier in
a gay-friendly environment.

Speaker A could have responded to this suggestion in several ways: by ignoring the gay content entirely; by indicating his own familiarity with the Mocha
House and its ambience; by objecting to the distance and the walking time. What
he did (line 5) was shift the discussion away from the Mocha House and back to
the locale that initiated the conversation: *We can go there, but you people are more
fun.* This comment transfers to the bookstore the allusions to gay ambience
brought into the conversation by the maitre d's reference to the Mocha House; if
I want fun, says speaker A, I can find it right here. And, by referring to the bookstore and its gay opportunities in personalized terms (e.g., you people) rather than
with some form of place deixis (e.g. *this place), speaker A's comment radically
shifts the maitre d's position within the dialogue. Instead of being the knowledge-
able bystander who proposed action to another, the maitre d' , in line 5, is made
into a coparticipant in the proposal and its implementation.

The physicality of the maitre d's presence changed noticeably, beginning
with these lines. His posture shifted, he stood less rigidly, he leaned slightly
over the podium, he moved his head slightly to one side, he lowered his voice,
and he barely concealed a trace of a smile—all of which reminded me of mo-
tion-picture stereotypes of a coquettish southern belle gently displaying her
passion to her gentleman caller. After giving a brief reply (line 6), the maitre d'
paused, interrupting the rapid-fire pace of his presentation in the preceding exchange and allowing speaker A to assume control over the next segment of the
conversation.

Speaker A's reply acknowledges the maitre d's display of a friendlier tone in two ways: his wording (*You're right, maybe the Mocha House is more fun*) responds to the referential point of the preceding comment, and his use of eye contact responds to the maitre d's shift in physical presentation. But the comment also allows speaker A to restate line 5 in a more forceful fashion: It is no longer *you people* but *your desert drinks* that attract him to the bookstore's cafe. *Desert drinks* identifies a type of the refreshment that both conclude a meal and act as a prelude to (not yet specified) after-dining activities. The comment maintains the maitre d's presence in the conversation and implies his continuing presence in the events to come, whatever those events might entail.

Both levels of meaning made the maitre d's next comment (line 9) a deliciously appropriate way to end the conversation. By duplicating Mae West's classic *Why doncha' come up and see me sometime*, speaker B addresses the erotic possibilities implied in speaker A's use of the *you* pronoun and his desert drinks trope, but he also maintains the playfulness—of language and of public practice—that has run throughout the whole of the conversation and that was also brought into clearer focus by line 5.

Certainly, a comment like *But you people are more fun* is not unique to Gay English conversations. And the reshaping of participation structure that this comment inspired can also be found in other forms of gendered conversation.[1] But recognizing these parallels does not change the fact that the appearance of this comment had gay-significant effects on the remainder of this conversation. It encouraged both speakers to address gay meanings in the midst of an objectively structured, service-centered conversation between strangers. It allowed each of them to begin to display what had initially been disguised gender identities. And it signaled "gay presence" to other persons in this seemingly "straight" environment who took notice of Gay English usage and were able to interpret its meanings.

What You See Is What You Get

Strategic placement of a single sentence also has gay significant effects on the conversation in my next example. As before, the conversation occurred in a service-oriented setting, but this time the participants were two gay male couples and a heterosexual woman, and the focus of this conversation very much revolved around participants' gender differences.

My source for this example is a conversation I had with a gay man (Paul) who was one of the participants in this exchange. He, his partner, and another gay couple had driven from Washington, D.C., into the Virginia suburbs to have dinner at a gourmet restaurant that was beginning to get rave reviews from local restaurant critics. The restaurant is one of several businesses in a shopping center, which also contains a grocery store, a drug store, and a series of specialty shops. Surrounding the shopping center is a neighborhood populated largely by retired military personnel and government workers. This is an unlikely place for a gourmet restaurant, Paul noted, and it is certainly an out-of-the-way, hard-to-find location.

(He later described the location as "on the other side of the moon"). In fact, it took
longer than they expected to find the restaurant and park the car. Still, when they
got inside, they found that their table was not ready. The maitre d' suggested that
they wait in the gourmet food store that adjoins the restaurant. Paul's narrative
(example 2) begins as he and his friends enter that store.

(2)   *What you see is what you get*

 1   The cashier was a large woman, in her thirties, who liked to
 2   talk (we later observed) and must have considered it her job
 3   greet customers as they came into the store, because she had
 4   something to say every time someone walked in.
 5   When the four of us walked in, she said, she did this
 6   loudly, so that everyone in the store could hear her: "Where
 7   are the wives?"
 8   No one answered. I mean, who expected this kind of opening
 9   remark from a saleswoman in a wine store?
10   So we just started looking at the stock and ignored the
11   question. Then she asked: "You men didn't leave them at
12   home?" One of us replied, quietly, "something like that," but
13   she didn't hear it. Now other customers in the store are
14   watching this whole thing; we are very much on the spot. She
15   continued: "Are they out parking the cars?"
16   At this point, I was ready to leave, except we had driven
17   about twenty-five miles to have dinner here and everyone was hungry.
18   Besides, why let this person's pushiness destroy our evening,
19   right?
20   So one member of the group walked up to the saleswoman and
21   said, to her face: "Look, lady, what you see is what you
22   get." Everyone in the store laughed—except the saleswoman,
23   who was thankfully at a loss for words.
24   We joked about this later in the evening, but at the time I
25   felt very strange. Was she teasing us ? Or did she really
26   think we were four straight guys and our wives were outside
27   in the parking lot ? I mean, we were the only gay people in
28   the store; it wasn't like shopping in Dupont Circle; no, not
29   at all.

This conversation, as Paul reported it, involves a use of language that is
somewhat different from that in example (1). At issue here is the cashier's persistent erasure of gay presence—*where are the wives?*—and a gay man's upstag-
ing of that erasure with a one-line response: *Look, lady, what you see is what you
get.* It is possible that the cashier knew that these men were gay and hoped to
demonstrate this awareness by constructing an "in-joke" reference to the absence
of women. But it is just as likely that the cashier assumed that all of the customers entering her store are (or should be) heterosexuals and treated these men
accordingly.

Either way, the result was the same: The gendered composition of this all-male grouping became a focus for public scrutiny. And this continued to be the case, until the appearance of the comment in lines 21–22.

Preliminary efforts to divert the cashier from this line of argument—the silence in lines 8–9, the quiet aside in line 12—were not successful. What was needed was a more forceful, dramatic reply, something that would terminate the cashier's line of questioning, whatever its motives. Lines 21–22 had precisely that effect. Moreover, besides leaving the cashier without reply, this statement shifted the center of discussion from the group of gay men to the cashier and made her the target of the other customers' laughter. And it also upstaged her repeated references to *the wives* (and the normalized heterosexuality that those references conveyed), not by avoiding the gendered message in her comment (as was the case in the first two responses) but by speaking directly to its gendered message. *What you see is what you get* said, in effect, there are no wives, so give up on this line of questioning. And that was, as Paul explained, exactly what happened.

I do not want to essentialize this experience; possibly, some gay men may never have been subjected to such teasing in a public place. But for others of us, such comments are part of "the context of oppression" that defines "the modern identity of being gay" (Plummer 1992: 4) as we know it in our daily lives. And for us, being able to silence such comments becomes a valuable linguistic skill, something we have to deliberately acquire and something we do not always master successfully. Events like these have additional value as language-learning experiences and as object lessons in gay resistance.

That's Mister Faggot to You, Punk

During the opening week of fall semester (1993) classes at my university, a comment appeared on the metal divider that separates the stand-up urinals from one of the toilet stalls in the men's restroom near my office (see figure 17-1). The comment was positioned at eye level, and that made the wording noticeable to any man approaching the urinals and provided momentary visual diversion for any man making use of those facilities.[2] When the comment first appeared, there were no other statements on the divider. Nor were there any drawings, diagrams, or "peepholes." The statement stood alone for two weeks; then some one replied, then someone replied to the reply, and soon the wall contained a whole sequence of linked messages.

I became interested in this exchange once I saw how others were reacting to the message presented in the initial comment. Rather than taking the writer to task for his antigay statement (or giving support to his homophobic comment), the second respondent moved away from message content altogether, focusing instead on his writing errors and inferred lack of intellectual skill (figure 17-2).

The second writer's neatly ordered, paragraph-like arrangement of commentary contrasted markedly with the first writer's irregularly placed wording. But the elegance of respondent 2's visual display did not prevent him from becoming, in turn, the target for an ad hominem attack. This time, instead of presenting a lengthy commentary, respondent 3 simply drew a circle around the spelling error

Figure 17-1. First graffiti on the bathroom wall. Reprinted from William L. Leap, *Word's Out Gay Men's English* (University of Minnesota Press © 1996), by permission.

in *appostrophies* in respondent 2's remarks, drew a line into the margin, and wrote: *wrong spelling* (figure 17-3). This comment shifted attention away from the antigay message in the initial comment. And the next three additions to this emerging text, each of which appeared at roughly one-week intervals between mid-October and mid-November 1993, continued to do the same.

Respondent 4—*shat up fucker*—(either deliberately or for other reasons) duplicates the mechanics of the initial writer's comment to reply to respondent 3. However, he does not make use of the writer's antigay remarks, and he keeps respondent 2 at the center of the exchange by drawing an arrow from his comment to respondent 2's statement. Respondent 5's generic comment on *happy pills* does not disrupt that focus; if anything, it appears to be making light of the whole exchange. And while respondent 6 responds harshly to respondent 5's attempt at levity—*KILL*—he draws arrows to ensure that respondent 2's comment are also addressed in his reply (figure 17-4).

At this point in the exchange, items 2–6 had become a distinct aggregate of comment: They shared a common location (on the right side of the wall); their content addressed similar themes (interconnected references to "standard lan-

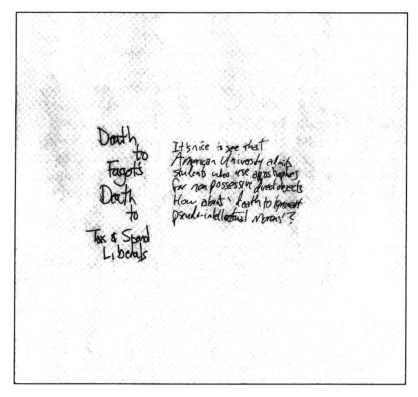

Figure 17-2. Addition to first graffiti. Reprinted from William L. Leap, *Word's Out Gay Men's English* (University of Minnesota Press © 1996), by permission.

guage" skills and violence, underscored by the network of arrows). The message of that aggregate jointly erased the first writer's antigay message. Now came item 7, the one-line comment of particular interest to this chapter: *That's Mr. Faggot to you, punk!* (figure 17-5).

This comment appeared on the left side of the wall, immediately above item 1 and at some distance from items 2–6. Its location directly reflects its meaning. Instead of continuing the evasion of homophobic message maintained by items 2–6, item 7 returned the focus of the discussion to its initial antigay sentiment and then upstaged that sentiment in several ways.

First, and as was the case in item 1, item 7 is also a hortatory ("let it happen") construction, but the intended recipient of this comment is much more tightly focused than is the case for item 1. *Death to fagot's* speaks to an open-ended audience—anyone who cares to read and respond to the statement. The phrase *That's Mr. Faggot to you, punk!* addresses a specific individual—the author of item 1, identified in this comment with a personal deictic marker (*punk*) that is less than complementary. Item 7 also personalizes the target of item 1's death threat by giving the target a more concrete identity, *Mr. Faggot*, rather than *fagots*, and by linking that identity to the author of item 7.

Figure 17-3. The next addition. Reprinted from William L. Leap, *Word's Out Gay Men's English* (University of Minnesota Press © 1996), by permission.

Besides personalizing the reference, item 7 also replaces the derogatory meaning of *fagot* with a set of more positive associations. Correcting the spelling and capitalizing the first letter of the term enhances the sense of dignity now present in the discussion. Adding *Mr.* in front of *Faggot* calls to mind the messages of self-assertion and struggle explored in films like *They Call Me Mr. Tibbs*. It hints at other parallels between African American and lesbian/gay experiences in U.S. society—and suggests that the punk's antigay remark has broader political meanings, as well. Combining *Mr.* with *Faggot* also implies an obligation to show respect to the individual simply because of this person's status as faggot. Using an appeal to appropriate verbal etiquette to respond to a death threat is an especially delicious moment of queer phrase-making. At the same time, by recasting item 1's *Death to Fagot's* into a more precisely stated paraphrase, *Death to Mr. Faggot*, item 7's reference to politeness makes the seriousness of item 1's suggestion very difficult to ignore.

The introduction of item 7 had a noticeable effect on the construction of this text. Item 7 appeared in mid-November 1993, but nothing was added in response

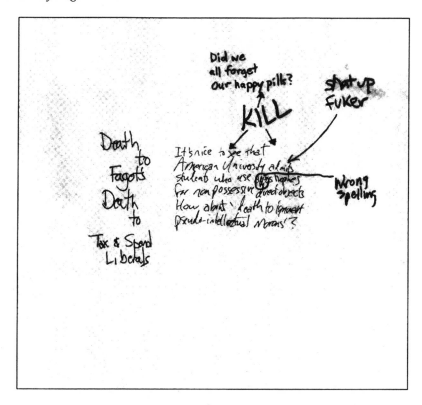

Figure 17-4. Three more additions. Reprinted from William L. Leap, *Word's Out Gay Men's English* (University of Minnesota Press © 1996), by permission.

to it until late January 1994. (Previously, as I mentioned, comments had been added to this display roughly once a week.) Thanksgiving break (four days at the end of November) and winter recess (two weeks between late December and early January) do not explain this disruption. Other graffiti'd comments (unrelated to the issues in this exchange) continued to appear on other walls in this bathroom throughout the end of the fall semester and during winter recess; yet no new comments appeared in this exchange.

Items 8 and 9 on *pickiness* (see figure 17-6) appeared in late January. As before, their writers placed these comments on the right-hand side of the wall, not in the area of items 1 and 7. And, as before, these items continued the debate over appropriate punctuation that items 2 and 3 had begun. Item 8, like item 3, challenged item 2's claims to written language correctness. Item 9 challenged item 8's claims to correctness. Neither comment acknowledged the gay-positive content that item 7 had introduced into this exchange.

Item 10, about *Red necks*, appeared on the wall in mid-February. Initially, given its location, I thought that this comment was addressed to item 1, but the

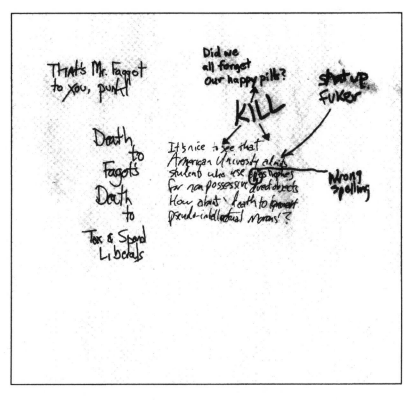

Figure 17-5. The gay-positive addition. Reprinted from William L. Leap, *Word's Out Gay Men's English* (University of Minnesota Press © 1996), by permission.

placement of the arrows (linking item 10 to items 7, 8, and 9) suggested that another message was at issue here. My observation of graffiti'd language in this men's room, and elsewhere on campus, has shown me that this expression can be associated with any number of gendered or political statements on bathroom walls and that its message is more emphatic (shows strong support or strong disapproval) in content than explicitly referential. Hence, I have learned, drawings of erect penises may be labeled *redneck*, and so can comments that attack women, on-campus fraternities, or freedom for the Palestinian people.

In this case, item 10 may not ignore the antigay sentiment of item 1 but may not necessarily support it. Whatever the writer's intention, the ambiguity of his comment sustains the erasure of gay themes that items 8 and 9 restored.

Two weeks after item 10 appeared, item 11, the top line, joined the display (see figure 17-6). The position of this comment allows it to function as a caption for this whole display, and in an ironic way it does summarize some of the issues that previous comments had explored. For example, item 11's reference to white men addresses a racial theme not previously explored in the text but suggested by the stereotypically nonstandard English spellings in items 1 and 4. The phrase

Figure 17-6. Final addition before erasure. Reprinted from William L. Leap, *Word's Out Gay Men's English* (University of Minnesota Press © 1996), by permission.

fucked in the ass contains an implied reference to violent action and to an enjoyment of violence, which complements references to power and punishment displayed in items 1, 4, and 6.

I do not read item 11 as a gay-friendly comment, but I am unable to report how others reacted to the statement. Shortly after it appeared, the university's building services staff repainted all of the walls in the bathroom and erased the whole exchange.

Discussion: Sentence Construction, Gay Practice, and Performative Effect

I did not know whether the author of item 7 was a gay man when I read his contribution to this exchange, but I certainly hope he was. Unlike the other participants, he responded directly and powerfully to the homophobic commentary in item 1. I would like to think all gay men would do the same, under similar circumstances.

My own experiences teach me that gay men are not automatically skilled in verbal retort and may not know "what to say" or "how to say it" when faced with the pressures of the political moment. To solve this problem, some gay men amass a small inventory of replies and draw from that inventory according to the particulars of each occasion. Sources for these replies include friends' joyful retelling of their own linguistic successes, catchy statements from television programs or cinema classics, punch lines from gay-positive jokes, and slogans displayed on bumper stickers, buttons, and t-shirts.

Overhearing comments like *But you folks are more fun* (example 1) and reading graffiti'd messages like item 7 provides additional materials that gay men can include in these inventories. By doing so, gay man increase their awareness of the politics of Gay English sentence construction, particularly in the context of heterosexual discourse. The exchange of messages in this example, for instance, shows how easily people overlook homophobic remarks as well as any gay-assertive commentary that is given in response to it. Such erasure is similar to the cashier's assumption (as inferred in my second example) that all of the male customers in the food store were heterosexual men and, accordingly, were out to dinner with their wives. And as both examples confirm, such erasure is, in itself, another form of homophobia.

It is difficult for gay men to sustain gay-positive discussion when coparticipants are unwilling even to acknowledge the presence of gay concerns within the exchange. If anything gay men say is likely to be overlooked, then gay men have to turn to alternative formats to establish gay presence in such settings. Gay men's use of silence in the context of an erasive discourse (as happened in the earlier segments of example 2) is quite understandable, in this regard. So is the popularity of "freedom chains" (rainbow-colored rings worn around the neck on silver or leather chains), pink triangle pins, and t-shirts with gay messages.[3]

Silence and wearable iconography are forms of gay practice, "ways of operating and doing things" that "appear as merely the obscure background of social activity" but in reality orient and organize the content of everyday experience, to cite de Certeau's definition (1984: xi, ff.). Gay graffiti—both isolated statements and comments directly linked to heterosexually oriented messages—are another viable form of gay practice. And, as in the judicious use of silence or the wearing of gay-pride paraphernalia, writing gay graffiti allows gay men to lay claim to the site of the practice and to create a sense of gay space in the midst of an otherwise open-ended, unformed, and (by assumption) heterosexual place.[4] Reading gay graffiti, like hearing gay silence or interpreting the freedom chains and t-shirt messages, allows the reader to become a coparticipant in the construction of gay space, whatever his gender or sexual interests.

In this sense, these examples make an important point about performativity in Gay English discourse—that is, about the power to "produce that which it names," to use Judith Butler's phrasing (1993: 19). Austin's initial discussions of this topic (1962, 1970) highlight connections between the actor and performative action; for example, by saying "I dub thee Sir Gerald of the Green Hand," the sovereign inducts the candidate into knighthood; by saying "I now pronounce you husband and wife," the officiant confirms the candidates' mutually affirmed marital bond. Sedgwick's depiction of queer performativity as "a strategy for production of meaning and being in relation to the affect shame and the later and related fact of stigma" (1993: 11) continues this trend, since it is the queer actor who experiences shame and converts those feelings into stigma.

In this chapter, rather than focusing on the constriction of performative acts by speakers, I have explored the performative effects (or what Austin 1962 once termed the *perlocutionary force*) that certain sentences elicit from listeners. I realize that a listener-centered analysis departs from the more orthodox linguistic treatments of performativity. But, just as Sedgwick is intrigued by the "potential interest that might also lie in speculations about versions of performativity . . . that might begin by placing some different kinds of utterances [e.g., other than first-person singular constructions] in the position of the exemplary" (1993: 3), I am intrigued by the idea of studying performativity as a multipartied, dialogic process. That is, to use one of Judith Butler's examples, a statement like *shame on you* has the performative effect of imposing shame on the listener—unless the listener chooses to overlook the authority of the speaker and to disregard the potential impact of his message.

Similarly, in example 1, speaker A's *but you people are more fun* would have been nothing more than a clever response within a turn-taking dyad had the maitre d' not been willing to play around with the comment and to react to its several levels of meaning. The maitre d's reaction established the validity of speaker A's comment within the conversational moment. Whether the staff and patrons at the coffee house are really "more fun" than the staff and patrons elsewhere is now of secondary importance, given the coconstructed understandings that both participants were beginning to share. As Austin himself observed, the performativity of a statement has nothing to do with its truth value (Austin, 1962; see also discussion in Levinson 1983: 227–230).

What you see is what you get and *That's Mr. Faggot to you, punk!* also produced exactly what they named in each context: Specifically, both statements affirmed gay presence in the face of oversight and insensitivity, and both statements prompted a termination of the expressions that had perpetuated conditions of erasure until that time. I cannot prove, in example 2, that the cashier's silence signaled an awareness that she was addressing gay men or, in example 3, that the two-month pause in follow-up commentary reflected other men's endorsement of item 7's claims to respect. What is at issue in these examples are the linguistic practices, not the surrounding conditions of truth; the termination of erasure is just as "real" in each setting as is the candidate's elevation to knighthood or the creation of the marriage ties in Austin's examples—though this is so, as I have explained, for entirely different reasons.

ACKNOWLEDGMENTS   I read a preliminary version of this paper at the Second American University Conference on Lavender Languages and Linguistics (17–18 September 1994). Comments from Keith Walters, John Martin, Birch Moonwomon, Arnold Zwicky, Anna Livia, and Kira Hall helped greatly in the development of this version of the text. I discuss these examples in greater detail in Leap (1996).

NOTES

Example (1) *But you people are more fun*, example (2) *What you see is what you get*, and Figures 17-1–17-6 are reprinted with permission from William Leap, *Word's Out: Gay Men's English*, © 1996, University of Minnesota Press, Minneapolis.

1. See, for example, Goodwin's descriptions (1990: 75–140, 239–243) of African American children's negotiation of participation frameworks in games and storytelling activities and Tannen's discussion (1994: 53–84) of the communicative significance of interruptions in men's and women's speech.

2. While I have not been able to reproduce the configuration exactly in these figures, each display suggests the placement of the statements in relation to each other and shows how writers used additional markers to connect their comments to materials others had already presented. The texts in these figures also retain the spelling, syntax, and other formal details contained in the original text.

3. Colleagues at the Second Lavender Languages and Linguistics Conference (fall 1994) advised me that t-shirts bearing the slogan *That's Mr. Faggot to you, punk!* have been popular gay-pride items for some time.

4. On this point, de Certeau writes, "Space is composed of intersections of mobile elements. . . . . Space occurs as the effect produced by the operations that orient it, situate it, temporalize it, and make it function in a polyvalent unity of conflictual programs or contractual proximities. . . . In short, space is a practiced place." (1984: 117, italics his).

REFERENCES

Austin, J. L. (1962). *How to Do Things with Words*. Oxford: Clarendon Press.
——— (1970). "Performative Utterances." In Austin, *Philosophical Papers*. Oxford: Oxford University Press, pp. 233–252.
Barrett, Rusty (1995). " 'Supermodels of the World Unite!' Political Economy and the Language of Performance among African American Drag Queens." In William L. Leap (ed.), *Beyond the Lavender Lexicon*. Newark: Gordon & Breach.
Butler, Judith (1993). "Critically Queer." *GLQ* 1: 17–32.
Cromwell, Jason (1995). "Talking within without Talking About: The Use of Protective Language among Transvestites and Transsexuals." In William L. Leap (ed.), *Beyond the Lavender Lexicon*. Newark: Gordon & Breach.
de Certeau, Michel (1984). *The Practice of Everyday Life*. Berkeley: University of California Press.
Doty, Alexander (1993). *Making Things Perfectly Queer: Interpreting Mass Culture*. Minneapolis: University of Minnesota Press.
Gaudio, Rudolph (1994). "Sounding Gay: Pitch Properties in the Speech of Gay and Straight Men." *American Speech* 69: 30–57.
Goodwin, Joseph (1989). *More Man than You'll Ever Be: Gay Folklore and Acculturation in Middle America*. Bloomington: Indiana University Press.
Goodwin, Marjorie Harness (1990). *He-Said-She-Said: Talk as Social Organization among Black Children*. Bloomington: Indiana University Press.
Joans, Barbara (1995). "Dykes on Bikes Meet Ladies of Harley." In William L. Leap (ed.), *Beyond the Lavender Lexicon*. Newark: Gordon & Breach.
Leap, William L. (1993). "Gay Men's English: Cooperative Discourse in a Language of Risk." In Deborah Blincoe and John Forrest (eds.), *Prejudice and Pride: Lesbian and Gay Traditions in America. New York Folklore* 19, no. 1–2: 45–70.

——— (1994). "Learning Gay Culture in 'a Desert of Nothing': Language as a Resource in Gender Socialization." *High School Journal* 77, no. 1–2: 122–131.

——— (1996). *Word's Out: Gay Men's English.* University of Minnesota Press.

Levinson, Stephen C. (1983). "Speech Acts." In Levinson, *Pragmatics.* Cambridge: Cambridge University Press, pp. 226–283.

Miller, Edward David (1995). "Inside the Switchboards of Desire: Storytelling on Phone Sexlines." In William L. Leap (ed.), *Beyond the Lavender Lexicon.* Newark: Gordon & Breach.

Moonwomon, Birch (1995). "Lesbian Discourse, Lesbian Knowledge." In William L. Leap (ed.), *Beyond the Lavender Lexicon.* Newark: Gordon & Breach.

Murray, Stephen O. (1979). "The Art of Gay Insulting." *Anthropological Linguistics* 21: 211–223.

Plummer, Ken (1992). "Speaking Its Name: Inventing a Lesbian and Gay Studies." In Ken Plummer (ed.), *Modern Homosexualities.* New York: Routledge, pp. 3–25.

Read, Kenneth E. (1980). *Other Voices: The Style of a Male Homosexual Tavern.* Novato CA: Chandler & Sharp.

Sedgwick, Eve Kosofsky (1993). " 'Queer Performativity': Henry James's *The Art of the Novel. GLQ* 1:1–16.

Tannen, Deborah (1994). "Interpreting Interruption in Conversation." In Tannen, *Gender and Discourse.* New York: Oxford University Press, pp. 53–84.

Weston, Kath (1991). *Families We Choose: Lesbians, Gays, Kinship.* New York: Columbia University Press.

18

$\mathcal{H}$omophobic Slang as Coercive Discourse among College Students

JAMES D. ARMSTRONG

An article in the 24 August 1988 issue of the *New York Times* reported that two men attacked by armed teenagers were also verbally degraded with "anti-homosexual epithets" (Wolinsky and Sherrill 1993: 53). Physical attacks on gay men (i.e., "gay bashing") are often accompanied by verbal assaults. On my campus and on others, "Take Back the Night" rallies sponsored by women's groups and activities organized by gay men and lesbian women sometimes evoke verbal assaults from male bystanders, who express their hostility with homophobic language. This is not so surprising given that language is an act that can be violent, exclusionary, and coercive. Furthermore, America's history of religious intolerance, stigmatization, and prejudice against homosexuals creates a context in which open derogation of homosexuality and homosexuals might be expected. In recent years, after some progress toward mainstream acceptance occurred during the 1970s, there has been an upturn in hostility toward gays and lesbians. This hostility has been accompanied by increased violence toward homosexuals and reinforced both by the fear generated by the AIDS pandemic and by the political power of the religious right (Blumenfeld and Raymond 1988; Perrow and Guillen 1990; Peters 1991). Against this background, gays and lesbians are likely to be "bashed" by both homophobic words and deeds.

Homophobia, however, is not limited to physical and verbal attacks on homosexuals and overt intolerance toward individuals suspected of being gay. Often in public interactions, people who might not think of openly attacking homosexuals use language that derogates homosexuality. Often those who employ this language in public are males, usually young, and presumably heterosexual. Use of such language creates an atmosphere of uncritical acceptance of intolerance toward homosexuality, while reinforcing stereotypical attitudes toward gays. At the same time, as this paper demonstrates, in some contexts this language asserts male (heterosexual) dominance by confirming presumed masculine values, while degrading presumed feminine gender attributes. Sociolinguists and feminists theorists have noted that the language used by men, including much of the slang, carries negative implications for the status of women in this society, and that male speech styles and language usage serve to reinforce male dominance (Lakoff 1975; Schultz 1975; Sutton 1995). They have not considered, however, that the language men sometimes direct toward one another also serves to maintain their hegemonic power over women.

In this chapter I explore the usage of some common slang terms that refer to homosexuals, especially when these terms are clearly used in derogatory or pejorative ways as a means of coercing others into behaving in a manner deemed appropriate by their users. The communicative acts that constitute the basis for my analysis are generally limited to situations where the target of the derogation is present. Usually in these situations the target is not suspected of being a homosexual. Rather, the usage is based on the linkage of some act or object to presumed attributes of homosexuals. Thus, this type of usage amounts to a connotative extension of the culturally based schema defining homosexuality to the referent. From an extensionist semantic view, focal types or prototypical schemata are defined in terms of attributes or features. In order to sensibly apply (or extend) a term to an object or person, the user evokes the relationship between the features that define an exemplar and the behavior, form, or function of the person or object to which the term is applied. In actual usage the similarities between exemplars and targets are not absolute but are influenced by contexts and by the cultural implications of one usage as opposed to another (Kronenfeld, Armstrong, and Wilmoth 1985).

Two more specific examples will clarify this process. Sweet (this volume) reflects on the usage of *feygele*, a Yiddish word meaning 'little bird'. American Jews might use this term to refer to gay or effeminate males. Such usage illustrates the process of metaphoric extension. This class of extension is metaphoric because a gay or effeminate male is not a little bird, but the user presumes that somehow the target possesses or exemplifies an attribute of "little birdishness," such as delicacy. In contrast, application of the slang term *homo* to an individual is a connotative extension because a person may actually be a homosexual. The extension of the term in this case is based on the user's presumption that the target shares some connotative attribute(s) with the prototype of the category "homo."

In the discussion that follows I will treat all terms under consideration as semantic equivalents,[1] although there are differences in their connotations. All of them, however, do connote effeminacy and nonconformity to the prevailing cultural code regarding appropriate sexual choice and behavior. As will be shown, in most cases the extension of these terms to a person is based on the linkage between the person's behavior and effeminate or nonconformist attributions concerning homosexuality.

For the purposes of this chapter, homophobic slang is any adaptation and extension of terms referring to homosexuals that can be interpreted as derogatory in the sense that the quality, action, attribute, or individual to which the term refers is being devalued (Pei and Gaynor 1975). For example, use of the slang term *homo* to refer to an individual is the result of the adaptation and extension of the term *homosexual*. Its usage is almost inevitably derogatory. As John Boswell, the noted historian of homosexuality, argues in his affidavit in the case of *Joseph C. Steffan v. Richard B. Cheney, Secretary of Defense*:[2]

> "[H]omo" became a widespread obloquy, especially among adolescents and those openly hostile to homosexuals. It is almost an exact lexical equivalent of the anti-Semitic "Hebe": both are abbreviations of terms applied by a suspicious majority to the minority in question ("homo" from "homosexual"; "Hebe" from "Hebrew"), as opposed to the terms used by the groups themselves ("gay" and "Jewish," respectively) and by those who are not hostile to them. Apocation of names is a common mode of intensification: ... for groups, especially suspect groups, the foreshortening usually betrays intensified hostility. (Boswell 1993: 51)

The hostility and the devaluation implicit in the usage of homophobic terms, as illustrated by Boswell's discussion of the term *homo*, occur by virtue of the assumed correctness of anything heterosexual. Thus, associating anything or anybody with the "other" category (i.e., homosexual) automatically makes it nonconformist at best.

Methodology

With the assistance of several students, I have been collecting instances in which terms that fit our definition of homophobic slang have been used in our presence.[3] In each instance we have attempted to describe the social context of the usage as completely as possible, paying special attention to the relationship of the user to others present, especially to the referent. The overwhelming majority of our examples were taken from conversations involving white male college students on this campus, although in some instances women and minority students were present. In addition, I conducted a number of interviews with students to explore the usage of this terminology more generally in the student culture of SUNY Plattsburgh. Since my student assistants had little access to the gay subculture in our area, I also interviewed several gay men and lesbian women about the usage of this terminology among gays and about their reaction to such usage by heterosexuals. The interviews were used to inform the other data and to fill in gaps in these data, not as a primary source of cases.

Social Context and Meaning

Homophobic language is used in a variety of ways. For example, it is not unusual to hear someone use a term, such as *fag*, to refer to another individual who is not within earshot. One of my students heard a classmate refer to the members of a local fraternity as a "bunch of fags." In cases such as this it is not possible for the observer (or often even for the speaker) to know if this represents some kind of denotatively "accurate" attribution about the referent, nor is it always possible to ascertain the attribute of the individual(s) on which the extension is based. Even though the terms are usually intended to be derogatory in these cases, they are not very interesting from a semantic point of view, since the referent is not present and there is usually no clear action that elicits these usages. Thus, although I have a number of instances of this type, they will not be considered in the analysis.

When the referent is present, it is relatively easy to identify both the intention of the user and the attribute on which extension is made. In this research the most frequently recorded homophobic usage was to employ the term *gay* to refer to any object, possession, attribute, or behavior of others, in their presence or not, deemed by the user to be nonnormative.[4] For example, I was present when a male friend of my daughter referred to another friend, who was also present, as "gay" because he spilled catsup on his shirt. I questioned those present about this usage and its relationship to conceptions we have about homosexuality. The young man who used the term in this case said, somewhat defensively, "I didn't mean anything by it. It's got nothing to do with homosexuals. I just kinda thought Jim acted sorta uncool." It seems from such examples that many young people will refer to almost anything or anybody as "gay" if they disapprove of it or find it "uncool" or odd. Thus, in this region, at least, young people have expropriated the preferred neutral sexual identity marker for males with a homoerotic orientation and, through connotative extension, given it a negative value.

Next to the usage of *gay* just described, the most frequently observed homophobic language occurs in multimale groupings, where one participant refers to another with a slang term synonymous for homosexual. This is pervasive behavior. Every student we interviewed has witnessed usages of this type on more than one occasion. Generally, the context is predominantly male, but it need not be limited to males. These usages usually occur in small groups of friends, with others within earshot. Usage of homophobic terminology in these contexts is often part of what is termed "busting" or "ranking." According to Moffatt, "In male locker-room talk the term [to bust] was short for 'to bust their chops' or 'to bust their balls'" (1989: 67). These speech acts are a form of verbal aggression in which the user mocks the victim, usually to challenge the victim's authority or to undermine his pretensions. It is characteristically an all-male activity in which the participants know each other. Still, in current student culture, women are allowed to participate, although their participation is contingent on sticking to the male-defined rules of the game (Moffatt 1989). In the situations under consideration here, one participant will refer to another as a "fag," "homo," "queer," or other term intended to be even more derogatory from the point of view of the user. The reference is usually generated by some action of the target, such as refusing to join in a homosocial activity. In interviews, students claimed that such exchanges also occurred in cross-sex interactions, but we have only one example of a female employing a term in this way.

1. A group of four male students sitting in a dorm lounge is discussing plans for the evening, which include the usual drinking and carousing. One of them claims that he needs to study. The others "bust" on him. His closest friend in the group pleads, "Don't be a *fag*, you can study any time."
2. A student, whom I know well, is in my office after an afternoon class with another student we both know. We are chatting sociably. He invites me "downtown" for a beer. I decline his offer, explaining that I have to go home to cook dinner and watch my kids. In reaction to my refusal of his invitation, he says, "Come on, you big *homo*. You can have one beer."
3. A man in a relatively quiet residential neighborhood observes a car speeding down the street. He runs to the curb and yells at the driver to slow down. The driver slams on his brakes and backs up to within earshot of the man. The man, in a stern tone, tells the driver to be more careful because of the kids playing in the area. The driver responds, "Fuck you, you *faggot*."

These examples represent the range of speech acts that serve as the corpus of my data. They share two main features. In each case (and in all the collected cases) the action being labeled by the derogatory term has nothing to do with the denotative meaning of the term employed. In each case the usage takes its meaning from extension to the effeminate connotation of the term. From the speaker's point of view, the actions of studying, cooking, and being concerned about the welfare of neighborhood kids are unmasculine (conversely, the actions they are justifying are manly and virile).

These examples also indicate a means by which young men affirm their masculinity. By referring to others as "homos" or "fags" in these contexts, the speakers are referencing their own heterosexuality and masculinity, while coercing the referents to adopt the same values. Peggy Sanday, in her book *Fraternity Gang Rape*, discusses the process by which fraternity hazing rituals symbolically make boys into men. She claims, "These rituals stamp the pledge with two collective images: one image is of the cleansed and purified 'manly' self bonded to the brotherhood; the second image is of the despised and dirty feminine, 'nerdy,' and 'faggot' self bonded to the mother" (1990: 157). Most boys and young men in American society are likely to experience this kind of affirmation process as part of membership in all male groups. Insiders remake newcomers in their "manly" image by frequently and often ritualistically referencing the "loser" status of outsiders (Sanday 1990: 136). From our observations, for example, we discovered that in the hazing rituals of one of the fraternities on this campus, the "brothers" routinely refer to the pledges as "faggots," even when they weren't present. In doing so, the "brothers" aren't merely indexing the "otherness" of the pledges, they are announcing to themselves that they are heterosexual men.

Each of these examples, especially the first one, illustrates how young men affirm their maleness. The speakers in each case are saying to themselves and to the others present, "I am a man because my behavior is not contaminated by the feminine quality of 'homos' and 'faggots.'"

Neither of the first two examples is particularly derogatory. In neither case was the intent to insult. Rather, the students in both cases were trying to coerce the referents by appealing to the culturally salient fear of being feminine with which most American males are raised. Students I interviewed felt that these kinds of usages mark the "take-it-for-granted" attitude that words are just words, similar to my daughter's friend's defense that his use of "gay" didn't really mean anything. Furthermore, in both these cases and in most other examples of this kind, the speakers are indicating their affection for and equality to the referent in a joking manner that is especially common in locker-room discourse. In all three examples the usage stems from the association of stereotypically feminine behavior with homosexuality. Thus, the basis of the extension of the term is the connoted feminine quality of the refusal to join in the carousing, the need to look after one's children, and the warning about speeding. The extension in each of these cases represents the common confusion in American culture of gender-role behavior (studying, performing childcare, and being careful) with sexual orientation (homosexuality).

The first example is a classic "bust" in which it is acceptable to degrade a friend. Usage, in this almost ritualistic context, reinforces referent group values, broadcasts the manliness of the user, defines what the group expects of its members, and establishes boundaries for the group (Moffat 1989).

The second example, which, by the way, motivated my interest in this research, has "busting" qualities, but the power asymmetry between the student and me makes it interesting for other reasons. The student had to assume a sufficient degree of familiarity and equality with me in order for him to "bust" me. "Busting" is a form of one-upmanship, but it requires a certain level of equality among those who engage in it. The student also had to assume that I wouldn't take offense, that I was one of the guys, and that I wouldn't view his attribution as "fighting words." In the indirect style characteristic of male interactions, he was telling me that he liked me. This assumption indexes the heterosexist ethos of American culture. If I am a heterosexual and I am "cool," I won't misinterpret his "bust." I'll let it slide. In fact, he assumed that our male bond would be affirmed. He wouldn't have called me a "homo" if he assumed I was one.

The final example is clearly more derogatory. It shares some of the violent overtones possessed by verbal and physical attacks on gay men. The speaker intended to hurt the referent with his language. He presumably did not know the target, nor did he appreciate the warning, although it was well deserved, according to the observer. Still, the use of the term *faggot* is generated by the association between caring about the well-being of children and being effeminate, in contrast to the manliness of speeding down a residential street (i.e., risk taking).

In student interviews it was unanimously agreed that terms like *homo, fag,* and *queer* were routinely used to refer to behaviors that didn't conform to what was considered "manly," such as playing sports, drinking, and general risk-taking behavior. In one of the cases collected, for example, preferring to go out with a girlfriend over playing touch football with male friends evoked a homophobic response. I find it particularly noteworthy and ironic that the speaker could "demean" his friend for preferring to go out with a woman (a fairly heterosexual thing to do) in an attempt to coerce the victim into engaging in a homosocial activity, such as playing touch football. However, in all-male groups, hanging around with the guys is often valued above heterosocial activities like dating. What all these instances share in common is the implication that "manly" behavior (i.e., drinking, playing sports, driving fast) is valued, while stereotypically feminine behavior should be avoided.

Conclusions

To conclude, I would like to make several points about the material discussed in this chapter. First, most of the examples cited demonstrate how particular usages (homophobic slang) or styles ("busting") signal inclusion in reference groups. If individuals value inclusion in groups where homophobic language is commonly employed, they will be likely to employ it in order to signal their inclusion. Second, for the social contexts that are the focus of this research, this type of language functions to define for some and confirm for others appropriate gender attributes and behaviors.

Third, this language is coercive in a number of ways. The link between homosexuality and nonconformity, gender-inappropriate behavior, and femininity pressures members of reference groups to act in ways they might not wish to in order to avoid labeling, even if the underlying tone is friendly. This coercion is not limited to the referents but includes all potential participants in these exchanges.

Use of homophobic language is coercive in other, less obvious ways. First, degrading homosexuality in public contexts serves to maintain the invisibility of homosexuals. All the gay men and lesbian women I interviewed made this point in one way or another. Their main reaction to my examples of homophobic usage was to point out that this language makes them feel excluded, devalued, and invisible. Implicit in these usages is the assumption that all those present are heterosexual and share a negative evaluation of homosexuality. The pervasiveness of such language is another indication to gays and lesbians that "mainstream" American culture remains intolerant of homosexuality. For young men on college campuses, who are often unsure of their sexuality and who usually want to be included in reference groups, it is, at least, uncomfortable, if not dangerous, to oppose these assertions of the value of heterosexuality. Usage of this kind of language, therefore, by disregarding the hurt that it may cause to some, indicates how unimportant the feelings of these people are. That is, homophobic slang implicitly disregards the existence of homosexuals. Furthermore, since, in most everyday contexts, gays and lesbians are not particularly identifiable, their presence does not constrain the usage of derogatory terminology. In most contexts on college campuses, gay and lesbian identities remain hidden. The sexual orientation of some activists may be known by many, but the sexual identities of most gays and lesbians are known only to those relatively familiar to them. In contrast to gays and lesbians, Asian and African Americans and women, by virtue of their identifiability, constrain the use of racist and sexist language in many contexts (Smith 1982).

Finally, this language usage affirms male dominance and defines the terms, at least in certain contexts, for gender equality. This last point was driven home to me by one of the examples I collected. Two teenage sisters were preparing to walk over to a friend's house on a rainy day. One of the sisters was less than enthusiastic because of the rain. The other sister called her a "homo" for not wanting to go out in the rain. Thus, as this example indicates and female participation on male terms in "busting sessions" confirms, the hegemonic language of males defines the terms for equality. Women may be permitted to participate in male groups if they talk like males, willingly "bashing" homosexuality and by extension the qualities traditionally associated with women. Of course, when women opt in, they are often degraded for being too "butch."

NOTES

1. I limit my discussion to terms that denote a homosexual orientation. There are differences among such terms, mainly in their severity and, as a consequence, in the contexts in which they are used and the behaviors that evoke them.

2. Joseph Steffan brought suit against the U.S. government because of his dismissal from the U.S. Naval Academy. Steffan admitted that he was gay. Defense Department regulations required that he be discharged, even though he was singled out as a model cadet and ranked at the very top of his class (Wolinsky and Sherrill 1993).

3. I wish to acknowledge the help of Matt Zeitler, Doug Leonard, and Jennifer Mesiano, whose contribution to this project was invaluable.

4. I do not put much stock in the frequency with which usage classes or terms occurred in the data set. I overheard or had reported to me more than one hundred instances of the "gay" usage and ceased collecting them because there was so little variety. Further, since neither my assistants nor I had easy access to the kinds of contexts where male-male "busting" takes place, this class of usage is probably underrepresented.

REFERENCES

Blumenfeld, Warren J., and Diane Raymond (1989). *Looking at Gay and Lesbian Life.* Boston: Beacon Press.
Boswell, John (1993). "Affidavit II of John Boswell: On the Use of the Term 'Homo' as a Derogatory Epithet." In Marc Wolinsky and Kenneth Sherrill (eds.), *Gays and the Military.* Princeton, NJ: Princeton University Press.
Kronenfeld, D., J. Armstrong, and S. Wilmoth (1985). "Exploring the Internal Structure of Linguistic Categories: An Extensionist Semantic View." In Jane W. D. Dougherty (ed.), *Directions in Cognitive Anthropology.* Urbana: University of Illinois Press.
Lakoff, Robin (1975). *Language and Woman's Place.* New York: Harper & Row.
Moffat, Michael (1989). *Coming of Age in New Jersey.* New Brunswick: Rutgers University Press.
Pei, Mario, and Frank Gaynor (1975). *Dictionary of Linguistics.* Totowa, NJ: Littlefield, Adams.
Perrow, Charles, and Mauro Guillen (1990). *The AIDS Disaster.* New Haven: Yale University Press.
Peters, Jeff (1991). "When Fear Turns to Hate and Hate to Violence." *Human Rights* 18: 1.
Sanday, Peggy R. (1990). *Fraternity Gang Rape.* New York: New York University Press.
Smith, Barbara (1993). "Homophobia: Why Bring it Up?" In Henry Abelove, Michele Barale, and David Halperin (eds.), *The Lesbian and Gay Studies Reader.* New York: Routledge.
Schultz, Muriel R. (1975). "The Semantic Derogation of Women." In Barrie Thorne and

Nancie Henley (eds.), *Language and Sex: Difference and Dominance.* Roxbury, MA: Newbury House.

Sutton, Laurel A. (1995). "Bitches and Skankly Hobags: The Place of Women in Contemporary Slang." In Kira Hall and Mary Bucholtz (eds.), *Gender Articulated: Language and the Socially Constructed Self.* New York: Routledge.

Wolinsky, Marc, and Kenneth Sherrill, eds. (1993). *Gays and the Military.* Princeton, NJ: Princeton University Press.

19

"Falling Short of God's Ideal"

Public Discourse about Lesbians and Gays

ELIZABETH MORRISH

Since consenting homosexual acts between men, in private, were made legal in Great Britain in 1967, gay sex and the gay lifestyle have been brought further and further within the remit of the criminal and civil law. Discriminatory reforms and accompanying public statements have been couched in a discourse that transmits and maintains homophobic attitudes. Lesbians and gays in Britain have not been slow to realize that public discourse, including the language of the law and pronouncements by politicians, journalists, educators, chief constables, and leading churchmen, has a powerful ideological effect. I shall take as a starting point Gunther Kress's (1988) definition of the effects of ideology as "imposing a prior and systematically organized set of values on nature and on the objects of other cultures—as though they too were nature" (69).

The purpose of this chapter is to trace the ideological structures represented in current and recent discursive practice. The tools of analysis are provided by "critical linguistics" and based on a framework suggested by Norman Fairclough (1992). Discourse can be viewed in this framework as a construct of many facets, including theme, interdiscursivity and intertextual relations, presupposition, transitivity, modality, and lexical choice—all revealed in the text and contributing to the ideological impact. In the case of discourse about lesbians and gays, there is a clear cumulative effect that leads to an atmosphere in which homosexuality is deemed "unnatural" and threatening to the dominant culture and in which homophobic acts are held to be justified and in the interests of the "general public."

The work of Michel Foucault has been highly influential in the development of this approach to discourse. "Discourses," in the sense that Foucault recognizes them, go beyond reflecting a social reality; the strength of his work is that he has shown how discourses shape and maintain prevailing perceptions of reality and dominant viewpoints. Discourse analysis, then, is essentially about an analysis of power and ideology in a society. Rather than a straightforward analysis of sentences or conversations, Foucault insists on the analysis of "discursive formations," or a kind of genealogical investigation into why, at a particular point in time, one set of sentences about a particular topic is more likely to occur than any other. Furthermore, people are positioned as "subjects" within a discursive practice, a corollary of which is that the discourse shapes not only ideology but also identity and the sense of self.

Another important concept for the critical discourse analyst is that of hegemony. Barry Smart (1986) offers this definition (after Foucault's reworking of Gramsci's formulation):

> Hegemony contributes to or constitutes a form of social cohesion not through force or coercion nor necessarily through consent, but most effectively by way of practices, techniques, and methods which infiltrate minds and bodies, cultural practices which cultivate behaviors and beliefs, tastes, desires, and needs as seemingly naturally occurring qualities and properties embodied in the psychic and physical reality (or "truth'" of the human subject. (160)

It is clearly a determining role of the dominant public discourse about lesbians and gays that it acts to provide a negative sense of identity and a set of hegemonically shared beliefs about gays, and their behaviors and values, as a group in society.

Since Foucault defines the rules of current discursive formation with reference to past discursive practice, it is necessary that we examine the linkage between hegemony and interdiscursivity. Hegemony is never total or complete; it is always informed and contested by current and past texts and discourses. This chapter details some important intertextual chains that contribute to current discourse about lesbians and gays.

In preparing this chapter I have selected for analysis legal texts and also reports from British quality newspapers. I have chosen not to include samples of the more overtly defamatory discourse from the British tabloid press, since the object is to illustrate the hegemonic construction of gays through mainstream "establishment" discourse. The aim is to identify prevailing discursive patterns and linkages and the way in which these construct subjectivity and reveal the thematic sites of hegemonic struggle and discourse change. For each text, or group of texts, I will look at some of the following elements of discourse:

Themes: discourse themes, as well as what appears initially in clauses, and the assumptions underlying these choices.

Presuppositions: information treated as given or implied in the text.

Interdiscursivity and *intertextuality*: relations between other discursive formations or explicit references to another text or texts, which may then form an intertextual chain.

Modality: the signification of the speaker/writer's authority about the text and the degree of certainty, generality, or "truth" of the utterance. Hodge and Kress (1993) write that "a speaker uses modalities to protect his utterance from criticism" (125). Modality within an utterance can be revealed by a number of devices in the text, e.g., tense (present tense suggesting universal validity), plurality (plurals suggest generalization about a category), negation, and adverbial choice.

Transitivity: the speaker's perception of agency and causality, e.g., active or passive verbs, nominalizations, types of verb (action), event, relation, mental process.

Lexical choice: the way in which the speaker/writer classifies and categorizes by lexical choice. Adjectives, particularly, carry a heavy ideological burden. Meaning is not made only by reference and denotation; connotations also construct meaning. Words may also change their meaning according to context of situation and to who is using them.

Legislative Discourse in Britain

It is commonly believed that homosexuality was legalized by the 1967 act, although this in fact served merely to decriminalize consenting homosexual acts between men over twenty-one years, in private. Britain has spent the intervening thirty years overseeing the progressive recriminalization of gay sex, and presently many types of sexual act and sexual encounter remain illegal. In 1967 Lord Reid (a Law Lord) said, "There is a material difference between merely exempting certain conduct from criminal penalties and making it lawful in the full sense. . . . (I)ndulgence in these practices . . . is corrupting" (Gooding 1992: 214). We can perhaps identify a discourse theme of ambivalence about legality, with a presupposition that these acts naturally fall outside the law and that the legal system is doing gays something of a favor. We note the transitivity feature of the nominalization "indulgence," which prevents the reader from constructing an agent. The lexical choice connotes a scene of dissolute intemperance. The sinful theme is underlined by the adjective "corrupting," which is predicative and generalized to all instances by the present tense copula.

The law in Britain has continued in this equivocal spirit. In 1989 police charged 2,022 men with "gross indecency between males," the highest figure since 1955, when the number was 2,322 (Gooding 1992: 215). The threat of entrapment is a constant fear for many gay men who cruise parks, public bathrooms (cottages), or gay porno theaters.

Clause 25 of the Criminal Justice Bill of 1991 defines many victimless gay "offenses" as "corruption of youth," "gross indecency," and "serious sexual assault." This section of the British legal apparatus encompasses even consensual acts (when not in strict privacy) of buggery (anal sex), gross indecency (anything else), soliciting for immoral purposes, and procuring and draws them into the purview of the criminal law. By categorizing most forms of gay sex as serious sexual offenses, they are inviting an interdiscursive linkage with offenses like heterosexual sex with an underage girl (i.e., one under sixteen years old) and indecent conduct with young children. Soliciting can be interpreted to mean chatting someone up in a gay bar; procuring can mean introducing two friends in the hope that they might hit it off for the evening. Word choice here is quite deliberately emotive hyperbole. The legislation draws attention to what are perceived to be immoral and distasteful acts. Anal sex is classified by the verb *buggery*, with its inherent actional transitivity emphasizing the action rather than the relation of mutual pleasure. It is a term that is frequently used for coercive effect in British public discourse. Furthermore, the semantic space of verbs such as *soliciting* and *procuring*, when appearing in this legislation, is widened for a purpose that discriminates uniquely against gays.

Section 28 of the Local Government Act, 1988 states that a local authority (in charge of schools, facilities) shall not:

a) intentionally promote homosexuality or publish material with the intention of promoting homosexuality
b) promote the teaching in any (publicly) maintained school of the acceptability of homosexuality as a pretended family relationship.

Nothing in subsection (1) above shall be taken to prohibit the doing of anything for the purpose of treating or preventing the spread of disease. (Colvin and Hawkesley 1989: 38)

This legislation has a purely ideological intent, and at present there have been no challenges based on an alleged contravention. Many local authorities, however, have used Section 28 as a justification for banning certain books, school discussions, plays, and gay and lesbian youth groups—anything presenting a positive image of gays—using threats of prosecution as an excuse. The not-so-hidden agenda is to stir up homophobia. Again, the semantic domain of a verb is extended in the context of its application to gays; "promoting" homosexuality is most often read as acknowledging it. A theme of invisibility can be recognized; homosexuality is restricted to the sphere of the "private" and must not be "promoted" into the public sphere. "Promotion" has dual meanings of "elevation" and "publicizing." Evidently, gays must be kept firmly in the lower echelons of society. Intertextual echoes appeared in 1994 in the Smith-Helms amendment passed by the U.S. Senate (but not the House) which would cut federal aid to schools that "promote" homosexuality as "a positive life style alternative." Two themes occur that are recurrent ones in public discussion of homosexuality: family life and disease.

The presupposition laid out in Section 28 is that the category of "family" is a rigid and impermeable one. It is unambiguously heterosexual, while the attributive adjective "pretended" declares the gay family to be invalid. Some families are based on homosexual relationships, however, and by implication the section derides these by evoking a childish game of "let's pretend." Gays and lesbians have shown their resilience to this act, not only by resisting legislation aimed at making them invisible, even vilified, but also by reclaiming the language of the act. People are bidden to gay events by posters declaring "bring the whole pretended family."

It appears that most often in contemporary discourse, the term *family* has become a codeword for the exclusion of homosexuality. Susan Reinhold (1994) points out that *family* is never defined except in relation to what it is not (i.e., the gay couple raising children together); instead, it remains an idealization in the minds of Conservative traditionalists and is reinforced by metaphors of "family life." Reinhold quotes a member of the House of Lords speaking during the 1988 debate on Section 28: "Indeed I am totally opposed to spending public money on promoting encouraging homosexual and lesbian relationships, particularly as happy family units, thereby in the eyes of our young people making our proper established family institution look odd or queer" (Reinhold 1994: 69).

This statement both acknowledges a priori that gays and lesbians do live in groups that are recognizable as family units and perversely seeks to undermine their "happiness." The sense of fragility of the traditional family is incongruously relayed by the use of the adjective *queer*, as if the mere existence of gay families involves incorporating traditional families into their "queerness." The lack of any definition of *family* might be seen to indicate a securely hegemonic concept; however, the very need to dispute the boundaries of its meaning reveals establishment fears of a slippage of a previously uncontested meaning.

In other legislation, too, we find that "the family," although bounded by convention and ideological certainty, is exposed as an extremely fragile edifice. A clause in the Human Fertilization and Embryology Act, 1990 is a transparent attempt to outlaw the possibility of donor insemination for lesbians, with the instruction that treatment services should act with regard to "the sanctity of family life." Once again, *family* is undefined and assumed to conform to a shared assumption of two parents of opposite sexes. The choice of the term *sanctity* is extraordinary, endowed as the word is with biblical and legal force.

The theme of "the spread of disease" mentioned in Section 28 draws on much previous and current discourse, which sees the gay subject solely in terms of the likelihood of transmission of AIDS. Nominalization of "spread" deletes agency and obscures the subject. This message is implicitly recoverable from the text; homosexuals spread disease. Interestingly, AIDS is not named—presumably to reinforce the notion that homosexuality is generally unhealthy. The sense becomes clearer when we contrast "the doing of anything for the purpose of treating or preventing the spread of disease" with perhaps another more neutral choice of words "AIDS/HIV prevention education."

Reporting of the Case of Jane Brown 1994

Legislation in Britain sets the frame for the discussion of homosexuality. The gay or lesbian subject must, then, engage in a continual process of contestation, not just of a personal identity, but of the public representation of the whole category of *lesbian* and *gay*.

The case of Jane Brown stands as an example of the public vilification of a lesbian, faithfully transmitted by politicians and the press.

Jane Brown is a headteacher (principal) of a primary (grade) school in Hackney, London. Her "crime" was to reject an offer of subsidized tickets to the Royal Opera's performance of *Romeo and Juliet*. Allegedly Ms. Brown gave as a reason that the play was "entirely about heterosexual love." The episode ignited a media frenzy in January 1994, with many calls for Ms. Brown's resignation, despite her popular leadership at the school and the support of the majority of the parents.

A full set of reports from the *Times* (a right-of-center daily) and the *Guardian* (a left-of-center daily) reveals shared themes and a surprising lack of hegemonic struggle. They run from 20 January 1994 to 15 February 1994.

The *Times* refers to Ms. Brown as a "headmistress" (O'Leary 1994: 1). Not only is this a gendered term; it is also overlaid with connotations of primness and prudishness, the implication being that a headmistress should not be thinking in sexual terms at all.

Two major themes emerge in the newspaper reports of this case, and both activate interdiscursive relations: political correctness and the portrayal of the "lesbian" as stereotype.

The *Times* makes immediate reference to "the damaging effects of creeping political correctness" (O'Leary 1994: 1). The *Guardian* refers variously to "a saga" and "a banquet" of political correctness (Katz 1994a: 2). The lexical choice of "saga" is clearly intended to conjure up meanings of an entire mythology, while "banquet" has connotations of self-indulgent excess. "Political correctness" has obvious interdiscursive relations with all the other reports of this so-called movement. Interestingly, "political correctness" is never defined, merely inserted as a general bugaboo. Political correctness has no meaning in itself and ultimately no reference, because it is never contrasted with anything. Meaning is implied, however, simply by the interdiscursive chains that are woven into the reports throughout the duration of the media interest in the case. Ms. Brown's actions, for example, are explicitly linked both to her lesbianism and to Hackney council's "loony left image." Reference is made to the school's Equal Opportunity policy, which covers racism, sexism, and homophobia. All are seen to be part of the same package. An ideological feature prominent in the 1990s also appears in the chain—fundamentalism. The *Guardian* writes of "spurious and fundamentalist dogmatism" (Katz 1994b: 3) and also quotes the director of education in Hackney as saying "Equal Opportunities is too serious an issue to be hijacked by the fundamentalism tendency" (Katz 1994a: 2). This utterance contains subtle echoes of Middle Eastern terrorism and Muslim militancy with its choice of "hijack" and "fundamentalism." *Fundamentalism*, like its ally *political correctness*, is never defined or challenged. Its function is ideological—threading one set of textual references into another. *Tendency* is another pejoratively loaded choice. The prevailing discourse about both Marxists and lesbians is that they have or form "tendencies." The lexical selection here reinforces the impression of subversion, perversion, and unpleasant radicalism, made all the more sinister by the attribution of the adjective "persuasive" earlier in the same article to describe Jane Brown's leadership (Katz 1994a: 2).

Through the unwitting vessel of Jane Brown, society's stereotype of lesbianism is invoked. One *Guardian* writer characterizes the headteacher thus: "She posed awkwardly for photographers yesterday" (Meikle 1994: 3), while another *Guardian* description reads, "With her short hair, heavy coat and workman style boots, she seemed to fit every stereotype of political correctness. Even her sullen, plainly unrepentant, expression seemed to match" (Katz 1994a: 2).

The emphasis on clothing and hairstyle, and especially those "workman"-style boots encourage the presupposition that these are inappropriate for a woman. The prevailing image of the inelegant and humorless lesbian is intact, and the statutory reference to "political correctness" is made in order to activate all previous discursive formations about gays and loony lefties. The adverbial clause that details Jane Brown's appearance is foregrounded in the sentence, giving the impression that conformity to this description is an essential part of being a lesbian.

Lesbianism as portrayed by the *Times* is not an intrinsic and healthy part of one's identity. Their writers describe "yesterday's admission by Ms. Brown that she is a lesbian" (Ellis 1994: 13) as if this were a sin or a guilty secret. The *Guardian* reports a statement by the director of education that he was "embarrassed to enquire about such personal matters" (Katz 1994a: 2). Clearly, then, lesbianism should remain invisible, relegated to the private sphere, lest it affront those who might encounter it.

Reporting the Parliamentary Vote on the Age of Consent for Gay Men 1993/1994

In February 1994 British Members of Parliament voted to lower the age of consent for gay men from twenty-one years of age, where it had been since 1967, to eighteen. The original proposal before Parliament was that the age of consent should be lowered to age sixteen to bring it into line for the age of consent for heterosexual sex and, indeed, for lesbian sex. This was the first time that gays and lesbians had rallied together since the battles over Section 28 in 1988. Here we can see the hegemonic struggle played out in the newspapers surveyed, with churchmen and right-wing commentators framing the debate in terms of prurient judgments about sexual behavior and the gay community adopting the stance of a human rights issue.

The *Observer* (the *Guardian*'s Sunday sister paper) comments that maintaining the status quo of age twenty-one is a popular option and adds with heavy irony, "This in spite of the increasing integration of homosexuals throughout society and public life and the best efforts of the liberal media to present homosexual men as ordinary, likeable and human, like their heterosexual counterparts" (Wroe 1994: 23). It is not evident from the data presented earlier that gay people have been thus portrayed. That the *Observer* feels the need to comment on the humanity of gays is extremely telling.

The issue of behavior is laid out graphically for the readership of the quality dailies. The Church of England reveals itself as the height of delicacy, describing homosexual sex as "falling short of God's ideal" (Wroe 1994: 23). Simon Raven, a right-wing novelist, interviewed in the *Guardian*, writes, predictably, about "buggery" as "thoroughly nasty, messy, painful, cruel business" and of a boy being "feeble enough" to "be enticed into being buggered" (Bennett 1994: 5). The presupposition of the word *entice* is that the desire for sex with another man would never occur to a younger one without prior suggestion. Another presupposition, signaled by the transitivity choice of the verb, is that the sexual act will be experienced entirely passively by the teenage partner and that there can be no other possibility. This is a widely expressed presumption and is repeated in several of the reports of the period. Furthermore, the adjectives assign an unpleasant tone to an act of mutual gratification. This latter meaning has been excluded from the reader's contemplation. An M.P., Robert Spink, announces that "the buggery of teenage boys is the only issue on the table" and refers to the "pro-buggery lobby" (Bates 1994: 1). The insistent use of the action verb *to bugger* reinforces the concept of homosexuality as synonymous with, and confined to, the act of anal sex.

Feebleness, penetration, and questionable manhood are all recurring discourse themes from the anti-sixteen side of the debate. Donald Campbell, a psychoanalyst, comments on the action of having "an older man put his penis in the boy's anus." The *Guardian* summarizes his assertion that girls may find penetration at sixteen frightening, but it will have less impact on their overall development. The law must "cushion a boy from the risk of penetration," however, as that may "drastically influence his future sexuality by altering his image of what kind of a man he is" (Pilkington 1994: 4). The uncertainty betrayed by the choice of modal "may" is superceded by the extreme lexical choices made—the influence may be "drastic," the event may "alter" the boy's whole self-concept. This concept is limited, of course, to the notion of manhood, which we are led to infer is incompatible with the act of being penetrated. Gay sex, then, in this discourse is not a consensual and rewarding experience; it acts purely to create a subjectivity of victimhood and of being "another kind" of man.

This discursive production of the subjectivity of the "other" appears frequently. In the following instance it is embedded within the now-familiar "I don't think we should encourage homosexuality" from Gary Bushell, a tabloid columnist quoted in the *Guardian* (Bennett 1994: 5). The pronoun "we" is at once inclusive but also exclusive of gays, inviting the reader to identify with the heterosexual majority. The negative "don't" is used for the purpose of polemic as it incorporates all the other discourse formations around "promoting" or "encouraging" homosexuality in order to reject them. Bushell goes on to assert, "You can discriminate between homosexuality and heterosexuality because one is absolutely normal . . . and the other isn't" (Bennett 1994: 5). The inference is clearly that we should need no further detail to determine which sexual identity is "normal."

The theme of the family, which traverses several texts and discursive formations ranging from abortion to homosexuality, also features in these reports. Tony Higton, a member of the General Synod of the Church of England, pronounces that "any lowering of the age of consent is going to be yet another nail in the coffin for marriage and the family" (Bennett 1994: 5). The modality of "is going to be" suggests the speaker's certainty, a certainty that is syntactically linked with the threat to "the family." We note the complete absence of any intellectual steps between the two processes identified. The metaphor of "yet another nail in the coffin" assumes that the process is already under way—the family is mortally wounded. This metaphor functions to make a connection with other texts impacting on "the family," while at the same time refuting the notion of gay families.

The Reverend Ian Paisley, who for years has vented his apocalyptic convictions in the province of Ulster (Northern Ireland), reserves some of the same for homosexuals. "The cement that holds society together is the family. As goes the family, so will go the nation. If we don't have the cement of the family, society will disintegrate and be destroyed" (White & Bates 1994: 6). No inductive discontinuities in this statement! The only imponderable is that of which agent to supply for the passive "be destroyed." The metaphor of cement reveals the belief in the family as an impregnable and durable structure. There is a transitivity feature of hypotheticality in the third sentence, "If we don't have the cement of the family, society will disintegrate and be destroyed," to maximize the effect of his intimidating rhetoric. Here, as with the discourse elicited in the context of the Section 28 debate, we view with irony Paisley's simultaneous assertion of the weakness and the instability of society and the family unit.

Other themes from the right-wing side of the debate cluster around the notion of the immaturity and the supposed vulnerability of boys. We note that there is never any mention of a need to protect girls of the same age, whether lesbian or heterosexual. The impression, then, is of a society that places a high value on its young men. An editorial writer for the *Times* (1994) offers this opinion: "Protecting this minority from acts which they may later regret and a sexual path which may leave them isolated and unhappy should remain a priority. It is a mark of a civilized society that it values the interests of young people more than abstract liberties" (15). The grammatical theme is expressed by the gerundive "protecting." The use of a verbal form rather than a nominalization indicates that society and the forces of protection should be active. The lexical choices "regret" and "unhappy" represent the gay subject as an unfortunate one. The group noun "minority" traces a lexical cohesion with "isolated." The last sentence skillfully deflects the core of the debate from the issue of "liberty," which has interdiscursive relations with "equality," to the foregrounded issue of "civilization" and that of the protection of the young.

The gay leaders in this debate wisely do not try to counter the cascade of arguments hurled at them by the opposition. Instead, they confine the discussion to the issue of equality and discrimination. Peter Tatchell, a highly vocal organizer of the group Outrage in Britain, writes: "It is wrong that the law singles out gay men for discriminatory treatment" (Bennett 1994: 5), while "out" gay MP Chris Smith refers to "a basic piece of inequality and discrimination" (Wroe 1994: 23).

Interestingly, nearly all participants overlook the key word "consent." Only David Starkey, a Conservative, who supports the lowering of the age of consent to sixteen, points out that "the key issue is consent" (Bennett 1994: 5), and a liberal psychiatrist, Jean Harris Hendricks, chooses to attenuate the emphasis on sexual identity and age with this statement: "Young people are individuals who are able to give consent according to their relative understanding" (Pilkington 1994: 4).

Hegemonic Struggle: A Discussion

The stated aim of this chapter was to identify discursive formations—the rules by which sentence and thematic patterns are made more likely by the occurrence and combination of previous discursive practice. The legislation and media cases that have been examined here affirm that the same leitmotifs are reworked time and again whenever the topic of homosexuality is mentioned in public. Collectively, the statements analyzed in this chapter form a pattern of discourse whose effect is to create an atmosphere where there can be legitimate censure of the open expression of homosexuality. The public image of gays and lesbians is framed by the linguistic activation and chaining of the themes of indecency, corruption, buggery, the threat to the family by "pretended families," and dread terror of "fundamentalism" and "political correctness." These are all imaginary moral concerns and are devoid of argument value. We can see at work here what Stuart Hall calls the "reality effect" (Turner 1992: 205). The "real" is socially constructed by those with cultural power, and their discourse establishes itself as the only legitimate account. This is known as *naturalization*—the process by which the discourse starts to be seen as legitimated by nature, rather than open to contest and debate. The recurrent discursive patterns identified in this article have no role other than to reinforce a hegemonic perception of lesbians and gays and to block the creation of new discourse by distracting from any discussion of themes that reflect the reality and the true concerns of gays. It could also be argued that this is effected not necessarily by conscious design but almost by default, inasmuch as it can seem as if there is no other language to talk about gays. In the habitual rules of this discourse, the words *gay* and *lesbian* are collocated with the themes mentioned earlier. This is the architecture of internal and external homophobia.

There are, however, points of contradiction within the discourse of the right. References to "nails in the coffin" of the family and the "disintegration" of society suggest that we might foresee impediments to the growth of conservative discursive authority. Despite many ideological defeats in the late 1980s and early 1990s in Britain, we are now beginning to see signs of a struggle for the discursive highground. Kress (1988) remarks about discourse patterns that, "as material and social processes alter, that ideologically-constructed common sense is always out of phase with these practices. There is thus a constant tension between social reality and social practices and the way in which they are and can be written and talked about in language" (83). So as social change becomes a reality, and the right-wing depicts gay behavior as buggery and corruption, the gay lobby endeavors to promote the themes of equality and antidiscrimination.

Patterns of discourse and interdiscursive relations maintain a forceful effect. Amplified by the mainstream media, it is an effect that is proving difficult to override. Fairclough, however, asserts that we are not hegemonic prisoners. He regards the relationship between subjects and discursive practices as a dialectical one in which subjects can also shape and restructure the discourse in continuity with their own evolving identity. Such an ideological shift seems to have penetrated the establishment most notably when, in the context of the debate on gays in the military, President Clinton is quoted as saying (and I paraphrase) that you should be excluded for something you do, not for something you are. In emphasizing gayness as a matter of "being," and thus as immutable, Clinton has countenanced a discourse that seeks to redefine homosexuality as a matter of identity, not of behavior. Despite Clinton's subsequent failure to enact the promised social change, perhaps his discourse has signaled a departure from the linguistic demonization of lesbians and gays. We in Britain await discursive endorsement from our own government.

REFERENCES

Bates, Stephen (1994). "Teenage Gay Sex Charges Unlikely." *Guardian*, 15 March, p. 1.
Bennett, Catherine (1994). "Consent or Coercion: 'A Bad Enough Mess as It Is'." *Guardian*, 14 January, p. G2T 5.
Colvin, Madeleine, and Jane Hawkesley (1989). *Section 28: A Practical Guide to the Law and Its Implications.* London: Liberty.
Ellis, Walter (1994). "A Voice from Hackney for Middle England." *Times*, 28 January, p. 13.
Fairclough, Norman (1992). *Discourse and Social Change.* Cambridge: Polity.
Gooding, Caroline (1992). *Trouble with the Law.* London: Gay Men's Press.
Hodge, Robert, and Gunther Kress (1993). *Language as Ideology.* London: Routledge.
Katz, Ian (1994a). "Head on the Block." *Guardian*, 27 January, p. G2T 2.
————— (1994b). "School Heads Get 'Dogma' Warning." *Guardian*, 4 February , p. 3.
Kress, Gunther (1988). *Linguistic Processes in Sociocultural Practice.* Oxford: Oxford University Press.
Meikle, James (1994). "Head Sorry for Refusing Romeo and Juliet Trip." *Guardian*, 21 January, p. 3.
O'Leary, John (1994). "Teacher Bans Romeo and Juliet for Being Heterosexual; Kingsmead School, Hackney, East London." *Times*, 20 January, p. 1.
Pilkington, Edward (1994). "Consent or Coercion." *Guardian*, 14 January, p. G2T 4.
Reinhold, Susan (1994). "Through the Parliamentary Looking Glass: 'Real' and 'Pretend' Families in Contemporary British Politics." *Feminist Review* 48: 61–79.
Smart, Barry (1986). "The Politics of Truth and the Problem of Hegemony." In David Couzens Hoy (ed.), *Foucault: A Critical Reader*. Oxford: Blackwell, pp. 157–174.
Times (1994). "Voting for Change," editorial, 21 February, p. 15.
Turner, Graeme (1992). *British Cultural Studies.* London: Routledge.
White, Michael, and Stephen Bates (1994). "Gay Consent 'Will Return to Commons.'" *Guardian*, 22 February, p. 6.
Wroe, Martin (1994). "Vexed Question of Gay Consent." *Observer*, 9 January, p. 23.

III

LINGUISTIC GENDER-BENDING

20

$\mathcal{D}$isloyal to Masculinity

Linguistic Gender and Liminal
Identity in French

ANNA LIVIA

Since the second wave of feminism began in the late 1960s, linguistic issues have been subject to intense scrutiny by feminist theorists. Participating in the discussion of language and gender, and of the relationship between language and worldview, a discussion that crosses national and linguistic boundaries to span Western Europe and North America, feminist writers have experimented with innovative solutions to the problem of creating a feminine subject position in languages that encode the masculine as the unmarked, the generic, the universal. This debate has been complicated by an examination of the language used by and about communities whose gender is not stable, or who use the linguistic gender system to different ends at different times.

The specific challenge to feminist orthodoxy posed by transsexuals has been taken up, often bitterly, by American theorists and radical feminists, and part of the ensuing discussion has centered around the use of gendered pronouns. Janice Raymond's *The Transsexual Empire* (1979) is subtitled, "The Making of the She-Male," a phrase that, says the author, illustrates her point that while transsexuals may be fundamentally masculine or feminine, they are not fundamentally men or women. With this distinction, she is drawing a line between the biological trappings of femininity (and masculinity—though she is principally concerned with male-to-female transsexuals) and true womanhood, which, though culturally based, is inculcated from birth onward and cannot be replicated in voice workshops and afternoon sessions on how to speak like a woman.[1]

When referring to male-to-female transsexuals, Raymond refuses to use the pronouns *she* and *her* unmodified, putting them in quotation marks: "she," "her," instead, to emphasize their anomalous status. Femininity is not, according to Raymond, simply a question of anatomical configuration. Feminine pronouns and, in French, feminine gender concord, confer a status on the referent that existential statements like *vous êtes une femme* (you are a woman), comforting though they may be, cannot. The use of a feminine pronoun presupposes the femininity of the referent; it does not assert it. The difference between an assertion and a presupposition of importance here is the fact that the truth of an assertion can be questioned or denied simply by putting the clause containing it in the interrogative or the negative. *Etes-vous une femme?* (are you a woman?) and *vous n'êtes pas une femme* (you are not a woman) explicitly question and negate the proposition that you are a woman. On the other hand, the interrogative and negative versions of the proposition *elle est venue* (she has come)—*est-elle venue?* (has she come?) and *elle n'est pas venue* (she hasn't come)—do not throw into doubt the gender of the referent of *elle* but question only the fact of this person's arrival, since the use of the feminine pronoun presupposes the referent's femininity. Cooperative speakers do not question presuppositions, and social commerce relies on cooperation.[2] Raymond is explicitly refusing to cooperate with the transsexual worldview.

The fight over the right to pronominally feminine (or masculine) status has not been restricted to theoretical works. A heated debate has arisen between the lesbian and gay community and the transsexual community over the correct way to refer to Billy Tipton and Teena Brandon, two people who were both anatomically female but lived their lives and were accepted by society as men. Billy Tipton was a jazz musician who married a woman and adopted and brought up children with her. At his death in 1989 it was revealed that he was anatomically female. While the gay community has claimed Billy Tipton as a lesbian and a passing woman, *TNT*, the *Transsexual News Telegraph*, a transgender 'zine of the Bay Area, claims Billy Tipton as a transsexual man. Where the gay community uses the pronoun *she* to refer to Tipton, *TNT* uses *he*: "Billy Tipton was transsexual. He lived and died as a man. . . . Hands off! He's one of ours!" (*TNT* Summer 1993). Feelings are even more heated when discussion turns to Teena Brandon. The *San Francisco Bay Times*, a gay paper, ran an article on the murder of Teena Brandon headlined "Queers Have No Right to Life in Nebraska" (13 January 1994). It tells how Teena Brandon, calling herself Brandon Teena, passed as a man in Falls City, Nebraska, dating girls and playing pool "just like any straight man would." On Christmas Eve 1993 she was raped by the ex-boyfriend of her female lover and a friend of his; on 31 December she and two friends, including her lover, were found murdered. In the *Bay Times* of 27 January 1994 there were two letters criticizing the portrayal of Brandon's life. Gail Sondegaard, editor of *TNT,* complains, "[Y]ou kept referring to Brandon Teena as 'she' and as a 'cross-dressing lesbian.' . . . Brandon went to a lot of effort to be taken seriously as a male. I think you should have respected that choice and referred to him as he obviously wished to be addressed: as a man." Max Wolf, another letter writer, makes a similar point: "[I]t appears Brandon had made the choice to live his life using the male pronoun to refer to himself. . . . Mindy Ridgway [the *Bay Times* journalist] should . . . respect his choice by referring to him not as 'she' but as 'he.'" This wording is telling. Wolf equates the assignment of male pronouns with living as a man, as though it were the pronoun itself that confered manhood.

In a provocative argument, Susan Stryker, a male-to-female transsexual, has stated that transsexuality is a linguistic problem: "[T]ranssexual genders, by virtue of their temporality, exceed language's static capacity to represent them" (abstract submitted to *Queerly Phrased*—to our regret, the article itself was never written). A change of grammatical gender is a mark not of a change of identity but of a lack of identity. How, Stryker asks, does one speak of the pubescent experience of a female-to-male transsexual, of the periods she used to have as a woman but, as a man, is incapable of having? "When he got his period"? "When he got her period"? Or, to give a French example, how does one speak about the pregnancy of a female-to-male-transsexual? Does one use the anatomically incorrect *Quand elle était enceinte* (when she was pregnant)?[3]—one is after all speaking of a person with male genitalia—or the grammatically incorrect *Quand il était enceinte* (when he was pregnant)?

In the French school of discourse analysis known as the *théorie de l'énonciation* there exist two useful terms to distinguish between the speaker of an utterance and the presentation of the speaker as created by that utterance. Oswald Ducrot (1984) coined the terms *locuteur-L* (the speaker as such) and *locuteur-λ* (the speaker as a being in the world) to articulate the difference between the person narrating a story (*locuteur-L*) and the identity the person creates for him or herself in the story (*locuteur-λ*). He applies these terms, for example, to Rousseau's *Confessions*, in order to explain how the Rousseau writing (*locuteur-L*) can construct the younger Jean-Jacques (*locuteur-λ* as brash and even vulgar (peeing in a saucepan) in order to gain the reader's belief in his honesty, even though this is at the expense of Jean-Jacques's reputation (or 'ethos'). An arch-conservative of fifty may tell a story about herself as an eighteen-year-old radical; someone who has lost a leg may tell a story from before the accident, using the same pronoun *je* without fear of being misunderstood, narrating in a historic present tense feats of athleticism of which he is visibly no longer capable. The contrast between oneself at the time of speaking and oneself at a previous time is immediately apprehendable, the gap between the two resolved by a concept of the self changing through time, whereas a change in the gender of the narrator causes a rupture, a sense of discontinuity, as though a second person must be involved. Time is understood as inherently changeable while gender is stable, immutable. Perhaps we need to add to our set of analytical terms the possibility of a *locuteur-L* speaking about a *locutrice-λ*. To the subscript notation $_{i, j, k,}$ . . . denoting the same or different referents, we should add i_f and i_m to denote coreference but change of gender.

The problem of how to refer to transsexuals was considered so important that the publishers of *Appelez-moi Gina* (1994), the autobiography of Georgine Noël, a Belgian male-to-female transsexual, placed the arresting question "Il ou Elle? *Il* puis *Elle*?" at the top of their cover blurb. The fact that the question may be asked is newsworthy in itself, whatever answer is given. Another male-to-female transsexual titles her autobiography *Je serai elle* (Sylviane Dullak 1983), signifyng her determination not only to be accepted as a woman but to pass as female without

question, her gender presupposed, not asserted. An analysis of the way Georgine
Noël refers to herself in her autobiography demonstrates the versatile uses to
which the linguistic gender system may be put. Although I concentrate on *Appelez-moi Gina* , my research show similar results for four additional autobiogra-
phies of male-to-female transsexuals writing in French, *Né homme, comment je suis
devenue femme* by Brigitte Martel (1981), *Alain, transsexuelle* by Inge Stephens
(1983), *Diane par Diane* (1987), and *Je serai elle* by Sylviane Dullak (1983), and for
two biographies, *Histoire de Jeanne transsexuelle* by Catherine Rihoit (1980) and *Le
Combat de la mère d'un transsexuel* by Marie Mayrand (1986). In each case, although the transsexual asserts that she has been female since birth, she alternates
between masculine and feminine gender concord with regard to herself, indicating
that the situation was in fact far more complex. The two third-person accounts
(Rihoit 1980 and Mayrand 1986) also switch gender reference. Mayrand, for example, whose son changed from a masculine to a feminine identity, describes her
offspring in the masculine until the moment she herself accepted that *he* was a *she*.
After this point in the narrative she uses feminine concord, except when describing a photograph of her child at her second wedding, where she writes of *him* in
the masculine, because for this occasion *he* was wearing a man's suit (60).

As we will see, the changes of grammatical gender in *Appelez-moi Gina* are
even more complex, suggesting that Gina's gender identification is not stable but
varies according to social situation and role. Since she presents herself as always
having been female, despite the facts of her body, Noël might have referred to herself in the feminine throughout her autobiography. Or, since her sex-change operation gave her anatomically correct female genitalia, she might have used masculine concord up to that point and feminine thereafter. Nine years after the
operation, her sex was legally changed on her birth certificate from "male" to "female," another possible demarcation point between masculinity and femininity.
Though she insists that her sex-change operation, which took place when she was
thirty-nine, had merely "rétabli la correspondance entre (s)on corps et (s)on esprit"
(reestablished the correspondence between her body and her mind)[4] (1994: 10),
Noël uses the binary opposition of the French linguistic gender system throughout
her autobiography to express or underscore many of her changes of mood, attitude, and identification.

The reader first sees Noël "allongée" (lying down[f]) (9) on her hospital bed in
Lausanne after her operation. "Avant j'étais un transsexuel, maintenant j'étais une
femme" (before I was a transsexual[m], now I was a woman) (10), she announces,
using the masculine form of the noun *transsexuel* to emphasize the fact that it was
as a male that her gender identity was abnormal. Before recounting, in chronolog-
ical order, the main episodes of her life, Noël describes the life that might have
been hers had she had the operation at fifteen. "Placée dans un environnement
scolaire exclusivement féminin (j'aurais pu) participer normalement aux sports"
(Placed[f] in an exclusively feminine school environment [I could have] played my
part in sports in the normal way), "Heureuse d'être femme et épouse, j'aurais aimé
adopté les enfants " (Happy to be a woman and a wife, I would have liked to adopt
children) (11). The contrary-to-fact conditional is used for the experience she
would have liked, in contrast with the imperfect, which describes the events she

lived through. "Comment le petit garçon pouvait-il un jour se révéler dans la femme adulte? Il allait vivre bien des souffrances" (How could the little boy show himself one day in the adult woman? He was going to/ would experience much suffering) (22). This pattern of using the imperfect for past lived events and the conditional for future time is repeated to underscore the tenuousness of both positions. As well as for habitual and durative events in the past, the imperfect is also used by children playing make-believe to establish unreal conditions: "moi j'étais le médecin et toi tu étais la petite fille" (I'll be the doctor and you'll be the little girl; lit. I was the doctor and you were the little girl). There is a tinge, then, of the unreal in Noël's description of herself in the masculine. "J'ai appris ce qu'on enseignait à qui j'étais et à qui je deviendrais" (I learned what was being taught to the person I was and to the person I would become) (32), Noël recounts. The impermanent nature of the person she was and the uncertain character of the one she was to become underline her precarious sense of identity.

After lengthy *prolégomènes* (prolegomena), in which Docteur Georgine Noël, as she is called on the title page, explains to the reader the medical facts of transsexualism, establishing herself as an authority rather than a victim by virtue of her medical expertise, the story begins with Georges's birth. At first Noël's choice of tense allows her to fudge the gender issue. For the announcement of her birth she uses the *passé simple*, avoiding the *passé composé*, which would have identified her as male: "je naquis par un bel après-midi" (I was born [passé simple] on a fine afternoon) (26). The *passé simple* also conveys a lack of connection to the present, categorizing the event as firmly part of the past with no relevance to the moment of utterance, downplaying the link between the baby boy who was born and the sixty-year-old woman who is telling the story.

Recalling how, during the dangerous years of the Nazi occupation, she and her mother were left at home while her father went off to work, Noël describes them as "*seuls toute la journée*" (alone[mpl] all day long) (27), using the masculine plural form of the adjective. Since Noël's mother is clearly a woman, it must be Noël's own masculinity that prevents the adjective taking the form of the feminine plural. Although, for most of the narrative, she insists on the isolation and loneliness of being a girl trapped in a male body, there are moments when Noël sees a certain heroism in her masculinity. She and her mother cannot be described as two females alone at the mercy of wandering German soldiers, for she at least has the body of a boy, hence the adjective "*seuls*" in its mascuine form. When her father learns that the Gestapo has set out to arrest her cousins for refusing to work in a German arms factory, it is she who pedals furiously on her bicycle to warn them and almost certainly saves their lives. "J'enfourche mon vélo héroïque" (I jump on my heroic bicycle) (35), Noël reports, using the historic present, which, not requiring gender agreement, does not make clear whether she performs this action as a boy or a girl. The bicycle has, however, been introduced in some detail in the previous paragraph as an instrument for masculine independence—"je pourrais aller seul à l'école" (I could go to school alone[m]) (35)—preventing Noël from walking home from school in the company of her girlfriends, picking flowers, chasing butterflies, and reveling in other girlish activities. At first Noël resents the present of the bicycle because it reinforces her masculinity and autonomy at the expense of her camaraderie with the girls. It becomes heroic, however, when it enables her to go, boyishly, to the rescue of her cousins. Throughout the autobiography, Noël's alternation between masculine and feminine forms encodes often quite subtle changes of attitude.

From this point in the narrative, until she begins to write a secret diary, Noël describes herself solidly in the masculine: "j'étais un enfant souffreteux" (I was a sickly^m child) (27); "Elève absent . . . assis au dernier banc" (a distracted^m pupil . . . sitting^m on the last bench); "j'étais bon élève" (I was a good^m pupil) (29); "engoncé dans mon costume trois pièces" (stuffed^m into my three-piece suit) (40; "j'étais encore trop jeune et maladroit" (I was still too young and clumsy^m) (43). The adjective "*seul*" (alone^m) is used to describe her seven times in thirteen pages, always in the masculine, emphasizing Noël's unease with her gender status and suggesting that had she been accepted as a girl, she would not have been so isolated. Indeed, she asserts, "la fille cherchait à naître isolée au milieu de tant de garçons" (the girl was struggling to be born, isolated^f among so many boys) (46). The feminine form of the adjective *isolée* (isolated), after a litany of *seul*, in the masculine, underlines the fact that Noël is alone despite the companionship of other boys because she is fundamentally different from them.

With the idea not only of writing a diary but of writing it in a secret code decipherable only by herself comes the possibility of describing herself in the feminine. Noël records that she did not trust her parents to respect her privacy and accept that she "(s)e sente étrangère dans (s)on corps et désire transporter (s)on âme dans la chair d'une autre" (felt like a stranger^f in her body and wanted to transport her soul into the flesh of another^f) (51). This is the first time in the story of her childhood that Noël has used feminine markers for herself. Creating her own private code with which to recount her thoughts and feelings, a code very different from the one in which she is obliged to live her life, gives her sufficient distance from the masculine persona forced upon her to begin to tell her story differently. Her journal recounts "je suis revenue dans la cour avec Edgard" (I went back^f into the playground with Edgard) (51) and tells of her watching the little girls from the local boarding school and feeling that her place was among them. Unfortunately, her mother finds her diary and reads it aloud to her father: "Le voilà maintenant qui gribouille n'importe quoi" (now he's scribbling any old rubbish) (51). They laugh scornfully at the idea of their son writing in code, while Noël, described in the feminine, listens in the dark: "[P]as encore endormie, j'avais tout entendu" (not yet asleep^f, I had heard everything) (52). After this violation, Noël realizes that the journal can no longer offer her solace. Her secret code is useless, and she returns to the masculine, resolving never to share anything with her parents: "[P]our ne pas être tenté je bloquerais tout" (so as not to be tempted^m, I would block out everything) (52).

The narrative now continues with masculine concord and, as though striving once again to make the best of her enforced masculinity, Noël informs the reader, "[J]'étais entré chez les scouts" (I had joined^m the scouts) (53). For a while masculine gender and masculine exploits seem to achieve a concord that is more than merely grammatical. As before, during her heroic race to save her cousins, Noël's masculinity allows her to do things and go places forbidden to girls. The description of her delight in the scouts' blue uniform, group loyalty, and *esprit de corps*, as well as their speleological adventures, which she sums up in the grandiose phrase "On en rentrait marqué du sceau de l'absolu" (we returned marked^m by the seal of the absolute) (54), where her own participation is consistently narrated in the masculine, demonstrates that here at least the use of masculine grammatical gender coincides nicely with her own self-concept.

The next change in grammatical gender occurs when Noël's friend Edgard is expelled from school for reading Baudelaire's *Les Fleurs du mal*.[5] Throughout her autobiography Noël insists that transsexuals are not homosexual. "Le transsexualisme est fondamentalement différent du transvestisme et de l'homosexualité" (transsexuality is fundamentally different from transvestism and homosexuality) (15), she announces, in the guise of filling the reader in on necessary medical theory. When deciding which cases are right for treatment and surgical reassignment, she insists, the medical practitioner must automatically exclude three groups: "(l)es travestis, (l)es homosexuels, (l)es transsexuels utilitaires" (transvestites, homosexuals, and professional transsexuals) (21). (It is amusing to note that added to this list of undesirables are "les psycopathes et les tordus sexuels de tous bords" [psychopaths and sexual deviants of all hues]). To express her own attraction to Edgard and her sadness at his expulsion, Noël has to swap to a feminine self-presentation; otherwise, her feelings might be dubbed homosexual: "J'étais attirée par cet ami, ne voyais que ses yeux, mais je ne lui en fis jamais l'aveu" (I was attracted^f by this friend, could see nothing but his eyes, but I never let him know it) (58).

Throughout her account of the next few years, the narrative shifts between masculine and feminine gender marking. It is not until Noël moves away from the confining isolation of her village school and the little cottage in the middle of the forest where she has lived with her parents and siblings and enters the sophistications of Louvain, where she will study to be a doctor, that a feminine identity becomes stable and the masculine markers disappear. Until then she must be content with her secret wardrobe of women's clothes, which, like the coded diary of her childhood, permit her the trappings of another sexual identity. "J'étais heureuse" (I was happy^f) (58), she recalls, dressed in a woman's blouse, skirt, and shoes, as she walks in the middle of the forest, far from the eyes of her family and schoolmates. The adjective *seul*, which dominated the account of her childhood, reappears, but this time it is in the feminine and has an entirely positive meaning: "(Je) savourais le plaisir d'être enfin pour moi seule" (I savored the pleasure of finally being for myself alone^f) (59). For Noël in her feminine persona, solitude means not isolation but peace and freedom. At the end of the book, after she has achieved both a sexchange operation and the rectification of her *état-civil*—the declaration of sex on her birth certificate—she reflects, "[C]'est seule avec moi-même que j'étais dans la joie" (it was alone^f with myself that I felt joyful) (157). Lonely and isolated as a boy surrounded by other boys, as a woman alone she feels complete.

In the scene of Noël's lone wandering in the forest, the adjective *seules* is picked up from "je savourais le plaisir d'être pour moi seule" and repeated in the following sentence, this time applied to the wild animals that roam, unafraid, among the trees: "Seules les biches et les sangliers passaient par là" (only^f the does and the wild boar passed by there) (59). Of particular interest in the phrase "seules

les biches et les sangliers" is the fact that the adjective *"seules"* has the feminine form. While it is grammatically correct for the adjective to take the gender of the nearest noun it qualifies (*les biches* [the does] is feminine), this rule is more often overlooked in favor of a competing one that states that where both masculine and feminine nouns are qualified by the same adjective, the masculine should prevail. Since *les sangliers* (the wild boar) is masculine, one might have expected *seules* to show masculine concord. Instead, the feminine form is used to imply a sense of fellowship—or rather sisterhood—in solitude between Noël and the animals, emphasizing the naturalness of Noël's femininity. In contrast to this bucolic scene is the description of Noël's return home in "normal clothes." Now the adjective *seuls* reappears in the masculine: "seuls les fleurs, les champignons . . . méritaient attention" (Only[m] the flowers, the mushrooms were worth attention) (59). Where before *seul* has agreed with the gender of the nearest noun, here, though it immediately precedes the feminine *les fleurs* (the flowers), it shows masculine concord, for Noël is no longer dressed as a girl. A sense of pathetic fallacy unites Noël's feminine identity with the innocence of nature and is recorded in the choice of grammatical gender. Her return to the masculine is marked by the masculine form of the adjective *sûr* (sure[m]) in an expression of disgust at the conformation of her body: "sûr que ce n'était pas à moi ce machin-là" (sure[m] that it was not mine, that thingummy-jig there).

At last Noël leaves home, and the narrative of her medical studies in Louvain and her establishment in Rwanda and then the Congo stabilizes in the feminine. The adjectives and past participles that describe her life in Africa read as follows: *engagée, attristée, habituée, innocente, gênée, happée, prête, seule, égarée, seule, envoyée, seule, voisine, seule, démunie, estimée, affectée, étonnée* (hired[f], saddened[f], accustomed[f], innocent[f], embarassed[f], snapped up[f], ready[f], lost[f], alone[f], sent[f], alone[f], neighboring[f], alone[f], running out of [f], esteemed[f], transferred[f], astonished[f]) (100–114). Suddenly, in the middle of this thoroughly femininized environment, the masculine returns, only to disappear again immediately. The point at which it makes its reentry into the text is highly significant. In the course of a small dinner party with another doctor and his wife, as well as some of the local white farmers, Noël gets a little drunk, disappears into her room, and returns wearing a dress: "Je me retirai dans ma chambre, puis revins en robe. J'en fus moi-même étonnée" (I withdrew to my bedroom, then returned in a dress. I myself was surprised[f])(114). This is the only time she shows her feminine self to other people during the whole of her stay in Africa. After her account of this incident, she turns to a series of racist reflections on the "hypersexual" habits of the Congolese men she has to treat and the observation that their promiscuity has led to the spread of AIDS. It is at this juncture that she describes herself in the masculine once again: "Né homme, je devais continuer à manifester ma supériorité sociale et sexuelle" (born[m] a man, I had to continue to show my social and sexual superiority) (114). The revelatory past participle *né* appears here in its masculine form, so carefully avoided at the outset of the narrative by the use of the *passé simple*, "je naquis," which, though gender neutral, is hardly colloquial. Masculine gender is needed to vouch for Noël's superior status and to claim her (his) birthright. Anxious lest her appearance in feminine garb has caused her to lose face among the white people she respects, she scornfully derides what she perceives to be the African sexual libido, emphasizing her own status and authority as a sexually abstemious white male. As soon as the moment of fear has passed, she presents herself as feminine once again. When Noël feels her back is up against the wall, a return to masculine gender presentation and masculine privilege is always possible.

Upon her reintegration into Belgian life, Noël speaks of herself in the masculine. The temporary license she had to present herself as she wanted in the exoticism and *dépaysement* of her African adventure is rescinded by the necessity to find her way through the bureaucratic process of reentry into the European way of life. Or perhaps the simple fact of going back to the place where she had grown up causes her to revert to the presentation of self of her earlier years. As before, when she was a child groping for a time, a place, a context in which to express her feminine nature, finding temporary solace in her coded diary entries and in solitary walks in the forest, it is not until she again finds a context in which to rethink her femininity that Noël begins to describe herself in the feminine once more. It is, ironically, in the newspaper account of the death of "Peggy," who died of an embolism ten days after her sex-change operation, that Noël discovers the address of an organization for transsexuals in Paris, the "A. Ma. Ho" (*Association d'aide aux malades hormonaux*—an association for aid to people with hormonal problems). In a little group of "amies . . . habituées à se retrouver à Neuilly" (friends[f] . . . accustomed[f] to meeting in Neuilly) (130), the grammatical feminine makes a comeback and, for the first time in the narrative, it is in the plural, for Noël has finally found other transsexuals like herself. Though she relates encounters with various women throughout the text, there has never before been the thread of mutuality, of activities undertaken together, that would generate a feminine plural.

After her account of the sex-change operation in Lausanne, though her sexual status is not changed on her birth certificate for another nine years, Noël sticks firmly to the feminine for the rest of her life story. There are, however, two final events described in the masculine before the operation is finally carried out. After painstakingly assembling all the documentation she needs, including psychiatric, psychological, and medical reports, provided at no small cost by Belgian professionals, she is told by the Swiss surgeon, "C'est très bien tout ça, mais ça vient de l'étranger" (That's all very well, but it's foreign) (134), and she is obliged to start over again with Swiss officials. In her frustration and disappointment, she resorts to her masculine persona, recalling "je suis retourné plusieurs fois" (I went back[m] several times) (134). It seems that, as before in her return to Europe, she finds her masculine identity best suited to deal with harassing bureaucracy.

Noël resumes the use of feminine qualifiers for the preparations that immediately precede the operation, but on the great day itself she recalls being "réveillé tôt le matin" (woken up[m] early in the morning) (136) and walking into the operating theater. As she leaves her bedroom she notices a sign saying "Monsieur Noël" hanging on the door. After the operation, she decribes herself in the feminine, "couchée sur le dos" (lying[f] on my back) (136); the sign now reads "Madame Noël." Noël has identified as a woman for the last twenty-five years, but she reintroduces the masculine the day of her operation to underline the difference between the person who wakes up that morning, and the one who lies in bed that night.

It is evident from Docteur Georgine Noël's skillful manipulation that the grammatical gender system may be utilized as a rich resource for expressing and exposing the inadequacies of the concept of natural gender. The meanings of the masculine and feminine forms of the adjectives and past participles used to qualify Noël at different stages of her life vary enormously. They depend for their significance on the context in which they are found, but it is their contrastive, oppositional nature that makes them so useful in expressing Noël's changes of mood, attitude, and mental state. At times the switch from the masculine to the feminine is indicative of a sense of triumph, of success, as when she manages to carve out a territory that will be wholly hers and where she may try out her chosen identity. It can also imply more negative emotions, however, such as fear of homosexuality. While the opposite movement, from a feminine to a masculine persona, often conveys a sense of frustration or failure, as when her diaries are read by her parents or when she is forced to deal with the endless demands for official documents on her return from the Congo, this is not always the case. It can also express an enjoyment of the authority and superiority of masculinity as well as a simple, if temporary, appreciation of the sexual identity she was born with, as when she goes pot-holing with the scouts.

Disloyal to Masculinity

At a time when gender distinctions in nouns and adjectives are tending to disappear (Bauche 1928; Brunot & Bruneau 1933; Durand 1936; Wagner 1968; Kneip 1985; Audiber-Gibier 1988; Blanche-Benveniste 1990),[6] many French gay men are still using feminine terms to address or refer to others in the community, including their lovers and themselves—indeed, this practice is a staple of drag comedy acts. A sociolinguistic survey conducted in Paris by Geneviève Pastre (this volume) lists some of the feminine epithets that gay men use when speaking to or about their lovers. These range from the hypocoristic and diminutive *ma fille* (my girl), and *ma petite chérie* (my[f] little[f] darling[f]) to the exaggeratedly offensive *folle pétasse* (crazy whore[f]), *mongolienne*[f] (mongol[f]), *salope* (bitch), and *conne* (cunt[f]) (Pastre 1995: 9).[7] Pastre quotes an article in *Exit*, a new Parisian magazine aimed at a mixed audience of gays and straights, "Le Pédé hors ghetto" (the faggot outside the ghetto) (12), which offers advice on how to attract a closet queer and includes two suggestions dealing specifically with the use of the feminine in gay speech. The first, "ne lui dites pas que vous êtes parti en vacances avec une bande de copines hystériques" (don't tell him you went on holiday with a bunch of hysterical girlfriends), draws attention to the use of the feminine *copine* (girlfriend) instead of the masculine *copain* (mate), which, coupled with the adjective *hystérique*, a cultural reference to women's supposed predisposition toward emotional instability, positions the speaker in a thoroughly feminine, if stereotypical context. The second, "ne parlez jamais au féminin" (never speak in the feminine), is a direct reference to gay men's use of feminine concord to designate themselves as radically different from other men.

In English, gay men often use the female pronoun *she* to refer to other gay men:

SPEAKER A   Speaking of fags, where is Miss Thing?
SPEAKER B   You mean Ron?
SPEAKER A   Yeah.
SPEAKER B   I don't know where she is. (Rudes and Healy 1979: 61)

In this example, Ron is first introduced as Miss Thing, a feminine designator that is then anaphorized as *she* from grammatical necessity There are also cases where no antecedent feminine is introduced to justify the use of feminine pronouns, as in the following, said in reference to a young man:

SPEAKER A   Who's that next to George?
SPEAKER B   I don't know but she's kind of cute. (Rudes and Healy 1979: 57)

In this case, *she* is deictic rather than anaphoric and therefore stands out as more marked. It presupposes the gender of the referent, requiring a homogeneous discourse context for reference to succeed. This use of female pronouns to refer to gay men is limited to specifically gay contexts; it can have dire social consequences if the device misfires.

It is important to note that this linguistic strategy is not intended to reflect a feminine persona so much as to dissociate the speaker from heterosexual alliance. As such, it is a statement of sexual orientation rather than of sexual identity. The men who use these feminine forms to refer to themselves or to other gay men are designating themselves, as well as the referents, as traitors to heterosexual masculinity. The very fact of referring to another man in the feminine, even if the speaker never uses feminine designators in reference to himself, indicates participation in this countercultural, antiheterosexual discourse mode. Speakers thereby underline their own alliance with the sissy, the nelly, the drag queen, and in fact create this alliance by their use of the feminine gender. As Pastre points out, while *fille*, meaning a girl or a prostitute, is used frequently by gay men to refer to themselves and each other, *femme*, meaning both a woman and a wife, is much rarer, indicating that it is not mature womanhood that is envisaged by the use of feminine terms and concord but the image of the young, the vulnerable, and the sexually available.

In an attempt to go beyond the simplistic gender binary, Patrizia Violi (1987: 15–35) argues that the contrary (or opposite) of masculine is not feminine but nonmasculine, while the contrary of feminine is nonfeminine. In terms of the theory of markedness, this argument fails to take account of the fact that, while two terms of an opposition may refer to different positions on a continuum, subjectively they will be transformed into an opposition (Trubetzkoy 1975). In the normal run of male-female relations, the hierarchic opposition is observed (in which *feminine* is the contrary of *masculine* as well as the marked constituent of the dyad), but, faced with the conundrum of a man addressing another man in the feminine, discourse participants will search for an explanation; in this context, Violi's theory of contraries, involving the negative of the term rather than its contradictory, will come to the fore, and discourse participants will accept feminine designation as a sign not of femininity but of opposition to (orthodox) masculinity—that is, heterosexuality. While the male-to-female transsexuals attending workshops on speaking like a woman (like those organized by Alison Laing—see note 1) aim toward a plus-feminine identifiation, the gay men in Pastre's survey aim toward a minus-masculine identification. There are many similarities in the verbal performance of the two groups, but their motivation is strikingly different: The transsexuals are constructing themselves around notions of femininity, the gay men around notions of masculinity. The efforts of the former are sincere attempts to sound like women; the gossip and banter of the latter are intended to establish in-group rapport, to *épater les hétéros* (shock straight outsiders), and their ludic and parodic aspect is inescapable.

While Pastre's survey did produce a few masculine forms used by lesbians to address their lovers, such as *mon chéri* (my[m] darling[m]) and *je suis ton petit mec* (I'm your little bloke, your little fella), none were used to refer to women in the third person; thus, the addressee was always present and the clash between her sex and the gender designation evident. It is also worth noting that while men are never addressed in the feminine unless some comment on their sexual orientation is intended, one frequently hears mothers replying to their daughters *oui, mon grand* (yes, my big[m] [one]), *oui, mon petit* (yes, my little[m] [one]), *oui, mon chéri* (yes, my darling[m]), *oui, mon vieux* (yes, my old[m] [one]) without any suggestion of homosexuality. Because the masculine is the unmarked term (as discussed earlier), it may be used generically, that is, with a zero interpretation as regards the mark of femininity, as in *les grands doivent aider les petits* (the older ones must help the little ones), with a minus interpretation, as in *les grands hommes font de mauvais pères* (great men make bad fathers), or with a plus interpretation, as in the example of *oui, mon grand* said to one's adolescent daughter. This may explain why the lesbians in Pastre's survey reported such minimal use of the masculine: It may have been considered unmarked or generic, rather than specifically masculine. The feminine, on the other hand, being the marked half of the dyad, is usually restricted to a plus interpretation and, if applied to a masculine referent, implies femininity or a homosexual orientation.

The use of feminine lexical items, feminine concord, and feminine pronouns to connote male homosexuality is a strategy used not only by gay men among themselves but also by heterosexuals commenting on the perceived homosexuality of men of their acquaintance. Thus, in *Zazie dans le métro* (Queneau, 1959), Zazie asks a female bystander whether she thinks Zazie's Uncle Gabriel is "hormosessuel ou pas" (hormosessuel[m] or not) (101). "Y a pas de doute" (there's no doubt), the woman replies, turning to Uncle Gabriel. "Vous en êtes une" (you are one[f] of them). The adjective *hormosessuel* is in the masculine, so the *une* of the bystander's reply must be interpreted either as an existential "you are one of the female kind" or as exhibiting concord with one of the grammatically feminine French terms for a homosexual: *une tante* (a pansy) or *une pédale* (a faggot). The humor of the bystander's reply lies in the fact that in either interpretation Uncle Gabriel stands condemned without the bystander's ever having to state explicitly what she means.

Grammatical Gender

Since the use of the feminine in reference to men in order to indicate homosexuality is a fairly common phenomenon in French literature, I will content myself with only a couple of examples. While exclamations like "la pauvre fille!" said of a person who is clearly male, as in the Pastre survey, are intended to provoke reaction by the evident dissonance between the term used and the referent described, other uses of the feminine are more subtle. In an article on Michael Jackson in *Paris-Match* (17 July 1987: 43–45), Olivier Royant plays with grammatical gender to underline Jackson's bizarre sexual status and way of life. The piece opens

> Qu'arrive-t-il à mon idole? Il paraît qu'elle est en train de devenir raide dingue et c'est Michael Jackson . . . roi du disco. . . . C'est elle et lui mon idoleᶠ
>
> (What is happening to my idol? It seems she is going raving mad, and it's Michael Jackson . . . king of disco. . . . She and he are my idol.)

The presentation of the singer as an *idole* (a grammatically feminine term) allows the journalist to use the feminine pronoun *elle* to refer to Jackson. Since it is not immediately clear who his idol is, Royant explains that "it's Michael Jackson," supplying the further designator *roi du disco*. *Roi* is, of course, a grammatically (and culturally) masculine term. Jackson has now been designated by terms both feminine (*une idole*) and masculine (*un roi*), justifying Royant's use of both genders in the phrase that follows: *c'est lui et elle mon idole*. The rest of the article describes Jackson's phobia of microbes, the hours he spends each day in an oxygen tank, the countless operations he has undergone to become white. Throughout the account, pronouns switch back and forth between feminine and masculine, depending on whether they anaphorize *idole*, *star* (also grammatically feminine in French), or the singer's proper name. In this way, Royant makes it clear that he finds Jackson extremely weird, beyond prevailing gender norms (a sentiment he expects his readers to share), but without ever stating this explicitly.[8]

It is interesting to compare this use of grammatical gender with that of more canonical texts. When they want to personify inanimate objects as sexed beings, French authors frequently introduce nouns that will allow the referent to be anaphorized by pronouns of the sex imputed to it. In Emile Zola's "*L'Attaque du moulin*" (The attack on the mill) (1969), a short story set during the Franco-Prussian war, the mill of the title comes to stand for France herself (feminine pronoun intended—France is grammatically feminine in French). The mill is personified as "une fidèle servante viellie dans la maison" (aᶠ faithfulᶠ female servant who has grown oldᶠ in the household). In order to write of the mill using feminine pronouns and adjectives, Zola replaces the masculine *le moulin* (the mill) with various feminine substitutes: *une gaieté* (a gay thing), *la bâtisse* (the old building), *la partie du moulin* (the part of the mill) (85–86). He writes, for example, "[L]a bâtisse, faite de plâtre et de planches, semblait vieille comme le monde. Elle trempait à moitié dans la Morelle" (the old building, madeᶠ of plaster and planks, seemed as old f as the world. It f was half dipping in the Morelle) (86). The use of the feminine *bâtisse* allows Zola to anaphorize the mill as *elle* in the second sentence. Evidently, if the gender of nouns were perceived as a purely grammatical phenomenon, Zola would not have had to go to such lengths to introduce feminine pronouns. *Il* and *elle* are considered first and foremost to be *personal* pronouns, in the sense that they designate *animate* referents. Their use with inanimate referents, although it appears to share equal status according to the traditional grammatical rules of gender concord, is in fact far less common, since the hierarchy of animacy in French places animate referents much higher on scales of saliency and accessibility. Animate referents are far more likely to be pronominalized than inanimate referents. Put simply, *il* and *elle* are assumed to designate animate referents unless there is clear contextual evidence to the contrary.

Lesbian Gender

The use of masculine terms and concord to connote lesbianism or mannishness among women is much rarer than the opposite, as we have seen, in large part due to the fact that the masculine may so easily be taken for a generic. Christiane Rochefort (1963) plays with the use of masculine concord to designate lesbian orientation in her description of the relationship between Céline and her fifteen-year-old sister-in-law, Stéphanie, in *Les stances à Sophie.* The feminine *une,* used to describe Uncle Gabriel in *Zazie,* comes almost out of the blue, and yet its homosexual signification is immediately apprehended. Rochefort, on the other hand, has first to set up a complicated game of rôle-play for the masculinization of Céline to be read as an implication of homosexuality and not simply as a grammatical error. Stéphanie, still a young *lycéenne,* positions herself as Socrates' friend and pupil Phèdre (Phaedrus), calling her sister-in-law Platon (Plato) to highlight the unequal power dynamic betwen them. The schoolgirl declares her love for Céline but receives no corresponding avowal. After a classical commentary on the nature of love, the lover, and the loved from Céline, Stéphanie sighs,

Alors, c'est moi qui aime?	So, I'm the one who loves?
C'est ce que tu as dit.	That's what you said.
Et toi qui es aimée?	And you who are loved f?
Grammaticalement obligé. . . .	Grammatically obliged. . . .
Si je t'ai bien compris . . .	If I have understood m you correctly . . .
Comprise.	Understood f.
Platon.	Plato.
Pardon	Sorry. (169).

Grammatically, if *je t'aime* (I love you), then *tu es aimée* (you are loved), as Céline points out. Stéphanie tries to push the grammatical one step further by addressing Céline in the masculine, using masculine concord for the past participle *compris* in order to suggest a homosexual orientation: "Si je t'ai bien compris." For Céline to accept this masculinization of herself without demur would be to implicate herself in Stéphanie's declaration. Instead, she immediately corrects

Stéphanie, insisting on feminine concord: *comprise*. In order to diffuse the situation and wave aside the rebuff, Stéphanie explains that she is speaking to Céline as Plato, an explanation Céline gracefully accepts, though, given the homosexual nature of the subject matter of the Phaedrus dialogue, this only continues the ambiguity.

Performative Gender

Speakers are not passive with regard to language and the possibilities its system of distinctions and similaritites sets up. As we will see, they may use the conventions of linguistic gender to create different gender identities. An analysis of the linguistic gender play in Marcello Danon's *La Cage aux folles* (1979) provides a clear example of why gender should be considered performative in the Austinian sense, as Judith Butler argues (1990). This film centers around the complicated adventures of the proprietors of a transvestite cabaret in St. Tropez named *La Cage aux folles*, a pun on *la cage à poules*, which is both a henhouse and a police station—where many unfortunate transvestites end up—as well as on *folles*, whose unmarked meaning is "crazy females" but which may also be used to mean "gay men / queens." The proprietors in question are a gay couple who have been together for more than twenty years. Albin is a drag queen who performs his stage act as "the fabulous Zaza Napoli," while Renato manages the club. Albin and Renato thus provide a parody of heterosexual roles; Albin is femme, commonly dressing in drag off-stage, while Renato is butch (comparatively—and the butch/femme dyad is purely comparative, each item defined in terms of its relational opposite). Their performances show that gender is not an essential identity derived from the body of the speaker but constructed from codifiable rules recognized by society as a whole. Albin performs femininity (understood as nonmasculinity, as I have argued; if viewers believe that Albin is a woman, they have completely missed the humor of the film), while Renato performs masculinity, in speech, in dress, in gait, and in mannerisms.

In the opening scene of *La Cage aux folles*, all the drag queens are addressed and referred to using feminine gender concord. "Très bien mes cocottes" (Nice work, my little chicks / my sweets); "Et voici la grande, la merveilleuse Mercedes" (And here is the^f great^f, the^f marvellous^f Mercedes), the master of ceremonies announces, using the feminine forms of the adjectives and the definite article. This usage extends to Albin, who is lying in bed refusing to get up: "C'est pas vrai. Qu'est-ce qu'elle fait? Je vais la chercher" (It's not true / I don't believe it. What is she doing? I'll go and get her), the stage manager complains. This usage is continued throughout the sequence by Renato, by the maid, Jacob, and by the other theatrical employees. It is used to signal ingroup membership.

STAGE MANAGER	Il faut qu'elle descende maintenant	She must come down now.
RENATO	Occupe t'en. Je vais la tuer.	See to it yourself. I'm going to kill her.

RENATO TO DOCTOR	Elle ne veut pas se lever. Il faut qu'elle entre en scène en cinq minutes, elle n'est même pas maquillée.	She won't get up. She has to be on stage in five minutes, she isn't even made up[f]
JACOB	Je vais lui dire que tu fais de petits soupers d'amoureux pendant qu'elle travaille	I'm going to tell him/her that you have romantic little dinners while she's working.
ALBIN	Je suis affreuse. Je suis affreuse. Je suis si malheureuse	I am hideous[f]. I'm so hideous[f] I am so unhappy[f].

The doctor, on the other hand, who has been called in from outside the theater and who therefore does not participate in the same cultural norms, uses a different system of address and reference. He calls Albin by his stage name, *Zaza*, but accompanies this by referring both to himself and to Albin in the third person, as though playing a child's game: "On va se montrer. On va vite se montrer pour que le docteur voie Zaza" (One is [you are] going to show oneself [yourself]. One is [you are] going to show oneself [yourself] quickly so that the doctor can see Zaza). He uses no gendered pronouns, participles, or adjectives while in Albin's presence. In this way, he avoids a confrontation between his own set of values and those of the *Cage aux folles*.

This use of gender markers does not remain consistent throughout the film, however. Or rather, it represents only part of the system. When Renato follows the doctor out after his examination, he switches gender reference. In the scene where he called the doctor away from his dinner to come and treat Albin, he had announced, "[E]*lle ne veut pas se lever*" (she won't get up), constructing Albin as female and thereby letting the doctor know what attitude to take toward her: She is a temperamental prima donna who is holding up the show. While Renato is seeing the doctor out, after the consultation is over, on the other hand, he asks, "[Q]u'est-ce que je fais s'il tombe malade? Je ferme la boîte?" (what do I do if he falls ill? Do I close the club?) The gender switch marks a change in attitude. Before, Renato had regarded Albin's behavior as part of the drag queen act, a theatrical fit of pique. In the later consultation, he is concerned that his lover may be really ill and worried about the effect this will have on the box office. His use of the masculine pronoun *il* allows the doctor to reply using the masculine, "[S]oyez gentil avec lui" (be nice to him), instead of the impersonal constructions he has used before in his careful avoidance of gender assignment: "[I]l lui reste des calmants?" (are there any tranquilizers left [to him/her]?).

With his son, Laurent, Renato is scrupulous in his use of masculine gender to refer to both Albin and himself. For his part, Albin refers to himself in the feminine when speaking to the boy, using the polysemic *tatie*, whose unmarked meaning is "auntie" but which is also employed to designate a gay man. Laurent refuses this gender play and addresses his father's lover by his masculine first name:

| ALBIN | Tu embrasses quand même ta tatie | You're still going to kiss your auntie. |
| LAURENT | Bonjour Albin. | Hello, Albin. |

Laurent constructs not only himself but his world as inalienably heterosexual, his refusal of Albin's feminization as strong an indictment as Janice Raymond's refusal to refer to male-to-female transsexuals as *she*. Laurent endeavors to enforce his heterosexual ideology on his father's household. His father's lover and the maid, Jacob, resist this rigid gender assignment just as forcefully. Renato, on the other hand, accepts and returns the use of masculine designators, thereby expressing his collusion with heterosexual norms. He gives in to his son's demand that they straighten up the apartment when Laurent's fiancée's parents come to dinner, even to the extent of asking Albin to leave.

In the end, however, Renato explodes, and his anger is expressed not only in the content of his speech but also in his use of a feminine term to refer to himself. "Oui je mets du fond de teint. Oui je vis avec un homme. Oui je suis une vieille tata. Mais j'ai trouvé mon équilibre" (Yes, I wear foundation. Yes, I live with a man. Yes I'm an old faggot. But I'm happy with myself). In this outburst, he reintroduces a variation of the term *tata* (aunt/fag), which Laurent had rejected in Albin's speech, showing solidarity with his lover and expressing a covert reprimand to his son's earlier reproof.

The dyadic structure of the linguistic gender system in French lends itself to a multiplicity of meanings, which may have little to do with biological or cultural gender attributes. It can express ingroup solidarity or outsider status, sympathy, or antagonism. Its avoidance may signify a refusal to commit or a fear of offense. While the linguistic marks of gender are on the decline in modern French, they may be used by groups whose sexual orientation or whose gender identity is at odds with societal norms. Sexually liminal communities use linguistic gender in ways both paradoxical and ironic, for the very system whose simple binary excludes them is called into play to generate their own meanings and construct the communities' own network of alliances.

While feminist writers who invent their own conventions of nongendered language are part of a movement toward a more egalitarian society in which distinctions of natural gender will be seen as less and less crucial, others, describing individuals whose anatomical or psychological configuration outlaws them from the traditional categories, make use of the system feminists decry. This championing of the traditional by outlaw or liminal figures (or their advocates) may seem at first paradoxical, or at the least a sign of false consciousness. Because of his/her ambiguous status, however, the hermaphrodite, the transsexual, or the drag queen may be said to act as a troubleshooter for gender, revealing resources available in the gender system to which more traditional identities may have scant recourse. Grammaticalized gender, which many feel acts as a trap to limit people in their gender roles, also provides linguistic devices to express gender fluidity.

NOTES

1. Alison Laing, herself a male-to-female transsexual, offers courses for transsexuals in Philadelphia who want to learn more feminine speech patterns. Laing has produced a voice-training video entitled "Speaking as a Woman with Alison Laing" (1992).

2. There is an extensive body of work on presupposition in linguistics, of which only the most elementary thesis is discussed in this chapter. For more ample information, see, for example, Strawson 1964; Stalnaker 1973, 1974, 1978; Clark and Haviland 1977, Ducrot 1972.

3. Marina Yaguello describes another *contretemps* involving the grammatically invariable but semantically feminine adjective *enceinte* (pregnant). Captain Prieur, who had been placed under house arrest on a Polynesian island for her part in the sinking of the Greenpeace ship Rainbow Warrior, was sent home to France when it was discovered she was pregnant. French journalists who reported this event found themselves in a dilemma as to how to refer to Captain Prieur. Because *le capitaine* is grammatically masculine in French, it cannot be anaphorized by the feminine pronoun *elle*. There is, on the other hand, a common-sense objection to this person being referred to as *il*, especially when the attributive adjective used to qualify the referent is *enceinte*, which only exists in the feminine, for obvious reasons (1988: 73–77).

4. All translations are my own.

5. In 1857 Charles Baudelaire and his publisher were tried for affronts against pubic decency after the publication of *Les Fleurs du mal*, which included poems on lesbian themes. Poet and publisher were found guilty and obliged to pay a hefty fine and remove six poems from the collection.

6. At the same time, the feminist movement, backed by ministerial decree, is hard at work finding suitable feminine terms for women in traditionally male occupations (Moreau 1991, Gervais, 1993), reforming and thereby revitalizing the grammatical gender system. It would therefore be an oversimplification to say that gender concord and lexicalized gender distinctions are on the road to extinction.

7. I presented some of the material discussed here at the national conference of the American Association of Applied Linguistics in Long Beach, California, in 1995. One participant, a newly out gay man who was clearly sympathetic to feminist principles, asked anxiously whether the use of feminine designators by gay men was considered politically correct these days, and didn't I find the practice misogynist. The question is an important one. It is hard to imagine a context in which terms like *mongolienne* (mongol[f]) and *folle pétasse* (crazy[f] whore) would not be both pejorative and misogynist, but this is not to say that the use of the feminine to refer to men is per se misogynist. We need to be careful to state precisely what we are talking about; otherwise, we risk miscategorizing, misunderstanding, and overgeneralizing the whole phenomenon. In French, gay men are compelled by morphosyntactic necessity to position themselves as either male or female; the choice of femininity is, at base, a choice against the masculine rather than for the feminine. I do not believe the gay men in Pastre's survey were thinking of women at all. Now, a complete lack of interest in women may well constitute a form of misogyny in itself, but this is not a topic I can discourse on here. See also Judith Butler's discussion of the possible misogyny of drag (1992: 126–128).

8. Readers may also like to look at the use of the grammatically masculine term *monstre* and the grammatically feminine *bête* in reference to the *Bête* of Jean Cocteau's film *La Belle et la bête*. Discussing her new "domestic partner" with her father, Belle uses the term *bête*, anaphorized as *elle* (she) to express her sense of the beast's vulnerability and nobility. Her father, in contrast, uses the term *monstre*, anaphorized as *il* (he) to maintain his stance that the creature is evil and inhuman.

REFERENCES

Audibert-Gibier, Monique (1988). "Etude de l'accord du participe passé sur des corpus de français parlé." Mémoire de maîtrise. Département de Linguistique Française, Université de Provence.

de Balzac, Honoré (1970). "Sarrasine." In *S/Z*. Paris: Editions du Seuil, pp. 227–258.

Barbin, Herculine (1978). "Mes souvenirs." In Michel Foucault (ed.), *Herculine Barbin dite Alexina B.* Paris: Gallimard.

Bauche, Henri (1928). *Le Langage populaire. Grammaire, syntaxe et dictionnaire du français populaire tel qu'on le parle dans le peuple de Paris*, vol. 1. Paris: Payot, p. 256.

Blanche-Benveniste, Claire (1990). *Le Français parlé*. Paris: Editions du CNRS.

Bornstein, Kate (1994). *Gender Outlaw*. New York: Routledge.

Brunot, Ferdinand, and Charles Bruneau (1933). *Précis de grammaire historique de la langue française*, vol. 1. Paris: Masson.

Butler, Judith (1990). *Gender Trouble*. London: Routledge, Chapman, Hall.

—— (1993). *Bodies that Matter*. London: Routledge, Chapman, Hall.

Chawaf, Chantal (1976). "La Chair linguistique." *Nouvelles Littéraires*, (26 May): 18.

Cixous, Hélène (1975). "Le Rire de la Méduse." *L'Arc*, no. 61: 39–54.

Clark, H., and S. Haviland (1977). "Comprehension and the Given-New Contract." In R. Freedle (ed.), *Discourse Production and Comprehension*. Newark, NJ: Ablex.

Delarue-Mardrus, Lucie (1930). *L'Ange et les pervers*. Paris: Ferenczi et Fils.

—— (1995). *The Angel and the Perverts*, trans. Anna Livia. New York: New York University Press.

Diane (1987). *Diane par Diane*. Paris: Acropole.

Ducrot, Oswald (1972). *Dire et ne pas dire*. Paris: Hermann.

—— (1984). *Le Dire et le dit*. Paris: Minuit.

Dullak, Sylviane (1983). *Je serai elle*. Paris: Presses de la Cité.

Durand, Marguerite (1936). *Le Genre grammatical en français parlé à Paris et dans la région parisienne*. Paris: D'Artrey.

Foucault, Michel (1978). *Herculine Barbain dite Alexina B.* Paris: Gallimard.

—— (1980). *Herculine Barbin*, trans. Richard McDougill. New York: Random House.

Garréta, Anne (1986). *Sphinx*. Paris: Gallimard.

Gervais, Marie-Marthe (1993). "Gender and Language in French." In Carol Saunders (ed.), *French Today: Language in Its Social Context*. Cambridge: Cambridge University Press, pp. 121–138.

Gordon, Rebecca (1994). "Delusions of Gender." A Review of Kate Bornstein's *Gender Outlaw: On Men, Women and the Rest of Us*. *Women's Review of Books* 12, no. 2. (November): 18–19.

Hervé, Jane, and Jeanne Lagier (1992). *Les Transsexuel(le)s*. Paris: Bertoin.

Kneip, Nadine (1985). "Quelques réflexions sur l'accord des participes passés en français écrit et en français parlé." Mémoire de Maîtrise. Département de Linguistique Française, Université de Provence.

Livia, Anna (1995a). "The Gender Trap." In Joachin Knuf (ed.), *Proceedings of the Third Kentucky Conference on Narrative*. Lexington, KY: University of Kentucky Press.

—— (1995b). " 'I Ought to Throw a Buick at You': Fictional Representations of Butch/Femme Speech." In Kira Hall and Mary Bucholtz (eds.), *Gender Articulated*. New York: Routledge.

Martel, Brigitte (1981). *Né homme, comment je suis devenue femme*. Montreal: Québecor.

Mayrand, Marie (1986). *Le Combat de la mère d'un transexuel*. Montreal: Editions le Cercle International des Gagnants.

Moreau, Thérèse (1991). *Dictionnaire masculin-féminin des professions, des titres et des fonctions*. Geneva: Metropolis.

Noël, Docteur Georgine (1994). *Appelez-moi Gina*. Paris: Lattès.

Pastre, Geneviève (this volume). "Linguistic Gender Play among French Gays and Lesbians."

Queneau, Raymond (1959). *Zazie dans le Métro*. Paris: Gallimard.

Raymond, Janice (1979). *The Transsexual Empire: The Making of the She-Male*. Boston: Beacon.

—— (1981). *L'Empire transsexuel*, trans. Jeanne Wiener-Renucci. Paris: Seuil.

Rihoit, Catherine (1980). *Histoire de Jeanne transsexuelle*. Paris: Mazarine.

Rochefort, Christiane (1963). *Les Stances à Sophie*. Paris: Livre de Poche.

Rudes, Blair, and Bernard Healey (1979). "Is She for Real? The Concepts of Femaleness and Maleness in the Gay World." In Madeleine Mathiot (ed.), *Ethnolinguistics: Boas, Sapir and Whorf Revisited*. The Hague: Mouton.

Stalnaker, Robert (1973). "Presuppositions." *Journal of Philosophical Logic* 2: 447–457.

—— (1974). "Pragmatic Presuppositions." In Milton K. Munitz and Peter Unger (eds.), *Semantics and Philosophy*. New York: New York University Press, pp. 197–213.

—— (1978). "Assertion." In Peter Cole (ed.), *Pragmatics* (= *Syntax and Semantics*, vol. 9). New York: Academic Press.

Stephens Inge (1983). *Alain, transsexuelle*. St. Lambert, Quebec: Heritage.

Strawson, Peter (1964). "Identifying Reference and Truth Value." *Theoria*, vol. 30. Reprinted in D. Steinberg and L. Jacobivitis (eds.), *Semantics*. Cambridge: Cambridge University Press.

Trubetzkoy, Nikolaj (1975). *Letters and Notes*, (ed.) Roman Jakobson . The Hague: Mouton.

Violi, Patricia (1987). "Les Origines du genre grammatical." *Langages* 85 (March): 15–35.

Wagner, Robert-Léon (1968). *La Grammaire française*, vol. 1. Paris: SEDES.

Yaguello, Marina (1987). *Les Mots et les femmes*. Paris: Payot.

—— (1988). "L'Elargissement du capitaine Prieur." *Contrastes: La Différence sexuelle dans le langage*. Actes du colloque ADEC-Université Paris III (December), pp. 73–77.

Zola, Emile (1969). "L'Attaque du moulin." In Zola, *Contes choisis*. London: Hodder & Stoughton, pp. 85–111.

21

Linguistic Gender Play among French Gays and Lesbians

GENEVIÈVE PASTRE

The question of homosexuality has long been neglected in feminist studies of sex and linguistic gender. This neglect has created a serious gap in the field of sociolinguistics: How does the classification *masculine/feminine* function in language when an individual's sexuality does not conform to the general rules of heterosexual patriarchy that regulate grammar? What effect does the fact of having a partner of the same sex as oneself have on the way one speaks? How do gay men and lesbians refer to themselves and each other?

Social differentiation, which tends to superimpose itself on sexual difference, insofar as it serves as an instrument of classification and order, assigns indivduals a representation of themselves to which they believe they must conform. Individuals acquire their first language by imitating those around them, a knowledge that is then developed through active learning and consolidated via grammatical rules and the values they encode and naturalize. Throughout a person's life his or her use of language is tested in interactions with others, revealing the mobility and the complex variability of linguistic phenomena.

Language continually enriches itself throughout its historical development by drawing on the resources of different spheres and registers, both private and public, and on those of other languages. It thus offers great flexibility, but also strong resistance. The French tend to consider their language a form of personal property, an inalienable right, an object that must be defended, as may be seen from the reactions to the proposed spelling reforms put forward by Monsieur Jacques Toubon, Minister of Culture (Pastre 1992; Catch 1993; Délégation Générale 1994). The French language cannot undergo the least modification without provoking an emotional response, and every attempt to intervene in matters of language is taken as an intrusion. The average speaker's linguistic judgment depends on ideas of social acceptability, as may be seen from the rich vocabulary of frequent critical discourse comments. Categories of criticism range from judgments of usage: *ça ne se fait pas* (that's not done); to taste: *ça fait mauvais genre, tu parles mal* (that's in poor taste, you don't speak nicely); to appropriateness: *ça n'est pas convenable, c'est grossier, c'est choquant* (that's inappropriate, that's vulgar, that's shocking); to morality: *c'est mal* (that's bad); to reasonableness, relevance, and good sense: *ça fait tout drôle, à quoi ça ressemble? à quoi ça rime?* (that sounds weird, that's ridiculous, that's nonsense). The average speaker has a view of language, and its correct use, that is overgeneralized, static, and emotionally charged. This situation produces a peculiar contradiction: While language constitutes, on the one hand, a sort of personal property that is not to be tampered with, speakers also believe that it is something they can command with complete freedom. The use speakers make of language is experienced, at least at the moment of speech, as an individual process, not a collective one.

Language offers, then, an excellent arena for the observation of social and individual functioning. But it also participates in the domain of performance, that is, it is the production, and even the creation, of an individual. Speech is a contextual act, driven by the specific conditions of the context. Although the moment of speech appears to repeat itself, for the social actor the moment is always new and can modify endlessly—endlessly creating the unforeseeable, the unexpected, the previously unheard of, *at least for the partners to the speech act themselves*. It is in this sense that the capacity for creation is limitless. But this capacity is also due to the choices made by speakers from the existing stock of language, taking what seems most suitable and deforming, reforming, transforming those elements that do not suit their purpose or in which they do not recognize themselves. There are constraints on how much the subject can innovate, but they leave much room for manoeuver.

French grammar, vocabulary, and morphosyntax place particular constraints on gay men and lesbians. These constraints are not simply the product of a relationship of dominance and subordination, to the detriment of one of the two officially recognized gender categories, constraints against which the only recourse is to demand equality by raising the status of women. While the category *woman* represents a recognizable social division, homosexuality is a reversal of expected behavior, a reversal that is neither inscribed in grammar nor reproduced through it. Feminist linguistic campaigns have concentrated on the derogation of women and the effort to relieve this by creating feminine equivalents for masculine job titles, rather than on the grammatical gender system as a whole, which not only assigns the category *woman* a lower step than *man* on the gender hierarchy but displaces *homosexual* and *lesbian* entirely. Nevertheless, gay men and lesbians can learn something from the feminist campaigns, which are essentially political and proactive, if only from their mistakes. These campaigns have met with a measure of success, as may be seen by the formation of language commissions in the broader

European community, including France, Belgium and Switzerland, which have published recommendations and lists of preferred usages (Gervais 1993; Houdebine 1989). However, the feminist movement has ignored an essential dimension of language: the will of the speaker, which is at the origin of all linguistic change. Nothing is more democratic than the phenomenon of language. Groups or individuals can attempt to give it direction or alter its form, but the success of these attempts depends in the end on the speaker. Political correctness has made little headway in France, perhaps due to the influence of the *Académie Française* and the long tradition of respect for the language of the socially eminent, a group that tends toward linguistic conservatism.

These cautionary remarks concerning grammar and linguistic change are necessary in order to clarify the context in which gay and lesbian speakers find themselves. Magnus Hirschfeld, writing at the turn of the century, invented the concept of the third sex in order to break out of the prison imposed by the inescapable differentiation and complementarity of the sexes. Although his is a biological hypothesis, provoking loud objections from those convinced of the cultural and historical origins of sexual identity, from a modern theoretical perspective we can see the idea of the third sex as an attempt to conceive an *anthropogenesis*, or an attempt to break down the imagined and imposed importance of the opposition and complementarity of the two sexes. There is not yet a grammatical category for this third sex, and it is precisely in this empty space that one may play with linguistic gender.

The survey described in the following sections does not claim to be representative (particularly from a statistical point of view) but is intended more as an ethnological study. Because the position of women on the sociopolitical and cultural playing fields differs so much from that of men, I have used separate questionnaires for each sex. The data were collected from both personal conversations and questionnaires distributed at the Gay and Lesbian Center in Paris in 1994 and given to friends and acquaintances in Paris. Respondents ranged in age from nineteen to forty. Some additional information comes from the text and advertisements of gay and lesbian newspapers and magazines, although this is not the principle focus of this chapter.

Questionnaire Distributed to Gay Men

The gay men's survey (see Appendix 1) was distributed at the Gay and Lesbian Center and received twenty-three responses.

QUESTION 1. Do you use the feminine when addressing (or talking about) your boyfriend or a male friend? Have you heard other people using the feminine?

Responses: Seventeen out of twenty-three respondents (almost two-thirds) replied in the affirmative. Several nuanced their responses, saying *ah oui!* (yes of course!); *non/oui* (yes and no); or *parfois* (sometimes). Without exception, all respondents had heard the feminine used by other gay men in reference to both self and others.

QUESTION 2. What terms, expressions, phrases do you use or hear used?

Responses:

Feminine designators alone:
chérie (darling[f]);[1] *ma petite chérie* (my[f] little[f] darling[f]); *ma fille* (my[f] girl); *copine* (girlfriend); *salope* (bitch[f], as opposed to masculine *salaud*); *conne* (lit.: cunt[f]—also exists in the masculine *con*; fig.: idiot); *mongolienne* (mongoloid[f]); *folle pétasse* (crazy[f] whore[f]—formed from the verb *péter*, to fart, ejaculate).

Full sentences:
comment ça va ma chérie (how are you, my[f] darling[f]?); *elle est toujours pareille celle-là* (she's always the same[f], that[f] one); *elle est folle* (lit.: she's mad[f]; fig.: she's such a queen); *tu es une vraie folle!* (you're a[f] real[f] queen[f]!); *elle est trop folle* (lit.: she is too crazy[f]; fig.: she's a flaming queen); *quelle folle* (what a queen!); *elle est folle[f], la pauvre fille* (the[f] poor[f] girl is crazy[f]/such a queen); *je suis complètement folle[f]* (I'm a total queen); *appelez-moi la[f] X* (call me Miss X); *dire 'elle'* (say *she*).

Lesbians who chose to answer this questionnaire in reference to gay men listed:
elle est toute belle aujourd'hui (she's made herself quite[f] beautiful[f] today); *elle a la tête dans le cul ce matin* (she has her head up her ass this morning); and *elle est gentille, la pauvre fille* (the[f] poor[f] girl's quite sweet[f]).

These expressions range from terms of endearment (*elle est gentille, ma petite chérie*) to terms of abuse (*mongolienne, folle pétasse*). The term *folle*, used either as an adjective or as a noun, occurs most frequently in survey responses; it is commonly used to designate an effeminate gay man by both the gay community and the straight world at large. *Folle* is occasionally spelled *fol* in the data, an archaic masculine form that used to be required before a vowel. The responses *appelez-moi la X* (call me Miss X) and *dire 'elle'* (say *she*) are interesting in that they indicate that simply referring to a man in the feminine is enough to label him homosexual. While the youthful term *fille* (girl) occurs frequently in the data, the adult *femme* (woman) never occurs.

One respondent indicated another type of feminization, in which the speaker feminized himself in relation to his partner, referring to him as *mon chéri* (my[m] darling[m]), *mon mari* (my[m] husband[m]), and *mon ami* (my[m] boyfriend). Since the partner of a husband is a wife, these terms feminize the speaker by association.

QUESTION 3. Is this use intimate, private, a group practice, or public?

Responses: Respondents reported that they use or hear these expressions in private, within closed groups, and in public—or, as one respondent specified, in *"lieux gays"* (gay places). Another subject stated that he used these terms standing in line at the market when recounting his adventures of the previous night. Thus, although use of these expressions is variable as to context, the practice of referring to gay men in the feminine is generalized throughout the gay community.

QUESTION 4. For what reasons do you use the feminine? Try to be as specific as possible.

Responses: Some respondents replied that they used feminine expressions *par provocation* (as a form of provocation), while others stated that they were used *par inadvertance* (unintentionally), a disparity that suggests that different speakers have different motivations, depending on the context. Other reasons given for the use of the expressions were: *une marque d'amitié* (a mark of friendship); *un jeu de dérision* (a mark of scorn); *une plaisanterie entre nous* (an in-joke); *un jeu* (a game); a way to *jouer sur le stéréotype du pédé hystérique* (play on the stereotype of the hysterical faggot); a desire to *avoir un langage propre à sa communauté* (have a language of our own); or as *provocation contre l'ordre établi* (provocation against the established order). Other respondents insisted that the use of feminine terms was humorous in intent and either affectionate or a sign of a negative reaction toward someone. One man remarked that he used feminine expressions with good-humored, ironic intention, to tease rather than to annoy.

Another respondent, "a researcher on Genet," provided the following elaboration of his reply:

Elle + V/ la grande + prénom/ la mère + nom ou prénom, X, c'est une salope (critique ou admiratif!), je suis qu'une pauvre fille/t'es qu'une etc. (trad. je/tu cherche(s) désespérément un mâle)/ Miss X / une copine (pour un ami)

She + Verb/ the[f] great + first name/ old mother + last name or first name, X, is a slut (critical or admiring)/ I'm just a poor girl/ you're just a[f] etc (trans. I am /you are desperately looking for a man) /Miss X/ a girlfriend (for a friend[m]).

This respondent provided the following commentary:

- Seems to me more common among men a little older than myself (i.e., over thirty-five), belonging to a different generation and a different gay sensibility. In any case, I don't recognize myself in it (or don't want to recognize myself in it!).
- The 1970s, rue Sainte Anne.[2]
- Political activists use the feminine to denigrate someone, particularly a heterosexual (*la mère Charvet*, for example) or someone in authority.
- Can be used in an affectionate way, as in *la grande X* said in a slightly patronizing tone of voice. The use of the feminine is linked in any case to the desire to put down the other person (which corresponds with Guiraud's analyses[3]). It may also be used playfully among friends: an assumed transgression of social and linguistic codes and the pleasure that produces.

This feminine irritates me because it seems to hark back to

1. An emphasis on the split between the genders (with the derogation or subordination of the feminine)
2. An internalized homophobia (although it does perhaps correspond to certain sociopsychological realities).

This respondent's rejection of the practice of feminization and his dismissal of it as a custom belonging to an older generation clash somewhat with his obvious grasp of the subject and his alacrity at providing both examples and rules.

Observations made in the course of casual conversation also bring to light interesting information. A heterosexual woman journalist, working with the editorial team of *Gai Pied Hebdo*, a popular gay weekly that appeared from 1979 to 1993, was not familiar with the way gay men speak. She was surprised by the fact that most of the journalists at the magazine had given themselves women's names, like "Marilyn," and used them in front of her without hesitation. Shocked by what she heard, she dismissed the men as "pathetic."

Many of my gay men friends have said to me in serious confidential tones, and with a tender smile, "J'ai rendez-vous avec mon mari" (I'm meeting my husband) or "Heureusement que j'ai mon petit mari" (Thank Heavens, I have my little husband). One day I overheard a gay man in Paris complaining on the telephone, "[I]l fait trop froid, je me sens complètement méditerranéenne" (it's too cold, I feel totally Mediterranean[f]).

The relatively new monthly magazine *Exit*, which has a mixed (gay and straight) readership, published an article entitled "Le Pédé hors ghetto" (the faggot outside the ghetto). This article offers lighthearted advice concerning the use of feminine gender, noting that gay men who do not want to be picked out by straights nevertheless give themselves away by a small detail that even the worst of screaming queens would have checked. How does one approach a closet queen? "N'appartenez à aucune des catégories suivantes: folles ringardes, butch techno queen, pédé militant, minet disco" (Don't belong to any of the following categories: screaming queen, butch techno queen, militant faggot, disco fag). "Ne lui dites pas que vous êtes parti en vacances avec une bande de copines hystériques" (Don't tell him you went on holiday with a bunch of hysterical girlfriends). How do you leave him? "Décidez d'adopter un look de pédale" (Decide to dress yourself up like a fairy).

In their quote-of-the-month column, *Exit* ran a postvacation special in which it cited a "phrase dite par une femme de sexe masculin totalement déchignonée" (a phrase said by a woman of the male sex having a bad hair day on a beach in the south): "J'en ai assez de ce plagiste de merde" (I've had enough of this crappy beach attendant[m]). Ten minutes later, same place, same person: "[J]'en ai assez de ces connes. Demain j'amène mon copain, Alex, le mannequin, pour donner une leçon de beauté à toute cette plage" (I've had enough of these silly bitches. Tomorrow I'm bringing my friend Alex, the model, to give the whole beach a beauty lesson). Evidently the phenomenon of feminization is widespread enough to be recognized and (gently) derided in a mixed magazine. It seems to be particularly connected to an image of fashion-conscious frivolity.

Questionnaire Distributed to Lesbians

The lesbian survey (see Appendix 2) was distributed at the Gay and Lesbian Center in the same manner as the one for gay men but received only seven responses.

The Center attracts lesbians in their thirties and forties, as well as a group of about forty young lesbians who don't belong to feminist groups but frequent the trendy bars and clubs in the neighborhood. The low response is therefore significant, as is the one hostile remark, *c'est con* (this is dumb), scrawled on a questionnaire, suggesting that lesbians resent the implication that they use the masculine gender to refer to each other.

QUESTION A. 1. Gay men often feminize their lovers. Do you do the same, or have you heard the masculine used by other lesbians?

Responses: one definitive *non* (no), without further details, concluded the questionnaire. One *non* without explanation was given by another respondent (who did reply to a later question about the feminization of job titles). Two others replied *oui*.

QUESTION 2. What terms, expressions, phrases do you use or hear used?

Responses: *mon chéri* (my^m darling^m), *mets-la-moi* (give it^f to me, i.e., fuck me— the feminine direct object pronoun *la* refers to *la verge* (the penis), which is grammatically feminine in French); *je suis ton petit mec* (I'm your little fella).

QUESTION 3: Is this use intimate, private, a group practice, or public?

Responses: (masculine terms are used) in situations that are *intimes et amoureuses* (intimate and romantic).

QUESTION 4. For what reasons do you use the masculine? Try to be as specific as possible. If not, why not?

Responses: for *excitation* (sexual excitement) and to express the *tendance masculine dans mon comportement* (masculine tendency in my behavior).

The use of masculine adjectives to describe women, used as terms of endearment, is not specific to lesbians but common practice in more general social situations that do not fall under the scope of this article (see Livia, this volume). Lesbians might not perceive the practice as typically lesbian, and this may account for the low response rate among lesbians in this survey.

The second part of the questionnaire related to the feminization of grammatically masculine job titles, a campaign that has received ministerial recognition, leading to the creation in 1986 of a *Commission de terminologie*, headed by the feminist writer Benoîte Groult, under the direction of Yvette Roudy, *ministre des droits de la femme* (minister of the rights of women).

QUESTION B.1. Are you in favor of the feminization of masculine words that refer to us (in your professional lives, etc.)?

Responses: Respondents were much more cooperative in this part of the questionnaire, perhaps because of the media attention this subject has received. Three respondents in particular seemed to be highly aware of the issues at stake: a thirty-one-year-old social worker, a twenty-four year-old student, and a forty-year-old sculptress. They offered the following examples of job titles that should be feminized:

Conservatrice (curator); *écrivaine* (writer); *fliquette* (cop); *quelqu'une* (someone, formed fom the masculine *quelqu'un*; *quelqu'une* is not accepted by traditional grammarians); and both *auteure*[4] and *auteuse* (author).

> QUESTION 2. Do you do this spontaneously or do you prefer to follow the official rules? Give specific examples. Explain why.

Responses: Some respondents expressed reservations about the method to be followed in the feminization of masculine terms and were concerned that it be etymologically correct.

For the most part, the lesbians surveyed did not comment on the connection between the use of masculine terms of endearment on the one hand and the feminization of job titles on the other. This is a sign of the complex imbrication of lesbians in society. Positioned on the side of women, defending women's rights to linguistic recognition on the one hand, they simultaneously occupy a second position, playing with masculine gender in the context of their sexuality and intimate relations.

This is not so much a contradiction as a double identification, reflecting the complexity of the sociopolitical situation of lesbians. Lesbians who like to play the part of *les petits mecs* (little fellas) are also calling for the feminization of job titles: *auteure, inspectrice* (inspector[f]), *madame la Ministre, postière* (postal employee[f]), *sculptrice* (scuptress). On the other hand, the honor and the prestige of the masculine fascinate many women, who are happy to accede to honors that have until now been reserved for men. These women fear that when such honors are accorded feminine titles, they may lose something they had won by themselves and at high cost. When the writer Hélène Carrère d'Encausse was accepted into the *Académie Française*, for example, her daughers made it clear that they did not consider her *une écrivaine* (a woman writer) and did not approve of the feminization of job titles. Similarly, Monique Wittig's famous declaration "lesbians are not women" (1992) must be taken as an attempt at provocation, rather than a psychosexual reality in the self-representation of lesbians—at least in the context of this survey.

Conclusions

Despite repeated refusals from both lesbians and gay men to be assimilated into the same social category, an analogy may nevertheless be established. There is a similarity not only of social situation—the fact of, in some sense, "sharing the same misery," as one man put it—but also of language and, to a certain extent, terms: *cuir, SM, amour, sentiment, visibilité, fierté gaie* (leather, S/M, love, emotion, visibility, gay pride). There is a common language, a common questioning, a rivalry around innovation and daring, a double gender that belongs to both sexes in their sexual indifferentiation, the analogous position of the genders, not their complementarity.

Will this situation produce new linguistic usages beyond the grammatical identification of gay men and lesbians with the members of a heterosexual couple? Perhaps, in the manner of the dual case of ancient and classical Greek, which was used to indicate things that come in pairs, such as eyes and feet, grammatical forms will be created that are better suited to describing gay male and lesbian pairings. If these new forms do not yet exist, the need for them clearly does. Within the constraints of French morphosyntax, gay and lesbian speakers are trying to establish a new equilibrium, neither masculine nor feminine in the traditional sense of a bipolar opposition or complementarity.

The appearance of new grammatical forms would allow us to create a linguistic space that does not further deepen the rift between the sexes. It would offer an alternative, enriching humanity by giving expression to a fundamental form of sexuality that otherwise has to confine itself to cultural registers inadequate to it. These new forms would also serve to show the relative nature of the opposition between the sexes and their conflict. We are at a turning point at which a tripolar, or even multipolar, system must replace the battle of one sex against another. Language, the conveyer of desires, feelings, and ideas, must break out of its old shell and refuse to submit to the old laws in order to give birth to new morphological possibilities to which the overthrow of the gender system is only a prelude. We are on the threshold of a catastrophe or a renaissance.

Appendix 1

Le jeu du féminin/masculin dans le langage gay et lesbien
Questionnaire à l'usage des gays

1. Utilisez-vous le féminin en parlant à (ou de) votre ami ou d'un ami? Avez-vous entendu employer le féminin par d'autres?
2. Quels termes, quelles expressions, quelles phrases employez-vous ou entendez-vous?
3. S'agit-il d'un usage intime, privé, de groupe, public?
4. Quelles intentions mettez-vous dans ce féminin? Essayez d'être le plus précis possible.

Vous pouvez utiliser le verso de cette feuille. L'enquête est anonyme. Veuillez toutefois indiquer votre âge ou votre tranche d'âge et votre profession.

(The play of masculine and feminine in gay and lesbian language
Questionnaire for gay men

1. Do you use the feminine when addressing (or talking about) your boyfriend or a male friend? Have you heard other people using the feminine?
2. What terms, expressions, phrases do you use or hear used?
3. Is this use intimate, private, a group practice, or public?
4. For what reasons do you use the feminine? Try to be as specific as possible.

You can use the back of this piece of paper. This study is anonymous. Please do, however, indicate your age or age group, and your profession.)

Appendix 2

Questionnaire à l'usage des lesbiennes

A. 1. Les gays féminisent souvent leurs amants, faites-vous de même, ou avez-vous entendu employer le masculin par d'autres lesbiennes?
  2. Quels termes, quelles expressions, quelles phrases employez-vous ou entendez-vous?
  3. S'agit-il d'un usage intime, privé, de groupe, public?
  4. Quelles intentions mettez-vous dans ce masculin? Essayez d'être le plus précis possible. Sinon pourquoi?
B. 1. Etes-vous favorable à la féminisation des mots masculins qui nous désignent (dans nos professions etc.)?
  2. Le faites-vous spontanément ou préférez-vous suivre la règle officielle? Donnez des exemples précis. Dites pourquoi.

Vous pouvez utiliser le verso de cette feuille et des feuilles agrafées. L'enquête est anonyme. Veuillez indiquer votre âge ou votre tranche d'âge et votre profession

(Questionnaire for Lesbians

A. 1. Gay men often feminize their lovers. Do you do the same, or have you heard the masculine used by other lesbians?
  2. What terms, expressions, phrases do you use or hear used?
  3. Is this use intimate, private, a group practice, or public?
  4. For what reasons do you use the masculine? Try to be as specific as possible. If not, why not?
B. 1. Are you in favor of the feminization of masculine words that refer to us (in your professional lives, etc.)?
  2. Do you do this spontaneously or do you prefer to follow the official rules? Give specific examples. Explain why.

You can use the back of this piece of paper. This study is anonymous. Please do, however, indicate your age or age group, and your profession.)

NOTES

The chapter was translated from the French by Leslie Minott with input from Anna Livia.

1. Superscripts ^{f} and ^{m} indicate that a noun, adjective, or determiner is grammatically feminine or masculine in French.

2. Rue Sainte Anne is a street crossing Avenue de l'Opéra that was famous in the 1970s and 1980s for its gay clubs.

3. Pierre Guiraud is a French linguist, known particularly for his work on slang.

4. Although still controversial in France, the term *auteure* is widely accepted in Quebec.

REFERENCES

Catach, Nina (1993). "The Reform of the Writing System." In Carol Sanders (ed.), *French Today: Language in its Social Context*. Cambridge: Cambridge University Press.

Délégation générale à la langue française (1994). *Dictionnaire des termes officiels*. Paris: Government of the French Republic (January).

Gervais, Marie-Marthe (1993). "Gender and Language in French." In Carol Sanders (ed.), *French Today: Language in Its Social Context*. Cambridge: Cambridge University Press.

Guiraud, Pierre (1978a). *Dictionnaire historique, stylistique, rhétorique, étymologique de la littérature érotique*. Paris: Payot.

——— (1978b). *Sémiologie de la sexualité: essai de glosso analyse*. Paris: Payot.

——— (1980). *L'Argot*. Paris: Payot.

Houdebine, Anne-Marie (1989). "La Féminisation des noms de métier en français contemporain." *Contrastes: La Différence sexuelle dans le langage*. Paris: Z'éditions: Actes du Colloque ADEC-Université Paris III).

Livia, Anna (this volume). "Disloyal to Masculinity: Linguistic Gender and Liminal Identity in French."

Pastre, Geneviève (1992). *Le Nouveau manuel d'orthographe*. Paris: Editions Geneviève Pastre, coll. les Octaviennes.

Wittig, Monique (1992). "The Straight Mind." In Wittig, *The Straight Mind and Other Essays*. Boston: Beacon.

22

Surrogate Phonology and Transsexual Faggotry

A Linguistic Analogy for Uncoupling Sexual
Orientation from Gender Identity

BRUCE BAGEMIHL

It is interesting to speculate how gay men will deal with female-to-male transsexuals who are gay male identified . . . gay men are now faced with women
becoming men, who may or may not have male genitals whose origins are
undetectable. I hope gay men meet the challenge of accepting gay FTMs with
balance and good grace.

— Gayle Rubin, "Of Catamites and Kings: Reflections on
Butch, Gender, and Boundaries" (1992)

There are aspects of the sound structure of Language that cannot be explained
simply by models of the social uses to which humans put their apparatus for
respiration, mastication, deglutition, and general concept formation.

— Stephen Anderson, "Why Phonology Isn't 'Natural'" (1981)

Language, like gender and sexuality, is an intersection of biological and cultural influences. As a result, linguistic analogies have often proven to be useful heuristic devices for teasing apart the intricate relationships among biological sex, gender identity, and sexual orientation. Money (1988), for example, draws a parallel between
language acquisition and the complex interplay between environmental and biological influences on sexual orientation. In order to explain how something can
have both a genetic *and* a social component—and thereby challenge the false dichotomy of "nature versus nurture"—he points to the fact that humans acquire
their native language as a result of both the particular environment they are raised
in and the organization of the brain's linguistic faculty (i.e., an innate predisposition
toward language). Another linguistic analogy is offered by MacCowan (1992), who

illuminates the autonomy of lesbian butch-femme identities from heterosexual gender roles through a sociolinguistic example. She points to Yiddish, which is based on German and yet has become the unique idiom of its Jewish speakers, in order to illustrate how an oppressed culture can adopt and transform symbols that originate in the oppressor's culture. Just as speakers of Yiddish have molded the German language to their own culture, combining it with elements of Hebrew to create a new and linguistically rich vernacular (whose German origins are nevertheless readily identifiable), so too have butch-femme lesbians constructed a new language of gender by reshaping and subverting traditional symbols of masculinity/ femininity, as well as combining them with the uniquely queer elements that arise out of the context of two women together. To say that butch-femme is nothing more than an imitation of heterosexuality is, therefore, as reductionist as saying that Yiddish is nothing more than a dialect of German.

This chapter offers an extended linguistic analogy for one of the most significant developments emerging in queer culture: the uncoupling of sexual orientation from gender identity by transsexual gays and lesbians. Transsexual or gender-described individuals who identify as gay, lesbian, or bisexual have begun to claim their identities (see, for example, Chapkis 1986, Sullivan 1990, Bornstein 1991, 1994, Gene 1993, Phillippa 1993, Deva 1994, among others). In the process, they are challenging the received view that in order to be a (gay) man, you must have been born male, or that in order to be a (lesbian) woman, you must have been born female. However, nontranssexual communities have typically responded to such individuals with a mixture of incredulity, confusion, and hostility (cf. Rubin 1992, Gene 1993, Walworth and Davina 1993). This stems in large part from a lingering mentality of biological determinism, as well as an inability to separate the domains of biological sex, gender identity, and sexual orientation, which are traditionally conflated.

It is not the primary purpose of this chapter to "document" the existence or numbers of transsexual gays and lesbians, to "explain" their "origin," or to treat transsexual queers as a "study group" whose language or other characteristics are to be analyzed. While the reader may wish to consult a number of references (briefly summarized in the next section) that address these topics, she or he should also question the problematizing and "analyzing" of such individuals in the first place—and listen directly to the voices of self-identified transsexual gays and lesbians, both in writing and in person. The primary object of scrutiny in this chapter is not transsexual queers but the *response* of the lesbigay and other communities *to* transsexual queers, since it is here that the bulk of misunderstanding, misinformation, and rejection has occurred. Not only will this response be documented, an antidote will be offered.

I propose that linguistics offers an excellent analogy for understanding how something that at first appears to be biologically determined or derivative of other domains can in fact have an autonomous existence. There are a number of languages throughout the world that dispense with the larynx altogether, using instead an alternate sound-producing mechanism such as whistling or musical instruments; such systems are usually called SURROGATE LANGUAGES.[1] An extensive body of literature has documented the structure and function of a wide array of such languages (see, for example, Sebeok and Umiker-Sebeok 1976 and Busnel and Classe 1976). In this chapter (and drawing on the work in Bagemihl 1988) I examine the interrelationships among source language phonologies, surrogate language phonologies, and surrogate language phonetics. Surrogate languages display a number of initially puzzling phonological properties that have traditionally been ascribed to the demands imposed by their new modalities. The failure of some surrogates to represent intonation, for example, is often erroneously attributed to the nature of the musical instruments that are used to articulate the surrogate language. However, I demonstrate that the physical realization of the surrogate language clearly has nothing to do with these properties.

This has important implications for an understanding of the interrelationships of gender identity, sexual orientation, and biological sex: It constitutes a linguistic example of several related domains that are often thought to be heavily dependent on one another and at the mercy of biological/physical constraints, when in fact they are largely autonomous. Just as phonology is independent of the particular physical/biological apparatus used to articulate it (mouth, hands, or drum), so too is gender identity independent of biological sex and sexual orientation.

Nothing is "proven," of course, by drawing this analogy, any more than pointing to dual influences of biology and environment in language acquistion "proves" that parallel forces are at work in determining sexual orientation. This chapter simply demonstrates, from a fresh perspective, how concepts that have traditionally been collapsed can in fact be autonomous (albeit related) entities. As noted earlier, the analogy to be offered here is an extended one: Since we are dealing with complex (and relatively unfamiliar) phenomena in the domains of both language and gender, a fair degree of explication is required. In the process, though, the reader will gain an appreciation for a rarely discussed (and fascinating) linguistic phenomenon, at the same time as its relevance to the transgender issues is made apparent.

A Gay Man without a Penis?

The very existence of transsexual individuals who are erotically attracted to members of their own (reassigned) sex poses significant challenges to our understanding of fundamental concepts like sex, gender, and sexual orientation. On a more individual level, nontranssexual members of the lesbian and gay communities are called on to reexamine their definitions of "gay man" and "lesbian woman" and the way that they interact with individuals who claim these identities. In this chapter, the response of the gay men's and other communities to female-to-male transsexuals is of primary concern, for a number of reasons. Historically, female-to-male transsexuals have been overlooked, and gay male-identified transsexuals doubly so (for various speculations on the reasons for this, see Sullivan 1990, Lorber 1994, and the references cited in these works). In addition, the lesbian community has already begun to address the issue of gay transsexuals and its (often less than congenial) response (cf. Rubin 1992, Walworth and Gabriel 1993), while the gay men's community has barely acknowledged the issue, much less begun to grapple with it. Finally, gay male-identified transsexuals continue to encounter confusion and misguided attempts to "explain away" their desires (especially by the medical/professional communities) in ways that lesbian-identified transsexuals often do not. I hope to show that this perplexity is symptomatic of a mistaken conception of the interrelationships between sexual orientation and gender identity and, moreover, that this misconception can be amended with the help of several well-chosen examples from other domains of experience—in particular, linguistics.

Dismantling the dichotomies

The feminist and the gay liberation movements helped to establish that sexual orientation is independent of biological sex, through the simple observation that if you're female, for example, you're not necessarily attracted to men. The transgender movement (cf. Feinberg 1992) has uncoupled gender identity from biological sex by showing, for example, that if you're born male, you needn't necessarily consider yourself to be a man. The queer transgender movement is offering the next uncoupling, that between sexual orientation and gender identity: if you were born female and are attracted to men, you don't necessarily have to identify as a woman. The intuition here is that being a gay man doesn't involve simply being attracted to men (i.e., having the same "object choice" as a heterosexual woman) but involves being *a man* who's attracted to men.

Prior to the emergence of the queer transgender movement, it was assumed that all transsexual individuals were heterosexually identified (indeed, attraction to members of the "opposite" sex—after reassignment—was part of the clinical definition of transsexuality). As always, the realities of individual lives refused to be so neatly categorized. The following anecdote from Kate Bornstein, a self-identified transsexual lesbian, is a particularly good example of some of the misconceptions involved: "At voice lessons I was taught to speak in a very high-pitched, very breathy, very sing-song voice and to tag questions onto the end of each sentence. And I was supposed to smile all the time when I was talking. And I said, 'Oh, I don't want to talk like that!' The teachers assumed that you were going to be a heterosexual woman. No one was going to teach you to be a lesbian because lesbian was as big an outlaw as transsexual" (quoted in Bell 1993:112).

Transsexual gays and lesbians have begun to claim their identities in the face of severe clinical and popular opposition, both within the gender communities and beyond. As in other liberation movements, a profound act of autonomy is that of *naming*: Identities are affirmed by making them linguistically distinct, either by coining new terms or reclaiming old ones. Xanthra Phillippa offers one such radical lexicon in the following excerpt from "TS Words and Phrases":

- ... *gender described/determined men/wimmin/people* are ... transsexuals
- *genetics, genetically/chromosomally described/determined* are non transsexual people
- *gender oriented wimmin/men/people* are wimmin, men or people who are attracted to TS's
- *transsexual lesbians* are usually gender described wimmin who are attracted to genetic wimmin or possibly other gender described wimmin

- *trans dykes* are usually gender described wimmin who are attracted to other gender described wimmin or possibly genetic wimmin
- *transsexual gays/fags* are usually gender described men who are attracted to genetic or possibly other gender described men or both*

'we still haven't dealt with the many other complex realities such as female to male transsexuals who become gay transvestites or drag queens or male to female transsexuals who identify as lesbians & then cross dress as men, in order to pick up genetic straight wimmin or gay men. (Phillippa 1993:19)

As noted in the introduction, I am not interested in engaging in a dialogue about the ability of individuals to claim (and name) such identities or in attempting to "explain" or in any way determine "why" this is so. Anyone in the lesbigay community whose sexuality and/or existence has been questioned, analyzed, "explained," trivialized, medicalized, or otherwise problematized should be able to understand this. Gay-identified transsexuals exist: That is sufficient. As the next section shows, such individuals have been subjected to an enormous amount of resistance both in mainstream society and in the lesbigay and the transgender communities. The question is not why are there queer-identified transsexuals but why do so many nontranssexual individuals have trouble coming to terms with this, and how can such gender oppression be overcome?

Why bother?

Gay-identified transsexuals face a litany of incomprehension, disapproval, and outright hostility from individuals whose notions of gender and sexuality they challenge. One of the most common questions posed by friends and strangers is some version of "Why bother?" Judith Lorber summarizes this state of incredulity as follows: "If genitalia, sexuality, and gender identity are seen as a package, then it is paradoxical for someone to change their anatomy in order to make love with someone they could easily have had a sexual relationship with 'normally'" (Lorber 1994: 86).[2] The misconception here, of course, is that transsexuals undergo sex reassignment only in order to make love with someone who would be a member of the "same" sex if reassignment were not performed (see, for example, "Gender Myth #8" in Walworth and Gabriel 1993). Under this view, for someone to take on a stigmatized homosexual identity *after* sex reassignment becomes utterly inexplicable.

The inability of many individuals to countenance the possibility of transsexualism, and gay identified transsexualism in particular, is due largely to two factors: a biologically deterministic worldview that refuses to separate gender identity from either sexual orientation or biological sex, and an assumption of the primacy of heterosexuality. When an individual who was born female wants to become a man, for example, it is usually immediately assumed that such an individual wants to be a *heterosexual* man; this is then erroneously ascribed to the fact that such a person is "really" a woman who is unable to accept her lesbian orientation and can therefore relate to women only heterosexually. On the other hand, when such an individual comes out as gay (i.e., a female-to-male transsexual who is attracted to men), this person's attraction to men is then ascribed to the fact that he is "really" a heterosexual woman after all.

This mentality becomes particularly destructive when wielded by medical professionals, research scientists, and clinicians who decide what transsexuality "is" and who "qualifies" as transsexual. As Califia (1983a), Sullivan (1990), and Rubin (1992), among others, point out, if individuals seeking sex reassignment do not present a "normal" heterosexual orientation (i.e., an erotic interest in the soon-to-be "opposite" sex), sex-reassignment surgery, hormone therapy, counseling, and so on are often denied. And while more progressive members of the medical community are beginning to recognize the existence of transsexual lesbians, gay male-identified transsexuals still face a formidable set of obstacles. Lou Sullivan, a self-identified female-to-gay male transsexual and a pioneering scholar and educator on gender issues, was repeatedly denied treatment at numerous "gender-dysphoria" clinics: "They told me that I must not really be transsexual. After all, they thought, if I just wanted to sleep with men, why go to all the trouble?" (Sullivan, quoted in Bloom 1994).

A particularly revealing example of the heterosexist and genetically biased reasoning of medical professionals can be found in the language used to categorize and pathologize transsexuality. Clinical studies and definitions have traditionally employed a confusing terminology in which, for example, a female-to-male transsexual who is attracted to women is labeled a "homosexual transsexual," while a female-to-male transsexual who is attracted to men is labeled a "heterosexual transsexual." In other words, the point of reference for "heterosexual" or "homosexual" orientation in this nomenclature is solely the individual's genetic sex *prior* to reassignment (see, for example, Blanchard et al. 1987, Coleman and Bockting 1988, Blanchard 1989). These labels thereby ignore the individual's personal sense of gender identity taking precedence over biological sex, rather than the other way around. With this clinical terminology, people can be conveniently described as "escaping" a stigmatized homosexual identity when they become involved with members of the opposite sex following reassignment (erroneously assumed to be "the norm"). The myth of the heterosexual imperative and the primacy of biology is thereby reasserted and rebuttressed, while the transgressive status of *all* transsexuals is trivialized.

Unfortunately, gay and lesbian communities have also been reluctant to show a welcoming attitude towards lesbian- and gay-identified transsexuals. Because several different stigmatized identities are involved, and because women and men experience sexism, violence, economic oppression, and so on differentially, this has become a very complex and multilayered issue with different ramifications in the lesbian and the gay men's communities.[3] Nevertheless, the underlying misunderstanding is the same: Gender identity, sexual orientation, and biological sex are by and large seen as inseparable, even in homosexual communities. And because of the way that "manhood" is defined (in both dominant cultures and subcultures), the problems are particularly acute for gay male-identified transsexuals. In society at large, the equation *penis = man = heterosexual/attracted to women* is considered the ultimate diagnostic of masculinity/maleness; in the gay men's community, the importance of the phallus is often exaggerated even more. Since many female-to-male transsexuals do not undergo full genital surgery to construct a flesh-and-blood penis, they are destined to fail this "test" in the eyes of most gay men.

Lou Sullivan succinctly captures this dilemma: "A gay man without a penis? But isn't the penis the most important thing to gay men?" (Sullivan 1990: 80). He rightly points out that not all genetic gay men are as phallocentric as this, but the experience of other female-to-gay males has not been encouraging. Gene (1993) explains, "I fear I will never be accepted by the gay male community where I feel I belong. . . . Most recently I have been depressed over the realization that many gay men are quite superficial, and measure a man by the size of what's in his pants" (pp. 15, 17). He goes on to describe how his genetic gay male boyfriend tried to manipulate him with the admonition "There will never be any gay man in the world who will accept a gay man who doesn't have a penis." We can only hope that this attitude is not typical of the entire community.

It is clear that there is a serious misunderstanding of women who become gay men. However, somewhat surprisingly, neither this prejudice nor the phenomenon that has inspired it are unique to transsexuality, as I show in the next section.

Faghaggotry and the Kirk/Spock connection

There is nothing new about women identifying as gay men or eroticizing and idealizing sexual relationships between men. In fact, striking parallels to the sentiments expressed by many female-to-gay male transsexuals can be found in two unlikely areas: "fag-hagging" and K/S "slash" fanzines. These phenomena also share, along with gay transsexuality, the fact that they are often either much maligned or ignored altogether.

First, consider the phenomenon of K/S zines. K/S stands for Kirk/Spock and describes an extraordinary genre of popular science-fiction writing in which an overt sexual relationship is created between the two male Star Trek characters. K/S stories also often have sadomasochistic and mystical overtones and are sometimes illustrated with explicit homoerotic drawings (for further details, see Penley 1991, Lamb and Vieth 1986, and Russ 1985). Such stories are written almost exclusively by straight women, who have developed a flourishing underground network for the distribution of such fanzines (which are often code-named "slash" zines since the slash between the K and S is used to indicate to readers that an explicit sexual relationship between the characters is involved). Joanna Russ, a science-fiction writer and self-identified K/S zine enthusiast, describes the appeal of this material as follows:

> [N]ot only are the two characters (Kirk and Spock) lovers . . . they are usually bonded telepathically in what amounts to a life-long, monogamous marriage. . . . If you ask "Why two males?" I think the answer is that . . . no one . . . can imagine a man and woman having the same multiplex, worthy, androgynous relationship, or the same completely intimate commitment. . . . What is so striking in K/S is the raw sexual and emotional starvation the writers are expressing so openly. (Russ 1985: 81, 84)

Next, consider the phenomenon of "fag-hagging"—or "faghaggotry," as De-carnin (1981) calls it. This word (which both she and I use in its radical, reclaimed sense rather than in its derogatory sense) is employed as a cover term for a large and complex set of interrelationships between women and gay men, which have a long history in our communities. Many (genetic) women who associate with fags articulate their interest in gay men in strikingly similar ways, such as Solo, a self-identified queer fag-hag interviewed in Decarnin (1981):[4]

> A straight man can look good to me but . . . when I know a man is gay, when he's picked up some of the gay male cultural tricks and mannerisms, I don't know, it just turns me on. . . . I think [what] turns me on is the idea of two men having an emo-tional relationship. It's like the only way I could imagine having an egalitarian rela-tionship with a man would be to be a man. . . . Since I was 19 or so I've fantasized about being a beautiful boy in a loving or hating relationship with a man. (quoted in Decarnin 1981: 10, 11)

Compare both of these quotations to the words of "HF," a self-identified fe-male-to-gay male transsexual:

> My first sexual fantasies were of a man hugging and caressing a boy, and thinking of men kissing each other. . . . What made gay men more sexually attractive than straight men? Simply the fact that they were aroused by other men. All kinds of gay men ap-peal(ed) to me romantically and sexually—old, young, leather and muscle types, lithe femmy queens, clean-cut men in business suits. If they loved men, I loved them! (quoted in Blanchard 1989: 330)

I do not mean to equate all of these women's and men's experiences (thereby minimizing the actual differences between them) or even to suggest that they are part of a continuum, nor do I want to imply that they are necessarily representative of their "communities." Rather, I want to draw attention to the way that these three phenomena have inspired the same type of negative response: trivialization, incredulity, and reanalysis. Just as female-to-gay male transsexuals (and transsex-uals in general) have been pathologized and ridiculed, so too have fag-hags and K/S enthusiasts been subjected to an unending attempt to "explain" their inter-ests—that is, when they haven't been completely overlooked. Like Decarnin and Penley, I am interested in revalorizing these often demonized individuals and ex-ploring what their ostracism tells us about the devaluation of homosexuality and transgender more broadly.

One common "explanation" of K/S literature is to deny that it is about gay men at all, or even about two men together. Lamb and Vieth (1986: 252–253) re-veal more about their own misconceptions concerning gay male relationships than about K/S when they claim that "these stories are not about two gay males" be-cause they involve "two loving equals," neither of whom is more masculine or fem-inine than the other. Similarly, Russ (1985: 82–83, 98), while recognizing the genuine erotic appeal of two men together, goes on to assert that "K/S is not about two men . . . their subject is not a homosexual love affair"; she seems to think that because "the two men are masculine, even macho figures," they can't possibly be gay. Apparently none of these people has ever heard of butch/butch relationships. Some theorists are so confounded by the absence of women in the writing of K/S enthusiasts that they often try to claim—all appearances to the contrary—that K/S-ers actually *are* writing about women, in some vague sort of symbolic way (cf. Lamb and Vieth 1986, Russ 1985). But if K/S enthusiasts want the "equality"of homosexual relationships, they ask, why then aren't K/S-ers eroticizing female characters directly or imagining lesbian relationships? While some of the explanations they offer have a certain plausibility (e.g., the marginalization of women's sexuality, both in general and in science-fiction writing; alienation from the body), one rather obvious point seems not to have occurred to them. If someone is attracted to men (as the majority of K/S enthusiasts are, being primarily heterosexual women), it is entirely logical (to quote Spock!) to eroticize gay men, not women, when imagining a homosexual/egalitarian relationship and to enjoy the erotic possibilities of a male-only universe.[5]

Similarly, fag-hags, when not reviled or psychoanalyzed, have also had to endure continual attempts to "explain" their interest in gay men as the symptom of some deeper motivation (or pathology).[6] For example, Decarnin (1981), in an otherwise ground-breaking presentation (and reclaiming) of the fag-hagging phenomenon, cannot help but offer the "explanation" that "women whose primary erotic objects are gay men have consciously or otherwise recognized men's valued position in society and desired to be valued as men are valued." While this may be partly true, it simply recapitulates the tired heterocentric view that the only reason someone would be attracted to homosexuals or homosexuality is out of a negative reaction to heterosexuality and/or sexism. Apparently one can only walk *away from* heterosexuality, never *toward* homosexuality. She seems to ignore the possibility that there might also be something intrinsically appealing about gay men, something—dare I say it?—*good* about homosexuality that would draw someone to it regardless of his or her experiences with heterosexuality. As one of her interviewees proclaims unproblematically (and unapologetically), "I'm turned on to queerness. I think queers are gorgeous!" (Decarnin 1981: 10). The same holds for female-to-gay male transsexuality: Most people find it incomprehensible that there might actually be something valuable in gay male relationships, something that would make it desirable to be involved with a man *as another (gay) man*— even with all the attendant stigma. As Sullivan (1990: 79) puts it, "If a female is attracted to men, wouldn't life be easier if she just remained a heterosexual woman? It should be obvious that being a straight woman is a lot different than being a gay man! . . . She may want to relate to men as another man would." This is as much a positive statement about embracing the unique dynamics of being two men together as it is a negative one about escaping the inherent power imbalances of being a man and a woman together.

Also ignored in this entire discussion is the possibility that the transgressive nature of homosexuality—regardless of the gender(s) of the people involved— can itself be inherently appealing in a way that heterosexuality rarely is. As Lizard Jones explains in *Her Tongue on My Theory*, "I saw a performance by Christine Taylor, a bisexual woman, in which she talked about her lust for gay men, and her distaste for straight ones. I am a lesbian, but I could relate. How can you lust after a straight man? But a man whose sexuality endangers him and you? Aaah." (Kiss & Tell 1994: 57). Carol A. Queen expresses similar sentiments in her essay "Why I Love Butch Women," a moving homage to butches and other queers. As she eloquently describes in the following passage, the very fact that an individual is crossing a supposedly inviolable boundary, in either identity or relationship, can yield an unsurpassable experience: "I love butch women because, in their big black boots, they step squarely across a line. I love butch women for the same reasons I love sissy men, the transgendered, the slutty, the outrageous queers of every stripe; the women and men who sell sex, and the ones who use sex to heal; the fetishists whose eroticism is more complicated than anyone ever let on to us eroticism could be" (Queen 1994: 22). Is any more compelling "explanation" necessary?

In all of these examples, we see that (once again) any deviation from a strictly heterosexual object choice or orientation—whether by a female-to-gay male transsexual, a fag-hag, or a "straight" K/S enthusiast—becomes problematized and subject to analysis. The issue here is not whether these analyses are correct (there may very well be a grain of truth in at least some of them)—but why so many people seem to feel that these phenomena need to be "explained" in the first place. In other words, if we took as a given that sexual orientation, gender identity, and biological sex are not necessarily connected, would we feel such an overwhelming need to explain instances where they don't "coincide"?

Part of our difficulty in separating these domains from one another is that we have so few other models of apparently biological phenomena that are in fact autonomous from biology. In the next section, I show how the example of surrogate languages can provide us with just such a model.

Spoken Language without a Larynx?

Just as the phallus has traditionally assumed a central position in the definition of maleness/masculinity, so too the larynx has been privileged in relation to the definition of language. The fact that language is usually *spoken* (i.e., vocalized) is often thought to have an overriding influence on linguistic structure, to the extent that it is sometimes considered impossible for languages to be realized through other means. Moreover, phonology (the overall sound system of a language)[7] is often considered to be directly dependent on its physical realization, that is, the vocal apparatus. Surrogate languages (as well as other languages that use different production-perception mechanisms, like sign languages) show that this cannot be the case: The basic organization of the phonological systems of such languages is strikingly similar to that of spoken languages, even though they are realized through a vastly different articulatory apparatus.[8]

This is really a question of the influence of the MODALITY of a language on its form (cf. Anderson 1993). MODALITY refers to the articulatory and perceptual channels that a language employs: Spoken language uses a vocal/auditory modality because it is articulated with the vocal apparatus and perceived through the ears; sign language uses a manual/visual modality because it is articulated with the hands and perceived through the eyes. As noted in the introduction, surrogate languages make no use of the larynx to generate the primary sound stream, relying instead on some other mechanism such as whistling or musical instruments; thus, surrogates employ a nonlaryngeal/auditory modality. As such, they constitute a fascinating example of language "exteriorized," something that is simultaneously both members of a traditional dichotomy: language versus music, biology versus culture, body versus technology.

One class of surrogate languages employs external resonators—typically, some kind of musical instrument—as its sound source. These languages are traditionally known as "drum languages," but this is something of a misnomer, since a wide variety of nonpercussive instruments, including flutes, trumpets, lutes (both plucked and bowed), and bells, are also used to translate linguistic structures; I call them INSTRUMENTAL LANGUAGES. Typically, instrumental languages represent the "suprasegmental" properties of their source languages—pitch, stress, rhythm, number of syllables, and duration—and are based on tone languages. In most intrumental languages, one beat on a drum/pluck of a string/note on a trumpet corresponds to one syllable in the spoken language; its pitch, duration, and loudness is correlated—often in subtle ways—with the tone, length, and stress of the spoken syllable.

Another class of surrogate languages is known as WHISTLE LANGUAGES because a whistle pitch is substituted for the laryngeal activity (fundamental frequency) of ordinary speech, often with segmental articulation superimposed on the whistling. A variety of whistle articulations are used, ranging from simple bilabial whistles to complex linguo-dental articulations with one or more fingers inserted into the mouth, but they all share the property that the pitch stream is produced by forcing air through a constriction at the anterior portion of the vocal tract rather than at the larynx. Whistled languages can reproduce both segmental and suprasegmental properties of their source languages. In tone languages, the whistle pitch corresponds directly to the spoken tones, while in nontone languages, the whistle pitch reflects spoken intonation, vowel quality, and consonant articulations (e.g., high vowels tend to have a higher pitch, voiced consonants tend to induce a dip in the whistle pitch).

Surrogate languages are found throughout the world in nearly all major language families, ranging from the drum talk of Jabo (Liberia), the hand-fluted[9] language of Kickapoo (an Algonquian language of Oklahoma and Mexico), the slit-log gong speech of the Chin languages (Burma), and the whistle languages of Chepang (Nepal), Pirahã (Brazil), La Gomeran Spanish (Canary Islands), Mazateco and Tepehua (Mexico), Turkish (Kusköy), and Wahgi (New Guinea). Moreover, their sociolinguistic uses are as diverse as those of any spoken language: In many cultures surrogate languages constitute a fully developed form of communication used by all individuals on a daily basis, while in others they take the form of a type of "secret language" understood by only a select group of individuals. The amount of descriptive literature devoted to this topic—spanning nearly a century of research—is enormous; yet (with the exception of Bagemihl 1988) its implications for linguistic theory and our understanding of the human linguistic capacity have gone virtually untapped. Paralleling the long overdue incorporation of transgender issues into discussions of sexuality and gender, only now is linguistics beginning to countenance these "ambiguous" and alternate-modality languages.

Unnatural phonology

Because phonology is influenced in many ways by phonetics (i.e., its modality), many researchers have been tempted to explain all aspects of phonology on the basis of phonetics (or other functional and/or extralinguistic considerations). This is entirely parallel to the way that *all* aspects of gender and sexual orientation are commonly reduced to biological influences. In linguistics, one of the few explicit defenses of the autonomy of the phonological component is a seminal article by Stephen Anderson, "Why Phonology Isn't Natural" (from which the quotation at the beginning of this chapter is taken; see also Anderson 1993). On the basis of a wide range of evidence drawn primarily from the domain of spoken language, Anderson argues for the independence of phonology from modality effects and other extralinguistic influences. He also points out the importance of alternative linguistic systems for establishing the autonomy of phonology, particularly languages realized through a different modality from that used in spoken language; the particular systems Anderson draws attention to are sign languages.

In recent years, a burgeoning literature has established the existence of SIGN LANGUAGE PHONOLOGY, a seemingly contradictory term that refers to the structural organization of the meaning-less components of gestures that, added together, form a meaning-ful sign. What this work shows is that sign language phonology shares many fundamental properties of organization with spoken language phonology, in spite of being realized through a radically different modality; these similarities include things like syllable structure, stress, distinctive features, sonority, and assimilation processes (see, for example, Sandler 1993 and Coulter 1993 for recent overviews). Because these languages have no connection to the vocal apparatus, they are a cogent example of the autonomy of the phonological component from its modality. As Anderson (1981: 535) states, they show that "Language is *not* governed by forces implicit in human vocalization and perception. . . . In this sense, then, phonology is clearly not 'natural.'"

Surrogate languages provide an even more compelling case for such autonomy, since by their very existence they show that spoken language can exist independent of the human vocal apparatus. Moreover, surrogate systems take this notion of autonomy one step further, since such languages also exhibit a striking independence from their *own* physical articulatory apparatus.[10] An excellent example of this is the way that instrumental languages deal with intonation, which is explored in the next section.

Modality is not destiny

There are a number of asymmetries in the organization of surrogate sound systems that are related to whether the surrogate is an instrumental or a whistled language and whether its source language is a tone or a nontone language. One of the more striking of these asymmetries concerns how INTONATIONAL ELEMENTS are represented. By intonational elements I refer to a cluster of different sentence-level pitch phenomena, including the following:

Intonation proper: the pitch pattern on entire sentences in nontone and pitch-accent languages

Downdrift: the (cumulative) lowering of the pitch of a high tone after a pronounced low tone

Downstep: the lowering of the pitch of a high tone after an unpronounced, i.e., floating, low tone

Tonal intonation: in tone languages, other sentence-level pitch changes such as sentence-end tones correlated with clause type, prepausal high or mid tones, and other modifications of lexical tone contrasts at the end of pause groups

As it turns out, only some surrogate languages represent intonational elements, while others dispense with them entirely, and this distinction is correlated in systematic ways with the type of spoken and surrogate language involved. Specifically, whistle surrogates of tone languages represent intonational elements, while instrumental surrogates do not (cf. Hasler 1960, Nketia 1971, Umiker 1974).[11] Thus, Nketia (1971: 728) notes explicitly that Akan speech drumming reproduces neither downdrift nor downstep; similarly, Ames et al. (1971: 25–26) take great pains to point out that Hausa speech drumming fails to represent downdrift. The same absence of phonetic pitch gradations is also characteristic of Efik bell-speech, Kele, Ewondo, and Chin slit-gong speech, Banen hand-fluted speech, and many others. In contrast, whistle languages always reproduces downdrift: see, for example, the instrumental evidence and descriptions of whistled Gurma presented in Rialland (1981).

This discrepancy between the two surrogate types is puzzling: Why should instrumental languages eliminate a significant aspect of their source languages' sound systems? Owing to the correlation with the type of modality, a number of functional explanations have been proposed; the one that is of interest to us appeals to *modality limiting effects*. The essence of this explanation is that the instruments used to articulate surrogate languages are somehow ill suited to realizing intonation; therefore, surrogate languages represent only those tonal elements that their modalities will allow. Intonational systems with downdrift and/or downstep involve a potentially unbounded number of pitch levels, since lowering of high tones is cumulative across an utterance. Instrumental languages are in a number of cases confined to musical instruments that have a range of only two or three distinctive pitches, which is not conducive to representing an unlimited number of tone levels. Some researchers have suggested, then, that the modality of the language—the particular musical instrument or physical apparatus used to articulate the language—exerts a powerful limiting effect on the structure of that language. According to this line of thinking, such surrogates would represent intonational elements if they could but are simply prevented from doing so by the physical limitations of their instruments. In fact, although this explanation initially sounds quite plausible, a careful consideration of the full range of surrogate properties shows that it cannot be true. Three types of evidence argue against a modality-deterministic view of surrogate sound structure.

First, a number of instrumental surrogates employ musical instruments that most definitely *can* produce a (potentially infinite) continuum of pitch levels; yet these surrogates still do not represent downdrift. A prime example is the hourglass drum, widespread in West Africa and used for speech drumming in Hausa (where it is called *kàlànguu*). Pitch differences on this type of drum are produced by holding the drum under the arm and squeezing with the armpit the cords joining the two drumheads. The greater the tension on the cords, the higher the pitch, so that a gradient of an essentially unlimited number of pitch values can be produced (Ames et al. 1971: 26, Nketia 1963:791–792, Armstrong 1955: 870). Ames et al. (1971: 25–26) note that these drums "can easily accommodate the pitch resources of practically all utterances . . . [and] could imitate not only the lexical tones but even the intonation of most Hausa utterances." Yet they most definitely do not, as noted earlier. There are numerous other examples of gradient pitch production being possible but nonoccurring in talking instruments used for surrogate languages, such as Yoruba hourglass drums (*dundun*), Akan skin-covered drums, and Akan elephant tusk or antelope horn trumpets (see Bagemihl 1988: 81–82 for further details).

A second argument against a modality-deterministic explanation is that while in principle the number of phonetic pitch levels in a downdrift system is infinite, in practice the number is quite small. The number of discrete pitch levels that have been reported for a typical sentence is in fact remarkably consistent across many languages, ranging from a low of five reported for Hausa declarative sentences (Welmers 1973: 94), through six to eight for Akan, Tiv, Efik, Igbo, and Gã (Schachter 1961: 235, Welmers 1973: 82), up to a maximum of nine posited for Yoruba and Zulu. Furthermore, as Hyman (1986) and a number of other investigators have noted for downstep systems, even where lowering effects should in principle be unbounded and cumulative, (spoken) languages often place severe restrictions on the number of (lowered) levels that are actually allowed to occur.

Thus, no more than an average of five to eight levels would need to be represented in surrogates. This range is certainly not too great to be accommodated by the tonal resources of many African fixed-pitched instruments, for example, which are considerably richer than the two- or three-pitch limit for percussion systems that is usually cited. Yet in all cases where instruments with a greater pitch range are found, they are either not used for surrogate purposes at all or else their full pitch range is not exploited for instrumental speech. Thus, the Akan *seperewa* or harp-lute, which is occasionally used for surrogate speech, has a five- to seven-note capability, but this is not utilized for representing downstep or downdrift (Nketia 1971: 70; 1963: 97). Further examples are Bijago long drums (Wilson 1963: 809), Luba wedge-shaped slit-log gongs (Carrington 1949: 607–608), Banen hand-fluting (Dugast 1955: 712), and Hausa bowed lutes (Ames et al. 1971: 12), all of which have tonal ranges that exceed the number actually employed for surrogate purposes.

A related point is that even for instruments that do indeed have a fixed two-

or three-tone limit, a technique known as HOCKET PLAYING is available for overcoming these limitations; yet it is never applied to surrogate speech. In this technique, individual instruments with fixed pitch ranges but different registers are
played sequentially, each sounding in turn the note or notes of the melody that fall
within its range (Nketia 1962). The result is that a greater combined total of distinct pitches is available than could be produced by any one of the instruments in-
dividually; for example, Akan trumpet ensembles produce up to five distinct
pitches (each trumpet is limited to two tones), while flute ensembles in northern
Ghana pool together seven notes, and it is reported that South African flute ensembles combine as many as fifteen flutes (Nketia 1962: 44, 49–51). The increased tonal inventories of these ensembles can certainly accommodate the range
of actually occurring downdrift levels, yet surrogate languages never take advantage of them.

An essential claim of the modality-deterministic explanation is that surrogate
languages should represent whatever intonational elements their particular modalities will allow. A third argument against this explanation, then, is that other intonational elements in tone languages that do not involve a potentially unbounded
number of pitch levels (and hence are well within the limits of the instrumental
modalities involved) are not reproduced in instrumental surrogates, either. The
first of these is, of course, downstep, which often simply adds a third surface-
contrastive tone level to the language (often equivalent to a "mid" tone). It would
be quite plausible for a language such as Akan to ignore downdrift in its surrogate
while still representing downstep by using a drummed mid tone. In fact, Nketia
(1963: 97ff) reports that the most typical drum ensembles in Akan contain three
drums producing high, mid, and low tones, which would appear ideal for the
three-way contrast of high, downstepped high, and low in this language. Once
again, these are not exploited for surrogate purposes.

Furthermore, a number of other intonational phenomena are found in tone
languages that involve only limited tonal resources but that are nevertheless omit-
ted in instrumental surrogates. In spoken Hausa questions, for example, the final
high tone of the sentence is raised in pitch. This raising is well within the means of
the hourglass drum, yet it is not represented (as stated explicitly by Ames et al.
1971: 28). Similarly, in Sizang and Kamhau Chin, lexical tones are modified before pauses, typically being replaced by low tones (Stern 1963: 232–233). This
change could readily be represented by the slit-gong drums used for surrogate
speech in these languages, since they are otherwise able to represent low tones, but
it is in fact not represented (Stern 1957: 137). Finally, in Kickapoo, three basic
sentence-final pitch changes are found: lowering for declaratives, final high-rising
for interrogatives, and high level or high falling for emphatics (Voorhis 1974: 9).
Yet these are not carried over to the surrogate, even though hand-fluting is readily able to represent these pitch modulations (Taylor 1975: 360).

From this discussion it is clear that instrumental modalities are in most cases
quite capable of reproducing intonational elements but simply do not. In other
words, this aspect of surrogate structure cannot be attributed to the physical demands imposed by the instrumental modality.[12] In Bagemihl (1988) I offer an alternative explanation for this phenomenon, based on the internal organization of

the surrogate phonological system: Because of the modularization of the surrogate component, instrumental surrogate languages only have access to the phonological representation prior to the introduction of intonational elements. For our purposes, however, the exact explanation is not important. What is significant in this discussion is that "modality is not destiny"; that is, a surrogate's modality does not exert an overriding influence on its sound structure.

So what does all this have to do with gay-identified transsexuals? Surrogate languages provide us with a model of several related domains of human/cultural/biological/physical experience that are autonomous from each other in a way that is parallel to what transsexual gays and lesbians reveal about sexual orientation, gender identity, and biological sex. Queer transgenderists offer this challenge: Just because a person who was born female identifies as a man, that individual doesn't have to be attracted to women (i.e., the heterosexual object choice "appropriate" for that gender identity). Surrogate languages offer this analogy: Just because a language that is usually spoken is realized through an alternate modality, the form it takes doesn't have to be entirely dependent on that new modality. Surrogate languages have numerous properties that spring from their own authentic phonological systems, rather than from the constraints of the particular mechanisms of sound production they employ. And just as spoken language can be realized without a vocal apparatus, so too can a given gender identity be realized in individuals with different sexual biologies, without such an identity being derivative of that person's biology or sexual orientation (or vice versa).

Conclusion: Men with Cunts, Chicks with Dicks

> I wondered . . . Would there be more hermaphrodites entering the world? Would there be a new community emerging, one of men with cunts? Would they become a new political force—women taking over the world, but as men? Would men now be able to get pregnant? . . . Would we eventually develop a new awareness of "transgender," of looking beyond a person's gender to his spirit, wherein society would no longer try and mold us into being plain, old heterosexuals? (Annie Sprinkle, "My First Time with a F2M-Transsexual-Surgically-Made Hermaphrodite" 1992)

In the preceding discussion, I have tried to show why queers should care about surrogate languages. Such languages illustrate how an aspect of our daily lives that is rarely questioned—the use of the vocal apparatus for speech—is not the only way to do things. There are in fact many more ways of "speaking" than initially meet the eye (or ear). If this is possible for "spoken" language (which is often considered to be intrinsically bound to biological constraints), then it is also possible for gender identity and sexual orientation. There are many more ways of being a "man" or "woman" (including ways of being a gay man or lesbian woman) than one would initially suppose. More broadly, this analogy offers a challenge to those who would continue to advocate for the widespread relevance of biological determinism, be they religious fundamentalists or geneticists.

But why should gays and lesbians care about transsexual queers in the first place? For a lot of reasons. Whether we are aware of it or not, lesbian- and gay-identified transsexuals are in our communities—as coworkers, fellow activists and organizers, friends, lovers. Simple human decency calls on us to acknowledge and accept this reality, or else, as Rubin (1992: 474) points out, "FTMs are another witch-hunt waiting to happen." And while gay- and bisexual-identified transsexuals most definitely deserve the understanding and support of the lesbigay community, *the gay community needs transsexual queers as much as transsexual queers need the gay community.* Gay-identified transsexuals challenge society's most fundamental prejudices of heterosexism and homophobia in ways that genetic gays and lesbians often cannot. People in the lesbigay community often speculate idly about whether they would take a "magic pill" (if such a thing existed) to make them heterosexual, usually concluding that they would not. Gay-identified transsexuals have taken this line of thinking to its most profound conclusion, by renouncing heterosexuality in order to relate to men or women specifically *as* homosexual individuals. And while the debate rages on endlessly about whether homosexuality is a "choice" or not, no genetic gay man or lesbian woman can imagine the kind of "choice" required of an individual when changing his or her sex *in order to become* gay or lesbian.

Transsexual queers also defy all attempts to pathologize and "explain" homosexuality in a way that is indispensable for the continued progress of the lesbigay movement. A rampant and long-held misconception about male homosexuality, for example, is that it involves a kind of "feminization," a desire on the part of a man to be (more like) a woman, a reduction in the "maleness" of the individual engaging in gay activity (where "maleness" is variously defined by clothing, speech or other mannerisms, sexual behavior, or size of the hypothalamus). This idea would be laughable if it did not keep reappearing in the guise of "scientific theories" about the origin of homosexuality. While there is ample evidence within the gay community (as well as cross-culturally) that this cannot be true, gay male-identified transsexuals offer a particularly pointed challenge to this view. If gay men ultimately just wanted to be (or were) "like" women, then by rights no woman should ever want to become a gay man, since she already "is" more completely what he can only approximate imperfectly. Moreover, the homosexuality of female-to-gay male transsexuals involves "masculinization," not feminization, since women who become gay men do so partly in order to *increase* their maleness—often to the point of becoming more "masculine" than their (genetic) male partners. How confounding this must be for a worldview that equates and conflates sexual orientation, gender identity, and biological sex.

If any further reasons are required: Transsexual queers are creating new gender paradigms that genetic individuals would do well to emulate. Within transgender communities, there is a move toward a profusion of gender categories, ambiguity and simultaneity, intermediate or undefinable genders, and richly textured mixtures of cultural and biological gender signals (cf. Bornstein 1994, Bolin 1994, Phillippa 1993, Bell 1993, Feinberg 1992, Rubin 1992, among others). As Jason Cromwell observes, "To acknowledge the validity of 'men with vaginas' (and 'women with penises') would be to admit that men as well as women could resist and thus, subvert the social order, by approximating the 'other' but never fully becoming the 'other.'" (Cromwell n.d., quoted in Bolin 1994: 485). Lesbians, gays, and bisexuals already pride themselves on their ability to transcend outmoded gender stereotypes, as evidenced by the wonderfully dizzying permutations of gender, sex, and sexual orientation encapsulated in the following passage, from Trish Thomas's story "Me and the Boys": "What's a nice butch dyke like me doing fantasizing about a drag queen with a dick? . . . Simple. I don't want him the way a woman wants a man. I don't even want him the way a fag hag wants a fag. I want him the way a perverted, horny bulldagger wants a young, tender drag queen in a tight black slip and combat boots" (Thomas 1992a: 27; see also Thomas 1992b). This spirit of polymorphous perversity must continue to be encouraged and cultivated. Many transsexuals are now establishing their identities in spite of—or perhaps more appropriately, *because*—they do not pass for genetics. For their part, genetic gays, lesbians, and bisexuals can and should take this as an opportunity to help forge a new vision of society, one that is radically polygendered.

Finally, the lesbigay community must question not only its response to gay-identified transsexuals but its response to genetic gays and lesbians who are attracted to transsexual queers (what Phillippa 1993 calls "gender-oriented" people). Although the lesbian and gay community has often been a haven for those who cherish alternate gender expressions, it also has a long history of trivializing and problematizing men and women who are attracted to the differently or intermediately gendered. A lesson can be learned from the experiences of butch-femme lesbians: As Nestle (1984) and MacCowan (1992), among others, have pointed out, femme lesbians who are attracted to butch women have been either dismissed as not really "gay" or else vilified with a particularly hateful vehemence. This response stems from the fact that femme dykes appear to conform to the gender expectations of our society, while simultaneously subverting such expectations through their erotic preference for women—but women who appear "masculine." In *S/HE*, a powerful and evocative exploration of her relationship with Leslie Feinberg, Minnie Bruce Pratt has responded that they are not "traitors to their sex," as some have branded them, but rather "spies and explorers across the boundaries of what is man, what is woman" (Pratt 1995: 118). Where transsexual queers and their genetic or gender-described lovers are concerned, we can either choose to respond with intelligence and open-mindedness (as Gayle Rubin suggests in the introductory quote to this chapter) or else risk undermining the very foundation of our communities.

In this chapter, I have offered a linguistic analogy that can contribute to a better understanding of the relationships among sexual orientation, gender identity, and biological sex in general and of gay-/lesbian-/bisexual-identified transsexuals in particular. As noted, this analogy does not "prove" that gender identity and sexual orientation are autonomous—and, indeed, such autonomy does not *need* to be proven or analogized in order for queer transsexual identities to be made "legitimate." Rather, these parallel examples simply demonstrate (once again) that human beings are infinitely creative in their abilities to reimagine and reinvent what appear to be the most immutable aspects of culture and biology. It is hoped that this analogy will contribute, in some measure, to the continued imagination of such possibilites and to the continued celebration of pluralities—both linguistic and gendered.

NOTES

1. The use of the term *surrogate* is traditional for these languages and does not imply that they are in any way "inferior" to their source languages.

2. Unfortunately, Lorber succumbs to the same biological-reductionist thinking she is attempting to expose when she argues that transsexuals should be called woman-to-man/man-to-woman rather than female-to-male/male-to-female. She claims that transsexuals change only their social gender role, not their biological sex, because certain aspects of their sex (e.g., chromosomes) are not altered! See Phillippa (1993), who suggests that terms like female-to-male or man-to-woman be avoided altogether because of their genetic bias.

3. For some discussion of the response of the lesbian community, see Rubin (1992) and Walworth and Gabriel (1993); see also Valerio (1990) on the response of the lesbian community to female-to-male transsexuals who are heterosexually identified.

4. Faghaggotry is not restricted to straight women: several of the fag-hags interviewed in Decarnin (1981) identify as lesbian or bisexual; see also Califia (1983b) and Thomas (1992b) for some additional variations on this theme. Nor is the eroticization/idealization of homosexuality only done by women in relation to gay men: There are also "dag hags" (fags who idolize bulldaggers) and "dyke mikes" or "dyke daddies" (straight men who are attracted to lesbians); for some discussion of these parallel—albeit considerably different—phenomena, see Athey (1994) and Bright (1992). On a related issue, see Kiss & Tell (1994) on the politics of lesbian-produced lesbian pornography as opposed to straight-male produced (and consumed) lesbian pornography.

5. Outside of academic and/or feminist discussions, this phenomenon has of course been even further trivialized. Penley (1991) remarks on how David Gerrold, the author of *The World of Star Trek* (1984; NY: Bluejay), derides the slash zine enthusiasts by calling them "the K/S ladies," whom he considers to be a "nuisance" to the producers and the fans of the show.

6. Some theorists have even drawn attention to the similarities between the K/S phenomenon and fag-hagging specifically in order to dismiss K/S, thereby conflating even further the "inexplicability" of these stigmatized identities/activities (cf. Penley 1991 for a response to the comment that K/S is "just" fag-hagging).

7. For those readers unfamiliar with the basic principles of phonology, a good general introduction is Kenstowicz (1993).

8. Of course, individuals who have had their larynxes removed for medical reasons can often talk by means of esophageal speech. This type of larynx-less speech is not generally considered to be a distinct language, however, since it is not culturally transmitted or characteristic of entire communities (unlike surrogate and signed languages).

9. Hand-fluting—also used in the surrogate speech of Banen (a language of Cameroon)—involves cupping the hands in front of the mouth and blowing through a narrow aperture formed between them, thereby creating an external resonating chamber. Pitch modulations are achieved by opening and closing the fingers. For further details and pictures, see Dugast (1955) and Voorhis (1971).

10. Such languages display another type of autonomy as well: They are also independent of their source language phonological systems, since they have phonological processes that are not found in the spoken languages on which they are based; see Bagemihl (1988) for exemplification and discussion. Attempts to assign all aspects of surrogate structure to the influence of either the surrogate's modality or its source language—when in fact surrogates exhibit their own "third category" of phonology—parallel the attempts to categorize transsexual individuals as either completely male or completely female, when in fact they often occupy a third, independent gender space.

11. A related observation is that all surrogates of nontone languages represent intonation; for further discussion, see Bagemihl (1988).

12. Other possible modality-related explanations, such as the putative ability of intonational elements to disambiguate utterances, can also be refuted; see Bagemihl (1988) for a complete discussion.

REFERENCES

Ames, David W., Edgar A. Gregersen, and Thomas Neugebauer (1971). "*Taaken Sàmàarii:* A Drum Language of Hausa Youth." *Africa* 41: 12–36.

Anderson, Stephen R. (1981). "Why Phonology Isn't 'Natural.'" *Linguistic Inquiry* 12: 493–539.

———— (1993). "Linguistic Expression and Its Relation to Modality." In Coulter (1993), pp. 273–290.

Armstrong, Robert G. (1955). "Talking Instruments in West Africa." *Explorations* 4: 140–153.

Athey, Ron (1994). "Bulldagger Chic and the Beauty of Butch." *The Stranger* 3, no. 39 (20–26 June): 14–15. Reprinted from the *L.A. Weekly*.

Bagemihl, Bruce (1988). "Alternate Phonologies and Morphologies." Ph.D. diss., University of British Columbia.

Bell, Shannon (1993). "Kate Bornstein: A Transgender Transsexual Postmodern Tiresias." In A. Kroker and M. Kroker (eds.), *The Last Sex: Feminism and Outlaw Bodies*. NY: St. Martin's, pp. 104–120.

Blanchard, Ray (1989). "The Classification and Labeling of Nonhomosexual Gender Dysphorias." *Archives of Sexual Behavior* 18: 315–334.

————, Leonard H. Clemmensen, and Betty W. Steiner (1987). "Heterosexual and Homosexual Gender Dysphoria." *Archives of Sexual Behavior* 16: 139–151.

Bloom, Amy (1994). "The Body Lies." *New Yorker*, 18 July, pp. 38–49.

Bolin, Anne (1994). "Transcending and Transgendering: Male-to-Female Transsexuals, Dichotomy and Diversity." In G. Herdt (ed.), *Third Sex, Third Gender: Beyond Sexual Dimorphism in Culture and History*. New York: Zone Books, pp. 447–485.

Bornstein, Kate (1991). "Transsexual Lesbian Playwrite Tells All!" In A. Scholder and I. Silverberg (eds.), *High Risk: An Anthology of Forbidden Writings*. New York: Penguin, pp. 259–261.

———— (1994). *Gender Outlaw: On Women, Men, and the Rest of Us*. New York: Routledge.

Bright, Susie (1992). "Men Who Love Lesbians (Who Don't Care for Them Too Much)." In *Susie Bright's Sexual Reality: A Virtual Sex World Reader*. Pittsburgh: Cleis Press, pp. 93–98.

Busnel, René-Guy, and André Classe (1976). *Whistled Languages*. (Communication and Cybernetics 13.) Berlin: Springer-Verlag.

Califia, Pat (1983a). "Genderbending: Playing with Roles and Reversals." *Advocate*, 15 September, pp. 24–27.

———— (1983b). "Gay Men, Lesbians, and Sex: Doing It Together." *Advocate*, 7 July, pp. 24–27.

Carrington, John F. (1949). *Talking Drums of Africa*. London: Harry Kingsgate Press.

Chapkis, Wendy (ed.) (1986). "Betty" [writing by a self-identified transsexual lesbian]. In *Beauty Secrets: Women and the Politics of Appearance*. Boston: South End Press, pp. 147–151.

Coleman, E., and W. Bockting (1988). "'Heterosexual' Prior to Sex Reassignment—'Homosexual' Afterwards: A Case Study of a Female-to-Male Transsexual." *Journal of Psychology and Human Sexuality* 1, no. 2: 69–82.

Coulter, Geoffrey (ed.) (1993). *Current Issues in ASL Phonology*. New York: Academic Press.

Cromwell, Jason (ms.) "Fearful Others: The Construction of Female Gender Variance." University of Washington, Seattle.

Decarnin, Camilla (1981). "Interviews with Five Faghagging Women." *Heresies No. 12*, 3, no. 4: 10–14.

Deva (1994). "FTM/Female-to-Male: An Interview with Mike, Eric, Billy, Sky and Shadow." In L. Burana, Roxxie, and L. Due (eds.), *Dagger: On Butch Women*. Pittsburgh: Cleis Press, pp. 147–151.

Dugast, Idelette (1955). "Le Langage tambouriné ou sifflé chez les banen." Extract from I. Dugast, *Monographie de la tribu des Ndiki (Banen des Cameroun)* (= *Travaux et mémoires de l'institut d'ethnologie* 50), pp. 567–602 and Appendix I.

Feinberg, Leslie (1992). *Transgender Liberation: A Movement Whose Time Has Come*. New York: World View Forum.

Gene, Bobby (1993). "The Self-Discovery Process." *Gender Trash from Hell* 1, no. 1: 15–17.

Hasler, Juan A. (1960) "El lenguage silbado." *La palabra y el hombre* (= *Revista de la Universidad Veracruzana*) 15: 25–36.

Hyman, Larry M. (1986). "The Representation of Multiple Tone Heights." In K. Bogers, H. van der Hulst, and M. Mous (eds.), *The Phonological Representation of Suprasegmentals*. Dordrecht: Foris, pp. 109–152.

Kenstowicz, Michael (1993). *Phonology in Generative Grammar*. Oxford: Blackwell.

Kiss & Tell (Persimmon Blackbridge, Lizard Jones, and Susan Stewart) (1994). "Redemption and Transgression." In Kiss & Tell, *Her Tongue on My Theory: Images, Essays, and Fantasies*. Vancouver: Press Gang, pp. 45–58.

Lamb, Patricia F., and Diana L. Veith (1986). "Romantic Myth, Transcendence, and *Star Trek* Zines." In D. Palumbo (ed.), *Erotic Universe: Sexuality and Fantastic Literature*. New York: Greenwood, pp. 235–255.

Lorber, Judith (1994). *Paradoxes of Gender*. New Haven: Yale University Press.

MacCowan, Lyndall (1992). "Re-collecting History, Renaming Lives: Femme Stigma and the Feminist Seventies and Eighties." In J. Nestle (ed.), *The Persistent Desire: A Femme-Butch Reader*. Boston: Alyson, pp. 235–255.

Money, John (1988). *Gay, Straight, and In-Between: The Sexology of Erotic Orientation*. New York: Oxford University Press.

Nestle, Joan (1984). "The Femme Question." In C. S. Vance (ed.), *Pleasure and Danger*. Boston: Routledge & Kegan Paul, pp. 232–241.

Nketia, J. H. Kwabena (1962). "The Hocket-Technique in African Music." *Journal of the International Folk Music Council* 14: 44–52.

———— (1963). *African Music in Ghana*. Evanston: Northwestern University Press.

———— (1971). "Surrogate Languages of Africa." In T. A. Sebeok (ed.), *Current Trends in Linguistics*, Vol. 7, *Linguistics in Sub-Saharan Africa*. The Hague: Mouton, pp. 699–732.

Penley, Constance (1991). "Brownian Motion: Women, Tactics, and Technology." In C. Penley and A. Ross (eds.), *Technoculture*. Minneapolis: University of Minnesota Press, pp. 135–161.

Phillippa, Xanthra (1993). "TS Words & Phrases." *Gender Trash from Hell* 1, no. 1 (April/May): 19.

Pratt, Minnie Bruce (1995). *S/HE*. Ithaca: Firebrand Books.

Queen, Carol A. (1994). "Why I Love Butch Women." In L. Burana, Roxxie, and L. Due (eds.), *Dagger: On Butch Women*. Pittsburgh: Cleis Press, pp. 15–23.

Rialland, Annie (1981). "Le Sifflement des tons et les structures syllabiques en Gurma (parler de Botou)." In W. U. Dressler, O. E. Pfeiffer, and J. R. Rennison (eds.), *Phono-*

logica 1980. Innsbruck: Institut für Sprachwissenschaft der Universität Innsbruck, pp. 357–363.

Rubin, Gayle (1992). "Of Catamites and Kings: Reflections on Butch, Gender, and Boundaries." In J. Nestle (ed.), *The Persistent Desire: A Femme-Butch Reader.* Boston: Alyson, pp. 466–482.

Russ, Joanna (1985). "Pornography by Women for Women, with Love." In *Magic Mommas, Trembling Sisters, Puritans and Perverts: Feminist Essays.* Trumansburg, New York: Crossing Press, pp. 79–99.

Sandler, Wendy (ed.) (1993). *Sign Language Phonology. Phonology* 10, no. 2: 165–306.

Schachter, Paul (1961). "Phonetic Similarity in Tonemic Analysis." *Language* 37: 231–238.

Sebeok, Thomas A., and Donna J. Umiker-Sebeok (1976). *Speech Surrogates: Drum and Whistle Systems.* 2 vols. The Hague: Mouton.

Sprinkle, Annie (1992). "My First Time with a F2M-Transsexual-Surgically-Made Hermaphrodite." In D. Cooper (ed.), *Discontents: New Queer Writers.* New York: Amethyst Press, pp. 316–325.

Stern, Theodore (1957). "Drum and Whistle 'Languages': An Analysis of Speech Surrogates." *American Anthropologist* 59: 487–506.

Sullivan, Lou (1990). *Information for the Female to Male Cross Dresser and Transsexual.* 3d ed. Seattle: Ingersoll Gender Center, esp. "Female to Gay Male Transsexuals," pp. 78–83.

Taylor, Allan R. (1975). "Nonverbal Communication Systems of Native North America." *Semiotica* 13: 329–374.

Thomas, Trish (1992a). "Me and the Boys." *Frighten the Horses* 8: 26–31.

——— (1992b). "Dykes and Dicks." *Frighten the Horses* 10: 38–44.

Umiker, Donna J. (1974). "Speech Surrogates: Drum and Whistle Systems." In T. A. Sebeok (ed.), *Current Trends in Linguistics*, Vol. 12, *Linguistics and Adjacent Arts and Sciences.* The Hague: Mouton, pp. 497–536.

Valerio, Max Wolf (1990). "Leaving the Lesbian World." In Sullivan (1990), pp. 74–78.

Voorhis, Paul H. (1971). "Notes on Kickapoo Whistle Speech." *International Journal of American Linguistics* 37: 238–293.

——— (1974). *Introduction to the Kickapoo Language* (Language Science Monographs 13). Bloomington: Indiana University Press.

Walworth, Janis, and Davina Anne Gabriel (1993). "Transsexual Womyn Expelled from Michigan Womyn's Musical Festival; Results of 1992 Gender Survey at Michigan Womyn's Music Festival; and *Gender Myths #1–24. Gender Trash from Hell* 2, no. 1: 17–23+insert.

Welmers, William E. (1973). *African Language Structures.* Berkeley: University of California Press.

Wilson, W. A. (1963). "Talking Drums in Guiné." *Estudios essaios e documentos* 102: 201–219.

23

$\mathcal{T}$he Gendering of the Gay Male Sex Class in Japan

A Case Study Based on Rasen no Sobyō

NAOKO OGAWA AND

JANET S. (SHIBAMOTO) SMITH

In recent years, the speech patterns of gay and lesbian speakers have begun to receive a great deal of attention in U.S. language and gender studies, in part as a response to a heightened appreciation of the importance of the role of language in shaping our gendered understandings of society (Gal 1991; Tannen 1994a; Wood 1994). This chapter reports the results of an exploratory study of the discourses and the grammars of gay men in urban Osaka and Tokyo, in an attempt similarly to flesh out our understanding of the construction of a gendered Japan. Much is known of sex-class conventions of men and women in Japan, particularly in what we might consider to be gender-typical roles and settings (e.g., Shibamoto 1985; Ide and McGloin 1991; Miyaji 1993; Reynolds 1993); much less is known about the linguistic features of gendered social alignment in the atypical cases. Some work has begun on the speech patterns of women in gender-atypical roles (Smith 1992a, 1992b; Sunaoshi 1994[1]). Virtually no work has been done on the speech of men in gender-atypical roles in Japan (exceptions are Shibamoto 1986 and a brief section on the speech of "gay" male performers in Shibamoto 1985). Additional work in this area is long overdue.

Grammatical patterns covary systematically with speaker sex in many of the world's languages. In the United States, the linguistic expression of gender is less evident in surface lexico-morphological and syntactic differences than in differences in patterns of discourse. In Japanese, on the other hand, there are many surface lexical and morphological cues to speaker sex class (Shibamoto 1985), which, however, have yet to be characterized for the gay male sex class. Furthermore, Japan has a long tradition of female role-playing by men (*oyama*).[2] The relationship of the speech patterns of gay men participating in a contemporary, lived social class to those of the historical, performative category of "man-as-ideal-woman" deserves special attention. At least some of the culturally conventionalized views of the speech appropriate to the contemporary sex class may derive from this historical, performative category. *Oneekotoba*, the speech of gay men who imitate the speech and gestures of women (Hirano 1994: 93), is one area in which this influence is seen; Fushimi, in fact, warns against interpreting *oneekotoba* as a simple imitation of feminine speech, stressing its "performative" (*enshutsuteki*) nature (1991: 21).

These are empirical issues that require extensive empirical investigation of naturally occurring conversations of gay male speakers in a full range of speech settings. Another important, immediately accessible source of empirical data on gay male speech and writing is the small (but growing) set of recent publications and films produced by and for members of the gay community. Publications include KICK OUT, *Pokoapoko* (the house publication of Gay Front Kansai), *Barazoku*, and *Sabu*; movies include, in addition to *Rasen no Sobyō*, *Okoge* (1991) and *Hatachi no Binetsu* (1992). This chapter reports several features of gay male speech identified in an analysis of one of these sources.

The Movie

Rasen no Sobyō 'Rough Sketch of a Spiral' (1990) is the first documentary film about gay life in Japan. The film grew out of a student project of its director, Kojima Yasufumi.[3] With the encouragement of his teacher at the Japan Film School, the director Imamura Shōhei, Kojima expanded his project from a thirty-minute short on a gay couple into a full-length movie.

Not unexpectedly, Kojima ran into problems; although he originally intended to make his documentary in Tokyo, he had trouble finding cooperative subjects. Local gays were reluctant to appear openly, using their real names. Then he returned to Osaka and was introduced to Yano Yoshikazu, a young store clerk, and Hirano Hiroaki, a high school teacher. Both were willing to allow Kojima's camera into their lives.

Rasen no Sobyō begins rather crudely and conventionally, like a student attempt to imitate a "daring" TV special. Kojima shows us scenes of "typical" gay life—gays strolling in the Shinjuku 2-chōme district,[4] cruising at a porno theater, and having sex at a gay beach. The rest of the movie, however, is set in Osaka, the second largest city in Japan, located about six hundred kilometers southwest of Tokyo. Many of the scenes take place in the apartment where Yano and Takashi, the couple around whom the movie is centered, live. The apartment is also home to their private FM radio station; both are DJs for a program that deals with problems shared by homosexuals, who call in to ask for their advice. Yano also works part-time at a small *konbini* 'convenience store', and Takashi works at a florist shop. They met through ads in a gay magazine and have known each other for six years.

The film follows Yano and Takashi through various parts of their daily lives, among which are activities, such as meetings of the Osaka Gay Community,[5] that bring them into contact with other gay men, who form part of the cast of the film. Kojima, however, does more than interview his subjects; he also records their daily routines, holiday-making, and personal crises.

A major portion of the film is devoted to the production of a play by Yano that explores homosexual views of "common sense and order of the society" (Program, *Rasen no Sobyō* 1990: 4). This activity involves a varied cast, described in the next section, and the film traces the production of the play from its inception to its successful conclusion.

The Characters

Yano Yoshikazu (25): One of the two central characters. Yano begins the film as a bagger of groceries at a local convenience store. He is a dynamic, engaging presence—and completely outspoken about his lifestyle. Yano also has an ambition; he wants to write and produce a play that examines society's attitudes toward homosexuality from a gay viewpoint. Quitting his job, he recruits not only his roommate but a varied segment of the Osaka gay community for his cast and crew.

Yano confides that he has never suffered as a result of his sexual orientation but that he used to be frustrated due to lack of information concerning homosexuality. He was therefore happy and at the same time surprised when he learned about gay magazines and places such as the Shinjuku 2-chōme district in Tokyo, where homosexuals meet. He sees the need for more opportunities for gay men to inform themselves about relevant aspects of their sexual orientation and to expand the broader community's understanding (and acceptance) of the lives of gay men.

Kiyao Takashi (23): Yano's partner. He calls Yano *papa* 'daddy' and refers to himself as *mama* 'mommy'.[6] Takashi clearly takes a "feminine" role in the relationship, and is heavily dependent on Yano as "husband." Takashi is in charge of overall housekeeping duties such as cooking and doing the laundry. Their relationship thus replicates heterosexual gendered stereotypes of a typical couple. In the past both Yano and Takashi have had affairs with others. Once, they decided to break up over Takashi's infidelities; this breakup caused Takashi to suffer from depression. In most of the scenes in the film, the gentle, rather reserved Takashi stands in stark contrast to the dynamic and forceful Yano, thus providing us with an extended look at an extreme example of "gendering" within a same sex pair.

Yohito (20): Yohito appears suddenly on Yano's and Takashi's doorstep, having decided to leave home after an argument with his father. Yano and Takashi allow Yohito to live with them. In the middle of the film, a member of the play's cast discloses that Yano and Yohito are having a relationship. Takashi accuses Yano of infidelity and becomes irate with Yano when he realizes that Yano does not share his perception of infidelity as wrong. A quarrel ensues, but the three—Yano, Takashi, and Yohito—make up their differences and continue to live together at the movie's end.

Hirano Hiroaki (35): A teacher at an evening high school who tells his students that he is gay, an openness that does not sit well with some of his fellow teachers. Colleagues criticize Hirano for teaching his students that *gei tte iu no ga futsû da* 'being gay is normal' (interview with colleague of Hirano, *Rasen no Sobyô*). Hirano says that when he was young, he believed that gays were a minority of the society but that being in the minority meant being superior to other nonminority groups. He thinks that this idea was an inversion of his anxiety over the likelihood of his being isolated from society. After being convinced that being gay is neither a thing to be proud of nor to be ashamed of, however, he has been living in a serene state of mind (*"tantan to iu ka, kiraku ni gei no ikikata o shite imasu"* . . . [would one] say "serene"? I am comfortably living the gay way of life') (interview with Hirano, *Rasen no Sobyô*).

Hase Tadashi (61): A poet, unemployed at the time of filming. Hase recognized his own sexuality when he was twelve years old. He had to struggle through World War II, a time when Japan strongly emphasized the masculine elements of society. He suffered over his sexual identity while he was of *kekkon tekireiki* 'marriageable age',[7] but he chose not to get married, believing that marriage would simply perpetrate a deception on, first, the woman he married and, secondarily, on society. Hase believes that he was born gay and that, therefore, he must live as a gay person, although he claims that this has kept him permanently celibate.

Kibako: A young gay transvestite dancer in the chorus line at a local gay bar. Kibako has a boyfriend. The subject of Kojima's student documentary, he is by far the most flamboyant of Yano's cast, and he also is among the frankest talkers. Kibako says, *Otoko ga suki dattara dooshite mo onna no mane o sun no yo . . . daka onna ni naroo to wa omotte nai shi, natteru to mo omotte nai shi* (If one likes men, it can't be helped but to pretend to be like a women. . . . I don't consider myself a woman and I don't think about trying to become one.) This attitude contrasts with that of transvestite/transsexuals such as Hirahara Tetsuo, who has not only pursued a drag-queen club career for over two decades but who, in 1972, underwent a transsexual operation in Morocco (Ihara 1994: 9).

None of the attitudes expressed by these individuals may be particularly new to those acquainted with the gay movement. It is new, though, for Japanese gays to be so frank on camera and an indication that they are finally gaining the confidence to challenge societal prejudices and norms.

The Data

Taken together, these six men represent a rich cross-section of the range of gay male Osaka speech so far observed. Despite the heterosexual community's general impression that all gay men speak in *oneekotoba*, this is far from the case. From Hirano and Yano, whose speech patterns on the surface, at least, most closely approximate those of heterosexual male sex-class conventions, to Kibako, whose speech in the film can be best characterized as *oneekotoba*, we observe a continuum of variability. In this chapter, we focus on specific features of the speech of the two main characters in the film: Yano and Takashi. The data to be analyzed are drawn from four scenes in which Yano and Takashi talk to each other and the interviewer. In one of the scenes, Yohito is also present. The scenes cover discussions of how the couple met (S1), past problems (S2), Takashi's search for his mother (S3), and a quarrel over infidelity, triggered by Takashi's discovery of the relationship between Yano and Yohito (S4). The corpus consists of a total of 275 utterances (T=147, Y=128). The focus of the present analysis is on (1) terms of self- and other-reference and address and (2) sentence final particles. These two aspects of Japanese are central to language and gender stereotypes.[8]

Pronouns and terms of reference and address

Pronouns and address terms have received a great deal of attention in the literature on Japanese language use. Japanese uses zero forms where many languages, including English, require anaphoric first-, second-, or third-person pronouns; when pronouns do occur, however, they exhibit sex/gender differences. Furthermore, the use of nonpronominal terms of reference and address where languages such as English would use anaphoric pronouns is common as well. Whether these forms are, properly speaking, pronominal or not, their use is also clearly gendered (Kanemaru 1993: 109), and a great deal of attention has been paid to the specifics of sex/class/status-of-speaker, as well as of situational, constraints on the production of these forms (e.g., Ide 1979).

First- and second-person pronoun choice in Japanese differs according to sex of speaker, as shown in Table 23-1.

Use of third-person pronouns *kare* 'he' and *kanojo* 'she' is perhaps best summarized by Martin, who reports a study of pronoun use in interviews in popular journals: (1) Speakers use these pronouns to refer to foreigners more than to other Japanese; (2) *kanojo* is more common than *kare*, and 3) *kare* refers to young rather than older men (Martin 1975: 1075). In Kansai dialects, particularly in Osaka and Kyoto, both *kare* and *kanojo* are used as second-person pronoun forms.

Other terms of address and reference used in lieu of pronouns are many and various. We restrict ourselves here to reviewing what is known about gender (or, more properly, sex of speaker) differences in terms used to address and reference a domestic partner. Lee (1976) elicited common terms of address and reference from Japanese couples living in the United States. She reported the following

Table 23-1. First- and second-person pronouns used by men and women (adapted from Kanemaru 1993).

First-Person Pronouns		Second-Person Pronouns	
Men	Women	Men	Women
watakushi	*watakushi*	*anata*	*anata*
watashi	*watashi*	*anta*	*anta*
boku	*atakushi*	*otaku*	
ore	*atashi*	*kimi*	
jibun[a]	*atai*[b]	*omae*	
washi[c]		*kisama*	
		teme-	

a. As a first-person pronoun, *jibun* formerly had militaristic overtones and was restricted in use to workplaces, especially those characterized by strict vertical relationships, such as police stations and the offices of the National Defense Force; Martin notes the use of *jibun* by men when talking about themselves to themselves and, newly in the 1970s, as a substitute for second- and third-person pronouns (Martin 1975: 1077). Less is known about the use of *jibun* in Kansai (western Honshu, particularly Osaka and Kyoto) dialects.

b. Considered vulgar, lower class.

c. This form is considered overbearing; it is used toward subordinates. The use of *washi* is largely restricted to older men.

terms of address used between husband and wife, listed in descending order of frequency in example (1):

(1) HU → WI   WI → HU

    first name   first name + *san*
    kimi, omae   *otōsan* 'father'
    okāsan 'mother'   *papa*
    mama   *anata*

Little change has occurred in husband-wife address term practices since Lee's study. A 1992 survey of 101 women students at Miyagi-ken Sōgō Gakuin asked students to report on their parents' address practices (Kanemaru 1993).[9] The average age of the parents was between forty-eight and fifty, making them somewhat older than the couples in Lee's earlier study, but the terms used are strikingly similar. In example (2), again the terms reported are again given in descending order of frequency.[10]

(2) HU → WI   WI → HU

    okāsan   *otōsan*
    first name   *papa*
    oi 'hey'   first name + *san*
    kāsan   *anata*
    nickname   *tōsan*
    mama   *otōchan*

Two points are particularly notable. First, in both studies, wives tend to refer to their husbands as *papa* more often than husbands refer to their wives as *mama*. Second, where husbands tend to call their wives by their first names or nicknames, without any title, wives tend to use first name plus the most common, slightly respectful title *-san*. As we will see, these understandings of the sex-differentiated, or gendered, pronouns and address terms provide material that Takashi and Yano can—and do—use to represent themselves as participating in not sex but gender categories commonly held in Japanese culture to underlie the organization of domestic units (or couples). In Japan, sexually coupled pairs tend to be recognized less in terms of their interpersonal relatedness than in terms of their complementarily gendered unity within a family unit (Coleman 1991). Valentine makes the additional point that Japan has historically conflated sex, gender, and sexuality; where sexuality is recognized, he notes, it is subsumed under gender. Homosexuality can, then, be identified in terms of gender transgression (Valentine, this volume). It is possible that we may read Takashi's and Yano's self- and other-referencing practices as part of an attempt to be homosexual without transgressing gender, their linguistically gendered positioning enabling them to make "sense" of their respective roles in terms of the larger society.

How do Takashi and Yano do this? An examination of the corpus produced 134 instances of first-, second-, and third-person pronouns or pronoun substitutes (T = 60, Y = 74). When these instances were compared as percentages of the points in each corpus where a pronoun or other reference form could be used, they displayed clear patterns of "gendered" use similar to patterns exhibited or reported by heterosexual pairs (see Figures 23-1–23-3).[11]

What we see in these figures is the relatively clear sex/gender differentiation of pronouns and pronoun substitutes along well-known and highly conventionalized lines (again, for heterosexual domestic partners). Takashi self-refers occasionally in gender-neutral ways (*watashi, kocchi*), most commonly by first-naming himself (a practice women and female children are said to share). In addition, de-

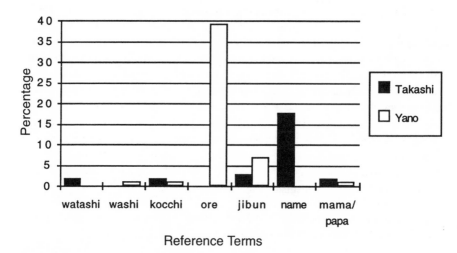

Figure 23-1.   First-person reference use by Takashi and Yano.

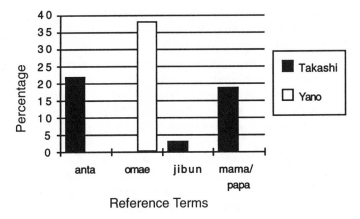

Figure 23-2. Second-person reference use by Takashi and Yano.

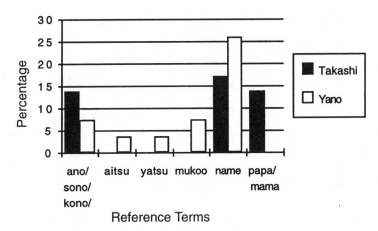

Figure 23-3. Third-person reference use by Takashi and Yano.

spite the fact that he and Yano have neither children nor any expectation of having children in the future, Takashi refers to himself as *mama*. This latter occurs rarely and, as we will demonstrate, in marked circumstances. Takashi also uses the term *jibun*, which carries some associations of masculinity, but only three times. In constrast, Yano exhibits a more stereotypical male pattern of self-reference. In all but two of forty-three instances of first-person reference, he uses terms with strong male-speaker associations: *ore* (n = 34), *jibun* (n = 6), and *washi* (n = 1). He uses the gender-neutral term *kocchi* once and the highly marked term (for self-reference) *papa* once, in a "quotation" of Takashi during their quarrel over Yano's relationship with Yohito (S4): *Saishūteki ni wa papa toko ni modotte ikimasu to yuu kimochi ga aru yaro* 'In the end, you feel [something like] "I'll return to papa," don't you?' Here, *papa toko ni modotte ikimasu* 'I will return to papa' is not something Takashi has really said but rather Yano's speculation about what Takashi might, at a later time, think to himself or say to Yano. Yano refers to himself as he imagines Takashi might in that circumstance, as *papa* 'papa'.

Takashi's use of the first-person pronoun substitute *mama* also occurs during this segment and is a particularly interesting indicator of his attempts to position himself simultaneously with respect to Yano and to Yohito. Yohito is present, although silent, throughout the quarrel between Takashi and Yano. In less sensitive conversational segments, with or without Yohito's presence, Takashi most consistently refers to himself as *Takashi* (and to Yano as *papa*). In Scenes 1–3, their partnership is not in question; suddenly, in Scene 4, it is. Now, for the first time, we see Takashi aligning himself with Yano as a domestic pair, in a way that, linguistically at least, is readily available from mechanisms of heterosexual couple alignment in Japanese households. He accomplishes this through strategic introduction of the self-referring term *mama* 'mama'.

(3) Takashi:

a. *Yohito ga mama ni zenbu yuu wa yuu kara sa. ##na.*
   Yohito SU mama to everything say TOP say because SFP SFP
   Because Yohito tells me (mama) everything, . . . you know?

b. *De,   ima   made   mama   o   damashite   kite,   anta*
   then now   until mama   DO   betray-GER come-GER   you

   kurushii   nakatta   ka   te   yuutara . . . "kurushikata
   [be] distressed   not-past   INT   QUO   say-when   [be] distressed-past

   te   yuu   nen.   ##na
   QUO   say   SFP   SFP

   So, when I say, "Don't you feel bad for having betrayed me up to now," you say, "I feel bad," you know?

Since parents most commonly self-refer as *mama/papa* or *okāsan/otōsan* when speaking to their children (Suzuki 1978), Takashi's use of *mama* in the midst of a quarrel over what is essentially a domestic love triangle allows the threesome to be reconfigured as a parental couple, with Yohito implicitly reconstrued as the child.

The same sort of reconstrual of the heterosexual domestic couple is seen in Takashi's and Yano's use of second-person pronouns; here, their usage conforms perfectly to heterosexual gender stereotypes. Takashi refers to Yano as *anta* (*n* = 7) or *papa* (*n* = 6), with one reflexive reference to Yano as *jibun* (Scene 4).

(4) *Anta   jibun   ga   uwaki   shiteru   kuse ni,   erasō ni.*
     you   yourself SU   infidelity do-GER-PROG though   self-importantly
     Where do you get off, all full of yourself, even though *you're* the one who's being unfaithful!

This use of *jibun* is reflexive rather than second-person pronominal and will not be considered further, since *jibun* is the only self-referential option in the reflexive case.

Third-person reference is more complex, and little can be said on the basis of such limited data. Of note, however, is the persistence of Takashi's use of *papa* in third-person reference (talking with the interviewer), as well as in second-person address; this is not echoed in Yano's third-person references. Yano refers to Takashi as *Takashi*. He also uses the colloquial and rather deprecatory forms *aitsu* and *yatsu*; these forms are loosely associated with male speakers and are considered highly informal. In contrast, Takashi uses *kono/sono/ano ko(ra)*, forms that are not associated with male speech, to refer to Yano; Yano uses the third-person *ko* forms as well, but less often and only as a distant or indefinite third-person, not in reference to Takashi.

In their use of pronominal forms, then, Takashi's and Yano's choices play an interesting part in their representation of themselves as a complementary pair, invoking the sexual division of interactional labor in the encoding of complementarity in heterosexual domestic pairs in the larger Japanese context. Much further work is necessary to assess how pervasive this strategy is among gay male couples in Japan and how address and reference practices generalize to settings other than the relatively "private."[12]

Sentence final particles

Japanese speakers do not like to end a sentence with a bare verbal (Kindaichi 1957, Martin 1975); this is well known, as is the fact that the class of sentence extensions (beyond the verb) called sentence final particles exhibits variability according to the sex of speaker.[13] Sentence final particles (SFP) are central to cultural stereotypes about gendered language in ways reflected in this SFP sample "continuum" (based on Shibamoto 1987, Kawaguchi 1987).

SENTENCE FINAL PARTICLE CONTINUUM

zo/ze	na/naa	yo		ne	sa	ka	na	no	yō	mon	wa
(Kansai)				wa/waa*	non		yan	nen			

relatively "masculine"   neutral   relatively "feminine"

*falling intonation

Takashi and Yano share their fellow Japanese speakers' liking for sentence extenders, in particular, for SFPs; roughly one third of their utterances contain SFPs (T = 37.4%, Y = 28.9%). We examined these instances of SFP use for their relationship to heterosexual sex-class conventions, in the first instance, and, in the second, for other differences across the two speakers.

Although Takashi and Yano employ somewhat different sets of SFPs, it is noticeable that they do *not* repeat the echo of male and female sex-class patterns seen in their use of pronouns and other naming terms. Virtually all SFPs used by both Takashi and Yano fall into the "masculine"-to-neutral categories (Table 23-2).

We cannot account for this difference at present but speculate that it may perhaps be explained, in part, by the relatively frequent use of SFP forms compared to the use of pronominal and other naming terms. When forms are used routinely, in

Table 23-2.   Sentence final particle use by Takashi and Yano.

Particle	Takashi		Yano	
	No. of tokens	*%*	*No. of tokens*	*%*
Relatively masculine	16/55	29.1	18/34	52.9
zo	1		0	
ya na	1		3	
na/naa	7		12	
na?/naa?	4		2	
yo	3		1	
Neutral	20/55	36.4	11/34	32.4
ka na/ka naa	4		0	
wa/waa	4		2	
sa/saa	3		0	
de/dee	4		5	
ne/nee	1		1	
non	4		1	
yan	0		2	
Relatively feminine	19/55	34.5	7/34	20.6
nen	4		3	
no yo	1		0	
no ne	1		0	
no	5		4	
##na?	8		0	

utterance after utterance throughout a discourse, it may be more difficult to break out of culturally conventionalized patterns of use. More work is needed in this area.

Again, although the differences are much more subtle, Takashi and Yano may be recreating a "hetero-gendered" scenario, but one much closer to the neutral-to-masculine particle zone on the SFP "continuum"; most of the forms produced by Yano (85.3%) fall in the neutral-relatively masculine zones, while most of the forms used by Takashi (70.9%) are neutral-relatively feminine. Limitations of sample size preclude statistical analysis, which would be of dubious utility in an assessment of differences between two speakers, in any event. The interesting differences appear to come in the area of the confirmatory particles *na/naa*, *ne/nee*, and *##na?*, both at sentence end, as in the data analyzed for this chapter, and as used interclausally. Not much is known about the *na/naa* forms and gender in Kansai dialects, but a nonrandom sample survey of native speakers suggests that both interphrasal and interclausal *na/naa* and *##na?* exhibit regularly gendered use. Kansai speakers casually surveyed report both to have "relatively feminine overtones," in contrast to the more masculine sentence final *na/naa*. Work on these forms is continuing. Although this preliminary sketch of SFP use in the dialogue of two speakers cannot be the basis for generalization, we might speculate on the basis of this evidence that sentence final particles appear to be nearer than pronouns to playing a part in the development of an independent gay male sex-class set of conventions.

Discussion

Social agents are not free agents. Speakers inherit a gendered system and can choose only from the options it makes available. What determines the expressive resources available to particular groups of speakers? Who or what produces the conventions that apply to their use? Tannen (1994b), borrowing from Goffman the concept of framing, suggests that speakers continually align themselves with particular (gendered) perspectives as they speak and that culture provides us with conventionalized ways of balancing status and connection within and across sex classes. But what if our culture's conventionalized sex classes do not fit an individual's or a group's reality?

The fixed categories *male* and *female* tend to reify an essentialist view of sex that fails to take into account how gender is linguistically constructed. Studies of grammatical production, then, require a sensitivity to the fluid cultural contexts in which speakers express their gender identity and create social alignments with other gendered speakers. It is necessary to be particularly attuned to the speech patterns of speakers for whom well-established sex-class conventions fail and to their dynamic interpretation, as these speakers adjust the conventions to their needs or as they invent new conventions. An analysis of a single set of speakers in a single setting is far from adequate as a basis for understanding, but it is hoped that this study will provide an empirical beginning for future investigation into the gendered nature of gay male speech.

NOTES

1. Horii (1993) is a study of women's speech in the workplace, but the study focuses primarily on women in "pink-collar" jobs.

2. Or, *onnagata*; male actors in kabuki theater specializing in female roles.

3. Japanese names throughout are cited in accordance with Japanese practice, that is, with last names first.

4. An entertainment area in Tokyo that has come to be a well-known gathering place for gays.

5. Established in 1988 as a break-off group from the Tokyo-based International Lesbian and Gay Association, Japan, OGC is a loosely organized group that meets monthly to discuss any issues of interest to the members. OGC operations are overseen by gay male members, but the organization is open to the participation of lesbians ("Dōseiai Kanren no Gurūpu, Minikomi, Supēsu Goshōkai" 1994: 78) and heterosexual men and women.

6. Although only under particular circumstances, as will be seen later.

7. Roughly, for men, the late twenties to early thirties.

8. There is considerable empirical verification of the sex/gender-differentiated use of the forms in these categories as well.

9. For a critique of the reliance on self-report rather than on observational studies in Japanese sociolinguistics, see Shibamoto (1987a).

10. The list is incomplete; for a complete report of the results, see Kanemaru (1993: 114).

11. Pronouns that did not occur in the data set are not listed.

12. Keeping in mind, of course, that these particular "private" conversations were being filmed.

13. At least in standard Japanese; the exploration of whether and how sentence final particles used in regional dialects exhibit similar variation is just beginning (see, for example, Kigawa 1991).

REFERENCES

Coleman, Samuel (1991). *Family Planning in Japanese Society*. Princeton, NJ: Princeton University Press.

"Dōseiai Kanren no Gurūpu, Minikomi, Supēsu Goshōkai" (1994). *Human Sexuality* [*Hyūman Sekushuariti*] 5, no. 2: 77–83.

Fushimi, Noriaki (1991). *Puraibēto Gei Laifu: Posuto-Ren'ai-ron*. Tokyo: Gakuyō Shobō.

Gal, Susan (1991). "Between Speech and Silence: The Problematics of Research on Language and Gender." In Micaela de Leonardo (ed.), *Gender at the Crossroads of Knowledge: Feminist Anthropology in the Postmodern Era*. Berkeley: University of California Press, pp. 175–203.

Hirano, Hiroaki (1994). *Anchi-Heterosekushizumu*. Tokyo: Pandora/Gendai Shokan.

Horii, Reiichi (1993). *Hataraku Josei no Kotoba*. Tokyo: Meiji Shoin.

Ide, Sachiko (1979). *Onna no Kotoba, Otoko no Kotoba*. Tokyo: Nihon Keizei Tsūshinsha.

Ide, Sachiko, and Naomi Hanaoka McGloin (eds.) (1991). *Aspects of Japanese Women's Language*. Tokyo: Kurosio.

Ihara, Keiko (1994). "Carousel Maki." *Japanese Times Weekly*, 15 October, p. 9.

Kanemaru, Hasumi (1993). "Ninshō Daimeishi-Koshō. 5-gatsu Rinji Zōkangō: Sekai no Joseigo-Nihon no joseigo." *Nihongogaku* 12: 109–119.

Kawaguchi, Yōko (1987). "Majiriau Danjo no Kotoba: Jittai Chōsa ni yoru Genjō." *Gengo Seikatsu* 429: 34–39.

Kigawa, Yukio (1991). "Hōgen ni okeru danjosa: Nishinihon Hōgen (Kansai)." *Kokubungaku Kaishaku to Kanshō* 722: 78–83.

Kindaichi, Haruhiko (1957). *Nihongo*. Tokyo: Iwanami Shoten.

Lee, Motoko Y. (1976). "The Married Woman's Status and Role as Reflected in Japanese: An Exploratory Sociolinguistic Study." *Signs* 1, no. 1: 991–999.

Martin, Samuel E. (1975). *A Reference Grammar of Japanese*. New Haven: Yale University Press.

Miyaji, Hiroshi (1993). "Sekai no Joseigo—Nihon no Joseigo." Special supplementary issue, *Nihongogaku* 12: 5.

Program, *Rasen no Sobyō* (1990). [Program handed out to moviegoers as they entered the theaters where *Rasen no Sobyō* played.] p. 4.

Reynolds, Katsue Akiba (ed.) (1993). *Onna to Nihongo*. Tokyo: Yūshindō.

Shibamoto, Janet S. (1985). *Japanese Women's Language*. New York: Academic Press.

———— (1986). "Japanese Women's Language: As Spoken by Women, as Spoken by Men." In Sue Bremner, Noelle Caskey, and Birch Moonwomon (eds.), *Proceedings of the First Berkeley Women and Language Conference*. Berkeley, CA: Berkeley Women and Language Group, pp. 171–182.

———— (1987a). "Japanese Sociolinguistics." *Annual Review of Anthropology* 16: 261–278.

———— (1987b). "The Womanly Woman: Manipulation of Stereotypical and Nonstereotypical Features of Japanese Female Speech." In Susan U. Philips, Susan Steele, and

Christine Tanz (eds.), *Language, Gender, and Sex in Comparative Perspective*. New York: Cambridge University Press, pp. 26–49.

Smith, Janet S. (1992a). "Linguistic Privilege: Just Stating the Facts in Japanese." In Kira Hall, Mary Bucholtz, and Birch Moonwomon (eds.), *Locating Power: Proceedings of the Second Berkeley Women and Language Conference*. Berkeley, CA: Berkeley Women and Language Group, pp. 540–548.

—— (1992b). "Women in Charge: Politeness and Directives in the Speech of Japanese Women." *Language in Society* 21, no. 1: 59–82.

Sunaoshi, Yukako (1994). "Mild Directives Work Effectively: Japanese Women in Command." Paper presented at the Third Berkeley Women and Language Conference, Berkeley, CA.

Suzuki, Takao (1978). *Japanese and the Japanese: Words in Culture*, trans. Akira Miura. Tokyo: Kodansha International.

Tannen, Deborah (1994a). *Gender and Discourse*. New York: Oxford University Press.

—— (1994b). "The Sex-Class-Linked Framing of Talk at Work." Paper presented at the Third Berkeley Women and Language Conference, Berkeley CA.

Valentine, James (this volume). "Pots and Pans: Identification of Queer Japanese in Terms of Discrimination."

Wood, Julia T. (1994). *Gendered Lives: Communication, Gender, and Culture*. Belmont, CA: Wadsworth.

24

*N*ot Talking Straight in Hausa

RUDOLF P. GAUDIO

Wai kuma shi ne Delu da Hansai! Ga shirme maganar ban haushi!

And he calls himself Delu and Hansai! Such nonsense, annoying talk!

—From the poem "Dan Daudu" by Aƙilu Aliyu (1976: 69)[1]

'Yan daudu, Hausa-speaking men who talk and act like women, employ so-called indirect forms of speech in ways that are widely perceived to be annoying and insulting, artful and clever. Although a number of sociolinguists have discussed indirectness in relation to women's politeness and powerlessness (e.g., Lakoff 1975; Brown 1993), the uses 'yan daudu make of certain so-called indirect speech genres, primarily *karin magana* 'proverbs' and *habaici* 'innuendo, insinuation', suggest that sociolinguists must broaden the scope of their analyses to investigate the resistive and confrontational qualities of indirectness as well. The familiar and humorous nature of many of 'yan daudu's indirect utterances supports Deborah Tannen's (1993) call to consider the ways in which indirectness enhances rapport and solidarity among speakers. Indeed, the (not always so) indirect insults that 'yan daudu throw at each other reflect their participation in a culturally situated conversational style that includes often intense sparring among friends (cf. Labov 1974; Tannen 1981; Schiffrin 1984; Hall this volume).

'Yan daudu's highly stigmatized position within conservative Muslim Hausa society compels us to keep in mind that solidarity among subordinate groups typically focuses as much on confronting and mitigating hegemonic—and sometimes violent—forces as it does on fostering ties of mutual understanding and affection. This paper thus engages Marcyliena Morgan's (1991) discussion of indirect communication as a form of "counterlanguage" devised by subordinate groups in response to the marginalization they experience in the dominant society. According to Morgan, whereas European-American speakers tend to see meaning and intentionality as emanating from a speaker-subject, the indirectness that she describes as characteristic of African American women's speech derives from traditional African understandings of meaning and intention as determined jointly by speakers and hearers. By focusing on the indirect ways of speaking used by marginalized speakers in one West African society, this paper seeks to contribute to an understanding of indirectness as a feature of language use in the African diaspora, at the same time as it critiques a notion of African communities as monolithic and homogeneous. Indeed, in concert with Rusty Barrett's proposal for a queer linguistics (this volume), I argue that 'yan daudu's linguistic practices call into question the very notion of a speech community—fundamental to both formal-linguistic and sociolinguistic theories—in which similar norms of membership and linguistic behavior are supposed to be understood and observed by all. As men who make use of "feminine" linguistic skills (including indirectness) as part of an ostentatious performance of their bigendered status, and who are occasionally persecuted for this behavior, Hausa-speaking 'yan daudu disrupt the expectations of sociolinguists as well as other Hausa speakers who subscribe to the idea that members of a particular gender, ethnicity, or other social category speak in objectively similar ways.

While 'yan daudu flaunt their womanlike behaviors in terms of speech, occupation (e.g., cooking and selling food), and, occasionally, attire, they are often evasive about their own sexuality. Their well-known association with the institution of *karuwanci* (often translated as *prostitution*, although Renée Pittin [1980] describes why this English term is inadequate and misleading with regard to Hausa women's sociocultural practices) is most often discussed by outsiders in terms of 'yan daudu's work as agents or intermediaries who put female *karuwai* 'prostitutes, courtesans' in touch with male patrons (Kleis and Abdullahi 1983). Less openly discussed, and only questionably understood, is the fact that 'yan daudu, many of whom are married to women and have children, are regularly sought out by men who desire their social and sexual companionship. While 'yan daudu call these men their "boyfriends" (*samari*) or "husbands" (*maza, mazaje*) and often refer to themselves as *karuwai*, social and Islamic religious injunctions against homosexuality prevent them from openly discussing same-sex relationships in contexts where the use of gender-crossing language is otherwise not so proscribed (e.g. 'yan daudu openly refer to each other using feminine terms of address such as *kawata* 'my girlfriend' and *uwata* 'my mother'). This paper thus investigates the cultural connections between the secrecy that shrouds 'yan daudu's (and other speakers') discussions of sexuality and the more canonical types of indirectness associated with 'yan daudu's use of *karin magana* and *habaici*. In particular, I suggest that discourses of deviant or condemned forms of sexuality constitute an important subtext to 'yan daudu's open transgression of gendered linguistic norms. By "hiding meanings" (*6oye ma'ana*) in proverbs and insinuations, 'yan daudu articulate a response to the marginalization they experience as gender and sexual deviants in Muslim Hausa society; indirect ways of talking allow them to appear to be playful and entertaining at the same as they address socially and/or personally sensitive topics that most other Hausa speakers would rather not discuss.

Academics have treated the subjects of *karin magana* and *habaici* very differently, in ways that reflect popular ideologies of language and gender. *Karin magana*, literally 'folding of speech', has attracted literary and linguistic scholars' attentions because of the important position proverbs are seen to have in Hausa oral traditions (Skinner 1980; Yahaya and Dangambo 1986; Gidley 1974), and because of their distinctive structural properties (Hill 1971).[2] Ibrahim Y. Yahaya and Abdulkadir Dangambo (1986: 169) echo the popular claim that women, praise-shouters, and 'yan daudu use proverbs more often than other speakers do, but they acknowledge that all kinds of people make use of them. They note that the use of *karin magana* requires wisdom (*hikima*), skill (*fusaha*), and cleverness (*azanci*). In school-sponsored debates that I observed during my fieldwork, Hausa girls and boys earned points for the skillful rhetorical use of proverbs. Scholars writing on *karin magana* typically provide lists of examples of individual proverbs, accompanied by a few explanatory sentences for each one. Very little scholarly attention has been paid to the use of proverbs in conversation, however.

While *karin magana* are used by a variety of speakers and enjoy a great degree of academic and popular respect, Aisha Rufa'i (1986: 90) reports that *habaici* "are regarded as a women's domain" because they "are characteristic of weakness and are as a result avoided by men." Conversations with nonacademic Hausa speakers revealed similar negative attitudes about *habaici* as the linguistic symptom of women's powerlessness (*rashin karfi*), fear (*tsoro*), or lack of sense (*rashin hankali*). Not suprisingly, *habaici* are in general not seen to have any literary value and do not appear in scholarly discussions of Hausa oral traditions. In this paper I argue that the skillful use of both *habaici* and *karin magana* by (some) 'yan daudu involves a highly attentive and creative command of sociolinguistic norms and processes. By considering the ways in which these indirect speech genres are used in conversation, I aim to show the multiple meanings that can be ascribed to them—meanings that relate to the complicated gender and sexual positionality of 'yan daudu in Hausa society.

The examples of 'yan daudu speech transcribed in this chapter are excerpts from a lively conversation involving four 'yan daudu and three other men that was recorded at a food shop in the northern Nigerian town of Ramiya. The primary speaker featured in these examples is Haruna, a dan daudu who took the lead throughout the conversation as the most forceful and boisterous speaker in the group.[3] Like the other 'yan daudu present, Haruna made his living (openly) by cooking and selling food and (discreetly) from men who sought his social and sexual companionship. He was in his late twenties and married and had children. Barbado, approximately seventeen years old, was the youngest dan daudu in the group. The non-'yan daudu included a Hausa friend/assistant of mine with whom I had traveled to Ramiya; Audu, a young man of about twenty who was the only one among us not known to be sexually interested in other men, and me. All those present knew of my interest in 'yan daudu's renowned language skills and of my particular desire to learn about *karin magana* and *habaici*.

In Excerpt 1 Audu intervenes in the conversation to try to direct Haruna and the others to provide specific examples of *habaici*. Haruna at first resists this request, insisting that to comply would be *aikin banza* 'nonsense' or 'useless work'. He buttresses this claim by citing a number of proverbs, which are underlined.[4]

Excerpt 1

1 AUDU   Akwai habaici wanda za ka ji an yi shi kamar karin magana=
        There's habaici that you'll hear, it was done like a proverb

2 HARUNA   =Aikin
                                    Useless

3 banza! To, ai (xx)
  work! OK, well (xx)
     [

4 AUDU   Akwai habaici wanda za'a yi cikin magana=
        There's habaici that'll done inside <in the course of> speaking

5 HARUNA   =Aikin banza.
                                 Useless work!

6 <u>Agwagwa tura ta cikin ruwa.</u>
  <u>*A duck, push it in water.*</u>

7 AUDU   Wannan karin magana ce=
        That is a proverb

8 HARUNA   =To, wane irin habaici? Habaici. Haba Allah.
                  OK, what kind of habaici? Habaici. For God's sake.

9 Ai tun kahin a daɗe ana yi. Billahillazi, <u>tun kahin a yi, duniya, Allah ya riga ya yi</u>
  People have been doing it since before a long time ago. By God, <u>since before the world was</u>
  <u>*made, God had already made*</u>

10 <u>manzon Allah.</u> (xx) shi na duniya. <u>Kuma tun kahin, a h[aih]i uwar</u>
  <u>*the Prophet of God.*</u> *(xx) him of the world.* <u>*And since before the mother of*</u>

11 <u>mai sabulu balbela take da farinta.</u>
  <u>*the one with soap was born, the buff-backed heron had its whiteness.*</u>
     [

12 BARBADO   Take da farinta ba? (.) **(slap)** Tun kahin a haihi uwar mai
        *had its whiteness, no? (.) **(slap)** Since before the mother of the one*

13 sabulu balbela (take da farinta)
  with soap was born the buff-backed heron (had its whiteness)

Audu attempts to elicit examples of *habaici* by comparing its use in conversation to the way people use proverbs (lines 1 and 4). He elicits instead Haruna's disdainful remark characterizing Audu's implied request as *aikin banza* 'useless work'. (*Banza,* an abstract noun, is commonly used as an epithet denoting meaninglessness and worthlessness; it appears frequently in proverbs [Skinner 1980: 17].) Haruna emphasizes this negative evaluation by citing a proverb (line 6) that is perhaps most familiar to Hausa speakers in its untopicalized form, *Tura agwagwa cikin ruwa* 'Push a duck in water.' This proverb epitomizes useless action in a manner similar to the English idiom "carry coals to Newcastle." Responding in a quiet, deliberate tone that contrasts with Haruna's volume and fast tempo, Audu ignores the pragmatic intent of Haruna's statement and instead focuses on its formal status as a proverb, as distinct from *habaici.* He treats the use of the proverb as an interactional mistake, as if Haruna has confused the two genres, although Audu's own initial statement also obscures the differences between proverbs and *habaici*. Audu thus fails to acknowledge the cleverness Haruna has displayed in making use, somewhat paradoxically, of a proverb at the same as he is criticizing Audu's request for a proverb-like example of *habaici*. Haruna's rejoinder, *To wane irin habaici?* 'OK, what kind of habaici?' (line 8), highlights the lack of clarity with which Audu has framed his request.

Haruna defends his resistance to producing examples of *habaici* with the claim that people have been doing *habaici*, that is, making insinuations, *tun kahin a dade*, 'since before a long time ago' (line 9). Such an age-old phenomenon, he implies, needs no comment or elaboration. He then cites two proverbs that speak to the theme of ancient truths. The first (lines 9–10) recounts the doctrine that God created the Prophet Muhammad before creating the physical world.[5] The second (lines 10–11) refers to one of God's more mundane creations, *balbela*, the buff-backed heron or cattle egret, a bird renowned for its whiteness. *Mai sabulu* 'the one with soap' refers to the putative individual who first brought or invented soap. That the buff-backed heron was white not just before the advent of soap but even before the birth of the mother of the one who brought or invented soap emphasizes the intrinsic nature of the bird's color. Both of these proverbs serve to buttress Haruna's critique of the business at hand, which is, broadly, to elucidate the phenomenon of *habaici* in Hausa for the sake of a foreign researcher. By appealing to long-standing aspects of God's creation, Haruna implies that *habaici*, like the primordial existence of Muhammad and the buff-backed heron's whiteness, is an immanent reality that does not lend itself to rational exposition.

Barbado's latched echo of the latter part of Haruna's statement (line 12) reflects both the call-and-response phenomenon that frequently characterizes the use of proverbs and the fact that the *balbela* proverb in particular forms part of the linguistic repertoire of many 'yan daudu. Using this proverb typically marks a male speaker as womanlike; the thigh slap that punctuates Barbado's utterance constitutes a stereotypically feminine gesture that reinforces the feminizing effect of his repetition of the proverb. Men who are not 'yan daudu (or who do not wish to be seen as one) are not likely to cite this proverb, lest they leave themselves open to accusations that they are "talking like a woman" or, significantly, "talking like a ɗan daudu." By citing the *balbela* proverb, therefore, Haruna and Barbado are affirming their identities as 'yan daudu before an audience that includes other 'yan daudu as well as non-'yan daudu. This sort of self-proclamation exemplifies the unabashedness that characterizes ɗan daudu identity generally and that conflicts with the culturally important Hausa notion of *kunya* 'shame', a virtue 'yan daudu are commonly said to lack.

At various points in the conversation excerpted here, Haruna makes several other seemingly incongruous references to *balbela*. Having offered up a toast and led the other 'yan daudu in a burst of *shewa*, a loud type of laughter typically associated with Hausa women, for example, Haruna invokes the buff-backed heron in the context of praising God's name:

14 HARUNA   Wallahi billahillazi la'ilaha illa huwa, Allah mun gode maka,
              (Ar. *By God, by God who there is no god but Him,*) *God we thank you,*

15 <u>tsakanin balbela da Ubangiji sai godiya,</u> a riƙa yin shewa
   between the buff-backed heron and the Lord [there is] only thanks, let one continue to do
   shewa
16 don Allah don kaset ɗin ya yi kyau.
   please so that this cassette will be good.

At another point, after failing to lure another ɗan daudu inside the shop to participate in the tape-recording session, Haruna apparently decides not to pursue the
matter any further:

17 HARUNA To wallahi shi ke nan. <u>Tsakanin balbela da Ubangiji sai godiya.</u>
           OK by God that's all. Between the buff-backed heron and the Lord, only
           thanks.

Expressions of thanks to God reflect and articulate the Muslim conviction that
everything one has or sees one enjoys only by the grace of God. Muslim Hausa
speakers thus make constant use of the phrases *da godiya* 'with thanks', *mun gode
Allah* 'we thank God', and its Arabic analogue, *alhamdulillahi* 'praise be to God',
in response to situations both mundane, as on concluding a meal or a journey
across town, and extraordinary, as on the birth of a child. Speakers also thank or
praise God as a way of expressing acceptance of God's will, even in uncomfortable
or unsatisfying circumstances. Thus, when asked *Yaya zafi?* 'How's the heat?' a
Muslim Hausa speaker will typically reply, *Zafi alhamdulillahi* 'The heat, praise be
to God', no matter how uncomfortably hot it is. In connected discourse, giving
thanks to God provides a gracious way of signaling acceptance of an unpleasant
situation.

The mention of the buff-backed heron in lines 15 and 17, where one might
expect a more conventional, first-person expression of thanks to God, suggests a
metaphorical association between *balbela* and 'yan daudu. In fact, the cultural
image of the buff-backed heron, which, as a grammatically feminine noun, is always referred to as *ita* 'she' or 'her', reflects the self-image of many 'yan daudu in
interesting ways. Whiteness, the bird's primary distinguishing characteristic, typically connotes goodness and beauty in Hausa. For example, *farin ciki* 'white
stomach' signifies happiness, while the phrase *ya yi fari* 'he has become white' indicates that the person referred to looks better and healthier than he did previously. The equation of whiteness with beauty is not just metaphorical; many
Hausa people consider a light complexion to be more attractive and desirable
than dark skin. Physical beauty is a matter of particular concern to many 'yan
daudu, whose efforts at enhancing their looks, like those of many Hausa women,
often include using chemicals to straighten their hair and lotions to bleach their
skin. The intrinsically white *balbela*, however, does not even need soap to maintain her beauty. Yet the image of the buff-backed heron has a less flattering side,
as well. The expression *balbela ci da motsin wani* 'the buff-backed heron [that]
eat[s] with the movement of someone else' refers to the bird's practice of eating
the insects that rise from the grass when other animals walk through it and connotes a person who sponges on others (Bargery 1934: 69). *Balbela*, therefore,
combines a beautiful appearance with an objectionable occupation, a striking par-

allel to the image of the ɗan daudu in Hausa culture—a feminized figure whom many find attractive and entertaining at the same time as they criticize him for the ways he lives and works.

Despite Haruna's initial resistance to the idea of reciting *habaici*, he quickly warmed to the task, providing a number of examples, three of which are featured in Excerpt 2. The elaborate structure of these examples (in lines 18–19, 22–23 and 24–28) illustrates Audu's contention (line 4) that *habaici* is done *cikin magana*, in the course of speaking. Indeed, although Audu speaks of a similarity between *habaici* and *karin magana*, Haruna's examples demonstrate that, at least in the idealized form in which he presents it, meaningful *habaici* is much more embedded in an ongoing discourse than proverbs typically need to be. Because proverbs constitute a canonized, albeit loosely defined, class of utterances, speakers can often recite and recognize them in isolation: one finds them written, for example, on the rear windows of public buses. In contrast, speakers typically describe *habaici*, which is a relatively undefined and stigmatized speech genre, as more context-dependent. This sense of *habaici*'s greater embeddedness in discourse may have been one of the factors that contributed to Haruna's initial unwillingness to provide examples of it.

Excerpt 2

18 HARUNA   Habaici kuma ke banza! Dinkin kasuwa. Yaushe ne? Ake ba ki
                    And habaici, you$_f$, useless! Market sewing! When is it?! You $_f$ were being given
19 takarda muke d- d- d- dariya muka ta- ta hana ki tahiya. Habaici (xx)
      <divorce> papers, we were l- l- l- laughing <so>we kept stopping you$_f$ from going. Habaici (xx)
                                                                                                  [
20 BARBARDO   Yo wai, ba ka ma
                                                                 Hey, you$_m$ don't even
21   sani ba!
                know!
                [
22 HARUNA   Tsaya. Kai don Allah, haba wawa. Zauna kurum. Zance ka zo, ba
                    Stop. You$_m$, please, come on, clown. Just sit down. You've$_m$ come to talk? I
23 ni da ruwa in cika ka. Wallahi tallahi sori ɗinka. Shi ne habaici.
      don't have any water to fill you$_m$. By God by God sorry for you$_m$. That's habaici.
24 Kai don Allah, in ka ga akuya ta zo, ke banza ce, na- nakiyan ruwa. Tcinanna
      You$_m$ please, if you$_m$ see a goat$_f$ has come, you$_f$! You're$_f$ useless, gravel under water. Damned$_f$
25 'yar iska. Allah haka yake son ganinki. Billahillazi sai dai ki yiwo titi=
      *good-for-nothing$_f$. That's how God wants to see you$_f$. By God just <you$_f$> come on
      over the street*
                                                                                [
26 ??   Heyi (laughs)
                                                                                 Heyi (laughs)
                                                                                [
27 HARUNA   =ki yi
                                                                                 <you$_f$>

28 kallo kuma ki ɗauki abinmu jama'a. Shi ne habaici. . . .
  take a look and get a thing of ours, the people. That's habaici. . . .

Haruna's opening remark, *Habaici kuma*. . . 'And habaici . . .' (line 18), and the coda *Shi ne habaici* 'That's habaici', which follows the last two examples (lines 23 and 28), frame his utterances as mini-performances executed at the request of his interlocutors. In the absence of any other situational motivation, prefatory expressions of abuse serve to set the stage in each case for the ensuing core *habaici* by positing a (changing) imaginary recipient of Haruna's insinuations. Because of their crafted, performative nature, therefore, Haruna's examples represent a kind of ideal type of *habaici*, rather than spontaneous instances of the genre. The three *habaici* he provides here display a common syntactic structure consisting of (1) a vocative, (2) one or more abusive epithets, (3) a mild put-down in the form of a monoclausal rhetorical question or command, and (4) a polyclausal element that constitutes the core of the *habaici*. The second *habaici* concludes with a sarcastic parting shot that combines a common Arabic-derived swear with the English loan *sori* to express mock sympathy for the rejected addressee. This structure is represented graphically in Table 24-1.

The first *habaici* represents an attempt to embarrass a fictive female addressee, whom Haruna mocks by referring to the time her husband allegedly served her with divorce papers. (Muslim Hausa men have the right to divorce their wives at will, whereas women must sue for divorce in court.) Locating himself in a group of onlookers, presumably the co-wife and/or female neighbors of the addressee, Haruna says that, although her husband had just banished her, "our" laughter so humiliated her that she could not leave the house. Divorce is a very common phenomenon in Hausa society, and jealousy and competition among women (especially co-wives, i.e., women married to the same man) with respect to men are frequent themes of popular discourse, including folktales, television shows, movies, and day-to-day conversation. These themes are also strongly associated with an archetypal notion of *habaici* as a speech genre through which co-wives and other women articulate their rivalries and mutual hostilities in a so-called indirect manner (Rufa'i 1986:91). The overtly mocking tone of this first example and the brusque reference it makes to the addressee's alleged divorce, however, show that the veil of indirectness under which speakers are said to hide their hostility when doing *habaici* can be quite sheer.

Because 'yan daudu frequently use feminine names and grammatical forms, including the second-person feminine pronoun *ki*, to refer to each other, the addressee of Haruna's first *habaici* is likely to be another ɗan daudu rather than a woman. 'Yan daudu also appropriate terms derived from mainstream heterosexual discourses (in which they also participate) to describe the socioeconomic and sexual relationships they establish with men. They speak of having "husbands" who marry and divorce them, rivalries abound over who attracts the most desirable men, and friendships founder when one party accuses another of "stealing" (*sata*) a man. As a result, this *habaici* could serve to mock a fellow ɗan daudu's humiliation at being dismissed (served "divorce papers") by a boyfriend (or "husband").

Table 24-1. Three examples of *habaici*.

	Voc.	*Epithet(s)*	*Put-down*	*Core*	*Parting comment*
1	Ke	banza	Yaushe ne?	Ake ba ki takarda, muke dariya, muka hana ki tahiya	
	You$_f$	*useless*	*When is it?*		
		Dinkin kasuwa		*When you got your divorce*	
		Market sewing		*papers, we were laughing so much we prevented you from leaving*	
2	Kai (don Allah)	Haba wawa	Zauna kurum.	Zance ka zo? Ba ni da ruwa in cika ka.	Wallahi tallahi sori dinka
	You$_m$ (please)	*Come on, clown*	*Just sit down.*	*You've come to talk? I don't have any water to give you (= anything to impress you with)*	*By God, by God, sorry for you.*
3	Ke	banza ce	Allah haka	Billahillazi, sai dai ki yiwo	
	You$_f$	*(you're) useless*	yake son ganinki.	titi, ki yi kallo kuma ki dauki abinmu jama'a.	
		nakiyan ruwa	*That's how*	*By God, you just come on over*	
		gravel in	*God wants*	*the street, take a look and get*	
		water	*to see you.*	*something of ours, the people.*	
		tcinanna			
		'yar iska			
		damned$_f$ good-			
		for-nothing$_f$			

NOTE: This table is intended not to represent the formal structural properties of *habaici* in general but simply to clarify the structure of three specific examples of *habaici*. *Habaici* can take a variety of forms other than those depicted here.

Yet the *habaici* need not, and typically does not, refer to an actual event. Because the mere utterance of such an insinuation in front of other people gives the speaker a rhetorical advantage vis-à-vis the addressee, the disparaging intent of the statement holds up even if it turns out that such a breakup never took place or the alleged relationship never existed at all. Because the sparring associated with *habaici* revolves around rhetorical one-upmanship and image-making rather than claims to an objective truth, the offended party (the "divorcée") is not able to defend himself simply by arguing that the insinuation is unfounded. The discursive situation compels him to respond in an equally performative manner, such as with a verbal comeback (e.g., a lewd insult or another *habaici*) or a dismissive gesture of the hands, hips, head, or eyes. The first *habaici* aims to embarrass the putative addressee not simply by referring to "her" divorce but, even more important, by emphasizing the embarrassment she felt with regard to her neighbors. Onlookers play a crucial role in affecting a person's status and self-esteem, both in the fictive

scenario alluded to in the *habaici* and in the real-time context in which an insinuation is made. The reactions of the secondary audience in the form of laughter,
jeers, gestures, or silence provide a measure of the sparring parties' relative standing in the court of public opinion, which for 'yan daudu typically consists of the
'yan daudu, *karuwai*, and other men in front of whom this kind of verbal competition takes place.

The disadvantaged position that 'yan daudu occupy in Hausa society provides
a basis for them to create and maintain bonds of group solidarity; at the same time,
it compels them to compete with each other over seemingly limited material and
symbolic resources, including both the admiration of other 'yan daudu and the attention of potential boyfriends and husbands. Because linguistic prowess is seen to
provide access to these social goods, language serves as an important site of such
competition. This is evident in Barbardo's interruption in lines 20–21, where he
disparages Haruna's knowledge of *habaici*. Haruna, however, fends off the challenge to his verbal dominance by quickly producing another example showing off
his rhetorical skills.

The second *habaici*, directed at a masculine recipient, exploits the vagueness
of certain words and expressions in order to forestall other listeners' understanding
of potentially inflammatory information. The vague import of this example derives largely from the indeterminacy of the word *zance*, whose generic meanings
include 'talk, conversation' and 'subject, matter.' *Zance* also has the additional, specific meaning of 'courting', the Hausa cultural ritual whereby a man visits a woman
he wishes to marry (normatively, at her father's home) and attempts to win her affection by engaging her in conversation. Just as they appropriate terms such as *aure*
'marriage' to refer to their relationships with men, 'yan daudu sometimes use *zance*
to describe the ways men go about seeking their sexual companionship. Yet the
term's inherent vagueness obscures its sexual-affectional implications when it is
used between a dan daudu and another man. As a result, the rhetorical question
Zance ka zo? 'You've come to talk?' does not specify what it is the addressee has
come to talk about, or even whether he has come to talk about anything in particular at all. In any event, Haruna's disdainful response, *Ba ni da ruwa in cika ka*, literally 'I don't have any water to fill you [with],' makes plain his unwillingness to
try to impress or satisfy his putative interlocutor. ('Yan daudu use the expression *ba
da ruwa* 'give water' to mean 'do something noteworthy, make an impression'.) In
the hypothetical exchange depicted in Haruna's second *habaici*, any listener would
understand that the addressee has been rejected in a rather offensive way. But listeners who are not acquainted with the ways "men who seek men" (*maza masu
neman maza*) communicate are not likely to notice the sexual-affectional connotation of the term *zance* when used between men. The vagueness of this and other
terms allows 'yan daudu to spar with other men over the taboo subject of homosexuality while maintaining a veneer of discretion.

The final *habaici* example also employs a term that has specialized ingroup
meaning. *Akuya* 'goat' is used by 'yan daudu as a pejorative term applied to an outsider, whether another dan daudu whom one wants to make feel unwelcome or a
person who is not known to be homosexual. In the latter case, *akuya* is not used as

an epithet directed at the person but typically serves as a warning for others to guard their speech in the outsider's presence. In this *habaici* the verbal abuse heaped on the newly arrived "goat," appropriately addressed in the second-person feminine (*akuya* is a feminine noun), suggests that the speaker's putative addressee is another dan daudu. By issuing a command for the "goat" to come have a look where the speaker is standing in a group of people (*jama'a*) and to take *abinmu* 'a thing of ours', the speaker of this *habaici* thus attempts to assert his social superiority by implying possession of some unspecified resource, whether material or symbolic, that the addressee ostensibly lacks.

Though only thinly veiled, the multiple possible meanings that can be attributed to these examples of *habaici* protect the speaker from having to accept responsibility for any particular one. In this way, one speaker can communicate different meanings to separate audiences at the same time. This ability is particularly important for speakers such as 'yan daudu, whose stigmatized social position as gender and sexual deviants requires them to be highly conscious of the way they present themselves to outsiders. 'Yan daudu know that many people consider their flamboyant ways of talking and acting to be frivolous and shameless (lacking *kunya*); yet their skillful use of *karin magana* and *habaici* shows that their discourse involves a careful combination of playfulness and hostility, of evasiveness and brusque confrontation. 'Yan daudu thus appear to share with Hindi-speaking *hijras* the ability to exploit linguistic ambiguity as a way of establishing and enhancing their seemingly paradoxical power to attract and criticize others in a society that demeans them (see Hall, this volume). The indirect speech forms used by 'yan daudu do not just convey multiple meanings in the referential sense; they also serve to position 'yan daudu in various ways in relation to each other and the society at large. The extent to which their language use manipulates the multiple audiences they might be addressing at any given time reveals their understanding of what Donald Brenneis (1986), drawing on Mikhail Bakhtin (1981), identifies as the "shared territory" of language, where speakers and hearers cooperate to give meaning to indirect forms of discourse.

This situation both resembles and differs somewhat from what Morgan describes as the way speaker responsibility is attributed in African American communities. For African Americans, she claims, "You are responsible for what you say as well as any consequences that may arise from saying it—whether you know it or not" (p. 425). 'Yan daudu's indirect linguistic practices similarly seem to locate a great deal of meaning-creation in their audiences. While Hausa-speaking hearers may believe that a speaker intended to offend them, however, the importance that Hausa society attaches to *kunya* 'shame' normatively compels people to avoid confrontation—to accept (at least outwardly) a benevolent interpretation of what someone has said by overlooking more disagreeable interpretations. When confronted, Hausa speakers can and do resort to such disclaimers as *Ba haka nake nufi ba* 'That's not what I mean' or *Ba ka gane ba* 'You$_m$ have not understood.' This is not to say, however, that speakers or hearers necessarily believe such excuses; it is simply that interactional calm is preferred to confrontation; offended parties are enjoined to *yi hakuri* 'be patient', rather than to create a stir. Language is valued more as the means for building and maintaining relationships than as a vehicle for conveying precise, objective meanings. The discursive production of 'yan daudu's social relationships crucially involves ambiguous and vague ways of talking, which represent the linguistic response to the contradictory positions they occupy in Hausa society as men who act like women and as people who are alternately admired and feared, desired and despised.

ACKNOWLEDGMENTS   Because of the social stigma attached to many of the themes discussed in this paper, I cannot acknowledge by name the individuals who have helped me the most in its preparation. Their patience and generosity both during and after my stay in Nigeria are the key factors that have made this research possible, and it is to them that I wish to express my deepest gratitude. In researching and writing this paper I have also benefited from the advice and support of many other smart and kind people, especially Usman Aliyu Abdulmalik, Renée Blake, Conerly Casey, Penelope Eckert, Kira Hall, Shirley Brice Heath, Clifford Hill, Alaine Hutson, William Leben, Norma Mendoza-Denton, Bonnie McElhinny, Haj. Fatimah Palmer, John Rickford, Haj. Aisha Rufa'i, Philip Shea, and John Works. *Allah ya saka da alheri.*

NOTES

1. Delu and Hansai are Hausa women's names. *Daudu* is an abstract noun referring to the phenomenon of men acting like women; *dan daudu* (pl. *'yan daudu*) 'son of daudu' refers to a man who does *daudu*. This paper draws on ethnographic-linguistic fieldwork carried out in north-central Nigeria in 1993-94.

2. Both *karin magana* and *habaici* are invariant with respect to number and so may be construed as either singular or plural.

3. All names for people and places are pseudonyms. Standard Hausa orthography is used in the transcription.

4. Transcription conventions are used as follows:

= represents a transition between speaker turns unaccompanied by a conversational pause.

[represents conversational overlap, with the bracket being located as closely as could be discerned to the point in a first speaker's utterance at which a second speaker's utterance begins.

( ) represents uncertainty regarding the transcription of the speech enclosed by the parentheses.

(xx)   represents undiscernable speech.

. represents falling, declarative-type intonation followed by a pause.

, represents a pause accompanied by even or rising intonation.

? represents sentence-final rising intonation followed by a pause.

! represents emphatic, sentence-final rising volume and/or intonation.

(.)   represents an extended pause.

(**slap**)   indicates a gesture or paralinguistic form such as laughter.

The English translations that accompany the transcription represent fairly literal interpretations of the original Hausa speech, with the exception of certain stylistic devices such as discourse markers (Hausa *to*, English 'OK') and contraction (Hausa *akwai*, English *'there's'*). Punctuation marks (period, comma, question, and exclamation marks) are used in the English translations according to commonly used methods of representing colloquial English speech, rather than the transcription conventions described. Line numbers are included for reference purposes and do not represent a single continuous segment of discourse.

5. This doctrine reflects the Sufi (Islamic mystical) veneration of the Prophet Muhammad as a metaphysical entity as well as a human being (Baldick 1989: 38). Sufi *tariqas*, or religious orders, have historically played a key role in the cultural and political organization of Islamic Hausa society (see, e.g., Paden 1973; Clarke 1982).

REFERENCES

Aliyu, Aƙilu (1976). "Dan Daudu." In Dalhatu Muhammad (ed.), *Fasaha Aƙiliya*. Zaria, Nigeria: Northern Nigerian Publishing, pp. 67–69.

Bakhtin, Mikhail (1981). *The Dialogic Imagination: Four Essays*, ed. Michael Holquist, trans. Caryl Emerson and Michael Holquist. Austin: University of Texas Press.

Baldick, Julian (1989). *Mystical Islam: An Introduction to Sufism*. London: I. B. Tauris.

Bargery, G. P. (1934). *A Hausa-English Dictionary and English-Hausa Vocabulary*. London: Oxford University Press.

Barrett, Rusty (this volume). "The 'Homo-genius' Speech Community."

Brenneis, Donald (1986). Shared Territory: Audience, Indirection, and Meaning. *Text* 6, no. 3, 339–347.

Brown, Penelope. (1993). "Gender, Politeness, and Confrontation in Tenejapa." In Deborah Tannen (ed.), *Gender and Conversational Interaction*. New York: Oxford University Press, pp. 144–162.

Clarke, Peter B. (1982). *West Africa and Islam*. London: Edward Arnold.

Gidley, C. G. B. (1974). *Karin Magana* and *Azanci* as Features of Hausa Sayings. *African Language Studies* 15: 81–96.

Hall, Kira (this volume). "'Go Suck Your Husband's Sugarcane!': Hijras and the Use of Sexual Insult."

Hill, Clifford A. (1971). "A Study of Ellipsis within *Karin Magana*." Ph.D. diss., University of Wisconsin.

Kleis, Gerald W., and Salisu A. Abdullahi (1983). "Masculine Power and Gender Ambiguity in Urban Hausa Society." *African Urban Studies* (n.s.) 16: 39–54.

Labov, William (1974). "Rules for Ritual Insults." In Labov, *Language in the Inner City: Studies in the Black English Vernacular*. Philadelphia: University of Pennsylvania Press, pp. 297–353.

Lakoff, Robin (1975). *Language and Woman's Place*. New York: Harper & Row.

Morgan, Marcyliena (1991). "Indirectness and Interpretation in African American Women's Discourse." *Pragmatics* 1, no. 4: 421–451.

Paden, John N. (1973). *Religion and Political Culture in Kano*. Berkeley: University of California Press.

Pittin, Renée (1980). "Marriage and Alternative Strategies: Career Patterns of Hausa Women in Katsina City." Ph.D. diss., University of London.

Rufa'i, Aisha A. (1986). "Sexism and Language." M.A. thesis, Bayero University, Kano, Nigeria.

Schiffrin, Deborah (1984). "Jewish Argument as Sociability." *Language in Society* 13: 311–335.

Skinner, Neil (1980). *An Anthology of Hausa Literature in Translation*. Zaria, Nigeria: Northern Nigerian Publishing.

Tannen, Deborah (1981). "Indirectness in Discourse: Ethnicity as Conversational Style." *Discourse Processes* 4: 221–238.

———— (1993). "The Relativity of Linguistic Strategies: Rethinking Power and Solidarity in Gender and Dominance." In Deborah Tannen (ed.), *Gender and Conversational Interaction*. New York: Oxford University Press, pp. 165–188.

Yahaya, Ibrahim Yaro, and Abdulƙadir Dangambo (1986). *Jagoran Nazarin Hausa* [Hausa research guide]. Zaria, Nigeria: Gaskiya.

25

"Go Suck Your Husband's Sugarcane!"

Hijras and the Use of Sexual Insult

KIRA HALL

> And always, licensed and provocative, hanging around the stalls, like a decayed
> reminder of Lucknow's past, were the transvestites and eunuchs of the ghetto,
> in women's clothes and with cheap jewelry, making lewd jokes and begging:
> the darkness of the sexual urge finding this ritual, semi-grotesque, safe public
> expression.
>
> —V. S. Naipaul, *India: A Million Mutinies Now*

Marginalized both socially and spatially, the *hijras*[1] have created an elaborate
network that spans all of India, establishing a divergent social space that both
parallels and opposes organizations of gender in the dichotomous system that
excludes them. Discussed variously in the anthropological literature as "transvestites," "eunuchs," "hermaphrodites," and even "a third sex,"[2] most of India's hijras
were raised as boys before taking up residence in one of the many hijra communities that exist in almost every region of India. In addition to appropriating
feminine dress and mannerisms, many hijras take male partners and choose to
undergo a ritualized castration and penectomy operation. Although relatively
untouched by police jurisdiction, hijras across the country have divided themselves according to municipal police divisions, in accordance with the demarcation of districts in mainstream society. They elect their own council of elders to
settle group disputes, referred to as *pancāyats*, who rule over a select group of
hijra communities within a particular region. They have regional meetings as
well: simply through word of mouth, tens of thousands of hijras have been
known to converge on a single area. Hijras in North India can now travel free of
charge on government trains,[3] knowing upon arrival in any new city precisely
where to go for hijra company. The extraordinary factor at work here is that the
estimated 1.2 million hijras now living in India (*Hindustan Times* 1994; Shrivastav 1986)[4] constitute a culture so diverse that all of India's myriad social and lin-

430

guistic groupings are represented within their numbers, and yet they are easily identified as part of one group by what might be referred to as a flamboyant and subversive semiotic system—a system identified through unique choices of dress, gesture, and discourse.

A number of European and American anthropologists have pointed to the existence of this network as evidence that a greater social tolerance of gender variance exists in India than in the West (see, for example, Bullough and Bullough 1993; Nanda 1990, 1992), but I argue instead that this network exists only because the hijras have created it in resistance to systematic exclusion. Ostracized by friends and family, the hijras have formed a parallel universe of sorts, its strength demonstrated by the hijras' loyal participation in local, regional, and national celebrations. Meetings that have won the attention of Indian journalists during the last two decades include the 1979 celebration in Ahmedabad for the 50th anniversary of a hijra named "Dada Guru" Shankar (*Times of India* 1979); a subsequent celebration in Panipat for the coronation of a successor to the Delhi *takia* (Mohan 1979); the 1981 All-India Hijra Conference in Agra, which is said to have brought together more than 50,000 hijras from throughout India and Pakistan (Singh 1982); the religious festival associated with the city of Koovagam, Tamil Nadu, where approximately 10,000 hijras gather on an annual basis to "marry" Aravan, the legendary husband of a female incarnation of Krishna (Shetty 1990); and the annual jamboree at the village of Bechraji, Gujarat, where hijras gather in mass to pay homage to their goddess, Bahucara Mata (Mitra 1984).

Likewise, it is the network, not the government, that is ultimately responsible for a number of landmark political decisions during the past fifty years regarding hijra rights in India and Pakistan. Some of the most notable gains for the hijra community include the 1936 decision to give hijras government pensions, ration cards, and the right to vote (Shrivastav 1986),[5] the 1952 and 1977 decisions to allow hijras to run for local office as women (Singh 1982), the decision in the 1950s to lift Ayub Khan's ban on hijra activities in Pakistan (Naqvi and Mujtaba 1992), and the 1994 decision to give hijras the right to vote as women in upcoming elections (*Hindustan Times* 1994). These gains were made only after lengthy protest from the hijra network, a fact not lost on the journalists and the sociologists who report them. Chandar Mohan, for instance, in his article titled "The Ambiguous Sex on the War-Path," offers a brief history of political platforms adopted by the hijras, mentioning in particular stances taken at two influential national conferences in 1969: an All-India Hijra Conference at Nadiad, where participating hijras demanded to be counted as females instead of males in the national census (Mohan 1979; Singh 1982), and a subsequent conference in Bhopal, where the hijras, who gain most of their income by singing and dancing at birth celebrations, launched an organized campaign against the anti-procreation stance of government-sponsored "family planning" (Mohan 1979; Singh 1982).

Indeed, the hijras have strategically exploited their perceived status as "neither men nor women" in their own campaigns for political office. Two events in particular exemplify this strategy: One took place in Gonda, India, in the late 1970s, the other in Abbottabad, Pakistan, after the collapse of the Benazir Bhutto government in the 1990s. In Gonda, the hijras urged President N. Sanjiva Reddy to invite them to form a government, arguing that as "neutralists" they would be able to serve the nation without the ingroup fighting typical of "men and women" (Mohan 1979); in Abbottabad, the hijras argued that because both "men and women" had failed as politicians, residents should try sponsoring a hijra instead (Naqvi and Mujtaba 1992). Credit for the visibility of the hijra in modern-day thinking, then, is perhaps best given to the hijras who participate actively in this network and who employ in-your-face tactics at public gatherings in order to make their positions heard. Hijras are not accorded respect in contemporary Indian society; they demand it.

In this chapter, I discuss how the hijras reclaim space normally unavailable to them through the use of verbal insult, a discursive practice that both accentuates and constructs the same sexual ambiguity for which they are feared. I begin by tracing the formation of a cultural ideology regarding the hijras' "verbal insolence," as evidenced in seventeenth- and eighteenth-century accounts of court eunuchs by European travelers, in nineteenth-century discussions of the hijras by British colonialists, and in contemporary portrayals of the hijras by South Asian journalists, poets, and novelists. I then move on to an analysis of the hijras' contemporary cursing strategies, referring to fieldwork I conducted with Veronica O'Donovan among four Hindi-speaking hijra communities in Banaras, India, during 1992 and 1993. I focus in particular on an ingroup speech event that the hijras perform in the presence of nonhijra outsiders. By employing what some Indian sociologists have named *aślīl evaṁ dviarthī bhāṣā* 'obscene and double-meaning language' (Singh 1982), the hijras are able to assume a position of control in their interactions with the public, inviting their nonhijra listeners to enter a linguistic space that questions dominant ideologies of gender and sexuality. Mapping their own sexual ambiguity onto linguistic ambiguity, India's hijras are able to locate themselves on an otherwise inaccessible social grid.

A History of Verbal Insolence

As a means of contextualizing the hijras' present-day social position as well as their use of verbal insults, I want first to offer a brief historical overview of the social and linguistic position of the "castrated eunuch" in India. Throughout their various incarnations in history, India's eunuchs have been portrayed as providers of verbal as well as sexual relief: as overseers of the king's harem in the fourth century B.C.E.; as "shampooers" in the Hindu courts during the second and fifth centuries; as protectors of the royal ladies of the harem in medieval Hindu courts; as administrators under the Khiljis of Delhi during the late thirteenth and early fourteenth centuries; as servants in the Mughal courts from the sixteenth to the nineteenth centuries; as slaves in the houses of Muslim nobility in Awadh (formerly called Oude) during the 1900s; and, finally, as the independent performers variously known since the early nineteenth century as *khojas, khusras, pavaiyas,* and *hijras.*[6]

Licentious tongues: The court eunuch in European travelogues

The eunuchs of the Mughal court, often referred to as *khwajas* in colonialist literature, are a very different entity from the hijras of the twentieth century, but because many of today's hijras conceptualize themselves as descendants of these earlier court eunuchs, frequently rattling off folk legends about sharp-tongued eunuch administrators, they merit attention here. The eunuchs' predilection for abusive language is documented in the literature over a span of several centuries, particularly in European travelogues. The lively stories narrated by the Italian physician Niccolao Manucci in the mid-1600s about his interactions with various eunuchs during the reign of the Mughal Emperor Aurangzeb provide some rather colorful examples. In his lengthy *Storia do Mogor* (translated by Irvine 1907), Manucci relates several stories regarding what he calls "that sort of brute" known as the eunuch, describing his greed, his vanity, and, most significant in terms of the present discussion, his "licentious tongue":

> Another of their qualities is to be friendly to women and inimical to men, which may be from envy, knowing what they have been deprived of. The tongue and the hands of these baboons act together, being most licentious in examining everything, both goods and women, coming into the palace; they are foul in speech, and fond of silly stories. Among all the Mahomedans they are ordinarily the strictest observers of the faith, although I knew some who did not fail to drink their little drop, and were fond of wine. These men are the spies for everything that goes on in secret, whereby they are always listening among the kings, princes, queens, and princesses. Fidā'e Khān, of whom I have spoken, aware of the character of these monsters, did not allow such to be employed in his house, although he retained two young men who acted as pages; he was indifferent to the fact that this sort of people are kept in the houses of princes and great men. This suffices for a brief notice of what the eunuchs are. (Manucci 1907: v. 2, 80–81)

The author's depiction of court eunuchs as "foul in speech and fond of silly stories" and as "spies for everything that goes on in secret" is significant, particularly as it reflects a perspective characteristic of narratives on the eunuch during the next three centuries.

Many of the stories told by Manucci portray the eunuch as a child wronged, rendered angry and miserable by an unwanted castration. Especially moving in this regard is a narrative about the faithful Daulat, who carried the bones of his deceased master 'Ali Mardān Khān all the way to Persia in order to bury them in the tomb of his forefathers, only to have his nose and ears cut off by the King of Persia in return (v. 2, 215–16). Hiding away in a house in Lahore full of shame, the deformed Daulat asks Manucci to make his nose and ears grow again, thinking that as a physician Manucci might be able to conjure a remedy. When Daulat finally comes to terms with the fact that there is no remedy for his deformity, he exclaims: "I know not what sins I have committed to be made an out-and-out eunuch twice over, first in my inferior part, and, secondly, in my upper half. Now there is nothing more to deprive me of, nor do I fear anything but losing my head itself" (v.2, 216–17). Yet in many of the stories told by Manucci, the eunuch will do anything in his power to revenge himself against his deprivation, as in the case of I'tibār Khan, a eunuch who figures prominently in Manucci's *Storio*. Sold into Mughal slavery at a very young age by his Hindu parents and bitter because of it, the "immeasurably stingy" I'tibār Khan takes great delight in helping Aurangzeb make his father, the elderly Shāhjahān, unconditionally miserable (v. 2, 76–77).

Of particular interest in Manucci's travelogue is a short narrative focusing on an unnamed "insolent" underling, a gatekeeper to Prince Shāh 'Ālam's seraglio, who tricks the author into giving away his money through a verbal slur on his family (v. 4, 225). It is not clear whether Manucci, even after recalling this exchange for his travelogue, recognizes that he has been duped, but the eunuch in question was clearly in control of the conversational encounter. After drawing blood from the prince Shāh 'Ālam, Manucci was given 400 rupees in payment, certainly a great sum of money in the seventeenth century. But when Manucci went to leave the seraglio, a eunuch at the gate remarked off the cuff: "It seems to me that you could never have had as much money in all your life." The statement was immediately interpreted as an insult by Manucci, the proud and prosperous son of a chief physician of the King of Spain. "At once I took the salver and emptied out on the ground all the money in it in the presence of the gatekeepers," Manucci angrily recalls, "telling them I made them a present of it. Then I turned to the eunuch: 'Do you not know that I am the son of the chief physician of the King of Spain, who is lord over half the world and owns the mines of silver?'" (225). Manucci appears to think that he is the winner in this dispute, but the verbal adroitness of his interlocutor cannot go unnoticed; the insolent eunuch, after all, became 400 rupees richer.

According to early accounts, many of the eunuchs who served the Mughal emperors were either kidnapped or sold into slavery by their Indian parents; others were brought from Ethiopia, Egypt, or Sudan as part of the Middle Eastern slave trade. Rajaram Narayan Saletore (1974, 1978) gives perhaps the most comprehensive historical account of the institution of eunuch slavery in India, although there are innumerable references to the practice in the memoirs of various Mughal rulers and European travelers. Francois Bernier (1891), for instance, a French physician in the court of the "Great Mogol" Shah Jahan during the seventeenth century, records one instance when the Ethiopian King sent the court "twenty-five choice slaves, nine or ten of whom were of a tender age and in a state to be made eunuchs. This was, to be sure, an appropriate donation from a Christian to a Prince!" (1891: 135). The practice apparently extended well into the mid-nineteenth century in certain areas of India: William Knighton (1855) identifies the eunuchs as "slaves" in his narrative on the household of Nussir-u-Deen, the King of Oude, and Richard Francis Burton (1886–1888, v. 1, 70–2n), who campaigned against the practice of slavery in general and took it upon himself to trace the development of pederasty in the Eastern world, provides an explicit account of the castration operation used on abductees from Darfur (i.e., "The parts are swept off by a single cut of a razor, a tube (tin or wooden) is set in the urethra, the wound is cauterised with boiling oil, and the patient planted in a fresh dunghill. His diet is milk; and if under puberty, he often survives").[7] The subject of court eunuchs in Indian history merits a full book in its own right; I mention it here as a means of contextualizing present-day ideologies about the hijras' language use.

Certain eunuchs, both before and during the Mughal period, did indeed rise to high positions in the royal courts, as suggested by several journalists and anthropologists when discussing the comparatively low status of hijras in modern-day society (e.g., *New Orleans Times Picayune* 1994; Claiborne 1983; Nanda 1990; Sharma 1984; Naqvi and Mujtaba 1992).[8] Their impotence was said to make them especially faithful servants, and some of them apparently became influential in court politics; these included Malik Kāfūr, Ala-ud-din Khilji's favorite eunuch, who led the annexation of Gujarat in 1297 and a raid on southern India in 1310 (see Rawlinson 1952: 226–27; Saletore 1974: 202); I'tibār Khan, who in the 1600s remained one of Aurangzeb's most trusted servants (as reported by Manucci); and Khwaja Saras Hilal, appointed in Agra as one of Sai'd Khan's 1200 eunuchs, who later joined the Emperor Jahangir and named the town Hilalabad after himself (see Saletore 1974: 203). Yet behind all these sporadic tales of valor is the awareness that the eunuch is an orphaned servant, and an emasculated one at that, who exists without family or genealogy. This point is made especially clear in one of Manucci's narratives, in which he gives an eyewitness account of how I'tibhār Khan reacted to two elderly visitors from Bengal who claimed to be his parents. After surmising that their claim was indeed true, I'tibhār Khan angrily ordered them to receive fifty lashes and cried: "How have ye the great temerity to come into my presence after you have consumed the price of my body, and having been the cause, by emasculating me, of depriving me of the greatest pleasures attainable in this world? Of what use are riches to me, having no sons to whom I could leave them? Since you were so cruel as to sell your own blood, let not my auditors think it strange if I betray anger against you" (v. 2, 78–79).

Yet it is this very emasculation that allowed I'tibhār Khan to become the gossiping governor of Aurangzeb's fortress, whose physiognomy, in the words of Manucci, betrayed the "vileness of his soul" (v. 2, 77). The eunuchs, in the minds of many European travelers, were thought to lead a contradictory existence: Their emasculation made them faithful, but their orphanhood made them cruel. Bernier, when reporting on a eunuch rebellion in Delhi provoked by an outgroup murder of one of the seraglio eunuchs, articulates this contradiction overtly:

> It seems nevertheless to be the general opinion that he cannot long escape the power and malice of the eunuchs. Emasculation, say the *Indians*, produces a different effect upon men than upon the brute creation; it renders the latter gentle and tractable; but who is the eunuch, they ask, that is not vicious, arrogant, and cruel? It is in vain to deny, however, that many among them are exceedingly faithful, generous, and brave. (Bernier 1891: 131–32)

Bernier's comparison of the court eunuch with "the brute creation," a phrase that when used in this context conjures the image of a male bullock feminized through castration, is telling, particularly as it points to several assumptions shared by European travelers regarding the "humanity" (or lack thereof) of the eunuch. In

many of the Europeans' travel accounts, the hijras exist somewhere between the
categories of man and beast, of man and woman, a liminality captured in
Manucci's more direct categorizations of the eunuch as "that sort of brute." Because of their neutered status, many Mughal eunuchs served as protectors of the
palace women; indeed, in many cases they were the only "nonwomen" allowed into
the women's quarters. But their association with feminine secrets won them simultaneous notoriety as court gossips, and cruel ones at that. Bernier, later in his
travelogue, describes the procession of the seraglio in Agra and Delhi, in which
the participating women were protected on all sides by eunuchs: "Woe to any un-
lucky cavalier, however exalted in rank, who, meeting the procession, is found too
near. Nothing can exceed the insolence of the tribes of eunuchs and footmen
which he has to encounter, and they eagerly avail themselves of any such opportunity to beat a man in the most unmerciful manner" (373).[9] The author's repeated
uses of the term *insolence* (formed from the Latin *in* 'not' +*solere* 'to be accustomed
to') serves to characterize the hijra as someone who is 'out of the usual', in voice as
well as deed. As in the descriptions quoted here, travel reports of the court eunuch
frequently conflate verbal insolence with physical cruelty, portraying the eunuch as
inhumanely adept at both.

Verbal abominations: The hijra in colonialist narratives

The historical connection between the *khwaja* of the Mughal courts and the *hijra*
of contemporary India is unclear. During the early 1800s, the status allotted to the
court eunuch was mapped linguistically onto the "natural" hijra; that is, the term
khoja, a derivative of *khwaja*, came to represent "hermaphrodites" in addition to
court eunuchs, and both were defined in opposition to the more vulgar, artificially
created *hijra* (see Ebden 1855: 522; Russel, Bahadur, and Lal 1916: 206).[10] Later
in the same century, the more prestigious term *khoja* was, for the most part, lost on
Hindi-speaking society, and natural eunuchs as well as castrated eunuchs were
conflated under the single term *hijra*. But the perception of the emasculated or-
phan as "insolent" remained constant, continuing through reports made by British
colonialists in the 1800s, who systematically objected to the hijras' vulgar manner
of acquiring alms at births and weddings. Indeed, Lawrence W. Preston (1987),
in his revealing discussion of the role of British colonialists in the oppression of
the hijras in the nineteenth century, explains that the vulgarity associated with
the hijras' begging techniques, particularly their predilection for verbal obscenity
and genital exposure, led the Collector at Pune to direct an edict against its realization. The Bombay Presidency ultimately denied the Collector's request for legislation on the grounds that education, not law, would eventually solve the problem, but it nevertheless declared itself in support of the sentiment behind the
request: "No doubt ... the evil will soon be mitigated, as far as it is susceptible of
remedy in the present state of society, and that it will ere long altogether cease to
exist, even in respect of the infatuated victims themselves, as other abominations
have done under the advantages of education, and under a Government which will
not tolerate them" (Webb 1837, quoted in Preston 1977: 379).

The hijras' verbal "abominations" continued to be central to colonialist narratives throughout the late 1800s. John Shortt (1873: 406), in his report on the *kojahs* of southern India (a term he uses for both natural and castrated eunuchs), identifies them as "persistent [and] impudent beggars, rude and vulgar in the extreme, singing filthy, obscene, and abusive songs"[11]; Fazl Lutfullah (1875: 95), in a short discussion of the hijras in Ahmedabad, refers to their "obstreperous sallies of witty abuse"[12]; and F. L. Faridi (1899: 22), in his entry on the Gujarat *híjdás* for the *Bombay Gazetteer*, remarks on their "indecent clamour and gesture." In a manner echoic of Bernier two centuries before him, Faridi exclaims: "Woe betide the wight who opposes the demands of a Hijda. The whole rank and file of the local fraternity [will] besiege his house."[13]

Contemporary Accounts

The designation of the hijra as a loose-tongued upstart has continued to the present day, although it is now Indian journalists and sociologists who carry on this descriptive genre. Authors frequently point to the hijras' idiosyncratic and nonconforming use of language, particularly to their mixing of feminine and masculine speech styles, as indicative of both gender dysphoria and sexual perversion. They contrast hijras with women by referring to the hijras' lewd jokes, their love of excessive obscenity, and their aggressive conversational style; they contrast them with men by referring to the hijras' penchant for gossip and their tendency to chatter excessively, to babble without content. Like the court eunuch described by Manucci in the 1600s, the hijra is portrayed as a foul-mouthed gossip; her dual nature, in the opinion of modern-day Indian authors, enables her to outdo the most negative verbal stereotypes associated with either side of the gender divide.

The work of Govind Singh, the author of a popular study entitled *Hijṛō kā Sansār* (The world of the hijras),[14] is but one example of this descriptive trend. Throughout his book, Singh portrays the hijra as a linguistically conflicted entity who, as he explains in the two excerpts reproduced here, shifts between positions of coquettish cursing and foul-mouthed flirting:

> When several hijras are together, they can never shut up. Even the hijra who lives alone can never be quiet. Some Don Juan will tease him, and with a clap he'll turn around and give him a quick answer. This answer is often very foul-mouthed and obscene. Hijras, together or alone, always speak and converse in this way. They can be identified by their effeminate gestures in a crowd of hundreds and even from a long way off, and moreover, their style of speaking is just as peculiar.

> They keep a storehouse of obscene words and they use metaphors that will shock all of those listening. The use of obscene words in Banaras is singularly unique and exceptional, but when face-to-face with the vocabulary of the hijras, Banaras speech pales in comparison. No one can keep up with the rhythms of the hijras' obscene pronunciations. On any particular day one of them might get angry at another hijra. When a hijra gets angry, he usually gesticulates in a coquettish manner and flares up. He is not

bent upon exchanging blows or serious mischief, but the hijra can't remain silent either. He will certainly begin to rave and babble. When they want something from someone in a crowd, they'll gossip about that man. (1982: 94–95, my translation)

In these passages, Singh employs certain Hindi terms that work together to portray the hijra's existence as linguistically troubling. In interactions with both the public and her own community, the hijra rebels against cultural ideologies of gendered language, assuming a linguistic position that is neither fully feminine nor fully masculine. She appropriates the masculine through her use of *kahā-sunī* 'verbal impropriety,' *garmāgarmī* 'heated verbal exchange,' and *apśabd* 'abusive words'; her speech is *phūhaṛ* 'coarse-grained' and *aślīl* 'obscene, vulgar.' Conversely, she appropriates the feminine through her use of effeminate *hāv-bhāv* 'gestures', as well as through her tendency to *maṭkānā* 'move in a coquettish manner' and *baknā* 'babble', 'chatter', 'make disjointed utterances.' The hijra, in the opinion of Singh, is a kind of a linguistic maverick, and her refusal to adhere to hegemonic notions of either feminine or masculine speech becomes almost an instantiation of her refusal to adhere to a particular gender.

Cursing as a corollary of impotence

The hijras' use of obscenity tends to interest commentators far more than their use of gossip; Indian journalists often devote full paragraphs to the hijras' abusive displays, not just at birth performances but also in their daily interactions with innocent bystanders. The hijras' strategy of shouting obscenities in front of outsiders appears to be just one contemporary realization of what has been traditionally identified as "the hijra curse." Since the early 1800s, and perhaps long before that, people in a variety of Indian communities have believed that the hijra, by virtue of her own impotence, has the power to prevent the birth of male children; her curse has therefore been viewed as a performative in the canonical Austinian sense, which, if uttered in the context of the birth celebration, serves to interrupt the family lineage. Because this belief is still extant in many communities, particularly in Indian villages, the hijras often provoke fear among their clients.

Rupa,[15] who shares a house with an Indian family in Banaras and considers herself to be the *pandit* 'priest' of the hijras living in the city, expands on this point. She explains that Banaras residents, fearing the pronouncement of a curse like "may your child die," will respond to the hijras with *izzat* 'honor', 'respect':

> They're very afraid of us. If someone has a child and we go to their door, they'll always talk to us with folded hands—whenever they talk to us. Why do they talk to us like that? Because they're afraid that something bad might come out of our mouths. And sometimes that really brings its fruits. They're afraid that we'll say something absurd, for example, *jā, terā baccā mar jāy!* 'may your child die!'. We say that sometimes in anger. And because they're always afraid that their child might die, they'll say, "Don't ever say anything to them, because if something bad comes out of their mouths, something bad will happen to us!" So they alway have fear in their hearts, and they always speak to us with respect. (personal communication, Rupa, Spring 1993, my translation)

But because this respect is motivated by fear, the hijras are situated precariously in the social structure. Even though many residents, as Rupa explains, still fear the curse of the hijra, an increasing number of Hindus and Muslims are angered at the hijras' manner of inspiring fear to collect alms, and they dismiss belief in the hijras' power over impotency as mere superstition. The modern-day hijra is left with little choice but to up the verbal ante with a sexual chip. And so it is that P. N. Pimpley and S. K. Sharma (1985: 41) depict the hijras as "making overtures to on-lookers" and "cracking sexually charged jokes at men"; Kavitha Shetty (1990: 52) describes them as "intimidating those who are wary of their queer appearance and outrageous behaviour"; and Nauman Naqvi and Hasan Mujtaba (1992: 89) focus on a hijra in Mazimabad who "hurl[ed] the most vociferous abuses" so that a man was "forced to disembark from the bus in shame."[16] Indeed, the United States Department of State (1992: 1–2) even commented on the hijras' use of sexual insult when officials answered a request for an advisory opinion on an asylum application made by a Pakistani "hermaphrodite."[17] Referring to information obtained from the United States embassy in Islamabad, Pakistan, the Department informed the San Francisco Asylum Unit of the U.S. Immigration and Naturalization Service that "[the hijras'] performances, despite the fact that they often involve crude sexual jokes, are considered more socially acceptable than real female dancers (who more often than not are also prostitutes)."

The hijras' predilection for obscenity has led a number of researchers, particularly those interested in the human psyche, to theorize on its psychological origins. Gautam N. Allahbadia and Nilesh Shah, who identify the hijras' collective existence as a "subhuman life," pose this question directly in their introduction to a brief article on the hijras in Bombay:

> The style of begging is very aggressive. In groups of three or four they confront individuals, clapping and making gestures with their fingers. Give them money and they will bless you and your family and pray for increased libido for you and for male heirs for your family. Refusal is followed by abuse, and obscene gestures, and some of them will lift their petticoats, exposing their genitals and cursing. . . . Why do they live like this? (Allahbadia & Shah 1992: 48)

While Allahbadia and Shah, for the most part, shy away from answering the question of "why," other researchers have tackled it head on, including Sumant Mehta, writing half a century ago, who offered a sociological explanation for the hijras' "indecent gestures" and "mincing and inviting gait": "It is not merely the lewdness which revolts," he explains, "but the fact that the Indian Society has so degraded and inhumanised these people that, without actually meaning to invite an unnatural sex intercourse, these people behave as lewdness-loving people expect them to behave, just in order to earn a pi[e]ce or two" (1945–1946: 47–48).[18]

But Mehta goes on to attribute the hijras' behavior (which he variously identifies as "malevolent," "unscrupulous," and "abased") to both the "inferiority complex" and the "resentment complex" (51), a claim more in sync with contemporary explanations. Satish Kumar Sharma, who conducted extensive research on the hijra community in the 1980s, works from the standpoint of Freudian psychology and links the hijras' sexual overtures to their "feeling of deprivation at the psychological level" (1984: 387). He is concerned less with the societal marginalization spoken of by Mehta than with the hijras' inability to perform sexual acts, a state that, in his opinion, logically leads to the use of obscene language:

> An interesting feature of eunuchs is that they pass on sexual overtures to the general population, especially to the males. Why do they do so? The enquiries revealed that though they are biologically incapable of performing sex, yet when they see couples in the society at large, they have a feeling of deprivation at the psychological level. The idea of sex and their imagination of performing sexual acts is gratified by passing sexual remarks, etc., on others. They do not have any physical sexual urge, but sex invades their mind. Thus they, in majority of the cases interviewed, have frustration of an unusual kind, i.e., no physical urge but psychologically they think of enjoying sex. This frustration, as revealed by some of the eunuchs, leads to the practice of sodomy, etc. (Sharma 1984: 387)

Sharma's claim that the hijras compensate for their own impotence by "passing sexual remarks" demands futher investigation. There is a long-standing folk association in northern India of foul language with sexual frustration; the work of many popular psychologists builds on the notion that a lack of sexual virility results in verbal degeneration. One need only turn to the scores of popular works on Indian sexuality to see the pervasiveness of this association. Dayanand Verma's (1971) *An Intimate Study of Sex Behaviour* offers but one example. In a chapter titled "Male Superiority by Sex Capacity," Verma attributes the verbal practices of both "name-calling" and "eve-teasing" to male impotency, explaining that a man who uses foul language "at least [proves] that he is potent and can have sexual relations with a number of women" (75). Verma is concerned primarily with the male employment of insult terms like "father-in-law" or "brother-in-law," which if used out of a sanctioned context imply that the speaker has had sexual relations with the addressee's mother or sister, respectively (see V. Vatuk 1969: 275). "A man's main asset is his virility," Verma proclaims, "if a man has all other qualitities like courage, patience, etc., but is impotent, that is, he is incapable of having sexual intercourse, he isn't worth being called a man" (74). By calling other men "brother-in-law" and "father-in-law," as well as by speaking sexually to women, the impotent man will "declare his manliness" and hence save face: "What he wishes to convey by narrating such incidents is—'Now at last you should believe that I am not impotent. I possess in abundance the main quality of manliness, namely a wolfish hunger for women. I may not be brave, courageous or patient but I can certainly handle a woman in bed. Whenever you want, I can furnish proof of this quality of mine'" (76).[19]

The connection between impotence and foul language is again expressed, albeit from a feminist perspective, by Mayah Balse (1976) in *The Indian Female: Attitude towards Sex*, apparently written as a companion piece to Jitendra Tuli's (1976) *The Indian Male: Attitude Towards Sex*. The book is replete with personal accounts of marriages that failed because of male impotence, among them that of Roopa, who had the misfortune of having an arranged marriage with an impotent

man who sported a "deformed sex organ," and Sheila, who had to live without sex
because she was married to a homosexual. To set the stage for these and other accounts like them, Balse hypothesizes about a group of men who in a cowardly way
left their wives on a sinking ship only to find themselves on a deserted island. Titling her narrative "A Male Dominated Society" followed by a question mark,
Balse points out that without women, men would be doomed to procreative
impotence:

> Know why women were the protected sex? Know why men always stood on sink-
> ing ships or "burning decks" and shouted: "Women and children first?" Know why
> they battled those urges to jump into the first available life-boat and make for dry
> land?
>   Men were bothered about the survival of the race. Suppose the ship went down
> with all the helpless women on board while the men swam merrily to shore, what
> would happen?
>   For a time the men would look at each other and cluck sympathetically. Then
> they would wring their hands, scratch their heads and say: "You don't say it's an in-
> habited island!" Next day they would sigh: "Oh for a woman!"
>   Then tell dirty jokes. Or become homosexuals.
>   It would not matter very much if it were only a question of sex. But the question
> of progeny made it a grave matter. Those men were doomed. It meant their race would
> end there.

Although Balse does not specifically mention the hijras in this passage, her suggestion that isolation ultimately provokes men to "tell dirty jokes" or turn to homosexuality echoes the opinion of Sharma, who asserts that impotence causes the
hijra to utter sexual remarks and to engage in sodomy. The image of the impotent
man as a shipwrecked entity, lost in a world of reproducing heterosexuals, is also
telling. The "question of progeny" referred to by Balse is precisely what distinguishes a hijra from a nonhijra—her inability to carry on the family lineage results
in a life of social marginalization.

A few American and European anthropologists have also connected the hijras' language use with their sexual confusion, frequently conflating the two as similar instances of perversion. Harriet Ronken Lynton and Mohini Rajan (1974), in
their short introduction to the hijras in Hyderabad, are a case in point. Reminiscent of Singh's and Sharma's analyses of the hijra's use of obscenity, the authors
draw a causal link between the hijras' "manner of speech" and what they perceive
to be the hijras' self-motivated withdrawal from the rest of society:

> The self-mutilation of these impotent wretches and their acceptance into the Hijra
> community is a kind of allegory of suicide and rebirth, while their manner of speech
> suggests a yearning for identity and identification with a social group. So together they
> have built a world for themselves. In Hyderabad, as in most of India, people are ad-
> dressed less often by name than by the title which shows their precise status and rela-
> tionship within the extended family. So also with the Hijras, with the added detail that
> the confusion of their terminology is a constant reminder of the sexual confusion
> which brought them into the group. (1974: 192)

While Lynton and Rajan are not referring to the hijras' obscene language per se, their description is in a way reminiscent of Balse's portrayal of the impotent man as shipwrecked. The terms *self-mutilation* and *suicide* imply that the hijras voluntarily choose to leave the "normal" world of women and men in order to be reborn into the "abnormal" hijra world—a world that, in the opinion of these authors as well as of many other social theorists, is identified by linguistic as well as sexual ambiguity. Isolation leads to a need for what M. D. Vyas and Yogesh Shingala (1987: 89) identify as "vicarious gratification"; many hijras can achieve sexual satisfaction, in the authors' opinion, only by *talking* about the "normal sex life" of men and women.

Hijra *as an abusive epithet*

Hijras do not have the corner on the Indian obscenity market; a variety of communities are notorious for breaking expectations of linguistic purity. These communities include, but are certainly not limited to, children in Western Uttar Pradesh who invoke a "triad of sex, shit, and sadism" in play-group humor (Vatuk 1969); female singers of *gālī* songs in Eastern Uttar Pradesh who provide ritualized entertainment at weddings (Henry 1976); Oriya-speaking male "charioteers" at the Bhubaneswar Chariot Festival who chant sexually obscene limericks and songs to the devotees of Lord Lingaraj (Freeman 1978); and Rajastani village women who at annual festivals and life cycle celebrations sing of sexual engagement with spouses and lovers (Raheja and Gold 1994). But what sets the hijras apart from these communities is the fact that obscenity is critical to the hijras' own survival. The Hindi-speaking hijras I spoke with in Banaras see their use of verbal insult not as a logical consequence of a self-motivated withdrawal from society but as a necessary survival technique in a society that enforces their marginalization.

In this sense, the hijras' curse is comparable to that of the Hindu widow who, because of the extremity of her marginalization, is given free range to defy the social order through her language use. This point is made clear in Shivarama Karanth's novel *Mukajjī*: The novel's main character is a widow who, in many ways, is the most powerful woman in her village.[20] Since she has already suffered the worst curse possible, namely widowhood, she has nothing to lose if the other villagers curse her back; the other villagers, afraid of her curse, try desperately to remain on her good side. The hijra and the widow have much in common in this respect; not only are both of these unmarried states considered to be a curse, but the words for *widow* and *hijra* in a variety of Indian languages are considered curses in themselves. M. N. Srinivas's observation more than half a century ago that "the worst word of abuse in the Kannada vocabulary is to call a woman, married or unmarried, a widow" (1942: 117) points to the pervasiveness of *widow* as derogatory epithet, his words reminiscent of the well-known Hindi proverb *rāḍ se pare koī gālī nahī̃* (there is no curse greater than calling someone a widow). But to call a nonhijra a hijra is no minor transgression either, especially since it implies that the addressee is sexually impotent and therefore incapable of continuing the family lineage.

Nanda (1990: 14) incorrectly states that the word *hijrā*, unlike its Telegu and

Tamil counterparts *kojja* and *pottai*, is "rarely used" as a derogatory term in Hindi; in fact, its employment as such has been well recorded since the 1940s, when Mehta (1945–1946: 52) wrote that "timid people are often abused as 'Hījaḍā' in Gujarat." Mitra (1983: 25) implies that the term is used throughout India in reference to more "effeminate" men, in a way that is perhaps comparable to the use of *faggot, fairy,* or even *sissy* in contemporary American slang (i.e., "Even before turning into a eunuch, a passive homosexual in Gujarat would be referred to as a *hijra.* This is also true of the rest of India"). Alyssa Ayres (1992), who also notes the prevalence of this epithet in her research among hijras in Gujarat,[21] suggests that the term is used among nonhijra men as part of a "male-bonding" ritual, in a manner that approximates the use of *homo* among the American heterosexual men discussed by James Armstrong (this volume).

The use of *hijra* as a derogatory epithet is affirmed by the hijras I spoke with in Banaras, who explained how they were repeatedly dubbed *hijra* when young because of their fondness for dolls and other girls' games. In the commentary reproduced here, Sulekha, a thirty-eight-year-old hijra who now lives with a male partner in a small village outside of Banaras, recalls how her childhood peers rejected her with the label *hijra,* refusing to allow her into their gendered playgroups:

> There were a few boys at my school who I used to study with. When I sat with them, they used to tell me that I was a hijra. Then they started telling other people, "This is a hijra! This is a hijra! Don't sit near him! Sit separately!" If I sat with the girls, the girls would say, "This is a hijra! This is a hijra! Don't sit near him! Sit separately!" So I felt very ashamed. I thought, "How is it that I've become a hijra? The girls don't talk to me; the boys don't talk to me. What terrible thing has happened to me?" I wanted to go and play with them, but nobody wanted to play with me. So life was going like that. Nobody would help me. (personal communication, Sulekha, Spring 1993, my translation)

The story of the reaction of Sulekha's peers to her interest in girls' activities (e.g., dancing and playing with dolls) is reminiscent of a narrative that appears in Bapsi Sidhwa's (1992) novel *The Crow Eaters,* written in English. When the father, Freddy, discovers that his son, Yadzi, has been writing love poetry (an enterprise Freddy categorizes as "emasculated gibberish"), he angrily pronounces him a *eunuch.* "If you must think and act like a eunuch," Freddy exclaims "in a cold rage," "Why don't you wear your sister's bangles?"[22]

Sulekha's distress at the use of *hijra* as an epithet is echoed by Charu, a hijra who lives with three other hijras in a small Muslim-identified community on the outskirts of Banaras. In the passage reproduced here, Charu explains how difficult it is for a hijra to return home to her family after joining a hijra community, encapsulating society's disgust in the final two lines by referring to their use of the epithet "*E HIJRĀ! e hijrā!*" (HEY HIJRA! Hey hijra!)[23]

hijrā cāhē, (1.5) apne ghar par calā jāe - vah sambhav nahī hai. iske- ye hijrā ke jariye hai- dekhiye samāj, aur asamāj kā bāt hai. (2.0) asamāj ho gayā- alag ho gayā, - agar ye jānā cāhēnge, - hijrā jānā cāhēnge, - parīvār vāle nārāz hōge. (1.0) khuś bhī hōge, (2.5) khuś bhī hōge ((softly)) ki ye hamārā parivār hai, (1.5) hamārā beṭā hai, - yā hamārā laṛkā hai, - yā hamārā bhāī hai. ā gayā royēge. - magar ek cīz kā nārāzgī āyegā, duniyā vāle bolēge ki "uphu. ye hijṛā ā gayā. (1.5) iske ghar hijṛā ātā jātā hai. - isse hijṛā kā riśtā hai. - iske ghar śādī nahī karēge." (3.0) to ye duniyā ne asamājik banā diya. (2.5) duniyā burī nazar se dekhne lagā. (2.5) "E HIJṚĀ, (2.0) e hijṛā."

(Even if the hijra wants to go home, it wouldn't be possible. The hijra is the dividing line—you see, it's a matter of social versus asocial. He has become asocial. If they want to go [back into society]— if the hijras want to go [back], the family members will get very upset. They'll also be happy—they'll also be happy [and think], "He's our family; he's our child; he's our son; he's our brother." But even though they might cry when he arrives, they'll still be angry about one thing: The worldly people will say, "Oh no! A hijra has come here! A hijra visits that household, so they must be related to a hijra! We won't arrange a marriage with anyone in that household!" So the world has made him an outcast; the world has looked at him with an evil eye: "HEY HIJRA! Hey, hijra!")

The family is, after all, what distinguishes the hijra from most other members of Indian society, who are intimately involved in the extended families so instrumental to social organization. But since the hijra is thought to act as a curse on this very family structure—a belief based on the idea that her impotence will spread to her siblings and prohibit procreation (see, for example, Mehta 1945–1946: 27; Vyas & Shingala 1987: 75; Pimpley & Sharma 1985: 42; Sharma 1989: 51–59)— she is, in the words of Sulekha, a "black spot," an existence that brings shame to the family's potency. It is perhaps this fact that leads Charu to describe the hijras as occupying the dividing line between society and nonsociety: If they were to cross this line by returning home, their appearance would be met with anger, fear, even hatred.

Recent employments of the term in derogatory reference to the Muslim community by the conservative Bharatiya Janata Party, commonly referred to as the *BJP*, suggests that *hijra* is used as a derogatory epithet more generally. In Anand Patwardhan's 1994 documentary *Father, Son, and Holy War*, to name but one example, a female BJP leader says scathingly of the now former chief minister of Uttar Pradesh, Mulayam Singh Yadav, *ek hijṛe par golī kyō bekār kī jāye* 'Why would you want to waste a bullet on a hijra?' Indeed, some Hindi poets and novelists have used the term metaphorically to suggest the ineffectiveness of the referent in question, including the Hindi poet Ved Prakash Vatuk in a number of political critiques (1977a, 1977b, 1987, 1995), such as in his poem *maĩne āj īsā ko marte hue dekhā* 'Today I saw Jesus dying' (1977a), when he identifies India as a country of *pacpan karoṛ hijṛe* '550 million hijras'.[24] Khushwant Singh similarly exploits this metaphor in his novel *Delhi* in order to indicate the ineffectiveness of his narrator (who, incidently, has an extended affair with a hijra named Bhagmati): "I was disowned by the Hindus and shunned by my own wife. I was exploited by the Muslims who disdained my company. Indeed I was like a *hijda* who was neither one thing nor another but could be misused by everyone" (1989: 55).

The notion of shamelessness

Both hijras and widows, then, are perceived to be outside the reproducing hetero-sexual mainstream, and because death would be a more welcome existence than life for those in such an unfortunate state, or so mainstream society thinks at any rate, the destitute have nothing to lose through verbal defiance. As illustrated by a well-known epithet from Kabir (दुर्बल को न सताइये, जाकी मोटी हाय, बिना जीव की स्वास से, लोह भसम हो जाय 'Do not torment the weak, their sigh is heavy; Breath from a bellows can re-duce iron to ashes', the sigh of the weak, or in this case their "voice," is thought to have the power to destroy the lives of those situated higher in the social hierarchy. Central to the hijras' narratives is the idea that because their existence is merely tangential to the world of women and men, they are a people without *śarm* 'shame'; that is, a people freed from the constraints of decency that regulate the rest of society. Sulekha identifies the lack of *śarm* not only as the primary trait that distinguishes hijras from women but also as the motivating factor behind their use of obscenity:

> We just speak from the mouth. Hijras aren't counted [in the polls] as women, after all. Hijras are just hijras, and women are just women. If there's a woman, she'll at least have a little *śarm* ['shame']. But compared to the hijras, how open can a woman be? No matter how openly a woman walks, she'll still have a little *śarm*. But hijras are just hi-jras. They have no *śarm*. They'll say whatever they have to say. (personal communica-tion, Sulekha, Spring 1993, my translation)

Sulekha considers her own status to be so low that she is completely outside the so-cial order, a fact that gives her free range to defy the propriety associated with caste and class affiliation through her language use. Several anthropologists report simi-lar observations from hijras in other communities. G. Morris Carstairs, for in-stance, notes that the hijras in the community he studied "had the security of know-ing that they had no vestige of dignity or social position to maintain; and their shamelessness made people reluctant to provoke their obscene retaliation in pub-lic" (1956: 60–61). Likewise, Nanda remarks that the hijras she worked with in South India, "as a group at the lowest end of the Indian social hierarchy, and hav-ing no ordinary social position to maintain within that hierarchy . . . are 'freed from the restraints of decency' and they know that their shamelessness makes people— not all, but surely most—reluctant to provoke them in a public confrontation" (1990: 51).[25] Like the Hausa-speaking Muslim 'yan daudu studied by Rudolph Gaudio (this volume), who as "men who act like women" are said to be shameless in their employments of sacreligious proverbs, the hijras push their hearers to the ver-bal limit, leaving them with no other choice but to pay the requested alms.

The fear of hijra shamelessness is nicely articulated by the Hindi novelist Shani (1984) in his book *Sāre Dukhiyā Jamnā Pār*. When describing his frustration with the city of Delhi, the narrator refers to an incident involving hijras, who ar-rive at his door unexpectedly and demand an *inām* 'reward'. Although the narrator initially refuses to succumb to the hijras' requests, their *gāliyō kī bauchār* 'shower of abuses' is too much even for him. When they threaten to expose themselves in front of onlooking neighbors, he is compelled to pay the requested 51 rupees in order to preserve his *izzat*:

> The first day in Mayur Vihar, the night somehow passed and morning came. But it was a very strange morning; as soon as it arrived, it seemed that evening had begun. I hadn't yet finished my morning tea, when someone rang the bell. The door opened, and I heard the sound of bells, clapping, dancing, and singing, and, behind that, the sound of drums. They were hijras. They came to get their reward. Reward? What for? You've come to a new house. House? Whose house? We' re just renters; go find the owner. We were answered with louder claps, faster drum beats; we were showered with curses instead of songs. When we protested, they began to strip naked, and in a few minutes there was such a spectacle in front of our gate that all of the people in the neighborhood came to their windows and doors. If you care about your honor, please quietly give them whatever they demand and get rid of them, even though you know you're being blackmailed.
>
> We paid them 51 rupees and got rid of them, even though we knew that if someone asked us what we celebrated, we would have nothing to say. (Shani 1984: 64–65, my translation)

Shani's account is paralleled by a diary entry written by Vatuk (1985), who recalls an actual incident in which the hijras came to his door in Meerut: *hijre āte hai. ve beśarm hai. unkī koī izzat nahī ve kisī ke prati uttardāyī nahī. unkī zabān par koī niyamtraṇ nahī. atah ve har avasthā mē vijyī hai* 'The hijras came. They are shameless. They have no honor. They are answerable to no one. Their tongue has no restraint. They are victorious in every exchange'.

Contemporary Cursing Strategies

Yet both of these accounts, written from a nonhijra perspective, are not particularly flattering. Sulekha offers a different perspective on the hijras' begging technique at birth celebrations, discussing it as a strategy for survival. Also concerned with the notion of *izzat*, she explains that the hijras use obscenity during their performances as a means of reclaiming respect:

> *Suppose you went to sing and dance somewhere and people didn't show you any respect, or they didn't give you money. Then you'd curse them and they'd be afraid of you, right? They'd be afraid of the hijras?*

> Yes, yes, yes! . . . Yes, yes, yes, yes. If they don't give us money, we'll feel sad in our hearts. So we'll swear at them, we'll curse them, we'll wish them evil, we'll cut them down to size.

> *Does society give hijras a lot of respect, then?*

> Yes, a lot of them do.

> *So how do you feel about that? Do you like it?*

If they give hijras respect, we feel good. If they don't give hijras respect, we feel bad. Then we'll strip down and start to fight with them. We'll shout *gālīs* 'obscenities' in order to get some money. But if someone gives us respect, touches our feet, and lets us sit down with him, even if he gives us less money than the others, we won't fuss about it. If someone gives us respect we'll leave him alone. If someone doesn't give us respect, we'll fight with him like crazy. (personal communication, Sulekha, Spring 1993, my translation)

Throughout the passage, Sulekha identifies the hijras' linguistic behavior with a variety of different verbs, among them *gālī denā* 'to utter obscenities, swear,' *sarāpnā* 'to curse', *kosnā* 'to wish someone evil', and *kaṭnā* 'to cut someone down to size'.[26] It is significant, however, that she consistently uses the Hindi term *sarāp dena* 'to curse' (with an inital alveolar [s] as in 'sip') instead of the more traditional *śarāp dena* (with an inital palatal [ś] as in 'ship'), distinguishing the former from the latter as a matter of referential perspective. The term *sarāp* differs from its Sankrit counterpart *śarāp* in that it is associated with the powerless as opposed to the elite; while a *śarāp* is given by saints and those in power, a *sarāp* is considered to be an instrument of the poor, uttered by people who are otherwise helpless, such as widows, outcasts, or, in this case, hijras. Although both terms mean 'to curse' or 'to imprecate', *śarāps*, according to Sulekha, are uttered by people in respected positions as a means of maintaining the social hierarchy, while *sarāps* are uttered by the marginalized as a means of fighting against it. Forced to live on the outskirts of Banaras both socially and spatially, Sulekha and her fellow hijras employ *sarāps* (i.e., curses used by those in inferior positions) in an effort to save face in a society that has, in her own words, unmasked them. When offered inadequate payment for their song and dance performances, a gesture that the hijras interpret as disrespectful, they shame their clients with a series of verbal abuses that quickly escalate from mild to severe. And if the most severe of these abuses also fails to bring the expected reward, the more aggressive members of the group will threaten to lift up their saris and expose their genitals, a practice that has been associated with the hijra community for well over a century (cf. Goldsmid 1836, as reported in Preston 1987; Bhimbai 1901; Russel, Bahadur, and Lal 1916). The hijras, as interlocutors without *śarm*, are uniquely skilled in the art of ridicule and insult, their curses winning them financial—and, indeed, a certain kind of social—respect. (I should add that, in the passage just quoted, Sulekha uses the expression *naṇgā honā* 'to become naked,' which can be interpreted both figuratively as 'to become shameless' and literally as 'to expose oneself'.)

The "fighting" behavior Sulekha alludes to in the excerpt just quoted, which occurs both in and out of the birth celebrations, consists of the overt employment of *gālīs* 'verbal abuses', as well the more subtle employment of semantically ambiguous puns, rife with sexual innuendo. The invective reproduced in the next excerpt serves as an example of the former. Shouted by a Banaras hijra to the owner of a tea shop who had made sarcastic reference to her promiscuity (Singh 1982: 33), its derogatory meaning is clear. What distinguishes this expression from the many other genres of *gālī*-giving in India is not so much the individual terms themselves but rather the concentration of these terms in a single utterance:[27]

nāspīṭe, mue, harāmī ke jāe, terī bībī kuttā khāe, kalmunhe, khudā-kahar barsāe tujh par, randue!

('You worthless fool, good-for-nothing, son-of-a-bastard, may your wife be eaten by a dog, may you be dark-faced, may god shower calamities on you, you widower!')

This series of invectives is, of course, not without some suggestion of sexuality. The phrase "may your wife be eaten by a dog" indirectly implies (1) that the addressee is not able to satisfy his wife sexually, (2) that the addressee's wife is potentially unfaithful, and (3) that the addressee's wife has no discrimination with respect to sexual partners. Similarly, although the common interpretation of *mue* is 'one who is dead' and therefore a 'good-for-nothing', the term is occasionally used to suggest impotence or emasculation. Finally, the term *randu* 'widower' suggests promiscuity, pointing up the instability between the Indian identities of 'widower' and 'pimp' (compare, for instance, the Hindi proverb *rāṇḍ to raṇḍāpā kaṭ le, raṇḍuve kāṭṭnā dē to* which translates roughly as 'The widow would be true to her widowhood if only the widower would allow it'). But these are all familiar Hindi insults, and the sexual references they were founded upon are not necessarily salient to present-day users.

The hijra insults reproduced in Table 25-1, however, are performed in a manner quite different from those in this example. Like the ritualized insults identified for some gay male communities in the United States (Murray 1979), the hijras direct these sexualized insults to each other for reasons of solidarity. Yet this speech event differs from that reported for English-speaking gay males in that the hijras issue these slurs to each other *when in the presence of nonhijras.* There is a strong element of performance in this vituperative banter, as the hijras create scripted quarrels among themselves to shock and embarrass their eavesdropping bystanders. Indeed, some hijra communities have a special *thālī* 'clap' used expressly for signaling the onset of this discursive activity (referred to by ingroup members as *ḍeḍh tālī* 'one-and-a-half clap'), which they perform by producing a 'full clap', where the palms are brought together with straight, spread, raised fingers, followed directly by an *ādhī tālī* 'half clap', where the palms are brought together in the same manner but no sound results (see Hall 1995). When one of the hijras gives this signal, the uninitiated nonhijra becomes witness to a rowdy display of put-downs that demand a highly sexualized interpretation.

Representative of what Singh (1982) calls the hijras' *aślīl evaṁ dviarthī bhāṣā* 'obscene and double-meaning language', these expressions contain words that, with the exception of the vocative *mue* 'good-for-nothing', are inherently inoffensive when uttered alone. The majority of these insults, as in the first five examples reproduced in Table 25-1, involve an extended metaphor of the marketplace: the buying and selling of fruits and vegetables, the exchange of wares, the satisfaction and dissatisfaction of voracious customers. The bazaar is one of the most public sites in the community and is traditionally a man's domain. The sociomoral geography of the community is such that the bazaar is off limits to "respectable" women, as illustrated by the existence of the Hindi term *bāzārū aurat* 'market woman', which translates variously as 'loose woman,' 'woman of low morals,' 'woman who has no shame', even 'prostitute.' Hijras often supplement the income

Table 25-1. Selected examples of hijra verbal insults

Expression used by the hijras	Literal translation into English
(a) khasam kā gannā cūs	'Go suck your husband's sugarcane!'
(b) khasam ke yār sāre bāzār ke kele cāṭ le, peṭ bhar jāyegā	'Husband's lover, go and lick all the bananas at the bazaar, *then* you'll get full.'
(c) pattal kuttā cāṭe hai, terā bhāī hai	'The dog who licks the leaf-plate is your brother' (i.e., 'You are just like a dog who eats other people's leftovers').
(d) thūktā jā aur laḍḍū khātā jā, mue	'Keep on spitting and eating *laḍḍū* (ball-shaped sweets), you good-for-nothing'.
(e) lakṛī bec lakṛī	'Sell that stick!' (Singh 1982 glosses this expression as follows: "In other words, the addressee should open up a store for selling his private parts").
(f) gilās mē pānī bharkar soyā rah, mue	'Fill the glass with water and go to sleep , you good-for-nothing'.
(g) terī saut ko kutte kā bāp rakhe thā. tab to kuch na bolā. ab ṭirr ṭirr kare hai.	'When that father-of-a-dog kept your co-wife you never said a word. Now you're complaining?'

Source: Singh (1982)(recorded in Delhi, Uttar Pradesh, and Madhya Pradesh).

that they receive from public performances at births and weddings by servicing men sexually in secret, despite popular perceptions of the eunuch as a sexless ascetic. The metaphors employed here by the hijras about the bazaar are meant to be understood ambiguously in sexual terms. These images—which, of course, carry euphemistic reference to male genitalia, as in the case of *gannā* 'sugarcane', *kele* 'bananas', *laḍḍū* 'sweets', and *lakṛī* 'stick'—highlight the hijra's own knowledge about the closed and open spaces of the social geography. By referring to secret domains, in this case the male body and indirectly prostitution, the hijras embarrass their male listeners and shamelessly collapse traditional divisions of the secret and the known, private and public, home and market, feminine and masculine.

At this point it would be appropriate again to consider Rupa's comment that the hijras "even give curses like women." After insisting that hijras always speak like women when together, Rupa asserts in the next excerpt that they additionally refrain from using those curses that involve insulting reference to the addressee's mother or sister. These kinds of curses, she explains, are *mardānā* 'manly' curses and oppose the more feminine variety of curses used by women:

gālī bhī dēgī, to aurat jaisā. (7.0) mardānā gālī nahī dete haī hijṛā. - auratō jaisā. auratō jaisā dete haī. (2.0) abhī nahī kahēngī "terī mā kī, terī bahan kī," nahī kahēngī, - ye gālī nahī dēngī. - ye gālī nahī dēngī. jaise chinrī, bucrī, ganjī, kanjrī, ye sab banaēgī auratō kī tarah. (3.0) mardānā log kahte haī, "terī mā kī, terī bahan kī, - bhosṛī vāle, ye- vo- coṭṭā, sālā," (1.0) uṭāēgī vo nahī.

(We'll even give curses like women. Hijras don't give *mardānā* curses; they curse like women. Like women. We won't say "*terī mā kī* [your mother's . . .], *terī bahan kī* [your

sister's . . .]," we won't say them. We won't give these curses. We won't give these curses.
[We'll say,] for example, "*chinrī* [loose one], *bucrī* [earless one], *ganjī* [hairless one], *kan-jrī* [low-caste loose woman]," we'll form all of these in the same way that women do.
Mardānā people give curses like "*terī mā̃ kī* ['your mother's...'], *terī bahan kī* [your sister's
. . .], *bhosrī vāle* [vagina-owner], *coṭṭā* [thief], *sālā* [wife's brother]." We won't say those.)

In Hindi-speaking Banaras, the genre sometimes referred to as *mardānā gālī*
'men's curses' is thought to involve mention of sexual violence to women, in opposition to 'women's curses' that generally only wish the hearer ill. The curses that
Rupa identifies as *terī mā̃ kī* 'your mother's. . .', *terī bahan kī* 'your sister's. . .', and
sālā 'brother-in-law' are known in Hindi as *mā̃-bahan kī gālī* 'mother and sister
curses', and because the speaker who utters them asserts his own sexual prowess
with respect to the addressee's female relatives, women do not tend to use them.
Oddly enough, these are precisely the terms that Verma (1971) claims are used by
impotent men to make themselves seem more potent to the rest of society, a facade
that is clearly meaningless to hijras, who collectively identify as nonmasculine.
Even in the structure of their curses, according to Sulekha, the hijras assert their
identity as feminine, employing "softer" curses that focus on either physical defect
or sexual immorality, such as *chinrī* 'loose one', *bucrī* 'earless one', *ganjī* 'hairless
one', and *kanjrī* 'low-caste loose woman'.

Yet in contrast to Rupa's claims, the hijras in Banaras do in fact employ *mardānā* curses in everyday conversation, as evidenced by Shashi's angry employments
of the term *mādar cod* 'mother fucker' in reference to her birth parents. Shashi, now
a seventy-eight-year-old guru of a small hijra community in Banaras, ran away
from home at the age of seven and joined a troupe of *bāī*, women dancers who are
often perceived to be prostitutes: "I renounced my mother; I renounced my father;
I renounced everybody!" But what was initially grief later turned into contempt,
and Shashi, adamant about the notion that hijras have no ties to the world of men
and women, whether of caste, class, or religion, blasphemes her own parents:

> As far as I'm concerned, my mother and father were all cremated on *Maṇikarṇikā*. I
> cremated them. I hit them four times with a stick and then I let their ashes flow down
> the Ganges river. I said, "You *mādar cod* 'mother fuckers' flow down the river! Don't
> ever show your face here again! If you come to my little town, I'll beat the hell out of
> you!"

Moreover, one of the hijras' favorite in-group insults is the term *bhosrī vālā*
'vagina-owner', an epithet so offensive to middle-class Hindi speakers that the
Banaras resident who typed my transcripts refused to include this word, typing an
ellipsis in its place. When used among nonhijras, the term is generally used between men and implies that the referent, although male, has somehow been de-
masculinized. The epithet is used differently from the American insult *cunt*, then;
for one, *bhosrī vālā* is itself grammatically masculine and its referent must be so as
well (the feminine counterpart *bhosrī vālī* does not exist in contemporary usage[28]).
When used among hijras, the insult lies not in the accusation of demasculation,
since the very definition of *hijra* depends on the notion of impotence, but in the

suggestion of maleness. In the next two excerpts, Sulekha recreates two different scenarios in which the term might be used among ingroup members, and while she clearly considers both uses somewhat humorous in retrospect, she nevertheless indicates that the accusation is a serious one. In both narratives, Sulekha illustrates how the term is used as both an attention-getting device and a means of expressing anger: in the first example it is used to convince her friend Megha to go to the movies with her, and in the second example it is used to reprimand initiates for speaking like men instead of women:

> puliṅg bhī hotā hai. bāt karne mē, jaise Megha se hamārā bāt hotā hai, "Megha suno, calogī nahī̃ kā sinemā mere sāth? <u>cal</u> sinemā dēkhe. cal nahī̃ Megha. (1.5) E! na calbe kare, bhosṛī vālā!" ((laughs)) (4.0) gussā mē ho jātā hai, is tarah mazāk mē ho jātā hai. "are sun re!" is tarah ke ho jātā hai.

> The masculine occurs, too. For example, if I'm talking with Megha, [it's], "Megha, listen! Won't you come with me to the movies? C'mon, let's go see a movie. Won't you come on, Megha? (1.5) Hey! Won't you come on? The *bhosṛī vālā* [vagina-owner]!" ((laughs)) It happens when we're angry. And it also happens when we're joking. "Hey, listen to me!" We'll use it like that.

> sikhāyā nahī̃ jātā hai. - anu<u>bhav</u> ho jātā hai. - <u>dekh</u>kar ke, - koī baccā to nahī̃ hai, usko sikhlāyā jāyegā. . . . kaise kar rahe haī, - is tarah hamko bhī karnā cāhiye. - nahī̃ karēge to hijṛā log hamko hansegā. - to kahegā ki "are baṛī kuḍhaṅgā hai, baṛī batta<u>mīz</u> hai." ((laughs)) hā. - "apne man se kah rahā hai bhosṛī vālā" ((laughs)) sab mārne uṭh jātā hai cappal se. ((3.0)) <u>hūā</u>. (5.0) dekhte dekhte ādat paṛ jātā hai, - tab vaisā svabhāv ho jātā hai.

> It's not taught. It's experienced, by watching. After all, he's not a child who needs to be taught. . . . [The new hijra will say,] "I should also act just like they're acting. If I don't, hijra people will laugh at me." [The hijra people] will say, "Oh, he's very ill-mannered! He's very ill-behaved." ((laughs)) Yes! "He's just saying whatever comes to mind, the *bhosṛī vālā* [vagina-owner]!" ((laughs)) Then everybody will get up to beat him with their sandals. ((laughs)) Really! So gradually, after watching for a long time, it becomes a habit. Then it just becomes his nature.

The older hijras' employment of the masculine-marked epithet in the second example is particularly telling, as it reflects their dissatisfaction with the initiate's attempts at discursive femininity. Refusing to grant the initiate the feminine reference so expected within the community (see Hall and O'Donovan 1996), the more experienced hijra veterens refer to the "ill-behaved" initiate with masculine-marked verb and noun phrases. Their use of the epithet *vagina-owner*[m], in this context, ironically implies that the addressee is acting too "masculine," a behavior that merits retribution in a community that wishes to distance itself from male representations. The initiate is categorized, in essence, as a vagina-owning want-to-be, the grammatically masculine *bhosṛī vālā*[m] being used to betray her essential (i.e., anatomical) masculinity.

As with the term *bhosṛī vālā*, the ingroup examples recorded in Table 25-1 also carry an overt and, I would argue, deliberate confusion of feminine and masculine reference. The authors of expressions (d) and (f) address their fellow hijras not with the feminine *muī* but with the masculine *mue*, a term that is itself generally thought of as a "soft curse" used primarily by women. The first six of these examples point to the addressee's insatiable sexual appetite, which in (a) can be satisfied only through size (i.e., sugarcane), in (b), (c), (d), and (e) only through quantity (i.e., the bananas at the bazaar, regular supplements of sweets, leftover leaf-plates, a store of stick-buying customers), and in (f) only though pacification (i.e., a cold glass of water at bedtime). Yet while the first four examples attribute an aggressive femininity to the hijra addressee, placing her squarely in the feminized role as the husband's lover or wife, examples (e) and (f) highlight the addressee's masculinity and point disdainfully to her machismo, referring to her insatiable *lakṛī* 'stick' on the one hand and her need to subdue an erection on the other. The final insult reproduced in (g) again points to the addressee's femininity, criticizing her for passively allowing her male lover to take a co-wife.

Conclusion

With these verbal shifts of perspective, the hijras who participate in this insulting banter are able to challenge dominant cartographies of gender and sexuality. In order to make any sense of the hijra's seemingly innocuous and nonsensical utterance, the passer-by must enter into what he believes to be the hijra's frame of reference, a linguistic space involving sexual innuendo, crudity, and gender fluidity. Yet by doing so, the hearer must also admit to himself that he in many ways inhabits that same space. Through this verbal play, then, the hijras, who have a precarious status in the Indian social matrix, are able to compensate for their own lack of social prestige by assuming linguistic control of the immediate interaction, creating alternative sociosexual spaces in a dichotomously gendered geography.

For the hijra, who either is born an intersexed infant or undergoes castration in order to adopt the hijra lifestyle, it is the body itself that determines her ambiguously situated linguistic position, a body that has been interpreted as something outside and therefore inferior to the female/male dichotomy. Because the hijras have a kind of between-sex status in contemporary India, their very existence serves as a theoretical challenge to previous characterizations of women's speech and men's speech as discursive styles indexically derived from the sex of the speaker. The hijras, liminal to the world of women and men, have a privileged position with respect to the linguistic gender system, their experiences on either side of the gender divide allowing for strategies of expression unavailable to the monosexed individual. Indeed, the hijras collectively exploit their liminality, subverting the linguistic ideologies associated with both femininity and masculinity in order to survive in a hostile world.

ACKNOWLEDGMENTS   I would like to thank Veronica O'Donovan for her help in Banaras, Ved Prakash Vatuk for his wisdom in Berkeley, and Anna Livia for her comments in San Diego. Above all, I would like to express my gratitude to the hijras I met in 1993, who are the best cursers I know.

NOTES

1. The correct English spelling for the Hindi हिजड़ा, according to the transliteration conventions adopted throughout the remainder of this chapter, would be *hijṛā*; I have chosen to use the spelling *hijra*, however, for easier reading. (Throughout this chapter, I use the transliteration system adopted by Snell and Weightman 1989: 7).

2. As I remark in a previous article on the hijras' alternating uses of feminine- and masculine-marked verb phrases (Hall and O'Donovan 1996), the choice of terminology used to identify the hijras in Indian, European, and American scholarship merits a full article in its own right. While contemporary sociologists and journalists who live in India and write in English generally refer to the hijras as "eunuchs" (e.g., Bobb and Patel 1982; Allahbadia and Shah 1992; Lakshmi and Kumar 1994; Mitra 1983, 1984; Mohan 1979; Mondal 1989; Patel 1983, 1988; Raghuramaiah 1991; Sayani 1986; Sethi 1970; Sharma 1984; Shetty 1990; Sinha 1967; Vyas and Shingala 1987), European and American researchers refer to them variously as "transvestites" (e.g., Freeman 1979; Preston 1987; Ross 1968), "an institutionalized third gender role" (Bullough and Bullough 1993; Nanda 1985, 1990), "hermaphrodites" (Opler 1960; Ross 1969), "passive homosexuals" (Carstairs 1956), and "male prostitutes" (Carstairs 1956). The inconsistency of these translations underscores the inherent difficulty of translating the concept *hijṛā* into Western scholarship. Other English terms besides *eunuch* that are occasionally employed by South Asian writers are "abominable aberrations" (Raghuramaiah 1991), "ambiguous sex" (Mohan 1979), "hermaphrodites" (Mohan 1979; Pimpley and Sharma 1985; Sethi 1970; Singh 1956; Srinivas 1976), "castrated human male" (Mohan 1979), "hermaphrodite prostitutes" (Sanghvi 1984), "labelled deviants" (Sharma 1989), "male-homosexual transvestites" (Rao 1955), "sex-perverted male, castrated or uncastrated" (Sinha 1967), "sexo-aesthetic inverts coupled with homosexual habits" (Sinha 1967), "sexual inverts," "sexual perverts" (Rao 1955), and "third sex" (Mondal 1989).

3. The Indian Railway often gives discounts to citizens who are traveling to national meetings; those traveling to and from All-India conferences, for instance, are routinely given a 50 percent discount on train fares.

4. Estimates on the number of hijras living in India during the past decade vary significantly, ranging from 50,000 (Bobb and Patel 1982), through 200,000 (Associated Press 1994) through 500,000 (*Tribune* 1983, referring to both India and Pakistan), through 1.1 million (Sharma 1989, quoting Bhola, president of the All-India Hijra Welfare Society) to 1.2 million (*Hindustan Times* 1994; Shrivastav 1986, quoting Bhola, president of the All-India Hijra Welfare Society). I have chosen the latter estimate, as it is most consistent with the results of my own fieldwork in North India.

5. This information was provided by Khairati Lal Bhola, the chairman of the Akhil Bhārtiy Hijṛā Kalyāṇ Sabhā (The All-India Hijra Welfare Society) in a public interview on 13 October, 1986. The article reporting this information, authored by V. K. Shrivastav and titled "Hijṛõ Kī Alag Duniyā, Dhan Kamāne Kā Kutsit Dhandhā" (The Separate world of the eunuchs: A vile profession for earning money), is highly inflammatory, asserting that older hijra gurus kidnap innocent bystanders and trick them into undergoing castration.

6. Other terms used in reference to the hijras since the mid-1800s include *khunsā*, *khasua*, *fātādā*, and *mukhanna*.

7. Burton also explains in his article "How to Deal with the Slave Scandal in Egypt" (recorded in Wright 1906, v. 2, 195–210) that castration increased the value of the slave by anywhere from five to eighty pounds, depending on the age of the boy in question.

8. Ayres (1992) and Preston (1987) attribute this loss of status to British colonialists, who launched moral and political campaigns against the hijras during the eighteenth and nineteenth centuries.

9. This passage points to an additional association of the eunuch with physical cruelty, which probably developed in response to the fact that they were often assigned the unpleasant task of inflicting royal punishments on offending persons. The eunuchs' penchant for physical cruelty was recorded even in the nineteenth century; William Knighton, for instance, comments that they carried out this task with "*gusto* and appetite": "Whether it was that I felt an antipathy to the class, or was prejudiced against them by the accounts I heard, I can not now tell; but my impression is, that the greater part of the cruelty practised in the native harems is to be attributed to the influence and suggestions of the eunuchs. They were usually the inflicters of punishment on the delinquents; and this punishment, whether flogging or torturing, they seemed to inflict with a certain degree of *gusto* and appetite for the employment" (1855: 161).

10. True hermaphrodites (or those thought to be so) were apparently considered more deserving of respect than castrated hijras, and so Edward Balfour's *Enclopaedia Asiatica* defines *khoja* as a "corruption of Khaja, a respectable man, a respectable term for a eunuch," apparently in opposition to terms that were perhaps not so "respectable" (1976, v.5, 564). John Shortt (1873: 404), however, reverses the semantics of *hijra* and *khoja* in his article on the "kojahs" of southern India (which is later quoted extensively by Thurston 1901 in *Castes and Tribes of Southern India*) and identifies the "artificially created" eunuch as *kojah* and the "natural" eunuch as *higra*. Ibbetson, MacLagan, and Rose (1911, v. 2, 331) delineate the linguistic distinction between court eunuchs and hijras as follows: "a eunuch, also called *khunsá, khojá, khusrá, mukhannas*, or, if a dancing eunuch dressed in woman's clothes, *zankhá*. Formerly employed by chiefs and people of rank to acts as custodians of their female apartments and known as *khwaja-sará, nawáb* or *názir*, they are still found in Rájputána in this capacity. In the Punjab the hijra is usually a *ḍeradár, i.e.,* attached to a *ḍera.*" W. Crooke (1896: 495) identifies the term *khoja* (or rather, "khwâja") as a Muslim subclass of *hijra*, a distinction that further points to an association of the khoja with Muslim courts.

11. "They go about the bazaars in groups of half-a-dozen or more singing songs with the hope of receiving a trifle. They are not only persistent but impudent beggars, rude and vulgar in the extreme, singing filthy, obscene, and abusive songs to compel the bazaarmen to give them something. Should they not succeed they would create a fire and throw in a lot of chillies, the suffocating and irritative smoke producing violent coughing, etc., so that the bazaarmen are compelled to yield to their importunity and give them a trifle to get rid of their annoyance, as they are not only unable to retain their seats in the bazaars, but customers are prevented from coming to them in consequence. With the douceur they get they will move off to the next bazaar to resume the trick" (Shortt 1873: 406).

12. "At Ahmedabad not only the Hijdás but some of the Bhawayyás, or strolling players, claim presents on the birth of a boy with a pertinacity that is not satisfied till the whole of their demand is paid. The person claiming the gift is generally the clown or fool of the troop. He does not dance or sing, but by his obstreperous sallies of witty abuse tries to make

his stay so annoying that to get rid of him no expense is thought to great. To avoid the nuisance some people satisfy his demands at his house by going and making a present of one or two shillings" (Lutfullah 1875: 95).

13. This turn of phrase is repeated verbatim by R. V. Russel, Rai Bahadur, and Hira Lal: "The hijras [artificial eunuchs] are beggars like the Khasuas [natural eunuchs], and sometimes become very importunate. Soon after the birth of a child in Gujarāt, the hated Hijras or eunuchs crowd round the house for gifts. If the demand of one of them is refused the whole rank and file of the local fraternity besiege the house with indecent clamour and gesture" (1916: 209). K. Bhimbai similarly comments on the hijras' abusive techniques: "In begging they stand in front of some villager, clap their hands, and offer him the usual blessing, 'May Mother Bahucharáji do you and your children good' or 'Ado Bhaváni,' that is 'Rise goddess Bhaváni.' If anyone fails to give them alms they abuse him and if abuse fails they strip themselves naked, a result which is greatly dreaded as it is believed to bring dire calamity" (1901: 507).

14. The existence of this book was pointed out by Rupa, the only hijra I spoke with who had learned to read and write. Unlike other hijras in Banaras, Rupa became a hijra at a very late age after receiving a childhood education. When showing this book to my research partner Veronica, Rupa enthusiastically explained that "everything you need to know about hijras will be in this book."

15. To preserve the hijras' anonymity, I have chosen pseudonyms for all of the hijras who appear in this article and have avoided giving the names of the four hijra communities I visited.

16. Naqvi and Mujtaba narrate the story as follows: "Hijras are appalled when they are ridiculed by 'normal' people. They maintain that such an attidude is not merely irrational, but sacrilegious. 'God has made us like this,' says one hijra. 'So if anyone ridicules me I swear at them.' When a hijra boarded a bus in Mazimabad, a young man clapped mockingly in imitation of the standard hijra practice. The hijra in turn proceeded to hurl the most vociferous abuses at the man, who was eventually forced to disembark from the bus in shame" (1992: 89).

17. The hermaphrodite, raised as a girl in an upper-class Muslim family in Pakistan, had undergone medical treatment in the United States in order to enhance his masculinity. In his application for asylum, he argued that if he returned to Pakistan as a man, his anatomy would be considered defective, and he would be forced to join the hijras against his will.

18. Mehta's decision to use the term *lewdness* in reference to the hijras is clearly influenced by their exhibitionism as well. He later remarks, "I once saw four handsome Pavaiyā youth about 20 years old expose their backsides in the most crowded locality of Bhadra in Ahmedabad." As with Manucci and Bernier in their descriptions of the court eunuchs, however, Mehta also notes the hijra's faithful and trustworthy nature: "But on the whole the Pavaiyas have the reputation of being particularly honest, loyal, reliable and incapable of betrayal. Their life is simple, their wants are simple, and they have no wife and children to worry about. It is an account of this well-known trait of honesty that they flourish as sellers of milk, because it is believed that they would not adulterate it. Usually their instinctive behaviour and mode of thought is masculine" (1945–1946: 51).

19. I should add that Verma also asserts that women have their own verbal strategies for indicating "sex-superiority," namely, what he refers to as "pleading innocent" (1971: 85).

Regarding women who claim to be victims of rape, he argues: "It is for her own good that she denies having felt any pleasure, even if she has actually felt it. It is in her interest to declare that the entire act was loathsome to her and that she had been forced to submit. Therefore, pleading innocent, she demands all those rights which the society gives to a respectable woman" (85).

20. I am grateful to Ved Vatuk for bringing this novel to my attention.

21. In Ayres's own words: "People tend to casually employ the word *hijra* in jest to describe rather effeminate men who appear to dress and identify as men but perhaps associate with hijras" (1992: 8).

22. The full passage is narrated as follows:

> Freddy could feel an angry vein throb in his forehead. He was furious and horrified that a son of his should write such emasculated gibberish. As for poetry, "The Charge of the Light Brigade" he could tolerate, but this!
>
> In a cold rage, he scribbled beneath the last line of the poem: "If you must think and act like a eunuch, why don't you wear your sister's bangles? And don't tear pages from your notebook!"
>
> He tucked the notepaper into a fresh envelope and addressed it to Yazdi. (Sidhwa 1992: 146)

23. The transcription conventions I have used in the transliterated Hindi passages are adapted from Jefferson (see Atkinson and Heritage 1984: ix–xvi); they include the notable additions of a superscripted *f* or *m* to designate feminine and masculine morphological marking. (I have not used these conventions in the English translations, since extralinguistic features like intonation and emphasis are not parallel.) Other transcription conventions include the following:

(0.4)   indicates length of pause within and between utterances, timed in tenths of a second

a - a   a hyphen with spaces before and after indicates a short pause, less than 0.2 seconds

but-   a hyphen immediately following a letter indicates an abrupt cutoff in speaking (i.e., interruption or self-interruption)

(( ))   double parentheses enclose nonverbal movements and extralinguistic commentary

( )   single parentheses enclose words which are not clearly audible (i.e., best guesses)

[ ]   brackets enclose words added to clarify the meaning of the text

<u>what</u>   underlining indicates syllabic stress

CAPS   small caps indicate louder or shouted talk

:   a colon indicates a lengthening of a sound (the more colons, the longer the sound)

.   a period indicates falling intonation

,   a comma indicates continuing intonation

?   a question mark indicates rising intonation at the end of a syllable or word

...   deletion of some portion of the original text

"a"   quotation marks enclose quoted or reported speech

24. The complete text of Vatuk's poem is as follows (my translation):

> Today I saw Jesus dying.
> Every inch of his body was pierced by nails.
> I saw all of India seething with pain,
> lying in a cot in the shape of an old man.

Onlookers are making noises all around the dying man,
pointing their bayonets toward him.
He's a fascist. Beware of him.
He can overturn the the government with his disarmed hands.
Every breath of truth is poisonous.
I have seen it suffocated by the smoke of propaganda.
I have seen non-violence being shot.
The fire is going out,
And all of India is locking the doors of their houses,
lest a flame engulf them.
I have seen today how, like vultures,
people eat up their own father raw.
I have seen on the fires of the cowards
a dying bravery
and a frightened witch trying to perform magical rites from afar.
Today I have seen my history being buried
and over its grave
I have seen dancing
550 million hijras.

25. Nanda also discusses how the hijras exploit their shamelessness for financial gain, drawing the important conclusion that "this stigma functions as an effective strategy of economic adaptation" (1990: 51).

26. The verbs *sarāpnā* and *kosnā* are very close in meaning, except that the former activity is generally associated with nonverbal cursing and the latter with verbal cursing (e.g., "May your two sons die tomorrow!"). The verbal activity subsumed under the verb *kosnā* is stereotypically associated with women instead of men.

27. See Raheja and Gold (1994) for an engaging discussion of research on women's insult traditions in North India.

28. Ved Prakash Vatuk (personal communication) offers a succinct explanation as to why this curse is never used in reference to a woman: "A woman already has one, so why would it be a curse to tell her so?"

REFERENCES

Allahbadia, Gautam N., and Nilesh Shah (1992). "India: Begging Eunuchs of Bombay." *Lancet* 339, no. 8784: 48–49.

Armstrong, James D. (this volume). "Homophobic Slang as Coercive Discourse among College Students."

Ayres, Alyssa (1992). *"A scandoulous breach of public decency... "Defining the decent: Indian hijras in the 19th and 20th centuries.* Honors Essay. Cambridge, MA: Harvard-Radcliffe College, April 1992.

Balfour, Edward ([1858]1976). "Khoja." *Encyclopaedia Asiatica*, vol. 5. New Delhi: Cosmo, p. 564.

Balse, Mayah (1976). *The Indian Female: Attitude Toward Sex.* New Delhi: Chetana.

Bernier, Francois (1891). *Travels in the Mogul Empire, A.D. 1656–1668*, trans. Archibald Constable. Westminster: A. Constable.

Bhimbhai, K. (1901). "Paváyás in Gujarat Population, Hindus." *Gazetteer of the Bombay Presidency*, vol. 9, pt. 1. Bombay: Government Central Press, pp. 506–508.

Bobb, Dilip, and C. J. Patel (1982). "Eunuchs: Fear Is the Key." *India Today*, 15 September, pp. 84–85.

Bullough, Vern L., and Bonnie Bullough (1993). *Cross-Dressing, Sex, and Gender*. Philadelphia: University of Pennsylvania Press.

Burton, Richard Francis (1886–1888). *Supplemental Nights to the Book of the Thousand and One Nights and a Night. With Notes Anthropological and Explanatory by Richard F. Burton*, 6 vols. Printed by the Burton Societ (for private subscribers only).

Carstairs, George Morrison (1956). "Hinjra and Jiryan: Two Derivatives of Hindu Attitudes to Sexuality." *British Journal of Medical Psychology* 29: 128–138.

Claiborne, William (1983). "India's Eunuchs Have Fallen in Esteem." *Washington Post*, 7 August, p. 14.

Crooke, W. (1896). "Hijra, Mukhannas." *Tribes and Castes of the North-Western Provinces and Oudh*, vol. 2. Calcutta: Office of the Superintendent of Government Printing, pp. 495–497.

Ebden, H. (1855). "A Few Notes, with Reference to 'the Eunuchs,' to Be Found in the Large Households of the State of Rajpootana." *Indian Annals of Medical Science* 3: 520–525.

Faridi, Khan Bahadur Fazalullah Lutfullah (1899). "Híjdás in *Gujarat Population, Musalmans.*" *Gazetteer of the Bombay Presidency*, vol. 9, pt. 2. Bombay: Government Central Press, pp. 21–22.

Freeman, James M. (1977). "Rites of Obscenity: Chariot Songs of Eastern India." *Journal of Popular Culture* 10, no. 4: pp. 882–896.

Freeman, James M. (1979). "Transvestites and Prostitutes, 1969–72." In *Untouchable: An Indian Life History*. Stanford: Stanford University Press, pp. 294–315.

Gaudio, Rudolph P. (this volume). "Not Talking Straight in Hausa."

Hall, Kira (1995). "Hijralect." *Hijra/Hijrin: Language and Gender Identity*. Ph.D. Diss., Department of Linguistics, University of California at Berkeley.

Hall, Kira, and Veronica O'Donovan (1996). "Shifting Gender Positions among Hindi-Speaking Hijras." In Victoria Bergvall, Janet Bing, and Alice Freed (eds.), *Rethinking Language and Gender Research: Theory and Practice*. London: Longman.

Henry, Edward O. (1976). "Vindicating Gali Songs: Insult Songs Which Promote Social Cohesion." *Journal of Social Research* 19, no. 1: 1–13.

Hindustan Times (1994). 7 November.

Ibbetson, D. C. J., M. E. MacLagan, and H. A. Rose (1911). "Hijra." *A Glossary of the Tribes and Castes of the Panjab and North-West Frontier Province*, vol. 2. Lahore, Pakistan: Civil and Military Gazette Press, pp. 331–333.

Karanth, Kota Shivarama (1984). *Mukajji: Eka Atindriya Kathaloka*. New Delhi: Bhārtīya Jñānpiṭh.

Knighton, William (1855). *The Private Life of an Eastern King. By a Member of the Household of His Late Majesty, Nussir-u-Deen, king of Oude*. New York: Redfield.

Lakshmi, N., and A. Gururaj Kumar (1994). "HIV Seroprevalence among Eunuchs." *Genitourinary Medicine* 70, no. 1: 71–72.

Lutfulláh, Fazl (1875). *Gujarát Musalmáns; Written for the Bombay Gazatteer*. Bombay: Government Central Press, pp. 95–98.

Lynton, Harriet Ronken, and Mohini Rajan (1974). "The Unworldly Ones: The Hijras." *The Days of the Beloved*. Berkeley: University of California Press, pp. 190–206.

Manucci, Niccolao (1907). *Mogul India, 1653–1708*, vols. 1–4, trans. William Irvine. London: John Murray.

Mehta, Sumant (1945–1946). "Eunuchs, Pavaiyās, and Hijaḍās." *Gujarat Sahitya Sabha*, Part 2: 3–75.

Mitra, Nirmal (1983). "The Making of a 'Hijra.'" *Onlooker*, 18 February, pp. 14–25.

——— (1984). "Bahuchara Mata and Her Rooster." *India Magazine*, April, pp. 44–53.

Mohan, Chander (1979). "The Ambiguous Sex on the War-Path." *Hindustan Times Weekly Sunday*, 26 August, p. i.

Mondal, Sekh Rahim (1989). "The Eunuchs: Some Observations." *Journal of Indian Anthropology and Sociology* 24: 244–250.

Murray, Stephen O. (1979). "The Art of Gay Insulting." *Anthropological Linguistics* 21: 211–223.

Nanda, Serena (1985). "The Hijras of India: Cultural and Individual Dimensions of an Institutionalized Third Gender Role." *Journal of Homosexuality* 11, no. 3–4: 35–54.

Nanda, Serena (1990). *Neither Man nor Woman: The Hijras of India*. Belmont, CA: Wadsworth.

Nanda, Serena (1992). "The Third Gender: Hijra Community in India." *Manushi* 72: 9–16.

Naqvi, Nauman, and Hasan Mujtaba (1992). "Neither Man nor Woman." *Newsline*, December, pp. 80–89.

New Orleans Times Picayune (1994). "India's Eunuchs Marry Mythical Demigod," 28 April.

Opler, Morris E. (1960). "The Hijarā (Hermaphrodites) of India and Indian National Character: A Rejoinder." *American Anthropologist* 62: 505–511.

Patel, Haribhai G. (1983). "The Hijada (Eunuch) Culture-Complex: Urgent Research Needs." *Bulletin of the International Committee on Urgent Anthropological and Ethnological Research* 25: 121–126.

——— (1988). "Human Castration: A Study of Hijada (Eunuch) Community of Gujarat in India." *Man and Life* 14, no. 1–2: 67–76.

Patwardhan, Anand (1994). *Father, Son, and Holy War*. Documentary film.

Pimpley, P. N., and S. K. Sharma (1985). "Hijaras: A Study of an Atypical Role." *Avadh Journal of Social Sciences* 2: 41–50.

Preston, Laurence W. (1987). "A Right to Exist: Eunuchs and the State in Nineteenth-Century India." *Modern Asian Studies* 21, no. 2: 371–387.

Raghuramaiah, K. Lakshmi (1991). *Night Birds: Indian Prostitutes from Devadasis to Call Girls*. Delhi: Chanakya.

Raheja, Gloria Goodwin, and Ann Grodzins Gold (1994). *Listen to the Heron's Words: Reimagining Gender and Kinship in North India*. Berkeley: University of California Press.

Rao, I. Bhooshana (1955). "Male Homosexual Transvestism: A Social Menace." *Antiseptic* 52: 519–524.

Rawlinson, Hugh George (1952). *India: A Short Cultural History*. London: Cresset.

Ross, Allen V. (1969). *Vice in Bombay*. London: Tallis Press.

Russell, R. V., Rai Bahadur, and Hira Lal (1916). "Hijra, Khasua." *Tribes and Castes of the Central Provinces of India*, vol. 3. London: Macmillan, pp. 206–212.

Saletore, Rajaram Narayan (1974). *Sex Life under Indian Rulers*. Delhi: Hind Pocket Books.

——— (1978). *Sex in Indian Harem Life*. New Delhi: Orient Paperbacks.

Sanghvi, Malavika (1984). "Walking the Wild Side." *Illustrated Weekly of India*, 11 March, pp. 25–28.

Sayani, Sanjay A. (1986). "Understanding the Third Sex" [Interview with Siddharth Shah]. *Sunday Observer*, 9 November, p. 14.

Sethi, Patanjali (1970). "The Hijras." *Illustrated Weekly of India*, 13 December, pp. 40–45.

Shani (1984). "Sāre Dukhiyā Jamnā Pār." *Ek śahar mē sahne bikte haī.* Delhi: National Publishing House.

Sharma, Satish Kumar (1984). "Eunuchs: Past and Present." *Eastern Anthropologist* 37, no. 4: 381–389.

——— (1989). *Hijras: The Labelled Deviants.* New Delhi: Gian.

Shetty, Kavitha (1990). "Eunuchs: A Bawdy Festival." *India Today,* 15 June, 50–55.

Shortt, John (1873). "The Kojahs of Southern India." *Journal of the Anthropological Institute of Great Britain and Ireland* 2: 402–407.

Shrivastav, V. K. (1986). "Hijṛō Kī Alag Duniyā, Dhan Kamāne Kā Kutsit Dhandhā." Source unknown.

Sidhwa, Bapsi (1992). *The Crow Eaters.* Minneapolis: Milkweed Editions.

Singh, Govind (1982). *Hijṛō Kā Sansār.* Delhi: Anupam Books.

Singh, Khushwant (1956). *Mano Majra.* New York: Grove Press.

——— (1989). *Delhi.* New Delhi: Viking Penguin Books.

Sinha, A. P. (1967). "Procreation among the Eunuchs." *Eastern Anthropologist* 20, no. 2: 168–176.

Snell, Rupert, and Simon Weightman (1989). *Hindi (Teach Yourself Books).* Kent: Hodder & Stoughton.

Srinivas, M. N. (1942). *Marriage and Family in Mysore.* Bombay: New Book Co.

——— (1976). *The Remembered Village.* Berkeley: University of California Press.

Thurston, Edgar (1909). "Khōjas." *Castes and Tribes of Southern India,* vol. 3, Madras: Government Press, pp. 288–292.

Times of India (1979). "A National Get-Together of Eunuchs." 2 February, p. 5.

Tribune (1983). "5 Lakh Eunuchs in India, Pak." 26 August, p. 5.

Tuli, Jitendra (1976). *The Indian Male: Attitude towards Sex.* New Delhi: Chetana.

United States Department of State (1992). Letter to Director, Asylum Unit, Immigration and Naturalization Service, San Francisco, 6 July.

Vatuk, Ved Prakash (1969). "Let's Dig Up Some Dirt: The Idea of Humor in Children's Folklore in India." *Proceedings of the Eighth International Congress of Anthropological and Ethnological Sciences, Tokyo and Kyoto* 2: 274–277.

——— (1977a). Maīne Āj Īsā Ko Marte Hue Dekhā. *Āpāt Shatak.* Minakshi Prakashan, pp. 79.

——— (1977b). "Patā Nahī̃ Kal Kyā Hogā." *Āpāt Shatak.* Minakshi Prakashan, pp. 43–44.

——— (1985). Unpublished diary entry. Meerut, 30 January.

——— (1987). "Hijṛō Kī Tarah." Unpublished poem.

——— (1995). "Yugadriṣṭā Manīṣiyō Kī Is Puṇyabhūmi Mē." Unpublished poem.

Verma, Dayanad (1971). *An Intimate Study of Sex Behaviour.* New Delhi: Star Publications.

Vyas, M. D., and Yogesh Shingala (1987). *The Life Style of the Eunuchs.* New Delhi: Anmol Publications.